COLONIAL AMERICA
to 1763

COLONIAL AMERICA
to 1763

Thomas L. Purvis

Richard Balkin
General Editor

☑®
Facts On File, Inc.

Facts On File, Inc.
11 Penn Plaza
New York NY 10001

Library of Congress Cataloging-in-Publication Data
Purvis, Thomas L., 1949–
        Colonial America to 1763 / Thomas L. Purvis.
            p. cm. — (Almanacs of American life)
        Includes bibliographical references and index.
        ISBN 0-8160-2527-4 (acid-free paper)
        1. United States—History—Colonial period, ca. 1600–1775.
    2. United States—Social life and customs—To 1775. 3. United
    States—History—Colonial period, ca. 1600–1775—Statistics.
    4. United States—Social life and customs—To 1775—Statistics.
    I. Title. II. Series.
    E188.P86 1999
    973.2—dc21   98-29007

Facts On File books are available at special discounts when purchased in
bulk quantities for businesses, associations, institutions, or sales
promotions. Please call our Special Sales Department in New York at
(212) 967-8800 or (800) 322-8755.

You can find Facts On File on the World Wide Web at
http://www.factsonfile.com

Text design by Fred Pusterla
Cover design by Cathy Rincon
Illustrations on pages 2, 18, 23, 43, 131, 134, 145, 152, 161, 165, 276,
280, and 281 by Jeremy Eagle

Printed in the United States of America

VB Hermitage 10 9 8 7 6 5 4 3

This book is printed on acid-free paper.

To

Joseph Lee Purvis

"A young gentleman of great expectations"

Note on Photos

Many of the illustrations and photographs used in this book are old, historical images. The quality of the prints is not always up to modern standards, as in many cases the originals are from glass negatives or the originals are damaged. The content of the illustrations, however, made their inclusion important despite problems in reproduction.

Contents

List of Maps

Acknowledgments

Contributing to this volume's completion were many people whose help deserves recognition and my thanks. The staff of the Campbell County, Kentucky, Library at Newport obtained numerous, hard-to-find sources by forwarding what must have seemed like a never-ending stream of interlibrary loan requests. Dr. Conard "Sandy" Carroll likewise afforded me help on some critical occasions by gaining me access to services at Northern Kentucky University's Steely Library.

Very much of the credit for the high-quality illustrations that grace this volume is due to dedicated curators and idealistic administrators who helped me to locate appropriate artwork and to avoid unnecessary delays. I wish in particular to acknowledge Michael Sherbon's exceptional efforts to complete a very difficult order for nine illustrations from the Pennsylvania State Archives and to expedite its completion through its lab facilities. The Commonwealth of Pennsylvania has a very valuable civil servant in Mike. Special thanks are also due to Elizabeth Dickinson for her generosity in making available several prints from the Delaware Art Museum's Howard Pyle Collection at an affordable price. Georgia B. Barnhill was extremely helpful in making excellent suggestions on suitable materials from the holdings of the American Antiquarian Society.

For offering helpful assistance and special considerations in a variety of ways, I also wish to thank Carolyn Singer of the Haverhill, Massachusetts, Historical Society; Jill Burns of the Worcester, Massachusetts, Art Museum; Karin Stanford of Historic St. Mary's City Commission in Maryland; Mimi Dornack of the National Geographic Society; Susan Newton of the Winterthur Museum and Gardens; Lt. Col. Leonid Kondratiuk from the Association of the National Guard; and the following staff members from the Smithsonian Institution's National Museum of American History: Thomas Bower (Rights and Reproduction Committee), Peter Daniel (curator of the Agriculture and Natural Resources Department), Douglas Mudd (curator of the Numismatics Department), and Sarah Rittgers (curator of the Military History Department).

I finally wish to give credit to series editor Richard Balkin for numerous valuable suggestions that improved my chapters and to the high standards shown by Nicole Bowen in bringing the manuscript to press at Facts On File. I also wish to thank them for the exceptional understanding and patience they extended during the impediments that delayed this volume long past its initial deadline.

Preface

The period since 1960 has seen an explosion of research in the field of early American history. Although scholars have generated a wealth of data about the colonial period, the vast majority of their output remains widely scattered among a wide variety of journal articles, books, and unpublished dissertations. Consequently, few libraries, except for leading university centers, have collections large enough to conduct in-depth research on more than a few of this era's topics.

The full extent of the problems entailed in finding quick answers to questions about colonial America can be illustrated through the work that currently stands as the best reference source on U.S history, the U.S. Census Bureau's two-volume *Historical Statistics of the United States: Colonial Times to 1970* (Washington, D.C., 1975). Of 1,200 pages, the *Historical Statistics* devotes just thirty-three pages to the entire period from 1607 to 1789. This work includes next to nothing on such subjects as immigration, agriculture, education, crime, and most sectors of the economy.

Colonial America to 1763 provides libraries with a compendium of basic quantitative data from the most important government sources and scholarly studies. It includes more than statistical tables. It places this data in scholarly perspective with brief sketches or extended essays (as are appropriate) summarizing current ideas on the broadest range of topics about early American society and culture. To enhance the reader's appreciation of this period, the text includes more than 100 illustrations and maps.

Whenever possible, information has been selected or essays added that give insight to everyday life. It should be understood, however, that many experiences that are nearly universal in the twentieth century were less common before 1763, and vice versa. This book attempts to provide as much information as possible, depending on what historical records have survived, into numerous circumstances affecting the widest range of people. The terminal date chosen for this volume, 1763, conforms with a common view among the historical profession, which usually sees the Revolutionary era (see *Revolutionary American, 1763 to 1800,* Facts On File) as taking shape immediately after then as the British government began to spark widespread resistance to its taxation policies, beginning with the Stamp Act in 1765.

Certain considerations governed the presentation of tables and other descriptive information. Although perhaps most scholars of early America have arranged statistical tables in descending order from the earliest date (at top) to the most recent (at bottom), this book presents most columns of numbers in ascending order. In doing so, it follows the example of the Census Bureau's previously mentioned *Historical Statistics of the United States,* which has the best claim to serve as a model for standardizing the organization of quantitative materials. Ascending style has primarily been used in tables of data for which a table listing like statistics from a later period will or may appear in a subsequent volume of this series (such as annual temperatures or price indexes). In many cases where a table's subject pertains solely to the colonial period, however, descending style has been retained if the table originally appeared in that format when published.

As a reference work, this series necessarily incorporates phraseology that is long dated. Some terms of earlier ages, especially concerning race or ethnicity, have now fallen out of use, either because they carry disparaging connotations or simply because newer words have become fashionable. As a rule, this work retains original labels when reprinting quotations or tables; it does so not in order to endorse "politically incorrect" or dated language but only to ensure a historically accurate context. Otherwise, this series uses interchangeably the terms *Anglo-American* and *white, African American* and *black,* and *Native American* and *Indian.*

Thomas L. Purvis

COLONIAL AMERICA
to 1763

CHAPTER 1 Climate, Natural History, and Historical Geography

Climate

Weather conditions varied considerably during the millennium prior to 1763. Dendrochronology, the study of tree rings, and other archaeological research indicate that warm, moist air dominated the North American climate from about 700 to 1200. Because conditions were highly favorable for agriculture in most of the modern United States, Indian societies increasingly relied on farming. This warming trend encouraged the formation of large-scale, sedentary communities in the Rio Grande, the Colorado, and the Mississippi watersheds; it also stimulated tribes on the Great Plains to rely less on hunting and more on crops.

The Northern Hemisphere's temperatures gradually cooled after 1200. This new weather regime, known as the Little Ice Age, made agriculture far more difficult than it had been in much of central North America. Colder, drier air greatly reduced rainfall on the Great Plains and the prairies, forced many groups to migrate southeastward, and increased the Indians' reliance on hunting. Drought spurred the residents of many pueblos in high southwestern altitudes to migrate south into the Rio Grande valley. Worsening weather conditions also contributed to the abandonment of large-scale communities that were characteristic of the highly developed Mississippian (or Mound-Builder) culture in the Midwest and the upper South, where the growing season shrank and crop losses due to early frosts became more common.

The years 1550 to 1700 constituted the most severe period of the Little Ice Age. Temperatures dropped sharply as glaciers advanced in the northern latitudes, winter lengthened by two to four weeks, and increased precipitation often caused grains to rot because fields were too wet for them to ripen properly. The Little Ice Age climaxed at precisely the moment when European colonization commenced in North America, and it created a harsh environment that sorely tested the endurance of the earliest English, Dutch, and Swedish settlers.

Seventeenth-century weather conditions were least severe in the southern colonies. Early accounts of Chesapeake Bay's climate usually declared its summers to be as hot as Spain's. Twentieth-century Annapolis, Maryland, has a mean summer temperature of 75° Fahrenheit and an average maximum of 102°, compared with the mean of 73° and average maximum of 102° in Madrid, Spain. It consequently seems that southern summers have not changed drastically in the four centuries since Jamestown's founding. The Little Ice Age nevertheless produced far colder winters below Pennsylvania than are now typical. Snow and frost were common from December to February, and observers usually described the air as sharp. During the winters of 1641–42 and 1645–46, ice covered much of Chesapeake Bay. Although not recorded, it is also likely that the bay froze over in 1657 when Swedish colonists near Wilmington, Delaware, reported that a mass of arctic air froze the Delaware River in a single day.

Frigid conditions were a regular feature of climate north of the Hudson River's mouth. On one of his early explorations to the continent's interior, Samuel de Champlain found ice on the edge of Lake Ontario as late as June. Ice on the Hudson River landlocked Dutch colonists at Albany in most years, and in 1645 the river froze as early as November 25. The first English attempt to settle New England at Sagadahoc on Maine's Kennebec River was abandoned after its initial winter (1607–08) proved unexpectedly harsh.

Extremes of both cold and heat characterized New England's climate during the seventeenth century. In 1637, for example, the summer was so hot that sunstroke killed a number of Puritans newly arrived from England, but the following winter froze Boston Bay and carpeted the ground with 3 feet of snow from November to early April. Boston harbor appears to have frozen over at least once every seven years from 1630 to 1700. Late frosts or excessively wet springs also compounded the difficulties of raising crops; these conditions led to poor harvests and grain shortages in the early 1640s, 1658, 1673, and the late 1690s.

About half of the winters from 1630 to 1650 brought either heavy snowfalls that blocked transportation between towns or else bitterly frigid temperatures. The winter of 1641–42 was probably that century's second coldest. Prevailing winds shifted from 1650 to 1679 and brought three decades of generally moderate winters, but they also created wet springs and summers that made farming more difficult. A colder climate suddenly reappeared with the winter of 1680–81, which was apparently the third worst in the seventeenth century. During the next twenty years, temperatures plunged to the lowest levels of the century, several heavy snowfalls unleashed destructive floods, and a number of droughts occurred. This phase of the Little Ice Age peaked in the winter 1697–98, the century's worst, which kept New England in a deep freeze from December 24 to mid-March and produced snow accumulations that measured up to 42 inches in Massachusetts.

The winter of 1697–98, long renowned as the worst ever experienced in Anglo-America, was followed by very severe winters in 1699–1700, 1704–05, and 1705–06. This cycle of intensely frigid climate marked the Little Ice Age's culmination in North America. A warming trend then ensued that dramatically improved conditions for agriculture and has dominated the continent's atmosphere to present times. This new climatic era can be examined with some precision because systematic weather data first came to be collected within the United States in the early 1700s.

The earliest recorded attempt to collect meteorological data came to naught about 1684 when Rev. John Clayton, who was embarked for Virginia to make a scientific survey of its natural phenomena, lost his thermometer and barometer in a shipwreck. The first thermometer to arrive safely in the colonies was brought to Philadelphia in 1715 by Cadwallader Colden. By the 1740s, regular tables of weather conditions were being compiled in Philadelphia, Pennsylvania, Charles Town, South Carolina, and Cambridge, Massachusetts. Climatic record-keeping depended on a small number of amateur scientists who could seldom coordinate their activities; consequently, they left an incomplete and haphazard body of statistics. Because surviving tables of temperature are rare and measurements of precipitation are almost nonexistent before 1800, the handful of remaining records merit special scrutiny as the sole source of documentation about atmospheric conditions in colonial times.

The shift from the Little Ice Age to more temperate conditions apparently occurred within a brief span of time. The earliest recorded temperatures for Philadelphia, Williamsburg, and Charles Town reveal that yearly averages for the mid-eighteenth century were within 1° Fahrenheit of twentieth-century norms. In the Mid-Atlantic region, winter was 2° warmer at Philadelphia during the years 1738 to 1763 than it would be during 1951 to 1980. That same season also moderated considerably in New England, where mean temperatures at mid-eighteenth-century Cambridge, Massachusetts, averaged just 1° less than averages for Boston winters during 1951 to 1980.

Despite the shift toward more temperate weather, several notable winters burst on the eighteenth-century colonies. The eighteenth-century's heaviest snowstorm occurred in the nine days from February 27 to March 7, 1717; sweeping from Pennsylvania through New England, this "great snow" paralyzed transportation for two weeks, dropped 5 feet of flakes north of the Charles River, produced drifts up to 14 feet, and melted into deep slushes that left the roads impass-

EXTENT OF GLACIATION OVER NORTH AMERICA

Bering Strait land bridge

Ice cap during Wisconsin glaciation

Possible coastline during glaciation

Variations in North America's climactic conditions have been extreme over millennia. The weather's greatest impact on the environment occurred during the Great Ice Age of Wisconsin glaciation, lasting from about 80,000 to 8000 B.C., when ice caps extended below the Great Lakes. A far less severe cooling period character-ized the Little Ice Age, from about A.D. 1200 to 1720, when the territory south of Canada was nevertheless free of glaciers. (Jeremy Eagle)

able for a fortnight. During early 1720, temperatures plunged to their lowest levels in twenty-two years, the Hudson River froze solid from Manhattan to New Jersey, Boston Harbor froze many miles out to sea, and ice trapped ships at Philadelphia from January 12 to March

6. After the exceptionally severe winter of 1732–33, snow stood 4 feet deep in the woods near Portland, Maine, as late as April 9. The hard winter of 1740–41 froze the northern coast so thoroughly that Francis Lewis (later a signer of the Declaration of Independence)

drove a sleigh on the ice 200 miles from Barnstable, on Cape Cod, to New York City, and the York River froze near Williamsburg, Virginia. The winter of 1747–48 blanketed New England with about thirty snows that deposited 60 to 66 inches of flakes on much of the region.

Because approximately a quarter of all Anglo-Americans lived within 125 miles of Philadelphia by 1760, meteorological data from that city provide an important indication of weather's impact on agriculture. The chance of losing crops to early or late frosts seems to have been slight because none of the twenty-six springs from 1738 to 1763 averaged less than 50°, and just five averaged under 52° (compared to a mean of 53.9°); the coldest autumn was only 53.8° (compared to a mean of 56.0°). The probablity of ground being too wet at planting time was low, for winter and spring's combined precipitation never exceeded the mean of 19.2 inches by more than 2.5 inches in the same period. The likelihood of crops being spoiled before harvest by excessive rain was also slim because total precipitation in summer and autumn surpassed the average of 22.2 inches by 2.5 inches once (and never exceeded that amount). The driest summer received just 1.3 inches of rain less than the average of 12.8 inches. Farmers enoyed optimal advantages for maximizing output and stood minimal risk of losing a year's crop.

By 1750, the climate of the thirteen colonies basically resembled that of the modern United States. Compared to western Europe, the eastern seaboard experienced hotter summers and colder winters, a more abrupt change from winter to summer, shorter—but more intense—rains, and exceptionally violent thunderstorms. The end of the Little Ice Age created atmospheric conditions ideal for maximizing agricultural yields and consequently underlay much of the eighteenth century's prosperity and rapid population growth.

TABLE 1.1 REPORTED WEATHER CONDITIONS IN NEW ENGLAND, 1607–1699

Year	Spring	Summer	Winter[a]
1607	…	…	Severely frigid
1620	…	…	Frigid until Jan., then mild & rainy
1623	…	Long drought	…
1629	…	…	Mild, little snow & frost
1630	…	…	Mild until Jan., then frigid through Feb. 20
1632	Cold, wet	Cold, wet	Frigid, much frost & snow
1633	…	Hot, dry	Mild, but snowy
1634	…	Hot[b]	Came early, much frost & snow
1635	…	Violent hurricane[c]	Frigid, very snowy
1636	…	…	…
1637	…	Extremely hot	Frigid, with more than 3 ft. snow
1638	Very cold	Warm[d]	Frigid
1639	…	Hot, dry	…
1640	…	Cool, wet	Cold, snowy
1641	…	Cool, wet	Extremely frigid
1642	…	Cool, wet	Mild, but very snowy
1643	…	…	Mild, dry
1644	…	Drought	Mild, dry until Feb.
1645	…	Drought	Early freeze, then frigid
1646	…	…	Mild
1647	…	Severe drought	…
1648	…	…	Frigid in Jan.
1649–1653	…	…	…
1654	…	…	Frigid
1655	…	…	"Normal" to Feb., then cold
1656–1657	…	…	Mild, little snow
1658	Very wet, cold	…[e]	Cold, stormy
1659	Cold, rainy	Warm[f]	Frigid, snowy
1660	Cold, late snow	…	Mild, little snow or frost
1661	Cold, wet	Warm[f]	Snowy

Year	Spring	Summer	Winter[a]
1662	Cold, wet	Drought	Mild, but deep snow from Jan. to March
1663	Cold, wet	…	Mild
1664	Cold	Late drought	Mild to Feb., then cold
1665	Cold	Late summer	Cold
1666	Cold, wet	Late summer, hot & dry	Cold, snowy
1667	Early spring	…	Mild, little frost or snow
1668	Early spring	Late frost	Mild, snowy
1669	Mild	Wet through Aug.	Snowy, cold
1670	…	Mild drought	Mild
1671	Rainy	…	Mild
1672	…	Began dry, late rains	Mild
1673	Very cold	Rainy late summer	Mild, wet, snowy
1674	…	…	Mild until Feb., then frigid
1675	Very cold	Warm[f]	Sharp & stormy until Jan., then warm
1676	Early spring	…	…
1677	…	…	Mild, several snowstorms
1678	Stormy	…	…
1679	…	…	…
1680	…	…	Severely frigid
1681	…	Drought	Frigid
1682	…	Warm[f]	Cold
1683	…	…	Cold
1684	…	…	Severely frigid
1685	…	…	Severely frigid
1686	…	Drought	…
1687	Rainy	…	Warm, rainy
1688	Dry	…	…
1689	…	…	…
1690	…	…	Very cold in Dec.
1691	…	…	Cold in Dec.–Jan., then warm
1692	…	Drought	Mixed weather
1693	…	Dry, hot	Mixed weather
1694	…	Mixed	Cold, great snowstorms
1695	…	…	Frigid
1696	Snowy	…	Frigid
1697	Very cold	Late frost, drought	Severely frigid, snowy[g]
1698	Wet	…	Mild
1699	…	Hot, wet, stormy	Freezing rain in Dec., then frigid until March

[a] Winter is dated from November of calendar year to March of next year.
[b] Hurricane in September ruined corn crop.
[c] In August.
[d] Followed by rainy, stormy fall.
[e] Very wet fall.
[f] Good for crops.
[g] Reputed to be century's coldest winter.
Source: Karen Ordahl Kupperman, "Climate and Mastery of the Wilderness in Seventeenth-Century New England," in Colonial Society of Massachusetts, ed., *Seventeenth-Century New England* (1984), 5–9, 21–25, 30–33. David M. Ludlum, *Early American Winters, 1604–1820* (1966), 1–60.

TABLE 1.2 CLASSIFICATION OF NORTHERN WINTERS, 1700–1763

Year	Weather
1763–64	severe
1762–63	average or mild
1761–62	severe
1760–61	severe
1759–60	average or mild
1758–59	average or mild
1757–58	average or mild
1756–57	severe
1755–56	very mild
1754–55	very mild

(continued)

TABLE 1.2 (continued)

Year	Weather
1753–54	very mild
1752–53	very mild
1751–52	severe
1750–51	average or mild
1749–50	average or mild
1748–49	average or mild
1747–48	very severe
1746–47	average or mild
1745–46	very mild
1744–45	very mild
1743–44	average or mild
1742–43	very mild
1741–42	average or mild
1740–41	very severe
1739–40	average or mild
1738–39	average or mild
1737–38	average or mild
1736–37	average or mild
1735–36	average or mild
1734–35	severe
1733–34	average or mild
1732–33	very severe
1731–32	average or mild
1730–31	average or mild
1729–30	average or mild
1728–29	average or mild
1727–28	severe
1726–27	severe
1725–26	severe
1724–25	average or mild

Year	Weather
1723–24	average or mild
1722–23	average or mild
1721–22	average or mild
1720–21	average or mild
1719–20	very severe
1718–19	average or mild
1717–18	average or mild
1716–17	average
1715–16	average or mild
1714–15	average or mild
1713–14	average or mild
1712–13	average or mild
1711–12	severe
1710–11	average or mild
1709–10	average or mild
1708–09	average or mild
1707–08	severe
1706–07	average or mild
1705–06	very severe
1704–05	very severe
1703–04	average or mild
1702–03	average or mild
1701–02	average or mild
1700–01	average or mild

Source: David M. Ludlum, *Early American Winters, 1604–1820* (1966), 39.

TABLE 1.3 AVERAGE ANNUAL TEMPERATURES ALONG ATLANTIC SEABOARD, 1738–1763

Year	Philadelphia, Pa.	Cambridge, Mass.	Nottingham, Md.	Williamsburg, Va.	Charles Town, S.C.
1763	53.4	44.7	...	...	...
1762	53.8	46.6	...	57.1	...
1761	54.7	46.0	...	59.3	...
1760	54.9	46.0	...	59.7	...
1759	53.8	45.8	...	...	64.7
1758	53.8	44.7	...	...	63.9
1757	55.2	...	58.0	...	65.3
1756	56.3	...	60.9	...	66.6
1755	53.6	45.3	59.0	...	62.2
1754	55.9	47.4	57.6	...	67.4
1753	55.2	46.7	...	...	66.4
1752	55.2	45.9	...	...	66.9
1751	55.0	46.1	...	...	66.3
1750	55.0	46.5	...	...	64.7
1749	53.6	46.2	...	...	...
1748	55.0	47.0	...	...	...
1747	55.6	46.8	...	...	...
1746	55.9	46.6	...	...	...
1745	54.9	...	...	...	...
1744	56.5	...	...	...	...
1743	55.0	...	...	...	...
1742	54.7	...	...	...	64.7
1741	...	...	...	...	...
1740	54.0	...	...	...	63.9
1739	54.7	...	...	...	64.8
1738	56.5	...	...	...	66.0

Note: Temperatures given in Fahrenheit. See Table 1.4 for averages during 1951–80.
Source: H. H. Lamb, *Climate: Present, Past, and Future, II, Climatic History and the Future* (London, 1977), 577. Helmut E. Landsberg, C. S. Yu, and Louise Huang, "Preliminary Reconstruction of a Long Time Series of Climatic Data for the Eastern United States," Technical Note BN–571, Institute for Fluid Dynamics and Applied Mathematics (Univ. of Md., Sep. 1968), 14–15. Charles A. Schott, *Tabulation of Resulting Mean Temperatures from Observations Extending Over a Series of Years, . . . for Stations in North America* (1876), 290.

TABLE 1.4   AVERAGE MONTHLY TEMPERATURES[a] ALONG ATLANTIC COAST, 1743–1777, COMPARED WITH AVERAGE MONTHLY TEMPERATURES IN 1951–1980

Month	Cambridge, Mass.[b]			Philadelphia, Pa.		
	1743–1759	1760–1773	1951–1980	1748–1749[c]	1758–1777	1951–1980
Jan.	29.5	28.0	29.6	33.5	32.1	31.2
Feb.	32.0	30.6	30.7	40.0	35.4	33.1
Mar.	37.5	34.8	38.4	50.0	40.4	41.8
Apr.	45.7	44.7	48.7	62.0	51.0	52.9
May	55.1	52.9	56.5	75.0	60.0	62.8
June	61.6	60.9	68.0	81.0	69.6	71.6
July	64.4	65.1	73.5	87.5	74.1	76.5
Aug.	61.6	63.5	71.9	85.0	73.0	75.3
Sep.	54.3	55.9	64.6	80.5	64.0	68.2
Oct.	45.5	46.9	54.8	64.0	54.6	56.5
Nov.	37.6	38.8	45.2	54.7	43.9	45.8
Dec.	29.9	31.2	33.2	49.5	34.7	35.5
Year	46.2	46.1	51.5	63.6	52.7	54.3

Month	Nottingham, Md.[d]		Williamsburg, Va.		Charles Town, S.C.	
	1753–1757	1951–1980	1760–1762	1951–1980	1760–1778	1951–1980
Jan.	42.8	32.7	35.6	38.4	49.3	47.9
Feb.	41.5	34.7	41.6	40.2	53.7	49.8
Mar.	49.2	43.3	46.3	47.9	58.4	56.7
Apr.	55.5	54.0	61.1	58.1	65.2	64.3
May	66.1	63.4	68.4	66.3	72.9	72.2
June	73.9	72.2	77.9	73.4	78.9	77.6
July	77.1	76.8	82.6	77.5	80.2	80.5
Aug.	76.2	75.6	80.0	76.7	79.5	80.0
Sep.	72.1	68.9	71.1	70.9	74.2	75.7
Oct.	57.2	56.9	56.5	59.8	65.3	65.8
Nov.	47.9	46.3	44.9	50.4	57.3	56.7
Dec.	46.0	36.5	38.5	41.6	51.3	50.0
Year	58.9	54.5	58.7	54.3	65.5	64.8

[a] Given in Fahrenheit.
[b] 1951–80 data from Boston.
[c] October 1748–September 1749.
[d] 1951–80 data from Baltimore.
Source: Charles A. Schott, *Tabulation of Resulting Mean Temperatures from Observations Extending Over a Series of Years, . . . for Stations in North America* (1876), 74–75, 76–77, 86–87. Helmut E. Landsberg, C. S. Yu, and Louise Huang, "Preliminary Reconstruction of a Long Time Series of Climatic Data for the Eastern United States," Technical Note BN–571, Institute for Fluid Dynamics and Applied Mathematics (Univ. of Md., Sep. 1968), 14–15. James A. Ruffner, ed., *Climates of the States* (1985 ed.), 506, 521, 957, 1162.

TABLE 1.5   COMPARISON OF AVERAGE SEASONAL TEMPERATURES (FAHRENHEIT) RECORDED ALONG ATLANTIC COAST FOR 1743–1777 AND 1951–1980

Period	Cambridge, Mass.[a]			Philadelphia, Pa.		
	1743–1759	1760–1773	1951–1980	1748[b]–1749	1758–1777	1951–1980
Spring	46.1	44.1	47.9	62.3	50.5	52.5
Summer	62.5	63.2	71.1	84.5	72.2	74.5
Autumn	45.8	47.2	54.9	66.4	54.2	56.8
Winter	30.5	29.9	31.2	41.0	34.1	33.3
Yearly	46.2	46.1	51.5	63.6	52.7	54.3

Period	Nottingham, Md.[c]		Williamsburg, Va.		Charles Town, S.C.	
	1753–1757	1951–1980	1760–1762	1951–1980	1738[d]–1761	1951–1980
Spring	56.9	53.6	58.6	57.4	65.5	64.4
Summer	75.7	74.9	80.2	75.9	79.5	79.4
Autumn	59.1	57.4	57.5	60.4	65.6	66.1
Winter	43.4	34.6	38.6	40.1	51.5	49.2
Yearly	58.9	55.1	58.7	58.4	65.5	64.8

[a] 1951–80 data from Boston.
[b] October 1748–September 1749.
[c] 1951–80 data from Baltimore.
[d] January 1738–October 1761.
Note: Seasonal divisions were as follows: Spring (March, April, May), Summer (June, July, August), Autumn (September, October, November), Winter (December, January, Feburary).
Source: Charles A. Schott, *Tabulation of Resulting Mean Temperatures from Observations Extending Over a Series of Years, . . . for Stations in North America* (1876), 74–75, 76–77, 86–87. Helmut E. Landsberg, C. S. Yu, and Louise Huang, "Preliminary Reconstruction of a Long Time Series of Climatic Data for the Eastern United States," Technical Note BN–571, Institute for Fluid Dynamics and Applied Mathematics (Univ. of Md., Sep. 1968), 14–15. James A. Ruffner, ed., *Climates of the States* (1985 ed.), 506, 521, 957, 1162.

TABLE 1.6 AVERAGE SEASONAL AND ANNUAL TEMPERATURES (FAHRENHEIT) AT PHILADELPHIA, PA., 1738–1763

Year	Winter[a]	Spring[b]	Summer[c]	Autumn[d]	Annual
1763	36.0	51.6	71.6	54.9	53.4
1762	33.4	51.0	74.3	54.1	53.8
1761	34.3	54.1	75.7	55.9	54.7
1760	36.0	53.2	74.8	55.9	54.9
1759	34.0	50.5	74.3	56.8	53.8
1758	36.2	51.3	73.2	56.5	53.8
1757	35.8	53.6	73.2	56.8	55.2
1756	38.8	53.6	73.4	56.8	56.3
1755	37.6	51.0	72.3	55.6	53.6
1754	39.4	54.0	73.2	57.4	55.9
1753	38.5	53.6	73.4	56.5	55.2
1752	34.9	54.1	73.6	57.0	55.2
1751	37.4	55.8	73.6	55.2	55.0
1750	34.5	54.7	73.8	55.8	55.0
1749	36.2	54.1	73.0	53.8	53.6
1748	35.1	54.3	74.1	56.5	55.0
1747	36.9	54.7	74.5	56.5	55.6
1746	36.5	54.9	76.5	57.6	55.9
1745	35.4	56.5	76.3	58.3	54.9
1744	35.4	55.2	73.6	55.9	56.5
1743	34.7	54.7	73.9	55.9	55.0
1742	…	54.7	75.2	54.9	54.7
1741	30.0	…	…	…	…
1740	36.0	53.6	74.5	54.9	54.0
1739	34.9	54.9	74.1	55.6	54.7
1738	…	56.8	75.2	55.9	56.5
Mean	35.7	53.9	74.0	56.0	54.9

Note: See Table 1.5 for modern comparison with 1951–80.
[a] December, January, February.
[b] March, April, May.
[c] June, July, August.
[d] September, October, November.
Source: H. H. Lamb, *Climate: Present, Past, and Future,* II, *Climatic History and the Future* (1977), 577.

TABLE 1.7 ANNUAL PRECIPITATION (INCHES) AT CHARLES TOWN, S.C., 1738–1759

1759	36.37
1758	30.62
1757	44.44
1756	31.69
1755	43.29
1754	37.22
1753	47.36
1752	42.88
1751	50.82
1750	56.16
1749	54.42
1748	51.60
1747	44.56
1746	39.65
1745	50.15
1744	48.32
1743	39.75
1742	36.01
1741	52.07
1740	39.81
1739	65.96
1738	49.27
Mean	45.11

Note: Data includes snow's equivalent in rainfall. During 1951–80, precipitation in this area averaged 51.59 inches annually.
Source: Charles A. Schott, *Tables and Results of the Precipitation in Rain and Snow, in the United States* (1872), 102.

TABLE 1.8 SEASONAL AND ANNUAL PRECIPITATION (INCHES) AT PHILADELPHIA, PA., 1738–1763

Year	Winter[a]	Spring[b]	Summer[c]	Autumn[d]	Annual
1763	8.31	9.88	12.28	9.21	40.51
1762	8.90	9.29	11.50	9.09	40.98
1761	8.70	9.88	11.89	9.29	42.09
1760	8.31	9.41	12.09	9.61	41.69
1759	8.70	9.69	14.13	9.80	41.42
1758	9.02	9.41	15.00	9.09	41.50
1757	8.90	10.20	12.09	9.02	41.52
1756	8.11	10.00	11.89	9.21	40.00
1755	8.82	10.39	12.20	9.21	40.98
1754	8.90	9.09	14.21	9.09	42.01
1753	8.70	10.31	13.58	10.12	42.40
1752	8.31	10.00	12.40	9.29	41.10
1751	9.69	10.00	15.39	9.29	43.11
1750	8.51	10.71	14.09	9.09	42.20
1749	9.21	11.50	12.91	9.21	42.80
1748	8.82	10.51	12.40	9.80	42.48
1747	9.09	10.31	11.69	9.80	41.61
1746	8.82	10.59	12.72	9.21	40.91
1745	9.80	10.91	13.50	9.21	42.28
1744	8.90	10.59	12.40	9.41	42.09
1743	8.82	10.79	11.69	9.41	40.98
1742	8.70	11.18	11.50	9.29	40.51
1741	9.21	11.18	12.09	9.61	42.48
1740	9.21	10.79	11.89	9.29	40.98
1739	9.02	11.10	14.61	9.61	44.29
1738	…	10.91	12.09	9.69	42.20
Mean	8.86	10.33	12.78	9.38	41.73

Note: Data includes snow's equivalent in rainfall. During 1951–80, precipitation in this area averaged 9.44 inches in winter, 10.51 inches in spring, 11.90 inches in summer, 9.57 inches in autumn, and 41.42 inches annually.
[a] December, January, February.
[b] March, April, May.
[c] June, July, August.
[d] September, October, November.
Source: H. H. Lamb, *Climate: Present, Past, and Future,* II, *Climatic History and the Future* (1977), 625, 626.

TABLE 1.9 COMPARISON OF MONTHLY PRECIPITATION (INCHES) AT CHARLES TOWN, S.C., AND WILLIAMSBURG, VA., IN EIGHTEENTH AND TWENTIETH CENTURIES

Period	Williamsburg, Va.		Charles Town, S.C.	
	1760–1762	1951–1980	1738–1761	1951–1980
Jan.	3.2	3.7	2.2	3.3
Feb.	2.0	3.5	2.9	3.4
Mar.	3.9	4.2	2.8	4.4
Apr.	3.7	3.0	1.8	2.6
May.	2.9	4.4	3.3	4.4
June	3.7	4.2	4.7	6.5
July	4.5	5.3	6.1	7.3
Aug.	9.1	4.7	7.2	6.5
Sep.	4.8	4.4	5.6	4.9
Oct.	3.6	3.6	3.1	2.9
Nov.	2.6	3.2	2.2	2.2
Dec.	2.9	3.4	3.1	3.1
Spring	10.5	11.6	8.0	11.4
Summer	17.4	14.1	18.0	20.4
Autumn	11.0	11.2	10.9	10.0
Winter	8.1	10.7	8.3	9.8
Year	47.0	47.6	45.1	51.6

Note: Data includes snow's equivalent in rainfall.
Source: Charles A. Schott, *Tables and Results of the Precipitation, in Rain and Snow, in the United States* (1872), 40–41. Thomas Jefferson, *Notes on the State of Virginia* (1955 ed.), 74.

Natural History

Environmental Change

Aside from climate, the most powerful factor influencing environmental change in North America has been human modification of the natural habitat. This process accelerated after Native Americans migrated throughout the continent, multiplied into sizable hunting bands, and developed more lethal weapons. By 9000 B.C., aboriginal peoples were becoming increasingly numerous in the Southwest and the Great Plains and had begun to make a significant impact on the animal life of those regions.

Hunting during this early period was primarily a collective activity rather than an individual pursuit. Groups of men armed only with spears found that their most vulnerable prey were large, lumbering mammals that moved awkwardly, such as mastodons, woolly mammoths, ground sloths, giant beaver, and giant bison. Such animals—often termed the Pleistocene megafauna—came under increasing attack by human predators as glaciers receded north rapidly after 10,000 B.C.

The Indians' growing social sophistication enabled them to organize big kills that were highly effective but terribly wasteful of animal resources. Hunters would panic entire herds with fire or another danger and drive them to their death over cliffs or into natural barriers where they would be slaughtered. These techniques placed great pressure on the large animals just as a new weather regime of dry, warm air reduced the plant life on which their survival depended. From 9000 to 5000 B.C., both factors contributed to the extinction of the Pleistocene megafauna, along with other species, such as the saber-toothed tiger and a breed of midget horses. This "Pleistocene overkill" was the first environmental disaster engineered by humans in North America.

As Native Americans acquired better weapons, particularly the bow and trapping snares, they abandoned collective hunts and became skilled at the solitary stalking of swift prey. Through close observation of the seasonal rhythms of different species, they learned how to take game at different times of year without disturbing critical cycles of reproduction and how to maximize their kills in winter when the animals faced the greatest danger of starvation. Such skills enabled the Indians to hunt without unduly disturbing the balance of nature, especially after they had lessened their reliance on wild game through farming.

As the Indians developed a complex economy based upon subsistence agriculture and seasonal hunting, they introduced a major transformation of the landscape. They established semipermanent village sites (ranging from 160 acres to a square mile) that could be occupied sequentially about every dozen years so that abandoned fields could regain their fertility. These clearings, opened up with either fire or crude stone axes, began the slow process of domesticating the North American wilderness.

Woodland tribes also made profound alterations in the forest cover. To ensure abundant supplies of game and to eliminate the difficulty of trailing animals through dense vegetation, the tribes regularly burned the forest undergrowth. Their fires replaced tangled brushes, tree seedlings, and other ground clutter with a better quality of forage grass, berry bushes, and nut trees to which deer, bears, buffalo, and turkeys flocked. Once thick vines, weeds, and shrubbery were eliminated, subsequent fires usually climaxed well below the leaf canopy and expired without destroying the large trees. Except along river or creek bottoms, where the moisture made it difficult to burn off tangled ground plants, the woodlands became open, unencumbered expanses that allowed in large amounts of light and facilitated travel by human and beast.

As the forests became thinner, it became possible to create large open meadows through repeated firings that denuded the ground of tree cover. Successive burnings left great expanses of succulent grasslands—of which the Shenandoah Valley was the most spectacular—that not only attracted deer, elk, moose, and buffalo but also enabled the herds to multiply in greater numbers by increasing their forage supply. Centuries of systematic firings created broad plains and savannas that teemed with game animals for nearby villages. This process gradually enticed the buffalo to expand their grazing territory from the Great Plains eastward over the Mississippi River, which they crossed into the Midwest about A.D. 1000; they migrated to the Carolinas by the 1400s and reached New York by the 1600s. By making the forests less dense and spawning vast expanses of grassland, the Indians created perhaps the greatest hunter's paradise ever seen on Earth.

At the time of European contact, the luxurience of North America's eastern forests was far beyond any natural setting known to Europeans. Even today, an ecological survey of a 400-acre stand of virgin forest in the Kentucky mountains, known as Lilly's Woods, revealed a variety of plant life approximately as rich as that of the Amazon Valley. Repeated burnings created an environment that was dominated by hardwood trees (principally oak, maple, hickory, yellow poplar, chestnut, birch, beech, and hemlock) that shed broad leaves each fall. The dead leaves formed a dense layer of mulch in various stages of decay that steadily enhanced the soil's fertility.

At the moment of European contact, the deciduous woodlands sustained a complex web of flora and fauna. Within a circle of just 10 square miles (26 square kilometers) would stand a quarter of a million trees that housed perhaps 15,000 squirrels. A hunter located at the center of this circle, whose diameter measures only 3.57 miles, would be within a radius of less than 2 miles of perhaps 5 bears, 3 wildcats or mountain lions, 3 wolves, 200 turkeys, and 400 deer. The number of insects, invertebrates, and anthropods visible to the naked eye numbered in the thousands of millions. Europeans found themselves overwhelmed

TABLE 1.10   PLANTS AND WILDLIFE IN 10 SQUARE MILES (26 KM²) OF DECIDUOUS, HARDWOOD FOREST IN EASTERN UNITED STATES, ABOUT 1600

Vegetation
750,000 trees[a] (3 in. + in diameter, 4 ft. high)
786,000 tree seedlings[b]
2,810,000 shrubs[c]
230–460 million herbaceous plants[d]

Wildlife
5 black bears
2–3 mountain lions
1–3 gray wolves
30 red foxes
2 elk
400 deer
10,000–20,000 squirrels
160,000–320,000 mice
200 turkeys
20–50 pairs of hawks, owls, and other predatory birds
7,680 pairs of small nesting birds[e]
8,960 million anthropods[f] in soil and ground litter
26,880 million insects, spiders, and other invertebrates

[a] Mainly oak, maple, basswood, hickory, walnut, chestnut.
[b] Mainly sugar maple, basswood, buckeye, ash.
[c] Mainly spicebush, pawpaw, strawberry bush, Virginia creeper.
[d] Including bloodroot, wild ginger, squirrel corn, violets, false Solomon's seal, jewelweed, nettle.
[e] They consume 386 million insects in a 60-day period.
[f] Including snails, millipedes, centipedes, earthworms, and larvae.
Source: Victor E. Shelford, *The Ecology of North America* (1963), 26–28.

Of the many environmental changes resulting from European colonization, the depletion of numerous animal species was one of the most important. Wolves and other predators declined especially rapidly. In this painting, artist Howard Pyle shows the consternation produced by the unexpected appearance of a wolf in a late seventeenth-century New England town where wolves had not been seen for a generation. (Howard Pyle Collection, courtesy Delaware Art Museum, Wilmington, Delaware)

by the New World's extraordinary richness. As Col. Henry Bouquet, a British army officer, enthusiastically wrote from Pennsylvania in 1758, "This continent teems with life."

The pace of ecological change accelerated after significant numbers of Europeans occupied the Atlantic seaboard during the seventeenth century. The Indians' forest clearings and extensive grasslands greatly eased the settlers' task of preparing fields for plowing and meadows. By some estimates, the Atlantic coastal region may have contained 30 to 40 acres of cleared ground or grassland per Indian in 1600, with such openings especially characteristic of sites near the ocean or along rivers. If so, there may have been 4,375 square miles of open land (more than half the size of modern Massachusetts) in New England below Maine, which then contained about 80,000 aboriginal peoples; 175,000 acres (273 square miles) of cleared ground possibly lay within an easy two-day trek of Jamestown at its founding in 1607 when Capt. John Smith estimated that 5,000 Virginia Indians lived within 60 miles.

What appeared to Europeans as a wilderness was actually a land already cleared for immediate occupancy at numerous strategic sites. White colonists selected such locations for their initial outposts whenever possible. As seaboard tribes became decimated by foreign diseases and found themselves with surplus lands, they sold their excess clearings to whites, who recognized them as valuable locations for plantations, milldams, and towns. In much of seventeenth-century New England and the Chesapeake, frontier expansion essentially entailed a process by which whites bought and then occupied barrens, meadows, cropfields, or other open ground abandoned by Indians. During the earliest decades of European colonization, surprisingly little deforestation resulted from the influx of English and Dutch, who preferred to purchase clearings from the Native Americans rather than carve fields from woodland.

The most immediate and drastic ecological consequence of the new European presence in North American resulted from the fur trade. The cold climate of New England and New York provided the best source of peltries, of which beaver was the most prized. By the 1640s, overtrapping had seriously depleted the beaver population everywhere below Maine along the New England coast and as far north in New York as Albany. By the 1670s, New England's sources of fur-bearing animals were nearing exhaustion, and the Iroquois of New York were seeking access to supplies of peltry in Illinois. So eagerly did Indians seek trade goods that they abandoned traditional restraints on overhunting and began to trap beaver to extinction as far west as Wisconsin. Sharp declines also occurred in the populations of animals that were valued for their skins: martens, otters, foxes, minks, and muskrats.

As the white population grew, it also disturbed the ecological balance of species by overhunting and severely decimating major game stocks, such as elk, moose, mountain lions, bears, and turkeys. Unfortunately typical of many white hunters was the Thomas Walker party that discovered Cumberland Gap in 1750; in just 130 days, its 6 men killed 4 wild geese, 8 elk, 13 buffalo, 20 deer, 53 bears, and 150 turkeys—"besides small game." To conserve its remaining deer, Massachusetts enacted its first closed season on them in 1694, again prohibited their hunting from 1718 to 1721, and began to appoint game wardens ("deer reeves") to preserve their numbers by the 1740s. By the mid-eighteenth century, not only had beaver and other fur-bearing animals virtually disappeared from the region east of the Appalachian Mountains, but wild game had also been drastically reduced, and sometimes eliminated, from most areas within 60 miles of the Atlantic coast.

The place of game and fur-bearing wildlife was taken by creatures from overseas. After most wild turkeys were killed off, the English brought over domesticated European turkeys, whose own breed originally came from Mexico. Gray rats, house mice, black flies, and cockroaches stowed away on ships and landed with the cargo. Europeans introduced chickens, goats, cattle, swine, sheep, horses, oxen, and honeybees. Because hogs, cows, and even horses were usually allowed to forage at large in both New England and the Chesapeake during the sixteenth century, they blended into the natural landscape, competed for food with the indigenous fauna, and sometimes fell prey to larger predators.

European draught animals permitted a far greater modification of the environment than had been characteristic of Indian agriculture. Whereas Indians had cultivated the soil lightly with hoes and sticks, horses and oxen enabled colonial plowmen to cut deeply into the earth. By eradicating all native plant species from cropland and substituting an alien habitat of domesticated cereals such as wheat, rye, oats, peas, or foreign clovers, European tillage accomplished perhaps the most thorough ecological transformation possible in early America. The natural habitat was modified similarly, if not so completely, by widespread cultivation of European garden vegetables—onions, carrots, parsnips, turnips, cabbage, various herbs—and the planting of foreign fruit trees—pear, cherry, plum, and various apple varieties.

The colonists' intensive agricultural practices also threatened the environment with long-term degradation. Unlike the Indians, who abandoned village sites for long periods so that fields could regain their full fertility, white settlers merely left fields fallow for short periods or rotated crops among them. Because deep plowing accelerated the loss of soil and nutrients, it eroded the land far more than the Indians' surface cultivation.

As more Indians sold lands, abandoned them in search of better hunting territories, or were pushed out in the aftermath of warfare with other Indians or with settlers, white colonists assumed control of vast tracts of woodland. Given that the English came from a country in which just one-eighth of its original forest still remained in 1600 and that the Dutch had completely deforested their homeland, it is clear that these settlers lacked any practical knowledge of how to maintain the pristine character of the eastern woodlands, even had they been so

inclined. The forests inevitably deteriorated after Europeans assumed their stewardship from Native Americans.

The earliest settlers found the woods majestically open and uncluttered, like royal game parks, due to the Indians' customs of firing the woods periodically. Once Indians sold or relinquished a territory, however, the underbrush resumed its growth and began the steady process of strangling the ground. The woods became less hospitable for herbivores like deer, which no longer congregated in such great number to keep the ground clear by eating the vegetation.

The increased density of the woods not only made travel and hunting more difficult but also magnified the danger of uncontrollable, accidental fires. Once the ground clutter reached a critical mass, fires set by lightning or human carelessness could readily become major combustions during the dry months of late autumn. A burning layer of thick ground clutter could easily achieve an intensity capable of reaching the leaf canopy and setting the largest trees aflame. This situation created the conditions for a growing incidence of devastating conflagrations known as black days because of the thick smoke that darkened the skies.

The first black day occurred in New England after a severe drought in the summer of 1697; in October, the dried underbrush suddenly ignited a blaze that simultaneously spread in several directions, lasted over a week, and burned hundreds of square miles. Another major fire left New England's air thick with smoke in 1716. In the summer of 1761, another enormous fire seared the earth eastward from New Hampshire to the vicinity of Casco Bay, Maine; this disaster caused such total destruction that it destroyed the local lumber-and-mast industry.

The cumulative result of forest fires, plowing new fields, and clearing new meadows was to cut back the ground cover, increase water runoff, and quicken the pace of soil erosion. As European settlement steadily decreased the extent of the deep-rooted native grasses and forest canopy, which facilitated the soil's ability to absorb a high quantity of water, a growing proportion of rainfall flowed into watercourses. This development occurred simultaneously with the flushing into streams of a rising amount of topsoil from cropland, roads, and

European occupation of the Atlantic seaboard dramatically changed the landscape. The terrain was denuded of tree cover in many thickly settled areas by the 1760s, such as in this countryside scene sketched near Wilmington, Delaware. (Courtesy Library of Congress)

TABLE 1.11

TABLE 1.11 WOODLAND CONSUMED TO PROVIDE FUEL IN UNITED STATES, 1700–1760

Decade	Cords Consumed for Heating Family Homes[a]	Cords Consumed for Iron Production[b]	Acres of Woodland Required[a]
1760–69	100,000,000	67,500,000	5,583,333
1750–59	74,000,000	54,000,000	4,266,666
1740–49	55,000,000	43,200,000	3,273,333
1730–39	41,000,000	34,600,000	2,520,000
1720–29	30,000,000	27,700,000	1,923,333
1710–19	22,000,000	…	733,333
1700–09	16,000,000	…	533,333
Totals	336,000,000	227,000,000	18,833,331

[a] Final estimate assumes that an acre could yield 30 cords.
[b] 300 bushels (225 cords of wood) yielded a ton of iron. Annual output averaged 30,000 tons in the 1760s. Earlier estimates assume a 25% rise in output per decade since the 1720s, when production began to increase rapidly.
Source: Extrapolated from Michael Williams, *Americans and Their Forests: A Historical Geography* (1989), 77–81, 104–109.

paths. This discharge progressively choked smaller waterways with silt or other sedimentation. Greater levels of siltation caused rivulets and small brooks in densely populated areas to fill up and disappear eventually. "Our runs dry up apace," wrote a Pennsylvanian in 1753, who added, "several which formerly wou'd turn a fulling Mill, are now scarce sufficient for The Use of a Farm." Larger creeks continued running but were unable to carry the same volume of water as before without overflowing their banks. This situation eventually created a new environmental hazard: flooding.

Floods afflicted New England, the most densely populated region of Anglo-America, as early as the 1680s. Damaging floods hit Massachusetts after heavy spring rains in 1683 and recurred in spring 1687. Summer rains swelled the rivers of Massachusetts and New Hampshire to dangerous levels in 1698, and violent storms produced the worst deluge yet endured by New Englanders that October. Because their settlements were dispersed over a larger area than New England, the Mid-Atlantic and southern colonies did not encounter flooding until later in the eighteenth century. (Virginia would suffer its first major innundation in May 1771.)

The most significant environmental development of the colonial era was the removal of tree cover from large areas along the Atlantic seaboard. This process proceeded slowly during the seventeenth century because the colonists often managed to settle in former Indian clearings that contained much open space for crops and livestock. Because most early farmers preferred to let livestock run wild in the woods rather than build barns, and because they fenced little more than their cropland and vegetable gardens, they needed relatively little wood to build their farmsteads: about 80 logs between 20 and 30 feet for their homes, plus shingles and floor.

Far more significant as a source of deforestation were the many industries that exploited lumber as an economic commodity. By 1680, New England fishers required 50,000 large and 250,000 small trees per year to dry their catches, and during the next decade they evidently burned 2,700,000 trees. At least fifty sawmills operated north of Boston by 1675, and their annual production might have reached 9,000,000 feet of boards. The thirteen colonies sent vast quantities of lumber to the West Indies; became a major exporter of tar, pitch, turpentine, and masts; and developed a large industry in wooden-ship construction. These enterprises resulted in large-scale forest destruction in New England, the Carolinas, and Georgia.

The greatest demands on woodland arose from the population's rising need for fuel. The average family burned perhaps 30 cords of wood, an amount equal to an acre of trees, because its open-air chimney was so inefficient that about 80% of all warmth generated was wasted; its total consumption can be appreciated if one imagines a stack of wood 4 feet high, 4 feet wide, and 300 feet long. As the colonies developed a large-scale iron industry after 1720, the rising number of furnaces and forges generated an enormous demand for charcoal, which required 750 acres of trees for every 100 tons of pig iron manufactured. By the 1760s, average annual production of 30,000 tons denuded approximately 225,000 acres every year.

Table 1.11 provides a conservative estimate of the amount of land deforested to provide firewood or charcoal during the colonial era. Total needs remained relatively small through the first century of colonization. During the earliest decades of settlement, forest regeneration offset most fuel usage because a clear-cut tract could produce wood suitable for fuel within eight years and trees suitable for boards within another ten. Larger, older settled communities by the seashore nevertheless experienced shortages of easily accessible firewood well before 1700. As early as 1638, fuel was reported in short supply near Boston, which had been built just eight years earlier in an area where Indians had cleared the forest to an extensive degree.

By 1745, when Benjamin Franklin noted that firewood, which had formerly been "at any man's door," had become a scarce commodity, most large population centers on the coast had to import wood from a considerable distance. New England farmers could no longer spare wood for their fences and had begun the laborious process of bounding their lands with stone. By the 1760s, demand for firewood had begun to reach an acute stage in the thirteen colonies. In that decade, colonial homes and ironworks cut enough firewood to cover the size of Massachusetts. During the entire period through 1769, the acreage needed to satisfy Anglo-American fuel consumption equaled an area slightly smaller than the modern states of Massachusetts, Connecticut, New Hampshire, and Vermont.

Natural Disasters

Because early Americans had to carry on their trade and other business with Europe in crude, small, wooden ships, the greatest cause of natural catastrophes was bad weather at sea. Colonial ships conducted a heavy trade with the West Indies, where the risk of hurricanes was highest. Losses in lives sometimes numbered in the hundreds, as when the British navy's HMS *Winchester* sank off Florida in 1695. Hurricanes also posed a threat to residents on the North American mainland after a significant population became established in South Carolina and Georgia.

Hurricanes devastated Charles Town, South Carolina, more than any other city. When raging winds tore through the city in 1713, they destroyed twenty-three ships anchored within the protection of its harbor. The great hurricane of 1752 wreaked more destruction than any other cataclysm of the colonial era; it slammed Charles Town with a huge tidal wave that crashed twelve ships on the docks, drowned ninety-five persons, and swept houses off their foundations with their terrified inhabitants still inside.

The Atlantic seaboard was a far more active earthquake zone in the colonial era than in the twentieth century. New England was the greatest center of ground tremors because of its proximity to the St. Lawrence valley, whose subterranean structure was highly unstable, but Anglo-Americans felt the earth shake as far south as Virginia. The two greatest colonial earthquakes occurred in 1727 when Newbury, Massachusetts, was the center of a disturbance that could be felt over 75,000 square miles, and in 1755 when violent shocks extended outward from Boston over an area of 300,000 square miles. During the 125 years from 1638 to 1763, an earthquake or major ground tremor occurred an average of once a decade in the thirteen colonies.

The environment also presented a number of less dramatic dangers that created a regular cycle of small tragedies. American winters were more intense than those of western Europe were, especially before 1700, and the most frigid of these took its toll in frozen travelers. Flooding grew into a serious menace by the late seventeenth century, especially because a large proportion of the population evidently never learned to swim.

Because thunderstorms occur four to five times more frequently in the Mid-Atlantic region than in western Europe, an immigrant's chance of being struck by lightning rose significantly after crossing the ocean. Colonial newspapers printed lurid stories of death by lightning bolts with an unsettling frequency. This danger stimulated Benjamin Franklin to develop the lightning rod, which he began to market in about 1749. So successful were the lightning rods in reducing the risk of being burned in a house set afire from the sky that a decade later, an English traveler in Virginia, Rev. Andrew Burnaby, wrote, "[N]o country has certainly proved the efficacy of electrical rods, than this."

TABLE 1.12   NATURAL DISASTERS IN EASTERN NORTH AMERICA, 1576–1763

Date	Event	Lives Lost
1576	A tempest sinks 1 ship in the Bahama Channel off Fla.	scores
Nov. 3, 1579	A tempest sinks 1 ship off the east coast of Fla.	scores
Sep. 9, 1589	Hurricane sinks 4 ships in the Bahama Channel off Fla.	scores
Jul. 27,1591	Violent sea storms sink at least 29 ships off the Fla. coast.	hundreds
Jan. 7, 1608	Fire destroys Jamestown, Va.	...
Sep. 6, 1622	Hurricane sinks at leat 9 ships off the Fla. Keys.	scores
Apr. 26, 1623	Sea storm sinks 2 ships in the Bahama Channel off Fla.	scores
1628	First major fire in New Amsterdam, N.Y.	...
Jun. 11, 1638	Earthquake centered in St. Lawrence valley is felt as far away as Conn. and R.I. At Plymouth, Mass., people clutch objects to avoid falling, and ships are swayed at sea.	...
Sep. 27, 1641	Hurricane sinks 5 ships 30° north of Fla.	scores
Jun. 11, 1643	Earthquake strongly shakes Newbury, Mass.	...
Jul. 5, 1643	A tornado strikes Essex Co., Mass.	1
1645	Gunpowder explosion destroys a third of Boston, Mass.	...
Apr. 14, 1658	Violent earthquake shakes New England.	...
Feb. 10, 1661	Violent earthquake centered in St. Lawrence valley is felt as far away as Roxbury, Mass.	...
Aug. 27, 1667	Hurricane off Jamestown, Va., produces 12-foot waves that destroy numerous buildings and livestock.	...
Sep. 7–8, 1675	Hurricane strikes New England.	...
Sep. 18, 1678	The *Griffin*, a French ship of 40 tons, sinks on its maiden voyage in a severe gale off Green Bay, Wisc.	31
Spring 1683	Damaging floods throughout New England.	...
Spring 1687	Floods throughout New England	...
Mar. 4, 1692	Violent wind-and-rain storm hits New Haven, Conn., followed by another a week later.	...
Sep. 1695	HMS *Winchester*, a 60-gun English naval ship, sinks off Key Largo, Fla.	400
Oct. 1697	Large forest fire burns for more than a week and darkens New England sky with smoke.	...
1697	Hurricane strikes the Atlantic coast of the English colonies.	scores
Oct. 1698	Worst flooding of seventeenth century strikes N. H.	...
1699	Violent sea storm strikes Charles Town, S.C.	scores

Date	Event	Lives Lost
Dec. 25, 1699	Violent earthquake shakes area of Chickasaw Bluffs (Memphis) on Mississippi River.	...
Sep. 3, 1700	Scottish frigate *Rising Sun* founders and sinks off Charles Town, S.C.	97
1704	Privateer *Castle del Rey* is wrecked off Sandy Hook, N.J., on voyage from New York.	132
Oct. 1706	Sea gale sinks 1 ship at St. Augustine, Fla.	...
Dec. 25, 1709	HMS *Solebay*, 32-gun British naval ship, founders off Boston, Mass.	43
Sep. 16–17, 1713	Hurricane sinks many ships at Charles Town, S.C., and causes great loss of buildings and life on N.C. coast.	70+
Jul. 30, 1715	Hurricane wrecks 11-ship Spanish flotilla off Florida coast.	1,000+
1716	Massive forest fires destroy large areas of New England.	...
Feb. 18, 1717	Blizzard strikes New England and results in numerous deaths by freezing.	scores
Sep. 12, 1722	Hurricane strikes New Orleans, La.	24
Aug. 12, 1724	Hurricane strikes mouth of the James River in Va. and sinks several ships.	scores
Nov. 9, 1727	Sharp earthquake is felt from the Kennebec to Delaware Rivers, with center at Newbury, Mass., where ground heaves, houses rattle violently, the flow of spring water alters, and chimneys and stone walls collapse.	...
Aug. 13–14, 1728	Hurricane strikes Ocracoke Inlet, N.C., and sinks 1 ship.	...
Sep. 14, 1728	Hurricane strikes Charles Town, S.C., and sinks 23 ships.	scores
Sep. 16, 1732	Sharp earthquake centered in St. Lawrence valley kills 7 persons at Montreal, damages houses at Piscataqua, N.H., produces tremors at Boston, and is reported as far south as Annapolis, Md.	...
Jul. 14, 1733	Hurricane strikes the Fla. Keys and sinks 17 ships.	scores
Feb. 17, 1737	Earthquake shock is reported at Boston.	...
Dec. 18, 1737	Earthquake shakes area from Boston, Mass., to New Castle, Del., and throws down chimneys in New York City.	...
1738	Immigrant ship *Princess Augusta* wrecks off Sandy Point of Block Island, R.I.	250
Jan. 1739	Unidentified German immigrant ship founders and sinks near Cape Henry, Va.	290
1739	British merchant ship *Adriatick* founders and sinks off Cape Hatteras, N.C.	100+
Jun. 24, 1741	Earthquake tremor is felt at Boston, Dedham, and Walpole, Mass.	...
Jun. 14, 1744	Sharp earthquake is felt from Falmouth, Me., to Boston, Mass., with reports of bricks being thrown from chimneys in Boston and stone walls shaking down in such towns as Ipswich and Newbury, Mass.	...
Oct. 7, 1749	Hurricane strikes Ocracoke Inlet, N.C., and sinks 11 ships.	scores
Oct. 8, 1749	Hurricane strikes Martha's Vineyard, Mass., and sinks 7 ships.	scores
Aug. 18, 1750	Hurricane strikes Cape Hatteras and Ocracoke Inlet, N.C., and sinks 5 ships.	scores
Aug. 18, 1750	Hurricane strikes Norfolk, Va., and sinks 14 ships.	scores
1751	Storms sink the ship *Greyhound* off the Chowan River, N.C.	...
Mar. 12, 1751	Violent sea gales strike New England.	scores
Sep. 15, 1752	Hurricane devastates Charles Town, S.C., and sinks 23 ships.	95

(continued)

Climate, Natural History, and Historical Geography   **11**

TABLE 1.12 (continued)

Date	Event	Lives Lost
Sep. 30, 1752	Hurricane strikes Charles Town, S.C., and sinks 12 ships.	...
Oct. 22, 1752	Hurricane sinks 12 ships in Gulf of Fla.	scores
Oct. 24, 1752	Violent sea storm with heavy waves hits New England.	scores
Nov. 18, 1755	Major earthquake centered at Cambridge, Mass., strikes New England and is felt as far away as Lake George, N.Y., Chesapeake Bay, Annapolis, Nova Scotia, and by a ship 200 mi. east of Cape Ann; it greatly damages buildings, kills many fish, and fissures the ground.	...
Nov. 22, 1755	A strong aftershock of the Nov. 18, 1755, earthquake is felt in New England.	...
Dec. 19, 1755	A strong aftershock of the Nov. 18, 1755, earthquake is felt in New England.	...
1756	St. Simon's Island, Ga., is flooded by ocean gale.	...
1757	*The Duke of Cumberland*, a British merchant ship, wrecks off Cape Henry, Va.	25
1758	Tropical cyclone strikes St. Mark's, Fla.	40
Apr. 24, 1758	Earthquake shock is felt for 30 seconds at Annapolis, Md., after subterranean noises and lesser tremors occur in Pa.	...
Mar. 20, 1760	Fire at Boston destroys 176 warehouses and makes 10% of families homeless.	...
Jun. 22, 1760	British slave ship *Racehorse* wrecks on Frying Pan Shoals on voyage to S.C.	100+
May 4, 1761	Hurricane sinks 5 ships near Charles Town, S.C.	...
Summer 1761	Enormous forest fire spreads from N.H. east to Casco Bay, Me., and devastates local logging industry.	...
1761	Flooding Monongahela and Allegheny rivers force evacuation of Pittsburgh and Ft. Pitt, Pa.	...
1762	Fires destroy large forested areas in southeast Me. and force lumber industry to relocate northward along coast.	...
1763	The *Pitt*, a British packet, founders in Delaware Bay.	100+

Source: Jay R. Nash, *Darkest Hours: A Narrative Encyclopedia of Worldwide Disasters from Ancient Times to the Present* (1976), 654–750. U.S. Coast and Geodetic Survey, *Earthquake History of the United States* (rev. ed., 1965), 11–16, 29. James Cornell, *Great International Disaster Book* (1982), 144, 145, 217. Helmut E. Landsberg and M.K. Douglas, "Fragmentary Accounts of Weather and Climate in the Americas (1000–1670 A.D.) and on Coastal Storms to 1825," Technical Note BN–1029, Institute for Physical Science & Technology, University of Maryland (Nov. 1984), 52–55. Stephen J. Pyne, *Fire in America: A Cultural History of Woodland and Rural Fire* (1982), 55, 56. Karen O. Kupperman, "Climate and Mastery of the Wilderness in Seventeenth-Century New England," in Colonial Society of New England, *Seventeenth-Century New England: A Conference Held by the Colonial Society of Massachusetts* (1984), 30–32.

Historical Geography

Exploration

Following Christopher Columbus's discovery in 1492 that the western Atlantic contained unknown lands populated by numerous peoples and seemingly valuable commodities, the exploration of North America proceeded far more slowly than that of South America. This lack of interest largely resulted from the disappointing reports of early navigators such as England's John Cabot and France's Giovanni da Verrazano who described the northern coast as sparsely inhabited and the aborigines as possessing few riches. Europeans primarily hoped to exploit the wealth of vulnerable native societies, but North America seemed to offer few prospects for plundering on the scale practiced by Spain in Mexico and Peru.

The great accomplishment of seventeenth-century European seafarers was to demonstrate that North America was a continuous landmass, rather than an extended archipelago. This fact proved to be a further deterrent to exploration because it revealed the continent as a barrier blocking merchants from an easy trade route to Asia. After 1570, the most ambitious voyages of discovery by England involved futile efforts to find a "Northwest Passage" around Canada to China and the Spice Islands.

Europeans were remarkably slow to appreciate the principal fact revealed by successive voyages along the North American shoreline: that because it contained a widely dispersed population of mutually antagonistic peoples, the continent was ideally suited for the establishment of large colonies of farmers, fishermen, and craftsworkers who were eager to escape the Old World's poverty and religious intolerance. Permanent English and Dutch settlements of this type—as opposed to military outposts like Spanish St. Augustine, Florida—took root quickly after 1600. Because so little prior exploration had been accomplished, however, the colonists often lacked the detailed geographical information necessary to avoid "starving times," ruinous economic setbacks, and other disasters after being founded. Having invested so scantily in exploration before 1600, England and the Netherlands doomed many of their earliest settlers to a harrowing existence as they tried to survive in a land that remained fundamentally unknown more than a century after its discovery. Most of what was learned about the North American mainland derived, in fact, from unheralded voyages by generations of obscure mariners who reconnoitered the fishing banks east of Newfoundland and by a few aristocrats like Sir Humphrey Gilbert and Sir Walter Raleigh who privately sponsored exploration.

The mapping of North America's interior advanced in fits and starts, depending on the curiosity of Spain, France, or England in uncovering its secrets. Beginning with the swashbuckling efforts of Pánfilo de Narváez, Hernando de Soto, and Francisco de Coronado to find cities of gold in the Southeast and Southwest, Spaniards pioneered the mapping of central North America. Spain nevertheless had approached the limits of its colonizing potential by the 1680s and thereafter made few discoveries beyond the Rio Grande valley and California.

France colonized the St. Lawrence River, the most accessible route to the American interior from the Atlantic coast, and so occupied the best position from which to explore the continent's interior. During the seventeenth century, French missionaries and coureurs de bois rapidly learned the major waterways and terrain features between the Mississippi River and the Appalachians. In the next century, they rambled across the trans-Mississippi plains and reached the easternmost ranges of the Rockies. During the seven decades from 1673 to 1743, a time when they were often distracted by wars with the English, the French accomplished one of history's greatest geographical challenges: mapping the basic outline of the Mississippi watershed, a drainage area covering 1,243,000 square miles.

Despite the enormous expansion of geographical knowledge provided by the French, the information acquired was far more notable for its breadth than its depth. The task of replacing the generalized, crude maps produced by the French with more detailed, accurate information increasingly fell to English discoverers in the late 1700s. Of all the major European powers to colonize North America, none had previously contributed less to exploring the continent than the English, whose expeditions of discovery covered relatively small areas in the area east of the Appalachians until 1750. In that year, Dr. Thomas Walker discovered Cumberland Gap, and Christopher Gist traversed Kentucky's bluegrass region after descending the Ohio River. Walker and Gist were the first of a growing number of Anglo-American woodsmen who would become the dominant force in exploring the wilderness from the Revolutionary era through the nineteenth century's conclusion.

TABLE 1.13 MAJOR EXPLORATIONS WITHIN PRESENT UNITED STATES BORDERS, 1497–1756

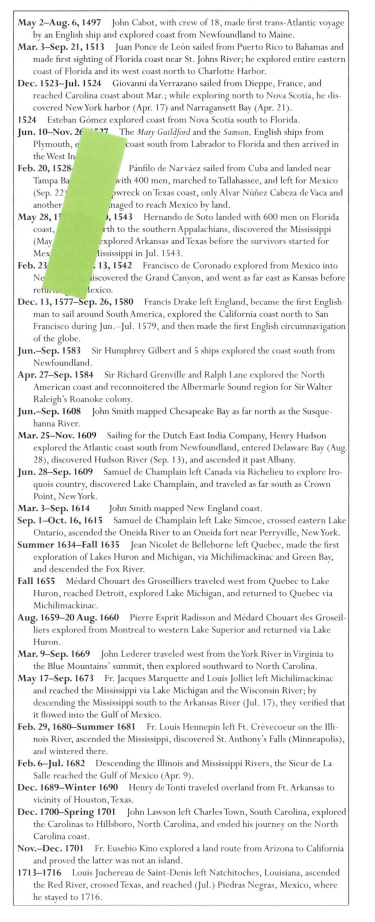

May 2–Aug. 6, 1497 John Cabot, with crew of 18, made first trans-Atlantic voyage by an English ship and explored coast from Newfoundland to Maine.

Mar. 3–Sep. 21, 1513 Juan Ponce de León sailed from Puerto Rico to Bahamas and made first sighting of Florida coast near St. Johns River; he explored entire eastern coast of Florida and its west coast north to Charlotte Harbor.

Dec. 1523–Jul. 1524 Giovanni da Verrazano sailed from Dieppe, France, and reached Carolina coast about Mar.; while exploring north to Nova Scotia, he discovered New York harbor (Apr. 17) and Narragansett Bay (Apr. 21).

1524 Esteban Gómez explored coast from Nova Scotia south to Florida.

Jun. 10–Nov. 26, 1527 The *Mary Guildford* and the *Samson*, English ships from Plymouth, explored coast south from Labrador to Florida and then arrived in the West Indies.

Feb. 20, 1528– Pánfilo de Narváez sailed from Cuba and landed near Tampa Bay with 400 men, marched to Tallahassee, and left for Mexico (Sep. 22); after shipwreck on Texas coast, only Alvar Núñez Cabeza de Vaca and another managed to reach Mexico by land.

May 28, 1539–1543 Hernando de Soto landed with 600 men on Florida coast, went north to the southern Appalachians, discovered the Mississippi (May); he explored Arkansas and Texas before the survivors started for Mexico down Mississippi in Jul. 1543.

Feb. 23, 1540–Oct. 13, 1542 Francisco de Coronado explored from Mexico into New Mexico, discovered the Grand Canyon, and went as far east as Kansas before returning to Mexico.

Dec. 13, 1577–Sep. 26, 1580 Francis Drake left England, became the first Englishman to sail around South America, explored the California coast north to San Francisco during Jun.–Jul. 1579, and then made the first English circumnavigation of the globe.

Jun.–Sep. 1583 Sir Humphrey Gilbert and 5 ships explored the coast south from Newfoundland.

Apr. 27–Sep. 1584 Sir Richard Grenville and Ralph Lane explored the North American coast and reconnoitered the Albermarle Sound region for Sir Walter Raleigh's Roanoke colony.

Jun.–Sep. 1608 John Smith mapped Chesapeake Bay as far north as the Susquehanna River.

Mar. 25–Nov. 1609 Sailing for the Dutch East India Company, Henry Hudson explored the Atlantic coast south from Newfoundland, entered Delaware Bay (Aug. 28), discovered Hudson River (Sep. 13), and ascended it past Albany.

Jun. 28–Sep. 1609 Samuel de Champlain left Canada via Richelieu to explore Iroquois country, discovered Lake Champlain, and traveled as far south as Crown Point, New York.

Mar. 3–Sep. 1614 John Smith mapped New England coast.

Sep. 1–Oct. 16, 1615 Samuel de Champlain left Lake Simcoe, crossed eastern Lake Ontario, ascended the Oneida River to an Oneida fort near Perryville, New York.

Summer 1634–Fall 1635 Jean Nicolet de Belleborne left Quebec, made the first exploration of Lakes Huron and Michigan, via Michilimackinac and Green Bay, and descended the Fox River.

Fall 1655 Médard Chouart des Groseilliers traveled west from Quebec to Lake Huron, reached Detroit, explored Lake Michigan, and returned to Quebec via Michilimackinac.

Aug. 1659–20 Aug. 1660 Pierre Esprit Radisson and Médard Chouart des Groseilliers explored from Montreal to western Lake Superior and returned via Lake Huron.

Mar. 9–Sep. 1669 John Lederer traveled west from the York River in Virginia to the Blue Mountains' summit, then explored southward to North Carolina.

May 17–Sep. 1673 Fr. Jacques Marquette and Louis Jolliet left Michilimackinac and reached the Mississippi via Lake Michigan and the Wisconsin River; by descending the Mississippi south to the Arkansas River (Jul. 17), they verified that it flowed into the Gulf of Mexico.

Feb. 29, 1680–Summer 1681 Fr. Louis Hennepin left Ft. Crèvecoeur on the Illinois River, ascended the Mississippi, discovered St. Anthony's Falls (Minneapolis), and wintered there.

Feb. 6–Jul. 1682 Descending the Illinois and Mississippi Rivers, the Sieur de La Salle reached the Gulf of Mexico (Apr. 9).

Dec. 1689–Winter 1690 Henry de Tonti traveled overland from Ft. Arkansas to vicinity of Houston, Texas.

Dec. 1700–Spring 1701 John Lawson left Charles Town, South Carolina, explored the Carolinas to Hillsboro, North Carolina, and ended his journey on the North Carolina coast.

Nov.–Dec. 1701 Fr. Eusebio Kino explored a land route from Arizona to California and proved the latter was not an island.

1713–1716 Louis Juchereau de Saint-Denis left Natchitoches, Louisiana, ascended the Red River, crossed Texas, and reached (Jul.) Piedras Negras, Mexico, where he stayed to 1716.

Sep. 22, 1738–Jan. 1739 Pierre Gaultier de Varennes, Sieur de La Vérendrye, left Ft. Maurepas (Lake Winnipeg) and explored North Dakota.

1739–Summer 1740 Pierre and Paul Mallet explored the Arkansas River west to Colorado, viewed the Rockies (Jun.), and reached Santa Fe (Jul. 22); they returned to Louisiana on May 1, 1740.

Apr. 29, 1742–Jun. 1743 Louis-Joseph Gaultier de La Vérendrye explored from Portage La Prairie, Manitoba, to northwest Wyoming, and returned via Pierre, South Dakota.

Mar. 6–Jul. 13, 1750 Dr. Thomas Walker, of the Loyal Land Company, discovered Cumberland Gap (Apr. 13), found the Cumberland River (Apr. 17), and proceeded as far as Barbourville, Kentucky.

Oct. 31, 1750–May 18, 1751 Christopher Gist, of the Ohio Land Company, left Cumberland, Maryland, descended the Ohio until just east of its falls, traversed central Kentucky, and walked to Yadkin Valley, North Carolina, via southwest Virginia.

Source: Richard B. Morris, ed., *Encyclopedia of American History* (1961), 19–24, 60–62.

Colonization and Regional Settlement Patterns

European settlement of North America east of the Mississippi River derived from five sources: fortifications and missions built in Florida and the Gulf of Mexico after 1565 by Spain, French fur-trading stations established in the St. Lawrence valley after 1608, communities of English farmers and fishermen planted in the Chesapeake after 1607 and New England after 1620, the Dutch West India Company's colony that expanded along Hudson River after 1614, and outposts of Swedish fur traders founded in the Delaware River valley after 1638. Aside from Florida's small Iberian population and a few thousand French Acadian exiles who became the progenitors of Louisiana's "Cajuns" after 1755, the French and Spanish contributed relatively little to peopling the eastern half of the United States. The French and Spanish nevertheless indirectly influenced the thirteen colonies' development by creating two military buffer zones that inhibited English expansion; Spain deterred English settlement south of Albemarle Sound until 1670 and then south of the Savannah River until 1733, while the French kept New Englanders closely bottled up along the coast north of the Merrimack River for most of the colonial era.

English settlement at first proceeded at a glacial pace. As late as 1624, the English numbered just 1,275 in Virginia and no more than 250 at Plymouth Harbor on Cape Cod. The decisive event that ultimately enabled the English to dominate North America was the Great Migration, which brought 25,000 Puritans to New England and 50,000 persons to the Chesapeake. Emigration from England's rivals remained at a trickle, as it would continue to do for much more than a century. By increasing the mainland's Anglo-Saxon population from under 5,000 in 1630 to more than 70,000 in 1660, this influx gave England the advantage of superiority in numbers over its imperial rivals, and it also bequeathed to the United States its founding stock.

Because England's earliest colonies on the Atlantic coast began as commercial outposts for trading companies, settlement sites were selected whenever possible at harbors that gave access to the interior via broad rivers. The first major geographical zone to be occupied was the southern tidewater, the coastal plain east of the first line of riffles that would block seagoing ships from further inland travel. The geography of the Chesapeake tidewater decisively influenced the manner in which the English used the land, expanded their frontiers, and dispersed themselves across Virginia, Maryland, and North Carolina in the seventeenth century.

Extending nearly 200 miles long and from 3 to 72 miles in width, Chesapeake Bay contained about 150 rivers and lesser watercourses—many of them navigable by seaworthy vessels for distances ranging up

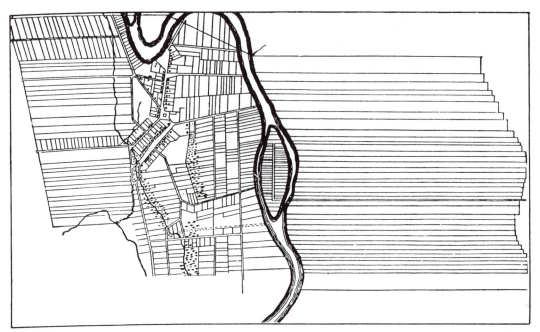

This map of land divisions in Wethersfield, Connecticut, shows how most first-generation New England towns allocated land to founding families. Grantees received not a single farmstead but a house lot (2 or 3 acres) in the town center, a small plot nearby for penning animals or raising corn for home consumption, and long strips of plowland in the outlying fields for growing wheat or some other grain with commercial value. (Frontispiece for Charles M. Andrews, *The River Towns of Connecticut* [1889])

to 100 miles. Its total shoreline stretched about 5,600 miles, of which nearly 2,000 miles was open to oceangoing ships. (By comparison, the entire remaining coast of the continental United States is almost 1,000 miles less than Chesapeake Bay.) The bay's extraordinary accessibility allowed the settlers to spread out widely in search of the best tracts of tobacco land, which generally lay in small plots of 3 to 10 acres along the bay's waterways and resulted in a landscape dotted with isolated plantations (a term initially used to describe any agricultural unit, not just those worked by indentured servants or slaves).

The easy availability of water transportation also eliminated the need to haul hogsheads of tobacco, which weighed a half-ton or more, overland long distances to market. Tobacco merchants could instead dispatch ship captains throughout the bay to buy hogsheads at wharves built by the larger planters on their property, where neighboring small planters would likewise deposit their own crops to be loaded for export. This maritime system of merchandizing tobacco inhibited the development of sizable towns in the tidewater for most of the colonial period. When significant towns later emerged in the Chesapeake, they appeared at or beyond the fall line that marked the beginning of the Piedmont, or the upland district where waterfalls or shallow water prevent seagoing vessels from further progress inland. Where ship captains could not sail up and load hogsheads at the planters' backdoors, towns grew at locations like Richmond, Virginia, at the James River falls; Fredericksburg, Virginia, where the Rappahannock became unnavigable; Petersburg, Virginia, the limit of inland travel along the Appomattox; and Baltimore, Maryland, where the Patapsco River narrowed. Even after these towns developed, the Chesapeake in particular and the southern colonies in general remained the most rural society in all of Anglo-America. The county served as the basic unit of local government rather than towns or villages, and most county seats remained mere hamlets containing little more than a courthouse, an Anglican church, a tavern, a country store, and a few homes.

New England's terrain provided little encouragement for the scattered pattern of settlement typical of the South except for Narragansett Bay, which resembled a miniature Chesapeake Bay and was

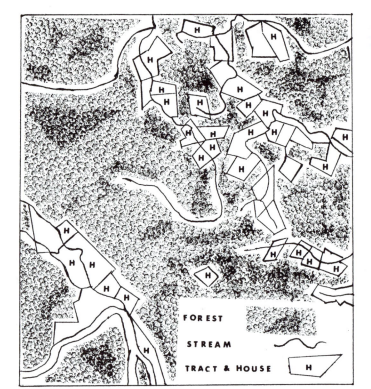

This map of a northwestern New Jersey community portrays the dispersed settlement patterns typical of settlement formation in the Mid-Atlantic hinterland. Rural communities consisted of collections of self-contained, irregularly shaped farms, often bordering one another, that were usually situated along a watercourse that would provide an adequate water supply. (Adapted from Robert D. Mitchell and Paul A. Graves, *North America: The Historical Geography of a Changing Continent* [1987], 128)

initially occupied in a similarly diffuse manner. Unlike the Chesapeake, New England contained few waterways with sufficient depth to carry oceangoing ships more than a few miles inland. This situation created a need for inland market towns to function as regional merchandizing centers linking the hinterland to numerous small harbors developed by fishermen on the Atlantic coast. The relatively cramped size of New England's coastal plain, wherein lay the most valuable tracts of flat and open land best suited for crops and meadows (then called champion land), likewise limited the degree to which Yankee farmers could spread themselves widely across the countryside before having to occupy areas with inferior soils and less desirable topography.

Aside from early Rhode Island and Plymouth Colony, both of which initially developed a landscape characterized by individual farmsteads scattered aross the countryside, the dominant style of land use in New England was settlement in tightly nucleated towns. New England's first and second generations replicated the basic structure of their mother country's agricultural villages. In accordance with a 1635 Massachusetts law requiring all houses to be built within a half-mile of the meetinghouse, families occupied small, adjacent house lots and owned one or more separate fields laid out in long strips beyond the town center. Rather than living on the land they farmed, the men walked out to their fields in the morning and returned nightly. The town, not the county, consequently emerged as the primary social institution in rural New England.

Such reconstituted English villages became increasingly awkward and inconvenient for succeeding generations of Yankee farmers. (The 1635 statute outlawing homes a half-mile beyond a town's center had to be rescinded as early as 1640.) Whereas most fields allocated to a town's founding families had lain within an easy walk of a half-mile from their home lots, later divisions of town lands distributed fields so far distant that a man might have to travel 3 or 4 miles from his home in the town center to work his outlying strips. This situation eventually led many farmers to exchange their various plots for a consolidated tract on the town's periphery and relocate their family on it. That process led to a significant dispersal of population away from the town centers by the late seventeenth century and the creation of a landscape

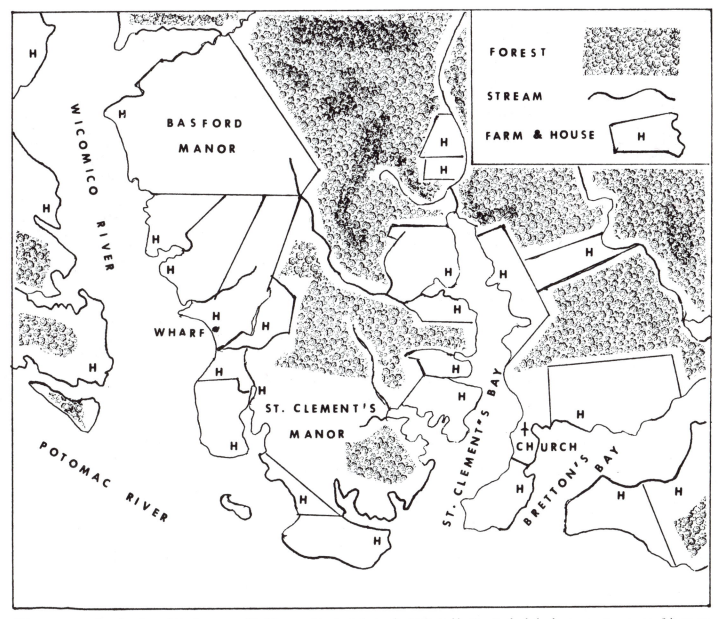

This map portrays farm locations within the manor of St. Clements, Maryland, during the 1660s. Unlike New England, the dominant pattern is one of dispersion into self-contained farmsteads along the two inlets of the Potomac River that form the manor's borders. (Adapted from Lois Green Carr, Russell R. Menard, and Lorena S. Walsh, *Robert Cole's World: Agriculture and Society in Early Maryland* [1991], 7)

divided among true family farms. By 1700, probably 80% of New Englanders lived outside the villages and port towns on their own farms, and they consequently lived a far more solitary, individualistic existence than had been typical of rural life in either old or New England. The town nevertheless remained a major social institution by serving as the focal point for local religious, political, and economic activity.

Colonization of the Mid-Atlantic region proceeded slowly in the seventeenth century under the Dutch and Swedes but accelerated rapidly after England conquered the area in 1664. The English established the township, an extended rural area usually about 25 to 30 miles square, as the basic unit of settlement. Unlike New England towns—which often included as much land—Mid-Atlantic townships did not evolve from a nucleated community but rather represented an agglomeration of numerous rural neighborhoods that grew up in scattered fashion along creeks or other sources of water. While the middle colonies' townships resembled the South's settlement patterns in their spatial dispersion, they nevertheless resembled the New England landscape by spawning numerous small merchandizing and distribution centers, usually at fords or important crossroads that economically connected the interior's rural population to the local metropolises of New York and Philadelphia. The Mid-Atlantic settlements consequently fused a highly decentralized type of agricultural community with a significant degree of urbanization as local market towns proliferated and prospered.

Expansion of Settled Area and Population Density

As of 1629, England's presence in North America consisted of two fragile toeholds separated by 600 miles of wilderness. Nine hundred Puritans clung to a series of small harbors dotting Massachusetts Bay from Plymouth to Salem, and 2,500 Virginians guarded a chain of small plantations stretching 40 miles up the James River beyond Jamestown. Virginia had nearly suffered extinction in a bloody massacre unleashed on Good Friday of 1624, and the desperately weak New Englanders could have been driven out by the local Algonquians at any time. It was from these tiny nuclei that successive waves of immigrants fanned out and eventually settled the entire Atlantic coast.

Within a mere two decades after 1630, Virginians founded eight counties in the tidewater and dotted Chesapeake Bay with tobacco plantations ranging from Norfolk to halfway up the Potomac River. During this period, population density in the Virginia tidewater multiplied almost 10 times, from 0.29 persons per square mile to 2.4. English Catholics had meanwhile not only founded the first communities north of the Potomac but also had pushed the line of settlement three-quarters up Chesapeake Bay to Annapolis. In the same period, Puritans founded fifty-nine towns near the New England coast from southern Maine to eastern Connecticut. Settlement was so rapid in the easternmost counties of modern Massachusetts that their population density was 4.5 English (almost one family) per square mile in 1650, or almost twice that of Virginia's tidewater.

English colonists had not yet entered North Carolina in 1650, but they thinly occupied almost half the shoreline from Norfolk, Virginia, to southern Maine. They numbered about 45,600, compared to 4,600 Dutch in New Netherland, 200 Swedes along the Delaware, less than 1,000 Spaniards in Florida, and just 675 French in all of Canada. By the mid-seventeenth century, the English had become the dominant European presence on the Atlantic coast; they were only outnumbered by the Indians, whose population still remained well in excess of 100,000 east of the Appalachians.

The quarter-century of 1651 to 1675 marked the high point of English expansion in the seventeenth century. Sixteen new counties were created in the Chesapeake, and forty-three new towns were founded in New England. Migration to North Carolina commenced in earnest around Albemarle Sound in the early 1650s, and settlement of South Carolina began near Charles Town in 1670. After England conquered New Netherland in 1664 during the Second Anglo–Dutch War, Yankees began to pour into East Jersey, and English Quakers founded West Jersey and Pennsylvania. Within the quarter-century preceding 1675, the Anglo-American population more than doubled to perhaps 110,000.

The English colonial frontier essentially stagnated—and in some areas actually contracted—for more than forty years after 1675 because of the disruption caused by King Philip's War in New England, Bacon's Rebellion in Virginia, the Yamasee and Tuscarora Wars in the Carolinas, and almost uninterrupted warfare against France and its

TABLE 1.14 FOUNDING OF COUNTIES, TOWNS, AND TOWNSHIPS, 1607–1762

Colonies/ States	1607–1650 New Towns[a]	1607–1650 New Counties[b]	1651–1675 New Towns	1651–1675 New Counties	1676–1700 New Towns	1676–1700 New Counties	1701–1725 New Towns	1701–1725 New Counties	1726–1750 New Towns	1726–1750 New Counties	1751–1762 New Towns	1751–1762 New Counties
Maine	...	...	5	1	...	...	4	...	2	...	7	2
New Hampshire	4	...	...	...	2	...	8	...	72	...	39	...
Massachusetts	30	3	20	1	9	5	29	...	35	1	32	1
Plymouth	9	...	5	...	8	...	...	...	...	...	...	...
Rhode Island	4	...	3	...	2	...	1	2	14	2	3	1
Connecticut	14	...	10	4	8	...	17	...	14	1	2	1
New York	4	...	13	...	8	10	4[c]	...	2[c]	...	4[c]	...
New Jersey	...	...	8	...	30	9	14[c]	1	21[c]	2	10[c]	2
Pennsylvania	...	...	...	...	...	3	...	...	...	2	...	3
Delaware	...	...	...	1	...	2	...	...	...	...	...	...
Maryland	2	2	...	8	...	1	...	1	...	2	...	...
Virginia	5	8	...	8	4	3	...	6	...	14	...	10
North Carolina	...	...	...	4	...	...	...	5	...	10	...	6
South Carolina	...	...	1	...	...	...	...	...	...	...	...	...
Georgia	...	...	...	...	...	...	...	...	3	...	...	...
Total	72	13	65	27	71	33	77	15	163	34	97	26

[a] Before 1626, six towns were founded in Virginia, New York, and Plymouth.
[b] The earliest counties were established in Virginia in 1634.
[c] Townships

Source: Joseph N. Kane, *The American Counties* (4th ed., 1983), 411–415. David Grayson Allen, "Both Englands," in Colonial Society of Massachusetts, *Seventeenth-Century New England* (1984), 79. Alice Eicholz, ed., *Ancestry's Redbook: American State, County, and Town Sources* (1989). John P. Snyder, *The Story of New Jersey's Civil Boundaries, 1606–1968* (1969). John H. French, *Historical and Statistical Gazeteer of New York State* (1860).

TABLE 1.15   POPULATION DENSITY (PER SQ. MI.) AND NUMBER OF ACRES PER FREE RURAL FAMILY IN BRITISH COLONIES, 1650–1760

Colony	1650 Pop. Dens.[a]	1650 Acres/ Family[b]	1700 Pop. Dens.[a]	1700 Acres/ Family[b]	1760 Pop. Dens.[a]	1760 Acres/ Family[b]
Maine	.03	118,783	.2	23,814	.6	5,555
Area of 8,129 sq. mi. settled by 1800	.1	31,153	.5	6,245	2.5	1,457
New Hampshire	.1	27,277	.5	7,158	4.3	882
Massachusetts	2.0	2,797[m]	7.1	620[m]	25.9	157[m]
Seacoast counties	4.5	1,241[m]	14.2	317[m]	43.8	95[m]
Interior counties[c]	...	...	1.5	2,600	11.6	321
Rhode Island	.7	5,316	5.6	724	43.1	126
Connecticut	.8	4,545	5.3	733	29.2	140
New York	.1	50,284[n]	.4	14,440[n]	2.5	1,715[n]
New York–Long Island	.8	11,400[n]	7.2	990[n]	28.1	249[n]
Hudson Valley[d]	.2	20,600	.5	8,662	5.2	772
New Jersey	.1	57,600	1.9	2,177	12.6	318
Pennsylvania	...	...	.4	13,772[o]	4.1	1,020[o]
Southeast counties[e]	...	...	8.2	669[o]	37.9	129[o]
Northeast counties[f] and Lancaster Plain	...	...	...	...	10.4	359
Southwest counties[g]	...	...	...	...	2.0	1,881
Delaware	.1	39,886	1.3	3,179	17.2	239
Maryland	.5	7,486	3.0	1,193	16.5	311
Tidewater[h]	.6	5,324	4.2	849	21.1	249
Piedmont[h]	...	...	...	...	5.2	804
Virginia[i]	.3	11,145	.9	4,843	5.3	1,231
Tidewater[h]	2.4	1,345	7.6	584	20.0	483
Piedmont[h]	...	...	...	...	8.2	680
Shenandoah Valley	...	...	...	...	3.9	1,036
Mountainous areas	...	...	...	...	.3	11,550
North Carolina	...	...	.2	15,167	2.7	2,277
Coastal Plain[h]	...	...	.5	6,536	3.3	1,791
Piedmont[h]	...	...	...	...	1.5	2,864
South Carolina	...	...	.2	48,325[p]	3.1	3,700[p]
Lowcountry[h]	...	...	.5	17,070[p]	6.9	3,498[p]
Upcountry[h]	...	...	...	...	1.0	3,820
Georgia	...	...	...	...	.2	33,444
Area settled by 1800[j]	...	...	...	...	.5	10,277
Thirteen Colonies						
Within modern boundaries[k]	.1	28,856,820[q]	.7	6,924[q]	4.3	1,111[q]
Within coastal districts[l]	.5	8,207[q]	2.3	1,969[q]	10.7	486[q]

[a] Persons per sq. mi.
[b] Acres per free, rural family.
[c] Worcester, Hampshire, Berkshire.
[d] 12,858 sq. mi.
[e] Boundaries of Bucks, Philadelphia, and Chester in 1775.
[f] Boundaries of Northampton, Berks, Lancaster, and York in 1775.
[g] Boundaries of Cumberland, Bedford, and Westmoreland in 1775.
[h] See Sutherland, cited below, pp. 202, 219–220.
[i] Boundaries as of 1800, including present West Virginia.
[j] 17,841 sq. mi.
[k] 366,166 sq.mi.
[l] 104,136 sq. mi., including southern Maine, all remaining New England, lower Hudson Valley, southeast-central Pennsylvania, New Jersey-Delaware, and southern tidewater regions.
[m] Minus Boston.
[n] Minus New York City.
[o] Minus Philadelphia.
[p] Minus Charles Town.
[q] See notes m–p on urban populations excluded.
Source: Stella H. Sutherland, *Population Distribution in Colonial America* (1936), xii, 34, 174, 175, 231, 240. Bureau of the Census, *A Century of Population Growth, 1790–1900* (1909), 54–56, 58–59. *Ibid., Historical Statistics of the United States: Colonial Times to 1957* (1960), 756. Herman R. Friis, "A Series of Population Maps of the Colonies and the United States, 1625–1790," *Geographical Review*, XXX (1940), 463–470. Evarts B. Greene and Virginia D. Harrington, *American Population Before the Federal Census of 1790* (1932), passim.

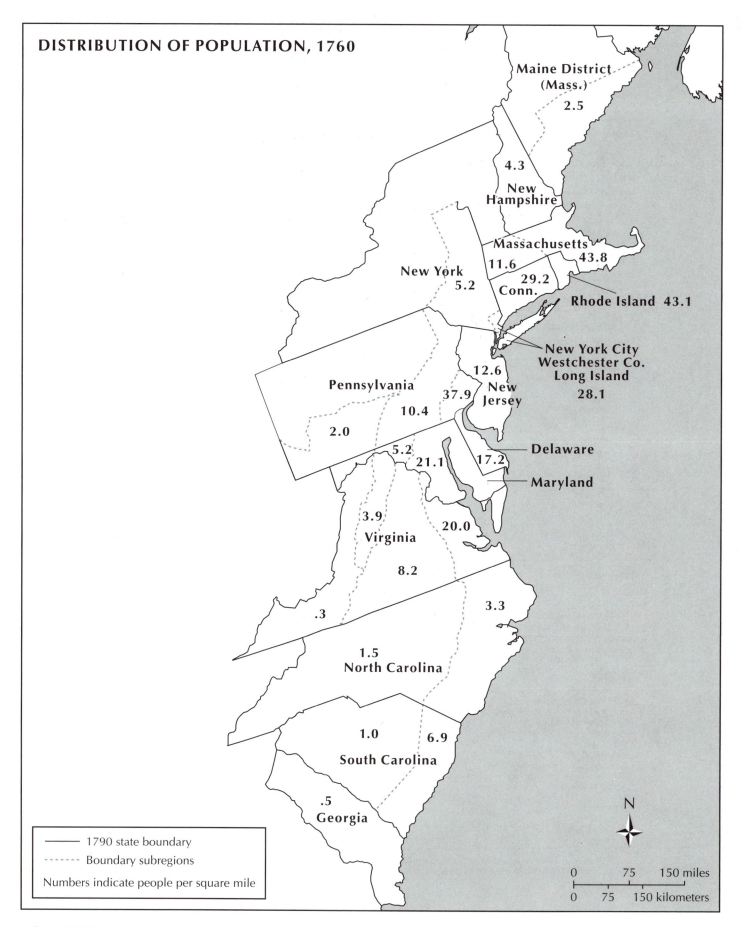

DISTRIBUTION OF POPULATION, 1760

Maine District (Mass.) 2.5

4.3 **New Hampshire**

Massachusetts 11.6

43.8

New York 5.2

29.2 **Conn.**

Rhode Island 43.1

New York City Westchester Co. Long Island 28.1

12.6 **New Jersey**

Pennsylvania 37.9

10.4

2.0

5.2

21.1

17.2 **Delaware**

Maryland

3.9 **Virginia**

20.0

8.2

.3

3.3

1.5 **North Carolina**

1.0 **South Carolina**

6.9

.5 **Georgia**

N

—— 1790 state boundary

- - - - Boundary subregions

Numbers indicate people per square mile

0   75   150 miles
0   75   150 kilometers

As late as 1760, few American colonists lived more than 75 miles from the coastline of the Atlantic Ocean or deepwater estuaries such as Chesapeake and Delaware Bays. During the next three decades, an enormous internal migration would redistribute the population away from the coastal districts and into the hinterland of the Appalachian Mountains. (Jeremy Eagle)

Indian allies from 1689 to 1713. During the four decades after 1675, the outermost limit of white settlement rarely stretched more than 50 miles from the coastline, except for two thin bands of settlement: one along the Hudson River to Albany and the other up the Connecticut River to Northampton, Massachusetts. The expansion of the thirteen colonies entered its final phase east of the Appalachians after 1720, when Anglo-Americans began to people the interior counties of New England, New York's Mohawk valley, Pennsylvania's Lancaster plain, the Chesapeake Piedmont, the Shenandoah Valley, the Carolina backcountry, and the thirteenth province of Georgia.

In 1748, Virginians planted the first English outpost west of the Appalachian crest at Draper's Meadows on the New River, at modern Blacksburg. It had taken 141 years after Jamestown's founding for Anglo-Americans to cross the summit of the Appalachians. By 1755, the outermost settlements reached 70 miles miles past Albany, 140 miles beyond Philadelphia, 220 miles west of Jamestown, and 55 miles upriver from Savannah. There they essentially remained until 1763, when Britain's victory in the Seven Years' War permitted the frontier to resume expanding.

The present area of the thirteen colonies in 1760 contained approximately 1,600,000 persons distributed (on average) at 4.3 individuals per square mile. The coastal districts held a far greater proportion of all inhabitants, however, and so averaged 10.7 persons (nearly two families) per square mile. Considering that improved farms in New England usually held from 40 to 80 acres and about 125 acres in southeastern Pennsylvania, the amount of land per free rural family—which then averaged 486 in counties along the Atlantic shore—remained theoretically greater than what each farm family needed to support itself. Although rural New England was very thickly settled, its population had risen to just 50% of the maximum level at which it would peak during the next century in Rhode Island, 38% in Massachusetts, and only 30% in Connecticut. Even in districts with high ratios of pop-

ulation density, it was rarely necessary for families to travel more than 80 miles (four to six days by wagon) to reach areas where land might be twice as accessible and far less expensive. After a century and a half of frontier expansion and rapid population growth, the thirteen colonies remained a highly rural society, with sufficient land to accommodate a population many times greater than its level at the colonial era's end.

TABLE 1.16   MEASUREMENTS OF LAND UTILIZATION BY COLONY, 1700–1750

Colony	Percent of Colony Settled[a], 1700	Percent of Colony Settled[a], 1750	Square Mileage of Modern State
New Hampshire	2%	10%	9,304
Massachusetts[b]	11%	38%	8,257
Rhode Island	9%	50%	1,214
Connecticut	7%	30%	5,009
New York	1%	3%	49,576
New Jersey	3%	13%	7,836
Pennsylvania	1%	4%	45,333
Maryland	5%	22%	10,577
Virginia[c]	4%	14%	40,815
North Carolina	1%	4%	52,712
South Carolina	1%	5%	31,055
Georgia	0%	1%	58,876

[a] Measured as a percent of the maximum number of persons living in rural areas when each state's nonurban population initially peaked.
[b] Does not include Maine.
[c] Does not include West Virginia.
Source: Lee J. Alston and Morton Owen Shapiro, "Inheritance Laws Across Colonies: Causes and Consequences," *Journal of Economic History,* XLIV (1984), 286.

CHAPTER 2 Native American Life

Origins and Cultural Development

Beginning perhaps as early as 50,000 B.C., migratory bands of scavengers traversed the Bering Strait across a frigid land bridge created during the last great ice age. The majority probably came from 28,000 to 12,000 B.C., when conditions were most favorable for tracking animals who drifted east from what is now Siberia to Alaska. Their descendants ultimately dispersed throughout the Americas to adapt themselves to a wide variety of ecological environments.

The earliest Native Americans organized their way of life around big-game hunting. They began to fashion more sophisticated tools and weapons to replace heavy choppers and crude projectile points about 10,000 B.C. During the two millennia after 7000 B.C., when they first began to forage natural plants and to experiment with seed germination, occupants of what is now the southwestern United States and northern Mexico successfully bred a hybrid of wild grass into corn. Corn became the Indians' agricultural staple and stimulated experimentation with other crops, particularly beans. Because corn and beans provide protein when eaten together, they were an excellent dietary alternative to meat and allowed their cultivators to form settled villages that were capable of supporting much larger populations than family-based hunting bands could.

Because Native Americans survived as members of small, isolated, kinship groups—without trade or other significant cross-cultural contacts—for unknown thousands of years after leaving Asia, a bewildering variety of mutually unintelligible languages proliferated among them. Within the eastern half of North America, for example, at least 128 different languages (divided among seven major linguistic stocks) existed when Europeans arrived in the Western Hemisphere. Scholars have been unable to establish any link between them and any languages spoken elsewhere in the world.

Cultural progress varied greatly among Indian groups. The most intricate societies and complex systems of economic exchange evolved within the area of modern Latin America, particularly along the Gulf of Mexico and South America's western coast. Native Americans achieved their first great cultural milestone, the acquisition of agricultural skills, about 7000 B.C., a date just 2,000 years after similar developments in the Middle East. From then on, the Indians increasingly lagged progress among other human societies. Farming seems not to have contributed more food than hunting or foraging among any Indians until 2000 B.C., whereas agriculture already provided the dominant means of subsistence 4,000 years earlier in Middle Eastern civilizations. The Near East possessed cities with more than 10,000 residents as early as 3000 B.C., but urban centers did not reach that size for another 4,000 years in the Western Hemisphere. Indians did not smelt their first metallic ore, bronze, until A.D. 1150 (in Peru), approximately 4,500 years after this skill was mastered by Semitic peoples, and they never learned how to make iron. Whereas hieroglyphs appeared in the eastern Mediterranean about 3000 B.C., followed by an alphabet about 1000 B.C., Indians did not start using hieroglyphs (in Latin America) until after the Christian era commenced, and none devised an alphabet in the precontact period. When the English colonized the North American coast in the early 1600s, they encountered Indians whose technology and social organization approximated the stage of civilization occupied by eastern Mediterranean peoples about 6000 B.C.

By at least 15,000 B.C., aboriginal peoples had migrated to the eastern half of North America, where their oldest campsite discovered so far has been excavated southeast of Pittsburgh, Pennsylvania. After millennia of subsisting primarily by hunting while they learned to exploit the area's natural resources, the Indians east of the Mississippi entered a lengthy period of sustained progress in agriculture, craftmanship, and social organization. The eastern Ohio River valley spawned the earliest such outburst of civilization when the Adena Culture emerged about 700 B.C.

Adena Culture flourished from 700 B.C. to A.D. 200 and was most characteristic of southwestern Ohio. It was the first Indian society east of the Mississippi to settle in sedentary towns, establish widespread trade networks, and construct large earthworks for burial sites. It coexisted with, and was succeeded by, the Hopewell Culture.

Hopewell Culture emerged about 300 B.C. and endured until A.D. 700; it was most highly developed in the eastern Ohio River valley. The Hopewell people differed from the Adena in four main respects: (1) their villages fed larger populations by more intense agriculture; (2) their trading network extended over a far greater territory (from the Great Lakes to the Gulf of Mexico); (3) their earthworks were built on a larger scale and with greater elaboration; and (4) their artifacts demonstrated higher levels of craftsmanship. The Hopewell civilization was supplanted by the Mississippian, or Mound Builders, Culture.

The Mound Builders flourished from A.D. 800 to 1400 in the Mississippi watershed and areas north of the Gulf of Mexico. At certain ceremonial centers, they constructed large urban communities around huge earthworks, burial complexes, and temple mounds. They developed an elaborate trading system that linked the Great Plains with Florida, and they supported a class of craftspeople who mastered the skill of conveying both realism and subtlety. The greatest expression of the Mound Builders' civilization was their city at Cahokia, Illinois, which extended 6 miles, contained eighty-five burial or religious mounds (including one temple that rose 100 feet off a base of 16 acres), and may have held up to 75,000 people.

Approximately one century before Christopher Columbus first came to the Western Hemisphere, the Mound Builders abandoned their communities for unknown reasons. A major factor that contributed to their demise was undoubtedly the onset of the climactic phase of the "Little Ice Age," which sharply reduced the Northern Hemisphere's growing season and undermined the viability of agricultural communities. The Little Ice Age also forced large numbers of desperate tribespeople who formerly occupied marginal farming areas beyond the Mississippi to drift eastward and invade the Mound Builders' homeland—in a migration similar to that of the German barbarians' onslaught on the Roman Empire—and consequently may have set in motion a spiral of cultural decline similar to the Dark Ages that followed the Roman Empire's disintegration. The central Ohio valley evidently experienced a steady decrease in population—through out-migration, increased mortality, or both—because many parts of this once densely inhabited area had become thinly occupied when the first French explorers arrived in the seventeenth century.

After 1400, the indigenous peoples underwent a slow cultural retrogression. Their struggle for subsistence and survival became so pressing because of adverse weather conditions that they could no longer spare the energy formerly devoted to improving their agricultural and artistic skills, developing complex urban societies with specialized occupational functions, and widening trade networks. The demise of the Mound Builders ended the most promising period of cultural progress in eastern North America and precluded the possibil-

The Great Serpent Mound, in Adams County, Ohio, is the largest serpent effigy earthwork in the United States. It stretches nearly a quarter-mile, shows a snake uncoiling to swallow an egg, and probably was constructed between the years A.D. 800 to 1200. (Courtesy Library of Congress)

ity that Indians along the Atlantic coast might have imitated their example by creating an equally sophisticated way of life before Europeans arrived.

Two major divisions of Indian life evolved within the eastern United States by 1600: the Northeast and Southeast cultural areas. The Northeast cultural area extended as far south as Albemarle Sound in the east and the Tennessee River in the west. Its inhabitants primarily spoke Algonquian and Iroquoian languages, and the further north they lived, the more heavily they depended on hunting rather than growing food for sustenance. The peoples of the Southeast cultural area primarily spoke Muskogean and Siouan, and they relied far more on agriculture than hunting. Indians of both areas were members of kinship groups defined by matrilineal descent, lived in villages that periodically shifted as fields lost their fertility, and organized their lives around seasonal patterns of farming, fishing, and hunting.

TABLE 2.1 INDIAN LANGUAGE GROUPS IN THE EASTERN UNITED STATES ABOUT 1600

Gulf Coasts and Tidal Swamps

Hokan-Coahuiltecan Group

Coahuiltecan

Coahuiltecan
Karankawa
Tonkawa

Muskogean Group

Timucua	Acuera
Mobile	Ais
Houma	Apalachee
Natchez	Calusa
Pascagoula	Chatot
Acolapissa	Mococo
Avoyel	Pensacola
Bayogoula	Seminole
Okelousa	Pohay
Quinipissa	Potano

Muskogean Group

Taensa	Tekesta
Tangipahoa	Tacobaga

Siouan–Yuki Group

Siouan

Biloxi

Tunican Group

Atakapa	Opelousa
Chawasha	Washa
Chitimacha	Koroa

Iroquois-Caddoan Group

Caddoan

Adai
Eyeish
Natchotoches Confederacy

Eastern Woodlands

Algonquian

Abnaki	Niantic	Delaware (Lenni Lenape)
Nauset	Massachuset	Mahican
Mohegan	Passamaquoddy	Nanticoke
Pocomtuc	Narranganset	Montauk
Nipmuc	Noquet	Pennacook
Ottawa	Penobscot	Potawatomi
Pequot	Wampanoag	Wappinger
Conoy		

Iroquoian

Erie	Mohawk	Susquehanna
Cayuga	Seneca	Oneida
Onondaga	Wenrohronon	Neutral
Wyandot (Huron)		Honniasont

Siouan

Mosopelea

Southeastern Woodlands

Muskogean

Chakchiuma	Tuskegee
Chickasaw	Apalachicola
Choctaw	Chiaha
Alabama	Guale
Creek Confederacy	Hitchiti
(Muskogee)	Cusabo

Tunican

Tunica
Yazoo

Iroquoian

Cherokee	Meherrin
Tuscarora	Nottaway

Algonquian

Shawnee
Chowanoc
Powhatan

Siouan

Catawba	Winyaw	Woccon
Congaree	Moneton	Yadkin
Peedee	Cape Fear Indians	Manahoac
Santee	Cheraw	Monacan
Sewee	Eno	Nahyssan
Sugaree	Keyauwee	Occaneechi
Waccamaw	Shakori	Saponi

Siouan

Wateree	Sissipahaw	Tutelo
Waxhaw		

Central Prairies and Woodlands

Algonquian

Illinois	Chippewa (Anishinabe)
Kickapoo	Sauk
Menominee	Mesquakie
Miami	

Siouan

Winnebago	Quapaw
Iowa	Osage
Missouri	

Muskogean

Kaskinampo

Source: John U. Terrell, *American Indian Almanac* (1971), 98, 152, 183, 231.

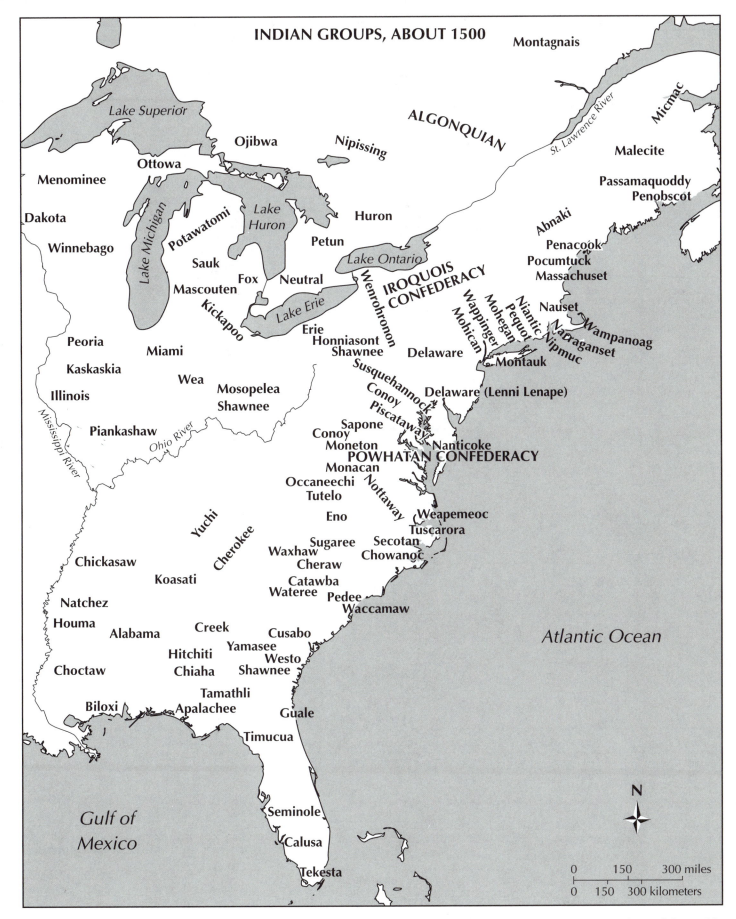

INDIAN GROUPS, ABOUT 1500

Montagnais

Lake Superior

ALGONQUIAN

St. Lawrence River

Micmac

Ojibwa

Nipissing

Malecite

Ottowa

Passamaquoddy
Penobscot

Menominee

Lake Michigan

Huron

Abnaki

Dakota

Lake Huron

Penacook
Pocumtuck
Massachuset

Winnebago

Potawatomi

Petun

Sauk

Lake Ontario

Nauset

Fox   Neutral

Niantic

Mascouten

Wenrohronon

IROQUOIS
CONFEDERACY

Wappinger
Mohegan
Pequot
Mohican
Nipmuc

Wampanoag

Kickapoo

Lake Erie

Narraganset

Peoria

Erie
Honniasont
Shawnee

Delaware

Montauk

Kaskaskia

Wea

Mosopelea

Susquehannock

Delaware (Lenni Lenape)

Illinois

Shawnee

Conoy
Piscataway

Sapone

Miami

Piankashaw

Ohio River

Conoy
Moneton

Nanticoke

Mississippi River

Monacan

POWHATAN CONFEDERACY

Occaneechi
Tutelo

Nottaway

Eno

Weapemeoc

Yuchi

Cherokee

Sugaree

Secotan

Tuscarora

Waxhaw
Cheraw

Chowanoc

Chickasaw

Koasati

Catawba
Wateree

Pedee

Natchez

Waccamaw

Houma

Creek

Atlantic Ocean

Alabama

Cusabo

Hitchiti
Chiaha

Yamasee
Westo
Shawnee

Choctaw

Tamathli

Biloxi   Apalachee

Guale

Timucua

N

Gulf of
Mexico

Seminole

0   150   300 miles

Calusa

0   150   300 kilometers

Tekesta

This map shows the most numerous Native American groups inhabiting the area east of the Mississippi. Most groups in the South spoke Muskogean dialects, while those in the North predominantly used Algonquian dialects. Iroquoian dialects were mostly concentrated along the St. Lawrence River and Lake Ontario. Sizable groups of Iroquoian and Siouan speakers could also be found in the Chesapeake and Carolinas. (Jeremy Eagle)

TABLE 2.2   LOCATION OF INDIAN NATIONS EAST OF MISSISSIPPI RIVER BEFORE 1600

Maine			
Nation	Linguistic Group	Locations	Tribal Subdivisions
Abnaki	Algonquian	Kennebec, Androscoggin, & Saco Rivers	Aroosaguntacook, Amaseconti, Ossipee, Missiassik, Pequawkek, Norridgewock, Sokoki, Rocameca, Wawenoc
Malecite	Algonquian	NE Maine	…
Passamaquoddy	Algonquian	Passamaquoddy Bay, St. Croix Riv., Schoodic Lakes	…
Pennacook	Algonquian	SW Maine	Accominta, Newickawanoc
Penobscot	Algonquian	Penobscot Riv. watershed	…

New Hampshire			
Nation	Linguistic Group	Locations	Tribal Subdivisions
Abnaki	Algonquian	Grafton Co.	Ossipee, Pequawkek
Pennacook	Algonquian	central & S N.H.	Amoskeag, Coosuc, Newichawanoc, Souhegan, Piscataqua, Squamscot, Winnecowet, Winnepesaukee

Vermont			
Nation	Linguistic Group	Locations	Tribal Subdivisions
Abnaki	Algonquian	Missisquoi Riv.	Missiassik
Mahican	Algonquian	SW & W Vt.	…
Pennacook	Algonquian	bordering N.H.	…
Pocumtuck	Algonquian	bordering Mass.	…

Massachusetts			
Nation	Linguistic Group	Locations	Tribal Subdivisions
Mahican	Algonquian	Housatonic Riv.	…
Massachuset	Algonquian	Massachusetts Bay (Salem to Brockton)	Cato, Chickataubut, Cutshamakin, Nahaton, Manatahqua, Nanepashmet
Nausett	Algonquian	Cape Cod	Iyanough, Nauset, Manomoy, Wiananno (or Hyannis)
Nipmuc	Algonquian	S Worcester Co.	Acoomemeck, Chabanakongkomun, Chachaubunkkakowok, Hassanamesit, Magunkaquog, Manchaug, Medfield, Menemesseg, Metewemesick, Missognonnog, Muskataquid, Nashobah, Nichewaug, Okommakamesit, Pekachoog, Quabaug, Tatumasket, Wacuntug, Wenimesset
Pennacook	Algonquian	NW Mass.	Agawam, Nashua, Naumkeag, Pentucket, Wachuset, Wamesit, Weshacum
Pocumtuck	Algonquian	Franklin, Hampshire, & Hampden Counties	Agawam, Mayawaug, Nonotuc, Pocumtuck, Squawkeag
Wampanoag	Algonquian	Plymouth, Bristol, & Dukes Counties	Annawon, Corbitant, Coneconam, Mankutquet, Nohtooksaet, Piowant, Pahkepunnasso, Totoson, Tewanticut, Tispaquin, Tyasks, Weetamoe

Rhode Island			
Nation	Linguistic Group	Locations	Tribal Subdivisions
Narraganset	Algonquian	W of Narraganset Bay	…
Niantic, Eastern	Algonquian	W of Narraganset Bay	…
Nipmuc	Algonquian	W of Blackstone Riv.	Coweset
Pequot	Algonquian	bordering Conn.	…
Wampanoag	Algonquian	E of Narraganset Bay	…

Connecticut			
Nation	Linguistic Group	Locations	Tribal Subdivisions
Mahican	Algonquian	Housatonic Riv.	Wawyachtonoc
Mohegan	Algonquian	upper Thames Riv.	…
Niantic, Western	Algonquian	seacoast from Niantic Bay to Connecticut Riv.	…
Nipmuc	Algonquian	Quinebaug Riv. watershed	Attawaugan, Manexit, Mashapaug, Quadic, Quantisset, Quinebaug, Quintusset, Wabaquasset
Pequot	Algonquian	coast from Niantic Riv. to R.I.	…
Wappinger	Algonquian	W of Connecticut Riv. to N.Y.	Hammonasset, Kitchawank, Massaco, Menunkatuck, Podunk, Paugusset, Poquonock, Quinnipiac, Sicaog, Siwanoy, Tankiteke, Tunxis, Wangunk

New York			
Nation	Linguistic Group	Locations	Tribal Subdivisions
Delaware	Algonquian	bordering N.J.	Munsee, Unami
Erie	Iroquoian	Chatauqua & Cattaragus Counties	…
Iroquois	Iroquoian	Mohawk Valley & Finger Lakes	Cayuga, Mohawk, Oneida, Onondaga, Seneca

Nation	Linguistic Group	Locations	Tribal Subdivisions
Mahican	Algonquian	Hudson Riv. watershed from Catskills to Lake Champlain	Mahican, Mechkentowoon, Wawyachtonoc, Wiekagjoc
Montauk	Algonquian	E & central Long Island	Corchaug, Manhasset, Massapequa, Merric, Matinecock, Montauk, Nesaquake, Patchogue, Rockaway, Secatogue, Setauket, Shinnecock
Neutrals	Iroquoian	W N.Y.	Ongniaahra, Ounontisaston
Wappinger	Algonquian	E bank of Hudson N to Poughkeepsie	Kitchawank, Siwanoy, Sintsink, Nochpeem, Wappinger, Wecquaesgeek
Wenrohronon	Iroquoian	Allegany Co.	…

New Jersey

Nation	Linguistic Group	Locations	Tribal Subdivisions
Delaware	Algonquian	all of N.J.	Munsee, Unami, Unalatchtigo

Pennsylvania

Nation	Linguistic Group	Locations	Tribal Subdivisions
Delaware	Algonquian	Delaware Riv. watershed	Munsee, Unami, Unalatchtigo
Erie	Iroquoian	upper Ohio Valley	…
Honniasont	Iroquoian	upper Ohio Riv.	…
Iroquois	Iroquoian	Allegheny Riv.	Seneca
Shawnee	Algonquian	W Pa.	…
Susquehanna	Iroquoian	Susquehanna Riv.	…
Wenrohronon	Iroquoian	bordering N.Y.	…

Delaware

Nation	Linguistic Group	Locations	Tribal Subdivisions
Delaware	Algonquian	N Del.	Munsee, Unami, Unalatchtigo
Nanticoke	Algonquian	S Del.	Cuscarawaoc, Nanticoke

Maryland

Nation	Linguistic Group	Locations	Tribal Subdivisions
Conoy	Algonquian	western shore	Acquintanacsuak, Conoy, Mattapanient, Moyawance, Nacatchtank, Pamacocack, Patuxent, Potapaco, Secowocomoco
Erie	Iroquoian	upper Potomac	…
Delaware	Iroquoian	bordering Pa.	
Nanticoke	Iroquoian	eastern shore	Annamessicks, Choptank, Cuscarawaoc, Manokin, Nanticoke, Nause, Ozinies, Tocwogh, Wicocomoco, Wicomese
Piscataway	Iroquoian	western shore	
Powhatan	Iroquoian	Worcester Co.	Accohanoc
Susquehanna	Iroquoian	Susquennah Riv.	…

Virginia and West Virginia

Nation	Linguistic Group	Locations	Tribal Subdivisions
Cherokee	Iroquoian	SW Va.	…
Conoy	Algonquian	Kanawha Riv.	…
Manahoac	Siouan	Rappahannock watershed	Hassinunga, Manahoac, Ontponea, Shackaconia, Stegaraki, Tanxnitania, Tegninateo, Whonkentia
Meherrin	Iroquoian	Meherrin Riv.	…
Monacan	Siouan	upper James Riv.	…
Moneton	Siouan	lower Kanawha Riv.	…
Nahyssan[a]	Siouan	Appomattox Riv.	…
Nottaway	Iroquoian	Nottaway Riv.	…
Occaneechi	Siouan	Roanoke & Dan Rivers	…
Powhatan	Algonquian	lower tidewater	Accohanoc, Accomac, Appomattoc, Arrohattoc, Chesapeake, Chickahominy, Chiskiac, Cuttatawomen, Kecoughtan, Mattapony, Moraughtacund, Mummapacune, Nansemond, Nantaughtacund, Onawmanient, Pamunkey, Paspahegh, Pataunck, Piankatank, Pissasec, Potomac, Powhatan, Rappahannock, Secacawoni, Tauxenent, Warrasqueoc, Weanoc, Werowocomoco, Wicocomoco, Youghtanund
Tutelo	Siouan	upper Roanoke Riv.	…

North Carolina

Nation	Linguistic Group	Locations	Tribal Subdivisions
Bear River	Algonquian	Pamlico Sound	…
Cape Fear	Siouan?	Cape Fear	…

(continued)

TABLE 2.2   (continued)

North Carolina

Nation	Linguistic Group	Locations	Tribal Subdivisions
Catawba	Siouan	Catawba Riv.	...
Cherokee	Iroquoian	mountains	...
Chowanoc	Algonquian	Chowan Riv.	...
Coree (Coranine)	Algonquian	Craven & Careret Counties	...
Eno	Siouan	Orange & Durham Counties	...
Hatteras	Algonquian	Cape Hatteras	...
Keyauwee	Siouan	Deep & Haw Rivers	...
Machapunga	Algonquian	Pamlico & Albemarle Sounds	...
Meherrin	Iroquoian	Roanoke Riv.	...
Moratok	Algonquian	Roanoke Riv.	...
Neusiok	Algonquian	lower Neuse Riv.	...
Occaneechi	Siouan	Roanoke & Haw Rivers	...
Pamlico	Algonquian	Pamlico Riv.	...
Shakori	Siouan	upper Roanoke Riv.	...
Sissipahaw	Siouan	Haw Riv.	...
Sugeree	Siouan	Mecklenburg Co.	...
Tuscarora	Iroquoian	Roanoke, Pamlico, Tar, & Neuse Counties	Katenuaka, Akawantca, Skarure
Wateree	Siouan	upper Yadkin Riv.	...
Waxhaw	Siouan	Union & Mecklenburg Counties	...
Weapemoc	Algonquian	Albemarle Sound	Pasquotank, Poteskeet, Perquiman, Yeopim
Woccon	Siouan	Wayne Co.	...
Yadkin	Siouan	Yadkin Riv.	...

South Carolina

Nation	Linguistic Group	Locations	Tribal Subdivisions
Catawba	Siouan	Catawba Riv.	Catawba, Iswa
Cheraw	Siouan	head of Saluda Riv.	...
Cherokee	Iroquoian	mountains	...
Congaree	Siouan	Congaree Riv.	...
Creek	Muskogean	Savannah Riv.	...
Cusabo	Muskogean	N of Savannah Riv.	Cusabo, Coosa, Etiwaw, Wando, Kiawa, Stono, Edisto, Ashepoo, Combahee, Wimbee, Escamacu
Pedee	Siouan	Great Pedee Riv.	...
Saluda[b]	Algonquian?	Saluda Riv.	...
Santee	Siouan	Santee Riv.	...
Sewee	Siouan	between Santee & Ashley Rivers	...
Shawnee	Algonquian	Savannah Riv.	Hathawekela
Sugeree	Siouan	York Co.	...
Waccamaw	Siouan	Waccamaw & Lower Pedee Rivers	...
Wateree	Siouan	Wateree Riv.	...
Waxhaw	Siouan	Lancaster Co.	...
Winyaw	Siouan	Winyaw Bay, Black & Lower Pedee Rivers	...
Yamasee[c]	Muskogean	Savannah Riv.	...

Georgia

Nation	Linguistic group	Locations	Tribal Subdivisions
Apalachicola	Muskogean	Chattahoochee & Flint Rivers	...
Cherokee	Iroquoian	mountains	...
Chiaha	Muskogean	Atlantic coast	...
Creek	Muskogean	coast & interior	Osochi, Sawokli, Tamathli
Guale	Muskogean	N of St. Andrews Sound	...
Hitchiti	Muskogean	Ocmulgee and lower Chattahoochee Rivers	...
Oconee	Muskogean	Oconee Riv.	...
Okmulgee	Muskogean	Ocmulgee & upper Chattahoochee Rivers	...
Shawnee	Algonquian	Savannah Riv.	Hathawekela
Yamasee	Muskogean	Ocmulgee Riv.	Upper & lower towns

Florida

Nation	Linguistic Groups	Locations	Tribal Subdivisions
Acuera	Muskogean	upper Ocklawatha Riv.	...
Ais	Muskogean	Indian Riv.	...
Apalachee	Muskogean	Tallahassee	...
Calusa	Muskogean	W coast of Fla. peninsula	...
Chatot	Muskogean	W of Apalachicola Riv.	...
Chine	Muskogean	mouth of Apalachee Riv.	...
Creek	Muskogean	bordering Ga. & Ala.	...
Freshwater	Muskogean	E Fla. from St. Augustine to Cape Canaveral	...
Guacata	Muskogean	St. Lucie Riv.	...

Nation	Linguistic Groups	Locations	Tribal Subdivisions
Guale	Muskogean	S of Ga. on coast	Northern, central, & southern Guale
Hichiti	Muskogean	N Fla.	...
Icafui	Muskogean	N Fla.	...
Jeaga	Muskogean	Juniper Inlet, SE Fla.	...
Mikasuki	Muskogean	Miccosukee Lake, Jefferson Co.	...
Mococo	Muskogean	Hillsboro Bay	...
Ocale	Muskogean	N of Withlacoochee Riv.	...
Osochi	Muskogean	Apalachicola Riv.	...
Pawokti	Muskogean	W of Choctawhatchee Riv.	...
Pensacola	Muskogean	Pensacola Bay	...
Pohoy	Muskogean	S shore of Tampa Bay	...
Potano	Muskogean	Alachua Co.	...
Saturiwa	Muskogean	mouth of St. Johns Riv.	...
Sawokoli	Muskogean	N Fla.	...
Surroque	Muskogean	Cape Canaveral	...
Tacatacura	Muskogean	Cumberland Island	...
Tekesta	Muskogean	Miami	...
Timucua	Timucuan	from St. Johns Riv. to Suwanee Sound	Onatheaqua, Hostaqua
Tocobaga	Muskogean	Old Tampa Bay	...
Utina (see Timucua)			
Yui	Muskogean	St. Mary's Riv.	...
Yustaga	Muskogean	from Aucilla to Suwannee Rivers	...

Alabama

Nation	Linguistic Group	Location	Tribal Subdivisions
Alabama	Muskogean	upper Alabama Riv.	Alabama, Pawokti, Tawasa
Apalachee	Muskogean	bordering Fla.	...
Apalachicola	Muskogean	bordering Fla.	...
Chickasaw	Muskogean	NW Ala.	...
Choctaw	Muskogean	SW Ala.	...
Creek	Muskogean	Coosa, Tallapoosa, & Chattahoochee Rivers	Abihka, Atasi, Coosa, Coweta, Eufala, Fushatchee, Hilibi, Holiwahali, Kanhatki, Kasihta, Kealedji, Kolomi, Okchai, Okmulgee, Pakana, Pilthlako, Tukabahchee, Wakokai, Wiwohka
Hitchita	Muskogean	bordering Ga.	...
Koasati	Muskogean	upper Alabama Riv.	...
Mobile	Muskogean	W of Mobile Bay	...
Muklasa	Muskogean	Montgomery Co.	...
Muskogee (see Creek)			
Napochi	Muskogean	Black Warrior Riv.	...
Sawokli	Muskogean	Chattahoochee Riv.	...
Tawasa	Muskogean	upper Alabama Riv.	...
Tohome	Muskogean	lower Tombigbee Riv.	Big & Little (Naniaba) Tohome
Tuskegee	Muskogean	lower Chattahoochee & middle Tennessee Rivers	...
Yuchi	Yuchi	lower Chattahoochee Riv. & Mussel Shoals	...

Mississippi

Nation	Linguistic Group	Location	Tribal Subdivisions
Acolapissa	Muskogean	Pearl Riv.	...
Biloxi	Siouan	lower Pascagoula Riv.	(Capinans?)
Chakchiuma	Muskogean	lower Yalobusha Riv.	(Sabougia?)
Chickasaw	Muskogean	N Miss.	...
Choctaw	Muskogean	S Miss.	Northeastern, southern, & western Choctaw
Choula	Muskogean	Yazoo Riv.	...
Grigra	Tunican?	Yazoo Riv.	...
Houma	Muskogean	lower Mississippi Riv.	...
Ibitoupa	Muskogean	Holmes Co.	...
Koroa	Tunican	bordering La.	...
Natchez	Muskogean	lower Mississippi Riv.	...
Pascagoula	Muskogean	Pascagoula Riv.	...
Taposa	Muskogean	Yazoo Riv.	...
Tiou	Tunican	upper Yazoo Riv.	...
Tunica	Tunican	lower Yazoo Riv.	...
Yazoo	Tunican	lower Yazoo Riv.	...

Louisiana

Nation	Linguistic Group	Locations	Tribal Subdivisions
Acolapissa	Muskogean	lower Pearl Riv.	...
Adai	Caddoan	middle Red Riv.	...
Atakapa	Tunican	E of Tex. on coast	...
Avoyel	Muskogean	mouth of Red Riv.	...
Bayogoula	Muskogean	S of Baton Rouge	...
Chawasha	Tunican	mouth of Mississippi Riv.	...
Chitimacha	Tunican	SW La.	...
Houma	Muskogean	lower Mississippi Riv.	...

(continued)

TABLE 2.2 (continued)

Louisiana			
Nation	Linguistic Group	Locations	Tribal Subdivisions
Natchitoches	Caddoan	NW La.	Capiche, Doustioni, Natchitoches, Ouachita, Yatasi
Okelousa	Muskogean	Pointe Coupee Par.	…
Opelousa	Tunican?	St. Landry Par.	…
Quinnipissa	Muskogean	lower Mississippi Riv.	…
Taensa	Muskogean	Tensas Par.	…
Tangipahoa	Muskogean	Tangipahoa Riv.	…
Washa	Tunican	Bayou La Fourche	…

Tennessee[d]			
Nation	Linguistic Group	Locations	Tribal Subdivisions
Cherokee	Iroquoian	bordering N.C. & S.C.	…
Chiaha	Muskogean	Burns Island	…
Chickasaw	Muskogean	bordering Miss.	…
Kaskinampo	Muskogean	Cumberland Riv.	…
Shawnee	Algonquian	Cumberland Riv.	Chillicothe, Hathawekela, Kispokotha, Mequachake, Piqua
Tali	Muskogean	middle Tennessee Riv.	…
Yuchi	Yuchi	SE mountains	…

Kentucky[e]			
Nation	Linguistic Group	Locations	Tribal Subdivisions
Cherokee	Iroquoian	upper Cumberland Riv.	…
Chickasaw	Muskogean	lower Tennessee Riv.	…

Ohio			
Nation	Linguistic Group	Locations	Tribal Subdivisions
Erie	Iroquian	NE Ohio	…
Honniasont	Iroquian	bordering Pa.	…
Mosopelea	Siouan	SW Ohio	…
Shawnee	Algonquian	S Ohio	Chillicothe, Hathawekela, Kispokotha, Mequachake, Piqua

Indiana			
Nation	Linguistic Group	Locations	Tribal Subdivisions
Illinois	Algonquoian	bordering Ill.	…
Kickapoo	Algonquoian	bordering Ill.	…
Mosopelea	Siouan	bordering Ohio	…

Illinois			
Nation	Linguistic Group	Locations	Tribal Subdivisions
Illinois	Algonquoian	on Mississippi & Illinois Rivers	Cahokia, Kaskaskia, Peoria, Tamaroa, Mascouten, Albivi?, Amonokoa?, Chepoussa?, Chinko?, Coiracoentanon?, Espeminka?, Tapouaro

Michigan			
Nation	Linguistic Group	Locations	Tribal Subdivisions
Chippewa (Anishinabe)	Algonquian	Sault Ste. Marie	…
Miami	Algonquian	St. Joseph Riv.	…
Neutrals	Iroquoian	SE Mich.	…
Ottawa	Algonquian	NW Mich.	Kishkakon (Bear People), Nassauaketon (Fork People), Sable People, Sinago (Grey Squirrel People)
Potawatomi	Algonquian	lower peninsula	…
Sauk	Algonquian	Saginaw Bay	…

Wisconsin			
Nation	Linguistic Group	Locations	Tribal Subdivisions
Dakota	Siouan	NW Wisc.	…
Mesquakie	Algonquian	Fox Riv.	…
Illinois	Algonquian	bordering Ill.	…
Kickapoo	Algonquian	Fox & Wisconsin Rivers	…
Menominee	Algonquian	Menominee Riv.	…
Potowatomi	Algonquian	Green Bay	…
Sauk	Algonquian	Green Bay, lower Fox Riv.	…
Winnebago	Siouan	S Green Bay	…

[a] Contracted from Monahassano.
[b] Possibly a branch of Shawnee.
[c] Primarily in Georgia before 1700.
[d] Little is known of Tennessee's precontact Indians, and many of the groups listed seem to have been temporary residents.
[e] Little is known of Kentucky's precontact Indians, most of whom seem to have been temporary residents, but it seems to have been sparsely occupied for a century after 1600 and eventually abandoned by Indians for unknown reasons.
Source: John R. Swanton, *The Indian Tribes of North America,* Bureau of American Ethnology Bulletin 145 (1953).

This scale model shows the typical organization of an Algonquian village about 1700, with its framed, bark houses protected by a palisade and the cornfields just outside the walls. (Record Group 12 [Photographic Unit, Department of Highways] Courtesy Pennsylvania State Archives)

Indian-White Relations

The earliest European colonists on the Atlantic coast encountered Native Americans whose cultural attainments and social organization were far less advanced than those of the empires conquered by Spaniards throughout Latin America. With no system of writing, limited architectural skills, and a Stone Age technology, these Indians lived at a level of civilization unknown in England since that country entered the Bronze Age about 2000 B.C. Such an immense gulf between themselves and the Indians could only have predisposed Europeans to assume an attitude of superiority—if not outright derision—toward the continent's original people. The Native Americans, moreover, held animistic religious beliefs that Christian Europeans invariably misinterpreted as paganism at best or devil worship at worst. Given the enormous cultural and religious chasm separating Europeans and Indians and the imperious behavior it engendered among whites, it was as inevitable as it was tragic that violence would ensue when Native Americans began to confront large-scale immigration from the British Isles and the Netherlands.

Europeans saw the critical difference between themselves and Native Americans as cultural rather than racial. The earliest English who studied Indians described them as having darker complexions (either brown or tawny) than their own but did not characterize them as a distinct race. Virginia's Indians, wrote Captain John Smith in 1624, were "of a color brown when they are any age, but they are born white." (The term *redskin* is first known to have been coined by New Englanders in 1699, during King William's War, in reference to warriors' use of blood-color paint while fighting enemies.) English observers at first speculated that Indians colored their bodies artificially by wild dyes, grease, and exposure to the sun. New England's earliest settlers thought it entirely plausible that the local Algonquians were descendants of Israel's ten lost tribes and that their conversion could fulfill the prophecy that the millennium might commence after Jews became Christians.

Anglo-Americans long regarded Indians as a unique branch within the white family rather than as an alien race physiologically dissimilar from themselves. Intermarriage between these groups was never outlawed nor considered socially degrading to whites in the the colonial era, although most whites with Indian spouses were either children captured and raised among Indians or fur traders (mostly Scots or Irish) who lived for long periods outside settled areas. The only objections voiced by Virginians to the first marriage between an Englishman and Indian—that of John Rolfe and Pocahantas in 1614—was that because Rolfe was a commoner but she a king's daughter, he was her inferior and thus unfit to be her spouse. Thomas Jefferson, who strongly opposed miscegenation with blacks, nevertheless wrote several times that the amalgamation of whites with Indians would strengthen American society.

The initial relations between European colonists and North American Indians were anxious and often confrontational but remarkably free of violence. Large-scale English and Dutch settlements in North America derived not from conquest, as in Latin America, but from the willingness of Native Americans to welcome them as trading partners and potential military allies against their own Indian enemies. Despite many minor tensions and sporadic bloodshed, Virginia existed for fifteen years before its settlers first came under Indian attack, New England was free of any major violence with Indians for seventeen years after Plymouth's founding, and New Netherland passed seventeen years after New Amsterdam's establishment before its earliest war with Indians.

Indian warfare occurred far less often in the thirteen colonies than is commonly assumed by twentieth-century Americans. English and Dutch settlers fought just fourteen major conflicts exclusively against Indians from 1607 to 1763, not counting wars between France and Britain that involved Indians merely as allies. (The U.S. Army fought the same number of Indian campaigns in just thirty years from 1862 to 1891.) Indian wars disrupted colonial society so infrequently that they totaled no more than the number of major earthquakes recorded in the colonial period of Anglo-America.

A major reason why relatively few Indian wars erupted was that so many ended in decisive white victories. Europeans owed these triumphs far less to their weaponry than modern Americans would imagine. Because the matchlock and arquebus (early seventeenth-century Europe's primary firearms) provided little accuracy and needed several minutes of awkward reloading before they could be fired again, colonial militias primarily fought with swords after shooting an initial volley at

This eighteenth-century Algonquian Indian shows the influence of the fur trade on Native American life. The warrior wears his hair in a style traditional to his people, and his dress includes traditional native decorations made from feathers, quills, and shells, but his blanket and leggings are of European manufacture; his weapons include both a European musket for skirmishing and a traditional ball-head, war club for hand-to-hand combat. (Painting by David Wright, available from Gray Stone Press of Nashville at 1-800-252-2664)

ground for English expansion in North America, and every generation of British colonists drew upon this ancestral experience when their own homes and families came under Indian assault.

Much of the Europeans' military success over Native Americans stemmed from their willingness to prosecute war brutally, but equal credit should be given to the assistance of their Indian allies. Except for the Powhatan Wars of Virginia and the conflicts engaging the Dutch in New Netherland, Europeans generally emerged victorious over Indian nations by exploiting intertribal rivalries and enlisting warriors to join the onslaught against their enemies. In numerous instances, such as the Pequot, Yamasee, and Tuscarora Wars, whites may have killed fewer of the defeated Indians than did their own Native American allies. The Indians' own disunity all too often provided Europeans with the wedge they needed to solidify their Atlantic beachheads and expand their control inland.

While competing to control the fur trade, the Dutch and French spawned other cycles of intertribal warfare. In the bloodiest of these struggles, the Iroquois waged near-genocidal campaigns against rival Indians in which they exterminated entire villages and created floods of refugees who died of mass starvation after fleeing their homes in midwinter to escape the fury of the Five Nations. Even the English at their worst never pursued enemies more ferociously nor snuffed out lives so remorselessly as did the Iroquois while they ravaged the trapping grounds of the Great Lakes Algonquians.

Warfare between Europeans and Native Americans became more equal as the latter began to acquire firearms. Although the English colonies tried to keep guns out of Indian hands, their attempts degenerated into an exercise in futility after 1650. Not only were many private English colonists willing to trade or sell the Indians guns, but the Dutch did so readily, and Swedes even sold small artillery to the Susquahanna and the Delaware. Dutch officials estimated that by 1644, the Mohawk possessed 400 arquebuses (with powder and lead), which would have made them the third-best-armed military force in North America (behind the Virginia and Massachusetts militias). By 1670, as smooth-bore flintlocks—which were relatively light and could be reloaded rather quickly—were replacing heavy and inaccurate weapons such as matchlocks and arquebuses, Indians had widespread access to guns. The Indian forces in King Philip's War were nearly as well armed as the white militia. Muskets became so easily available to Native Americans during the Anglo-French intercolonial wars that bows and arrows virtually ceased being used as battlefield weapons after 1700, except as a means of firing buildings from safe distances.

Because of its dramatic nature, warfare has received the bulk of attention from scholars who examine relations between Indians and whites. War was nevertheless an exceptional situation to which a minority of tribes found themselves driven. More common was the strategy chosen by tributary tribes, who accepted English or Dutch authority and devised strategies that protected their property rights and cultural inheritance. Groups such as New York's Mahican, Maryland's Piscataway, the Delaware (Lenni Lenape) of Pennsylvania and New Jersey, and South Carolina's Catawba maintained a high degree of cultural autonomy without warfare and held onto their traditions well into the eighteenth century.

The tributary tribes avoided wholesale displacement and disintegration while accommodating themselves to the reality of white domination, but they paid a heavy cost. European diseases depopulated all of them at frightening rates. (See Population, this chapter.) The survivors either submerged their own tribal identities by amalgamating with groups linguistically related to themselves, as Maryland's Piscataway did in the early 1700s, or they eventually became trapped behind the advancing white frontier on modest reservations that gradually passed from their hands to settle debts owed to whites for hunting supplies, alcohol, and other trade goods. Most tributary tribes shared the fate of the Delaware, who succumbed to the temptation of selling portions of what originally seemed like a limitless supply of land for trade goods—sometimes for a pittance

the enemy. Native American tactics heavily depended on surprise, mobility, and whittling away an enemy by attrition, however, so they rarely gave Europeans a chance to inflict many losses in set-piece battles.

Frustrated by their inability to close combat with an elusive and dangerous foe, the English resorted to tactics pioneered in their campaigns to subjugate Elizabethan Ireland: invasions of enemy population centers, destruction of villages and food stocks, and the dispersal of noncombatants under conditions that threatened them with mass starvation. Such ruthless measures violated contemporary Christian attitudes on how to wage a "just war," but the English had rationalized them as the only means of pacifying the "savage" Irish, whose "barbarism" disqualified them from the rules of civilized warfare. English colonists exempted Indians from the rules of civilized warfare by the same logic, although it should be remembered that events such as the Good Friday Massacre of Virginians in 1622—when 347 men, women, and children were treacherously and indiscriminately slaughtered—demonstrated that Indians also viewed civilians as legitimate wartime targets who were not necessarily entitled to quarter. The Tudor-Stuart reconquest of Ireland consequently served as a testing to speculators who cheated them shamelessly—and wound up migrating as refugees to the Ohio River valley after 1750.

The demise of these nations typified the gradual disappearance of Native Americans from east of the Appalachian Mountains. Far more than war, epidemics and the steady loss of tribal lands through sales or treaties displaced Indians from their homelands. "That the lands of this country [Virginia] were taken from them [the Indians] by conquest, is not so general a truth as is supposed," wrote Thomas Jefferson in *Notes on the State of Virginia*, "I find in our historians and records, repeated proofs of purchase … made in the most unexceptionable form." After realizing too late that they had sold their birthright to land speculators for little more than a bowl of porridge, most of the tributary tribes dwindled to mere shells of their former selves or disappeared entirely, and by the mid-eighteenth century few Anglo-Americans east of the frontier had any regular contact with Indians.

Anglo-American attitudes toward the Indian began ambiguously but turned progressively negative during the colonial era. The English at first viewed Indians as culturally benighted but innately capable of acquiring European standards of civilization. The earliest colonists moreover encountered numerous tribes that gave much needed assistance and even formed military alliances against other Indians. During most of the seventeenth-century wars, aid from allied Indians was crucial in enabling whites to achieve victory over hostile forces. These circumstances forced whites to recognize, however begrudgingly, that Indians were not a monolithic threat to themselves but included numerous groups and individuals entitled to varying degrees of appreciation and esteem.

By the early eighteenth century, however, a steady population decline among pro-English tributary tribes had reduced the military value of these allies to virtual insignificance. As Native Americans slowly faded from the tidewater and the Piedmont of the Atlantic coast, the interior Indians who occupied the French and Spanish borderlands emerged as a potent force blocking Anglo-American expansion beyond the Appalachian Mountains. Unlike the Indians who confronted the initial waves of English colonists, all but a few of these nations lived well beyond the reach of military retaliation and could raid Anglo-American settlements with impunity. Realizing that English expansion threatened to overwhelm their traditional way of life under a human avalanche of farmers who would level their forests and destroy their hunting grounds, these Indians allied with the French, whose fur traders and missionaries not only left few scars on the land but also showed respect for aboriginal culture, and also with the Spanish in the Southeast.

By the 1740s, Anglo-Americans confronted an Indian challenge fundamentally different from the situation their grandparents faced before King William's War erupted in 1689. In the half-century after 1689, English colonists found themselves surrounded by a solid phalanx of hostile Indians who were allied with the French. Well armed with French muskets and living beyond the reach of military retaliation, these Indians not only terrorized frontier settlers with small raiding parties but also showed themselves capable of defeating large forces of British regulars at the Battle of Braddock's Defeat in 1755.

Because pro-British tributary tribes no longer possessed the human resources to supply any significant military force, and because the traditionally anti-French Iroquois remained neutral after King William's War, Native Americans rarely fought as comrades-in-arms with Anglo-Americans during their wars against the French. Even when contingents of pro-British Indians joined campaigns against the French, their help was too marginal to generate widespread gratitude or respect among whites. British settlers increasingly redefined all Native Americans as hostile and began to regard even Indians who professed to be their allies with suspicion.

The French and Indian Wars consequently proved to be the period when an implacable hostility toward all native peoples, without discrimination, crystalized among Anglo-Americans. Prior to these conflicts, whites were forced to judge Indian nations selectively because their own victories over hostile Indians had often depended on assistance by pro-English tributary tribes. Anglo-Americans found themselves bereft of any significant Indian support by the 1750s, however, and they began to stereotype all Indians as vicious enemies. Frustrated by their own inability to prevent the pillaging of their frontiers by stealthy raiders from afar, British settlers nursed a festering hatred for all Indians that increasingly exploded into wartime atrocities equal to any committed by their enemies. By the end of the Seven Years' War in 1763, the Anglo-American folk consciousness had demonized all Indians indiscriminately to such an extreme degree that murders of peaceful—or even Christian—Indians could be widely applauded among whites. This unrelenting hostility toward Indians set the scene for their redefinition by nineteenth-century Americans as "redskins," who were biologically different and racially inferior.

TABLE 2.3 CHRONOLOGY OF THE COLONIAL INDIAN CONFLICTS, 1622–1763

Dates	War and Location	Summary of Conflict
Mar. 22, 1622 to Apr. 1623	First Powhatan War of Virginia	After a surprise Powhatan offensive killed 347 colonists, the English forced the Indians to make peace by destroying their villages and food reserves in winter campaigns. The war left the English militarily superior over Virginia's Indians.
Aug. 24, 1636 to Fall 1637	Pequot War of Connecticut	When two Pequot villages were burned by Massachusetts militia in retaliation for attacks on English ships, the Pequot killed 30 Connecticut settlers. The English and allied Indians dispersed the enemy and killed 800 (versus 50 whites). The war established English military superiority over New England's Indians.
Aug. 1642 to Nov. 5, 1653	First Iroquois Beaver War	To win control of the fur trade, the Iroquois virtually exterminated Canada's Huron, Neutral, and Petun Indians and besieged French outposts.
Feb. 26, 1643 to Aug. 1644	Kiefft's War of New Netherland	In retaliation for a massacre of 100 Wesquaesgeeks by Gov. Kiefft's Dutch militia, nearby Algonquians annihilated most outlying white settlements. A counteroffensive by whites in early 1644 killed perhaps 600 Indians and saved the colony but left the Dutch far weaker than their enemies.
Mar. 18, 1644 to Oct. 1646	Second Powhatan War of Virginia	After surprise Powhatan attacks killed 500 whites, Virginians brought them to the verge of starvation by destroying their winter food stocks. The war ended Indian ability to check English expansion within Chesapeake Bay.
mid-1654 to 1656	Second Iroquois Beaver War	To gain control of western fur supplies and replace losses from the First Beaver War by prisoners, the Iroquois annihilated the Erie Indians of Ohio.
Sep. 15, 1655 to Mar. 6, 1660	Peach War of New Netherland	In retaliation for the death of a woman shot stealing peaches from a Dutch orchard, Algonquian looted New Amsterdam and burned settlements on Staten Island and New Jersey. Most Dutch prisoners were ransomed by Sep. 1657, and most settlements were reoccupied by 1658.

(continued)

TABLE 2.3 (continued)

Dates	War and Location	Summary of Conflict
1656 to Jun. 1667	Third Iroquois Beaver War	To win control of western fur sources and replace losses from earlier Beaver Wars by prisoners, the Iroquois dispersed
		Algonquian tribes along Lake Huron and raided French Canadian outposts but sought peace after French troops ravaged their own towns.
Sep. 20, 1659 to Jul. 15, 1660	First Esopus War of New Netherland	To avenge the death of a drunken Indian, Esopus warriors burned farms around Wiltwyck. After the Dutch destroyed several of their towns, Indians agreed to a truce but remained undefeated.
Apr. 1663 to 1675	Fourth Iroquois Beaver War	To monopolize the fur resources of Pennsylvania and replenish losses in other Beaver Wars by taking captives, the Iroquois inflicted heavy losses on the Susquehannocks and dispersed them south into Cheasapeake Bay.
Jun. 7, 1663 to May 16, 1664	Second Esopus War of New Netherland	After Esopus Indians burned Wiltwyck, Dutch militia destroyed nearby Algonquian towns and their winter food reserves. The Indians ceded much of the central Hudson River valley to obtain peace.
Jun. 20, 1675 to Fall 1676	King Philip's War of New England	A Narraganset attack against Plymouth colony mushroomed into a general war uniting 80% of New England's Indians. Before being defeated, the enemy attacked 52 towns, destroyed 12, and killed 600 English. The war broke the power of New England's Indians, of whom 40% were killed, starved, or sold overseas as slaves.
Sep. 1675 to Aug. 1676	Bacon's Indian War of Virginia	Following small-scale raids by the Susquehannock, the Virginia militia made unprovoked attacks on peaceful Occaneechi and Pamunkey and killed or enslaved unknown hundreds of Indians.
Summer 1680 to 1683	Westoe War of South Carolina	South Carolina declared war on the Westoe for attacking Indians that were valuable to the colony's fur trade. In three years, all but 50 Westoe had been killed or enslaved or had fled the province.
Sep. 1680 to Spring 1684	Fifth Iroquois Beaver War	To extend their control over western fur grounds and take prisoners to adopt in place of casualties lost in earlier Beaver Wars, the Iroquois terrorized the Illinois, Ottawa, and Miami Indians and besieged France's western trading outposts.
May 12, 1689 to Sep. 30, 1697	King William's War	Pro-French Indians destroyed Schenectady, N.Y.; Salmon Falls, N.H.; Casco, Me.; York, Me.; and Wells, Me.; and badly damaged Oyster Bay, N.H. Pro-English Iroquois raided Canada and lost perhaps 25% of their population from incessant invasions and raids by Franco-Indian forces.
May 4, 1702 to Apr. 11, 1713	Queen Anne's War	Pro-French Indians raided New England but captured only Deerfield, Mass. South Carolina militia destroyed Florida's Spanish missions and enslaved hundreds of Catholic Indians.
Sep. 22, 1711 to Jun. 8, 1713	Tuscarora War of North Carolina	To avenge numerous outrages by fur traders, Tuscarora wiped out New Bern but were soon thrown on the defensive by English militia and their Indian allies. After about 20% of the nation was slain or enslaved, the Tuscarora capitulated and joined the Iroquois. The war ended Indian resistance to white expansion in the colony until the Cherokee War.

Dates	War and Location	Summary of Conflict
Apr. 15, 1715 to Nov. 15, 1717	Yamasee War of South Carolina	Embittered by a long train of abuses by fur traders, the Yamasee and the Creek drove back the frontier to within 12 miles
		of Charles Town. With aid from allied Indians, whites counterattacked and drove the enemy to Spanish territory. The war ended Indian hostilities on the South Carolina frontier until the Cherokee War.
1722 to Dec. 15, 1725	Dummer's War in Maine	The governor of Massachusetts declared war on the Abnaki in 1722 after small-scale violence erupted over conflicting land claims with white settlers in the Kennebec River valley. Fighting intensified in 1724 when Yankee militia destroyed the Catholic mission center at Norridgewock, and hostilities largely ended by May 1725 when whites burned the the village of Penobscot. The conflict opened up south-central Maine for English expansion.
Nov. 29, 1729 to Fall 1730	Natchez War of Mississippi	Alienated by French military occupation of their territory, the Natchez killed or captured 600 whites at Ft. Rosalie but were dispersed when the French and Choctaw destroyed 9 of their villages, killed 1,000 warriors, and sent 450 as slaves to Haiti.
1732 to 1752	Chickasaw War of Mississippi	After the Chickasaw closed the Mississippi to French vessels in 1732, they withstood incessant raiding by pro-French Choctaw and withstood invasions by French armies in 1736, 1739, and 1752.
Mar. 15, 1744 to Oct. 18, 1748	King George's War	Pro-French Indians raided New England, where they captured Ft. Mass., Me., and N.Y., where they burned Saratoga. Some Iroquois raided Canada.
May 28, 1754 to Feb. 10, 1763	Seven Years' War	Pro-French Indians raided New England, New York, Pennsylvania, Maryland, and Virginia. Anglo-Americans destroyed the Delaware town of Kittaning, Pa., and Abnaki town of St.-François, Canada.
Winter 1760 to Dec. 17, 1761	Cherokee War of the Carolinas	After the Cherokee raided South Carolina to avenge several warriors murdered in Virginia, Highlanders and militia invaded their territory but could not prevent the fall of British Ft. Loudoun or further attacks on the Carolina frontier. A second British expedition ended the war after burning numerous Cherokee towns in mid-1761.

Source: Carl Waldman, *Atlas of the North American Indian* (1985), 88–105.

TABLE 2.4 INDIAN TREATIES NEGOTIATED IN THE COLONIAL ERA, 1607–1763

Date	Parties	Provisions
Autumn 1607	Powhatan Confederacy–Virginia	peace
Spring 1608	Powhatan Confederacy–Virginia	friendship, peace
Aug. 1608	Rappahannock–Virginia	peace
Aug. 1608	Mannahock–Virginia	friendship
Sep. 1608	Nansemond–Virginia	peace
Apr. 5, 1614	Chickahominy–Virginia	friendship, alliance
Apr. 10–15, 1614	Powhatan Confederacy–Virginia	friendship, allegiance
Nov. 19, 1619	Powhatan Confederacy–Virginia	alliance
Apr. 2, 1621	Wampanoag–Plymouth	friendship, land cession
Apr. 1623	Powhatan Confederacy–Virginia	peace
Mar. 1634	Indians[a]–Maryland	land cession
Nov. 1, 1634	Pequot–Massachusetts	land cession
Winter 1634	Narraganset–Providence Plantations	land cession
Spring 1636	Powhatan Confederacy–Virginia	boundary revision
Sep. 1, 1640	Mohegan–Connecticut	land cession
Aug. 27, 1645	Narraganset, Niantic–New England Confederation	peace, captives
Aug. 9, 1646	Wampanoag–Providence Plantations	peace, land cession
Oct. 1646	Powhatan Confederacy–Virginia	peace, land cession, return of captives
May 1650	Indians[a]–Maryland	land cession
Jul. 5, 1652	Susquehannock–Maryland	land cession
May 15, 1658	Plymouth Indians–Plymouth Plantation	land cession
1664	Jersey Indians[a]–New Jersey	land cession
Apr. 8, 1665	Narraganset–Massachusetts	land cession
Apr. 10, 1671	Wampanoag–Plymouth Plantation	allegiance, surrender of arms
Summer 1671	Sakonnet–Plymouth Plantation	allegiance
Sep. 29, 1671	Wampanoag–Plymouth Plantation	allegiance
1674	Seneca–Maryland	peace
Mar. 10, 1675	Kiawah–South Carolina	land cession
May 13, 1675	Delaware–New Jersey	peace
Jul. 15, 1675	Narraganset–Massachusetts	alliance
Sep. 20, 1675	Susquehannock–Great Britain	land cession
Jul. 3, 1676	Eastern Indians[a]–United Colonies of New England	peace, friendship
May 29, 1677	Pamunkey, Roanoke, Nottaway, Nansemond–Great Britain	peace, allegiance
Jul. 17, 1677	Eastern Indians[a]–Massachusetts	peace
Aug. 1677	Westoe, Cusabo–South Carolina	peace
Jul. 15, 1682	Delaware–Pennsylvania	land cession
Feb. 28, 1683	Wimbee–South Carolina	land cession
Jun. 23, 1683	Delaware–Pennsylvania	land cession
Jun. 25, 1683	Delaware–Pennsylvania	land cession
Jul. 14, 1683	Delaware–Pennsylvania	land cession
Jul. 14, 1683	Delaware–Pennsylvania	land cession
Sep. 10, 1683	Delaware–Pennsylvania	land cession
Oct. 18, 1683	Delaware–Pennsylvania	land cession
Feb. 13, 1684	Cusabo–South Carolina	land cession
Jun. 3, 1684	Delaware–Pennsylvania	land cession
Jun. 7, 1684	Delaware–Pennsylvania	land cession
Jul. 31–Aug. 5, 1684	Mohawk, Oneida, Onondaga, Cayuga–New York	land cession, allegiance
Apr. 10, 1685	Five Nations–Maryland	friendship
Jul. 30, 1685	Delaware–Pennsylvania	land cession
Oct. 2, 1685	Delaware–Pennsylvania	land cession
Jun. 6, 1687	Five Nations–New York	alliance
Aug. 6, 1687	Five Nations–New York	alliance
Feb. 25, 1689	Five Nations–New York	alliance, allegiance
Feb. 3, 1689	Five Nations–New York	alliance, allegiance
Nov. 29, 1690	Eastern Indians[a]–Massachusetts	peace
May 1, 1691	Five Nations–New York	peace, delivery of captives
Jun. 2–4, 1691	Five Nations–New York	alliance
Jun. 15, 1692	Delaware–Pennsylvania	land cession
Jul. 3–4, 1693	Five Nations–New York	peace
Aug. 22, 1694	Five Nations–New York, New Jersey, Connecticut, Massachusetts, Pennsylvania	peace
Oct. 2, 1696	Five Nations–New York	peace, alliance
Jul. 5, 1697	Delaware–Pennsylvania	land cession
Jul. 20–22, 1698	Five Nations–New York	peace
Nov. 23, 1699	Bear River Indians–North Carolina	land cession
Aug. 31, 1700	Five Nations–New York	friendship, religion, trade
Sep. 13, 1700	Susquehannock–Pennsylvania	land cession
Apr. 23, 1701	Susquehannock, Potomac, Shawnee, Onondaga–Pennsylvania	friendship, alliance, trade, land cession
Jul. 19, 1701	Five Nations–Great Britain	land cession, alliance
Aug. 1705	Creek–South Carolina	alliance, allegiance
Jun. 7, 1706	Conestoga, Potomac, Shawnee–Pennsylvania	trade regulation, friendship
Sep. 29, 1706	Five Nations–New York	alliance
Jul. 16, 1709	Five Nations–New York	alliance
Jul. 4–10, 1710	Five Nations, Ottawa–New York	alliance
Jul. 31, 1710	Five Nations, Shawnee, Delaware–Pennsylvania	peace, land
Aug. 22, 1710	Mohawk–New York	land cession
May 19, 1712	Delaware–Pennsylvania	friendship
Jun. 8, 1713	Tuscarora–North Carolina	peace
Jan. 16, 1714	Abnaki–Massachusetts	peace
Jul. 23–28, 1714	Abnaki–Massachusetts	peace
Sep. 20–27, 1714	Five Nations–New York	peace, friendship
Feb. 11, 1715	Coree–North Carolina	peace, land cession
Jun. 22, 1715	Susquehannock–Pennsylvania	friendship, trade
Jul. 30, 1715	Delaware, Shawnee, Conestoga, Potomac–Pennsylvania	peace
Nov. 15, 1717	Creek–South Carolina	peace
Jun. 16, 1718	Shawnee, Conestoga, Delaware–Pennsylvania	friendship
Sep. 17, 1718	Delaware–Pennsylvania	land cession
Summer 1721	Cherokee–South Carolina	land cession
Sep. 1721	Five Nations–New York	friendship
Aug. 20–Sep. 12, 1722	Five Nations–New York, Virginia, Pennsylvania	peace, boundary settlement
Sep. 1723	Six Nations–Massachusetts	alliance
Dec. 15, 1725	Eastern Indians[a]–Massachusetts	peace
Sep. 14, 1726	Seneca, Cayuga, Onondaga–Great Britain	land cession
Apr. 1, 1727	Mattamuskeet–North Carolina	land cession
Jul. 11, 1727	Eastern Indians[a]–Massachusetts	peace
Aug. 4, 1727	Eastern Indians[a]–Massachusetts, New York	peace, alliance
May 26–27, 1728	Delaware, Shawnee, Conestoga, Potomac–Pennsylvania	peace, friendship
Oct. 1–5, 1728	Six Nations–New York	land cession, alliance
Sep. 9, 1730	Cherokee–Great Britain	allegiance, return of slaves, peace
Aug. 31–Sep. 2, 1732	Six Nations–Pennsylvania	friendship
Sep. 7, 1732	Delaware–Pennsylvania	land cession
May 21, 1733	Lower Creek, Yuchi, Yamacraw–Georgia	land cession, amity, trade
Jun. 11, 1735	Creek–Georgia	boundary settlement, alliance
Aug. 1, 1735	Caughnawaga Mohawk, Western Abnaki, Housatonic, Scaghticoke, Mohegan–New York	commerce, amity
Aug. 27, 1735	Iroquois of Canada–Massachusetts	peace
Oct. 11, 1736	Seneca, Oneida, Onondaga, Cayuga, Tuscarora–Pennsylvania	friendship, land cession
Aug. 25, 1737	Delaware–Pennsylvania	land cession confirmation
Jun. 28–Jul. 6, 1738	Penobscot, Norridgewock–Massachusetts	friendship
Aug. 1, 1739	Shawnee–Pennsylvania	friendship, land cession confirmation
Aug. 21, 1739	Creek–Georgia	land cession, alliance
Aug. 1, 6, 1740	Delaware, Mingo–Pennsylvania	peace, friendship, trade regulation
Aug. 16–19, 1740	Six Nations–Great Britain	peace, covenant with southern Indians

(continued)

TABLE 2.4 (continued)

Date	Parties	Provisions
May 14, 1741	Seneca–New York	land cession
Jun. 15–18, 1742	Six Nations–New York	friendship, land cession
Jul. 2–12, 1742	Six Nations, Shawnee, Delaware, Nanticoke–Maryland, Pennsylvania	land cession, removal of squatters, trade
Aug. 4, 1742	Penobscot, Norridgewock, Pigwacket, Maliseet, St. Francis, Passamaquoddy–Massachusetts	trade problems
Aug. 1743	Six Nations–Virginia	peace, friendship
Jun. 18–20, 1744	Six Nations–New York, Connecticut, Massachusetts	friendship, alliance
Jun. 22–Jul. 4, 1744	Six Nations–Pennsylvania, Virginia, Maryland	land cession, boundary revision
Oct. 1745	Six Nations–New York, Massachusetts, Connecticut, Pennsylvania	friendship
Aug. 19–23, 1746	Six Nations, Mississauga–New York, Massachusetts	alliance
Nov. 13, 16, 1747	Shawnee, Six Nations, Miami–Pennsylvania	alliance
Jul. 1748	Six Nations, Miami, Shawnee–Pennsylvania	alliance
Jul. 23–26, 1748	Six Nations–New York, Massachusetts	friendship
Aug. 22, 1749	Six Nations, Delaware, Shamokin–Pennsylvania	land cession
Sep. 1749	Cherokee, Creek–South Carolina	trade regulation
Sep. 27, 1749	Penobscot, Norridgewock–Massachusetts	peace, return of prisoners
Jul. 1, 1751	Six Nations, Catawba–New York, Pennsylvania, Connecticut	peace, union
Nov. 29, 1751	Cherokee–South Carolina	trade regulation
Jun. 13, 1752	Six Nations–Virginia, Pennsylvania	friendship
Oct. 13, 1752	Eastern Indians–Massachusetts	peace
Sep. 21, 1753	Penobscot–Massachusetts	return of captives
Sep. 29, 1753	Norridgewock–Massachusetts	return of captives
Jul. 2, 1754	Norridgewock–Massachusetts	peace
Jul. 5, 1754	Penobscot–Massachusetts	peace

Date	Parties	Provisions
Jul. 11, 1754	Six Nations–Pennsylvania	land cession
Aug. 29, 1754	Catawba–North Carolina	friendship, land cession
Dec. 17, 1754	Six Nations–Great Britain	land cession
Nov. 24, 1755	Cherokee–Great Britain	land cession
Dec. 1755	Creek–Georgia	friendship
Jan. 1756	Creek–South Carolina	trade regulation, fort location
Jan. 8–9, 1756	Delaware groups–New Jersey	trade restrictions
Feb. 21, 1756	Catawba–Virginia	alliance, fort construction
Mar. 17, 1756	Cherokee–Virginia	alliance, Indian education
Jul. 1756	Delaware, Shawnee–Great Britain	peace
Apr. 1–May 22, 1757	Six Nations, Delaware, Nanticoke, Susquehannock–Pennsylvania	alliance
Apr. 1757	Mahican, Shawnee, Nanticoke–Great Britain	friendship
Aug. 7, 1757	Six Nations, Delaware, Shawnee, Nanticoke, Mahican–Great Britain	peace
Nov. 3, 1757	Creek–Georgia	land cession, friendship, peace
Apr. 22, 1758	Creek–Great Britain	land settlement
May 1, 1758	Creek–Great Britain	land cession
Aug. 7–8, 1758	Minisink–New Jersey	peace
Oct. 1758	Six Nations, Delaware, Mahican, Nanticoke, Minisink–New Jersey, Pennsylvania	peace, land cession
Dec. 21–28, 1759	Cherokee–North Carolina	peace, resumption of trade
Aug. 12, 1760	Six Nations–Great Britain	friendship
Aug. 3–12, 1761	Mahican, Tutelo, Nanticoke, Delaware, Conoy, Oneida, Onondaga, Cayuga–Pennsylvania	return of prisoners, land questions
Dec. 17, 1761	Cherokee–Great Britain	peace, boundary line, return of prisoners
Aug. 11–28, 1762	Delaware, Shawnee, Miami, Conoy, Kickapoo, Six Nations–Pennsylvania	land questions, return of captives
Nov. 5, 1763	Cherokee, Creek, Choctaw, Chickasaw–Great Britain	boundary definition, peace, land cession

Source: Compiled by George Chalou for Wilcomb E. Washburn, ed., *History of Indian-White Relations* (1988), 190–194.

Population

No agreement currently exists regarding North America's aboriginal population upon the inception of European contact. Although projections of this area's pre-Columbian inhabitants have ranged from 1,000,000 to 12,000,000, the best scholarly estimate would seem to be that 3,800,000 persons lived within the modern boundaries of the United States and Canada about 1492. Human density was highest along the shorelines of oceans, large lakes, and major rivers because abundant marine life enabled groups to survive a failed harvest or a bad hunting season without hunger. Demographers now assume that a significant depopulation afflicted the coastal regions along the Gulf of Mexico and Atlantic Ocean due to diseases contracted from European mariners and fishermen who visited those coasts in the 1500s; they also suspect that these contagions may have traveled along trade routes through the Mississippi and St. Lawrence watersheds but cannot determine how destructive they were prior to Jamestown's founding in 1607.

More than 400,000 persons might have lived in the territory east of the Appalachian Mountains around 1600. There may have then been 105,000 Indians in New England, 150,000 in the Mid-Atlantic region (including Chesapeake Bay), and 150,000 in the Southeast (not including Florida). The onset of English and Dutch settlement almost immediately precipitated a dramatic rise in mortality among native peoples due to "virgin-soil" epidemics (outbreaks of disease to which a population has no previous exposure) of smallpox, plague, chicken pox, mumps, measles, and influenza.

Europe's most deadly viral diseases initially infected almost 100% of afflicted groups and usually left more than half of the victims dead of the malady itself or secondary respiratory ailments. A mysterious plague, either bubonic or pneumonic, contracted from sailors exterminated perhaps 90% of the seacoast Algonquians from Cape Cod to Maine from 1616 to 1619. During the 1630s and 1640s, smallpox ravaged the Great Lakes region and killed perhaps half of the Huron and Iroquois peoples, including probably 75% of the Mohawk. Smallpox destroyed half of the Cherokee in 1738 and half of the Catawba in 1759. Indian populations frequently did not stabilize from recurring waves of virgin-soil epidemics until their losses reached 90% or higher. The Mahican of New York, for example, declined from perhaps 4,000 in 1600 to 227 in 1755, yet fought no major wars with whites.

A low rate of natural increase inhibited all but a few native populations from rapidly replacing such catastrophic losses. Because Indian mothers did not normally become fertile for four years after giving birth because of the prolonged suppression of ovulation caused by the custom of suckling infants past their third birthday, they spaced pregnancies four to five years apart (twice as long as white women) and bore half or less the number of children as European households. Along with the added impact of childhood mortality, Indian populations tended to grow slowly or remain stable under normal circumstances. Losses from epidemics consequently required very long periods to overcome.

The virulence of European pandemics eventually depopulated most of the eastern seaboard of its native inhabitants. Virginia's

TABLE 2.5 EARLIEST POPULATION ESTIMATES OF INDIAN NATIONS IN EASTERN UNITED STATES

Eastern Woodlands			Southeastern Woodlands			Central Prairies and Woodlands			Gulf Coasts and Tidal Swamps		
Group	Year of Estimate	Population	Group	Year of Estimate	Population	Group	Year of Estimate	Population	Group	Year of Estimate	Population
Abnaki, Passamaquoddy, and Penobscot	1600	3,000	Siouan tribes	1600	22,300	Miami	1650	4,500	Coahuiltecan	1690	15,000
Nauset	1600	1,200	Chakchiuma	1650	1,200	Quapaw	1650	2,500	Karankawa	1690	2,800
Pocomtuc	1600	1,200	Chickasaw	1600	8,000	Kaskinampo	1699	500	Tonkawa	1690	1,600
Narraganset and Niantic, Eastern	1600	4,000	Choctaw	1761	20,000	Illinois	1650	8,000	Acuera (in Timucua)		
Pennacook	1600	2,000	Tunica	1650	2,000	Missouri	1780	1,000	Ais	1650	400 (?)
Niantic, Western	1600	600	Yazoo (in Tunica)	...	...	Osage	1780	6,200	Apalachee	1650	7,000
Iroquois (Cayuga, Mohawk, Oneida, Onondaga, and Seneca)	1670	16,000	Creek Confederacy	1700	22,500	Iowa	1780	1,200	Calusa	1650	3,000
Neutrals	1600	10,000	Cherokee	1650	22,000	Fox	1650	3,000	Chatot	1674	1,500
Wenrohronon	1600	2,000	Guale	1650	4,000	Kickapoo	1650	2,000	Mococo (in Timucua)		...
Susquehanna	1600	5,000	Yuchi	1650	2,500	Menominee	1650	3,000	Pensacola	1726	160 (?)
Potawatomi	1600	4,000	Chowanoc	1650	1,500	Sauk	1650	3,500	Seminole	1800	2,000
Nanticoke	1600	2,700	Tuscarora	1600	5,000	Winnebago	1650	3,800	Pohoy	1680	300
Mosopelea	1700 (?)	200	Cusabo	1600	2,800	Chippewa (Ojibway)	1650	35,000	Potano	1650	3,000
Massachuset	1600	3,000	Meherrin	1600	700				Tekesta	1650	1,000 (?)
Nipmuc	1600	500	Nottaway	1600	1,500				Tacobaga (in Timucua)		...
Wampanoag	1600	2,400	Shawnee	1650	3,000				Timucua	1650	13,000
Delaware	1600	8,000							Mobile	1650	2,000
Mohegan	1600	2,200							Houma	1650	1,000
Pequot	1600	2,200							Natchez	1650	4,500
Mahican	1600	3,000							Pascagoula	1698	460
Montauk	1600	6,000							Acolapissa and Tangipahoa	1698	1,500
Wappinger	1600	4,750							Bayogoula and Quinipissa	1650	1,500
Honniasont	1638	4,000							Avoyel	1698	280
Ottawa (in U.S.)	1600	3,500							Washa, Opelousa, Okelousa, and Chawasha	1698	1,000 (?)
Conoy	1600	2,000							Taensa	1650	500 (?)
Erie	1650	14,500							Biloxi	1650	540
Wyandot (Huron)	1600	18,000							Atakapa	1650	2,000
									Chitimacha	1650	3,000
									Koroa (with three other small tribes)	1650	2,000
									Adai	1698	400
									Eyish	1779	300
									Natchitoches Confederacy		1,000
Total		105,950	Total		119,000	Total		74,200	Total		72,740
Grand Total	371,890										

Source: John U. Terrell, *American Indian Almanac* (1971), 93, 133, 200, 240.

Indian nations declined so rapidly that by 1697, just nine decades after the colony's founding, their bowmen numbered just 362, a figure indicating a total population of about 1,800. From a precontact population probably exceeding 100,000, New England's native peoples had fallen to 10,000 by 1675 and would number just a few hundred by 1750. South Carolina's governor noted in 1770 that although his colony had been "swarming with tribes of Indians" when first settled in 1670, "there now remain, except the few [hundred] Catawba, nothing of them but their names, within three hundred miles of our sea coast."

Knowledge about the population of Indian nations was extremely imprecise during the colonial era. The earliest figures derived from impressionistic estimates made by explorers or missionaries and represent little more than educated guesses. Most of the data was collected to

French and Spanish missionaries made many converts among Indians, but few clerics from the thirteen colonies followed their example. One of the exceptions was Rev. David Zeisberger, a Moravian minister who began to preach to the Delaware (Lenni Lenape) in the 1760s and established a congregation of several dozen Indian families on Pennsylvania's frontier. (Courtesy Library of Congress)

determine how many adult males could go to war, and relatively little information exists about how many women, children, and elderly belonged to various tribes, except that the total population of any group was most likely four to six times as high as the number of warriors.

The Indian depopulation proceeded so rapidly that the native peoples most likely became a minority east of the Appalachians during the late 1680s, when the total of Europeans and Africans in the English colonies surpassed 200,000. British subjects probably came to outnumber all Indians living east of the Mississippi sometime in the early 1720s, when the white and black population first exceeded 500,000. By the early 1760s, the number of Indians east of the Mississippi had fallen to around 150,000 persons, a figure dwarfed tenfold by the 1,500,000 white and black inhabitants of the thirteen colonies.

TABLE 2.6   ESTIMATES OF INDIAN WARRIORS IN VIRGINIA, 1607–1669*

Powhatans				
County	Chief Town	1607	1669	Tribes
Fairfax	About General Washington's	40	...	By the name of Matchotics. U. Matchodic. Nanzaticos. Nanzatico. Appamatox Matox.
Stafford., King George	Patowmac Creek	200	...	
King George	About Lamb Creek	20	60	
King Geo., Richmond	Above Leeds town	...		
Westmoreland	Nomony river	100	...	
Richmond County	Rappahanoc Creek	100	30	by the name of Totuskeys
Lancaster, Richmond	Moratico River	80	40	
Northumberland	Coan River	30	...	
Northumberland	Wicocomico river	130	70	
Lancaster	Corotoman	30	...	
Essex, Caroline	Port tobacco creek	150	60	
Mattapony River	...	30	20	

Powhatans				
County	Chief Town	1607	1669	Tribes
King William	Romuncock	300	50	
Gloucester	About Rosewell	40	...	
Piankatank River	Turk's Ferry, Grimesby	55	...	
Pamunkey River	...	60	...	
Chickahominy River	Orapaks	250	60	
Henrico	Powhatan, Mayo's	40	10	
Henrico	Arrohatocs	30	...	
Charles City	Weynoke	100	15	
Charles City, James City	Sandy Point	40	...	
York	Chiskiac	45	15	
Elizabeth City	Roscows	20	...	
Chesterfield	Bermuda hundred	60	50	1669
Surry	About Upper Chipoak	25	3 Pohics	Nottoways —
Isle of Wight	Warrasqueac			Meherrics 90
Nansamond	About the mouth of West. branch	200	45	Tuteloes 50
Princess Anne	About Lynhaven River	100	...	—

County	Chief Town	Warriors 1607	1669	Tribes
Accom. Northampton	Accohanoc River	40	...	
Northampton	About Cheriton's	80	...	

Mannahoacs

Area	Tribes	County	Chief Town	Warriors 1607	1669	Tribes
Between Patowmac and Rappahanoc	Whonkenties	Fauquier		...	...	Tauxenents
				...	...	Patówomekes
	Tegninaties	Culpeper		...	...	Cuttatawomans
				...	...	Pissasecs
	Ontponies	Orange		...	...	Onaumanìents
				...	...	Rappahànocs
	Tauxitanians	Fauquier		...	...	Moràughtacunds
				...	...	Secacaonies
	Hassinungaes	Culpeper		...	...	Wighcocòmicoes
				...	...	Cuttatawomans
Between Rappahanoc and York	Stegarakies Shackakonies Mannahoacs	Orange Spotsylvania		...	...	Nantaughtacunds Màttapomènts Pamùnkies
		Stafford Spotsylvania		...	...	Wèrowocòmicos Payànkatanks

Monacans

Area	Tribes	Country	Chief Town	Warriors 1607	1669	Tribes
Between York and James	Monacans	James R. above the falls	Fork of James R.	...	30	Youghtanunds Chickahòminies Powhatàns Arrowhàtocs Wèanocs Paspahèghes Chìskiacs Kecoughtáns
	Monasiccapanoes	Louisa., Fluvanna		...	...	
Between James and Carolina	Monahassanoes	Bedford., Buckingham Cumberland		...	...	Appamàttocs Quiocohànocs Wàrrasqeaks Nansamònds Chèsapeaks
	Massinacacs Mohemenchoes	Powhatan		...	...	
Eastern Shore				...	...	Accohanocs Accomàcks

* Original spellings used in table have been retained.
Source: Thomas Jefferson, *Notes on the State of Virginia* (William Peden, ed., 1955), 94–95.

TABLE 2.7 ESTIMATES OF IROQUOIS WARRIORS AND POPULATION, 1620–1763

Six Nations							
	1763	1746	1721	1697	1689	1677	1620
Mohawk	160	100	160	110	270	300	...
Oneida	250	100	200	70	180	200	...
Tuscarora	140	150	...	...	...	...	...
Onondaga	150	200	250	250	500	350	...
Cayuga	200	500	130	200	300	300	...
Seneca	1,050	700	700	600	1,300	1,000	...
On Ohio River	40	...	...	...	...		
Total Warriors	1,990	1,750	1,440	1,230	2,550	2,150	6,250[a]
Total Iroquois[a]	7,960	7,000	5,760	4,920	10,200	8,600	25,000

Refugees with Iroquois[b]							
	1763	1746	1721	1697	1689	1677	1620
Warriors	280	...	...	...	...	...	...
Total Refugees[a]	1,120	...	...	...	...	...	...

[a] Estimated by the ratio of 1:4 warrior to population ratio, as by Richter, cited below.
[b] 80 Oswegachie (at Ogdensburg, New York) and 200 Nanticoke, Conoy, Tutelo, Saponi, and Oka.
Source: Daniel K. Richter, *The Ordeal of the Longhouse: The Peoples of the Iroquois League in the Era of European Expansion* (1992), 17, 188, 355, 356. Evarts B. Greene and Virginia D. Harrington, *American Population Before the Federal Census of 1790* (1932), 194–197.

TABLE 2.8 ESTIMATES OF FIGHTING MEN AMONG MAJOR EASTERN INDIAN NATIONS, 1718–1763

Nations	1763	1757	1759	1755	1721	1718
Abnaki	100	...	...	...	...	...
Delaware	600	...	600	500	...	...
Wyandot (Huron)	250	150	300	...	...	100
Shawnee	300	300	500	500	...	...
Miami	230	1,600	500	2,900	2,000	1,500
Piankeshaw	100	...	300	...	...	...
Potawatomi	350	2,000	...	...	...	...
Kickapoo	180	...	600	...	...	...
Mascouten	90	...	...	...	...	200
Illinois	...	...	400	...	3,000	400
Sauk	300	...	200	...	200	...
Mesquakie (Fox)	320	...	200	...	...	570
Ottawa	700	650	2,000	...	500	100
Chippewa	4,720	...	...	...	...	...
Menominee	100	...	...	...	...	...
Winnebago	360	...	...	...	600	...
Wisconsin	110	...	...	...	...	...
Cherokee	...	...	1,500	3,000	3,800	...
Lower Creek	...	...	...	1,200	...	...
Upper Creek	...	...	...	1,180	...	...
Choctaw	...	...	2,000	3,600	...	...
Chickasaw	...	...	...	480	...	...
Chakchiuma	...	...	...	150	...	...
Catawba	...	...	...	320	...	...
Total	8,810	4,700	9,100	13,830	10,100	2,870

Note: For a rough estimate of each nation's total population, multiply number of Indians times five.
Source: Evarts B. Greene and Virginia D. Harrington, *American Population Before the Federal Census of 1790* (1932), 195–197. Wilbur R. Jacobs, ed., *The Appalachian Indian Frontier: The Edmond Atkin Report and Plan of 1755* (1967 ed.), 41–44. Charles F. Mullet, "Military Intelligence on Forts and Indians in the Ohio Valley, 1756–1757," *William and Mary Quarterly*, III (1946), 408–409.

CHAPTER 3 Chronology, to 1763

The following chapter provides a concise outline of colonial American history through 1763. Although limited to especially significant developments, the chronology also incorporates many dates concerning the first documented occurrence of miscellaneous social customs, law, the economy, and various curiosities among Native Americans, European colonists, and African Americans.

The timetable follows the change from Old Style to New Style dating adopted by the British Parliament in 1752. (See chapter on calendrical information.) Prior to this reform, Britain's year had begun on March 25. The dates below appear in New Style so that each year runs from January 1 to December 31. Dates that cannot be stated with exactness are preceded by *ca.* (meaning "about"). Many events cannot be identified with a precise day and so are listed by month or in some cases only by year.

ca. 2,000,000 B.C.   Beginning of the Pleistocene Ice Age, when an ice cap covered approximately 50% of North America.

ca. 80,000 B.C.   Last phase of advance by the polar ice cap (Wisconsin glaciation), during which a land bridge connected Siberia and Alaska at Bering Strait.

ca. 50,000 B.C.   Oldest conjectural crossing of Bering Strait to Alaska by migratory groups.

ca. 27,000 B.C.   Earliest evidence of human habitation in Arctic, as dated from slaughtered bones excavated in Canada's Yukon Territory.

ca. 18,000 B.C.   Wisconsin Glacier reached its southernmost limits above modern Ohio River.

ca. 15,000 B.C.   Earliest dating of human camp remains found in eastern North America (southeast of Pittsburgh, Pennsylvania).

ca. 10,000 B.C.   End of the earliest hunting culture, when heavy chopping tools and blunt projectile heads were replaced by more sophisticated tools and projectile points fluted according to Clovis and (after 9200 B.C.) Folsom styles.

ca. 9000–5000 B.C.   Many large animal species became extinct.

ca. 9000 B.C.   Wisconsin Glacier receded north of Great Lakes.

ca. 8000 B.C.   Rising ocean levels submerged the land bridge from Siberia to Alaska. (Bering Strait refilled to present depth ca. 2500 B.C.)

ca. 7000 B.C.   Seminomadic groups in northern and central Mexico began intensive foraging of wild vegetables and seed plants.

ca. 5000 B.C.   Corn (maize) widely cultivated in Mexico.

ca. 4000 B.C.   Bean cultivation developed in Mexico.

ca. 3000 B.C.   Ancestors of modern Aleut and Inuit began to cross Bering Strait to Alaska by boat.

ca. 3000 B.C.   Corn cultivation spreads north of Rio Grande.

ca. 2500 B.C.   Intensive foraging of vegetables and seed plants adopted by seminomadic groups in Mississippi Delta.

ca. 2000 B.C.   Settled village life emerged in central Mexico.

ca. 700 B.C.–A.D. 400   Adena and Hopewell cultures flourished in eastern woodlands, characterized by large earthworks, trade networks, and sedentary settlements.

ca. 300 B.C.–A.D. 300   Villages became fixed in American Southwest.

ca. 250 B.C.–A.D. 1000   Agriculture and sedentary life spread to grass prairies along Missouri River valley.

ca. A.D. 200   Seaborne migrants from Marquesas Islands first arrived at Hawaii.

ca. 800–1400   Large-scale temple complexes constructed in the Mississippi valley.

986   Norse Vikings under Eric the Red planted first European settlement in Western Hemisphere at Greenland.

986   Driven off course west of Greenland, Bjarni Herjulfson's Norse crew reported first probable European sighting of America.

ca. 1000   Leif Eriksson named North American coastline Vinland and explored southward to New England.

ca. 1000–15   Norse intermittently occupied a settlement at Vinland (now L'Anse aux Meadows, Newfoundland, Canada).

1007   Snorro, son of Thorfinn and Gudrid Karlsefni, was first child born of European parents in America.

1011   First instance of Christian missionary activity arose from the baptism of two Indians captured by Norse at Vinland.

1112   The first diocese including America was established when Eric Gnupsson became bishop of Greenland and Vinland.

1485–88   Portuguese monarchy twice declined opportunity to fund trans-Atlantic voyage of discovery by Christopher Columbus.

August 3, 1492   Financed by Spanish Kingdom of Aragon, Christopher Columbus sailed west into Atlantic from Palos.

October 12, 1492   Columbus landed at San Salvador in the Bahamas.

1493–1504   Columbus returned to the Caribbean on three voyages.

May 3–4, 1493   Pope Alexander VI issued two bulls awarding Spain title to all pagan lands 100 leagues west of the Azores. On June 7, 1494, Spain conceded possession of all territory less than 370 miles west of the Cape Verde Islands (i.e., Brazil) to Portugal.

June 24, 1497   Commissioned by Henry VII, the Italian John Cabot sighted North America (probably Newfoundland) and laid the legal basis for English claims in the Western Hemisphere. He then sailed southward and probably reached Maine.

April 1507   "America" was first used to describe the New World in Martin Waldseemüller's geography, *Cosmographiae Introductio,* in honor of Amerigo Vespucci, an Italian who claimed in 1501 that he had reached a new continent after twice sailing to South America.

April 2, 1513   Juan Ponce de León sighted Florida and then explored the coast from modern Georgia to the Florida Keys.

1519–21   Spanish under Hernando Cortés conquered Mexico.

1521   Attempting to colonize Florida, Ponce de León was driven offshore by Indians and later died of wounds.

ca. April 17, 1524   Giovanni da Verrazano, an Italian sailing for France, was the first European to locate New York harbor.

1526–27   The first European settlement to last a winter within the modern United States was founded in August, probably near the Pee Dee River in South Carolina by 500 Spaniards under Lucas Vásquez de Ayllón; the site was abandoned in 1527.

April 14, 1528   Four hundred Spanish colonists under Pánfilo de Narváez landed at Tampa Bay, Florida, from which they marched to Apalachee in a search for gold. The expedition sailed for Mexico on September 22 but lost virtually all hands in a shipwreck off Texas.

1535–36   French explorer Jacques Cartier located the mouth of the St. Lawrence River on May 19, 1535, sailed as far west as Montreal, and wintered at Quebec before returning to France.

1536   First autopsy was performed in what is now the United States on Felipe Rojamon in Florida.

1539–43   Landing in Florida on May 28, 1539, Hernando de Soto began a march of exploration to the foothills of the southern Appalachians, across the Mississippi, and into Texas. De Soto died in 1542, and the survivors sailed for Mexico in mid-1543.

1540   Earliest known baptism within present-day United States was performed on Peter, an Indian guide for de Soto, in Georgia's Ocmulgee River.

1540–42   Searching for gold, Francisco Vásquez de Coronado left Mexico on February 23, 1540, and explored through New Mexico, Texas, Oklahoma, and Kansas; he returned to Mexico City by October 1542.

The Vikings were the first Europeans to reach North America, and they may have explored its coastline as far south as Massachusetts before abandoning their settlements in the early eleventh century. (Courtesy Library of Congress)

ca. 1540 Earliest introduction of horses to America by Spanish occurred when many of Coronado's mounts escaped on the plains.

September 28, 1542 João Rodriques Cabrilho became first European to reach the California coast.

1559–61 Don Tristán de Luna y Arellano and 1,500 Spaniards landed at Pensacola, Florida, on August 14, 1559, after which they sent exploratory parties into Alabama and explored the Atlantic coast to North Carolina. The expedition returned home in 1561.

Spring 1562 Jean Ribault founded first French settlement on North America at Port Royal, South Carolina, which the French abandoned in early 1564.

June 25, 1564 French settlers built Fort Caroline near the mouth of St. John's River in Florida.

1565 First white child born in United States delivered at Fort Caroline, Florida.

August 28, 1565 Fifteen hundred Spanish founded first permanent European settlement in United States at St. Augustine, Florida.

September 8, 1565 St. Augustine's chaplain established the first Catholic parish within the United States.

September 20, 1565 Spanish troops destroyed French Ft. Caroline.

1565 First billiards shot in United States by Spanish at St. Augustine.

February 14–18, 1571 Indians kill Spanish Jesuit priests who had established Catholic missions on Chesapeake Bay in 1570.

1578–79 Sir Humphrey Gilbert led England's first trans-Atlantic colonizing expedition but returned, having failed to reach America.

1581 Spanish priests started the first systematic effort to convert Indians in New Mexico.

July 27, 1585 Ralph Lane landed colonists sent by Sir Walter Raleigh at Roanoke Island, North Carolina, England's first settlement to spend a winter in America, but they abandoned it in June 1586.

July 22, 1587 John White landed 117 settlers sent by Raleigh, including England's first female colonists, at Roanoke Island, North Carolina.

August 18, 1587 Virginia Dare, the first child of English parents delivered in America, was born at Roanoke Island, North Carolina.

Fall 1587 First beer brewed in United States at Roanoke Island, North Carolina.

August 17, 1590 Returning from England, John White found Roanoke abandoned and was unable to locate any survivors.

1595 Spanish began major effort to build missions in Florida and convert Indians, of whom 26,000 became Catholic by 1647.

1598 Juan de Oñate initiated Spanish settlement of New Mexico by leading 500 Spaniards to upper Rio Grande valley.

April 30, 1598 The earliest known play performed in the United States was a comedy about army life performed for Juan de Oñate's expedition near modern El Paso, Texas.

1604 Spain conceded England the right to settle areas of North America beyond Spanish control in the Treaty of London.

April 20, 1606 James I of England gave a patent authorizing the London and Plymouth companies to colonize "Virginia" (America).

April 26, 1607 The London Company's expedition to settle Virginia reached Chesapeake Bay with 105 colonists (39 others died at sea).

May 24, 1607 The first permanent English settlement in America was founded at Jamestown, Virginia. During the next four months, 46 of the 105 colonists died from various causes.

August 14, 1607 The Plymouth Company founded a settlement on Maine's Sagadahoc River, which was abandoned in September 1608.

September 17, 1607 First suit for slander filed by John Robinson at Jamestown, Virginia.

The first major exploration of the Southwest occurred during the Coronado expedition of 1540–42, which is here depicted marching through a stretch of desolate, semiarid terrain. (Courtesy Library of Congress)

December 1607 First attempted coup in what is now United States failed when George Kendall was discovered plotting against Virginia's Council and shot.

September 10, 1608 Captain John Smith given control of Virginia, which he governed until June 16, 1609.

October 1608 First glass factory established at Jamestown.

1608 The first book written by an American colonist, John Smith's *A True Relation of ... Virginia Since the First Planting of that Collony* was published in London.

1609 Santa Fe, New Mexico, founded.

Spring 1609 First Indian corn planted by English in Virginia.

July 8, 1609 Samuel de Champlain founded Quebec, Canada's first permanent settlement.

September 13, 1609 Henry Hudson located and explored the Hudson River.

1609 Anne Burrows and John Laydon were the first English couple to be married in America.

Winter 1609–10 Virginia's "starving time" reduced the colony's population by 80%, from about 500 to 100 by May 1610.

1610 Dr. Lawrence Bohune, the first English physician in present-day United States, arrived in Virginia.

May 1611 Earliest reported game of bowling in what is now United States played by Jamestown settlers, who used the town streets as throwing alleys.

September 11, 1611 The first significant geographic expansion of the Virginia colony occurred with the settlement of Henrico, about 40 miles upriver from Jamestown near modern Richmond.

1612 John Rolfe began first experiments with tobacco cultivation.

1613 Earliest armed conflict between English and French colonists resulted when Samuel Argall of Virginia captured French settlements on the Bay of Fundy.

March 1614 First Virginia tobacco exported to England.

April 14, 1614 John Rolfe married Pocahantas.

1614 First Dutch settlement in New York, Fort Nassau, built on Hudson River opposite modern Albany.

1616–19 An epidemic disease contracted from European sailors killed perhaps 90% of New England's coastal Indians as well as large numbers in the interior.

November 18, 1618 First plans made to build a college when the Virginia Company endowed 10,000 acres for a school to educate Indians.

August 1619 First African Americans known to arrive in the English colonies were landed by a Dutch privateer at Jamestown, Virginia.

August 9–14, 1619 First representative legislature in present-day United States met at Jamestown, Virginia.

1620 Construction began on the first colonial ironworks at Falling Creek, Virginia, which was destroyed by Indians shortly before it could start production in 1622.

November 9, 1620 The *Mayflower,* with 101 English "Pilgrims" sighted Cape Cod, Massachusetts, after 66 days at sea. The Pilgrims signed the Mayflower Compact on November 21 and landed at Plymouth on December 26.

1621 First windmill in United States was constructed to grind grain for Virginia's population.

June 18, 1621 First duel fought in English colonies at Plymouth by E. Leister and E. Dotey.

Fall 1621 Plymouth settlers held their first "Thanksgiving" celebration.

January 1622 Potatoes first introduced as a crop to North America.

March 22, 1622 Indians launched surprise attack that killed about 30% (347) of Virginia's colonists and began the first major war between English and Indians.

1623 First settlement within New Hampshire made at Rye.

1623 First attempt to promote silk industry taken when Virginia encouraged planting of mulberry trees for silkworms.

May 24, 1624 James I revoked the charter authorizing the London Company's authority over Virginia.

Summer 1624 Dutch established the first settlement in New Jersey on the Delaware River at Ft. Nassau (near Camden).

May 13, 1625 Charles I proclaimed Virginia a royal colony.

May 4, 1626 Peter Minuit and Dutch settlers arrived at Manhattan Island, where he founded New Amsterdam.

June 14, 1626 The Dutch abandoned their Delaware River settlements and relocated near New Amsterdam on the Hudson River.

1628 First Reformed Dutch church established at New Amsterdam.

1628 First primary school established at New Amsterdam.

March 14, 1629 Charles II granted land between Merrimack and Charles Rivers to Puritans of Massachusetts Bay Company.

1629 Virginia legislature passed earliest law restricting crop output by limiting tobacco production after a steep price fall.

June 12, 1630 First colonists sponsored by Massachusetts Bay Company arrived at Salem, Massachusetts, under Gov. John Winthrop.

September 17, 1630 Boston, Massachusetts, was given its modern name, in preference to Shawmut and Tramount.

April 1631 First European settlement in Delaware made by Dutch at Swanendael (near Lewes).

1631 Maryland first settled by English when William Claiborne of Virginia led 100 colonists to Kent Island.

Spring 1632 Delaware Indians killed all Dutch at Swanendael.

June 30, 1632 Cecil Calvert, second Lord Baltimore, received charter establishing proprietary colony of Maryland as Catholic refuge.

June 8, 1633 The first settlement in Connecticut was founded as a trading post by the Dutch at Ft. Good Hope (now Hartford).

September 1633 The first English settled in Connecticut at Wethersfield and Windsor.

1633 The first secondary school, Boston Latin School, began instruction.

March 25, 1634 Gov. Leonard Calvert landed with 200 proprietary colonists, including many Catholics, in Maryland.

August 1635 The Dutch reoccupied Ft. Nassau on the Delaware River after expelling a few English fur traders who had settled there.

June 1636 Roger Williams established first settlement in Rhode Island after buying land at Providence from Indians.

August 24, 1636 The Puritans' first major Indian war ensued when Massachusetts sent militia against the Pequots of Connecticut in response to the killing of English ship crew. By late 1637 perhaps a fourth of the 3,500 Pequot were dead and the Puritans had established their military supremacy in New England.

October 28, 1636 The first college in the New World was chartered by Massachusetts; it was named Harvard in 1638.

1636 The earliest military pensions were granted by Plymouth to soldiers crippled in the Pequot War.

Summer 1637 Puritans led by John Davenport founded settlements in modern Connecticut that became colony of New Haven on November 6, 1643, when several towns adopted the Frame of Government. New Haven established the most strict legal system of any colony by adopting Old Testament law and making no provision for jury trials.

November 12–17, 1637 New England's first major religious dispute, the Antinomian Controversy, ended when Anne Hutchinson of Boston was tried and banished from Massachusetts for sedition and heresy.

March 29, 1638 New Sweden first settled at Ft. Christina, Delaware.

1638 The first printing press in the United States was set up at Cambridge, Massachusetts.

1638 The first recorded American incident of what would later be known as a pub crawl was made by Anne Walker, who was expelled from her Boston church for "intemperate drinking from one inn to another and for light and wanton behaviour."

January 24, 1639 The Fundamental Orders of Connecticut were adopted as a frame of government for a separate colony.

1639 The first document printed in North America, *The Oath of a Freeman,* was published at Cambridge, Massachusetts.

May 30, 1639 Earliest school funded by public taxes was founded by the Dorchester, Massachusetts, town council.

June 16, 1639 Massachusetts granted Edmund Rawson land to build the first known gunpowder mill in North America.

ca. 1640 Margaret Brent of Maryland became first American woman to practice law by performing legal duties for Lord Baltimore.

April 17, 1640 The first Lutheran pastor, Rev. Reorus Torkillus, arrived at New Sweden.

1640 The first book printed in North America was *The Whole Booke of Psalmes Faithfully Translated into the English Metre,* published at Cambridge, Massachusetts.

October 1641 The earliest American patent was given to Samuel Winslow of Massachusetts for his process of producing salt.

1641 The press of Cambridge, Massachusetts, published America's first best-seller, Thomas Shepard's *The Sincere Convert,* which went through twenty editions.

August 1642 Earliest wave of Beaver Wars over fur trade began when Iroquois of New York raided the Huron in Canada and then attacked French settlements. Peace was not ratified until November 5, 1653.

September 23, 1642 First college commencement held at Harvard.

February 25, 1643 Kiefft's War broke out between the Dutch and the Algonquian in New Netherland and lasted until peace restored on August 9, 1645. Of 1,600 Dutch colonists, 900 were killed or fled the province.

May 19, 1643 Massachusetts, Plymouth, Connecticut, and New Haven formed the United Colonies of New England, a loose military alliance that lasted until the 1670s.

1643 The first fulling mill (mill that shrank and thickened wool) constructed for clothing production was built at Rowley, Massachusetts, by John Pearson.

1643 The first recorded restaurant, or "cook's shop," was licensed at Boston, Massachusetts, by Goody Armitage.

March 18, 1644 Powhatan Indians launched massive attacks against Virginia's 8,000 settlers, who registered 500 dead before defeating the Indians in 1646.

1644 The first successful ironworks was begun at Lynn, Massachusetts

1644–47 Protestant rebellion led by Richard Ingle and William Claiborne overthrew Catholic proprietary government in Maryland.

1646 The earliest anti-smoking legislation was passed by Massachusetts Bay, which forbade smoking in towns as a fire hazard.

January 1647 Martha Brent of Maryland became the first American woman to demand the right to vote; she was refused.

1647 First rice planted by colonists in America at Virginia, but crop failed.

November 11, 1647 Massachusetts passed the "Old Deluder Act," the first law mandating compulsory primary education.

1647 Florida Indians launched major attacks on Spanish missions.

June 6, 1647 Achsah Young became first person executed as a witch.

April 27, 1648 Governor Stuyvesant of New Netherland ordered Ft. Beversrede built on the Schuykill River (at modern Philadelphia) to compete in the fur trade with Swedish Ft. New Krisholm, on the opposite bank. A month later the Swedes burned the Dutch fort.

October 18, 1648 Massachusetts chartered Boston's shoemakers, the first officially recognized labor organization in the United States.

April 21, 1649 Maryland assembly enacted its Toleration Act, the first law protecting freedom to worship passed in United States.

1650 The first book written by an American woman, *The Tenth Muse Lately Sprung Up in America* by Anne Bradstreet of Massachusetts, was published in London.

Summer 1651 The earliest Indian reservation was established when Massachuset tribe was settled at "Praying Town" of Natick, Massachusetts. (It was later settled by colonists.)

October 9, 1651 The Interregnum Parliament passed England's first Navigation Law; it excluded foreign ships from colonial trade. After the Stuart monarchy's restoration, this statute had no force and so was reenacted with the royal signature on July 27, 1661.

November 5, 1651 Swedish colonists captured Ft. Casimir, a Dutch trading post built on the Delaware in the previous summer.

June 7, 1652 Massachusetts established the first Anglo-American mint, which coined "the pine tree shilling" until 1684.

ca. 1653 First permanent English settlements made in North Carolina.

Summer 1654 Erie Indians of Ohio attacked and dispersed by Iroquois warriors seeking domination of the fur trade.

September 1654 The earliest Jewish community in America originated when 23 Sephardim from Brazil immigrated to New Amsterdam, where they were awaited by Jacob Barsimon, who preceded them on August 22. They founded Congregation Shearith Israel.

October 30, 1654 Protestant majority in Maryland assembly repudiated Lord Baltimore's proprietary authority.

1654 Boston voted to purchase America's first fire engine, a wheeled water-pumping machine built at the Lynn ironworks.

March 25, 1655 Protestant forces defeated Lord Baltimore's forces at Battle of the Severn River.

September 26, 1655 New Sweden's governor surrendered the colony to a Dutch force under Peter Stuyvesant, who had captured Ft. Casimir.

1655 Lady Deborah Moody won the right to vote in her town meeting at Gravesend, Long Island, New Netherland.

September 22, 1656 The first women jury members were empaneled at Patuxent, Maryland; they found Judith Catchpole innocent of infanticide.

1656 Harvard College abandoned teaching Ptolemaic astronomy, which described the Earth as the universe's center, and accepted Galileo's research, then only 23 years old and still controversial, that the Earth and planets orbited the sun.

November 1657 England's Puritan government returned Maryland to Lord Baltimore's control.

September 30, 1659 Earliest mention of tennis in America was a decree regulating the days on which it could be played in New Netherland.

1661 John Eliot published the first Bible printed in America, the *Up-Biblum God,* an Algonquian translation of the New Testament. An Algonquian translation of the Old Testament appeared in 1663.

May 3, 1662 Connecticut's colonial status was recognized by English crown in a charter that annexed New Haven colony to it.

December 1662 Virginia passed the earliest law declaring that the children of a slave woman and free man would inherit the mother's status.

October 8, 1662 General synod of New England churches adopted the Halfway Covenant, which preserved Congregationalism's appeal to the majority by extending baptism to virtually all children, rather than limiting baptism to those whose parents had been born again.

April 3, 1663 Colony of Carolina (modern North and South Carolina) created by charter from Charles II.

June 7, 1663 The Esopus War began with a massacre of Dutch settlers at Wiltwyck. After the Dutch destroyed two Esopus villages, peace was negotiated on May 16, 1664.

July 18, 1663 Rhode Island's authority to govern itself was acknowledged by royal charter.

1664 Maryland passed the first law that unequivocally declared lifetime slavery as the status of all imported blacks.

1664 Maryland passed the first law forbidding marriage between whites and blacks.

April 2, 1664 Charles II ordered Col. Richard Nicolls to capture New Netherland with a force of regulars and Connecticut militia.

June 24, 1664 Charles II granted John Lord Berkeley and Sir George Carteret title to New Jersey, which was the object of an English miltary expedition ordered to America.

September 7, 1664 Gov. Peter Stuyvesant surrendered New Netherland to English task force under Richard Nicolls, who renamed both the colony and its major city, New York, after the Duke of York.

October 28, 1664 English settlement of New Jersey began with the purchase of 400,000 acres near Elizabeth from Indians.

1664 Newmarket Course, established at Hempstead Plains by New York's governor Richard Nicolls, was the earliest professionally organized racetrack to adopt standard rules for betting and to offer special purses. In 1668, it awarded the first trophy, a silver bowl, given for an American sporting event.

August 27, 1665 The first amateur play performed in Anglo-America was Philip Bruce's *The Bare and the Cubb,* given at Accomac, Virginia.

1665 The first Native American to earn a college degree, Caleb Cheeshateamuck, graduated from Harvard.

Fall 1666 A thousand French troops invaded the Mohawk lands in New York and burned four villages and their winter food supplies.

June 1667 The Iroquois and the French signed a peace treaty that ended fighting over fur trade until 1680.

April 1670 First English settlement made in South Carolina at "Old Charles Town" (relocated to modern Charleston in 1680).

1670 Virginia legislature declared all blacks brought to the colony subject to lifetime bondage, as Maryland had in 1662.

1671 South Carolinians defeated and enslaved many of nearby Kusso Indians, who were believed to be conspiring with the Spanish.

May 15, 1672 Massachusetts passed the first copyright law, which established exclusive publishing rights for seven years. The first copyrighted publication was John Usher's *The General Laws and Liberties of the Massachusetts Colony.*

August 12, 1672 A Dutch fleet recaptured New York, which was not restored to English control until November 10, 1674.

October 2, 1672 The Spanish began replacing wooden defenses at St. Augustine, Florida, with a stone fort, Castillo de San Marcos.

January 22, 1673 Regular mail delivery by horse commenced between Boston and New York over the Boston Post Road.

June 17, 1673 Fr. Jacques Marquette and Louis Joliet became first Europeans to find a route to the Mississippi River from Canada; they then traveled as far south as the Arkansas River.

1673 Josiah Winslow, the first native-born American to serve as governor of a colony, took office in Plymouth.

December 4, 1674 Fr. Jacques Marquette built a mission to convert Indians at what is now Chicago, Illinois.

August 24, 1675 The first priest ordained in the United States received Holy Orders at St. Augustine, Florida.

1675 The Susquehannah Indians of Pennsylvania and Maryland were attacked and dispersed by Iroquois raids.

May 10, 1675 Bacon's Rebellion began when Nathaniel Bacon led an unauthorized expedition to retaliate against Indian raids, for which he was declared a rebel on July 29. Bacon's forces burned the capital Jamestown on September 19, but the insurrection quickly disintegrated after Bacon died of disease on October 18.

June 1675 The first Quakers to settle the Delaware valley landed at Salem, New Jersey, under John Fenwick's leadership.

June 20, 1675 First battle of King Philip's War occurred when Wampanoag under Metacomet (King Philip) attacked Sawnsea, Plymouth. Indians ultimately attacked 52 of New England's

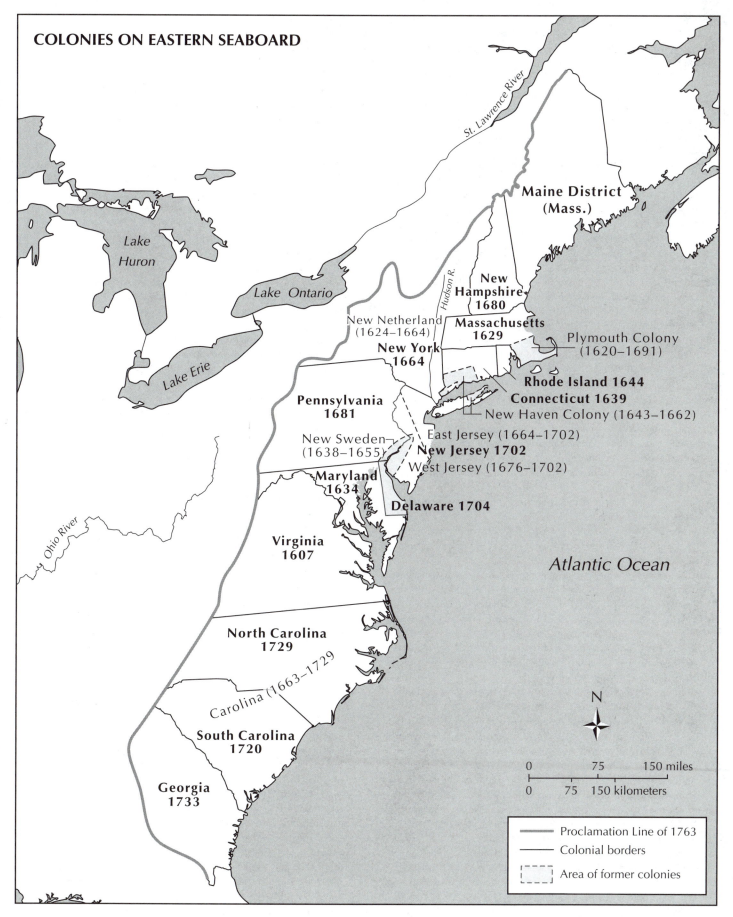

COLONIES ON EASTERN SEABOARD

Lake Huron

Lake Ontario

Lake Erie

St. Lawrence River

Maine District (Mass.)

New Hampshire 1680

New Netherland (1624–1664)

Massachusetts 1629

Plymouth Colony (1620–1691)

New York 1664

Hudson R.

Rhode Island 1644
Connecticut 1639
New Haven Colony (1643–1662)

Pennsylvania 1681

New Sweden (1638–1655)

East Jersey (1664–1702)
New Jersey 1702
West Jersey (1676–1702)

Maryland 1634

Delaware 1704

Ohio River

Virginia 1607

Atlantic Ocean

North Carolina 1729

Carolina (1663–1729)

N

South Carolina 1720

| 0 | 75 | 150 miles |
| 0 | 75 | 150 kilometers |

Georgia 1733

Proclamation Line of 1763
Colonial borders
Area of former colonies

Although the term *the thirteen colonies,* is popularly used to refer to pre-Revolutionary Anglo-America, seventeen British provinces were actually established within the present United States before 1763, plus two others founded by the Dutch and the Swedes. The above map gives dates of duration for those colonies that became defunct before 1763 and dates of settlement for the others. (Jeremy Eagle).

towns (destroying 12 entirely), burned 1,200 houses, slaughtered 8,000 cattle, and killed 600 colonists. By late 1676 the English had prevailed and perhaps 40% of New England's 10,000 Indians had perished.

July 11, 1676 New Jersey divided into separate colonies of East and West Jersey following sale of western half to Quakers.

September 1676 William Davyes and John Pate were hanged for inciting rebellion against Maryland's Catholic government.

October 1676 First coffee house was established at Boston by John Sparry.

December 3, 1677 The proprietary government of Carolina's Albemarle (northern) district was usurped in John Culpeper's Rebellion.

March 13, 1677 Massachusetts established undisputed title to Maine by purchasing rights of heirs to Plymouth Company shareholders.

January 1678 The first medical publication printed in Anglo-America was *A Brief Rule to Guide the Common-People of New-England How to Order Themselves and Theirs in the Small Pocks, or Measels* by Thomas Thacher, who was not a physician but a minister in Boston.

January 15, 1680 René-Robert Cavelier, sieur de La Salle built Ft. Crèvecoeur on the Illinois River.

April 1680 Westo Indians attacked South Carolinians, who defeated them by end of the year.

September 1680 A royal commission nullified claims of Massachusetts to govern New Hampshire, which became a royal colony.

September 1680 Iroquois captured several hundred prisoners in raids on the tribes of Illinois.

March 14, 1681 Pennsylvania created by royal charter.

April 1681 Josias Fendall instigated an unsuccessful rebellion against Maryland government and was banished.

November 15, 1681 Earliest use of shorthand made in transcription of court proceedings at St. John's, Maryland.

early 1682 The first Quaker settlers arrived at Philadelphia.

April 9, 1682 Having paddled south from the Illinois River, La Salle reached the mouth of the Mississippi River and claimed all land drained by it for France.

October 27, 1682 William Penn arrived in the Delaware valley to take title of his proprietary lands. He returned to England on August 14, 1684, and did not return until 1699.

June 23, 1683 Pennsylvania and the Delaware Indians signed a treaty of friendship at Shackamaxon that laid the basis for seven decades of peace between the colony and Native Americans.

March 1684 The Iroquois launched raids into Illinois and beseiged the French at Ft. St. Louis on Illinois River.

June 21, 1684 England's Chancery Court nullified the charter of 1629 establishing Massachusetts Bay, which became a royal colony.

January 1685 La Salle established a French camp at Matagorda Bay, Texas, and then explored inland until killed by his own men in 1687.

1686 Henry de Tonti built Ft. Arkansas on the Mississippi River.

August 17, 1686 Spanish troops invaded South Carolina and destroyed the Scottish settlement of Stuart's Town but were prevented from attacking Charles Town by a tropical storm.

December 20, 1686 Gov. Edmund Andros arrived in Boston to centralize royal authority over all New England colonies and to promote the interests of the Church of England.

June 28, 1687 James II conferred knighthood on the first American colonist to be so honored: William Phips of Massachusetts, who had made a fortune salvaging a sunken treasure.

Summer 1687 A French army of 1,600 invaded Iroquois lands in New York, defeated Seneca warriors, and burned Seneca towns.

April 17, 1688 Edmund Andros appointed governor of Dominion of New England, including all of New England, New York, and New Jersey.

April 18, 1689 Boston militia overthrew the Dominion of New England by disarming royal soldiers and arresting Governor Andros.

May 3–9, 1689 Insurrection against royal government began in New York when English towns on Long Island elected new officials to replace appointees of Lieutenant Governor Nicholson, who fled twelve days after militia under Jacob Leisler seized New York's fort on May 31.

May 12, 1689 England and France commenced the War of the League of Augsburg, termed King William's War by Anglo-Americans.

August 1, 1689 Maryland's proprietary government ousted by the "Protestant Association" under John Coode.

August 3, 1689 French and Indians seized Pemaquid, Maine.

February 3, 1690 The first paper money issued in what would become the United States was paid by Massachusetts to its soldiers fighting the French.

February 9, 1690 French and Indians destroyed Schenectady, New York.

March 27, 1690 French and Indians sacked Salmon Falls, New Hampshire.

May 11, 1690 Massachusetts troops captured Port Royal, Canada, the only major Anglo-American victory in King William's War.

May 20, 1690 Indians destroyed Casco, Maine.

July 31, 1690 French captured Ft. Loyal (Portland), Maine.

August 2, 1690 Connecticut regained its charter, which England's attorney general ruled had been illegally usurped by James II. The charter's form of government would continue until 1818.

September 25, 1690 Benjamin Harris printed *Publick Occurrences,* the first newspaper published in America, at Boston, but it was suppressed immediately for criticizing the government and not revived.

October 1690 Two thousand New Englanders under Sir William Phips besieged Quebec but failed for lack of ammunition and supplies.

1690 Spain established a Catholic mission in Texas on the Neches River. It was abandoned in 1693.

June 27, 1691 Maryland declared a royal province.

October 17, 1691 Massachusetts given a royal charter that continued its royal status and incorporated Plymouth within its borders.

January 23, 1691 Spain appointed first governor of the province of Texas.

March 18, 1692 The Crown ended William Penn's political authority in Pennsylvania but returned power to him on August 20, 1694.

April 4, 1692 Andrew Hamilton of New Jersey appointed deputy to England's postmaster general and directed to extend British system of mail delivery to America.

June 21, 1692 Wells, Maine, raided by Abnaki Indians.

February 29, 1692 First indictments charging witchcraft were issued at Salem, Massachusetts. By October, when Governor Phips forbade any further imprisonments, more than 100 persons had been jailed, 200 others had been accused, and 20 lives had been taken.

February 8, 1693 Virginia chartered the College of William and Mary.

December 7, 1693 Rhode Island regained its charter when England's attorney general ruled that it had been wrongly revoked by James II. The charter's form of government would continue until 1842.

June 23, 1694 French and Indians raided Durham, New York.

August 15, 1696 French recaptured Pemaquid, Maine.

March 15, 1697 French and Indians raided Haverhill, Massachusetts.

September 30, 1697 Treaty of Ryswick ended the state of war among Europeans in America but failed to end fighting between the Abnaki and New Englanders or between the French and the Iroquois.

1698 The first songbook to match words with musical notes was the ninth edition of *The Bay Psalm Book,* titled *Psalms, Hymns, and Spiritual Songs.* All previous editions appeared without tunes to guide congregations in song, so cacophony often resulted.

May 1698–March 1701 Dissatisfaction with proprietary government produced widespread attacks on sheriffs and judges in East and West Jersey. The proprietors thereafter asked the crown to assume responsibility for governing these provinces.

January 7, 1699   A peace treaty signed at Casco Bay, Maine, between the Abnaki and Massachusetts ended Indian raids on New Englanders.

May 4, 1699   Pierre Le Moyne, sieur d'Iberville, completed Ft. Maurepas at Biloxi, Mississippi, which was abandoned in 1702 when the settlers relocated to Mobile Bay.

July 6, 1699   Boston authorities arrested pirate Captain William Kidd; he was sent to England, where he was hanged on May 23, 1701.

1699   French priests built a Sulpician mission at Cahokia, Illinois.

1700   French built Ft. Mackinac in Michigan.

October 16, 1701   Connecticut chartered the Collegiate School, later designated as Yale. Its first graduates matriculated in 1716. Classes were held at Killingworth, Milford, and Saybrook before the college settled at New Haven in 1745.

July 24, 1701   French soldiers began to construct Ft. Ponchartrain at Detroit, Michigan.

August 4, 1701   The Iroquois negotiated a treaty with the French at Montreal that established peace but without repudiating their trade connections with the English. The Iroquois remained largely neutral in England's next three wars with France.

April 26, 1702   East and West Jersey became the royal colony of New Jersey.

May 4, 1702   England and France entered the War of the Spanish Succession (known to Anglo-Americans as Queen Anne's War).

1702   French built Ft. Louis at Mobile, Alabama.

December 1702   South Carolina troops pillaged St. Augustine, Florida, but failed to force Spanish troops holding the castle to surrender.

1703   French Jesuits founded a mission at Kaskaskia, Illinois.

August 10, 1703   Indians inflicted heavy losses at Wells, Maine.

1703   The first organ used in the English colonies was imported from Europe and played at Gloria Dei (Swedish Lutheran) Church in Philadelphia.

February 29, 1704   Indians destroyed Deerfield, Massachusetts.

April 17, 1704   The first colonial newspaper to be published on a regular basis was the *News-Letter* of Boston.

1704   South Carolina troops destroyed fourteen Spanish missions along Apalache River and enslaved the Christian Indians.

1704   French began work on Ft. Miami on Maumee River in Indiana.

1704   The first organ constructed in the English colonies was built by Thomas Witt at Philadelphia.

1704   The first underground sewer was built in Boston.

November 22, 1704   Delaware's first legislature met, as allowed by the Pennsylvania Charter of Liberties (November 8, 1701). Pennsylvania's governor served as chief executive for this province, which was technically termed the Three Lower Counties on the Delaware.

August 24, 1706   Spanish and French forces unsuccessfully attacked Charles Town, South Carolina.

1706   The earliest known gallstone operation was performed by Dr. Zabdiel Boylston at Boston.

September 21, 1707   Abnaki Indians raided Winter Harbor, Maine.

1707   South Carolina troops attacked Spanish at Pensacola, Florida.

August 30, 1708   Indians inflicted heavy losses at Haverhill, Massachusetts.

1709   The first copper mine in the English colonies was established at Simsbury, Connecticut.

1709   The first mental hospital in Anglo-America was opened in Philadelphia.

July 30, 1711   A naval task force of 5,000 redcoats, 2,000 colonists, and 6,000 sailors embarked from Boston for an attack on Quebec. After losing nearly a thousand men drowned in shipwrecks in the St. Lawrence River in late August, the attack was canceled.

September 22, 1711   Tuscarora Indians launched attacks on the North Carolina frontier and inflicted heavy losses. By March 1713,

when their last major stronghold was taken, more than a thousand Tuscarora had been killed or captured. Most surviving Tuscarora migrated to New York where they became the Sixth Nation of the Iroquois.

April 6, 1712   Two dozen slaves set fires in New York and killed nine whites trying to extinguish them. Eighteen slaves were later executed, and six others escaped hanging by committing suicide.

May 9, 1712   Separate governorships were established for North and South Carolina by the proprietors.

1712   The first fines for speeding were given to cart drivers who careened too fast through Philadelphia.

April 11, 1713   Treaty of Utrecht ended Queen Anne's War.

1714   The earliest play written and printed in the colonies was *Androborus* by Gov. Robert Hunter of New York. It was not produced.

1714   The French built Ft. Toulouse on the Alabama River (near Wetumpka, Alabama, and Ft. Tombecbe, at confluence of the Tombigbee and Black Warrior Rivers (near Demopolis, Alabama).

April 15, 1715   Yamassee and Creek Indians launched attacks that drove back the South Carolina frontier to Charles Town's outskirts. A counteroffensive by white militia, armed slaves, and Cherokee Indians decisively defeated the Yamassee by January 1716.

May 1715   George I restored Maryland to the fourth Lord Baltimore, a Protestant, and reinstituted the charter of 1632.

June 6, 1716   The first black slaves came to Louisiana. By 1732, slaves would compose about two-thirds of lower Louisiana's people.

September 14, 1716   The first lighthouse in the thirteen colonies began operation at Boston, Massachusetts.

November 26, 1716   The first African lion in the colonies was exhibited in Boston.

1716   The first theater was built at Williamsburg, Virginia, by William Livingston; it closed in 1723 and was later used for town offices.

1718   Parliament passed the Transportation Act, which authorized the sentencing of convicts to labor in the colonies for seven to fourteen years. From then to 1775, the colonies received about 50,000 convicts, most of whom left the colonies when freed.

November 1718   New Orleans founded by Jean-Baptiste Le Moyne, sieur de Bienville.

November 22, 1718   The pirate Blackbeard died at Pamlico Sound, North Carolina, when attacked by an armed ship under Lt. Robert Maynard of Virginia.

1719   French built Ft. Ouiatanon on Wabash River in Indiana.

November 1719   South Carolinians usurped the government from their proprietors and requested to be taken over by the Crown.

1720   The French built Ft. Niagara in New York.

May 29, 1721   George I proclaimed South Carolina a royal colony.

May 25, 1721   The first American marine-and-fire-insurance company commenced business under John Copson at Philadelphia.

1722–1725   Massachusetts fought Dummer's War against the Abnaki Indians of Maine.

1723   Interior plumbing was built into the Newport, Rhode Island home of John Headley, who received spring water via an underground pipe.

December 16, 1723   The earliest public concert in Anglo-America was performed at Boston.

1724   French built Ft. Vincennes on Wabash River in Indiana.

1724   The first flood levees on the Mississippi River were built in Louisiana.

Spring 1724   Earliest English settlement in Vermont made at Ft. Dummer, near modern Brattleboro.

September 19, 1727   First newspaper in the southern colonies, the *Maryland Gazette,* was published at Annapolis.

March 9, 1728   South Carolinians retaliated for Indian raids by destroying a Yamassee Indian village near St. Augustine, Florida.

1728   John Bartram established the first botanical gardens at Philadelphia.

November 29, 1729 Natchez Indians launched major attacks on French in Louisiana. After losing Ft. Rosalie and several hundred casualties, the French and their Choctaw allies prevailed in 1730, when they killed or captured perhaps 1,400 Natchez.

July 25, 1729 North Carolina became a royal colony.

1729 The first literary work to appear as a newspaper serial was Daniel Defoe's *Religious Courtship* in the *Philadelphia Gazette.*

1730 Daniel Coxe of New Jersey became the first American appointed as a grand master of Masonic lodges.

1731 French built Ft. Crown Point in New York.

July 31, 1731 Philadelphians led by Benjamin Franklin founded America's first circulating library. In November 1732, Louis Timothee became the first person paid to work as a librarian.

February 26, 1732 The thirteen colonies' first Roman Catholic church north of Maryland celebrated its premier mass in Philadelphia.

1732 The first regularly operating stagecoach line began to run between Burlington and Perth Amboy, New Jersey.

May 6, 1732 The first foreign-language newspaper in Anglo-America, the German *Philadelphische Zeitung,* was printed in Pennsylvania.

June 20, 1732 Georgia's charter was issued to twenty-one trustees, who were responsible for supervising its growth until 1753. The charter's provisions forbade slavery within the colony.

1732 Daniel Henchman and Thomas Hancock published the first American road atlas and travel guide, *Vade Mecum for America; or a Companion for Traders and Travellers.*

December 6, 1732 New York City's first theater, the New Theater on Nassau St., opened with George Farquhar's play, *The Recruiting Officer.*

December 19, 1732 Benjamin Franklin published the first *Poor Richard's Almanac* in Philadelphia.

1732 The first planetarium in America was established when Harvard College imported an orrery, a mechanical model that showed the position and movement of stars and planets.

February 12, 1733 James Oglethorpe founded Savannah, Georgia.

July 30, 1733 The first Masonic Lodge in the present-day United States organized on a permanent basis was chartered as St. John's of Boston, Massachusetts.

August 18, 1734 William Bull of South Carolina became the first native-born American to earn a doctor's degree from a medical school by graduating from the University of Leyden in Holland.

February 8, 1735 The first opera in Anglo-America, Colley Cibber's *Flora, or the Hob in the Well,* opened at Charles Town, South Carolina.

1735 The first medical society was organized at Boston.

February 5, 1736 John Wesley, early Methodism's most influential leader, landed at Savannah, Georgia, as minister to an Anglican parish. He departed on December 2, 1737, after a grand jury charged him with defaming a parishioner's reputation by denying her communion.

March 17, 1737 America's first St. Patrick's Day celebration was held in Boston by the Charitable Irish Society.

1737 The first greenhouse in the present-day United States was built by Andrew Faneuil at Boston.

August 25, 1739 Rev. George Whitefield, the man whose preaching sparked America's first widespread revival, the Great Awakening, arrived in Philadelphia from England.

September 9, 1739 The only large-scale slave revolt of the colonial era began with the theft of arms and ammunition from a store at Stono River Bridge 20 miles beyond Charles Town, South Carolina. About 100 slaves armed themselves, burned 7 plantations, and killed 20 citizens that day before being overwhelmed by local militia.

October 19, 1739 England commenced the War of Jenkins' Ear by declaring war on Spain.

1739 Pierre and Paul Mallet explored the Arkansas River as far west as Colorado and became the first Europeans to sight the Rocky Mountains from the Great Plains.

January 1740 James Oglethorpe's Georgia and South Carolina troops took Spanish forts at San Francisco de Pupo and Picolata, Florida.

May–July 1740 Spanish troops at St. Augustine, Florida, withstood a three-month siege by General Oglethorpe's colonial troops.

Spring–Summer 1741 Hysteria swept New York City, where rumors of an impending slave revolt led to the execution of thirty-five suspected conspirators (including four whites) and the banishment of seventy slaves to other colonies.

1741 The first genuine porcelain produced in America was made at Andrew Duche's pottery in Savannah, Georgia.

1741 Sailing under orders from Russia's czar, Vitus Bering prepared the way for Russian expansion by mapping the Aleutian Islands and Alaskan coastline.

June 9, 1742 An invading army of 3,000 Spaniards was defeated with heavy losses by 650 colonists and Scottish Highlanders under James Oglethorpe at the Battle of Bloody Marsh, on St. Simons Island, Georgia.

1742 The first cookbook written in the present-day United States was published at Williamsburg, Virginia.

1742 The first school for girls, the Moravian Seminary for Women, was founded at Bethlehem, Pennsylvania.

May 14, 1743 Benjamin Franklin and other Philadelphians founded the colonies' first chartered organization for promoting scientific knowledge, the American Philosophical Society.

March 15, 1744 France and England entered the War of the Austrian Succession (known to Anglo-Americans as King George's War).

1744 A Collegium Musicum, the thirteen colonies' earliest chamber orchestra, was organized at Bethlehem, Pennsylvania. By 1748 the ensemble had eight pieces in its string section, four in the brass, and two flutes.

June 17, 1745 Gen. William Pepperell of Maine and 4,000 Yankees captured the French fortress of Louisbourg and 1,500 prisoners.

November 29, 1745 French and Indians burned Saratoga, New York.

Fall 1746 Lucy Terry, a slave, composed the earliest known poetry written by an African American. The unpublished verse was a ballad titled "Bars Fight," which described the Indian raid of August 25, 1746, on Deerfield, Massachusetts.

1747 The first bar association was founded by New York lawyers.

1748 First English settlement west of the Appalachian crest founded at Draper's Meadows, Virginia.

July 1748 Pennsylvania and Ohio Valley Indians signed the Treaty of Lancaster, which allowed English merchants to share in the western fur trade that the French had traditionally dominated.

October 18, 1748 Treaty of Aix-la-Chapelle ended Anglo-French warfare in America and returned Louisbourg to France.

June 1749 The first waxworks museum was opened by James Wyatt in New York City.

October 26, 1749 Georgia's trustees ended the colony's ban on importing slaves.

1749 Benjamin Franklin invented the lightning rod.

April 13, 1750 While exploring for the Ohio Land Company, Dr. Thomas Walker discovered Cumberland Gap, Kentucky.

March 5, 1750 The first American acting company, founded by Thomas Kean and Walter Murray, gave *Richard III* at New York as its premier performance, with Kean in the title role.

1750 The first Arabian thoroughbred horse, Selima, was imported from England to Belair, Maryland, by Colonel Tasker.

February 25, 1751 The first trained monkey act performed in New York.

1751 Sugarcane cultivation was introduced to Louisiana by colonists from the French Caribbean.

February 6, 1752 The first general hospital (other than a pesthouse or quarantine center) opened in Philadelphia.

The mid-eighteenth century's most notable military campaign was the successful assault against the massive French fortress at Louisbourg. Here the Massachusetts troops are shown embarking for the siege under Governor Pepperell in 1745. (Courtesy Library of Congress)

June 21, 1752　A French attack on the Pennsylvania trading post at Pickawillany (near Piqua, Ohio) forced English fur traders to abandon the Ohio valley and reestablished French influence over the western Indians.

July 4, 1752　Georgia's parliamentary trustees tranferred control of the colony to George II.

1752　The first professional European actors to tour America, the Hallam Company, premiered at Williamsburg, Virginia, with *The Merchant of Venice.* The company's repertoire of forty plays was seen in New York, Philadelphia, and Jamaica by 1754, when it disbanded.

September 25, 1753　The first steam engine was brought from England by Joshua Hornblower to North Arlington, New Jersey, for use in the Schuyler copper mines. The pumping machine began operation in March 1755.

Spring–Summer 1753　French troops built Ft. Presqu'Ile (Erie, Pennsylvania), Ft. Le Boeuf (Waterford, Pennsylvania), and Ft. Machault (Franklin, Pennsylvania) to block English expansion in the Ohio valley.

April 17, 1754　French troops occupied the forks of the Ohio and began to build Ft. Duquesne at modern Pittsburgh.

May 19, 1754　The first newspaper cartoon was printed in Benjamin Franklin's *Pennsylvania Gazette;* it used a dismembered snake to symbolize colonial disunity in the face of French aggression.

May 28, 1754　First blood of Seven Years' War shed when Virginia troops ambushed a French scouting party 50 miles from Ft. Duquesne.

June 19–July 10, 1754　First meeting of representatives from most colonies, the Albany Congress, was held to devise responses to the French threat. It advised a Plan of Union that failed to gain approval from either colonial assemblies or British officials.

July 4, 1754　French troops capture Ft. Necessity, at Great Meadows, Pennsylvania, from Virginians and redcoats under George Washington.

May 27, 1755　The first pumping system to furnish piped city water was operated using a water mill at Bethlehem, Pennsylvania.

July 9, 1755　French and Indians killed 900 redcoats and colonists under Gen. Edward Braddock near Ft. Duquesne.

June 19, 1755　Massachusetts forces took Ft. Beauséjour and by June 30 had driven French troops from Nova Scotia's border.

September 8, 1755　Troops under William Johnson of New York defeated French and Indians at Battle of Lake George.

October 8, 1755　The first of several thousand Acadians, French civilians in Nova Scotia, underwent forced deportation to other English colonies for disloyalty to Britain. Many exiles went to Louisiana, where they became known as Cajuns.

April 1, 1756　French destroyed Ft. Bull, on Wood Creek, New York.

May 17, 1756　Britain declared war on France and officially began the conflict known as the Seven Years' War in Europe but the French and Indian War to Anglo-Americans.

July 3, 1756　Outnumbered colonial troops under Col. John Bradstreet defeated French and Indians near Ft. Oswego, New York.

August 14, 1756　French forces under the Marquis de Montcalm captured 1,600 British prisoners at Ft. Oswego, New York.

August 30, 1756　Pennsylvania militia rescued white prisoners and destroyed the Indian village of Kittaning.

July 22, 1757　Half of 350 New York and New Jersey provincials on a scouting mission were killed or captured by French and Indians near Ft. William Henry, New York.

August 9, 1757　The Marquis de Montcalm captured 2,000 British troops at Ft. William Henry, New York. Indians afterward

A major challenge to English land claims west of the Appalachians was the French construction of three forts along the portage route from Lake Erie to the beginning of the Ohio River in 1753. This picture shows a scale model of Fort Machault, built at the present location of Franklin, Pennsylvania. (Record Group 13 [WPA, Frontier Forts and Trails Survey] Courtesy Pennsylvania State Archives)

killed many of the disarmed soldiers as they marched from the garrison.

July 8, 1758 Montcalm repulsed British assault on Ft. Ticonderoga (Carillon), New York, and inflicted 2,000 casualties on the attackers.

July 26, 1758 Gen. Jeffery Amherst captured Louisbourg, a French garrison with 6,000 troops and civilians, after a two-month siege.

August 27, 1758 Col. John Bradstreet and 2,500 colonial troops took Ft. Frontenac and severed French supply lines to the Ohio valley.

September 11, 1758 French defeated 900 Highlanders and provincials under Maj. James Grant who made a surprise attack on Ft. Duquesne.

October 12, 1758 Colonial soldiers at Ft. Ligonier, Pennsylvania, beat off an attack by 1,000 French and Indians attempting to cut the supply line of British troops advancing on Ft. Duquesne.

November 25, 1758 Gen. John Forbes's Anglo-American army occupied the ruins of Ft. Duquesne, which the French had burned and deserted.

July 25, 1759 French garrison of Ft. Niagara, New York, surrendered to Anglo-American forces under Sir William Johnson of New York.

July 26, 1759 The French blew up and abandoned Ft. Ticonderoga (Carillon) as General Amherst's British army advanced on it.

July 31, 1759 Ft. Crown Point, New York, was blown up and abandoned by the French as General Amherst's British army advanced on it.

September 13, 1759 Gen. James Wolfe's British forces defeated Montcalm's army at Quebec. Both commanders fell mortally wounded.

October 6, 1759 American Rangers under Maj. Robert Rogers destroyed the Abnaki Indian village of St. François.

December 13, 1759 Michael Hillegas opened the thirteen colonies' first music shop at Philadelphia.

Winter 1760 The Cherokee War commenced with attacks on South Carolina frontier.

March 20, 1760 The colonial era's most destructive fire burned 176 warehouses and left every tenth family homeless in Boston.

August 10, 1760 Cherokee massacred disarmed British redcoats who had surrendered to them at Ft. Loudoun, Tennessee, three days earlier.

September 8, 1760 British army under Jeffery Amherst accepted the surrender of Canada following a siege of Montreal.

1760 The first poetry published by an African American, "An Evening Thought, Salvation by Christ, with Penitential Cries," was printed for Jupiter Hammon, a slave of Queen's Village, New York.

ca. 1760 The first bifocals were devised by Benjamin Franklin.

Summer 1761 The last expedition of South Carolina's Cherokee War was led by Lt. Col. James Grant, whose redcoats and provincials survived ambush at Echoee Pass and burned numerous Indian villages.

February 24, 1761 James Otis gave an impassioned, fiery, legal brief denouncing the Writs of Assistance (general search warrants) as unconstitutional before the Massachusetts Supreme Court. John Adams, who heard Otis, later wrote, "Otis was a flame of fire … Then and there the child Independence was born."

1761 The first Venetian blinds were installed at St. Peter's Church in Philadelphia.

1761 The first pile bridge was constructed at York, Maine.

January 2, 1762 Great Britain declared war on Spain. Yankee privateers swarmed into the Caribbean to hunt Spanish vessels.

Fall 1762 Regiments from Connecticut, Rhode Island, New York, and New Jersey fought at the two-month siege of Havana, Cuba, which surrendered to the British on October 5, 1762.

February 10, 1763 The Treaty of Paris ended the Seven Years' War. Britain gained possession of Spanish Florida and French Canada.

CHAPTER 4 The Economy

More statistical information has survived about the economy than any other topic in colonial history, but the existing data remains far from complete for any subject concerning the production, consumption, and distribution of early American wealth. The British customs service documented American trade in massive detail, for example; yet even its figures are incomplete because numerous goods were exempt from registration. Historians have still not undertaken a comprehensive examination of British customs ledgers, nor have they solved the problem of estimating the volume of undocumented trade, both legal and illegal. Scholars likewise have barely begun to exploit the vast stock of facts regarding farm production, commodity prices, consumption, and personal income compiled by colonial probate courts.

The English and colonial governments collected no set of statistics corresponding to modern economic concepts such as gross national product or per capita earnings. Historians have still not devised reliable calculations for the total value of agricultural, maritime, commercial, and industrial output prior to 1763. Comprehensive statistics describing economic activities rarely exist for all years prior to 1763, especially before 1700, and data are quite thin for most colonies. Because much of the best recent work by economic historians has involved studies of small localities in particular provinces, the data needed to build firm approximations of gross output and income levels will remain extremely fragmentary long into the foreseeable future.

This chapter's data are first organized according to type of economic activity (agriculture, maritime pursuits, etc.). Because of governmental regulation over oceanic trade, much more is known about the production of export goods than about the economy's purely domestic functions, which absorbed perhaps nine-tenths of colonial output. The latter sections of the chapter provide information on such general topics as gross measures of economic transactions, levels of wealth, price indices, and the use of unfree or contract labor.

A Note on Monetary Values

England's law forbade the export of that kingdom's gold and silver coins overseas during the colonial period. Anglo-Americans consequently obtained their main stock of circulating money through overseas commerce with the Spanish Empire. The prime coin was Spain's silver dollar, which equaled four shillings, six pence (4s, 6d) in British sterling, whose primary unit (the pound) was divided into twenty shillings (20s), each of twelve pence (12d). Because silver and gold always remained relatively scarce in North America, Spanish coins commanded more purchasing power there than their official exchange rate would have yielded in Europe. This premium of Spanish coinage to official English currency values became known as the proclamation rate, which expressed the local value of Spanish bullion in units of pounds, shillings, and pence. When colonial governments issued their own paper monies, they also set exchange values according to this proclamation rate. The following table gives an approximate indication of how exchange rates varied in the thirteen colonies and how mid-eighteenth-century American monetary values compared with modern U.S. dollars. (For more detailed information, see section entitled "Currency and Money Supply" and Table 4.194).

Agriculture

Although at least 66 percent of all colonists engaged in farming, surprisingly little is still known about early American agriculture. The most systematic series of data concern price fluctuations for major commodities, volume of exports, and rough estimates of yields per acre. Because few personal records have survived—and those mostly kept by wealthy planters who were untypical of average individuals—there remains a great lack of understanding of how most farms operated and how agricultural production changed over time. This section first provides information about the land, livestock, farm equipment, productivity, and work schedules of farmers; it then lists available data concerning prices, yields, and exports for twelve major agricultural commodities.

The Farm

Unlike their European counterparts, who were overwhelmingly tenants renting small properties from the aristocracy, colonial farmers generally owned their own land. American tenants were largely young men still accumulating savings for a down payment, and a majority seem to have negotiated a mortgage well before middle age. The acreage cultivated by an American farmer was furthermore significantly larger than the usual agricultural unit in Europe. American landowners consequently had more land than family members could sow in crops, often more than 100 acres, and so could afford luxuries beyond the means of most European peasants, such as planting orchards and breeding small herds of livestock. Few farms achieved self-sufficiency in its most literal meaning—that of providing every item needed to support their owners' families—but most became essentially self-sufficient by producing a surplus to sell or barter for foodstuffs or consumer goods that they needed.

The following tables and documents describe both the material context and labor situation of early American agriculture. Little research has been done to estimate the size of a typical farm, but the study of probate records is slowly providing more information on livestock holdings. Probate records have also been used to reconstruct the operation and hypothetical output of average farmers in several colonies. An appreciation for the daily and yearly rhythms of agricultural life can be gleaned from various work schedules and crop-rotation practices.

Colonial Currency of 1725–1738		British Sterling of 1725–1738		Equivalent Value of U.S. Dollars in 1991
£1 Massachusetts	=	5s, 6d	=	$26.60
£1 New York	=	12s, 1d	=	$58.25
£1 Pennsylvania	=	12s, 9d	=	$61.25
£1 Maryland	=	15s	=	$72.00
£1 Virginia	=	16s, 8d	=	$80.25
£1 South Carolina	=	2s, 10d	=	$13.60

TABLE 4.1 MEDIAN SIZE OF CONNECTICUT FARMS OWNED BY MEN AGE 40–60 DURING 1640–1699

Period	Farm Size
1640–1679	79 acres
1680–1689	80 acres
1689–1699	92 acres

Source: Probate records analyzed in Jackson T. Main, *Society and Economy in Colonial Connecticut* (1985), 68.

Richard Schlicht's painting of Martin's Hundred, Virginia, portrays a newly organized agricultural community in Virginia during the early 1620s. Fields of corn (lower left and upper right) and winter wheat (upper left) border the settlement, a large vegetable garden has been cultivated (lower left), and a fence surrounds the central stockade to corral cattle at night. After the settlers have cleared enough fields for their food needs and laid up a year's stock of grain and salted meat, they will turn their energies to the Chesapeake's main cash crop, tobacco. (Courtesy Richard Schlicht, National Geographic Image Collection)

TABLE 4.2 MEDIAN ACREAGE, COMPOSITION, AND VALUE (IN LOCAL CURRENCY) OF CONNECTICUT FARMS OWNED BY MEN AGE 40–60 DURING 1670–1754

	1670–1699	1720–1729	1750–1754
Value of buildings	£34	£45	£60
Improved lands[a]			
acreage	35 acres	34 acres	41 acres
value/acre	£3/acre	£4/acre	£4.10/acre
Uncultivated lands[b]			
acreage	70 acres	102 acres	105 acres
value/acre	£2.5/acre	£2.5/acre	£2.10/acre
Average of total			
acreage	100 acres	170 acres	137 acres
value/acre	£1.10/acre	£2/acre	£3/acre

[a] Home lots, plowland, orchards, and meadows.
[b] Fenced woodlands.
Source: Probate records analyzed in Jackson T. Main, *Society and Economy in Colonial Connecticut* (1985), 207.

TABLE 4.3 CULTIVABLE LAND (NOT INCLUDING PASTURE) AND LIVESTOCK OF FARMS AS REPORTED ON TAX LISTS OF LONG ISLAND IN 1675 AND BOSTON IN 1687

	Long Island, N.Y., 1675		Boston, Mass., 1687	
	Dutch Towns	English Towns	Muddy River [Brookline]	Romney Marsh [Chelsea]
Number of farms	146	259	30	33
Average acreage	38 acres	18 acres	13.5 acres	37.4 acres
Cattle				
percent of farms with cattle	97%	89%	100%	94%
average number	8.1	9.8	6.3	10.8
largest herd	36	37	13	40

(continued)

TABLE 4.3 (continued)

	Long Island, N.Y., 1675		Boston, Mass., 1687	
	Dutch Towns	English Towns	Muddy River [Brookline]	Romney Marsh [Chelsea]
Oxen (4 years old)				
percent of farms with oxen	24%	72%	29%	79%
average number	2.2	3.1	2.2	2.7
largest number	6	12	4	8
Swine				
percent of farms with swine	50%	64%	42%	85%
average number	2.4	6.7	2.2	3.3
largest herd	9	30	5	20
Sheep (year old)				
percent of farms with sheep	21%	43%	42%	88%
average number	5.9	12.7	16.5	51.5
largest flock	16	81	40	370
Horses				
percent of farms with horses	84%	85%	97%	80%
average number	3.0	2.4	1.9	2.5
largest number	8	9	4	8

Source: Percy W. Bidwell and John I. Falconer, *History of Agriculture in the Northern U.S., 1620–1860* (1925), 26–37.

TABLE 4.4 PRICES (IN STERLING) OF FARMLAND IN ANNE ARUNDEL CO., MD., 1660–1756

Period	Price
1660–1678	6.32s per acre
1679–1696	5.88s per acre
1697–1705	13.03s per acre
1706–1717	9.45s per acre
1718–1726	10.25s per acre
1727–1732	8.58s per acre
1733–1741	9.77s per acre
1742–1750	10.35s per acre
1751–1753	14.81s per acre
1754–1756	14.63s per acre

Source: Carville V. Earle, *The Evolution of a Tidewater Settlement System: All Hallow's Parish, Maryland, 1650–1783* (1975), 210.

TABLE 4.5 MEDIAN SIZES OF LANDHOLDINGS IN VIRGINIA, 1704, AND MARYLAND, 1707

Virginia, 1704		
County	Landholdings	Median Size
Charles City	94	200 acres
Elizabeth City	116	110 acres
Gloucester	381	230 acres
James City	287	180 acres
Middlesex	122	200 acres
Nansemond	376	200 acres
Princess Anne	215	298 acres
Warwick	122	155 acres
York	205	150 acres
Maryland, 1707		
County	Landholdings	Median Size
Anne Arundel	134	176 acres

Source: Thomas J. Wertenbaker, *The Planters of Colonial Virginia* (1922), 183–247. Carville V. Earle, *The Evolution of a Tidewater Settlement System: All Hallow's Parish, Maryland* (1975), 203.

TABLE 4.6 MEAN VALUE (IN LOCAL CURRENCY) OF FARM BUILDINGS AND REAL ESTATE IN CONNECTICUT, 1675–1754

	1675–1699	1700–1714	1720–1729	1750–1754
House	£20	£25	£30	£35
Barn	£14	£14	£14	£10
Price/acre	£2/acre	£2/acre	£2.10/acre	£4/acre

Source: Probate records analyzed in Jackson T. Main, *Society and Economy in Colonial Connecticut* (1985), 58–59.

TABLE 4.7 LAND AVAILABLE FOR FARMING, PER FAMILY, IN CONNECTICUT, 1680–1779

Decade	Land per Family
1680–89	486 acres
1690–99	414 acres
1700–09	404 acres
1710–19	397 acres
1720–29	314 acres
1730–39	242 acres
1740–49	208 acres
1750–59	166 acres
1760–69	131 acres
1770–79	106 acres

Source: Bruce C. Daniels, *The Fragmentation of New England: Comparative Perspectives on Economic, Political, and Social Divisions in the Eighteenth Century* (1988), 6.

TABLE 4.8 UTILIZATION OF FARMLAND IN EIGHTEENTH-CENTURY NEW ENGLAND

Massachusetts						
Place	Year	All Taxable Acreage	Percent Used in Tillage	Percent Used in English Hay	Percent Used in Meadow Hay	Percent Used in Other Pasture
Milton	1760	3,791	8.9%	20.7%	12.2%	54.7%
Chelsea	1760	2,896	6.4%	11.5%	2.1%	78.3%
Counties of Norfolk, Essex, & Middlesex	1767	328,000	12.8%	10.7%	18.0%	58.5%
Oxford	1781	4,062	16.4%	10.4%	30.4%	42.8%
Connecticut						
Place	Year	All Taxable Acreage	Percent Used in Tillage	Percent Used in English Hay	Percent Used in Meadow Hay	Percent Used in Other Pasture
Towns of Hadley, South Hadley, Amherst, and Granby	1773	9,086	49.5%	14.9%	22.6%	13.0%
Rhode Island						
Place	Year	All Taxable Acreage	Percent Used in Tillage	Percent Used in English Hay	Percent Used in Meadow Hay	Percent Used in Other Pasture
Newport	1761	3,672	4.1%	...	30.4%	63.4%

Note: The percent of acreage in orchards was: 1.7% in Chelsea, Massachusetts; 2.1% in Newport, Rhode Island; and 3.4% in Milton, Massachusetts.
Source: Max G. Schumacher, *The Northern Farmer and His Markets During the Late Colonial Period* (1975), 23.

A colonial farmer would slowly increase his homestead's value by constructing outbuildings for specialized functions, such as a smokehouse, various storage sheds, and perhaps a detached kitchen, besides covering his spring and digging root cellars. An example of how a prosperous husbandman might situate such improvements as these around his home can be seen in the above photo of the Joseph Gilpin house, which dates from 1745, at Chadd's Ford in Delaware County, Pennsylvania. A front view of this home and its outbuildings appears in photo on page 282. (Historic American Buildings Survey, courtesy Library of Congress)

TABLE 4.9 AVERAGE VALUE OF BUILDINGS AND REAL ESTAGE ON FARMS IN CONNECTICUT (IN POUNDS AND SHILLINGS, PROCLAMATION), 1765–1769

Property	Hartford	New Haven	Guilford	Fairfield	Average
House	£50	£35	£42	£50	£45
Barn	£15	£10	£9	£12	£12
Other buildings	£15	£10	£4	£4	£8
Meadow (1 acre)	£9	£6	£8	£6.12	£7
Tillage (1 acre)	£5	£5.3	£5.13	£8.5	£5.10
Woodland (1 acre)	12s	£1	13s	18s	15s
average value of 1-acre farm land	£3.10	£4.10	£4.10	n.a.	£4

Source: Jackson Turner Main, *Society and Economy in Colonial Connecticut* (1985), 59.

TABLE 4.10 PERCENT OF ESTATES OWNING LIVESTOCK IN ALL HALLOW'S PARISH, MD., 1660–1769

Period	Cattle	Horses	Hogs	Sheep
1660–79	71%	47%	56%	3%
1680–89	79%	81%	70%	21%
1690–99	67%	77%	72%	10%
1700–09	75%	84%	75%	23%
1710–19	80%	85%	78%	48%
1720–29	83%	90%	75%	44%
1730–39	78%	91%	83%	54%
1740–49	91%	97%	92%	72%
1750–59	83%	96%	77%	58%
1760–69	89%	90%	85%	63%

Source: Carville V. Earle, *The Evolution of a Tidewater Settlement System: All Hallow's Parish, Maryland, 1650–1783* (1975), 122.

TABLE 4.11 NUMBER AND VALUE (IN LOCAL CURRENCY) OF LIVESTOCK OWNED BY CONNECTICUT FARMERS AGE 40–60, 1670–1769

Livestock	Median Owned	Value per Head
Cattle	13	£2.3.5
Horses	3	£3.3.0
Sheep	16	5s
Swine	7	9s

Note: Size of livestock holdings changed little in this period.
Source: Probate records analyzed in Jackson T. Main, Society and Economy in Colonial Connecticut (1985), 236–238.

TABLE 4.12 AVERAGE NUMBER OF LIVESTOCK OWNED BY MARYLAND RESIDENTS, 1656–1719

Percent of population by wealth level	No. of Cattle	No. of Horses	No. of Swine	Percent with Swine	No. of Sheep	Percent with Sheep
Bottom 30%	9.8	2.2	8.6	(75%)	8.2	(27%)
Lower-mid 30%	21.2	3.3	19.2	(90%)	13.2	(45%)
Upper-mid 30%	34.2	4.9	24.0	(92%)	20.6	(58%)
Upper 10%	76.3	9.9	51.7	(100%)	32.2	(81%)

Source: Probate records analyzed in Gloria L. Main, Tobacco Colony: Life in Early Maryland, 1650–1720 (1982), 62.

TABLE 4.13 AVERAGE LIVESTOCK HOLDINGS IN ALL HALLOW'S PARISH, MD., 1660–1759

Period	Cattle	Hogs	Horses	Sheep
1660–79	14.88	11.85	1.68	.62
1680–89	19.47	16.45	2.67	3.63
1690–99	17.00	12.93	2.15	1.48
1700–09	17.22	16.53	2.55	3.96
1710–19	23.55	22.24	4.72	11.50
1720–29	22.56	21.58	4.48	8.04
1730–39	26.78	40.68	5.54	12.80
1740–49	25.85	38.56	5.34	15.27
1750–59	22.33	35.50	5.44	15.75

Source: Carville V. Earle, The Evolution of a Tidewater Settlement System: All Hallow's Parish, Maryland, 1650–1783 (1975), 124.

TABLE 4.14 AVERAGE LIVESTOCK OWNED BY RESIDENTS OF CHESTER AND LANCASTER COUNTIES, PA., 1713–1772

Period	No. of Cattle	Percent of Young	No. of Horses	Percent of Young	No. of Sheep	Percent of Young	No. of Swine
1713–16	8.6	(58%)	6.0	(21%)	15.6	(9%)	9.7
1728–37	9.6	(56%)	6.7	(33%)	12.0	(5%)	8.9
1750	8.3	(57%)	3.8	(22%)	12.3	(8%)	6.7
1761	9.3	(39%)	4.2	(22%)	12.3	(4%)	5.8
1772	9.4	(47%)	3.9	(19%)	14.9	(6%)	7.3

Source: Probate records analyzed in James T. Lemon, The Best Poor Man's Country: A Geographical Study of Early Southeastern Pennsylvania (1972), 162.

TABLE 4.15 AVERAGE LIVESTOCK HOLDINGS IN SHENANDOAH VALLEY, VA., ABOUT 1750

County	Cows	Steers	Swine	Sheep	Horses
Frederick County	11	3	7	5	9
Augusta County	11	3	14	7	7

Source: Probate records analyzed in Robert D. Mitchell, Commercialism and Frontier: Perspectives on the Early Shenandoah Valley (1977), 140, 148.

TABLE 4.16 PERCENTAGE OF COLONIAL HOUSEHOLDS OWNING PLOWS, 1636–1769

Place	1636–1664	1639–1648	1690–1699	1710–1719	1740–1749	1750–1759	1760–1769
Essex Co., Mass.	28%...	...	...	...	...	...	...
Hartford, Conn.	...	53%	...	...	...	...	...
Anne Arundel Co., Md.	...	...	8%	20%	66%	44%	61%
Augusta Co., Va.	...	...	...	...	33%	30%	35%
Frederick Co., Va.	...	...	...	...	40%	35%	48%

Source: Carville V. Earle, The Evolution of A Tidewater Settlement System: All Hallow's Parish, Maryland, 1650–1783 (1975), 122–123. Robert D. Mitchell, Commercialism and Frontier: Perspectives on the Early Shenandoah Valley (1977), 115. Percy W. Bidwell and John I. Falconer, History of Agriculture in the Northern United States, 1620–1860 (1935), 35.

TABLE 4.17 CROP YIELDS AND PROFITS PER ACRE IN CONNECTICUT, 1640–1774

	Yields per Acre			Value (Local Money) per Acre	
	low	high	average	1640–1740	1750–1774
wheat	4 bu.	12 bu.	6.5 bu.	24s/acre	28s/acre
corn	6 bu.	20 bu.	10 bu.	20s/acre	22s/acre
rye	4.5 bu.	5 bu.	4.75 bu.	13s, 3d/acre	14s, 9d/acre
oats	...	...	12 bu.	18s/acre	18s/acre
flax	...	...	...	20s/acre	20s/acre
meslin	...	...	...	20s/acre	20s/acre
peas & barley	...	...	...	18s/acre	18s/acre

Source: Probate records analyzed in Jackson T. Main, Society and Economy in Colonial Connecticut (1985), 239.

TABLE 4.18 ESTIMATED ANNUAL PRODUCTION OF AN AVERAGE FARM OF 120 ACRES IN THE SHENANDOAH VALLEY OF VIRGINIA ABOUT 1749

Crop	Acres Sown	Yield and Price per Bu.	Value (Local Money)
wheat/rye	8 acres	80 bu. @ 2s, 6d–3s	= £10.3.1
maize	5 acres	75 bu. @ 1s, 6d–2s	= £6.11.3
oats	3 acres	36 bu. @ 1s–1s, 3d	= £2.1.5
barley	¾ acre	9 bu. @ 1s–1s, 3d	= £0.10.4
flax	½ acre	7.5 bu.(225 lb.) @ 2s	= £0.15.0
Total value			£20.0.1

Livestock	Number	Yield	Volume (Local Money)
cattle	14	One 500 lb. steer slaughtered for 145 lb. beef	= £3.2.6
		One 500 lb. steer sold live @ 12s, 6d/100 lb.	= £3.2.6
swine	7	Two hogs @ 7 sh. each slaughtered for family use	= £0.14.0
Total value			£6.19.0
Conjectural Surplus for Sale			
Total value of crops and slaughtered livestock			= £26.19.1
Minus home consumption: 60% of grain			(–£12.15.¹/₂)
1 steer and 1 hog			(–£3.16.6)
Surplus for sale			= £10.7.6 ¹/₂

Source: Robert D. Mitchell, *Commercialism and Frontier: Perspectives on the Early Shenandoah Valley* (1977), 140–142, 148.

TABLE 4.19 ESTIMATED LAND USE AND CROP YIELDS OF A NONSLAVEHOLDING FARMER ON MARYLAND'S EASTERN SHORE, ABOUT 1760

Crop	Acreage	Yield
Tobacco	2.2 acres	1,110 lb.
Winter wheat	15.0 acres	90 bu.
Indian corn	4.0 acres	48 bu.
Pasturage	9.5 acres	…
Garden & orchard	3.0 acres	…

Source: Paul G. E. Clemens, *The Atlantic Economy and Colonial Maryland's Eastern Shore: From Tobacco to Grain* (1980), 197.

TABLE 4.20 ESTIMATED ANNUAL PRODUCTION OF AN AVERAGE FARM OF 125 ACRES IN LANCASTER OR CHESTER COUNTIES, PA., ABOUT 1760

Crops	Yields per Acre	Acres	Yield
Wheat	10 bu. (1 bu. sown)	8	80 bu.
Rye	12¹/₂	2	25
Oats	15	4	60
Barley	15	2	30
Buckwheat	15	2	30 (or green manure)
Indian corn	15	8	120
Total		26	345 bu.[a]
Flax and/or hemp	150 lb. hackled, 5 bu. seed	2	300 lb., 10 bu.
Potatoes, turnips	100 bu.	3	300 bu.
Fruit	6 bu. per apple tree at 70 trees per acre	2	800 bu.
Hay	1¹/₂ tons	20	30 tons
Other vegetables, tobacco	Amounts uncertain		

Livestock	Size (Live)	Number	Food Requirements for All Livestock			Yield
			Grain	Hay	Pasture	
Cattle	700 lb.	7:3 cows, 1 steer, 3 calves	100 bu. (13 acres)	20 tons (13 acres)	10–15 acres plus browse in forest and stubble	Meat: 450 lb. (1 carcass dressed) Dairy: milk, 300 gal.;

Livestock	Size (Live)	Number	Food Requirements for All Livestock			Yield
			Grain	Hay	Pasture	
Horses	1,000 lb.	3–4:1 young	80 bu. (5 acres)	9 tons (6 acres)	3 acres, etc.	cheese butter Plowing, road transport
Swine	175 lb.	8	30 bu. (2 acres)	…	Yes plus mast	Meat: 500–600 lb. dressed (4–5 carcasses)
Sheep	50 lb.	10:2 young (fall)	5 bu. (¹/₃ acre)	1 ton	1 acre	30 lb. wool
Poultry	…	…	…	…	…	Meat, eggs
Bees	…	1 or 2 hives	…	…	…	Honey, pollinated clover, etc.
Total			215 bu.	30 tons		

[a] Of which 30 bu. for seed and 215 for animals.
Source: James T. Lemon, *The Best Poor Man's Country: A Geographical Study of Early Southeastern Pennsylvania* (1972), 152.

TABLE 4.21 TRADITIONAL FIELD ROTATION USED IN EIGHTEENTH-CENTURY NEW JERSEY

	1st Year	2nd Year	3rd Year	4th Year
Field #1	corn	fallow	winter wheat	hay
Field #2	hay	corn	fallow	winter wheat
Field #3	winter wheat	hay	corn	fallow
Field #4	fallow	winter wheat	hay	corn

Source: John Rutherfurd, "Notes on the State of New Jersey," N.J. Historical Society, *Proceedings*, Ser. 2, I (1867–9), 78–89.

TABLE 4.22 ESTIMATED ANNUAL EXPENSES OF ESTABLISHING A SMALL FARM AND A RICE PLANTATION IN SOUTH CAROLINA, ABOUT 1710

Expense of a Small Farm in South Carolina, about 1710	
"2 Negro Slaves 40£ each	80£
4 cows and Calves, 1£. 5s each	5
4 Sows, 15s. each A Canoe 3£	6
A Steel Mill, or Pair of Querns	3
Axes, Hoes, Wedges, Hand-saws, Hammers, etc.	2
200 Acres of Land 4£. Survey and other Charges 2£	6
A small House for the first Year or two,	8
Corn, Pease, Beef, Pork, &c. for the first Year,	14
Expences and Contingencies	26
Total	150£

"This Calculation is made in the Money of the Province, which is just 100£ Sterling. The Things mention'd here of Necessity to one who would settle with any tolerable Decency. And from this small Begining, … a Man may get a competent Estate, and live very handsomly. But there are many who settle without any Slaves at all, but labour themselves."

"Here follows an Account of what is necessary to settle an Estate of 300£ *per Annum*, … [on a rice plantation]

"30 Negroes, 15 Men and 15 Women, 40£ each,	1200£
20 Cows and Calves, 1£ 5s. each	25
2 Mares, 1 Stone-horse, 10£ each, 6 Sows and a Boar 6£	36
1000 Acres of Land, 20£. Survey & other Charges 7£.	27

(continued)

TABLE 4.22 (continued)

A large Periagoe 20£. a small Canoe 2£. a Steel Mill 4£	26
10 Ewes and a Ram, 7£. 3 dozen Axes 6£.	13
Hoes, Hatchets, Broad Axes, Nails, Saws, Hammers, Wedges Maul Rings, a Froe, and other necessary tools	23
Ploughs, Carts, with their Chains and Irons,	10
A small House for the first Year or two, later a Kitchen	20
300 Bushels of *Indian* Corn and Pease, at 2s. 6d. *per* Bushel, with some Beef, Pork, &c. for the first Years Provision	50
Expences and Contingencies	70
Total	**1500£**

"This Sum of *Carolina* Money being reduc'd to Sterling, makes 1000£. The 30 Negroes begining to work in *September* or *October*, will clear 90 Acres of Land, plant and hoe it; half of which, that is 45 Acres, sowed with Rice, will, after the common Computation, yield 1000 Weight an Acre, which sold at 15s. a hundred, the middle Price, amounts to 337£ 10s. The other 45 Acres are to be sowed with *Indian* Corn, Pease, Pompions, Potatoes, Melons, and other Eatables, for the Use of the Family."

Source: Thomas Nairn Letter, 1710, in Jack P. Greene, ed., *Selling a New World: Two Colonial South Carolina Promotional Pamphlets* (1989), 63–65.

TABLE 4.23 VALUATION OF CROPS IN SPRINGFIELD, MASS., 1660–1670

Food Item	Price
apples	2s, 6d per bu.
barley	3s–4s per bu.
beef	$2^3/_4$d per lb.
cider	6d per qt. & 16s per barrel
corn	2s, 4d–2s, 6d per bu.
dung	8d per cartload
hemp	9d–10d per lb.
oats	2s per bu.
peas	2s, 6d per bu.
pork	$2^1/d$–3d per lb.
salt	5s–8s per bu.
sugar	8d–12d per lb.
turnips	12d–16d per bu.
turkeys	4s, 6d each
wheat	3s, 6d–3s, 10d per bu.

Source: Stephen Innes, *Labor in a New Land: Economy and Society in Seventeenth-Century Springfield* (1983), 464.

TABLE 4.24 PERCENT OF FARMS IN ALL HALLOW'S PARISH, MD., WITH AGRICULTURAL TOOLS NEEDED FOR SELF-SUFFICIENCY, 1660–1769

Period	Bee-hives	Fishing Items	Cider Items	Steel-yards	Planta-tion Tools	Spinning Wheels	Wool Cards	Wood-working Tools	Black-smith Tools	Shoe-maker's Tools	Tailor's Tools	Powdering Tubs, Milk Pans	Butter Pots, Butter	Butter Churns
1660–79	0	12%	27%	35%	29%	0	3%	24%	3%	0	0	0	6%	0
1680–89	0	9%	30%	36%	38%	4%	2%	26%	0	2%	0	21%	4%	8%
1690–99	3%	10%	39%	21%	49%	10%	5%	15%	3%	3%	8%	18%	8%	10%
1700–09	0	11%	41%	39%	45%	9%	14%	39%	5%	2%	7%	7%	7%	0
1710–19	0	15%	56%	28%	30%	15%	9%	30%	4%	4%	2%	4%	2%	0
1720–29	4%	4%	48%	31%	60%	33%	8%	23%	2%	2%	0	15%	2%	2%
1730–39	2%	13%	54%	31%	52%	39%	26%	35%	2%	6%	6%	11%	13%	6%
1740–49	8%	28%	75%	50%	80%	63%	47%	61%	2%	19%	8%	30%	25%	6%
1750–59	15%	15%	67%	42%	77%	50%	40%	46%	2%	21%	10%	19%	46%	6%
1760–69	13%	19%	66%	29%	71%	69%	39%	50%	5%	16%	2%	11%	29%	5%

Source: Carville V. Earle, *The Evolution of a Tidewater Settlement System: All Hallow's Parish, Maryland, 1650–1783* (1975), 122–123.

TABLE 4.25 ESTIMATED WORKDAYS (10 HOURS EACH) EXPENDED BY A FARM FAMILY WITH 3.25 FULL-TIME LABORERS IN VIRGINIA OR MARYLAND ABOUT 1750

Months	Tobacco Task	Days	Corn Task	Days	Wheat Task	Days
Jan.–Mar.	prepare 200 sq. yards of seed beds	18	…	…	hill, sow, harrow 10 acres	14
Apr.–May	prepare 4 acres of hills	40	hill 5 acres	30	roll & weed	2
May–Jun.	transplant seeds	8	sow 5 acres	2	…	
Jun.–Jul.	weed, rehill	30	weed	15	harvest	20
Jul.–Aug.	prime & top	10	weed	15	thresh & winnow	40
Aug.–Sep.	worm, sucker	48	sucker & top	15	…	…
Sep.–Oct.	cut, house, cure	32	harvest	15	…	…
Oct.–Nov.	strip, prize	40	…	…	…	…
Nov.–Dec.	…		husk	3	…	…
Total 10-hour workdays		226		95		76
Total workdays per worker		69		29		23
Total yields	2,000–4,000 lb. (1,230 lb. per laborer)		100 bu. (31 bu. per laborer)		60 bu. (18.5 bu. per laborer)	

Source: David O. Percy, "The Production of Tobacco Along the Colonial Potomac," "Corn: The Production of a Subsistence Crop on the Colonial Potomac," and "English Grains Along the Colonial Potomac," *National Colonial Farm Reseach Report No. 1, 2, and 3* (Accokeek, Md., 1979–1981).

TABLE 4.26 WORKDAY SCHEDULE OF FRANCIS PEPPER, A HIRED FARM LABORER IN SPRINGFIELD, MASS., ABOUT 1665

4:30–5:00 A.M.	rise and tend livestock
5:00–6:30 A.M.	field work
6:30–7:00 A.M.	breakfast
7:00–11:00 A.M.	field work
11:00–11:30 A.M.	cider or rum break
11:30 A.M.–2:00 P.M.	field work
2:00–3:00 P.M.	dinner
3:00–6:00 P.M.	field work, livestock, tool repair
6:00–7:00 P.M.	supper
8:30 P.M.	retire

Source: Stephen Innes, *Labor in a New Land: Economy and Society in Seventeenth-Century Springfield* (1983), 113.

Cattle Husbandry

Because North American Indians domesticated no animals as a source of meat, Europeans were obliged to import all livestock from abroad. Cattle in the seventeenth-century South became a mongrel mix of whatever bovine stock landed from England or the Caribbean. New England's "native," or "red," cattle were a hybrid of English Devonshire stock and various breeds obtained from the Dutch in New Netherland, the Spanish colonies, and Danish strains. Cattle in the Delaware Valley derived heavily from herds imported from Sweden before English settlement of that area commenced.

English and Swedish settlers often let cattle range freely for fodder and left them unsheltered during the winter. These practices helped develop a breed better suited to scanty fodder and harsh winters than European cattle but also one that produced less meat when slaughtered.

TABLE 4.27 YEARLY WORK ROUTINE OF SLAVES AT MT. VERNON, VA., PLANTATION IN EIGHTEENTH CENTURY

Spring–Summer Tasks	Autumn Tasks	Winter Tasks
plow	harvest corn	haul crops
harrow	harvest peas	strip tobacco
roll grain fields	thresh peas, rye	shell corn
make cornhills	thresh clover seed	cut straw
sow grains, oats, flax,	thresh wheat, oats	thresh grain
cabbage, carrots,	break flax	beat out hominy
barley, clover	swingle flax	kill hogs
plant potatos, peas,	chop in flax	fill icehouse
corn, pumpkins	clean oat seed	cut wood
weed corn and peas	clean wheat seed	split rails
harvest wheat, rye	dig carrots	trim timber
bind harvest	cut cornstalks	dig ditches
tie and heap wheat	pile cornstalks	build roads
shock wheat and oats	harrow	work new ground
thresh wheat, clover	plow	frame barn
cut hay and clover	sow winter grain	tend stables
shell corn	make livestock pens	tan leather
cut straw	make feed racks	make baskets
gather basket splits		make horse collars
tan basket bark		work on millrace
dig ditches		do odd jobs
clean swamp		
fill gullies		
grub fields		
seine fish		

Source: Lois G. Carr and Lorena W. Walsh, "Economic Diversification and Labor Organization in the Chesapeake, 1650–1820," in Stephen Innes, ed., *Work and Labor in Early America* (1988), 185–187.

New England farmers preferred to build their fences out of stone, with which their fields unfortunately abounded, such as this stone barrier surrounding a cornfield in Massachusetts. Elsewhere in the colonies, the settlers overwhelmingly preferred to build fences out of rails. (Courtesy National Museum of American History, Smithsonian Institution, negative 85–18146)

The primary reason that colonial cattle had a low proportion of meat to body weight was that North America lacked a native source of nutritious forage plants. During the 1700s, English Americans solved this problem by importing European pasturage plants, such as white and red clovers or timothy grass.

Cattle served as a primary source of meat for colonial adults, who probably ate a pound of beef per week, and they enriched the diet with dairy products. Farmers mainly used females to build up herds, and they would have been able to obtain adequate milk, butter, and cheese for an average family from two milk cows, which could could yield about 1,100 quarts during a nine-month milking season. Little dairying was done in winter because calving was arranged so cows would give milk while pastures were rich. Because only one bull sufficed to breed six or seven cows, most males were gelded for use as draft animals or fattened to be sold or slaughtered for family consumption. The primary export market for salted beef was in the Caribbean sugar islands, where demand remained strong from the 1640s through independence.

TABLE 4.28   TERMINOLOGY OF CATTLE BY GENDER AND AGE

> The female is first a *cow calf.*
> A *heifer* is a young female without a calf.
> A *cow* is a female that has calved.
> A *yearling* is a cow in its second year.
> The male is first a *bull-calf,* and if left intact becomes a *bull.*
> A castrated male is a *steer* and becomes an *ox* in two or three years.

Note: Male bovines fatten more readily once having been castrated, and they are easier to work under yoke after gelding.

TABLE 4.29   RATIO OF POPULATION TO CATTLE IN VIRGINIA, 1614–1664

Year	Cattle	Population	Population/Cattle
1614	200	350	1/1.7
1616	144	350	1/0.4
1620	500	890	1/0.5
1625	500	1,300	1/0.4
1629	3,500	2,600	1/1.3
1649	30,000	11,000	1/2.7
1664	100,000	24,400	1/4.1

Source: Lewis C. Gray, *History of Agriculture in the Southern United States to 1860* (1933), 19–29, 209. Thomas J. Wertenbaker, *The Planters of Colonial Virginia* (1922), 101. Edmund S. Morgan, *American Slavery, American Freedom: The Ordeal of Colonial Virginia* (1975), 404.

TABLE 4.30   PRICE OF CATTLE IN VIRGINIA, ABOUT 1650, IN TOBACCO AND STERLING

Cattle	Tobacco	Sterling @ 2d. per Lb.
calf	100 lb.	16s, 8d
yearling	100–200 lb.	16s, 8d–£1.13.4
bull	200–400 lb.	£1.13.4–£3.6.8
steer	200–600 lb.	£1.13.4–£4.7.0
mature cow	300–600 lb.	£2.10.0–£4.7.0

Source: Edmund S. Morgan, *American Slavery, American Freedom: The Ordeal of Colonial Virginia* (1975), 140, n. 28.

TABLE 4.31   PRICE OF A COW IN MARYLAND, 1650–1720, GIVEN IN PROCLAMATION MONEY

	Anne Arundel County	Baltimore County	Calvert County	Charles County	Kent County	Somerset County
Price	£2.62	£2.40	£2.29	£2.02	£2.30	£1.46

Source: Probate records analyzed in Gloria L. Main, *Tobacco Colony: Life in Early Maryland, 1650–1720* (1982), 278.

TABLE 4.32   PRICE OF A YOKE OF OXEN IN CONNECTICUT, 1640–1763

Period	Country Pay	Spanish Silver
1640–59	£14.10	£9.16
1660–69	£12.10	£8.15
1670–74	£11.10	£8.1
1675–99	£11.0	£7.10
1700–09	£11.0	£7.10
1710–14	£8.0	£7.4
1715–19	£10.0	£7.10
1720–23	£10.10	£7.7
1724–26	£11.10	£6.18
1727–29	£13.0	£6.10
1730–34	£17.0	£7.9.7
1735–39	£21.0	£7.17.6
1740–44	£30.0	£7.1
1745–47	£41.0	£7.3.6
1748–49	£60.0	£7.4
1750	£66.0	£7.5.2
1751	£69.0	£7.11.9$^{1}/_{2}$
1752	£77.0	£7.14
1753	£80.0	£8.0
1754	£84.0	£7.11.2
1755–58	...	£8.10
1759	...	£10.10
1760	...	£12.6
1761	...	£12.0
1762	...	£11.8
1763	...	£11.6

Source: Probate records analyzed in Jackson T. Main, *Society and Economy in Colonial Connecticut* (1985), 57.

TABLE 4.33   PRICES OF MATURE COWS IN VIRGINIA AND NEW JERSEY, ABOUT 1755

Place	Price	Date
Shenandoah Valley, Va.	£1.10 to £2 (proclamation)	1750s
Cape May County, N.J.	£2.10 to £3 (proclamation)	Oct. 1755

Source: Robert D. Mitchell, *Commercialism and Frontier: Perspectives on the Early Shenandoah Valley* (1977), 140, n. 28. William. A. Ellis, ed., "Diary of Jacob Spicer, 1755–6," New Jersey Historical Society, *Proceedings,* LVIII (1945), 115.

TABLE 4.34   WHOLESALE PRICES OF 31.5-GALLON (225-LB.) BARREL OF BEEF AT PHILADELPHIA, 1720–1763, IN SHILLINGS OF LOCAL CURRENCY

Year	Price
1720	30.00
1721	30.00
1722	30.67
1723	30.58
1724	30.65

Year	Price
1725	30.17
1726	...
1727	...
1728	36.72
1729	...
1730	...
1731	36.31
1732	...
1733	...
1734	30.56
1735	30.61
1736	33.50
1737	36.06
1738	36.67
1739	35.75
1740	35.63
1741	40.63
1742	36.63
1743	44.75
1744	41.94
1745	36.88
1746	41.13
1747	40.55
1748	44.29
1749	37.31
1750	38.17
1751	48.44
1752	51.01
1753	45.70
1754	45.13
1755	47.85
1756	48.96
1757	46.43
1758	48.18
1759	48.66
1760	53.72
1761	54.91
1762	58.04
1763	60.29

Source: Arthur H. Cole, *Wholesale Commodity Prices in the United States, 1700–1861* (1938), 5–77.

Corn was most commonly consumed as bread or pone that was milled from dried kernels in colonial times, not fresh from the cob as is most popular among modern Americans. Windmills, such as this replica of one built in southeast Virginia during the 1600s, sometimes provided the power to grind kernels into grist for corn meal. (Courtesy National Museum of American History, Smithsonian Institution, negative 86–6608)

TABLE 4.35   PRICE OF HAY (IN STERLING) IN RHODE ISLAND, 1753–1762

Year	Price per Hundredweight
1762	57d
1761	61d
1759	41d
1758	37d
1753	30d

Source: Max G. Schumacher, *The Northern Farmer and His Markets During the Late Colonial Period* (1975), 18.

TABLE 4.36   MEAT AND DAIRY YIELDS FROM CATTLE IN PENNSYLVANIA, ABOUT 1760

Average weight of fattened steer = 750 lb.
Dressed meat from 600 lb. steer = 300 lb.
Average milk production of a cow = 1 quart per day for 9 months
1 gallon milk yielded either 1 lb. cheese or ¹/₂ lb. butter

Source: James T. Lemon, *The Best Poor Man's Country: A Geographical Study of Early Southeastern Pennsylvania* (1972), 163.

Corn

Maize, or Indian corn, was grown almost immediately in the earliest settlements as soon as the first colonists learned its manner of cultivation from Native Americans. Unlike wheat, corn could be sowed without the use of a plow by planting seeds within individual hills made by hoeing, and so it was well suited to newly cleared fields still obstructed with stumps, partially buried roots, or stones. Maize was often planted with "Indian peas," or lima beans, which used the stalks as poles and helped maintain the soil's fertility. When cooked together as succotash or eaten within a quarter-hour of each other, corn and beans provided an individual with the essential protein needed for a healthy diet. The annual corn ration for an adult laborer was 28 to 30 bushels.

Protected by its husk, corn was relatively resistant to insects and diseases, and so it was less likely to fail than other crops unless destroyed by a severe drought. It ripened gradually from early summer through autumn, and consequently it offered a steady supply of food without interfering with the harvest of other staples. One worker tending about 7 acres was capable of growing up to 120 bushels, which would not only feed a family of six for a year but could also furnish winter fodder for animals in the form of its husk leaves and top growth. After being shelled and dried out, the kernels kept well until next year's crop began to ripen and were generally eaten as cornmeal or cornbread.

TABLE 4.37 ESTIMATED PRODUCTION OF CORN PER LABORER IN EARLY VIRGINIA

Year	Corn
1619	140 bu., plus beans intermixed (from 4 acres)
1635	100 bu., of corn and 20 bu. of beans
1669	50 barrels (about 150 bu.)

Source: Lewis C. Gray, *History of Agriculture in the Southern United States to 1860* (1933), 27.

TABLE 4.38 BARRELS OF CORN PRODUCED PER LABORER IN THE CHESAPEAKE, 1630–1763

Years	Lower Western Shore of Md.	Upper Eastern Shore of Md.	York River Basin of Va.	Lower Rappahannock River, Va.
1630–49	7.8	4.0	...	...
1650–69	7.0	...	8.6	...
1670–79	...	...	4.5	...
1680–99	5.8	...	9.5	4.5
1700–09	8.3	...	8.9	...
1710–19	6.6	...	5.2	8.2
1720–29	8.6	11.8	8.0	10.9
1730–39	12.2	16.3	10.6	9.3
1740–47	22.7	17.1	16.0	11.0
1748–53	9.0	25.2	18.6	2.5
1754–63	24.8	22.1	15.4	11.0

Note: Source does not specify volume of barrels (3 to 5 bu.).
Source: Lorena S. Walsh, "Plantation Management in the Chesapeake, 1620–1820," *Journal of Economic History,* IXL (1989), 398.

TABLE 4.39 YIELDS PER ACRE OF CORN IN EIGHTEENTH-CENTURY BRITISH AMERICA

Year	Corn	Place
ca. 1750	12 to 17 bu.	Augusta and Frederick Counties, Va.
ca. 1760	15 bu.	Chester and Lancaster Counties, Pa.
ca. 1760	10 bu.	Connecticut

Sources: Robert D. Mitchell, *Commercialism and Frontier: Perspectives on the Early Shenandoah Valley* (1977), 142. James T. Lemon, *The Best Poor Man's Country: A Geographical Study of Early Southeastern Pennsylvania* (1972), 152, 157. Jackson T. Main, *Society and Economy in Colonial Connecticut* (1985), 239.

TABLE 4.40 PRICE OF CORN, IN PENCE PER BARREL, IN KENT AND TALBOT COUNTIES, MD., 1680–1763

Year	Kent	Talbot
1763	114	113
1762	106	111
1761	97	108
1760	111	115
1759	114	101
1758	88	100
1757	97	93
1756	108	114
1755	106	106
1754	108	104
1753	108	114
1752	95	108
1751	108	124
1750	123	115
1749	106	115
1748	111	115
1747	97	96
1746	95	99
1745	95	94
1744	97	100
1743	112	114
1742	125	135
1741	119	118
1740	104	93
1739	107	100
1738	127	117
1737	112	110
1736	97	95
1735	97	97
1734	96	94
1733	98	87
1732	94	88
1731	85	84
1730	97	96
1729	98	92
1728	103	101
1727	96	90
1726	94	90
1725	104	94
1724	103	95
1723	91	99
1722	98	99
1721	97	99
1720	99	92
1719	...	98
1718	...	98
1717	...	93
1716	...	77
1715	...	81
1714	...	93
1713	...	84
1712	...	93
1711	...	81
1710	...	90
1709	...	91
1708	...	95
1707	...	91
1706	...	96
1705	...	94
1704	...	96
1703	...	95
1702	...	97
1701	...	99
1700	...	98
1699	...	108
1698	...	80
1697	...	88
1696	...	72
1695	...	75
1694	...	59
1693	...	60
1692	...	71
1691	...	71
1690	...	71
1689	...	71
1688	...	71
1687	...	78
1686	...	90
1685	...	99
1684	...	86
1683	...	...
1682	...	92
1681	...	100
1680	...	100

Source: Paul G.E. Clemens, *The Atlantic Economy and Colonial Maryland's Eastern Shore: From Tobacco to Grain* (1980), 226–227.

TABLE 4.41 PRICE OF CORN IN MARYLAND, 1705–1719, AND IN SHENANDOAH VALLEY, ABOUT 1750 (IN PROCLAMATION MONEY)

	Anne Arundel County	Baltimore County	Calvert County	Charles County	Kent County	Somerset County
barrel of 5 bushels =	8.16s	7.82s	8.01s	7.79s	7.91s	7.0s
Shenandoah Valley, Va., about 1750						
1 bushel =	1s, 6d to 1s, 8d					

Sources: Gloria L. Main, *Tobacco Colony: Life in Early Maryland, 1650–1720* (1983), 278. Robert D. Mitchell, *Commercialism and Frontier: Perspectives on the Early Shenandoah Valley* (1977), 141.

TABLE 4.42 WHOLESALE PRICE OF BUSHEL OF CORN AT PHILADELPHIA, 1720–1763, IN SHILLINGS OF LOCAL CURRENCY

Year	Price
1720	1.73
1721	1.76
1722	1.73
1723	1.86
1724	2.12
1725	2.13
1726	2.13
1727	2.02
1728	2.26
1729	2.15
1730	1.93
1731	1.65
1732	1.81
1733	2.10
1734	2.02
1735	1.58
1736	1.89
1737	2.08
1738	2.10
1739	1.41
1740	1.50
1741	2.74
1742	2.69
1743	2.14
1744	1.53
1745	1.69
1746	1.82
1747	1.92
1748	2.28
1749	2.63
1750	2.56
1751	2.79
1752	2.56
1753	2.91
1754	2.84
1755	2.16
1756	2.50
1757	1.72
1758	1.94
1759	2.99
1760	2.96
1761	2.42
1762	3.48
1763	3.75

Source: Arthur H. Cole, *Wholesale Commodity Prices in the United States, 1700–1861* (1938), 1–77.

Flax

Flax was minor crop from whose seeds linseed oil was extracted and whose stem produced fibers for linen thread. Although Virginia, Connecticut, and Maryland passed various laws to stimulate its cultivation between 1619 and 1671, flax output remained low until the 1740s. The major market for flax exports was Ireland, whose linen industry was required to use the stems before their seeds matured in order to obtain thread that was sufficiently supple to weave. Ireland consequently had to import from North America seeds for succeeding years' crops and also for linseed oil.

Farmers rarely sowed more than 2 acres in the crop. One bushel of seed would plant an acre, which would yield a harvest ranging from 80 to 200 pounds of hackled flax (i.e., cut and mangled so as to separate the fibers) and 4 to 10 bushels of seed. Settlers in the backcountry found flax a profitable crop because its transportation costs to market were relatively low. New York and Pennsylvania were its major centers of cultivation.

TABLE 4.43 WHOLESALE PRICE OF A BUSHEL OF FLAXSEED, IN SHILLINGS OF LOCAL CURRENCY, AT PHILADELPHIA, 1734–1765

Year	Price
1734	4.25
1735	4.95
1736	3.80
1737	4.30
1738	3.25
1739	3.51
1740	3.23
1741	4.23
1742	5.42
1743	5.90
1744	4.14
1745	3.00
1746	2.32
1747	2.75
1748	3.60
1749	7.87
1750	9.92
1751	5.83
1752	5.03
1753	5.47
1754	4.61
1755	4.06
1756	4.04
1757	4.91
1758	5.58
1759	5.95
1760	5.66
1761	4.70
1762	9.34
1763	9.08
1764	8.21
1765	8.79

Source: Anne Bezanson, ed., *Prices in Colonial Pennsylvania* (1935), 416.

This acquatint by W. Hincks shows how flax was beaten by a paddle to soften the plant, once its thick outer surface had been allowed to decompose by laying outside through the winter. After the outer core was pulverized, the inner fibers were combed out so that they could be spun into thread for clothing or twine. (Courtesy Library of Congress)

TABLE 4.44   EXPORTS OF BRITISH NORTH AMERICAN FLAXSEED TO IRELAND, 1732–1763

Year	Hogsheads[a]	Price per Hogshead
1732	498	30s
1733	1,310	43s, 4d
1734	1,113	40s
1735	3,121	40s
1736	3,167	40s
1737	5,000	40s
1738	9,045	40s
1739	5,933	34s
1740	10,408	33s, 4d
1741	5,771	34s
1742	10,360	34s, 4d
1743	9,929	34s
1744	11,252	33s, 4d
1745	11,828	30s
1746	6,841	33s, 4d
1747	8,602	34s

Year	Hogsheads[a]	Price per Hogshead
1748	12,074	30s
1749	17,777	30s
1750	3,719	30s
1751	12,909	30s
1752	16,488	30s
1753	22,146	30s
1754	20,743	30s
1755	20,335	30s
1756	18,538	30s
1757	19,662	30s
1758	18,907	30s
1759	26,604	30s
1760	21,226	30s
1761	22,738	30s
1762	19,448	30s
1763	19,745	30s

[a] Cask with capacity of 63 to 140 gal. (63 gal. most common size)
Source: Thomas M. Truxes, *Irish-American Trade, 1660–1783* (1988), 284.

TABLE 4.45 PROPORTION OF ALL FLAXSEED IMPORTED TO IRELAND PURCHASED FROM BRITISH NORTH AMERICA, 1735–1770

Year	Percent of Imports
1735	32.9%
1740	63.1%
1745	63.8%
1749	86.1%
1750	34.0%
1751	57.6%
1755	97.2%
1760	87.8%
1765	73.6%
1770	99.1%

Source: Thomas M. Truxes, *Irish-American Trade, 1660–1783* (1988), 284.

Hemp

Hemp was a fibrous crop used to manufacture ship rigging and other cordage. Virginia in 1619 and Connecticut in 1640 passed laws obliging farmers to cultivate small amounts of the plant, and Maryland encouraged its growth with a bounty in 1671, but these measures proved ineffectual. Output evidently increased after wartime demand for rigging by the Royal Navy temporarily raised prices to £33 per ton in 1693, but a steep fall in price to £14 per ton in 1694 discouraged further expansion of colonial output. Even after the English Parliament enacted a bounty of £6 per ton in 1702 and exempted it from importation duties in 1721, hemp exports remained low through 1764, when Parliament raised the bounty to £8.

Hemp yields were greatest on lowlands with a high content of moisture. Hemp production centered in the Chesapeake region, where the terrain was best suited for its cultivation and where the proximity of most planters to water transportation lowered carrying charges. A laborer could raise approximately a half-ton of hemp on an acre and adequately tend up to 4 acres per season. Because much labor had to be expended to make hemp marketable—a process of cutting, rotting, separating bark from core, and drying—curing hemp kept workers occupied at one of tobacco's busiest seasons. For this reason, many small farmers found it impractical to grow hemp, in spite of the bounty's attractiveness, and even large planters were reluctant to divert their slaves' energies away from tobacco.

Horses

Horses served British North Americans not only as riding mounts and draft animals but also as a commodity that could be sold abroad. The earliest export of live horses from North America occurred in 1647 from Massachusetts to the West Indies, where they were needed for transportation and powering sugar mills. Horse breeding was an especially economical use of hilly or unfertile land, and so it first became established in New England.

Horse raising spread southward from New England, and by the 1760s substantial exports were being sent to the Caribbean from the Delaware valley and South Carolina. Most colonial horses were of nondescript bloodlines, but two distinctive stocks emerged in British North America during the eighteenth century. In Rhode Island were raised the Narragansett Pacers, possibly of Andalusian origin, which were admired for their swift gait and solely used as saddle animals. A notably strong and large breed was developed in Pennsylvania for harness work, and it became known as the Conestoga (or sometimes German) horse.

TABLE 4.46 WHOLESALE PRICE OF A POUND OF HEMP, IN PENCE OF LOCAL CURRENCY, AT PHILADELPHIA, 1749–1764

Year	Price
1749	3.8
1750	3.7
1751	4.5
1752	4.5
1753	3.9
1754	3.9
1755	3.6
1756	4.8
1757	5.6
1758	4.9
1759	6.0
1760	4.9
1761	4.8
1762	6.7
1763	7.4
1764	6.2

Source: Anne Bezanson, *Prices in Colonial Pennsylvania* (1935), 417.

TABLE 4.47 PRICE OF A HORSE IN CONNECTICUT, 1640–1763

Period	Country Pay	Spanish Silver
1640–59	£10.0	£7.14
1660–69	£6.16	£4.14.6
1670–74	£2.17	£1.19.11
1675–99	£2.10	£1.15
1700–09	£2.7	£2.7
1710–14	£2.10	£2.5
1715–19	£3.10	£2.12.6
1720–23	£3.14	£2.11.9 $^{1}/_{2}$
1724–29	£4.16	£2.8
1730–34	£5.10	£2.8.6
1735–39	£8.3	£3.1.1
1740–44	£15.0	£3.10.6
1745–47	£26.0	£4.11
1748–51	…	…
1752–54	£40.0	£4.0
1755–58	…	£4.0
1759–62	…	…
1763	…	£4.12

Source: Probate records analyzed in Jackson T. Main, *Society and Economy in Colonial Connecticut* (1985), 57.

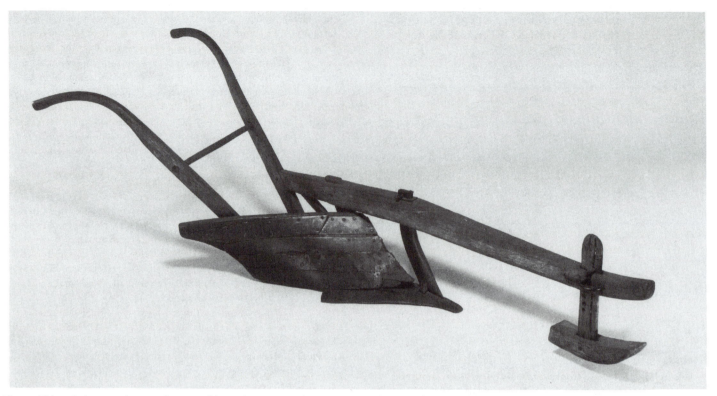

This mold-board plow was the typical type used by Anglo-American farmers to put in their crops during spring. This plow was made by Peter Hardy of Raymond, New Hampshire, about 1735. Compare it with the photo of the German wheeled plow on page 324. (Courtesy National Museum of American History, Smithsonian Institution, negative 95–20555)

Indigo

Indigo was a nonedible plant from which a bright blue, purple, or copper coloring agent could be extracted for dyeing textiles. A variant of the plant is native to South Carolina, where the first settlers experimented with it in the 1670s, but Carolinians overwhelmingly turned to rice cultivation despite the incentive of a provincial bounty on indigo in effect from 1694 to 1696. English planters in the Bahamas and a few Caribbean islands began to grow the crop after the English Parliament offered incentives to reduce the English textile industry's dependence on French and Spanish sources.

Eliza Lucas Pinckney, who had learned the craft of indigo cultivation on her father's Antigua plantation, took a leading role in popularizing the plant on the southern North American mainland. She moved to South Carolina in 1738 and for the next seven years drew attention to indigo's potential profitablity through her own experiments. The crop was particularly appropriate for South Carolina and Georgia

TABLE 4.48 INDIGO EXPORTS OF SOUTH CAROLINA AND GEORGIA, 1747–1763

Period	Unit	Charles Town	Savannah	Total
1747–1748 (Mar. 25–Mar. 25)[2]	pounds	138,334	…	…
1748–1749 (Mar. 25–Mar. 25)[2]	pounds	62,195	…	…
1749–1750 (Mar. 25–Mar. 25)[2]	pounds	138,299	…	…
1750–1751 (Mar. 25–Mar. 25)[2]	pounds	63,102	…	…
1751–1752 (Mar. 25–Mar. 25)[2]	pounds	19,891	…	…
1752–1753 (Mar. 25–Jan. 5)	pounds	3,787	…	…
1753–1754 (Jan. 5–Jan. 5)	pounds	28,474	…	…
1754–1755 (Jan. 5–Jan. 5)	pounds	129,645	…	…
1755–1756 (Jan. 5–Jan. 5)	pounds	303,531	4,508	308,039
1756–1757 (Jan. 5–Jan. 5)	pounds	222,805	9,335	232,140
1757–1758 (Jan. 5–Jan. 5)	pounds	876,393	18,150	894,543
1758–1759 (Jan. 5–Jan. 5)	pounds	563,025	9,600	572,625
1759–1760 (Jan. 5–Jan. 5)	pounds	695,661	555	696,216
1760–1761 (Jan. 5–Jan. 5)	pounds	507,584	11,746	519,330
1761–1762 (Jan. 5–Jan. 5)	pounds	384,053	1,552	385,605
1762–1763 (Jan. 5–Jan. 5)	pounds	255,305	9,133	264,438

Note: The variations in the fiscal years apply only to Charles Town, with the terminal dates for Savannah being January 5 for all years.
Source: Lewis C. Gray, History of Agriculture in the Southern United States (1933), 1024.

TABLE 4.49 WHOLESALE PRICE OF A POUND OF INDIGO (IN SHILLINGS OF LOCAL CURRENCY) AT CHARLES TOWN, S. C., 1747–1763

Year	Price
1747	18.50
1748	20.00
1749	18.30
1750	19.25
1751	19.70
1752	24.20
1753	30.10
1754	27.90
1755	30.30
1756	25.00
1757	26.25
1758	25.00
1759	24.90
1760	20.70
1761	22.50
1762	26.90
1763	28.90

Source: Arthur H. Cole, Wholesale Commodity Prices in the United States, 1700–1861 (1938), 28–123.

TABLE 4.50 BRITISH BOUNTIES PAID TO AMERICAN INDIGO PLANTERS, 1748–1763

Year	Price
1763	£7,695
1762	£4,415
1761	£7,159
1760	£10,905
1759	£3,728
1758	£5,122
1757–1750	no data
1749	£1,548
1748	£266

Source: Oliver M. Dickerson, *The Navigation Acts and the American Revolution* (1951), 28.

planters because land did not have to be taken out of rice cultivation to raise indigo; indigo developed best in higher, sandy elevations than the rice country's wet lowlands.

Exports of mainland indigo increased rapidly after 1744 because England's usual imports from the French Caribbean were disrupted by war. Indigo production became especially profitable in North America after British Parliament offered a bounty of 6 pence per pound in 1748 (reduced to 4 pence in 1763). Experienced slaves could reportedly tend at least 2 acres of common land and raise 120 pounds of dye worth £20 to £30 sterling, and an expert hand might cultivate up to 4 acres and harvest more than 300 pounds worth more than £60. Such yields made indigo one of the mainland's most lucrative crops, but its leaves could only be gathered twice yearly compared to four cuttings in the West Indies, and the quality of mainland dye was inferior to its competitors.

Pork

Pork was the meat most often consumed by colonial adults, who probably ate an average of 2 pounds per week. The prevailing taste preferred fat flesh, and so hogs were bred with a higher proportion of meat relative to body weight than cattle. Fattened hogs often weighed more than 200 pounds, sometimes in excess of 300 pounds, and yielded more than two-thirds of that total in dressed meat.

TABLE 4.51 PRICES (PROCLAMATION) OF LIVE HOGS IN CONNECTICUT AND VIRGINIA

Place	Date	Price
Connecticut	ca. 1650	6s, 6d
Connecticut	ca. 1750	4s, 6d
Shenandoah Valley	ca. 1750	7s to 10s

Source: Jackson T. Main, *Society and Economy in Colonial Connecticut* (1985), 213. Robert D. Mitchell, *Commericialism and Frontier: Perspectives on the Early Shenandoah Valley* (1977), 140, n. 28.

TABLE 4.52 WHOLESALE PRICE OF PORK, PER BARREL OF 31.5 GALLONS (200 LB.), AT PHILADELPHIA, 1720–1763 (IN SHILLINGS OF LOCAL CURRENCY)

Year	Price
1720	46.46
1721	45.00
1722	45.00
1723	40.48
1724	36.00
1725	39.29
1726	48.58
1727	47.79
1728	59.17
1729	51.65
1730	59.24
1731	55.97
1732	49.41
1733	47.54
1734	43.58
1735	37.59
1736	41.72
1737	54.44
1738	59.58
1739	54.88
1740	46.04
1741	49.83
1742	54.17
1743	68.52
1744	60.49
1745	53.02
1746	53.79
1747	57.66
1748	61.04
1749	60.16
1750	63.99
1751	69.97
1752	72.35
1753	63.20
1754	61.19
1755	65.94
1756	61.42
1757	60.94
1758	59.49
1759	69.19
1760	69.30
1761	73.92
1762	85.63
1763	86.95

Source: Arthur H. Cole, *Wholesale Commodity Prices in the United States, 1700–1861* (1938), 5–76.

Hogs could forage for a large portion of their food from nuts and roots if allowed to roam wild. Swine were also more economical to fatten than were cattle because equal amounts of grain would produce 50% more pork than beef. Annual feed for 8 swine, which was about normal for a farm family, required about 2 acres of corn, an amount that could be reduced significantly by planting a half-acre in potatoes for pigs. Because pork can be more tastefully salted or smoked than beef, hogs tended to be slaughtered in fall and eaten during the winter months. The West Indies became a highly profitable market for the mainland's surplus hog production.

Rice

South Carolina's proprietors had anticipated that rice might be an appropriate crop for their colony, and as early as 1674 some rice had been harvested near Charles Town. It was not until the mid-1690s, however, that the settlers mastered the culture of this difficult plant, and Carolina did not begin to export significant amounts of rice until 1698. Rice plantations initially were restricted to swampy regions along the Atlantic coast, but about 1724 irrigation began to be employed to ensure a continuous supply of water to low-lying areas further inland. Rice cultivation eventually spread from the Cape Fear in North Carolina to Georgia.

Rice became the economic mainstay of South Carolina and Georgia. Exceptionally strong export markets developed in southern

TABLE 4.53 **REPORTED YIELDS OF RICE PER ACRE IN THE EIGHTEENTH-CENTURY SOUTHERN COLONIES**

Year	Yield per Acre	Weight of Bu.	Total Weight
1710	45 bu.	about 65.5 lb.	2,947.5 lb.
1750	11.5 bu.	about 66.5 lb.	765 lb.

Source: Lewis C. Gray, *History of Agriculture in the Southern United States to 1860* (1933), 283–284.

TABLE 4.54   DESTINATION OF RICE (IN BARRELS) EXPORTED FROM CHARLES TOWN, S.C., 1717–1766

Year	Total	England	Scotland	Continental Colonies	British West Indies	Foreign West Indies	Countries South of Cape Finisterre
1766	85,862	39,468	2,862	3,297	11,730	3,369	25,136
1763	103,451	51,335	3,703	16,117	16,466	1,490	14,340
1762	82,159	33,217	4,573	10,921	20,239	1,970	11,239
1759	51,037	18,517	9,359	4,546	5,962	490	12,163
1758	61,501	30,687	7,214	4,611	6,432	…	12,557
1738	32,372	27,331	…	596	643	…	3,802
1737	37,896	32,322	…	511	594	…	4,469
1736	53,376	38,158	…	798	1,164	…	13,256
1735	44,418	28,345	…	667	713	…	14,693
1734	37,303	24,849	…	605	1,061	…	10,788
1732	38,942	26,766	…	1,417	1,504	…	9,255
1731	48,337	38,331	…	1,737	1,872	…	6,397
1724	19,908	16,452	…	2,199	1,257	…	…
1719	13,357	8,423	31	3,210	1,693	…	…
1718	8,421	6,187	…	1,005	1,229	…	…
1717	10,380	7,257	…	1,980	1,143	…	…

Source: Data of J. R. House in Bureau of the Census, *Historical Statistics of the United States* (1960), 768.

TABLE 4.55   RICE EXPORTS (IN HUNDREDWEIGHTS OF 112 LB.) TO ENGLAND BY COLONY, 1698–1763

Year	Total	Carolina	Georgia	New England	New York	Pennsylvania	Virginia and Maryland
1763	271,505	251,476	9,494	1,537	5,354	3,644	…
1762	148,754	138,777	7,786	750	408	1,033	…
1761	238,750	224,964	7,220	164	4,562	1,840	…
1760	108,673	95,773	11,628	…	309	958	5
1759	109,596	102,001	6,358	481	523	233	…
1758	102,794	95,741	…	305	4,819	1,929	…
1757	74,741	72,785	…	1,375	67	514	…
1756	167,261	156,279	5,931	1,359	3,621	71	…
1755	312,845	306,720	3,945	342	1,837	1	…
1754	276,935	273,862	2,782	62	204	25	…
1753	123,682	120,221	1,970	…	225	…	1,266
1752	267,210	261,387	1,047	1,815	1,387	174	1,400
1751	202,943	196,863	…	4,363	923	794	…
1750	166,672	164,378	1,783	505	…	6	…
1749	122,401	121,614	…	748	…	39	…
1748	144,068	143,515	…	…	209	344	…
1747	86,018	85,939	…	79	…	…	…
1746	51,736	50,202	…	1,094	431	…	9
1745	75,153	73,792	…	38	317	1,006	…
1744	196,968	195,249	…	1,323	156	240	…
1743	243,091	241,820	…	244	60	888	79
1742	136,117	134,368	1,518	52	…	179	…
1741	263,093	261,110	…	360	1,006	613	4
1740	313,571	308,178	798	1,597	1,374	1,624	…
1739	254,879	253,380	…	1,350	105	…	44
1738	128,337	128,187	…	149	…	…	1
1737	154,318	154,010	…	128	…	180	…
1736	151,234	150,797	…	…	…	437	…
1735	118,295	116,441	1,444	…	309	97	4
1734	80,263	79,448	…	286	222	300	7

Year	Total	Carolina	Georgia	New England	New York	Pennsylvania	Virginia and Maryland
1733	147,272	147,021	...	124	...	83	44
1732	101,838	101,387	...	401	...	50	...
1731	164,515	161,246	...	1,784	37	1,448	...
1730	139,384	136,578	...	1,365	507	922	12
1729	119,202	117,550	...	1,120	232	300	...
1728	100,466	95,973	...	1,986	1,918	589	...
1727	89,942	89,942	...	...	...	...	...
1726	69,092	67,041	...	499	1,465	87	...
1725	53,670	52,268	...	754	585	63	...
1724	63,383	59,385	...	3,115	556	327	...
1723	67,613	60,952	...	5,746	488	425	2
1722	76,034	72,238	...	2,457	366	940	33
1721	62,215	54,873	...	5,574	620	1,058	90
1720	50,669	44,915	...	5,444	175	118	17
1719	31,259	26,233	...	4,035	147	813	31
1718	23,097	19,530	...	2,303	1,130	129	5
1717	22,509	17,484	...	3,822	641	439	123
1716	35,820	27,555	...	5,709	871	1,424	261
1715	18,497	14,405	...	2,013	1,272	807	...
1714	24,527	22,264	...	1,620	210	433	...
1713	30,083	28,517	...	1,393	165	...	8
1711	9,231	8,678	...	174	379	...	...
1710	12,508	12,265	...	128	105	...	10
1709	11,802	11,274	...	289	232	...	7
1708	5,276	5,220	...	49	...	...	7
1707	4,385	4,120	...	173	83	...	9
1706	2,089	2,058	...	...	3	21	7
1704	5,933	5,550	...	217	79	28	59
1703	5,426	5,320	...	17	62	...	27
1702	4,786	4,568	...	...	218	...	...
1701	1,521	1,457	...	...	64	...	...
1700	3,079	3,037	...	26	4	...	12
1699	1,025	1,018	...	...	...	7	...
1698	81	81	...	...	...	...	...

Source: Data of Lawrence A. Harper in Bureau of the Census, *Historical Statistics of the United States* (1960), 768.

TABLE 4.56 AVERAGE PRICE OF RICE (IN SHILLINGS) PER HUNDREDWEIGHT OF 112 LB. AT CHARLES TOWN, S.C., 1722–1763

Year	Currency	Sterling
1763	46.57	6.50
1762	33.60	4.80
1761	38.50	5.50
1760	51.80	7.40
1759	65.80	9.40
1758	43.40	6.20
1757	33.61	4.80
1756	34.96	4.90
1755	40.60	5.80
1754	43.40	6.20
1753	66.50	9.50
1752	55.30	7.90
1751	45.50	6.50
1750	63.20	9.00
1749	62.38	8.60
1748	53.37	7.00
1747	36.51	4.80
1746	15.40	2.20
1745	16.10	2.30
1744	29.40	4.20

Year	Currency	Sterling
1743	34.30	4.90
1742	44.03	6.30
1741	51.12	7.40
1740	42.98	5.40
1739	49.10	6.20
1738	82.15	10.60
1737	72.30	9.60
1736	54.26	7.30
1735	58.10	8.30
1734	60.20	8.60
1733	39.90	5.70
1732	42.00	6.00
1731	37.23	5.32
1730	40.49	6.29
1729	44.66	6.38
1728	46.34	6.62
1727	56.21	8.03
1726	46.00	6.57
1725	37.78	5.62
1724	40.03	6.16
1723	40.56	6.01
1722	30.00	5.17

Source: George R. Taylor, "Wholesale Commodity Prices at Charleston, South Carolina, 1732–1791," *Journal of Economic and Business History,* IV (May 1932), 372. Peter A. Coclanis "Rice Prices in the 1720s and the Evolution of the South Carolina Economy," *Journal of Southern History,* XLVIII (1982), 538. Sterling adjusted to Carolina money using John J. McCusker, *Money and Exchange in Europe and America, 1600–1775* (1978), 222–224.

TABLE 4.57 RICE EXPORTS FROM THE LOWER SOUTH, 1740–1774

| Year | Total | | Charleston, S.C. | Beaufort and Georgetown, S.C. | Georgia |
	Pounds	Barrels			
1774	76,265,700	145,268	118,482	6,594	20,192
1773	81,476,325	155,193	126,940	6,681	21,572
1772	69,218,625	131,845	104,821	4,076	22,948
1771	81,755,100	155,724	125,151	5,209	25,364
1770	83,708,625	159,445	131,805	5,568	22,072
1769	73,078,950	139,198	115,582	6,900	16,716
1768	77,284,200	147,208	125,538	7,045	14,625
1767	63,465,150	120,886	104,125	5,480	11,281
1766	48,396,600	92,184	74,031	3,896	14,257
1765	65,710,575	125,163	107,292	5,647	12,224
1764	55,907,250	106,490	91,960	4,840	9,690
1763	61,959,450	118,018	104,800	5,516	7,702
1762	47,435,325	90,353	79,652	4,192	6,509
1761	58,480,275	111,391	101,389	5,336	4,666
1760	35,327,250	67,290	60,807	3,200	3,283
1759	30,472,575	58,043	51,718	2,722	3,603
1758	38,527,650	73,386	67,464	3,551	2,371
1757	33,976,950	64,718	58,634	3,086	2,998
1756	45,344,250	86,370	79,203	4,170	2,997
1755	59,057,775	112,491	104,682	5,510	2,299
1754	49,179,520	94,576	88,570	4,662	1,344
1753	19,747,675	38,345	35,523	1,870	952
1752	42,245,850	82,835	78,208	4,116	511
1751	32,751,270	64,854	61,611	3,243	...
1750	27,372,500	54,745	51,190	2,694	861
1749	21,381,030	43,194	41,034	2,160	...
1748	28,368,550	57,895	55,000	2,895	...
1747	27,643,060	56,996	54,146	2,850	...
1746	27,335,040	56,948	54,101	2,847	...
1745	29,813,375	62,765	59,627	3,138	...
1744	39,963,630	85,029	80,778	4,251	...
1743	35,935,200	77,280	73,416	3,864	...
1742	22,706,060	49,361	46,196	2,431	734
1741	38,720,955	85,101	80,846	4,255	...
1740	43,326,000	96,280	91,110	4,785	385

Note: Terminal dates for yearly statistics are primarily December 24, January 4 (of the succeeding year), and October 31. Weight of barrels varied by year (see source). *Source:* Compiled by Lawrence A. Harper for *U.S. Bureau of the Census, Historical Statistics of the United States* (1960), 767–768.

Europe, Scandinavia, and the West Indies. Prices increased by more than 50% from 1730 to 1775, and output more than doubled during the three decades after 1740. Although rice was unusually profitable, it was also exceptionally expensive to grow because of the cost of constructing waterworks and obtaining labor. More than any other commodity, rice was a rich man's crop, and it supported the most opulent plantocracy on the British mainland.

Sheep

Sheep husbandry was never as important in English North America as in England, where the demand for wool was greater and fewer people could afford a regular diet of beef and pork. Sheep became increasingly important in northern agriculture after 1700, when wolves had been driven from the more densely settled regions. Because mutton was difficult to preserve by salting or smoking, and because its taste was also unpopular among Anglo-Americans (perhaps due to poor slaughtering techniques), wool was the main object of sheep raising. The typical sheep yielded only 2 to 3 pounds of wool, and because the average weight was about 50 pounds, it would provide only 10 to 15 pounds of dressed meat or in some exceptional cases up to 20 pounds. Sheep nevertheless were economical because they cost relatively little to maintain; a flock of ten could be fed from the produce of a third of an acre of hay, a quarter-acre of grain, and an acre of pasture, plus

TABLE 4.58 NOMENCLATURE OF SHEEP (OVINES) BY GENDER AND AGE

A male is a *ram* or *tupp*.
A *wether* is a gelded male.
A *ewe* is a female sheep after being shorn twice.
A *lamb* is a young sheep from birth to a year old.
A *yearling* is a sheep in its second year, or its *fleece*.
Shearlings are sheep of either gender shorn once or twice.

TABLE 4.59 PRICE OF A SHEEP (IN SHILLINGS AND PENCE) IN CONNECTICUT, 1640–1763

Period	Country Pay	Spanish Silver
1763	...	6s, 4d
1759–62	...	...
1754–58	...	4s
1752–53	33s	3s, 4d
1748–51	...	...
1745–47	27s	4s, 8 1/2d
1740–44	18s	4s, 3d
1735–39	15s	5s, 7 1/2d
1730–34	12s	5s, 3d
1720–29	7s	4s, 11d
1715–19	6s	4s, 6d
1710–14	5s, 3d	5s, 8 1/2d
1700–10	5s, 3d	5s, 3d
1675–99	9s	6s, 4d
1670–74	8s	5s, 7d
1660–69	11s	7s, 8d
1640–59	24s	16s, 7d

Source: Probate records analyzed in Jackson T. Main, *Society and Economy in Colonial Connecticut* (1985), 57.

TABLE 4.60 OWNERSHIP OF SHEEP AND WOOLWORKING TOOLS IN PRINCE GEORGE'S COUNTRY, MD., 1730–1769

Percent of Households Owning Items Below				
Items	1730s	1740s	1750s	1760s
Sheep only	41%	52%	62%	50%
Cards or wheels only	45%	41%	57%	47%
Sheep & cards or wheels	28%	30%	41%	30%
Looms only	5%	2%	4%	7%
Sheep & looms	1%	2%	2%	5%
None of above	38%	43%	20%	24%

Source: Allan L. Kulikoff, *Tobacco and Slaves: The Development of Southern Cultures in the Chesapeake, 1680–1800* (1986), 102.

TABLE 4.61 PRICE OF A SHEEP (PROCLAMATION MONEY) IN THE 1750s

Year	Place	Price
1750	Shenandoah Valley, Va.	2s, 6d to 4s (proclamation)
1755	Cape May County, N. J.	7s, 6d to 8s (proclamation)

Source: "Diary of Jacob Spicer, 1755–6," New Jersey Historical Society, *Proceedings*, LVIII (1945), 85. Robert D. Mitchell, *Commercialism and Frontier: Perspectives on the Early Shenandoah Valley* (1977), 140.

whatever grass they consumed in woodlots and along fence rails. Because the islands of Narragansett Bay allowed animals to graze unthreatened by wolves, Rhode Island became the earliest and most prosperous center of sheep husbandry; the importance of sheep exports to the colony's prosperity was symbolized in 1696 when the town council of Newport chose to portray an ovine on its seal.

Silk

Projects to promote silk culture in North America began almost as soon as the first colonizing ventures. Virginia's royal governor received instructions in 1628 to encourage the planting of mulberry orchards for silkworms, and Edward Digges managed to make 8 pounds of silk after importing Armenian craftsworkers in 1654. Several bales were sent by South Carolina Huguenots to London in 1716, and that colony's legislature offered a bounty of 20 shillings per salable pound in 1736.

Not until the 1730s, when Georgia was settled, did significant progress occur in developing this industry. The colony's trustees initially required every landowner to plant mulberry trees, and they imported experts from France and Italy to supervise the collection and reeling of cocoons. Parliament offered a bounty of 3 shillings to stimulate production, and by the late 1740s several hundred pounds were being exported from Georgia. Some silk culture also occurred in South Carolina, which reported a crop of 118 pounds in 1750. Silk exports grew in volume through 1763, but the high level of skill required, along with the consequent high cost of labor, kept production low.

TABLE 4.62   EXPORTS OF SILK FROM GEORGIA AND SOUTH CAROLINA, 1742–1763

Year(s)	Exports from Ga. (Lb.)	Exports from S.C. (Lb.)
1763	953	…
1762	380	…
1761	332	…
1760	558	…
1759	734	…
1758	358	…
1757	358	…
1756	268	…
1755	438	5.5
1754	…	…
1753	…	11
1752	…	…
1751	…	…
1750	…	118
1749	…	46
1748	…	52
1743–1747	…	…
1742	…	18.5

Source: U.S. Bureau of the Census, *Historical Statistics of the United States* (1960), 762.

Tobacco producers packed their crop into large barrels called hogsheads, which came to be standarized into a routine size 4 feet high and could hold about 475 pounds of "prized" (that is, pressed) leaf. By running a small wooden axle through the center and fixing it to a frame, Chesapeake farmers could create a rolling hogshead that could be pulled by land to a wharf without undue damage to the leaf, as is illustrated in the next photo. (Courtesy National Museum of American History, Smithsonian Institution, negative 13173)

Tobacco

Virginians learned how to produce a salable variety of tobacco by 1618 when the colony first began to export it in significant amounts. Tobacco cultivation later became established in Maryland, the Carolinas, and briefly in Delaware. Soaring demand for the commodity resulted in steep profits until 1629 when tobacco prices fell 97%. Returns on tobacco remained modest but still were sufficient for a family's financial support until the 1660s when overproduction drove the price down to a penny per pound. The tobacco industry then sank into deep depression, at which time the quantity of leaf grown plateaued at about 28 million pounds from 1680 until about 1715.

During most of the half-century before the War of Independence, European demand for tobacco crept slowly upward and its cultivation stayed generally profitable. The greatest part of this demand came from consumers on the European continent, to which more than 70% of all mainland tobacco was eventually reexported by British merchants in

This sketch by Robert Gamble depicts how tobacco hogsheads, which usually weighed nearly a quarter-ton, were rolled to market in colonial Chesapeake. (Courtesy National Museum of American History, Smithsonian Institution, negative 3498)

TABLE 4.63 TOBACCO PRICES (IN PENCE STERLING PER LB.) PAID FARMERS IN THE CHESAPEAKE, 1618–1658, AND MARYLAND, 1659–1710

Year	Maryland Tobacco Price	Chesapeake Tobacco Price
1710	0.85	...
1709	.90	...
1708	.90	...
1707	.90	...
1706	.80	...
1705	.80	...
1704	.90	...
1703	.85	...
1702	1.00	...
1701	.95	...
1700	1.00	...
1699	1.05	...
1698	1.00	...
1697	0.90	...
1696	.85	...
1695	.75	...
1694	.75	...
1693	.75	...
1692	.80	...
1691	.80	...
1690	.80	...
1689	.70	...
1688	.75	...
1687	.85	...
1686	1.00	...

Year	Maryland Tobacco Price	Chesapeake Tobacco Price
1685	1.00	...
1684	0.80	...
1683	.80	...
1682	.80	...
1681	.90	...
1680	1.00	...
1679	1.05	...
1678	1.15	...
1677	1.15	...
1676	1.05	...
1675	1.00	...
1674	1.00	...
1673	1.00	...
1672	1.00	...
1671	1.05	...
1670	1.15	...
1669	1.15	...
1668	1.25	...
1667	1.10	...
1666	.90	...
1665	1.10	...
1664	1.35	...
1663	1.55	...
1662	1.60	...
1661	1.50	...
1660	1.50	...
1659	1.65	...
1658		2.10
1657		2.00
1656		2.25

Year	Maryland Tobacco Price	Chesapeake Tobacco Price
1655	...	2.00
1654	...	2.80
1653	...	2.60
1649	...	3.00
1648	...	1.50
1647	...	2.00
1646	...	2.20
1645	...	1.50
1644	...	2.55
1643	...	1.80
1642	...	4.20
1640	...	2.50
1639	...	3.00
1638	...	3.00
1637	...	3.00
1636	...	5.35
1635	...	5.00
1633	...	5.00
1632	...	3.40
1631	...	4.00
1624	...	13.00
1623	...	16.00
1622	...	18.00
1621	...	20.00
1620	...	12.00
1619	...	27.00
1618	...	27.00

Source: Russell R. Menard, "Farm Prices of Maryland Tobacco, 1659–1710," *Maryland Historical Magazine*, LXVIII (1973), 80–85, and "A Note on Chesapeake Tobacco Prices, 1618–1660," *Virginia Magazine of History and Biography*, LXXXIV (1976), 401–410.

TABLE 4.64 TOBACCO PRICES PAID TO MARYLAND FARMERS (IN PENCE PER LB., STERLING AND LOCAL MONEY), 1711–1763

Year	Current Money Mean	Sterling		
		Mean	High	Low
1711	.97	.97	1.00	.60
1712	1.00	1.00	1.00	1.00
1713	1.00	1.00	1.00	.95
1714	.94	.71	.75	.29
1715	.96	.72	.75	.45
1716	1.07	.80	1.44	.63
1717	1.05	.79	1.13	.75
1718	1.19	.89	1.35	.75
1719	1.39	1.04	1.50	.75
1720	1.58	1.19	1.50	.75
1721	1.29	.97	1.50	.45
1722	1.15	.86	1.13	.75
1723	1.42	1.07	1.13	.75
1724	1.20	.90	1.08	.72
1725	1.39	1.05	1.80	.54
1726	1.22	.91	1.13	.26
1727	1.09	.82	1.13	.75
1728	.89	.67	.75	.26
1729	.94	.70	.99	.38
1730	.90	.67	1.13	.27
1731	.87	.65	.90	.23
1732	.99	.74	.90	.36
1733	1.12	.84	1.13	.54
1734	1.29	.97	1.26	.54
1735	1.24	.93	1.50	.45
1736	1.36	1.02	2.25	.36
1737	1.24	.93	1.50	.45
1738	1.36	1.02	1.80	.45

Year	Current Money Mean	Sterling		
		Mean	High	Low
1739	1.34	1.01	1.50	.45
1740	1.61	.80	1.20	.30
1741	1.23	.62	1.05	.24
1742	1.33	.67	1.00	.30
1743	1.35	.67	1.20	.19
1744	1.25	.63	1.00	.15
1745	1.12	.56	1.20	.15
1746	1.21	.61	1.00	.30
1747	.90	.45	1.00	.00
1748	1.33	.67	1.00	.24
1749	1.53	.76	1.50	.00
1750	2.32	1.16	1.89	.60
1751	2.03	1.16	1.54	.31
1752	2.21	1.48	1.60	.80
1753	1.74	1.16	1.60	.60
1754	1.56	1.04	1.33	.60
1755	1.28	.85	1.60	.40
1756	1.76	1.07	1.21	.91
1757	1.83	1.16	1.90	.63
1758	2.12	1.29	2.73	.73
1759	3.07	2.05	3.00	1.28
1760	2.40	1.60	2.72	.80
1761	2.30	1.54	2.00	1.00
1762	2.08	1.39	3.00	.80
1763	1.65	1.10	1.44	.88

Source: Carville V. Earle, *The Evolution of a Tidewater Settlement System: All Hallow's Parish, Maryland, 1650–1783* (1973), 228–229.

TABLE 4.65 TOBACCO PRICES (IN GUILDERS PER DUTCH LB.) AT AMSTERDAM, 1674–1763

Year	Virginia	Dutch
1674	0.28	0.25
1675	0.26	0.16
1676	0.26	0.25
1677	0.30	0.19
1678	0.18	0.12
1682	0.18	0.16
1683	0.24	0.16
1686	0.29	0.19
1688	0.19	0.13
1691	0.25	0.17
1692	0.21	0.17
1694	0.24	0.14
1696	0.34	0.15
1697	0.35	0.18
1701	0.18	0.19
1703	0.37	0.20
1705	0.30	0.14
1706	0.43	0.16
1708	0.29	0.15
1709	0.33	0.16
1710	0.29	0.17
1711	0.32	0.19
1712	0.33	0.14
1713	0.33	0.14
1714	0.31	0.16
1715	0.37	0.17
1716	0.34	0.18
1717	0.33	0.25
1718	0.31	0.21
1719	0.28	0.13
1720	0.29	0.12
1721	0.29	0.10

(continued)

TABLE 4.65 (continued)

Year	Virginia	Dutch
1722	0.25	0.11
1723	0.24	0.13
1724	0.25	0.15
1725	0.33	0.15
1726	0.21	0.18
1727	0.21	0.13
1728	0.19	0.12
1729	0.18	0.10
1730	0.18	0.09
1731	0.18	0.14
1732	0.19	0.13
1733	0.21	0.13
1734	0.23	0.15
1735	0.24	0.13
1736	0.22	0.12
1737	0.21	0.12
1738	0.23	0.12
1739	0.24	0.12
1740	0.22	0.19
1741	0.22	0.18
1742	0.22	0.17
1743	0.18	0.17
1744	0.21	0.15
1745	0.21	0.15
1746	0.18	0.15
1747	0.20	0.15
1748	0.20	0.15
1749	0.20	…
1750	0.20	0.12
1751	0.20	0.11
1752	0.19	0.10
1753	0.18	0.08
1754	0.17	0.12
1755	0.18	0.14
1756	0.20	0.15
1757	0.21	0.14
1758	0.21	0.15
1759	0.26	0.18
1760	0.23	0.19
1761	0.27	0.13
1762	0.19	0.10
1763	0.18	0.11

Source: Jacob M. Price, France and the Chesapeake: A History of the French Tobacco Monopoly, 1674–1791, and of Its Relationship to the British and American Tobacco Trades (1973), 852.

TABLE 4.66 COMPARATIVE PRICES (IN PENCE STERLING PER LB.) PAID FOR SWEETSCENTED VERSUS ORINOCO TOBACCO IN THE CHESAPEAKE, 1670–1749

Period	Price (Ster.) of Sweetscented	Price (Ster.) of Orinoco	Premium Paid for Sweetscented over Orinoco
1670–1679	1.10d	1.06d	3.8%
1680–1689	1.08d	.86d	25.6%
1690–1699	1.10d	.85d	29.4%
1700	1.38d	1.00d	38.0%
1700–1709	1.34d	.90d	48.9%
1710–1719	1.40d	1.03d	35.9%
1717	1.34d	1.05d	27.6%
1720–1729	1.28d	1.18d	8.5%
1727	1.27d	1.13d	12.4%
1728	1.28d	1.06d	20.8%
1730–1739	1.46d	1.01d	44.5%
1740–1749	1.33d	1.17d	13.7%

Source: Darrett B. And Anita H. Rutman, A Place in Time, II, Explicatus (1984), 4.

TABLE 4.67 CYCLICAL PATTERN OF MARYLAND TOBACCO PRICES, 1659–1774

Period	No. Years	Average Price	Profitablity
1659–1663	6	1.53d	Profitable
1664–1680	16	1.06d	Unprofitable
1681–1697	17	.82d	Unprofitable
1698–1704	7	.98d	Unprofitable
1705–1718	14	.88d	Unprofitable
1719–1726	8	1.00d	Profitable
1727–1733	7	.73d	Unprofitable
1734–1739	6	.98d	Profitable
1740–1749	10	.64d	Unprofitable
1750–1753	4	1.24d	Profitable
1754–1756	3	.99d	Profitable
1757–1761	5	1.53d	Profitable
1762–1766	5	1.31d	Profitable
1767–1771	5	1.93d	Profitable
1772–1774	3	1.56d	Profitable

Source: Carville V. Earle, The Evolution of a Tidewater Settlement System: All Hallow's Parish, Maryland, 1650–1783 (1975), 18, 228.

TABLE 4.68 QUALITY OF MARYLAND TOBACCO HARVEST ACCORDING TO GRADES, 1740–1747

Top and Good Tobacco	Seconds	Trash, Grounds, and Scrub
53.3%	26.8%	20.3%

Source: Carville V. Earle, The Evolution of a Tidewater Settlement System: All Hallow's Parish, Maryland, 1650–1783 (1975), 26.

TABLE 4.69 COMPARISON OF FREIGHT CHARGES, IMPORT DUTIES, AND MERCHANT'S COMMISSION TO THE SELLING PRICE OF ORINOCO TOBACCO ABOUT 1710

Itemized Costs of Imported Tobacco	Pence	Percent
Sale price to American grower	1.12	14.9%
Freight and handling charges	.89	11.9%
Import duties paid in Britain	5.28	70.7%
Commission (2.5% of sale price)	.19	2.5%
Total	7.48	100.0%

Note: The import duty was 5.28d per lb. of leaf between 1704 and 1748 if paid by a merchant's bond, but 4.75d. if paid in cash. If the tobacco was reexported, most import duties were remitted.
Source: Paul G. E. Clemens, The Atlantic Economy and Colonial Maryland's Eastern Shore: From Tobacco to Grain (1980), 38.

The primary out-building on Chesapeake farms was a tobacco house, similar to this reconstruction of a late, seventeenth-century barn now maintained by Historic St. Mary's City of Maryland. As is obvious from the photo, southern tobacco farmers did not have to construct expensive, multi-story barns to cure and store their crop until it was sold. Because Chesapeake husbandmen typically did not build shelters for their livestock but rather let them range at large during the winter, it was a considerable economic advantage for southern farmers to be able to cure and store their region's main export crop without having to pay to erect large, costly barns like those used in such northern colonies as Pennsylvania (see, for example, photo on page 76). (Courtesy Paul Leibe, staff photographer for *St. Mary's Today*)

TABLE 4.71 AVERAGE POUNDS OF TOBACCO RAISED PER LABORER IN MARYLAND, 1656–1719

County	1656–1683 Mean	1684–1696 Mean	1697–1704 Mean	1705–1712 Mean	1713–1719 Mean
Anne Arundel	1501	1568	1662	1573	1361
Baltimore	1737	1778	1435	1605	1518
Calvert	1484	1549	1499	1590	1480
Charles	1626	1936	1616	1774	1820
Kent	1553	1436	1457	1582	1553
Somerset	1147	1122	1229	1512	1069
Averages	1547	1585	1522	1609	1515

Source: Probate records analyzed in Gloria L. Main, *Tobacco Colony: Life in Early Maryland, 1650–1720* (1983), 39.

TABLE 4.72 AVERAGE POUNDS OF TOBACCO RAISED BY CHESAPEAKE LABORERS, 1630–1763

Period	Lower Western Shore of Md.	Upper Eastern Shore of Md.	York River Basin of Va.	Lower Rappahannock River, Va.
1630–1649	781	400	938	...
1650–1669	1,539	...	1,087	1,625
1670–1679	1,534	2,583	1,366	1,355
1680–1699	2,167	2,584	1,453	1,395
1700–1709	1,621	1,750	1,175	1,408
1710–1719	1,120	1,831	806	881
1720–1729	1,347	1,277	717	611
1730–1739	1,009	1,352	635	622
1740–1747	1,275	1,055	864	787
1748–1753	1,078	1,026	980	968
1754–1763	820	902	849	778

Source: Lorena S. Walsh, "Plantation Management in the Chesapeake, 1620–1820," *Journal of Economic History*, IXL (1989), 395.

TABLE 4.70 PURCHASING AND MARKETING EXPENSES OF EXPORTING ONE HOGSHEAD OF TOBACCO FROM MARYLAND TO LONDON, ENGLAND, IN 1737

Purchase of one hogshead (790 pounds net) at 1 ½d. per pound (in Maryland)	£	s.	d.
	4	18	9
British duties[a]	16	18	2
Maryland export duty	0	2	9
Freight	1	15	0
Primage and petty charges	0	2	1
To entry inwards etc.	0	1	6 .
To entry outwards etc.	0	2	0
To cooperage etc.	0	2	0
To porterage etc.	0	1	0
To warehouse rent	0	3	6
To brokerage	0	2	0
To postage of letters	0	1	0
To drafts (4 pounds of tobacco)	0	0	9
To loss of weight (allowing 14 pounds for natural loss on shipboard 44 pounds of tobacco)	0	8	3
To commission of 2½% on duties and on selling price	0	12	0
Total charges	20	12	0
Total value in London	25	10	9

[a] British duties were rebated upon reexport from England.
Source: Lewis C. Gray, *History of Agriculture in the Southern United States to 1860* (1933), 224.

TABLE 4.73 POUNDS OF AMERICAN TOBACCO IMPORTED BY ENGLAND, 1616–1695

Year	Total	To London	To Other Ports
1695	...	19,937,400	...
1694	27,836,700	17,280,700	10,556,000
1693	27,464,100	19,866,000	7,598,100
1692	...	13,423,500	...
1691	...	14,830,500	...
1690	...	12,638,000	...
1689	...	14,392,600	...
1688	28,385,500	14,890,500	13,495,000
1687	27,567,000	14,072,000	13,495,000
1686	28,036,500	14,541,500	13,495,000
		[no data for 1685]	
1684	...	...	13,495,000
1683	...	...	13,495,000
1682	21,399,000	12,592,000	8,807,000
1681	...	14,472,000	...
1680	...	11,943,000	...
1679	...	12,983,000	...
1678	...	14,455,000	...
1677	...	11,735,000	...
1676	...	11,127,000	...

(continued)

TABLE 4.73 (continued)

Year	Total	To London	To Other Ports
		[no data for 1673–1675]	
1672	17,559,000	10,539,000	7,020,000
		[no data for 1670–1671]	
1669	15,039,600	9,037,300	6,002,300
		[no data for 1664–1668]	
1663	...	7,371,100	...
		[no data for 1641–1662]	
1640	...	1,257,000	...
1639	...	1,345,000	...
1638	...	3,134,000	...
1637	...	1,537,000	...
		[no data for 1632–1636]	
1631	272,300	209,700	62,500
1630	458,200	360,600	97,500
1629	178,700	89,000	89,700
1628	552,900	420,100	132,800
1627	376,900	335,300	41,600
1626	333,100	213,300	119,800
1625	131,800	111,100	20,700
1624	203,000	187,300	15,600
1623	134,600	119,400	15,200
1622	61,600	59,400	2,200
1621	73,800	73,800	...
1620	119,000	118,000	1,000
1619	45,800	45,800	...
1618	49,700	49,500	200
1617	18,800	18,800	...
1616	2,500	2,300	200

Source: Research by Jacob M. Price printed in Bureau of the Census, *Historical Statistics of the United States* (1975), 1191.

TABLE 4.74 BRITISH TOBACCO IMPORTS AND REEXPORTS (IN LB.), 1697–1763

Year	To England	To Scotland	Total Imports	Reexports	Percent
1763	65,179,000	32,839,000	98,018,000	64,692,000	66%
1762	44,111,000	26,708,000	70,819,000	61,600,000	87%
1761	47,075,000	26,262,000	73,337,000	65,814,000	90%
1760	52,347,000	32,183,000	84,557,000	64,388,000	76%
1759	34,782,000	14,886,000	49,668,000	50,326,000	101%
1758	43,969,000	25,693,000	69,662,000	43,171,000	62%
1757	42,232,000	17,860,000	60,092,000	45,977,000	77%
1756	33,291,000	12,214,000	45,505,000	37,880,000	83%
1755	49,084,000	15,201,000	64,285,000	44,741,000	70%
1754	58,867,000	16,712,000ᵉ	75,579,000	53,154,000	70%
1753	62,686,000	22,131,000ᵉ	84,817,000	50,484,000	60%
1752	57,250,000	20,089,000ᵉ	77,339,000	48,813,000	63%
1751	45,979,000	19,998,000ᵉ	65,977,000	39,297,000	60%
1750	51,339,000	17,951,000ᵉ	69,291,000	33,148,000	48%
1749	44,648,000	22,229,000ᵉ	66,877,000	44,144,000	66%
1748	50,695,000	16,922,000ᵉ	67,617,000	43,169,000	64%
1747	51,289,000	12,757,000	64,045,000	39,083,000	61%
1746	39,990,000	11,729,000	51,719,000	32,474,000	63%
1745	41,073,000	13,612,000	54,686,000	33,364,000	61%
1744	41,434,000	10,727,000	52,161,000	41,798,000	80%
1743	56,767,000	10,627,000	67,394,000	46,702,000	69%
1742	43,467,000	9,739,000	53,206,000	44,088,000	83%
1741	59,449,000	8,925,000	68,374,000	46,431,000	68%
1740	36,002,000	5,303,000	41,305,000	34,971,000	85%
1739	46,724,000	6,643,000	53,367,000	38,220,000	72%
1738	40,120,000	4,588,000	44,708,000	32,889,000	74%
1737	50,208,000	...	...	40,656,000	...
1736	37,904,000	...	...	31,823,000	...
1735	40,069,000	...	...	32,919,000	...
1734	35,563,000	...	...	26,891,000	...
1733	40,085,000	...	...	26,042,000	...
1732	30,891,000	...	...	30,846,000	...
1731	41,595,000	4,096,000ᵐ	45,691,000	28,930,000	63%
1730	35,080,000	5,526,000ᵐ	40,606,000	27,496,000	68%
1729	39,951,000	7,192,000ᵐ	47,143,000	31,273,000	66%
1728	42,588,000	7,234,000ᵐ	49,821,000	28,580,000	57%
1727	43,275,000	6,972,000ᵐ	50,247,000	26,448,000	53%
1726	32,311,000	3,858,000ᵐ	36,169,000	27,697,000	77%
1725	21,047,000	4,193,000ᵐ	25,239,000	13,366,000	53%
1724	26,634,000	5,717,000ᵐ	32,351,000	17,848,000	55%
1723	29,295,000	4,783,000ᵐ	34,078,000	22,333,000	66%
1722	28,542,000	6,720,000ᵐ	35,261,000	20,687,000	59%
1721	37,292,000	4,090,000ᵐ	41,382,000	26,416,000	64%
1720	34,526,000	...	...	23,372,000	...
1719	33,684,000	...	...	20,293,000	...
1718	31,840,000	...	...	18,675,000	...
1717	29,600,000	2,449,000ᵃ	32,049,000	19,392,000	61%
1716	28,316,000	2,449,000ᵃ	30,765,000	16,604,000	54%
1715	17,810,000	2,449,000ᵃ	20,259,000	13,476,000	67%
1714	29,264,000	...	...	19,650,000	...
1713	21,598,000	...	...	16,598,000	...
1712	30,523,000	...	...	19,391,000	...
1711	28,122,000	1,449,000ᵃ	29,571,000	15,108,000	51%
1710	23,498,000	1,449,000ᵃ	24,947,000	15,442,000	62%
1709	34,547,000	1,449,000ᵃ	35,997,000	20,703,000	58%
1708	28,975,000	1,449,000ᵃ	30,424,000	16,565,000	54%
1707	28,088,000	...	28,088,000	21,277,000	76%
1706	19,780,000	...	19,780,000	11,045,000	56%
1705	15,661,000	...	15,661,000	10,589,000	68%
1704	34,864,000	...	34,864,000	19,701,000	57%
1703	20,075,000	...	20,075,000	16,622,000	83%
1702	37,209,000	...	37,209,000	14,376,000	39%
1701	32,189,000	...	32,189,000	21,239,000	66%
1700	37,840,000	...	37,840,000	24,881,000	66%
1699	31,253,000	...	31,253,000	22,431,000	72%
1698	31,530,000	...	31,530,000	22,849,000	72%
1697	35,632,000	...	35,632,000	17,520,000	49%

ᵃ Average of several years.
ᵐ Year ending Michaelmas.
ᵉ Estimate based on partial data of Clyde ports (about 80% of total).
Source: Jacob M. Price, *France and the Chesapeake: A History of the French Tobacco Monopoly, 1764–1791, and of Its Relationship to the British and American Tobacco Trades* (1973), 843–844. Research of Jacob M. Price printed in Bureau of the Census, *Historical Statistics of the United States* (1975), 1190–1191.

TABLE 4.75 ANNUAL TOBACCO EXPORTS FROM EASTERN SHORE OF MARYLAND, 1696–1773

Period	Hogsheads	Weight	Total Weight
1770–1773	5,490	1,000 lb.	5,490,000 lb.
1760–1769	4,700	1,000 lb.	4,700,000 lb.
1750–1759	6,030	1,000 lb.	6,030,000 lb.
1740–1749	7,870	1,000 lb.	7,870,000 lb.
1730–1739	6,250	800 lb.	5,000,000 lb.
1720–1729	5,620	700 lb.	3,934,000 lb.
1717–1719	6,940	600 lb.	4,164,000 lb.
1696–1699	3,640	500 lb.	1,820,000 lb.

Source: Paul G. E. Clemens, *The Atlantic Economy and Colonial Maryland's Eastern Shore: From Tobacco to Grain* (1980), 171.

TABLE 4.76 NUMBER AND PERCENTAGE OF TOBACCO HOGSHEADS EXPORTED TO BRITAIN FROM VIRGINIA DISTRICTS, 1737–1768

Year	Upper James River	Lower James River	York River	Rappa- hannock River	South Bank of Potomac River
1768	16,838 (40%)	2,640 (6%)	6,258 (15%)	9,132 (22%)	6,817 (16%)
1762	21,993 (37%)	1,678 (3%)	11,504 (20%)	15,727 (28%)	7,761 (13%)
1761	16,919 (33%)	1,601 (3%)	11,389 (23%)	15,356 (30%)	5,294 (11%)
1758	13,219 (27%)	2,109 (4%)	11,980 (25%)	13,606 (28%)	8,015 (16%)
1750	13,397 (26%)	2,148 (4%)	13,235 (26%)	15,937 (31%)	6,465 (13%)
1745	10,181 (22%)	1,892 (4%)	12,439 (27%)	13,170 (29%)	8,320 (18%)
1744	9,121 (27%)	782 (2%)	8,350 (25%)	10,886 (32%)	4,689 (14%)
1743	7,179 (18%)	1,429 (4%)	12,433 (31%)	13,234 (33%)	5,735 (14%)
1742	9,154 (24%)	1,494 (4%)	9,672 (25%)	12,403 (33%)	5,161 (14%)
1741	7,887 (20%)	1,148 (3%)	15,469 (39%)	10,077 (25%)	5,241 (13%)
1740	7,120 (23%)	1,077 (3%)	8,243 (26%)	10,141 (33%)	4,597 (15%)
1739	6,060 (18%)	1,132 (3%)	11,910 (34%)	10,761 (31%)	4,834 (14%)
1738	6,808 (25%)	936 (3%)	10,079 (38%)	7,073 (27%)	1,797 (7%)
1737	8,689 (24%)	899 (3%)	12,720 (35%)	9,678 (27%)	4,001 (11%)

Note: Percentages do not always equal 100% due to rounding.
Source: Jacob M. Price, France and the Chesapeake: A History of the French Tobacco Monopoly, 1674–1791, and of Its Relationship to the British and American Tobacco Trades (1973), 669–670.

TABLE 4.77 COLONIAL ORIGIN OF TOBACCO EXPORTED TO ENGLAND (IN LB.), 1697–1763

Year	Virginia & Maryland	South Carolina	Northern Ports
1763	64,500,000	647,000	6,000
1762	41,862,000	2,226,000	10,000
1761	45,818,000	796,000	450,000
1760	51,283,000	989,000	17,000
1759	34,652,000	120,000	4,000
1758	43,623,000	273,000	...
1757	41,542,000	369,000	...
1756	32,943,000	289,000	1,000
1755	48,610,000	241,000	16,000
1754	57,977,000	836,000	46,000
1753	61,913,000	451,000	320,000
1752	56,591,000	83,000	573,000
1751	45,745,000	162,000	71,000
1750	50,785,000	12,000	481,000
1749	44,190,000	321,000	122,000
1748	49,646,000	393,000	385,000
1747	50,765,000	287,000	231,000
1746	39,567,000	81,000	228,000
1745	40,897,000	...	166,000
1744	41,119,000	35,000	162,000
1743	55,666,000	515,000	18,000
1742	42,838,000	558,000	30,000
1741	59,007,000	70,000	228,000
1740	35,372,000	49,000	475,000
1739	45,866,000	552,000	305,000

Year	Virginia & Maryland	South Carolina	Northern Ports
1738	39,868,000	...	226,000
1737	49,946,000	86,000	154,000
1736	37,682,000	108,000	100,000
1735	39,818,000	...	250,000
1734	35,216,000	...	339,000
1733	39,854,000	...	169,000
1732	30,847,000	...	35,000
1731	41,194,000	2,000	90,000
1730	34,860,000	16,000	73,000
1729	39,785,000	...	161,000
1728	42,328,000	1,000	156,000
1727	43,026,000	...	225,000
1726	32,159,000	...	143,000
1725	20,968,000	...	68,000
1724	26,612,000	...	14,000
1723	29,259,000	6,000	25,000
1722	28,383,000	8,000	141,000
1721	36,949,000	47,000	295,000
1720	34,138,000	8,000	370,000
1719	33,503,000	1,000	179,000
1718	31,740,000	4,000	95,000
1717	29,450,000	...	149,000
1716	28,305,000	...	3,000
1715	17,783,000	...	18,000
1714	29,248,000	...	10,000
1713	21,573,000	...	14,000
1712	30,502,000	...	15,000
1711	28,100,000	...	7,000
1710	23,351,000	2,000	119,000
1709	34,467,000	1,000	67,000
1708	28,716,000	7,000	242,000
1707	27,684,000	6,000	321,000
1706	19,379,000	5,000	116,000
1705	15,573,000	...	56,000
1704	34,665,000	7,000	97,000
1703	19,451,000	2,000	429,000
1702	36,749,000	3,000	371,000
1701	31,754,000	...	315,000
1700	37,166,000	8,000	433,000
1699	30,641,000	3,000	113,000
1698[a]	8,359,000	...	76,000
1698[b]	22,738,000	...	31,000
1697[b]	35,329,000	1,000	146,000

[a] For September 29–December 24 only.
[b] For fiscal year ending September 28.
Source: Data compiled by Jacob M. Price, printed in Bureau of the Census, Historical Statistics of the United States (1975), 1189.

TABLE 4.78 TOBACCO EXPORTED TO EUROPE BY NEW SWEDEN COMPANY, 1640–1660

Year	Tobacco (Lb.)	Price
1660	52,707	...
1659	39,036	...
1658	23,557	...
1657	19,201	...
1656	36,398	...
1655	28,758	...
1654	13,519	6,083 Fl.
1653	...	...
1652	...	...
1651	...	...
1650	...	...
1649	20,836	6,329 D.
1648	18,450	6,277 D.
1647	379	379 D.
1646	26,696	6,694 D.

(continued)

TABLE 4.78 (continued)

Year	Tobacco (Lb.)	Price
1645	11,886	5,517 D.
1644	20,000	...
1643	38,703	29,000 D.
1642	14,689	10,606 D.
1641	21,095	15,781 D.
1640	9,722	6,602 D.

Fl. = Dutch Florins (2.5 Fl = 1 Spanish dollar)
D. = Swedish Krone
Source: Amandus Johnson, *The Swedish Settlements on the Delaware, 1638–1664* (1911), I: 162, 292–295; II: 516, 639, 644.

the eighteenth century. After 1720, prices generally remained at profitable levels, in large part because increasing efficiencies in packaging and declining freight rates reduced the overhead charges for shipping the commodity to market. (See Table 4.97.) Tobacco not only dominated the Cheasapeake's economy but also ranked as English North America's leading export during the the colonial era. By the 1760s, the selling price of this crop equaled about one-quarter of the earnings gained from all goods shipped overseas from the thirteen colonies.

Wheat

Wheat was the second-most-commonly planted cereal crop (after corn, which was mostly raised for domestic consumption), and it accounted for a greater value of exports than any other commodity except tobacco. Although wheat was sowed at Jamestown in 1607, the

German immigrants became known in the colonies for building exceptionally large and sturdy barns. Observant travelers noted that a German farm family's barn was often better constructed and worth more than its house, which was usually a log cabin like that on page 278. This structure in Montgomery County (just west of Philadelphia), whose foundation probably dates from the late colonial period, shows the typical dimensions of a stone barn in the Pennsylvania Dutch country. Compare with the far more modest features of the "tobacco house" on page 73. (Record Group 12 [Photographic Unit, Department of Highways], Courtesy Pennsylvania State Archives)

grain was little cultivated in the seventeenth-century South because so few farmers owned plows. New Englanders initially grew large amounts of wheat. Yields became sharply reduced by black stemrust after 1710, and many farmers ceased growing it for the export market and substituted rye for family consumption. The Middle-Atlantic colonies emerged as the English mainland's breadbasket in the late 1600s and provided the great bulk of exported flour and packaged bread. The trade in breadstuffs primarily centered in the Caribbean and to a lesser extent involved southern Europe.

Although wheat required little work to sow, its harvest imposed heavy labor requirements within tight time constraints because the grain ripened within a very short period. Farmers could only produce the amount of wheat capable of being cut by by their families before it

TABLE 4.79   PRICE OF WHEAT (IN SHILLINGS AND PENCE) IN CONNECTICUT, 1640–1758

Year(s)	Country Pay	Spanish Silver
1755–58	n.a.	3s, 9d
1753–54	n.a.	n.a.
1752	38s	3s, 9d
1750–51	n.a.	n.a.
1748–49	36s	4s, 4d
1745–47	15s	2s, 7 1/2d
1740–44	12s	2s, 10d
1735–39	10s	3s, 9d
1730–34	8s	3s, 6d
1727–29	7s, 6d	3s, 9d
1724–26	6s	3s, 7d
1720–23	5s	3s, 6d
1715–19	4s, 6d	3s, 3 1/2d
1710–14	4s, 5d	4s
1700–09	6s	5s
1640–99	4s, 6d	3s, 2d

Source: Probate records analyzed in Jackson T. Main, *Society and Economy in Colonial Connecticut* (1985), 57.

TABLE 4.80   PRICE OF BUSHEL OF WHEAT IN MARYLAND, 1705–1719, IN SHILLINGS OF PROCLAMATION MONEY

	Anne Arundel Co.	Baltimore Co.	Calvert Co.	Charles Co.	Kent Co.	Somerset Co.
Wheat	3.44s	3.48s	3.49s	2.92s	3.17s	3.21s

Source: Probate records analyzed in Gloria L. Main, *Tobacco Colony: Life in Early Maryland, 1650–1720* (1982), 278.

TABLE 4.81   WHEAT PRICES, IN LOCAL PENCE PER BUSHEL, IN KENT AND TALBOT COUNTIES, 1680–1763

Year	Kent	Talbot
1763	49	46
1762	49	46
1761	57	45
1760	49	42
1759	47	41
1758	39	40
1757	37	37
1756	45	42
1755	46	44
1754	46	43
1753	43	45
1752	43	41
1751	43	44

Year	Kent	Talbot
1750	45	41
1749	45	45
1748	39	41
1747	35	39
1746	36	37
1745	34	34
1744	35	36
1743	39	47
1742	49	54
1741	48	51
1740	40	32
1739	40	39
1738	47	42
1737	44	34
1736	38	38
1735	37	38
1734	33	38
1733	34	42
1732	32	36
1731	30	30
1730	36	39
1729	36	41
1728	38	42
1727	34	38
1726	36	37
1725	35	38
1724	36	41
1723	35	40
1722	36	39
1721	36	43
1720	39	41
1719	…	38
1718	…	36
1717	…	38
1716	…	36
1715	…	31
1714	…	41
1713	…	39
1712	…	44
1711	…	37
1710	…	36
1709	…	39
1708	…	42
1707	…	41
1706	…	42
1705	…	38
1704	…	43
1703	…	48
1702	…	48
1701	…	47
1700	…	44
1699	…	39
1698	…	36
1697	…	48
1696	…	38
1695	…	…
1694	…	36
1693	…	…
1692	…	…
1691	…	…
1690	…	…
1689	…	…
1688	…	…
1687	…	38
1686	…	43
1685	…	48
1684	…	48
1683	…	42
1682	…	43
1681	…	39
1680	…	40

Source: Paul G. E. Clemens, *The Atlantic Economy and Colonial Maryland's Eastern Shore: From Tobacco to Grain* (1980), 226–227.

TABLE 4.82 AVERAGE PRICE OF WHEAT, BREAD, AND FLOUR AT PHILADELPHIA, 1700–1763

| | Wheat | Bread | | Flour |
| | | Middling[a] | Ship[b] | |
Year	Bu.	Cwt.	Cwt.	Cwt.
1763	6.06	30.18	17.82	16.94
1762	5.66	28.88	17.49	16.82
1761	5.03	25.18	12.67	14.82
1760	5.11	24.36	13.40	14.96
1759	4.96	22.14	14.33	14.59
1758	3.89	21.84	13.98	12.27
1757	3.79	21.24	14.16	11.31
1756	4.34	21.21	13.65	12.76
1755	4.49	21.42	14.50	13.76
1754	4.46	21.64	15.89	14.11
1753	4.48	21.52	13.87	12.80
1752	4.38	21.94	13.17	13.13
1751	4.28	22.37	14.20	12.34
1750	4.51	23.82	15.23	13.10
1749	5.66	26.30	17.60	16.59
1748	5.04	19.67	13.89	15.41
1747	3.29	16.48	11.53	10.01
1746	2.87	14.95	10.15	9.07
1745	2.60	13.06	8.81	8.01
1744	2.49	13.32	8.47	7.68
1743	2.84	14.31	9.06	8.69
1742	3.58	15.96	11.77	10.98
1741	4.47	19.58	15.83	13.66
1740	3.25	13.56	10.31	8.72
1739	2.82	13.01	9.60	8.03
1738	3.48	16.75	12.58	11.16
1737	3.88	15.21	11.78	11.71
1736	3.24	12.77	10.94	9.61
1735	3.85	14.58	12.33	11.47
1734	3.55	13.75	10.90	10.51
1733	3.06	12.85	10.39	8.84
1732	2.70	11.91	...	8.17
1731	2.47	11.72	...	8.02
1730	3.68	14.88	...	11.56
1729	3.70	14.00	...	10.65
1728	3.39	13.72	...	10.02
1727	3.27	13.46	...	11.46
1726	3.82	14.08	...	12.51
1725	3.87	12.79	...	12.12
1724	3.36	11.92	...	10.95
1723	2.73	11.67	...	8.80
1722	2.97	12.54	...	8.93
1721	3.05	13.00	...	8.83
1720	3.08	13.31	...	9.26
1719	3.20	...	...	11.30
1718	3.10	...	...	11.30
1717	2.70	...	...	8.30
1716	2.50	...	...	7.60
1715	2.70	...	...	10.30
1714	4.10	...	...	17.00
1713	4.40	...	...	16.30
1712	3.40	...	...	12.00
1711	3.30	...	...	11.30
1710	3.40	...	...	11.80
1709	3.80	...	...	13.50
1708	5.30	...	...	19.00
1707	5.00	...	...	...
1706	4.10	...	...	...
1705	3.80	...	...	15.00
1704	3.90	...	...	14.80
1703	4.10	...	...	15.90
1702	...	...	...	19.60
1701	...	...	...	21.80
1700	5.00	...	...	20.90

Note: Hundredweight (cwt.) equals 112 lb. Price in shillings.
[a] Middling was leavened bread baked in loaves.
[b] Ship was unleavened bread baked as very hard wafers that were resistant to spoilage for long periods.
Source: Arthur H. Cole, *Wholesale Commodity Prices in the United States, 1700–1861* (1938), 1–5. Anne Bezanson, et al., eds., *Prices in Colonial Pennsylvania* (1935), 422–424.

TABLE 4.83 YIELDS PER ACRE OF WHEAT IN BRITISH MAINLAND COLONIES

Locality	Period	Yields per Acre	Average Yield
Connecticut	1640–1750	4 to 12 bu.	6 bu.
Connecticut	1750–1774	4 to 12 bu.	7 bu.
Southeast Pennsylvania	1750–1760	8 to 15 bu.	10 bu.
Shenandoah Valley, Va.	1750–1760	8 to 12 bu.	10 bu.

Sources: Jackson T. Main, *Society and Economy in Colonial Connecticut* (1985), 239. James T. Lemon, *The Best Poor Man's Country: A Geographical Study of Early Southeastern Pennsylvania* (1976), 152–156, 265, n. 15. Robert D. Mitchell, *Commercialism and Frontier: Perspectives on the Early Shenandoah Valley* (1977), 142.

TABLE 4.84 AVERAGE WHEAT PRODUCTION PER LABORER IN THE CHESAPEAKE, 1720–1763

Year	Lower Western Shore of Md.	Upper Eastern Shore of Md.	York River Basin of Va.	Lower Rappahannock River, Va.
1720–1739	6.6 bu.	11.1 bu.	7.4 bu.	3.5 bu.
1740–1753	5.1 bu.	11.0 bu.	3.4 bu.	...
1754–1763	8.8 bu.	35.1 bu.	9.0 bu.	7.6 bu.

Source: Lorena S. Walsh, "Plantation Management in the Chesapeake, 1620–1820," *Journal of Economic History,* IXL (1989), 399.

spoiled in the fields, about 8 acres, unless they had the resources to hire day labor. Because the labor needs for grain were intensely seasonal, it was impossible to achieve economies of scale by raising wheat with large gangs of slaves or indentured servants who could not be profitably used year round. The production capabilities of farmers increased marginally after the cradle scythe came into wider usage after 1750, but technological limits on harvesting wheat delayed the development of large farms specializing in its cultivation until mechanical reapers were invented in the nineteenth century.

The Maritime Industries

The Fisheries and Whaling Industry

The fishing industry remained essentially a New England enterprise through the colonial era. New England predominated in this trade because of its proximity to the North Atlantic's major fishing grounds, which lay north of Cape Cod, and because the poor returns offered by the area's agriculture induced many marginal farmers to supplement their income by joining fishing crews for short voyages. Modest fisheries later grew up elsewhere to supply shellfish for New York, Philadelphia, and other coastal cities.

New England's fisheries developed rapidly because, by the time large-scale, Puritan migration began in the 1630s, mariners from England's West Country had already identified the nearest banks during trans-Atlantic voyages. Because the closest banks, those south of Nova Scotia, enjoyed two fishing seasons rather than one and numerous farmers were eager for winter employment, owners of small boats found it relatively easy to organize short voyages to bring in catches. Permanent settlements of commercial fishermen also sprang up to provide bases for preserving and packing catches. So quickly did the industry rise that in 1641 Gov. John Winthrop estimated that Massachusetts sold 300,000 cod overseas.

Hampered by small boats and inexperienced crews, New Englanders initially limited their fishing activity to grounds no more than 15 miles offshore, but by the mid-seventeenth century they had expanded their activity to deep-water banks east of Nova Scotia, where cod, hake, haddock, and mackerel were abundant. By the 1660s they were exploiting the Sable Island Bank, 200 miles east of Nova Scotia, and by the 1670s had extended operations to well east of Newfoundland. About 600 New England boats were hauling catches from Newfoundland waters by 1675, and within a half-century it was the Yankees rather than sailors making long-distance voyages from England's West Country who dominated the North Atlantic fisheries.

Dried cod or mackerel was the first major commodity exported from New England. The earliest market for colonial fish emerged in the West Indies, where salted mackerel and low-quality cod served as an inexpensive source of protein for slaves. American merchants soon discovered that a more profitable market existed in the Iberian Peninsula and the Spanish West Indies, whose population required large amounts of fish for Catholic days of abstinence from red meat. New Englanders could sell high-quality cod in the southern European market at premium prices and still dispose of their undersized or otherwise undesireable catch to West Indian sugar planters. By 1731, New England's fishing industry provided income for perhaps 5,000 full- or part-time sailors and enjoyed an annual catch of approximately 230 million fish (mostly cod).

Hunting whales for bone and oil also emerged as a highly profitable aspect of the fishing industry. By the 1690s, isolated centers of whaling existed along the Massachusetts coast, eastern Long Island, and southern New Jersey. The earliest whalers limited their pursuits to species migrating yearly from Greenland along the Atlantic shore and rarely ventured more than 50 miles from land.

In 1712, Captain Christopher Hussey of Nantucket Island, Massachusetts, located large schools of spermaceti, or sperm, whales in the mid-Atlantic. His discovery inaugurated the era of deep-sea whaling. Colonial whalers became the first mariners to identify and exploit the Gulf Stream, which enabled them to pursue their quarry to either southern Africa or the Falkland Islands. Sperm-whale hunting offered exceptional profits because the mammal's head yielded large amounts of rich oil that made the purest lighting fluid and finest candles then known.

About 1750, two major innovations enhanced the spermaceti industry's efficiency. Rhode Islanders devised improved methods to increase the yield of spermaceti separated from common whale oil. Captains gained freedom from the necessity of limiting voyages to four weeks because of the need to refine blubber before it spoiled by installing, on board ship, iron kettles built in brick furnaces that transformed ships into floating factories capable of ranging the seas for months. Nantucket became the foremost whaling center, and by 1740 its fleet numbered about 50 sloops, each manned by about 13 crew members, that could retrieve about 4,700 barrels of oil. By 1762, Nantucket had seventy-eight deep-sea whaling vessels, and an equal number of such ships probably sailed from other New England ports.

Information about the fisheries lacks precision. Estimates of the size and value of annual catches exist for barely a dozen years before 1764. No reliable price series distinguishing between types catches exists, and little is known about outfitting ships and marketing practices. Aside from

TABLE 4.85 PRICE OF 100 LB. OF JAMAICA COD AT BOSTON, MASS., IN SHILLINGS OF LOCAL CURRENCY, 1750–1763

Year	Price (in Shillings)
1763	13.70
1762	13.90
1761	15.30
1760	14.50
1759	13.50
1758	12.60
1757	10.70
1756	9.70
1755	9.10
1754	9.50
1753	9.00
1752	9.20
1751	7.50
1750	6.67

Source: Arthur H. Cole, *Wholesale Commodity Prices in the United States, 1700–1861* (1938), 31–50.

TABLE 4.86 VOLUME AND VALUE OF FISH EXPORTED FROM NEW ENGLAND, 1641–1763

Year	Exported From	Where Sold	Exports (Quintals)	Value (Sterling)
1641	Massachusetts	West Indies	3,000	£1,500
1675	New England	West Indies & Iberia	60,000	[£30,000?]
1686	Boston, Mass.	Iberia	11,000	£5,500
1700	Boston, Mass.	West Indies	25,000	£15,000
		Southern Europe	25,000	£15,000
1713	Boston & Salem	Iberia	60,000	[£36,000?]
1716–17	Salem, Mass.	Southern Europe	67,000	[£40,000?]
1719	New Hampshire	not stated	7,681	…
		not stated	318 hogsheads	…
1731	New England	Southern Europe	230,000	£172,000
1744	New England	West Indies & Iberia	80,000	£40,000
1747–48	Salem, Mass.	West Indies	20,000	[£7,000?]
		Southern Europe	32,000	[£16,000?]
1754	Boston, Mass.	Southern Europe	26,000	[£19,000?]
1755	Boston & Salem	Southern Europe	148,000	[£108,000?]
1763	New England	West Indies	137,794	[£90,000?]
		Southern Europe	102,265	[£102,000?]

Note: A quintal equaled about 100 lb. or about 100 dried cod.
Source: James G. Lydon, "Fish and Flour for Gold: Southern Europe and the Colonial American Balance of Payments," *Business History Review,* XXXIX (1965), 173–174, 181. Harold A. Innis, *The Cod Fisheries: The History of an International Economy* (rev. ed. 1954), 118, 161–162. Ralph G. Lounsbury, *The British Fishery at Newfoundland, 1634–1763* (1934), 142, 312. Joseph J. Malone, *Pine Trees and Politics: The Naval Stores and Forest Policy in Colonial New England, 1691–1775* (1964), 153.

TABLE 4.87 COST OF OUTFITTING A FISHING BOAT FOR THE COD SEASON, ABOUT 1760

Expenses	Price (in Pound Sterling)
To a Boat*	£20.0.0
To 1 New Road	2.0.0
To 1 Sute of Sails	4.10.0
To Rigging & Blocks	1.1.0
To Ropes for Sean Lines 3 hund[d]. weight	3.0.0

(continued)

TABLE 4.87   (continued)

Expenses	Price (in Pound Sterling)
To 1 Small Anchor of 40 lb. & 1 Cillick	1.10.0
To 3 dozen fishing Lines @ 6ce each	0.18.0
To 1 D⁰. Sand. Ditto @ 10ce	0.10.0
To fishing Leads 56 pounds	0.10.6
To Sheet Lead 12 pounds	0.4.0
To 6 Dozen Small Quarter hooks	0.1.9
To 1 Grose Middle Ditto	0.6.0
To 3 Dozen Bank hooks for Giggers	0.8.0
To 1 Boatmaster @ 23 £	23.0.0
To 1 Midshipman @ 18	18.0.0
To 1 Foreshipman @ 12	12.0.0
To 1 Captain @ 7	7.0.0
To 1 Splitter @ 20	20.0.0
To 1 Salter @ 16	16.0.0
To 2 Greenmen @ 5	10.0.0
To 4 Barrels Pork @ 50/pq	10.0.0
To 2 Barrels Beef @ 40/pq	4.0.0
To 1 m of Bread @ 12/pq	6.0.0
To 3 Gallons Sweet Oyl @ 5/pq	0.15.0
To 1 ferkin Butter	2.0.0
To 2 Bushels of Pease	0.10.0
To 2 Gallons Rum @ 3/pq	3.0.0
To 11 Gallons Molasses	1.10.0
To 1 Caplin Sain of 30 foot deep & 4 fathom Long	18.0.0
To 3 Netts	2.10.0
To 40 Hhds Salt @ 8 pq	16.0.0
Total	£205.4.3

* allowed to a Single Boat

{ Stage room 16 feet wide & 70 feet Long.
Flake room 50 Yards long & 40 yards wide
N.B.: 10 Hhds Salt allowed to Cure one hundᵈ.
Quintals of Fish.

Source: Harold A. Innis, *The Cod Fisheries: The History of an International Economy* (rev. ed. 1954), 181.

TABLE 4.88   TONNAGE AND ANNUAL PRODUCTION OF WHALING VESSELS OUTFITTED AT NANTUCKET, MASS., 1715–1763

Year	Number of Vessels	Average Tonnage	Barrels of Oil	Value (Sterling)
1763	60	75	9,238	…
1762	78	75	9,440	…
1756	80	75	12,000	£27,600
1748	60	50–75	11,250	£19,648
1730	25	38–50	3,700	£3,200
1715	6	38	600	£1,100ᵃ

ᵃ Includes value of 11,000 pounds of whale bones.
Source: Obed Macy, *The History of Nantucket* (1835), 54–55, 232–233.

Nantucket, most information on the whaling industry comes from anecdotal or antiquarian material. This lack of information is most regrettable because the colonial fisheries sustained a highly profitable overseas trade and they were long reckoned as the "nursery of seamen" for their role in training sailors and ship's officers for the merchant marine.

The Merchant Marine

An American-based merchant marine began to emerge in the 1640s when New England merchants began to invest in ships to carry foodstuffs and lumber for markets in the English West Indies. In 1700, when at least 171 ships engaged in oceanic commerce from New England's ports, New York's governor declared, "There are more good vessels belonging to the town of Boston than to all of Scotland and Ire-

land." With 124 trading vessels carrying cargo space for 6,443 tons, Boston possessed the most numerous merchant fleet in North America and the second largest of any English-speaking harbor; in terms of tonnage, Boston stood as the third-greatest port in England's dominions, behind London and Bristol.

Outside of New England, the Dutch dominated Anglo-American trade for most of the seventeenth century. Because perhaps three-quarters of western Europe's commercial vessels sailed from Holland, the Dutch controlled most seaborne traffic in the North Atlantic, including England's foreign trade. To encourage the growth of its own merchant marine, the English Parliament passed several statutes after 1649 prohibiting foreigners from carrying English exports or imports. These Navigation Laws inevitably forced the imperial economy to develop commercial shipping adequate for overseas trade. Because Parliament placed no restrictions on colonial shipowning, the Navigation Laws stimulated the growth of a merchant marine in English North America as well as England. By 1740, English officials estimated the size of the Anglo-American merchant marine at 1,330 vessels (exclusive of fishing and coasting ships), of which 76% were from New England.

Once freed of competition from the Dutch, merchants in the Mid-Atlantic colonies also enlarged their stock of shipping, with the result that New York City and Philadelphia eventually came to rival Boston as

The thirteen colonies were unique among Europe's American possessions in developing a sizable merchant marine that helped diversify the economy and retain shipping earnings that could be used for domestic investment. This scene recaptures the sense of economic activity along New York City's wharf during the mid-1700s. (*Harper's Magazine*, May 1892)

centers of trade. The colonial merchant marine initially expanded into niches for which they held a competitive advantage, or were unattractive to English shipowners, such as the North American coastal trade or provisioning the West Indies. By the mid-eighteenth century, however, colonial vessels were transporting a significant amount of freight to and from England, and only the trade of the southern provinces, whose major ports remained relatively small, was primarily in the hands of English shippers.

The only estimates of the Anglo-American merchant marine's size and earnings in the late colonial era date from about 1770, by which time a foundation had been laid for the later emergence of the U.S. martime fleet as the world's largest. Shortly before independence, every third ship in the imperial British merchant marine operated from North American ports, and critical segments of the empire's trade, especially the supply of foodstuffs and lumber to the West Indies, were primarily dependent on cargoes transported in colonial vessels. The rise of the merchant marine benefited American society enormously by helping maintain the country's balance of international payments through the retention of shipping earnings, by diversifying the economy through the creation of such varied industries as shipbuilding and insurance, by reducing the country's commercial dependence on outside nations, and by creating a reservoir of experienced mariners available for wartime naval service.

TABLE 4.89   MERCHANT MARINE OF BRITISH NORTH AMERICA, ABOUT 1700

New England	
State	Vessels
Massachusetts	171
New Hampshire	24
Connecticut	20
Rhode Island	30
Total	245
Mid-Atlantic	
State	Vessels
New York	124
New Jersey	…
Pennsylvania	…
Total	124
South	
State	Vessels
Maryland	41
Virginia	27
South Carolina	11
Total	79
Total Colonial Shipping	448 vessels

Source: Bernard and Lotte Bailyn, *Massachusetts Shipping, 1697–1714: A Statistical Study* (1959), 21–22, 79.

TABLE 4.90   AVERAGE TONNAGE OF TRADING VESSELS REGISTERED IN NEW ENGLAND DEPARTING OVERSEAS FROM BOSTON, MASS., 1661–1698

Periods	Number of Vessels	Average Tonnage
Aug. 16, 1661–Feb. 25, 1662	13	61 tons
Mar. 25, 1687–Sep. 29, 1687	119	43 tons
Mar. 25, 1688–Sep. 29, 1688	…	47 tons
Mar. 25, 1698–Sep. 29, 1698	163	49 tons

Source: Charles F. Carroll, *The Timber Economy of Puritan New England* (1973), 131.

TABLE 4.91   MERCHANT MARINE OF MASSACHUSETTS BAY IN 1698

Composition of Merchant Marine by Area				
Home Port	Vessels	Tonnage	Vessels Jointly Owned	Total Owners
Boston Bay				
Boston	124	6,443	94	261
Charleston	5	134	4	12
Cambridge	1	18	0	1
North Shore				
Salem	21	998	8	26
Ipswich	3	125	3	12
Newbury	2	60	1	4
Gloucester	2	40	1	4
Beverly	1	30	1	6
Lynn	1	15	1	6
South Shore				
Scituate	1	200	1	9
Plymouth	1	15	0	1
Cape Cod				
Yarmouth	2	55	2	5
Sandwich	1	20	1	2
Barnstable	1	15	1	2
Nantucket	3	65	3	3
"Mass. Bay"	2	220	2	9
Total	171	8,453	123	332

Composition of Merchant Marine by Ship Type, 1698	
Type of Ship	Percentage
Ships	41.3%
Sloops	22.5%
Brigantines	19.1%
Barks	8.2%
Ketches	5.8%

Source: Bernard and Lotte Bailyn, *Massachusetts Shipping, 1697–1714: A Statistical Study* (1959), 19, 79.

TABLE 4.92   MERCHANT SHIPPING OF THE LARGEST ENGLISH IMPERIAL PORTS, 1702

Home Port	Vessels	Tonnage
London	560	71,977
Boston, Mass.	124	6,443
Bristol	98	10,299
Yarmouth	85	5,889
New York, N.Y.	73	3,358
Exeter	72	4,222
Hull	68	4,493
Liverpool	61	5,120
Scarborough	59	4,075
Whitby	65	4,050

Source: Bernard and Lotte Bailyn, *Massachusetts Shipping, 1697–1714: A Statistical Study* (1959), 20–21.

TABLE 4.93   NUMBER AND TYPE OF SAILING RIG OF VESSELS REGISTERED AT ANNAPOLIS, MD., 1733–1750

Rig	Number (%)	Range in Tons	Tonnage of Majority
Ships	35 (13%)	50 to 400	100 to 250
Snows	15 (5%)	40 to 180	90 to 120
Brigs	34 (12%)	40 to 180	60 to 100
Schooners	69 (25%)	20 to 90	30 to 50
Sloops	123 (45%)	20 to 100	20 to 50

Source: Arthur P. Middleton, *Tobacco Coast: A Maritime History of Chesapeake Bay in the Colonial Era* (1953), 217, 242.

TABLE 4.94 PORT OF ORIGIN AND TYPE OF VESSELS TRADING TO MARYLAND, 1745–1747

Origin	Ships	Snows	Brigs	Schooners	Sloops
Great Britain	60	10	7	...	1
Maryland	7	1	2	16	23
Virginia	...	...	1	7	6
New England	7	4	10	32	38
Middle Colonies	1	...	2	1	2
Carolinas	...	...	...	5	...
West Indies	...	...	...	1	2
Bermuda	...	...	...	...	5
Totals	75	15	22	62	77

Source: Arthur P. Middleton, *Tobacco Coast: A Maritime History of Chesapeake Bay in the Colonial Era* (1953), 252.

TABLE 4.95 PORT OF ORIGIN AND TYPE OF VESSELS TRADING TO VIRGINIA, 1736–1766

Origin	Ships	Snows	Brigs	Schooners	Sloops
Great Britain	165	21	18	...	2
Virginia	6	12	24	20	38
Maryland	...	...	...	...	2
New England	1	...	...	9	15
Middle Colonies	...	...	...	...	4
Carolinas	...	...	5	2	5
West Indies	...	1	...	...	...
Bermuda	...	...	...	...	57
Totals	172	36	47	31	123

Source: Arthur P. Middleton, *Tobacco Coast: A Maritime History of Chesapeake Bay in the Colonial Era* (1953), 251.

TABLE 4.96 MERCHANT SHIPPING OF BRITISH NORTH AMERICAN PORTS, AUGUST 1740

Merchant Vessels Owned by Residents of American Colonies		British Merchant Vessels Trading with the American Colonies	
Colony	Vessels	Colony	Vessels
Massachusetts & New Hampshire Used in overseas trade	750	With Massachusetts, New Hampshire, & Nova Scotia	20
Sloops & schooners in fishing & coastal trade	350		
Rhode Island & Connecticut Used in overseas trade	260	With Connecticut & Rhode Island	6
Fishing & coasting sloops	150		
New York Foreign & coasting trade	50[a]	With New York and New Jersey	8
New Jersey Foreign & coasting trade	10[a]		
Pennsylvania	70[b]	With Pennsylvania[b]	10
Maryland	60	With Maryland	95
Virginia	80	With Virginia	120
North Carolina	25	With North Carolina	30
South Carolina	25	With South Carolina	200
Newfoundland	25	With Newfoundland	80
West Indies	105	West Indies	331
Bermuda	75	Guinea Slave Trade	150
Total	2,035	Total	1,050
Among colonial vessels are 1,065 ships, snows, & brigantines worth an average of £1,000 sterling each and 970 sloops & schooners worth an average of £400 sterling each.		Among British vessels are 900 ships, snows, & brigantines worth an average of £1,200 sterling each and 150 slaving vessels specially equipped worth £1,500 sterling each.	
Total value £1,453,000 ster.		Total value £1,305,000 ster.	

[a] Adjusted from Dinwiddie's Report of Aug. 1743, CO 5/5, f 242.
[b] Includes Delaware.

Source: Robert Dinwiddie, "Report on Colonial Trade, Aug. 1740," in Merrill Jensen, ed., *American Colonial Documents* (1955), 366.

TABLE 4.97 FREIGHT RATES, BY TON, FOR CARGOES SENT FROM BRITISH NORTH AMERICA

Tobacco: Maryland to London	
Years	Rate per Ton of 4 Hogsheads
1630–39	£12.0.0.
1654–60	£7 to £7.10.0
1675	£7.0.0
1677	£10.0.0
1678	£7. to £10.0.0
1680	£6. to £6.10.0
1684	£5.5.0
1685	£6.5.0
1689–91	£14. to £16.0.0
1692	£12.10.0 to £13.0.0
1696–97	£6.10 to £8.10
1705–06	£15.0.0
1707	£16.0.0
1708–09	£14. to £16.0.0
1711	£12. to £13.0.0
1712	£11. to £12.0.0
1713	£8.0.0
1714	£6.0.0
1715	£5. to £8.0.0
1716–19	£6. to £7.0.0
1720–21	£7. to £8.0.0
1722–23	£7.0.0
1724–25	£6. to £7.0.0
1726–29	£7.0.0
1730	£6. to £7.0.0
1731–39	£7.0.0
1740	£9. to £10.0.0
1741–43	£9.0.0
1744	£9. to £12.0.0
1745	£12. to £13.0.0
1746	£13. to £14.0.0
1747	£16.0.0
1748	£8. to £16.0.0
1749–55	£7.0.0
1756	£9.0.0
1757	£13 to £14.0.0
1758–60	£12.0.0
1761	£10. to £12.0.0
1762	£11. to £13.0.0
1763–75	£7.0.0

Flour: New York to Jamaica	
Years	Rate per Ton of 16 Half-Barrels
1699	£5. to £5.10.0
1700	£5. to £5.10.0
1701	£6.0.0
1702	£6. to £7.0.0
1704	£6.10.0 to £8.5.0
1705	£8. to £8.5.0
1719	£3.17.6
1720	£3.17.6 to £4.0.0
1721	£5.0.0
1722	£3.17.6 to £4.0.0
1723	£5.0.0
1729	£4.10.0
1768	£3.10.0

Oil: Boston to London	
Years	Rate per Ton of 8 Barrels
1700	£3.10.0
1701	£4.0.0
1702	£4.10.0
1724–25	£2.10.0
1732	£2.10.0
1739	£2.10.0
1754	£2.0.0
1764	£2.10.0
1767	£2.5 to £2.10.0
1768	£2.5.0
1771	£2. to £2.5.0
1774	£2.5.0

Coin & Bullion: New York to London	
Years	Percent Rate
1699	2.0% to 4.2%
1700	2.0%
1701	2.0% to 2.5%
1704–05	2.5%
1712	2.5%
1720–25	2.0%
1736	1.0% to 2.0%

Note: Rates express the charge of carrying a registered ton (or ton burden) of either 2,240 lb. or 60 cu. ft., in pounds sterling.
Note: 1736 route for bullion is Boston to London.
Source: Gary M. Walton, "A Measure of Productivity Change in American Colonial Shipping," *Economic History Review*, XXI (1968), 277–280.

Forestry Products

No natural resource was in more universal demand than wood, which served as the primary source of building material and heat. Because the earliest settlers usually sought out grassy meadows or lightly forested riverbanks and often depleted nearby trees after a few decades, financial incentives soon arose for specialists to locate, cut, and haul wood to more densely populated communities. Requirements for timber accelerated as new industries appeared such as fishing, which consumed perhaps 50,000 large and 250,000 small trees to dry each year's catch by 1690. Given the heavy demand for wood as construction material and fuel, forestry enterprises almost certainly ranked as the third-largest component of early America's gross national product, behind agriculture and the maritime trades.

Although a serious timber shortage encumbered seventeenth-century England, where few forests remained larger than 16 square miles, that country purchased little sawed lumber from its colonies because it could buy less expensive imports from Baltic countries. By the 1650s, however, England's Caribbean sugar islands had exhausted much of their indigenous woodlands, and they became a highly profitable market for North American planks, staves, and shingles. During the early 1700s, Parliament attempted to lessen British dependence on foreign masts, turpentine, tar, and pitch by encouraging their production in North America through the payment of cash bounties, and its policy stimulated a provincial naval-stores industry. During the 1750s, Anglo-Americans also began to sell to British manufacturers significant amounts of potash, a source of alkali leached from wood ashes.

During the seventeenth century, the primary center of the forestry industry lay in New England, particularly in Maine and New Hampshire. After 1700, the Carolinas and Georgia emerged as a second major center of lumbering and naval-stores production. Small-scale, decentralized timber production was also an important source of income in the upper South and the Mid-Atlantic, which exported a great volume of shingles, staves, posts, and rails split by individual farmers during the winter months. By the late 1760s, sales of forestry products comprised more than 7% of exports from the thirteen colonies and approximately equaled the overseas earnings of the fisheries. Despite this subject's importance, there is no comprehensive study of the volume or value of wood products sold overseas, and no one has yet attempted to measure the forestry industry's contribution to the domestic economy.

Lumber and Construction Materials

Although their initial need for lumber was immediate and pressing, almost every early settlement went many years without a sawmill. Such communities instead relied on crude, laborious sawpits in which planks were cut from logs resting over an excavated pit by two laborers—one standing in the pit and the other balanced above it on cross-rafters—who alternately pushed and pulled a handsaw from their respective positions. The Virginia Company apparently waited until 1619 to begin construction of water-powered sawmills. New England's two earliest sawmills both began operation in 1634 at Piscataqua, New Hampshire, and York, Maine.

A large need also existed for shingles, barrel staves, firewood, and fencing materials. Although some such items were fashioned by slaves or specialized commercial operations, most were split by small farmers seeking to supplement their income during the winter months. This component of the lumber trade became a major economic sideline for agriculturalists in every colony, but it was especially important in New England, where crop yields were often marginal.

The charge of transporting wood across the Atlantic prevented colonial lumber from competing successfully with inexpensive lumber imported to Britain from the Baltics. As early as the 1640s, however, strong demand for North American timber developed in the English Caribbean islands, which had rapidly used up their own woodlands. As the economy and population of the West Indies expanded, they served as the primary and most profitable market for the mainland's forestry products.

Most lumber exports originated in New England during the 1600s. By 1675, at least fifty sawmils were operating north of Boston. Their total production for a season of 180 days probably ranged from 4,500,000 to 9,000,000 feet of boards annually; their output might have been worth £6,750 to £13,500 at the mill and could have sold for twice that amount in the English sugar islands. Ten years later, Maine alone possessed twenty-four active sawmills, which in a year's season had the capacity to cut 2,000,000 to 4,000,000 feet, worth up to £3 per 1,000 feet in overseas markets.

American lumber production expanded greatly after 1700, in part to satisfy West Indian markets but increasingly to meet domestic demands arising from urbanization, shipbuilding, and the housing needs of a rapidly growing population. Timber production rose strongly in every colony, especially in the Carolinas and Georgia. New England nevertheless remained the center of lumbering, however, and exported about half the colonies' sawed timber as late as the 1760s.

GEORGIA.

SHIPS or VESSELS, of *any* Bur-then, may be laden at the *first* Bluff, on the *North* Side of St. *Mary's River*, with LUMBER and SCANTLING for *London*, the *West-Indies* or elsewhere, with Dispatch, at reasonable Rates for Money, or in Exchange for any Kind of Merchandize. For further Particulars enquire at Mr. WRIGHT'S Plantation, within a Mile of the said Bluff.

The Inlet lieth between *Cumberland* and *Amelia* Islands, is a safe Navigation, being an easy short Bar to pass over, with sufficient Depth of Water for large Ships; it is about thirty Leagues to the Northward of *St. Augustine* Inlet. The River is bold, the Bluff in sight of *Cumberland Island*, about five Miles up the River, where Ships may in Safety load in all Seasons of the Year.

Lumber was not an especially profitable commodity, but cutting shingles or other wood products allowed many farmers to supplement their income during the winter months between crops. This Georgia advertisement solicits lumber for export to the West Indies, its best market, or possibly to Britain. (Courtesy American Antiquarian Society).

TABLE 4.98 AVERAGE ANNUAL WHOLESALE PRICES FOR WOOD STAVES AT PHILADELPHIA, 1720–1763 (IN LOCAL CURRENCY, PER 1,200 UNITS)

Year	Barrel Staves	Hogshead Staves	Pipe Staves
1763	66.04s	£6.82	£12.79
1762	90.85s	£8.89	£13.12
1761	86.91s	£8.53	£13.30
1760	68.82s	£5.35	£11.60
1759	60.69s	£4.92	£8.81
1758	60.73s	£5.60	£6.91
1757	50.82s	£3.94	£5.87
1756	41.63s	£3.54	£5.87
1755	51.54s	£4.57	£7.17
1754	55.94s	£4.92	£7.70
1753	56.87s	£5.07	£8.33
1752	53.28s	£4.26	£6.60
1751	51.50s	£4.66	£6.50
1750	68.36s	£5.98	£8.89
1749	68.79s	£5.25	£9.60
1748	61.06s	£5.19	£9.03
1747	56.03s	£5.27	£6.91
1746	40.63s	£4.08	£5.17
1745	39.79s	£2.93	£4.96
1744	40.00s	£2.96	£5.40
1743	40.85s	£3.31	£5.34
1742	47.81s	£3.68	£7.4
1741	49.17s	£4.50	£6.08
1740	39.42s	£3.34	£5.50
1739	44.58s	£3.22	£5.58
1738	47.56s	£3.41	£5.42
1737	45.36s	£3.19	£5.54
1736	35.21s	£2.33	£4.73
1735	36.37s	£2.56	£5.38
1734	44.50s	£2.85	£5.00
1733	…	…	…
1732	…	…	…
1731	…	…	…
1730	…	…	…
1729	…	…	…

Year	Barrel Staves	Hogshead Staves	Pipe Staves
1728	20.00s	£1.75	...
1727	...	...	...
1726	...	...	...
1725	...	...	...
1724	20.00s	£2.00	£2.50
1723	22.50s	£2.25	£3.00
1722	22.50s	£2.25	£3.00
1721	22.50s	£2.25	£3.00
1720	22.50s	£2.25	£3.00

Note: Pipe staves measured 56 in. × 4 in. Hogshead staves measured 42 in. × 3.5 in. Barrel staves measured 28 to 32 in. × 3.5 in.
Source: Anne Bezanson, et al., eds., *Prices in Colonial Pennsylvania* (1935), 424, 364–374. Arthur H. Cole, *Wholesale Prices in the United States, 1700–1861* (1938), 9–17.

TABLE 4.99 PRICE OF MISCELLANEOUS LUMBER (IN POUNDS OF LOCAL CURRENCY) IN NEW JERSEY AND NEW YORK, 1755–1761

Date	Commodity	Price	Market
Aug. 1761	1,000 36-in. shingles	£2	at Cape May, N.J.
Feb. 1760	1,000 36-in. shingles	£2.2.6	at Cape May, N.J.
Sep. 1759	1,000 36-in. shingles	£2	at Cape May, N.J.
Sep. 1759	1,000 cedar rails	£2	at Cape May, N.J.[a]
Jun. 1759	1,000 cedar rails	£1 cash and £3 barter	at Cape May, N.J.[a]
Dec. 1758	1,000 oak rails	£1.2.8	at Cape May, N.J.
Dec. 1758	Cord of wood	10d	at Cape May, N.J.
Sep. 1758	1,000 cedar rails	£2	at Cape May, N.J.[a]
May 1758	1,000 shingles	£1.15	at Little Egg Harbor, N.J.
Oct. 1755	1,000 barrel staves	£1	near Burlington, N.J.[b]
Aug. 1755	1,000 shingles	£3.10–£3.15	at New Brunswick, N.J.
Aug. 1755	1,000 shingles	£2.15 (cash) or £3 (barter)	at New York

[a] If carted to wharf.
[b] To retail at market for £2.
Source: William A. Ellis, ed., "Diary of Jacob Spicer, 1755–6," *Proceedings of the New Jersey Historical Society,* LXIII (1945), 104, 114. "Memorandum Book of Jacob Spicer, 1757–1764,"*Cape May Magazine of History and Genealogy,* I (1934), 116, 162–167, 172, 187.

Naval Stores and Ships' Masts

The maritime industry needed specialized forest products to build ships and preserve their timbers: masts, yardarms, bowsprits, tar, pitch, resin, and turpentine. During the early 1600s, England had minimal need to stimulate these industries in North America, even though it was dependent on imports for domestic needs, because its own

TABLE 4.100 NEW HAMPSHIRE LUMBER EXPORTS, 1695–1752

Exports	1695	1718	1727	1742	1752
Pine Boards (ft.)	260,000	915,331	1,701,653	1,843,269	6,249,400
Staves[a] (no.)	235,000	252,710	17,500	452,844	898,200
Shingles (no.)	129,000	614,950	24,000	1,032,100	2,051,050
Hoops (no.)	1,700	6,000	6,000	31,550	26,400
Clapboards (no.)	...	11,000	10,000	...	3,000
Oak Planks (ft.)	...	26,880	...	3,889	7,600
[other units]	...	1,022 tons	...	14 pieces	107 tons
Ranging Timber[b] (ft.)	...	5,515	...	41,400	2,000
[other units]	73 tons	...	355 tons	32 tons	...
Oak Rafters (ft.)	...	13,905	...	26,532	3,132
Joists (ft.)	10,000	55,472	...	9	...

[a] Includes hogsheads, barrels, and pipes.
[b] Includes "ranging timber," "square timber," and "timber." Squared logs with each side greater than 6 inches and less than 12 inches were considered ranging timber.
Source: David E. Vandeventer, *The Emergence of Provincial New Hampshire, 1623–1741* (1976), 96, which also reports small exports of the following items in 1742 and 1752: dyewoods, firewood, walnut, lathe wood, house frames, boat frames, axes, oars, desks, tables, chairs, wheelbarrows, oxbows, drain spouts, handspikes, pails, and pumps.

TABLE 4.101 LUMBER EXPORTS FROM SOUTH CAROLINA AND GEORGIA, 1754–1763

Year	From South Carolina			From Georgia		
	Lumber (Ft.)	Shingles (No.)	Staves (No.)	Lumber (Ft.)	Shingles (No.)	Staves (No.)
1763	647,112[a]	1,225,160[a]	362,065[a]	917,384	1,470,120	594,356
1762	414,754	896,500	163,990	417,449	685,265	325,477
1761	610,952	1,354,500	236,327	307,690	606,650	50,969
1760	545,333	1,354,500	135,992	283,961	581,200	80,500
1759	1,018,490	1,204,890	146,172	273,066	808,580	102,959
1758	639,012	724,000	145,529	50,215	68,985	63,339
1757	234,303[b]	664,100[b]	83,617[b]	270,396	178,400	182,268
1756	202,316[c]	522,420[c]	109,890[c]	289,843	263,000	196,259
1755	780,776	952,880	168,121	387,849	240,690	203,225
1754	764,607	822,120	102,290	...	...	...

[a] Data for eleven months only.
[b] Data for ten months only.
[c] Data for nine months only.
Source: Charles J. Gayle, "The Nature and Volume of Exports from Charleston, 1724–1774," in *Proceedings of South Carolina Historical Association* (1937), 31. G. Melvin Herndon, "Forest Products of Colonial Georgia," *Journal of Forest History,* XXIII (1979), 134.

The production of naval stores became a major industry in the Carolinas and Georgia. The manufacture of these staples came to center at large-scale operations, usually worked by slaves, and were similar to this replica of a North Carolina turpentine still. (Courtesy National Museum of American History, Smithsonian Institution, negative 29595)

merchant marine and navy were yet modest in size and because it received adequate and inexpensive supplies from Baltic nations.

The term *naval stores* usually referred to turpentine, pitch, and tar. (Tar also had many minor uses such as greasing wagon wheels.) The earliest North American manufacture of these commodities took place near Jamestown in 1608 under Polish and Baltic supervisors hired by the Virginia Company. The company exported some tar to England that year and afterward, but its quality was poor and the company eventually abandoned efforts to develop this industry.

The production of ships' timber and stores developed in tandem with shipbuilding in New England. The first sector of this industry to export for overseas markets was the harvesting of white pines for masts. Mature white pines grew remarkable straight to a height of 120 feet, and substantial numbers grew north of the Piscataqua River. Cutting white pines entailed great skill in cushioning the trunk's fall to prevent splintering, carrying the behemoths to a navigable river took as many as seventy-two oxen, and sending them across the ocean required vessels of special construction. Small shipments of masts began to arrive in England by the early 1630s. The Royal Navy first began to buy New England masts in 1653, and by 1664 a mast with a 36-inch diameter commanded a price of £135. In the early 1670s London's great timber merchant, Sir William Warren, imported 250 white pines worth £35,000 (about £140 each).

After England adopted a policy of expanding its navy and merchant marine, it began to exercise greater control over the mast industry. In 1691, the crown laid claim to certain white pines in Massachusetts when it reissued that colony's charter. The White Pines Act of 1722 (amending an act of 1711) required a royal license to fell white pines whose diameter exceeded 24 inches unless they were privately owned, and in 1729 Parliament reserved all such trees to the government except those already in private hands before October 7, 1690. The high prices commanded by white pines, up to £156 for a trunk with a 36-inch diameter in 1700 and £153 in 1768, sparked sharp competition for permission to cut them and inevitably spawned much poaching by individuals denied licenses by the surveryor-general of the king's woods.

Concerned that naval stores from the Baltic had become more expensive and subject to disruption, Parliament in 1705 authorized cash bounties as an incentive for Americans to undertake their manufacture. The bounties induced many colonists to begin to refine sufficient turpentine, tar, and pitch for export. Production of turpentine, a natural oleoresin in conifers, expanded least because sap could not be extracted from pines already cut to clear fields and because the work could not be limited to winter, the only time when many farmers could engage in nonagricultural pursuits. Tar and pitch could be made from dead trees downed while expanding cropland or from pines unsuitable for the sawmill, and their manufacture could be restricted to winter when rural inhabitants eagerly sought seasonal employment. A cord of wood usually yielded a barrel of tar. Pitch was made by heating tar until it boiled, setting it afire, and burning it down to the required consistency.

Prior to the enactment of parliamentary bounties, the naval-stores trade had centered around Portsmouth, New Hampshire, and Portland (then Falmouth), Maine. The bounties of 1705 almost immediately stimulated large-scale manufacture of tar, pitch, and turpentine in the Carolinas, where the coastal districts abounded with pine. After these industries also became an important part of Georgia's economy, the lower South overtook New England as the primary exporter of resin-based naval stores, although New England continued as the near-exclusive source of masts. From 1706 to 1763, Anglo-Americans received £1,074,233 in British subsidies for exporting naval stores to Britain. By the 1760s, about one-third of exported forestry products were naval stores, exclusive of masts; domestic consumption of naval stores remains undetermined.

TABLE 4.102 PRICES FOR PITCH AND TAR IN BRITISH NORTH AMERICA, 1693–1704

Year	Tar (per Last)	Pitch (per Unit)
1693	£12. in New York	…
1694	£13.4.0 in New England £5.4.0 in Maryland	20s per cwt. in New England £4.16.0 per ton in Maryland
1699	£4.4.0 in Carolina £7.16.0 in New England	12s per cwt in Carolina …
1700	£2.4.0 in Carolina	£17.10.0 per last in Carolina
1703	£4.16.0 in Carolina	18s per cwt. in Carolina
1704	£21.12.0 in New England £6. to £7.4.0 in Virginia	23s per cwt. in New England 20s to 24s in Virginia

Note: last = 80 bu. cwt. = 112 lb. ton = 2,240 lb.
Source: Eleanor L. Lord, *Industrial Experiments in the British Colonies of North America* (1898), 140–141.

TABLE 4.103 PRICES OF PITCH, TAR, AND TURPENTINE (PER BARREL, IN LOCAL CURRENCY) AT PHILADELPHIA, 1720–1763

Year	Pitch	Tar	Turpentine
1763	14.93s	12.30s	13.56s
1762	13.47s	10.04s	13.27s
1761	14.06s	11.25s	14.11s
1760	14.47s	10.82s	14.29s
1759	16.07s	10.68s	16.75s
1758	15.11s	9.75s	16.12s
1757	15.19s	9.85s	14.88s
1756	13.93s	11.42s	13.53s
1755	14.92s	11.54s	15.01s
1754	15.71s	10.67s	17.90s
1753	16.05s	9.76s	18.71s
1752	20.06s	10.08s	25.37s
1751	21.56s	11.07s	24.81s
1750	18.91s	12.89s	19.50s
1749	15.41s	10.49s	17.12s
1748	14.76s	11.06s	15.86s
1747	13.19s	10.30s	14.81s
1746	11.42s	9.11s	13.83s
1745	13.50s	10.38s	12.51s
1744	13.90s	10.92s	10.98s
1743	14.25s	10.40s	11.82s
1742	16.21s	12.75s	19.95s
1741	17.54s	14.08s	21.30s
1740	14.29s	10.88s	19.41s
1739	11.42s	9.42s	13.26s
1738	11.33s	8.63s	11.91s
1737	10.85s	8.56s	12.90s
1736	12.25s	8.98s	16.80s
1735	12.83s	9.63s	19.23s
1734	12.92s	10.14s	23.94s
1733	17.17s	12.25s	25.20s
1732	13.75s	10.10s	29.19s
1731	14.31s	11.10s	10.50s[a]
1730	15.00s	11.04s	12.00s[a]
1729	12.08s	11.00s	9.45s[a]
1728	13.11s	11.92s	…
1727	18.40s	17.11s	…
1726	19.19s	17.61s	14.00s[a]
1725	18.42s	…	…
1724	15.50s	10.67s	…

Year	Pitch	Tar	Turpentine
1723	12.63s	11.38s	...
1722	13.50s	10.25s	28.50s
1721	12.00s	8.33s	25.14s
1720	14.17s	9.83s	24.00s

[a] Per cwt. of 112 lb.
Source: Anne Bezanson, et al., eds., *Prices in Colonial Pennsylvania* (1935), 366–367, 424. Arthur H. Cole, *Wholesale Prices in the United States, 1700–1861* (1938), 10–15.

Year	Bounties
1713	£5,783
1712	£3,934
1711	£3,170
1710	£4,259
1709	£5,840
1708	£1,370
1707	£4,410
1706	£554
Total	£1,074,233

Source: Robert G. Albion, *Forests and Sea-Power: The Timber Problem of the Royal Navy, 1652–1862* (1926), 418.

TABLE 4.104 BRITISH BOUNTIES PAID FOR COLONIAL NAVAL STORES, 1706–1763

Year	Bounties
1763	£18,753
1762	£17,963
1761	£19,961
1760	£14,689
1759	£21,402
1758	£20,507
1757	£14,059
1756	£24,041
1755	£23,587
1754	£22,109
1753	£32,609
1752	£35,669
1751	£23,218
1750	£20,325
1749	£18,314
1748	£12,059
1747	£15,382
1746	£11,199
1745	£12,726
1744	£21,094
1743	£22,237
1742	£21,560
1741	£16,005
1740	£15,097
1739	£10,999
1738	£19,199
1737	£18,048
1736	£14,612
1735	£22,698
1734	£28,459
1733	£19,008
1732	£16,868
1731	£10,804
1730	£11,148
1729	£423
1728	...
1727	£234
1726	£21,709
1725	£36,974
1724	£45,110
1723	£36,317
1722	£24,732
1721	£23,539
1720	£28,684
1719	£43,743
1718	£52,011
1717	£40,354
1716	£27,410
1715	£10,135
1714	£6,860

TABLE 4.105 PARLIAMENTARY BOUNTIES FOR COLONIAL PINE-RESIN PRODUCTS, 1705–1774

Years	Payments per 2,000 lb. (8 barrels, each of 31.5 qal.)			
	Pitch	Tar	Turpentine	Resin
1705–1716	£4	£4	£3	£3
1717–1724	£2	£2	£2	none
1725–1728	none	none	none	none
1729–1774[a]	£1 to £4	£2.4.0 to £4	£1.10.0 to £3	none

[a] Payment determined by quality of product.
Note: Import duties of 4s., 2d. per barrel were assessed 1669–1776.
Source: Lewis C. Gray, *History of Agriculture in the Southern United States to 1860* (1933), 153–156.

TABLE 4.106 EXPORTS OF NEW ENGLAND PITCH AND TAR TO BRITAIN, 1706–1713

Year	Lasts[a] Exported
1713	290
1712	72
1711	191
1710	164
1709	71
1708	208
1707	330
1706	412

[a] One last was a measure of weight equaling 80 bu.
Source: Joseph J. Malone, *Pine Trees and Politics: The Naval Stores and Forest Policy in Colonial New England, 1691–1775* (1964), 32.

TABLE 4.107 COLONIAL PINE-RESIN PRODUCTS IMPORTED BY ENGLAND, 1701–1718

Year Ending Dec. 25	Imports from Colonies			Percent of Total Imports from Colonies		
	Tar & Pitch (Barrels)	Rozen (Cwt.)	Turpentine (Cwt.)	Tar & Pitch (Barrels)	Rozen (Cwt.)	Turpentine (Cwt.)
1718	82,084	...	...	89%	...	...
1717	72,389	...	...	78%	...	...
1716	45,453	...	...	58%	...	...
1715	25,279	86	11,211	49%	56%	99%
1714	11,639	18	12,466	29%	6%	100%
1713	4,825	165	8,679	12%	10%	99%
1712	5,264	163	6,520	12%	9%	100%
1711	4,453	850	4,077	11%	35%	99%
1710	5,484	342	7,109	13%	49%	100%
1709	7,093	404	5,885	19%	38%	100%
1708	6,166	256	6,305	16%	24%	96%

(continued)

TABLE 4.107 (continued)

Year Ending Dec. 25	Imports from Colonies			Percent of Total Imports from Colonies		
	Tar & Pitch (Barrels)	Rozen (Cwt.)	Turpentine (Cwt.)	Tar & Pitch (Barrels)	Rozen (Cwt.)	Turpentine (Cwt.)
1707	9,358	276	3,035	23%	83%	100%
1706	6,755	293	801	18%	18%	94%
1705	2,346	105	2,907	5%	3%	98%
1704	872	95	11,245	1%	2%	96%
1703	483	48	5,498	1%	5%	98%
1702	271	26	3,713	2%	1%	72%
1701	177	124	3,162	1%	1%	34%

Source: Eleanor L. Lord, *Industrial Experiments in the British Colonies of North America* (1898), App. B.

TABLE 4.108 NEW HAMPSHIRE EXPORTS AND IMPORTS OF PINE-RESIN PRODUCTS, 1695–1752

Year	Turpentine (Barrels)	Resin (Barrels)	Pitch (Barrels)	Tar (Barrels)	Pitch & Tar (Barrels)
1752					
Exports	637	77	61	817	...
Imports	15	...	285	380	...
1742					
Exports	140	...	581	222	122
Imports	6	...	33.5	22	...
1727					
Exports	18	...	42	54	...
Imports	...	...	...	...	260
1725					
Exports	...	...	37	60	...
Imports	...	...	b	40	...
1723					
Exports	10	...	...	...	...
Imports	...	...	170	...	...
1718					
Exports	74	...	...	149	...
Imports	a	a	a	a	...
1695					
Exports	...	46.5	...	28	...
Imports	...	...	...	...	...

[a] No records for 1718.
[b] Item imported, but amount unrecorded.
Source: David E. Vandeventer, *The Emergence of Provincial New Hampshire, 1623–1741* (1976), 112.

TABLE 4.109 ESTIMATED PRODUCTION OF PITCH AND TAR IN VIRGINIA, 1704–1765

Year	Production
1704	3,000 barrels of tar produced for domestic use
1709	190 barrels exported (including some from Maryland)
1711	3,000 barrels of pitch & 3,500 barrels of tar exported
1743	10,000 barrels of pitch produced (8,000 barrels exported)
1764	1,866 barrels of pitch & tar exported from Upper James
1765	470 barrels of pitch & tar exported from Upper James

Source: Sinclair Snow, "Naval Stores in Virginia," *Virginia Magazine of History and Biography,* LXXII (1964), 75–93.

TABLE 4.110 PINE-RESIN PRODUCTS EXPORTED FROM SOUTH CAROLINA, 1717–1763

Year	Pitch (Bbls.)	Tar (Bbls.)	Turpentine (Bbls.)	Green Tar (Bbls.)
1763[a]	6,087	1,265	3,042	411
1762	6,315	1,244	1,438	289
1761[a]	6,626	1,438	4,874	...
1760	5,754	886	2,420	97
1759	7,813	2,236	1,333	405
1758	2,521	1,720	937	328
1757[b]	4,962	2,103	337	397
1756[c]	3,058	2,711	1,195	1,070
1755	5,869	2,596	2,171	547
1754	11,025	2,295	5,375	369
1753	15,220	6,008	6,496	...
1752	20,483	2,651	6,271	...
1751	11,441	5,070	1,401	...
1750[a]	11,157	3,858	812	...
1749	7,796	3,765	1,582	...
1748	5,521	3,075	2,397	...
1747	13,737	4,422	5,162	...
1746	18,016	1,519	4,262	...
1745	8,823	1,286	988	...
1744	7,678	17,552	1,245	...
1743	9,755	2,206	2,012	...
1742	15,808	3,115	1,986	...
1741	11,831	1,811	1,691	...
1740	11,377	2,436	577	...
1739	7,890	2,722	33	...
1738	16,088	5,417	845	...
1737	11,987	8,501	4,411	...
1736	11,736	1,491	5,193	...
1735	24,036	5,636	8,061	...
1734	28,874	7,336	4,552	...
1733	18,165	6,604	2,212	...
1732	32,593	4,575	2,466	...
1731	9,385	1,725	1,560	...
1730	10,825	2,014	1,073	...
1729	8,377	3,441	1,913	...
1728	3,186	2,269	1,232	...
1727	13,654	10,950	1,252	...
1726	29,776	8,322	715	...
1725	57,422	2,333	133	...
1724	32,720	12,220	469	...
1723	no data	...	...	...
1722	no data	...	...	...
1721	no data	...	...	...
1720	24,453	10,025	75	...
1719	17,489	25,495	1,245	...
1718	20,208	32,007	605	...
1717	14,363	29,594	669	...

[a] Data for four months.
[b] Data for ten months.
[c] Data for nine months.
Source: Converse D. Clowse, *Economic Beginnings in Colonial South Carolina* (1971), 257–258. Charles J. Gayle, "The Nature and Volume of Exports from Charleston, 1724–1774," *Proceedings of the South Carolina Historical Association* (1937), 31.

TABLE 4.111 EXPORTS OF COLONIAL PINE-RESIN PRODUCTS, BY REGION, 1729–1775

Years	From New England Pitch & Tar (Lasts)	From New England Turpentine (Cwt.)	From Virginia & Maryland Pitch & Tar (Lasts)	From Virginia & Maryland Turpentine (Cwt.)	From No. & So. Carolina Pitch & Tar (Lasts)	From No. & So. Carolina Turpentine (Cwt.)
1774–75	592	1,309	2,487	33,450	5,447	58,322
1767–68	1,102	3,308	1,450	12,108	14,728	35,436
1762–63	1,556	10,277	1,048	4,367	2,163	15,374
1759–60	582	7,013	295	621	1,409	12,950
1754–55	1,160	3,228	1,095	4,141	3,636	13,596
1749–50	1,032	2,467	608	768	3,764	3,166
1744–45	1,564	4,154	182	83	1,536	3,395
1737–38	874	6,288	292	…	2,698	2,068
1733–34	2,847	16,985	594	227	4,660	8,281
1729–30	1,140	8,965	487	…	1,024	…

Note: 1 last = 80 bu. cwt. = 112 lb.
Source: Joseph J. Malone, *Pine Trees and Politics: The Naval Stores and Forest Policy in Colonial New England, 1691–1775* (1964), 44.

TABLE 4.112 ROYAL NAVY SPECIFICATIONS FOR EIGHTEENTH-CENTURY MASTS

Mast	1st Rate, 120 Guns Diameter (Inches)	1st Rate, 120 Guns Length (Yards)	3d Rate, 74 Guns Diameter (Inches)	3d Rate, 74 Guns Length (Yards)	Frigate, 28 Guns Diameter (Inches)	Frigate, 28 Guns Length (yards)
mainmast	40	40	36	36	20	24
bowsprit	37	25	34	22	21	14
foremast	37	37	31	33	19	22
mainyard	25	35	23	33	14	21
mizzenmast	24	27	22	25	16	18
maintopmast	21	23	19	22	13	14
maintopsailyard	15	25	14	23	6	9
jib boom	15	17	14	16	9	11
maintopgallant mast	12	11	11	11	7	7

Source: Robert G. Albion, *Forests and Sea-Power: The Timber Problem of the Royal Navy, 1652–1862* (1926), 28.

TABLE 4.113 NEW HAMPSHIRE EXPORTS OF MASTS AND SPARS, 1695–1767

Exports in	1695	1718	1727	1742	1752
Masts	56	199	123	524	570
Spars	13	520	64	1,106	2,815
Bowsprits	16	151	82	171	42
Yardarms	4	…	30	102	51

Masts Exported in	1742	1743	1744	1745	1747	1752	1753	1754
To England	427	294	318	160	189	554	414	374
To Other Colonies	97	72	32	42	74	16	27	17

Masts Exported in	1755[a]	1756	1757	1758	1759	1762	1764	1767
To England	252	93	0	218	189	124	377	258
To Other Colonies	14	31	50	84	96	155	15	2

[a] Records incomplete.
Source: David E. Vandeventer, *The Emergence of Provincial New Hampshire, 1623–1741* (1976), 96, 104.

TABLE 4.114 PRICES PAID FOR MASTS, YARDS, AND BOWSPRITS BY ROYAL NAVY, ABOUT 1750

Masts[a] Diameter	Price[b]
32 in.	£74.13.4
31 in.	£59.14.8
30 in.	£46.13.4
29 in.	£37.6.8
28 in.	£30.13.4
27 in.	£24.0.0
26 in.	£21.6.8
25 in.	£18.8.0
24 in.	£14.8.0
22 in.	£10.0.0
20 in.	£6.0.0

Bowsprits Diameter	Price[b]
34 in.	£53.6.8
33 in.	£42.13.4
32 in.	£34.13.4
31 in.	£28.0.0
30 in.	£20.0.0
29 in.	£10.16.0
28 in.	£8.18.8
27 in.	£8.13.4
26 in.	£7.6.8

Yards Diameter	Price[b]
24 in.	£42.13.4
23 in.	£34.0.0
22 in.	£28.0.0
21 in.	£24.13.4
20 in.	£19.6.8
19 in.	£16.0.0
18 in.	£12.0.0
17 in.	£9.12.0
16 in.	£9.0.0

[a] Masts were hewn to have as many yards in length as the diameter had inches.
[b] Source did not specify if price was in sterling or local money.
Source: William A. Fairborn, *Merchant Sail* (1945), 243.

TABLE 4.115 BRITISH IMPORTS OF COLONIAL AND EUROPEAN MASTS, 1701–1760

Year Ending Dec. 25	No. of Masts Imported from Colonies Great	No. of Masts Imported from Colonies Midling	No. of Masts Imported from Colonies Small	Percent of All Imported Masts Provided from Colonies Great	Percent of All Imported Masts Provided from Colonies Midling	Percent of All Imported Masts Provided from Colonies Small
1760[a]	603	127	58	32%	6%	2%
1745[b]	419	…	…	21%	…	…
1718–27	2,615	1,148	2,748	30%	11%	12%
1715	101	18	4	14%	1%	…
1714	83	92	22	9%	5%	…
1713	261	27	6	12%	1%	…
1712	198	125	56	15%	9%	3%
1711	152	9	20	15%	1%	3%
1710	121	8	8	7%	1%	1%
1709	174	20	…	15%	2%	…
1708	169	…	…	14%	…	…
1707	48	…	…	3%	…	…
1706	…	…	2	…	…	…
1705	107	…	…	10%	…	…

(continued)

TABLE 4.115 (continued)

Year Ending Dec. 25	No. of Masts Imported from Colonies			Percent of All Imported Masts Provided from Colonies		
	Great	Midling	Small	Great	Midling	Small
1704	34	…	…	6%	…	…
1703	81	15	8	11%	10%	1%
1702	…	…	…	…	…	…
1701	74	19	30	65%	6%	3%

[a] All masts from New England, except three midling from Chesapeake.
[b] 224 greats from New England and 195 from Chesapeake.
Source: Eleanor L. Lord, *Industrial Experiments in the British Colonies of North America* (1898), App. B. Joseph J. Malone, *Pine Trees and Politics: The Naval Stores and Forest Policy in Colonial New England, 1691–1775* (1964), 55, 56.

TABLE 4.116 BRITISH GOVERNMENT EXPENDITURES FOR NAVAL CONTRACTS, 1705–1775

Navy Payments for Colonial Contracts, 1705–1775				
Contracts	Rozen	Turpentine	Pitch & Tar	Masts, Spars, & Bowsprits
New England Contracts	£82	£15,401	£8,492	£298,880[a]
Carolina Contracts	…	£130	£13,996	…
Va.–Md. Contracts	…	…	£800	…
New York Contracts	…	…	£494	…
Plantation Contracts[b]	…	£20,459	£107,220	…
Total Payments	£82	£35,990	£131,002	£298,880
Total Colonial Contracts				£465,954

Navy Bounties Paid to Colonists for Naval Stores, 1705–1775[c]	
Total Bounties Paid Colonists	£1,471,719

Total Payments to Colonists for Naval Stores & Bounties, 1705–1775	
Total Colonial Expenditures	£1,937,673

[a] On p. 55, source stated that total contracts for New England masts from 1694 to 1775 were £425,769 versus £509,586 for Baltic masts.
[b] "Plantation" contracts referred to goods bought from merchants in New England but produced in other colonies.
[c] Source also listed £268,155 paid for Baltic pitch and tar.
Source: Joseph J. Malone, *Pine Trees and Politics: The Naval Stores and Forest Policy in Colonial New England, 1691–1775* (1964), 45.

Potash

Potash (potassium carbonate) is an alkali compound leached from tree ashes. It served as the eighteenth century's leading industrial chemical and was essential for manufacturing crown (flint) glass, soft soap, saltpeter, many dyes, and various drugs. Potash was also the sole alkali used in bleaching linens, scouring woolens, and printing calicoes.

Although the colonies possessed abundant forest reserves from which to produce wood ash, several efforts to encourage potash manufacture were stillborn before 1750. Governor Bellomont failed to arouse any interest among New Yorkers in the early 1700s, as did offers of bounties by South Carolina from 1707 to 1712, legislative encouragements offered by Massachusetts in 1735, and monopoly privileges awarded by Connecticut in 1741. Not until Parliament exempted American potash from British import duties in 1751 did large-scale production of potash commence in the thirteen colonies.

During the 1750s, English and American entrepreneurs invested a minimum of £5,900 in ventures for refining potash. Centers of production emerged briefly at Boston, Lancaster, and Marlborough in Massachusetts, at Fredericksburg in Virginia, and at Philadelphia. The going

price for wood ash in Philadelphia in the year after December 26, 1754, was 6 pence per bushel or 7 pence if delivered free of transportation costs. The largest factory was at Philadelphia, and in 1755 it paid local farmers about £800 for 29,900 bushels of ashes, which yielded more than 30 tons of potash, worth perhaps £850 in Britain at £28 a ton. The narrow profit margins experienced by the Philadelphia enterprise were typical of the industry's early years, and all the largest partnerships ceased operations by 1761 when the Fredericksburg, Virginia, furnace exploded. Despite the initial failure of the industry to achieve profitablity, manufacture and exports of potash rose dramatically after 1763, and by 1775 Britain was receiving 66% of its imported potash from North America, including some bought from from Nova Scotia.

TABLE 4.117 TONS OF NORTH AMERICAN POTASH IMPORTED BY GREAT BRITAIN, 1753–1765

Year Ending Dec. 25	American Imports (Tons)	Total Imports (Tons)	Percent of Imports from North America
1765	596	1,624	36.7%
1763	50	1,727	2.9%
1762	21	…	…
1761	7	…	…
1760	10	2,424	.4%
1759	27	…	
1758	13	…	
1757	27	…	
1756	…		
1755	30.6[a]	…	
1754	2.4[a]	…	
1753	0.5[a]	…	

[a] Incomplete figures based on production data.
Source: William I. Roberts III, "American Potash Manufacture Before the American Revolution," *American Philosophical Society, Proceedings,* CXVI (1972), 385–390.

TABLE 4.118 PROFITABILITY OF SELLING AND MARKETING POTASH IN NEW ENGLAND, 1765

Expenses	Sales
£209.19.4 for 6,299 bu. of ashes @ 8d. per bu.	£173.6.2 received at Boston for 4 tons—9 hrd—2 gr—16 lb. of potash @ £38.13.4 per ton
£12.15.0 for 51 cords of wood to boil ashes @ 5s. per cord £10.4.0 for 51 barrels for packing potash @ 4s. each £30.0.0 to cart 5 loads to Boston [Mass.] @ £6 per load £7.0.0 to cart 4 loads to Norwich [Conn.] @ £1.15.0 per load	£149.6.8 received at Norwich [Conn.] for 4 ton @ £37.6.9
£303.18.4 in total expenses	£322.12.10 in final sales

Source: William I. Roberts III, "American Potash Manufacture Before the American Revolution," *American Philosophical Society, Proceedings,* CXVI (1972), 392.

The Fur Trade

Furs had long signified superior social status in Europe, especially among the nobility and higher clergy for whom they served as expensive garment lining and lush background for jewels. Western Europe's most suitable species of fur-bearing animals were overhunted in the Middle Ages, and the region then had to import large amounts of peltry. Because North America teemed with animals highly prized for their skins—deer, bear, otters, marten, foxes, and beaver, whose thick fur made the most water-resistant and durable hats—pelts became one of the colonies' earliest exports.

The first Europeans to engage in the fur trade were transient fishing crews who bartered them from Indians while laying over on shore to dress their catches. Because animals exposed to the coldest winters produced the heaviest and most luxurient pelts, the fur trade initially began and reached its greatest volume in northern colonies, where there existed the largest supply of animals most prized by consumers: beaver, otters, and marten. By the late 1600s, however, England's southern provinces were exporting many deerskins, which served as a source of high-quality leather.

The Peltry Trade

Heavily indebted to London merchants for capitalizing their colony at Plymouth, the Pilgrims relied primarily on profits from the fur trade to pay off their obligations. By situating trucking houses strategically from the Connecticut River to the Kennebec River, they garnered the main share of New England's fur business until about 1640, when their trade declined swiftly. The rapid extinction of suitable animals near the coast induced Puritan merchants from Massachusetts to tap inland sources through trading posts, which became an important vehicle for frontier expansion by serving as the nuclei for new settlements. The volume of skins bartered from Indians dropped sharply after 1660, and it dwindled steadily after King Philip's War in 1675. Although New England provided 18% of furs exported from English North America in 1700, its share of this trade steadily shrank as overhunting diminished the local stock of desirable animals.

Because the Hudson River offered the best access to the prime beaver territories of the St. Lawrence River and the Great Lakes, Dutch colonists made New Netherland the most successful center of the peltry business south of Canada in the early 1600s. As in New England, the small supply of furs nearest the coast was soon exhausted, the locus of trading moved steadily inland, and Ft. Orange (now Albany, New York) became the main site to which Indians brought their skins. New Netherland also hoped to tap the Delaware River as a source of furs, but Swedish colonists won most of that trade until the Dutch forcibly annexed their settlements in 1655.

After England acquired New Netherland in 1664, Albany's Dutch merchants continued to dominate the northern fur trade. The Dutch tried to divert western skins from Montreal, and they were aided by New York's Iroquois who waged a series of bloody "beaver wars" against rival Indians and raided New France. After 1701, economic competition largely replaced open warfare, and New Yorkers won a large share of western furs primarily by paying higher prices than the French, sometimes double the rate offered at Montreal; they even attracted a steady stream of furs that were being smuggled out of Canada.

New York provided 36% of England's fur imports in 1700 and sent a sizable amount of pelts to Holland as well. The Hudson's Bay Company's Canadian outposts soon became the leading supplier of skins for England, but New York continued to furnish about a quarter of England's fur imports from 1720 to 1755. In no other colony were furs more important to the local economy than in New York, where they often composed about 20% of exports to England from 1700 to 1755. Colonial beaver skins also added significantly to the economy of England, which forbade Americans from selling furs to other European nations in 1722; English hat exports increased from 5,786 dozen (worth £44,000) in 1700 to 45,000 dozen (worth £263,000) in 1750. The beaver trade furthermore stimulated a modest hat industry in the thirteen colonies that met much of the local demand; a surplus was exported to the West Indies.

Aside from Massachusetts, which established trucking houses as a public monopoly run by political appointees in 1694, the colonies regulated the peltry business by limiting participation to licensed traders. Albany became the preeminent fur market in the north, though after 1727 it acquired much of its skins via the provincial trading post constructed by New York on Lake Ontario at Oswego. Pennsylvanians rarely provided more than 5% of English fur exports, but after 1748 they briefly managed to outbid the French for much of the Ohio valley's fur trade. After 1750, the business of buying skins shifted away from Albany and other centers of the fur trade to the wilderness, as competition among merchants led them to take their wares to Indian towns and haul back the pelts themselves.

The thirteen colonies' fur trade faced stiff competition from French Canadians. Unlike the English and Dutch, who relied on Indians to bring them western furs for sale, the coureurs de bois went west, lived among Indians, set their own traps, and encouraged Indians to sell their furs exclusively to French traders. This diorama shows coureurs de bois unloading a boatload of furs at their wharf by Fort Duquesne. (Record Group 13 [WPA, Frontier Forts and Trails Survey], Courtesy Pennsylvania State Archives)

TABLE 4.119 FURS SHIPPED FROM PLYMOUTH COLONY TO ENGLAND, 1621–1638

Year	Beaver[a]	Otters[b]
1638	1,325 lb. (779 skins)	...
1636	2,528 lb. (1,487 skins)	209 skins
1635	1,150 lb. (676 skins)	200 skins
1634	3,738 lb. (2,199 skins)	234 skins
1633	3,366 lb. (1,980 skins)	346 skins
1632	1,348 lb. (793 skins)	147 skins
1631	400 lb. (235 skins)	20 skins
1628	...	1 barrel worth £78.12.0
1625	800 lb. (470 skins)	...
1621	2 hogsheads	...

[a] 100 beaver skins reportedly weighed about 170 lb. in 1623. Beaver sold in London for about 20s. per lb.
[b] Otters sold in London for about 15s. per skin.
Source: William Bradford (ed. by George F. Willison), The History of Plymouth Plantation (1948), 122, 150, 211, 343, 365.

TABLE 4.120 PELTRY ACCUMULATED BY MASSACHUSETTS BAY FUR TRADERS, 1630–1674

Years	Company or Trader	Beaver[a]	Otter	Muskrat
1630–33	Laconia Co.	500 lb. (333 skins)	...	...
1632–33	John Pynchon	400 lb. (267 skins)	...	...
1632–33	Miscellaneous	222 lb. (148 skins)	...	...
1652–57	John Pynchon	13,130 lb. (8,992 skins)	320	148
1658–74	John Pynchon	9,400 lb. (6,428 skins)	400	715[b]

[a] Beaver sold for 8s. to 10s. in Massachusetts.
[b] Also 415 moose, 317 raccoon and fox, and 101 sable.
Source: Bernard Bailyn, New England Merchants in the Seventeenth Century (1955), 27, 50, 53–54. Paul C. Phillips, The Fur Trade (1961), I, 135.

TABLE 4.121 FUR EXPORTS (BY NUMBER OF SKINS) FROM NEW NETHERLAND, 1624–1657

Year	Beaver	Otters, etc.	Total Furs	Value (florins)[a]
1657	...	...	40,940	...
1656	34,840	300	35,140	...
1636	7,000[b]	1,000[b]	8,000	...
1635	7,446[c]	707[c]	8,153[c]	...
1634	7,446[c]	707[c]	8,153[c]	...
1633	8,800	1,383	10,183	fl.91,375
1632	6,500[c]	835[c]	7,335[c]	...
1631	6,500[c]	835[c]	7,335[c]	...
1630	6,041	1,085	7,126	fl.68,012
1629	6,500	835	7,335	...
1628	6,951	734	7,685	fl.61,075
1627	7,520	370	7,890	fl.56,420
1626	7,258	857	8,115	fl.45,050
1625	5,295	436	5,731	fl.35,825
1624	4,000	700	4,700	fl.27,125

[a] 2.5 florins equaled 1 Spanish dollar.
[b] Beaver and otters estimated from year's total exports.
[c] Numbers derived from totals for several years.
Source: Van Cleaf Bachman, Peltries or Plantations: The Economic Policies of the Dutch West India Co. in New Netherland, 1623–1639 (1969), 94, 129, 131, 142. E. B. O'Callaghan, ed., History of New Netherland, or New York Under the Dutch (1855), II, 310n. E. B. O'Callaghan & B. Fernow, eds., Documents Relative to the Colonial History of the State of New York (1856–1887), XIII, 27n.

TABLE 4.122 FUR EXPORTS (BY NUMBER OF SKINS) FROM NEW SWEDEN, 1639–1648

Year	Beaver — Number of Skins	Beaver — Value	Otters — Number of Skins	Otters — Value	Bears — Number of Skins	Bears — Value
1648	1,240	d.5,318	63	d.118	...	...
1645	976	fl.15,000	...	...	...	...
1644	300	...	...	...	...	...
1643	675	fl.5,558	...	...	...	...
1641	1,558	...	101	fl.227	...	...
1640	737	fl.5,152	...	...	29	fl.350
1639	1,769	fl.12,365	314	fl.1,305	132	fl.1,594

Note: Values given in Swedish florins (fl.) and Swedish krone (d.)
Source: Amandus Johnson, The Swedish Settlements on the Delaware, 1638–1664 (1911), I, 119, 144, 157, 288, 289, 310, 317.

TABLE 4.123 ESTIMATED ANNUAL EXPENSES (IN FLORINS[a]) OF THE FUR TRADE SPENT BY THE DUTCH WEST INDIA COMPANY IN NEW NETHERLAND ABOUT 1631

Florins Spent	Expense
fl. 22,179[b]	Trading goods for bartering furs
fl. 500	5% spoilage of stockpile of fl. 10,000 in trade goods
fl. 12,750	Wages of 75 men @ annual average of fl. 170 each
fl. 7,500	Provisions for 75 men @ annual average of fl. 100 each
fl. 375	10% annual spoilage of rations stockpiled for 6 months, valued at fl. 3,750
fl. 600	10% annual depreciation on 2 light yachts, 2 sloops, & 2 shallops, valued in all at fl. 6,000 new
fl. 1,000	Naval stores for above vessels
fl. 225	25% annual depreciation of hand weapons for 75 men, valued in all at fl. 900 new
fl. 400	10% annual depreciation of 10 cast iron cannon and 20 light cannon for forts Amsterdam and Orange, valued all at fl. 4,000 new
fl. 420	1,200 lb. new powder yearly at fl. 35 per cwt.
fl. 225	600 lb. musketballs, 50 cannon balls, 600 lb. pig lead, 4 reams cartridge paper
fl. 7,700	Charter of a well-armed 150-last merchantman for 7 months @ fl. 1,100 per month
fl. 500	Storage and accounting costs in Netherlands

Subtotals

Florins Spent	Expense
fl. 22,679	Trading goods
fl. 20,625	Wages & rations
fl. 1,600	Colonial ships
fl. 1,270	Munitions
fl. 7,700	Oceanic cargo
fl. 500	Home expenses
fl. 54,374	Total Annual Cost

[a] Based on expenses of fl. 110,895 on trade goods from 1624 to 1628
Note: 2.5 florins equaled 1 Spanish dollar
Source: Van Cleaf Bachman, Peltries or Plantations: The Economic Policies of the Dutch West India Co. in New Netherland, 1623–1639 (1969), 94, 126–127.

TABLE 4.124 PRICE DIFFERENCES FOR TRADE GOODS AT ALBANY AND MONTREAL, 1689

Merchandise	Costs at Albany	Costs at Montreal
6 qts. rum/brandy	1 beaver	6 beaver
a musket	2 beaver	5 beaver
8 lb. gunpowder	1 beaver	4 beaver
40 lb. lead	1 beaver	3 beaver
red blanket	1 beaver	2 beaver
white blanket	1 beaver	2 beaver
6 pair stockings	1 beaver	2 beaver
4 shirts	1 beaver	1 beaver

Source: E. B. O'Callaghan & B. Fernow, eds., *Documents Relative to the Colonial History of the State of New York* (1856–87), IX, 408.

TABLE 4.125 COST OF SHIPPING A HOGSHEAD OF FURS FROM NEW YORK TO LONDON, 1751

Sales Price to London Agent	Shipping Expenses to London
£46.8.0 for misc. furs (fox, wildcat, wolf, mink, otter, marten, and muskrat)	£4.14.4 for 2.5% sales commission and 0.5% brokerage fee
	£17.18.3 for customs duties and entry fees @ 6d. per skin
£110.8.0 for 197 beaver @ 6s. per lb.	2s., 1d. for freight
£156.16.0 for hogshead	5s., 6d. to landwaiters, wharfage, porterage and cooperage
Net Return: £131.16.11[a]	£24.19.1 in total expenses

[a] Insurance premium of 2 to 2.5% of value was optional in peace. Small fees were owed to New York agent, plus packing expenses.
Source: Thomas E. Norton, *The Fur Trade in Colonial New York, 1686–1776* (1974), 107–108.

TABLE 4.126 NUMBER OF BEAVERSKINS EXPORTED FROM VIRGINIA AND CAROLINA, 1699–1715

Year Ending Dec. 25	From Virginia (No.)	From Carolina (No.)
1715	404	694
1714	407	533
1713	357	242
1712	4,800	314
1711	8,050	36
1710	491	125
1709	1,621	52
1708	590	…
1707	526	436
1706	2,679	258
1705	401	25
1704	2,481	540
1703	71	489
1702	1,063	2,724
1701	1,476	451
1700	2,104	1,486
1699	2,390	1,436

Source: Verner W. Crane, *The Southern Frontier, 1670–1732* (1928), 328.

TABLE 4.127 MISCELLANEOUS FURS EXPORTED FROM VIRGINIA, 1699–1701 AND 1713–1715

Fur	1699–1701	1713–1715
Black Bear	1,216	1,119
Wildcat	2,297	516
Fox	11,080	4,337
Fisher	339	104
Mink	4,770	2,750
Muskrat	1,886	901
Otter	2,398	418
Raccoon	44,064	12,911
Wolf	204	78
Woodchuck	272	206

Source: Paul C. Phillips, *The Fur Trade* (1961), I, 404–405.

TABLE 4.128 VALUE OF FURS BARTERED AT MASSACHUSETTS TRADING POSTS, 1726–1756

Year[a]	Value of Furs	
	Old Tenor	Sterling
1756	£6,686	£668
1755	£13,735	£1,373
1754	£21,412	£2,141
1753	£23,774	£2,438
1752	£21,292	£2,129
1750	£13,950	£1,354
1742	£3,917	£712
1740	£3,383	£644
1726	£1,417	£488

[a] No set fiscal year, periods vary from 9 to 15 months.
Source: Ronald O. MacFarlane, "The Massachusetts Bay Truck-Houses in Diplomacy with the Indians," *New England Quarterly*, XI (1938), 58

TABLE 4.129 PELTRY PRICES (LOCAL MONEY) IN CAPE MAY CO., N.J., JULY–NOVEMBER 1755

Fur	Price
otter	10s
mink	3s
wolf	3s
fox	2s, 8d
wildcat	2s, 8d
deerskin	2s, 3d in summer
deerskin	2s in fall
raccoon	2s
muskrat	5d

Source: William A. Ellis, ed., "Diary of Jacob Spicer, 1755–6," New Jersey Historical Society, *Proceedings*, LVIII (1945), 98, 176.

TABLE 4.130 VALUE (IN POUNDS STERLING) OF NORTH AMERICAN AND EUROPEAN FURS IMPORTED BY ENGLAND, 1700–1750

Market	1750	1739	1730	1725	1720	1710	1700
Hudson Bay	£8,143	£13,452	£12,335	£11,180	£9,839	…	£2,360
Newfndland.	£420	£551	£656[a]	£452	£457	£553	£223
N. England	£1,015	£2,481	£2,010	£1,862	£2,119	£1,595	£2,435
New York	£5,710	£5,073	£2,611	£6,952	£5,393	£2,148	£4,962
Penn.	£1,909	£329	£1,642	£923	£849	£88	£723
Va. & Md.	£282	£641	£493	£488	£467	£754	£2,433
Carolinas	£12	£9	£57	£46	£4	£27	£576
Subtotal	£17,491	£22,536	£19,804	£21,903	£19,128	£5,165	£13,712
European	£5,326[b]	£2,660[c]	£2,544[d]	£1,638[c]	£249[e]	£2,675[d]	£2,572[d]
All Furs	£22,817	£25,196	£22,348	£23,541	£19,377	£7,840	£16,284

[a] Includes £156 from Nova Scotia.
[b] Primarily Germany, Russia.
[c] Primarily Germany, Russia, Ireland.
[d] Primarily Ireland.
[e] Primarily British West Indies.
Source: Murray G. Lawson, *Fur: A Study in English Mercantilism, 1700–1775* (1943), 108–109.

TABLE 4.131 EXPORTS OF NORTH AMERICAN SKINS, BY TYPE, TO ENGLAND, 1700–1750

Type of Skin	1750	1739	1730	1725	1720	1710	1700
Beaver[a]							
Number	61,672	96,547	79,003	94,714	85,826	11,382	44,457
Value	£10,871	£16,970	£13,931	£16,658	£15,061	£1,992	£7,920
Bear							
Number	3,222	793	4,682	2,057	4,190	4,528	4,585
Value	£1,047	£258	£1,522	£669	£1,362	£1,472	£1,490
Fox							
Number	20,541	11,208	14,049	15,773	5,256	7,028	18,828
Value	£1,284	£701	£878	£992	£328	£439	£739
Marten							
Number	18,503	25,925	30,115	30,915	19,542	4,612	6,291
Value	£617	£864	£1,004	£1,031	£647	£147	£227
Mink							
Number	11,175	12,647	6,355	7,453	5,757	4,890	4,827
Value	£977	£1,119	£570	£656	£505	£428	£422
Muskrat							
Number	24,642	15,238	3,853	6,448	7,728	6,407	11,110
Value	£490	£291	£77	£151	£194	£42	£86
Otter							
Number	6,493	5,274	4,088	3,655	2,444	1,892	3,702
Value	£974	£842	£681	£579	£403	£340	£695
Raccoon							
Number	19,555	12,082	23,227	30,740	11,618	9,106	33,610
Value	£489	£302	£581	£769	£297	£228	£1,884
Wildcat							
Number	4,825	5,139	3,154	4,156	1,577	950	2,955
Value	£44	£148	£31	£39	£15	£8	£25
Wolf							
Number	1,507	844	718	400	204	152	483
Value	£374	£220	£200	£94	£55	£38	£180

Note: Includes furs from thirteen colonies, Newfoundland, Nova Scotia, and the Hudson's Bay Company.
[a] Value includes cut beaver, beaver womb, and beaver wool.
Source: Murray G. Lawson, *Fur: A Study in English Mercantilism, 1700–1775* (1943), 87–102.

TABLE 4.132 IMPORTS OF ENGLISH BEAVER HATS BY THIRTEEN COLONIES, 1700–1770

Colonies	1770	1765	1760	1750	1740	1730	1720	1710	1700
New England									
Number	5,256	10,308	25,848	7,848	3,972	13,008	11,220	11,304	5,520
Value	£1,209	£1,511	£3,360	£2,617	£1,324	£4,335	£3,976	£3,668	£2,577
New York									
Number	16,212	4,212	13,440	8,544	4,164	2,844	2,064	3,456	1,776
Value	£5,404	£1,404	£4,480	£2,846	£1,388	£947	£730	£1,151	£906
Pennsylvania									
Number	2,880	4,836	16,632	6,684	4,212	3,480	1,656	348	1,656
Value	£960	£1,612	£5,544	£2,228	£1,677	£1,161	£585	£115	£808
Va., Md.									
Number	43,404	27,456	64,872	41,532	22,116	8,148	9,264	6,816	6,660
Value	£12,658	£8,018	£26,650	£12,114	£6,451	£2,375	£3,292	£1,989	£2,778
Carolinas, Ga.									
Number	2,064	17,616	13,164	5,400	7,260	8,112	1,980	1,080	156
Value	£688	£5,870	£4,389	£1,800	£2,381	£1,965	£702	£360	£67
Total									
Number	69,816	64,428	133,956	70,008	41,724	35,592	26,184	23,004	15,768
Value	£20,919	£18,415	£44,423	£21,605	£13,221	£10,783	£9,285	£7,283	£7,136

Note: Values given in pounds sterling.
Source: Murray G. Lawson, *Fur: A Study in English Mercantilism, 1700–1775* (1943), 118–130.

TABLE 4.133 SIR WILLIAM JOHNSON'S ESTIMATE OF ANNUAL VALUE OF TRADE GOODS EXCHANGED WITH INDIANS IN THE NORTHERN COLONIAL FUR TRADE, 1764

Trade Goods and Prices	Value in N.Y. Money	Value in Sterling
20,000 blankets @ 13s	£13,000	£7,583.6.8
30,000 strouds @ 20s	£30,000	£17,500.6.0
40,000 shirts @ 10s	£20,000	£11,666.13.4
40,000 pair of stockings @ 5s	£10,000	£5,833.6.8
10,000 laps @ 5s	£2,500	£1,458.6.8
30,000 pieces of quartering @ 6s	£9,000	£5,250.6.0
20,000 lb. of vermillion @ 12s	£12,000	£7,000.6.0
20,000 M black wampum @ 40s per M	£40,000	£23,333.6.8
5,000 M white wampum @ 25s per M	£6,250	£2,645.16.8
20,000 knives @ 6d	£500	£291.13.4
60,000 awls @ 60d per 100	£100	£58.6.8
10,000 lb. of brass wire @ 4s	£2,000	£1,166.13.4
5,000 lb. of beads @ 4s	£1,000	£583.6.8
10,000 looking glasses @ 3s	£1,500	£875.6.0
10,000 razors @ 9d	£375	£218.15.0
50,000 gal. of rum @ 3s	£7,500	£4,375.10.0
80,000 lb. of gunpowder @ 3s	£12,000	£7,000.0.0
160,000 lb. of lead @ 6d	£4,000	£2,333.6.8
3,000 guns @ 30s	£4,500	£2,625.6.0
5,000 beaver traps @ 10s	£2,500	£1,458.6.8
10,000 axes @ 3s	£1,500	£875.6.0
10,000 weight of kettles @ 3s, 6d	£1,750	£1,020.16.8
misc. hair plates & silver trinkets	£20,000	£11,666.13.4
misc. gilt trunks	£400	£233.6.8
misc. calicoes & calimancoes	£4,000	£2,333.6.8
misc. ribbons	£1,000	£583.6.8
misc. silk handkerchiefs	£500	£291.13.4
Totals	£207,875	£121,260.18.4
To the foregoing may be added for the use of the Children of Each family at the most moderate computation Goods to the Amt. of…	£100,000	£58,333.6.8
Total Indians Goods Sold in Fur Trade[a]	£307,875	£179,594.5.0

[a] "Several small Articles such as Jews harps, Combs, Needles, Hawkbells, Flints, Steels, Worms, Worsted for Belts & Garters, & other Threads &ca are not inserted, being of small Value and their Quantity of uncertain computation."
Source: Alexander C. Flick, ed., *The Papers of Sir William Johnson* (1925), IV, 559.

TABLE 4.134 EXCHANGE RATES OF PELTRY AND TRADE GOODS ALONG THE GREAT LAKES, 1765

Trade Goods		Number and Type of Pelt
womens yarn stockings	=	1 marten
childrens stockings	=	2 muskrat
white blanket	=	2 large beaver
mens Penniston coat with gimps	=	2 beaver
boys (to 16) Penniston coat with gimps	=	2 medium beaver
childrens Penniston coat with gimps	=	1 medium beaver
mens coarse garlix shirt	=	1 medium beaver
mens ruffled shirt	=	2 medium beaver
shirt for childrens aged 2 to 5	=	2 otter or 7 raccoon
black wampum	=	1 small beaver or 2 large raccoon
white wampum	=	1 marten or 2 large raccoon
Cutteau large knive	=	3 muskrat or 2 large raccoon
womens small knive	=	2 muskrat or 1 small raccoon
1 ps best roll gartering	=	1 beaver or 6 raccoon
2 fathom ribbon	=	2 medium beaver
1 lb. vermillion	=	2 beaver
1 fathom calicoe	=	1 beaver
1 fathom calimanco	=	2 medium beaver
silver hairplate	=	1 small beaver
beaver trap	=	2 medium beaver
6 Jews harps	=	1 large raccoon
fathom of worsted serge	=	1 medium beaver
2 horn combs	=	1 mink, 1 raccoon, or 3 muskrat
medium looking glass	=	6 muskrat or 2 medium raccoon
large trunk	=	2 medium beaver
medium trunk	=	1 beaver
small trunk	=	1 marten or 6 muskrat
fathom of small wire	=	1 muskrat
fathom of thick wire	=	1 raccoon
6 brass rings	=	1 small raccoon or 2 muskrat
3 gallons rum	=	3 large beaver
10 quarts rum	=	2 large & 1 small beaver
8 quarts rum	=	2 large beaver
6 quarts rum	=	1 large & 1 small beaver
4 quarts rum	=	1 large beaver or 5 raccoon

Source: Alexander C. Flick, ed., *The Papers of Sir William Johnson* (1925), IV, 893–895.

The Deerskin Trade

The southern colonies were home to relatively few beaver or otters, which in any case bore fur of light and poor quality; however, the colonies abounded in deer. As late as 1682, Thomas Ashe of Virginia said deer in nearby Carolina formed "such infinite herds, that the whole country seems but one continuous park." Virginia's assembly forbade export of that colony's deerskins from 1631 to 1659 in an effort to stimulate a tanning industry, and it resumed this prohibition from 1677 to 1691. By 1699, Virginians were accumulating large amounts of deerskins and exported an annual average of 16,900 hides through 1709, but their role in this trade remained peripheral because the main deer country lay southward in the Carolina Piedmont.

The Carolina proprietors initially restricted trading rights to themselves, but they gave up their monopoly in 1691. Many unsavory individuals tried to get rich quick by intimidating or cheating Indians out of skins, and the accumulated weight of their abuses helped instigate the Yamasee and Tuscarora Wars between 1711 and 1717. South Carolina, the chief center for collecting hides, then began to regulate this business more closely through commissioners especially appointed to license and oversee the colony's traders.

By 1748, Charles Town merchants had revived the deerskin trade and doubled the volume of hides sent abroad from the level in 1715. This enterprise evidently paid high returns: in 1748 South Carolinians exported deerskins worth £36,000, representing a profit exceeding 250% of the average value of Indian wares that were imported for the trade, which reputedly was about £10,000. These substantial gains were nevertheless always at risk from Spanish or French agents who sowed disaffection among the Indians, and the supply of deerskins was consequently subject to sudden fluctuations, such as those after armed conflict erupted with Spain in 1739 and the Cherokee in 1760. Britain's expulsion of France and Spain from all territories east of the Mississippi in 1763 ended this element of uncertainty and it brought such unprecedented levels of exports by 1770 that the value of deerskins shipped overseas from the thirteen colonies exceeded that of beaver and peltry.

TABLE 4.135 DEERSKIN EXPORTS (NO.) FROM VIRGINIA AND SOUTH CAROLINA, 1699–1724

Year[a]	South Carolina (No.)	Virginia (No.)
1724	61,124	...
1723	64,315	...
1722	59,827	...
1721	33,939	...
1720	35,171	...
1719	24,355	...
1718	17,073	...
1717	21,713	...
1716	4,702	...
1715	55,806	6,843
1714	50,781	4,952
1713	60,451	3,019
1712	80,324	16,230
1711	33,409	22,927
1710	68,432	7,521
1709	52,014	28,511
1708	31,939	2,349
1707	121,355	12,037
1706	32,954	24,393
1705	10,289	1,958
1704	61,541	34,387
1703	57,881	849
1702	49,646	18,937
1701	51,086	15,107
1700	22,133	24,900
1699	64,488	22,678

[a] Years end on December 25.
Note: Deerskins probably worth 10s. each on the dock about 1700.
Source: Verner W. Crane, *The Southern Frontier, 1670–1732* (1928), 328–329.

TABLE 4.136 DEERSKIN EXPORTS FROM SOUTH CAROLINA, SEPTEMBER 1726–NOVEMBER 1763

Year Ending	Hogsheads[a]	Weight[b] (Lb.)
Nov. 1, 1763	633	...
Dec. 25, 1762	350	177,491
Dec. 25, 1761	276	155,902
Dec. 25, 1760	514	303,610
Dec. 25, 1759	609	355,207
Dec. 25, 1758	476	260,433
Dec. 25, 1757	450	239,817
Dec. 25, 1756	408	210,434
Dec. 25, 1755	512	263,586
Dec. 25, 1754	477	237,858
Dec. 25, 1753	424	206,990
Dec. 25, 1752	342	157,489
Dec. 25, 1751	444	186,916
Dec. 25, 1750	299	143,948
Dec. 25, 1749	618	227,363
Dec. 25, 1748	427	214,956
Dec. 25, 1747	607	277,545
Dec. 25, 1746	602	277,728
Dec. 25, 1745	661	305,717
Dec. 25, 1744	257	130,884
Dec. 25, 1743	519	264,844
Dec. 25, 1742	506	257,952
Dec. 25, 1741	298	153,180
Dec. 25, 1740	450	229,500

Year Ending	Hogsheads[a]	Chests	Loose Skins
Nov. 1, 1739	559	...	856
Nov. 1, 1738	441	...	1,465
Nov. 1, 1737	339	5	1,050

Year Ending	Number	Duties[c]
Mar. 25, 1736	81,017	£2,025
Mar. 25, 1735	84,958	£2,123
Mar. 25, 1734	96,523	£2,413
Mar. 25, 1733	74,483	£1,862
Mar. 25, 1732	86,771	£2,169
Mar. 25, 1731[d]	79,753	£1,495
Mar. 25, 1730[d]	79,753	£1,495
Mar. 25, 1729[d]	79,753	£1,495
Mar. 25, 1728[d]	79,753	£1,495
Mar. 25, 1727[d]	79,753	£1,495
Sep. 29, 1726[d]	79,753	£1,495

[a] Hogsheads weighed 500 to 515 lb.
[b] Average deerskin about 1.5 lb.
[c] In local currency.
[d] Average figures for 1726–1731.
Source: Verner W. Crane, *The Southern Frontier, 1670–1732* (1928), 330–331.

TABLE 4.137 EXPORTS OF DEERSKINS (IN LB.) FROM GEORGIA, 1755–1772

Year	Skins (Lb.)
1772	213,475
1771	270,860
1770	284,840
1769	288,870
1768	306,510
1767	205,340
1766	273,460
1765	200,695
1764	172,425
1763	184,737
1762	42,855
1761	13,140
1760	65,765
1759	7,380
1758	5,791
1757	26,357
1756	39,220
1755	49,995

Note: Deerskins probably weighed 1.5 lb. each.
Source: Lewis C. Gray, *The History of Agriculture in the Southern United States to 1860* (1933), 102.

TABLE 4.138   EXCHANGE VALUE OF DEERSKINS IN INDIAN TRADING GOODS, 1716–1718

Exchange Product	Savannah Town, 1716	Cherokee, 1716	Settlements, 1718	Creek, 1718	
	Buck Skins (No.)	Deerskins (No.)	Heavy Dressed (Lb.)	Heavy Dressed (No.)	Light Dressed (No.)
1 gun	30	35	16	25	35
1 pistol	20	20	…	12	18
1 lb. powder	a	a	1	1	b
bullets	1 per 50	1 per 30	1 per 4 lb.	1 per 40	1 per 30
flints	1 per 18	1 per 12	1 per 50	1 per 20	1 per 15
1 steel	1	1	…	…	…
1 hatchet	2	3	2	…	…
1 knife	1	1	1/2	…	…
1 hanger	…	…	…	7	10
pair scissors	1	1	…	…	…
1 axe	4	5	…	4	6
1 hoe, narrow	2	3	…	2	3
1 hoe, broad	4	5	3	4	6
brass kettle	a	a	2.5 lb. per 1 lb.	…	…
pipes	…	…	1 per 24	…	…
1 gal. rum	…	…	4	…	…
1 bottle rum	1	…	…	…	…
string of beads	1 per 3	1 per 2	3 per 1 lb.	…	…
vermillion paint	…	…	20 per 1 lb.	…	…
red lead paint	…	…	20 per 2 lb.	…	…
1 yd. strouds	7	8	4	6	9
1 yd. plains or half-thicks	3	3	2	2	3
1 white duffel blanket	14	16	8	…	…
1 blue or red duffel blanket	…	…	7 per 2 yds.	6	9
1 striped duffel blanket	…	…	…	6	9
1 yd. double striped cloth	…	…	3	…	…
1 shirt	4	5	3	…	…
1 coat, half-thick, laced	…	20	14	14	21
1 coat, plain half-thicks	…	…	12	12	18
1 hat, laced	8	…	3	…	…
1 hat, plain	…	…	2	…	…
flowered calico	…	…	4 per yd.	…	…
1 calico petticoat	12	14	4 per yd.	…	…
scarlet caddice	1 per yd.	…	1 per 3 yds.	…	…
1 red girdle	2	2	…	…	…

a "as you can"
b "in proportion"
Source: Verner W. Crane, *The Southern Frontier, 1670–1732* (1928), 332–333.

TABLE 4.139   EXCHANGE RATES OF DEERSKINS AND TRADE GOODS ALONG THE GREAT LAKES, 1765

Trade Good		Exchange Rate (in Deerskins)
white blankets of 24 blkts in a piece	=	1 large buck & a doe
white blankets of 30 blkts to a piece	=	2 does
mens Penniston coats with gimps	=	3 bucks
boys of age 16 Penniston coats with gimps	=	3 does
childrens Penniston coats with gimps	=	1 buck
mens coarse garlix shirts	=	1 buck
mens ruffled shirts	=	2 bucks
childrens shirts, age 2 to 5	=	1 doe
1 ps of best roll gartering	=	2 does
2 fathom of ribbon	=	1 buck
1 lb. vermillion	=	3 bucks
1 fathom calicoe	=	3 does
1 fathom calimancoe	=	2 does
1 fathom worsted serge	=	1 buck
large silk handkerchief	=	2 does
large silver hair piece	=	4 bucks
large trunk	=	2 bucks
medium trunk	=	1 buck

Trade Good		Exchange Rate (in Deerskins)
beaver trap	=	2 bucks
3 gallons rum	=	4 large bucks
10 quarts rum	=	3 bucks & 1 doe
8 quarts rum	=	3 bucks
6 quarts rum	=	1 bucks & 2 does
4 quarts rum	=	2 does

Source: Alexander C. Flick, ed., *The Papers of Sir William Johnson* (1925), IV, 893–895.

Manufacturing, Handicrafts, and Mining

English promoters of colonization hoped that manufacturing and mining would grow rapidly in North America. Sir Walter Raleigh was careful to have a Bohemian metallurgist, Joachim Ganz, accompany his first expedition to Roanoke Island in 1585–86. The earliest settlers often expended much energy in futile efforts to discover gold, silver, and other valuable ores. The Virginia Company began to construct an ironworks in 1621, and New Englanders formed a corporation to refine iron just four years after Boston's founding.

The industrial sector of Anglo-America's economy nevertheless developed slowly during the colonial era. Although agriculture was not immune to market disruptions and recessions, farming attracted most available capital because land was far less expensive and much less risky as an investment than were either factories or mines. The scarcity of labor also discouraged industrial activities, which experienced great trouble in finding the proper mix of skills and reliable personnel, even when high wages were offered. Although textiles and steel were discouraged by such parliamentary laws as the Woolen Act (1699) and the Iron Act (1750), their failure to prosper before 1763 arose from the high cost of labor, a local shortage of skilled workers, and a limited supply of investment capital, rather than from imperial prohibitions.

Mining remained in its infancy through 1763. The ore used by iron manufacturers was dug from deposits laying near the surface of bogs rather than from underground deposits. The little coal produced in the colonies came from pits dug into veins just below the ground and not from subterranean tunnels. Underground mines were rare in early America, except for a brief period when a small number of copper mines flourished in New Jersey and Connecticut.

Because Britain could provide its provinces with manufactures that were relatively inexpensive and yet of high quality, the colonial market provided little financial stimulus for large-scale production beyond the level provided by local craftspeople working alone or with apprentices. The only circumstance favoring the emergence of mass production in workyards or factories was the availablity of abundant, low-cost supplies of timber, molasses, and bog iron to Anglo-Americans. By 1763, a modest industrial base had consequently emerged in distilling, shipbuilding, and iron smelting, all of which could be more competitively produced in North America than imported from abroad.

Distilling

The manufacture of spirits from local grain dated from the earliest settlements. Demand for alcohol was long met by individual stills and imports of inexpensive West Indian rum. By the 1660s, North Americans began to import substantial amounts of Caribbean molasses and established large-scale distilleries to satisfy the local market. The production of liquor expanded into a major economic activity after 1700, especially in New England. Although a few breweries and numerous family stills produced beer, cider, and grain whiskeys for sale, only the distillation of rum developed into a major industrial enterprise by the 1760s.

Rum came in several varieties, depending on whether it was refined from molasses or the juice of sugarcane. After being mixed with water, molasses or cane juice was cooked into a mash and transformed through fermentation into alcohol and carbon dioxide. To separate the alcohol from water, the distillation process boiled off the alcohol and collected the vapors above the kettle in a long neck; it then condensed these gases in a spiral tube that cooled the steaming alcohol so that it could be collected in liquid form. Double distilling imparted body and character to the best rum, but North Americans often economized at this stage and produced liquors far inferior to Caribbean rum in taste and color.

Because much North American rum was mediocre, its consumers tended to be those with little inclination to discriminate on the basis of taste. Continental rum's best customers were fishing crews and lumberjacks, for whom the liquor provided a vital means of coping with prolonged exposure to harsh winter weather. A sizable market for New England rum developed in Africa, where it was bartered for slaves. Rum also flowed freely in the fur trade, in part to dim the Indians' bargaining skills, and by 1764 Sir William Johnson estimated that peltry merchants distributed 50,000 gallons to Indians along the Great Lakes. The contribution of early American distillers to colonial society was consequently checkered, for, as Lawrence A. Harper observed, their product served largely "to cheat the Indian, cheer the fisherman and enslave the Negro."

TABLE 4.140   WHOLESALE PRICE OF NEW ENGLAND RUM AT NEW YORK, N.Y. (IN STERLING PER GAL.), 1708–1763

Year	Price
1763	1.63s
1762	1.59s
1761	1.97s
1760	2.52s
1759	2.47s
1758	1.97s
1757	1.65s
1756	1.47s
1755	1.39s
1754	1.47s
1753	1.58s
1752	1.48s
1751	1.44s
1750	1.41s
1749	1.51s
1748	1.75s
1747	1.96s[a]
1746	1.50s[a]
1745	1.67s
1744	1.46s
1743	1.56s
1742	1.78s[a]
1741	1.69s[a]
1740	1.47s
1739	1.82s
1738	1.52s
1737	...
1736	1.31s
1735	...
1734	...
1733	...
1732	1.65s
1731	1.82s
1730	1.71s
1729	1.65s
1728	1.98s
1727	2.13s
1726	1.82s
1725	1.98s
1724	1.52s
1723	1.58s
1722	1.80s
1721	1.94s
1720	1.96s
1719	...
1718	...
1717	2.05s
1716	...
1715	1.82s
1714	1.77s
1713	...
1712	2.34s
1711	2.02s
1710	2.04s
1709	1.85s
1708	1.80s

[a] Price from Albany, New York.
Source: John J. McCusker, *Rum and the American Revolution: The Rum Trade and the Balance of Payments of the Thirteen Continental Colonies,* 2 vols. (1989), II, 1133–1135.

TABLE 4.141 WHOLESALE PRICE OF AMERICAN RUM (IN STERLING PER GAL.), 1763–1770

Year	Boston[a]	New York[a]	Philadelphia[b]	Charles Town[a]
1770	1.13s	1.49s	1.44s	1.54s
1769	1.14s	1.44s	1.36s	1.75s
1768	1.09s	1.37s	1.35s	1.82s
1767	1.08s	1.44s	1.26s	1.54s
1766	1.07s	1.51s	1.34s	1.87s
1765	1.11s	1.26s	1.20s	1.72s
1764	1.22s	1.52s	1.21s	1.76s
1763	1.28s	1.63s	1.44s	2.04s

[a] New England Rum
[b] Pennsylvania Rum
Source: John J. McCusker, Rum and the American Revolution: The Rum Trade and the Balance of Payments of the Thirteen Continental Colonies, (1989), 1133, 1134.

TABLE 4.142 PROFITABILITY OF RUM PRODUCTION IN THE THIRTEEN COLONIES, ABOUT 1765

Cost of importing 6,626,286 gal. of molasses[a]	£255,000
Gallons of rum distilled	4,807,000 gal.
Value of rum distilled @ 1.20s. per gal.[b]	£288,400
Average annual profits of 1.5d. per gal.	£33,000
Number of distilleries	143
Total capitalization @ £1,000 per distillery	£143,000
Average return on capitalization and production costs[c]	8%

Note: All values given in pounds sterling.
[a] Includes 2,690,000 gal. smuggled, which avoided £11,200 in duties.
[b] Price quoted from Boston.
[c] No data on cost of wages, fuel, etc.
Source: John J. McCusker, Rum and the American Revolution: The Rum Trade and the Balance of Payments of the Thirteen Continental Colonies (1989), Ch. 5.

Shipbuilding

The first colonial-built vessel was the 30-ton pinnace *Virginia*, launched in 1607 at the settlement of Sagadahoc, Maine; it was sufficiently seaworthy to cross the Atlantic twice. Shipbuilding began as an established enterprise when the New England Company sponsored the emigration of a half-dozen shipwrights to Salem, Massachusetts, in 1629. The early shipyards primarily made modest fishing craft, but from the beginning they turned out substantial craft. On July 4, 1631, ship carpenters at Medford christened an oceangoing bark, the 20-ton *Blessing of the Bay*. Medford launched a 60-ton vessel in 1633, Marblehead built another of 120 tons in 1636, and Salem outfitted one of 300 tons by 1641.

Massachusetts Bay enacted its first legislation regulating shipbuilding in 1641, and shipwrights organized their first guild in 1644. Massachusetts produced at least 30 vessels during the 1640s, including nine rated at more than 100 tons and 12 carrying capacity that exceeded 200 tons. From 1674 to 1696, New Englanders constructed 151 oceangoing vessels, about 6 each year, but from 1705 to 1714 they averaged 66 annually. Approximately 70% of New England's shipping originated in Boston, Scituate, Salem, and Charlestown about 1700. The major center of this industry was Boston, whose shipyards produced every fourth vessel and almost 30% of the tonnage launched.

Shipbuilding expanded in tandem with the rapid growth of New England's merchant marine. Despite a shortage of skilled labor and the necessity of importing specialized equipment such as blocking and tackling, colonial shipwrights produced vessels for about £4.5.0 per ton before 1700, or about 60% less expensively than they would have cost in England. British merchants bought 187 New England ships, averaging 110 tons each, from 1698 to 1714. American shipyards remained competitive by keeping construction expenses below £4 in the 1700s, and they attracted a large flow of orders from the British Isles. By 1724, colonial output of vessels had risen to the point where London's shipwrights complained to Parliament that their best carpenters were emigrating to America.

TABLE 4.143 TYPES OF SEAWORTHY VESSELS BUILT IN THE THIRTEEN COLONIES, 1700–1760

Type of Vessel	Average Tonnage (ca. 1750)	Number of Masts	Rig of Sails	Number of Decks	Crew Size
ship	130	3	all square	2 +	13
bark	90	3	2 square & 1 fore & aft	2	11–12
snow	90	2	square-rig on foresail, fore & aft-rig on main	1	11
brig[a]	60	2	square-rig on foresail, fore & aft-rig on main	1	7
schooner	35	2	square-rig, and fore & aft-rig	1	5
sloop	40	1	fore & aft mainsail with jib	1	5
ketch[c]	10–40	1	square	1	4
shallop[b]	10–15	1	fore & aft-rig	open	4
pinnace[a]	to 12	1	square or lateen	open	4

[a]Sometimes equipped with oars before 1710.
[b]Always with oars.
[c]"Pinkie" or "yacht" to Dutch.
Source: William A. Fairburn, Merchant Sail (1945), 236–240. William A. Baker, "Vessel Types of Colonial Massachusetts," in Colonial Society of Massachusetts, ed., Seafaring in Colonial Massachusetts (1980), 5–29. Joseph A. Goldenberg, Shipbuilding in Colonial America (1976), 150, 154, 170, 189, 236.

Major centers of ship construction emerged at Philadelphia, New York, and Baltimore after 1720, but New England's shipyards long dominated the industry. Shipbuilding served to diversify the economy by stimulating a wide range of ancillary activities such as lumbering; production of tar, pitch, and turpentine; ropewalks; canvas works; and smithies. On the Revolution's eve, American shipyards had outfitted a third of Great Britain's merchant marine, which was then the world largest, and the thirteen colonies ranked as a leading center of international ship production.

TABLE 4.144 COLONIAL SHIPBUILDING COSTS PER MEASURED TON, 1641–1764

Date	Ship Size	Cost per Ton	Location
1764	40 tons	£3.17.2 (currency)[a]	Massachusetts
1762	102 tons	£25.0.0 (old tenor)[b]	Massachusetts
1758	56 tons	£22.0.0 (old tenor)[b]	Massachusetts
1747	...	£24.0.0 (old tenor)[b]	Massachusetts
1735	80 tons	£3.5.0 (sterling)	Rhode Island
1729	122 tons (masts & yards)	£3.12.0 (sterling)	New York
1725	...	£3.5.0 (sterling)	New England
1721	...	£2.17.0 (sterling)	Rhode Island
1712	ship	£3.0.0 (sterling)	New England
1711	250–350 tons	£2.15.0–£3. (sterling)	New England
1711	150–250 tons	£2.0.0 (sterling)	New England
1701	45-ft. keel (full rig)	£2.13.0 (sterling)	New England
1700	72-ft. keel (full rig)	£3.12.0 (sterling)	New England
1695–1701	...	£4.5.0 (sterling)	New England
1697	82-ft. keel (full rig)	£2.10.0 (sterling)	New England
1676	ship	£4.0.0 (sterling)	New England
1661	190 tons	£3.10.0 (sterling)	Massachusetts
1660–69	20 tons	£4.0.0 (sterling)	New England
1641	40–50 tons (full rig)	£4.5.0 (sterling)	Massachusetts

[a] Valued at £1.333 to £1. sterling.
[b] Valued at 14% of Massachusetts currency.
Source: Gary M. Walton, "A Measure of Productivity Change in American Colonial Shipping," Economic History Review, 2d Ser., XXI (1968), 276–277.

TABLE 4.145 SHIPBUILDING IN MASSACHUSETTS, 1674–1714

Year	Vessels	Tonnage	Value
1714	44	2,885	£10,097
1713	79	5,134	£17,969
1712	67	4,135	£14,472
1711	62	4,412	£15,442
1710	76	4,913	£17,195
1709	69	4,813	£16,845
1708	54	4,045	£14,158
1707	54	2,887	£10,105
1706	77	4,805	£16,818
1705	75	4,931	£17,258
1704	63	3,627	£12,695
1703	43	2,280	£7,980
1702	48	2,357	£8,250
1701	47	2,365	£8,277
1700	68	3,653	£12,785
1699	73	4,192	£14,672
1698	67	3,881	£13,584
1697	29	2,400	£8,400
1674–1696	151	6,956	£24,346
Total	1,246	74,671	£261,348

Source: Bernard Bailyn and Lotte Bailyn, *Massachusetts Shipping, 1697–1714: A Statistical Study* (1959).

TABLE 4.146 AVERAGE SIZE OF VESSELS BUILT IN COLONIES, ABOUT 1750

Colony	Sloop (Tons)	Schooner (Tons)	Brig (Tons)	Snow (Tons)	Ship (Tons)	Average (Tons)
Massachusetts	43	39	63	88	136	59
New Hampshire	42	34	62	72	129	60
Pennsylvania	17	19	52	73	95	65
Maryland	31	36	83	97	147	70
South Carolina	20	22	59	97	127	35

Source: Joseph A. Goldenberg, *Shipbuilding in Colonial America* (1976), 150, 154, 170, 189, 236.

TABLE 4.147 SHIPBUILDING IN NEW HAMPSHIRE, PHILADELPHIA, AND MARYLAND, 1722–1763

Year	New Hampshire Ships Built	New Hampshire Average Tonnage	Philadelphia Ships Built	Philadelphia Average Tonnage	Maryland Ships Built	Maryland Average Tonnage
1763	...	...	...	...	27	85
1762	...	...	...	...	24	85
1761	...	...	26	76	18	85
1760	...	...	30	73	15	85
1759	...	...	28	61	21	85
1758	...	...	18	78	9	85
1757	...	...	21	78	11	85
1756	...	...	20	53	8	85
1755	...	...	17	62	10	85
1754	...	...	20	82	9	...
1753	...	...	16	74	9	...
1752	...	...	31	65	5	...
1751	...	...	30	60	6	...
1750	...	...	39	66	7	...
1749	...	...	...	...	3	...
1748	...	...	...	...	...	...
1747	...	...	...	...	2	...
1746	...	...	...	...	1	...
1745	26	90	...	...	...	...
1744	15	90	...	...	...	...
1743	33	90	...	...	...	...
1742	30	90	...	...	...	...
1741	18	90	...	...	...	...
1740	12	90	...	...	...	...
1727	17	118	...	...	...	...
1726	10	60	...	...	...	...
1725	22	51	...	...	...	...
1724	14	60	...	...	...	...
1723	24	60	...	...	...	...
1722	7	60	...	...	...	...

Source: David E. Vandeventer, *The Emergence of Provincial New Hampshire, 1623–1741* (1976), 105, 106. Paul H. Giddens, "Trade and Industry in Colonial Maryland, 1753–1769," *Journal of Economic and Business History*, IV (1932), 535. Billy G. Smith, *The "Lower Sort": Philadelphia's Laboring People, 1750–1800* (1990), 223.

Ironmaking

As early as 1610, just three years after Jamestown's founding, the Virginia Company considered erecting an ironworks and even advertised for "Iron-men for Furnasse and hammer." This project was delayed until 1621, however, when work on a furnace began at Falling Creek. Before the ironworks could be completed, it was destroyed by Indians on March 22, 1622. Almost a century was to pass before Virginians built another furnace.

New England became the first part of the colonies to smelt significant amounts of iron. In 1644, Massachusetts Bay chartered the Company of Undertakers of the Iron Works in New England, which agreed to sell iron in the province at no more than £20 per ton. The investors completed a furnace at Braintree that December but abandoned it in 1647 for lack of ore, although a forge at the site continued operating. By 1650, the company completed its Hammersmith plant at Lynn on the Saugus River. Hammersmith eventually consisted of a blast furnace (which measured 21 feet high and had a base 26 feet square), two fineries, a chaffery, a water-powered forge hammer, a rolling mill, and a slitting mill; it could produce 7 tons of cast iron per week. Few facilities in contemporary Europe were so completely equipped as the mature Hammersmith. By 1696, two other blast furnaces had been built in Connecticut and New Jersey, besides a minumum of six separate operating forges.

The most advanced ironworks included a blast furnace that burned charcoal to liquefy the ore and then flushed out the slag and dirt with a bath of limestone or another slow-melting rock. Three tons of bog ore and 400 bushels of charcoal usually yielded a ton of iron. The molten iron might be cast immediately into pots or pans, but it was usually carried off into a trench called the sow, from which it poured into a series of molds, called the pigs. The resulting pig iron contained up to 4% carbon, which had to be burned off at a finery forge through a complex process of melting and stirring that made a dumbbell-shaped ingot, or ancony. Workers at chafery forges heated and hammered the anconies into bars or plates known as bar or wrought iron, from which blacksmiths beat out tools and implements. A few ironworks had plating mills, which could use coal or waterpower, that rolled bar iron between two cylinders into thin rods suitable for cutting into nails at a slitting mill.

From 1676 when Hammersmith ceased operation until 1720, most colonial iron came from bloomeries, or large forges with deep and reinforced sides. Bloomeries extracted a slag residue, or bloom, out of metal oxide over a charcoal hearth. Blacksmiths then heated the bloom red-hot and consolidated the iron by hammering out the impurities. Although smaller in size and output than furnaces, bloomeries could meet the needs of smaller localities if nearby sources of ore were adequate; they also produced iron at less cost than it could have been bought from distant furnaces.

A Pennsylvania iron furnace dating from 1742 that has been taken out of commission and converted for other purposes. (The photo was unidentified but may have been Peter Grubb's Cornwall Furnace on Furnace Creek in Lebanon County.) Iron ore would have been poured from the top of the building at the right into the furnace at the left for smelting. (Photographs, Manuscript Group 23 [Arthur C. Bining Papers] courtesy Pennsylvania State Archives)

After 1715, the colonial iron industry grew at an accelerating pace as it attracted large infusions of investment capital, much of which came from England. Regular amounts of iron began to be exported in 1718, but the domestic economy consumed most output and continued to import a large volume of high-quality, cast-iron implements from Britain. The center of iron smelting quickly shifted to Pennsylvania and New Jersey after 1720.

As colonial ironmaking matured, the primary unit of production became an integrated complex built around a blast furnace. Besides a furnace, such "iron plantations" included one or more forges, storage facilities, store, sawmill, workers' homes, and fields sown with grain. These plantations had to be self-contained communities because they were located in isolated areas capable of supplying sufficient wood to refine ore, which needed 400 bushels of charcoal for each ton of pig iron. (Because plating and slitting mills could operate with coal or waterpower, they were often built in towns.) Transportation costs thus increased iron prices signficantly. Even in Pennsylvania, where more than half the ironworks were within 20 to 40 miles of Philadelphia by 1760, teamster expenses might add £3 to £6 to a ton of iron, which normally sold for £19 at the furnace. Iron manufacturing consequently experienced its birth in ironic circumstances, for although it was early America's premier example of heavy industry, it primarily flourished in rural rather than urban settings.

TABLE 4.148 COLONIAL IRONWORKS ERECTED, 1621–1696

Date	Type and Location	Erected by	Operational Until
1621	Falling Creek Furnace Chesterfield Co., Va.	Southampton Adventurers	burned 1622
1644	Furnace and Forge Braintree, Mass.	Co. of Undertakers of New England Ironworks	furnace to 1647
1645	Hammersmith Furnace Lynn, Mass.	Co. of Undertakers of New England Ironworks	to 1676
1652	Raynham Bloomery Taunton, Plymouth, Mass.	Henry and James Leonard	to 1876
1658	Furnace New Haven, Conn.	John Winthrop, Jr.	to 1680
1660	Assabet Bloomery Concord, Mass.	…	after 1682
1663	North Saugus Furnace Lynn, Mass.	John Gifford	after 1680
1670	Forge (3 hearths) Rowley, Mass.	Henry Leonard	about 1680
1672?	Forge Pawtucket, R.I.	Joseph Jenckes, Jr.	after 1721
1674	Tintern Furnace Shrewsbury, N.J.	James Grover, Henry Leonard, C. Steenwyck	about 1710
1680?	Whittenton Forge Taunton, Mass.	James Leonard	after 1807
1696?	Chartly Forge North Taunton, Mass.	Thomas and James Leonard	to late 1700s

Source: James A. Mulholland, *A History of Metals in Colonial America* (1981), 24–59. E. N. Hartley, *Ironworks on the Saugus: The Lynn and Braintree Ventures of the Company of Undertakers of the Ironworks in New England* (1957).

TABLE 4.149 IRONWORKS ERECTED IN VIRGINIA AND MARYLAND, 1715–1760

Date	Type and Location	Erected by	Operational Until
1715	Cecil Co. Furnace Perryville, Md.	Principio Co.	...
1720?	Germanna Furnace Spotsylvania Co., Va.	Alexander Spotswood	after 1861
1720?	Northeast Forge Cecil Co., Md.	Principio Co.	...
1726	Accokeek Furnace Stafford Co., Va.	Principio Co.	about 1753
1730?	Massaponax Furnace Spotsylvania Co., Va.	Alexander Spotswood	after 1861
1730?	Fredericksville Furnace Spotsylvania Co., Va.	Alexander Spotswood	before 1861
1731	Baltimore Furnace Gwynn's Falls, Md.	Charles Carroll and Benjamin Tasker	...
1731	Patapsco Furnace Gwynn's Falls, Md. Gwynn's Falls, Md.	Baltimore Co.	...

Date	Type and Location	Erected by	Operational Until
1738?	Neabsco Furnace Pr. William Co., Va.	John Tayloe	...
1742	Vestal's Furnace Frederick Co., Va.	Mr. Vestal	...
1745	Kingswood Furnace Baltimore Co., Md.	Principio Co.	...
1755?	Occoquan Furnace Pr. William Co., Va.	John Ballendine, John Tayloe, Jr., & Presley Thornton	...
1760?	Falling Creek Furnace Chesterfield Co., Va.	Archibald Cary	to 1760
1760	Mossy Creek Furnace Augusta Co., Va.	John Miller	...
1760	Marlboro Furnace Frederick Co., Va.	Isaac Zane	...

Source: Kathleen Bruce, *Virginia Iron Manufacture in the Slave Era* (1931), 454. Paul H. Giddens, "Trade and Industry in Colonial Maryland, 1753–1769," *Journal of Economic and Business History,* IV (1932), 522–523.

Typical of large-scale centers of iron production was Hopewell Furnace in Pennsylvania. William Bird began the operation as a forge at modern Union Township in Berks County in 1744, and Mark Bird built this furnace about two decades later. (Photographs, Manuscript Group 23 [Arthur C. Bining Papers] Courtesy Pennsylvania State Archives)

TABLE 4.150 IRONWORKS ERECTED IN PENNSYLVANIA AND DELAWARE, 1716–1762

Date	Name and Location	County	Erected by
1716	Rutter's Forge Matawny Creek	Berks	Thomas Rutter
1718	Coventry Iron Works French Creek	Chester	Samuel Nutt, Sr.
1720?	Colebrookdale Furnace Iron Stone Creek	Berks	Thomas Rutter
1722	Ball Bloomery White Clay Creek	Newcastle (Del.)	John Ball
1725	Keith Furnace Christiana River	Newcastle (Del.)	William Keith
1725	Pool Forge Manatawny Creek	Berks	Alex. Wooddrop
1725	Pine Forge Manatawny Creek	Berks	Thomas Rutter
1725	Glasgow Forge Manatawny Creek	Montgomery	George McCall
1726	Rock Run Furnace French Creek	Chester	Samuel Nutt, Sr., & William Branson
1726?	Kurtz Bloomery Octoraro Creek	Lancaster	Kurtz
1726	Abbington Furnace Christiana River	Newcastle (Del.)	S. James
1727	Durham Iron Works Delaware River	Bucks	Anthony Morris
1729	Spring Forge Manatawny Creek	Berks	Anthony Morris
1732	Coventry Steel Furnace French Creek	Chester	Samuel Nutt, Sr.
1733	Green Lane Forge Perkiomen Creek	Montgomery	Thomas Maybury
1733?	Reading Furnace No. 1 French Creek	Chester	Samuel Nutt, Sr., & William Branson
1736	Reading Furnace No. 2 French Creek	Chester	Samuel Nutt, Sr., & William Branson
1737	Warwick Furnace French Creek	Chester	Anna Nutt
1737	Grubb Bloomery Furnace Creek	Lebanon	Peter Grubb
1737	Mt. Pleasant Furnace Perkiomen Creek	Berks	Thomas Potts, Jr.
1739	Sarum Forge Chester Creek	Delaware	John Taylor
1740	Crum Creek Forge Crum Creek	Delaware	John Crosby & Peter Dicks
1742	Hopewell Forge Hammer Creek	Lebanon	Peter Grubb
1742	Cornwall Furnace Furnace Creek	Lebanon	Peter Grubb
1742	Mt. Joy–Valley Forge Valley Creek	Chester	Daniel Walker
1743	Mt. Pleasant Forge Perkiomen Creek	Berks	Thomas Potts, Jr.
1743	Windsor Forges Conestoga Creek	Lancaster	William Branson
1744	Oley (Spang) Forge Manatawny Creek	Berks	John Ross
1744	Hopewell Forge Union Twsp.	Berks	William Bird
1744	New Pine Forges Haw Creek	Berks	William Bird
1744	Darby Creek Plating Mill	Delaware	Solomon Humphreys
1745	Hereford Furnace Perkiomen Creek	Berks	Thomas Maybury
1746	Sarum Slitting Mill Chester Creek	Delaware	John Taylor
1746	Byberry Plating Mill Byberry Twsp.	Philadelphia	John Hall
1747	Charming Forge Tulpehocken Creek	Berks	J.G. Nikoll
1747	Paschall Steel Furnace Philadelphia	Philadelphia	Stephen Paschall
1747?	Branson Steel Furnace Philadelphia	Philadelphia	William Branson
1750	Union Forge Blue Mountains	Berks	…
1750	Elizabeth Furnace Middle Creek	Lancaster	John Jacob Huber
1750	Spring Forge No. 2 Pine Creek	Berks	…
1750	Boiling Springs Forge	Cumberland	…
1750?	Newmarket Forge Quittapahilla Creek	Lebanon	Gerrard Etter
1752?	Maria Forge Poco Creek	Carbon	G. M. Weiss
1752	Pottsgrove Forge Manatawny Creek	Berks	John Potts
1754	Offley's Anchor Forge Philadelphia	Philadelphia	Daniel Offley
1754	Martic Furnace & Forge Pequa Creek	Lancaster	T. & W. Smith
1755	Roxborough Furnace Heidelberg Twsp.	Berks	William Bird
1756	Dick's Bloomery Codorus Creek	York	Peter Dicks
1759?	Helmstead Forge	Berks	…
1760	Shearwell (Oley) Furnace Furnace Creek	Berks	Benedict Swope
1760	Speedwell Forge Hammer Creek	Lebanon	D. Caldwell & James Old
1760?	Rebecca Furnace Brandywine Creek	Chester	Mordecai Peirsol
1760	Moselem Forge Maiden Creek	Berks	J. Shoffer
1762	Mary Ann Furnace Furnace Creek	York	George Ross
1762	Carlisle Furnace Boiling Springs5	Cumberland	J. S. Rigby
1762	Vincent Steel Furnace French Creek	Chester	Thomas Potts
1762	Pottsgrove Steel Furnace	Montgomery	Samuel Potts
1762	Humphreys' Steel Furnace Philadelphia	Philadelphia	Whitehead Humphreys

Source: Arthur C. Bining, *Pennsylvania Iron Manufacture in the Eighteenth Century* (1938), 187–188.

TABLE 4.151 IRONWORKS ERECTED IN NEW JERSEY, 1710–1763

Date	Type and Location	Erected by	Operational Until
1710	Whippany Riv. Forge Morristown	John Ford	…
1715?	Rancocas Creek Forge Mt. Holly, Burlington Co.	Peter Bard	…
1716	Imlaystown Forge Monmouth Co.	…	by 1720
1725?	Black Creek Forge Bordentown	John Allen, Daniel Coxe, & Thomas Potts	to 1748
1725?	Assunpink Creek Forge Trenton	…	by 1790
1726	Pompton Forge Bergen Co.	…	…

(continued)

TABLE 4.151 (continued)

Date	Type and Location	Erected by	Operational Until
1730	Rancocas Creek Furnace Mt. Holly, Burlington Co.	Isaac Pearson, John Burr, & Mahlon Stacy	to 1778
1730?	Rockaway Riv. Forge Morris Co.	Job Allen	…
1732	Assunpink Plating Mill Trenton	Isaac Harrow	by 1790
1739	Pequannock Riv. Forge Bergen Co.	Cornelius Board	to 1853
1742	Pequannock Riv. Furnace Bergen Co.	Ringwood Co.	to 1853
1742	Oxford Furnace Greenwich, Sussex Co.	…	to 1882
1743	Allen-Turner Furnaces High Bridge, Hunterdon Co.	Wm Allen & Joseph Turner	to 1800s
1743	Troy Forge Parsippany Creek, Morris Co.	…	…
1745	Changewater Forge Musconetcong Riv., Sussex Co.	Jonathan Robeson	after 1834
1745?	Greenwich Forge Warren Glen, Sussex Co.	Jacob Starn	1830
1745?	Rockaway Riv. Forge Dover, Morris Co.	William Schooley	…
1749?	Middle Forge Rockaway Riv., Morris Co.	Jonathan Osborn	to 1850s
1749?	Assinpink Creek Furnace Trenton	Benjamin Yard	by 1790
1750	Burnt Meadow Forge Denmark, Morris Co.	Jacob Ford	to 1840s
1750?	Muthockaway Creek Furnace Norton, Hunterdon Co.	Wm Allen & Joseph Turner	…
1750?	Cohansie Forge Fairfield Twsp., Cumberland Co.	…	…
1750?	Jackson Brook Forge Dover, Morris Co.	John Jackson	to 1880s
1750?	Forge So. Branch of Raritan	Samuel Johnson	…
1750?	Mt. Olive Bloomery Morris Co.	Heaton Bros.	by 1760
1751	Beach Glen Brook Forge Whippany Riv., Morris Co.	John Johnston	to 1867
1752?	Chelsea Forge Finesville, Sussex Co.	David Miller	to 1790s
1753	White Meadow Forge Rockaway Riv., Morris Co.	David Beaman & Thomas Miller	after 1800
1753	Bloomsbury Furnace Musconetcong Riv., Sussex Co.	Samuel Johnson	after 1800
1754	Cokesbury Furnace Beaver Creek, Hunterdon Co.	Wm. Allen & Joseph Turner	by 1760
1755	Spotswood Forge Middlesex Co.	Peter Ten Eyck	by 1780
1758	Boonton Forge Morris Co.	…	to 1830s
1760	Andover Furnace Pequest Riv., Sussex Co.	Wm. Allen & Joseph Turner	to 1780s
1760?	Brooklyn Forge Little Pond, Morris Co.	Benjamin & Thomas Coe	to 1828
1760?	Pittston Forge Lockatong Creek, Hunterdon Co.	…	after 1780s
1760?	Squire Point Forge Sussex Co.	Martin Ryerson & Reading	by 1778
1763	Waterloo Forge Musconetcong Riv., Sussex Co.	Wm. Allen & Joseph Turner	after 1808
1763	Spotswood Forge Middlesex Co.	James Perry & Thomas Hays	by 1780
1763?	Hacklebarney Forge Pottersville, Hunterdon Co.	Christopher Beekman	after 1834

Source: Charles S. Boyer, *Early Forges and Furnaces in New Jersey* (1931).

TABLE 4.152 IRONWORKS ERECTED IN NEW YORK, 1734–1775

Date	Ironworks	Erected by	County
1734?	Lime Rock Furnace	Philip Livingston	Albany
1743	Ancram Creek Furnace	Philip Livingston	Albany
1751	Sterling Mountain Furnace	Ward & Colton	Orange
1752	Noble's Forge	Abel Noble	Orange
1755?	Marysburg & Sober Forges	Philip Livingston	Albany
1756?	Forest of Dean Furnace	…	Orange
1760?	Charlotte Furnace	…	Orange
1760	Sing Sing Furnace	…	Westchester
1760?	Amenia Ironworks	…	Dutchess
1770?	Cedar Pond Furnace & Forge	…	Rockland
1770?	Haverstraw Furnace & Forge	…	Rockland
1775?	Craigsville Forge	…	Orange
1775?	Riverhead Furnace	Solomon Townsend	Long Island
1775?	Patchogue Ironworks	…	Long Island

Source: Irene D. New, "The Iron Plantations of Colonial New York," *New York History,* XXXIII (1952), 3–24.

TABLE 4.153 IRONWORKS OPERATIONAL IN CONNECTICUT AS OF MAY 1751

Built	Ironworks	County	Erected by
1732	Plainfield Forge	Windham	William Dean
1732	Saybrook Forge	New London	Samuel Williams
1732	Stonington Forge	New London	John Dean
1742	Woodstock Forge	Windham	David Wallis
1744	Killingworth Steel Furnace	New London	Benj. Gale, Jared & Aaron Eliot
1746	Killingworth Forge	New London	Benj. Gale, Jared & Aaron Eliot
1747	New London Forge	New London	George Sheffield
1747	Groton Forge	New London	Thomas Pelton
1748	Norwich Forge	New London	Elijah Backus

Source: Connecticut Historical Society, *Collections,* VI, 312; VII, 174; VIII, 338; XVI, 74–75. Arthur C. Bining, *British Regulation of the Colonial Iron Industry* (1933), 15.

TABLE 4.154 IRON FORGES AND FURNACES OPERATING IN MASSACHUSETTS, 1758

Towns	Ironworks	Owners
Suffolk Co.		
Dedham	1 forge	William Avery
Walpole	2 forges	Mr. Morse, Capt. Clap
Stoughton	2 forges	Nathaniel Leonard, Elkanah Billings
Needham	1 forge	Oliver Pratt
Wrentham	1 furnace	Josiah Maxey
Essex Co.		
Salisbury	1 forge	Philip Rowell
Middlesex Co.		
Westford	1 forge	Mr. Keep
Hampshire Co.		
Springfield	1 forge	Joseph Dwight
Sheffield	1 forge	John Ashley
Worcester Co.		
Leicester	1 forge	David Keys
Uxbridge	1 forge	Nicholas Baylis
Western	2 forges	Keys, Blackmore, & Hayward
Western	1 furnace	David Keys
Bristol Co.		
Norton	3 forges	George Leonard, Ephraim Leonard, William Stone
Freetown	1 forge	Ebenezer Hathaway
Attleboro	1 forge	Sweet & Merrit
Taunton	3 forges	Zephary Leonard, James Leonard, Baylis & Laughton

Towns	Ironworks	Owners
Raynham	1 forge	Elijah Leonard
Taunton	1 furnace	Mrs. King
Raynham	1 furnace	Seth Leonard
Easton	1 furnace	Mrs. Williams
Plymouth Co.		
Middleboro	2 forges	Peter Oliver, Elkanah Leonard
Wareham	1 forge	Mrs. Lothrop
Rochester	1 forge	Amos Bates
Plympton	unstated	John Beecham, Warden & Goodwin
Bridgwater	5 forges	Capt. Bass, Mr. Codman, Iona Carver, John Miller, Daniel Hayward & Co.
Kingston	2 forges	Samuel Seabury, Jonathan Holmes
Hanover	2 forges	Thomas Jocelyn, Mr. Palmer
Pembroke	1 forge	Elijah Cushing
Plympton	2 furnaces	Joseph Scott, Mrs. Lothrop & Co.
Kingston	1 furnace	Gamaliel Badford & Co.
Halifax	1 furnace	Thomas Croade & Co.
Hanover	1 furnace	Thomas Jocelyn
Bridgwater	4 furnaces	James Bowdoin, Nicholas Sever & Co., Josiah Edson & Co. (1 unimproved)
Total	41 forges and 14 furnaces	

Source: Arthur C. Bining, *British Regulation of the Colonial Iron Industry* (1933), 126–127.

TABLE 4.155   OPERATING EXPENSES AND RETURN ON INVESTMENT AT GERMANNA FURNACE, SPOTSYLVANIA CO., VA., 1732

Capitalization
£12,000 for 15,000 a., 80 slaves, misc. animals
£700 for blast furnace & £200 for 2 bellows
£12,900 = initial investment (no interest due)

Unit Costs of Production	Annual Costs of Production
1s, 6d to cart 2,912 lb. ore	£138 for 2,400 tons[b]
2s per cord of wood (4'×4'×8')	£160 for 1,600 loads
5s per load of wood charred	£400 for 1,600 loads
2s, 6d per ton of limestone	£30 for 240 tons
1s, 6d to cart 2,912 lb. limestone	£14 for 240 tons
10s per ton for stoppages	£400 for 800 tons
7s, 6d per ton freight to wharf	£300 for 800 tons
3s, 9d per ton customs duties	£150 for 800 tons
18s, 9d per ton merchant fees	£750 for 800 tons
Wages up to £140 for manager	£600 for 9 staff
	£2,942 annual expenses[a]

Return on Equity
20 tons per week for 40 weeks = 800 tons[b]
Gross sales of £6 per ton = £4,800
Annual expenses = £2,942
Net profit = £1,858
Annual return on equity = 14.4%

[a] Assumes laborers will grow 1,600 barrels of corn (worth £160).
[b] All tons measure imperial weight of 2,240 lb.
Source: Louis B. Wright, ed., *The Prose Works of William Byrd of Westover: Narrative of a Colonial Virginian* (1966), 347–360.

TABLE 4.156   LABOR AND WAGE COSTS PER TON OF PENNSYLVANIA BAR IRON, 1730

	Woodcutter	Collier	Finer	Chafer	Total
Daily Task	3 cords	210 bu.	1 ton	…	…
Labor input for 1 ton	3.75 days	2.06 days	1 day	1 day	7.81 days
% of All Days	48%	26%	13%	13%	100%
Total Wages	£1.25	£2.47	£1.00	£1.00	£5.72

Note: Currency is Pennsylvania money.
Source: Paul F. Paskoff, *Industrial Evolution: Organization, Structure, and Growth of the Pennsylvania Iron Industry, 1750–1860* (1983), 13–14.

TABLE 4.157   IRON PRICES (PER TON OF 2,240 LB., IN LOCAL MONEY) AT PHILADELPHIA, 1738–1763

Year	Bar Iron	Pig Iron
1763	£26.25	£9.33
1762	£34.37	£13.00
1761	£34.00	£9.50
1760	£33.00	£9.00
1759	£26.66	£8.50
1758	£23.00	£8.00
1757	£22.63	£7.18
1756	£22.64	…
1755	£22.65	…
1754	£23.00	…
1753	£24.00	£7.00
1752	£25.25	…
1751	£25.00	£7.38
1750	£26.55	…
1749	£26.16	£6.13
1748	£27.17	£6.05
1747	£22.91	£5.50
1746	£19.50	£5.89
1745	£24.00	£6.00
1744	…	£6.13
1743	£25.00	£6.54
1742	£27.50	£6.78
1741	£28.19	£7.00
1740	£28.30	£7.00
1739	£30.00	£7.50
1738	£30.00	…

Source: Anne Bezanson, ed., *Prices in Colonial Pennsylvania* (1935), 378–415.

TABLE 4.158   TONS OF COLONIAL PIG IRON EXPORTED TO GREAT BRITAIN BY COLONY OF ORIGIN, 1723–1763

Year	Virginia & Maryland	New York & East Jersey	Pennsylvania & West Jersey	Other	Total
1763	2,325	108	132	…	2,566
1762	1,733	19	7	23	1,767
1761	2,512	76	149	29	2,766
1760	3,123	51	61	30	3,265
1759	1,429	103	128	12	1,596
1758	3,448	49	195	25	3,717
1757	2,462	157	80	…	2,699
1756	2,468	201	234	108	3,011
1755	2,133	457	836	15	3,441
1754	2,591	116	513	25	3,245
1753	2,347	97	243	51	2,738
1752	2,762	41	156	20	2,979
1751	2,950	33	200	27	3,210
1750	2,509	76	318	21	2,924
1749	1,575	17	167	…	1,759
1748	2,018	22	115	1	2,156
1747	2,119	13	25	…	2,157
1746	1,729	29	103	…	1,861
1745	2,131	19	97	27	2,274
1744	1,748	6	88	20	1,862
1743	2,816	81	63	45	3,005
1742	1,926	…	144	5	2,075
1741	3,261	…	153	43	3,457
1740	2,020	…	159	96	2,275
1739	2,242	…	170	6	2,418
1738	2,113	…	228	18	2,359
1737	2,120	…	169	27	2,316
1736	2,458	…	271	…	2,729
1735	2,362	…	196	3	2,561
1734	2,042	…	147	7	2,196

(continued)

TABLE 4.158 (continued)

Year	Virginia & Maryland	New York & East Jersey	Pennsylvania & West Jersey	Other	Total
1733	2,310	...	95	...	2,405
1732	2,226	...	107	...	2,333
1731	2,081	...	169	...	2,250
1730	1,527	...	189	1	1,717
1729	853	...	274	5	1,132
1728	643	...	243	...	886
1727	407	...	77	...	484
1726	263	...	33	...	296
1725	137	...	...	...	137
1724	202	...	...	...	202
1723	15	...	...	...	15

Note: Reporting year ends December 24. Tons equal 2,240 lb.
Source: Arthur C. Bining, *British Regulation of the Colonial Iron Industry* (1933), 126–133. Research of Lawrence A. Harper in Bureau of the Census, *Historical Statistics of the United States: Colonial Times to 1957* (1960), 762.

TABLE 4.159 TONS OF COLONIAL BAR IRON EXPORTED TO GREAT BRITAIN BY COLONY OF ORIGIN, 1718–1763

Year	Virginia & Maryland	New York & East Jersey	Pennsylvania & West Jersey	Other	Total
1763	234	39	21	3	310
1762	107	...	3	3	110
1761	36	...	3	...	39
1760	98	...	29	...	127
1759	74	...	199	...	273
1758	341	...	10	4	355
1757	35	19	19	...	73
1756	148	2	31	...	181
1755	299	12	79	...	390
1754	154	7	110	...	271
1753	98	...	148	...	248
1752	17	...	65	...	82
1751	3	2	...	...	5
1750	6	...	...	...	6
1748	4	...	...	...	4
1747	83	...	...	...	83
1746	193	...	3	...	196
1745	4	...	...	...	4
1744	57	...	...	...	57
1741	5	...	...	...	5
1740	5	...	...	...	5
1736	...	...	5	...	5
1735	44	...	11	...	55
1733	...	1	...	...	1
1730	...	...	...	9	9
1727	3	...	...	...	3
1726	...	...	...	1	1
1724	7	...	...	...	7
1721	15	...	...	...	15
1720	4	...	...	...	4
1719	1	...	...	...	1
1718	3	...	...	...	3

Note: Reporting year ends December 24. Ton equals 2,240 lb.
Source: Arthur C.Bining, *British Regulation of the Colonial Iron Industry* (1933), 128–133. Research of Lawrence A.Harper in Bureau of the Census, *Historical Statistics of the United States: Colonial Times to 1957* (1960), 763.

TABLE 4.160 TONS OF IRON EXPORTED FROM THE THIRTEEN COLONIES TO ENGLAND, 1763–1776

Year	Type	Virginia & Maryland	New York	Pennsylvania	Other	Total
1776	Pig Iron	208	43	...	60	303
	Bar Iron	28	...	...	...	28
1775	Pig Iron	1,467	1,015	385	130	2,997
	Bar Iron	462	361	88	5	916
1774	Pig Iron	1,458	1,533	323	131	3,445
	Bar Iron	244	284	114	...	642
1773	Pig Iron	1,581	984	209	163	2,937
	Bar Iron	289	498	137	5	929
1772	Pig Iron	1,879	756	706	364	3,705
	Bar Iron	382	561	...	18	961
1771	Pig Iron	2,624	778	1,553	379	5,334
	Bar Iron	709	1,493	18	1	2,221
1770	Pig Iron	1,572	1,031	1,381	248	4,232
	Bar Iron	598	984	93	41	1,716
1769	Pig Iron	1,616	864	634	288	3,402
	Bar Iron	659	861	208	51	1,779
1768	Pig Iron	1,718	520	665	50	2,953
	Bar Iron	712	909	357	10	1,988
1767	Pig Iron	2,070	357	785	101	3,313
	Bar Iron	569	401	342	13	1,325
1766	Pig Iron	1,741	548	299	...	2,588
	Bar Iron	744	400	88	24	1,256
1765	Pig Iron	2,071	564	301	29	2,965
	Bar Iron	639	194	85	160	1,078
1764	Pig Iron	1,837	371	307	40	2,555
	Bar Iron	247	241	272	1	761
1763	Pig Iron	2,325	108	132	...	2,565
	Bar Iron	234	39	21	3	297

Note: Reporting year ends December 24. Ton measures 2,240 lb.
Source: Research of Lawrence A. Harper in Bureau of the Census, *Historical Statistics of the United States: Colonial Times to 1957* (1960), 762, 763.

TABLE 4.161 TONS OF ENGLISH BAR AND WROUGHT IRON IMPORTED BY COLONIES, 1710–1758

Year	Type	Virginia & Maryland	New York	Pennsylvania	New England	Carolina	Total
1758	Wrought	506.4	314.0	434.4	172.8	342.5	1,770
1750	Wrought	434.2	219.2	238.3	394.2	186.7	1,473
	Bar	3.0	...	...	1.0	1.0	5
1735	Wrought	485.5	106.9	105.1	327.2	167.7	1,192
	Bar	3.0	108.0	...	101.0	6.0	218
1734	Wrought	432.1	114.6	157.5	309.6	144.1	1,158
	Bar	2.0	90.0	...	263.0	8.0	363
1733	Wrought	440.8	80.5	121.0	355.3	134.7	1,132
	Bar	12.0	55.0	2.0	371.0	25.0	465
1732	Wrought	372.3	119.0	110.4	429.9	108.4	1,140
	Bar	5.0	58.0	3.0	413.0	9.0	488
1731	Wrought	484.1	131.4	147.3	486.4	88.5	1,338
	Bar	4.0	102.0	5.0	243.0	11.0	365
1730	Wrought	319.5	138.8	131.5	366.5	74.0	1,030
	Bar	2.0	92.0	...	150.0	6.0	250
1729	Wrought	243.3	95.2	42.6	369.7	67.1	818
	Bar	1.0	58.0	4.0	338.0	4.0	405
1718	Wrought	336.8	69.8	44.4	155.5	48.5	655
	Bar	27.0	3.0	4.0	154.0	2.0	190

Year	Type	Virginia & Maryland	New York	Pennsylvania	New England	Carolina	Total
1717	Wrought	436.4	57.3	57.4	191.0	43.3	785
	Bar	10.0	43.0	9.0	141.0	4.0	207
1716	Wrought	372.3	54.7	48.2	269.9	33.5	779
	Bar	9.0	147.0	10.0	373.0	...	539
1715	Wrought	447.4	69.0	49.4	289.8	34.6	890
	Bar	17.0	111.0	8.0	373.0	2.0	511
1714	Wrought	329.9	56.9	46.2	231.7	52.6	717
	Bar	8.0	98.0	25.0	279.0	9.0	419
1713	Wrought	143.0	49.3	52.0	244.2	70.4	559
	Bar	8.0	49.0	7.0	211.0	27.0	302
1712	Wrought	282.7	32.0	27.0	267.3	77.6	686
	Bar	5.0	32.0	2.0	282.0	5.0	326
1711	Wrought	150.7	28.4	49.4	229.9	57.2	515
1710	Bar	2.0	10.0	13.0	201.0	...	226

Note: Reporting year ends December 24. Ton equals 2,240 lb. Wrought iron includes bars free from impurities and goods cast by molds.
Source: J. L. Bishop, *A History of American Manufactures from 1608 to 1860* (1861), 629. Research of Lawrence A. Harper in Bureau of the Census, *Historical Statistics of the United States: Colonial Times to 1957* (1960), 763, 765.

Glassmaking

Glassmaking began simultaneously with colonization. In 1608, the Virginia Company dispatched eight Dutch and Polish glassmakers to Jamestown, where they followed their trade for several years. Six Italian artisans manufactured beads and bottles at a second glass furnace for several years after 1622. Virginians thereafter gave up this trade, and for the next century it made slight progress.

Colonial craftsworkers manufactured glass from the silica in sand and such alkali compounds as lime, potash, or carbonate of soda. After being cleansed of impurities by washing and heating, these materials were liquefied in a furnace and skimmed of any scum that rose to the surface. High temperature eliminated carbonic acid and fused silica with alkalis into saltlike crystals. Colonial technology could not completely melt the raw materials, however, and the vitreous compound was usually bubble pocked and cloudy. The molten fluid was thickened through slow cooling until it could be blown, flattened out, or molded into finished articles.

Pre-Revolutionary glass included three major types: green glass for bottles and windows, soda glass for transparent or clear surfaces, and lead (flint) glass for the finest decorative or serving wares. Metallic oxides and other chemical agents added artificial color. Until the 1760s, the colonies produced little glass besides the sturdy, cheap, and unattractive green variety.

Large-scale glass manufacture only began in 1739 when Caspar Wistar built a factory at Alloway, New Jersey. The Wistar works imported German craftsworkers and eventually included two furnaces, two flatting ovens, a cutting house, two pottery mills, a store, and eleven dwellings for the manager and indentured servants. Wistar and his son Richard maintained production for forty years, and several of their employees then built Stanger's Glass House (nearby Glassboro) and carried on the South Jersey glassmaking tradition beyond 1800.

TABLE 4.162 GLASS PRODUCTION IN THE THIRTEEN COLONIES, 1608–1754

Dates	Proprietors and Location	Products
1608–1609?	Eight Dutch and Polish artisans work glasshouse for Virginia Co. at Jamestown. Works reported to have fallen into decay by 1617.	Unknown
1622–1625?	Capt. Norton and six Italians operated glasshouse at Jamestown to make goods for Indian trade.	Beads, Bottles?
1641–1643?	Obadiah Holmes, Lawrence Southwick, and Annanias Concklin operated glasshouse at Salem, Mass.	Unknown
1650–1674?	Johannes Smedes built glasshouse at New Amsterdam. Sold in 1664 and possibly continued by Jansens.	Unknown
1650?–1674?	Evert Duycking built glasshouse at New Amsterdam. Possibly succeeded by Jacob Milyer, whose family may have produced glass past 1700.	Unknown
1683–1693?	Free Society of Traders built glasshouse at Shackamaxson, Pa., 1 mile north of Philadelphia, to be run by glassblower Joshua Tittery.	Windows, bottles, hollow ware
1739–1780	Casper Wistar built glass furnace at Alloway Creek, Salem Co., N.J. Operation taken over by son Richard in 1752.	Windows, bottles, hollow ware
1750?–1756	Peter Etter, Joseph Crellins, and Norton Quincy build glasshouse at Braintree, Mass. Leased in 1752 to Joseph Palmer and burned in 1756.	Bottles
1752–1767?	Mathew Earnest, Ludwick Bamper, Samuel Bayard, and Christian Hertel built glasshouse at New York.	Bottles
1752–1785?	M. Earnest, L. Bamper, S. Bayard, and C. Hertel built glasshouse at New Windsor, Ulster Co., N.Y. Hertel managed works.	Windows, bottles
1754?	Ludwick Bamper built glassworks at Brooklyn, N.Y.	Bottles

Source: George S. and Helen McKearin, *American Glass* (1941), 584.

Gunmaking

Firearms production remained small scale and did not progress beyond the handicraft stage prior to 1763. Gunsmithing tended to pass from master to apprentice, and it often descended from father to son. When English gunmaker Eltweed Pomeroy emigrated to Massachusetts in 1630, for instance, he began a tradition of manufacturing weapons that continued in his family for two centuries. The Waters family of Millbury also made guns for about 200 years in Massachusetts.

Anglo-American arms production differed fundamentally from practices in Europe. European artisans specialized in making only a few gun components—such as stocks or barrels—at their own homes and then sold the pieces to an armorer who put the weapon together at the armorer's shop. American gunsmiths mastered every aspect of the profession and completed all necessary parts at their own workplaces. All work was done by hand because machine tools that could mass-produce parts had not yet been developed.

Colonial gunsmiths produced two basic types of firearms: smoothbore muskets and spiral-bore rifles. Despite their superior accuracy, rifles were rarely used outside Germany during the 1700s. Because few British gunsmiths had experience making rifled barrels, the gunsmithing tradition of most colonies was limited to musket production. Only three riflemakers have been identified as being established in New England prior to the Revolution.

Riflemaking developed almost exclusively in Pennsylvania because of the emigration of many riflesmiths among the large numbers of Germans and Swiss who settled there. Between 1725 and 1775, Penn-

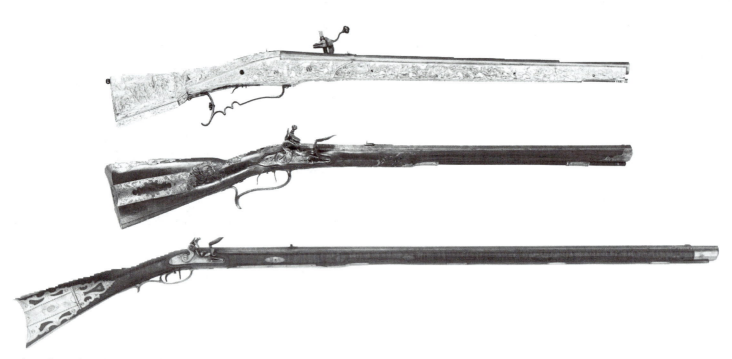

These photos show the ancestry of the Kentucky rifle. Typical of late sixteenth-century central European weapons is the Schnitzel wheelock rifle at top. Pennsylvania Dutch gunsmiths began to make more accurate firearms through improvements on early eigtheenth-century German Jaegar rifles, like that shown in the middle. The fully evolved Kentucky rifle at bottom is 58 inches long and has a 42-inch, .44-caliber octagon barrel, with curly maple stock and decorative brass work. (Courtesy National Museum of American History, Smithsonian Institution, negatives 60094–A, P64124, 75,940)

TABLE 4.163   EQUIPMENT NEEDED TO OPERATE A PENNSYLVANIA RIFLEMAKING SHOP

Blacksmithing Equipment	Gunsmithing Tools
1 forge	rifling engine
forging tools	bits and floats
2 bellows	2 small hacks
1 anvil	2 saw frames
1 beck iron	12 smooth files
5 pairs tongs	2 rasps
2 soddering irons	8 bench hammers
polishing leath	1 ax and hatchet
6 vises	2 saw frames
2 vise claps	12 large screw plates
3 vise wedges	1 small screw plate
	2 pairs nippers
	1 compass saw
	1 square
	6 double trickers
	2 casting tool picks
	1 grindstone
	reamers
	needsfoot oil
	britchen tools
	6 pairs pliers
	7 pairs compasses
	1 large stillyards
	2 draw knives
	4 rammer bits
	1 saw
	stocking tools
	stock drill
	tumbler tool
	2 pairs old shears
	boring mill
	boring rods
	3 saw plates
	1 bullet mold
	2 spring locks
	punches
	barrel guage
	9 planes

Source: Inventory of Matthius Roessor, 1771, in Henry J. Kauffman, *The Pennsylvania–Kentucky Rifle* (1960), 147.

sylvania gunmakers modified the Jaeger, the basic rifle used for hunting big game in central Europe, which had a short barrel of about 36 inches, a large caliber (.60–.75), and was very heavy at the breech. To meet the needs of American pioneers, this weapon's barrel was increased to about 48 inches, its bore was reduced below .60 (sometimes to .35), and the barrel's breech was decreased in bulk. Pennsylvania riflesmiths continued to use octagonal (eight-sided) barrels, extend stocks nearly to the muzzle, provide a covered recess for greased bullet-patches in the butt, and mount inlayed brass ornamentation. The resulting firearm was not only exceptionally accurate, well balanced, and functional but also charactized by superb craftsmanship in wood carving and metal decoration.

Originally known as a Dutch or Pennsylvania gun, this firearm later became popularized as the Kentucky long rifle for its vital role in the settlement of that frontier. The Kentucky rifle's development represented a remarkable achievement of the areas of ballistics, graceful design, and artistic ornamentation. As the colonial era ended, Pennsylvania's gunmakers were the world's most technologically advanced riflesmiths. "I never in my life saw better rifles (or men who shot better)," observed English officer George Hanger during this golden age of gunmaking, "than those made in America."

Papermaking

Domestic demand for paper remained inadequate to justify the expense of establishing mills, which required waterpower, some relatively complex machines, a steady supply of rags or linen, and more employees than a family could usually muster by itself. William and Klaus Rittenhouse built the earliest colonial paper mill in 1690 at the urging of a printer, William Bradford, who needed a steady supply of newsprint. The Rittenhouse works on Wissahickon Creek near Philadelphia washed away during a flood in 1700, but they were rebuilt, later expanded by Gerard DeWees, and operated by DeWees's descendants past 1800.

Even as American presses and newspapers grew in number, the construction of paper mills lagged behind the need for printing materials. Seventeen paperworks were built in the seventy years after the Ritten-

TABLE 4.164 PAPER MILLS ESTABLISHED IN THE THIRTEEN COLONIES, 1690–1761

Built	Location	Proprietors	Ceased Operations
1690	Wissahickon Creek Philadelphia Co., Pa.	William and Klaus Rittenhouse	sold 1710
1710	Wissahickon Creek Philadelphia Co., Pa.	Gerard DeWees bought and expanded Rittenhouse mill	1815?
1726?	Elizabeth, N. J.	William Bradford	1740?
1728	Dorchester (now Milton), Mass.	Daniel Henchman, Gillam Phillips, Thomas Hancock, Benjamin Faneuil	1776+
1731	Falmouth, Me.	Samuel Waldo, Thomas Westbrook, Richard Fry	1736
1736	Ephrata, Pa.	Jacob and Samuel Funk	...
1739	Sandy Run Montgomery Co., Pa.	Jacob Calliday	...
1744	Archer's Hope Creek James City Co., Va.	William Parks	1752?
1747	Springfield Twsp., Bucks Co., Pa.	Anthony Newhouse	1752
1747	Amity Twsp., Berks Co., Pa.	Daniel Womelsdorf	1784
1750?	Lower Merion Twsp. Philadelphia Co., Pa.	William Sheetz	1771?
1752	Whitemarsh Philadelphia Co., Pa.	Jacob Hagy	...
1757	Montgomery Co., Pa.	Nicholas Hasselbach	...
1758	Montgomery Co., Pa.	John and Christopher Roberts	...
1758	Spotswood, N. J.	Frederick Roemer	...
1760	Whitemarsh Philadelphia Co., Pa.	Andrew Katz	1812
1760	Springfield Twsp., Bucks Co., Pa.	Michael Schlatter	1776
1761	Mill Creek, Montgomery Co., Pa.	Frederick Bicking	...

Source: Dard Hunter, *Papermaking in Pioneer America* (1952), 140–169.

house mill's construction in 1690, and most of these failed after a few years. By 1763 there were two primary centers of paper production in the colonies, near Boston, Massachusetts, and around Philadelphia, Pennsylvania. As the Revolutionary era began, Americans remained essentially dependent on British imports for their writing and printing needs. Although still in its infancy, papermaking would shortly begin a period of major expansion in response to the growing readership of newspapers and political pamphlets during the Revolutionary era.

Shoemaking

Shoemaking remained a highly decentralized industry through the colonial period. In 1648, Massachusetts Bay awarded a legislative charter to Boston's cobblers, who then gained the right to set and enforce professional standards. Cordwainers outside major metropolises normally worked free of any external constraints aside from the need to satisfy their clients. Most shoemakers labored at home, and their busi-

TABLE 4.165 PRICES OF SHOES IN SPRINGFIELD, MASS., 1648–1688

Date	Price per Pair	Type Footwear
1672–1688	7½–8½s	men's shoes
1672	7s	girls' shoes
1666–1671	7½–8½s	men's shoes
1660–1666	4½–5s	women's shoes
1660	3½s	boys' shoes
1653	6⅓s	shoes
1648	½–1s	shoes

Source: Stephen Innes, *Labor in a New Land: Economy and Society in Seventeenth-Century Springfield* (1983), 229–459.

ness varied according to customer demand, but some masters operated small shops with apprentices and journeymen who produced a surplus that was marketed by itinerant peddlers in the countryside. An experienced cobbler seems to have been able to make a pair of common shoes in a day and to produce a pair with linings in an extended workday.

Like most other types of small-scale manufacturing, shoemaking's economic aspects have been little studied for the years before 1763. Little effort has been expended to determine how much capital was needed to open a cobbler's shop, the costs of overhead and wages, prices fluctuations for footwear, average profit margins for the trade, and the division of the domestic market between imports and home manufactures. This lack of knowledge is highly unfortunate because, although the British colonies remained net importers of footwear until after independence, shoemaking constituted one of early America's largest occupational groups outside of agriculture.

TABLE 4.166 THE ESSENTIAL TOOLS AND PROCEDURES OF COLONIAL SHOEMAKING

Two Basic Parts of Shoe
a sole and an upper.
Nine Essential Tools
last (foot-shaped block), knife, awl, needle and cord, pincers, hammer, nails or pegs, lapstone, stirrup.
Four Basic Processes
1. *Cutting.* After pounding leather upon lapstone with a hammer, cut out sole and upper from leather.
2. *Fitting.* Bore holes through sole and upper with an awl, and then sew together.
3. *Lasting.* Slip sewed parts over a foot-shaped block, or last—which had an insole tacked to it—form tightly with pincers, and fasten temporarily with nails. (Last was held in place by a stirrup or strap passing between cobbler's knees, where shoe rested, to his feet, which held the stirrup firm.)
4. *Bottoming.* Permanently fix upper to sole by sewing or pegging.

Source: Blanche Evans Hazard, *The Organization of the Boot and Shoe Industry in Massachusetts Before 1875* (1921), 3–4.

Woodworking Industries

Early Americans depended so heavily on timber for their building materials, storage containers, and furniture that they could truly be described as inhabiting a "wooden age." Because the rapidly growing English colonies required a constant expansion in their stock of housing and home furnishings, and because virtually all their exports were shipped in barrels or hogsheads, carpentry and cooperage must have been especially vital components of their domestic economy. Few

TABLE 4.167 ESTIMATED HOUSING CONSTRUCTION IN THE THIRTEEN COLONIES, 1650–1759

Decade	Population Increase	Dwellings Added	Dwellings Replaced (10% of Existing Stock)	Total
1750–59	422,865	83,400	26,200	109,200
1740–49	265,197	52,300	17,860	70,160
1730–39	276,118	54,460	12,410	66,870
1720–29	163,260	32,200	9,190	41,390
1710–19	134,474	26,520	6,540	33,060
1700–09	80,823	15,940	4,950	20,890
1690–99	40,516	7,990	4,150	12,140
1680–89	58,865	11,610	2,990	14,600
1670–79	39,572	7,800	2,200	10,150
1660–69	36,877	7,270	1,480	8,750
1650–59	24,690	4,870	990	5,860

Source: Estimate of 5.07 persons per dwelling from Samuel Blodget, *Economica: A Statistical Manual for the United States of America* (1806), 58. Jack P. Greene, ed., *Settlements to Society, 1584–1763* (1966), 238.

studies nevertheless examine the cooperage or construction industries, and these few generally approach their subjects in an antiquarian fashion that ignores questions about gross levels of production, the monetary value of total output, and the size of their respective workforces. Housing and barrel making employed more artisans than any other trades, and until these topics are examined systematically, one of the largest sectors of early America's economy will remain a mystery.

TABLE 4.168 CARPENTRY WAGES AND HOUSING COSTS IN SPRINGFIELD, MASS., 1655–1694

Year(s)	Wages and Costs
1694	£4.15.0 to groundsill barn
1679	£14 to build 22×17×8 foot school
1678	£1 to lay barn floor
1678	£20 to build 28×20×10 foot house
1678	£14 to build 24×18 foot log house
1677	£140 to build meeting house with gallery
1674	£25 and 2 gal. rum to build 46×24 foot barn
1674	2s per day for daubing chimney
1673–74	£20 to build and shingle 46×24 foot barn
1672	£4.10.0 to build small room & groundsill parlor
1663	6d per foot to groundsill barn
1663	3s per day for plastering
1662	£18 & two weeks board to build 46×11 foot barn (with carpenter providing most materials)
1661–72	£5–£7 for building brick chimney
1661	1s per day for apprentice's work
1659–69	17$\frac{1}{2}$s–20s per 1,000 bricks
1659–69	13s–14s per 100 pavements
1658–72	2$\frac{1}{2}$s–5s per day for finishing work & carpentry
1658	2s–2$\frac{1}{2}$s for daubing chimney
1657	£21 for building 50×24 foot barn
1655–59	2$\frac{1}{2}$s–4s for building brick oven

Source: Stephen Innes, *Labor in a New Land: Economy and Society in Seventeenth-Century Springfield* (1983), 229–459.

TABLE 4.169 EXPENSES OF WOODEN CONTAINERS IN SPRINGFIELD, MASS. 1658–1664

Year(s)	Expenses
1659–80	2$\frac{1}{2}$s–4 1.2s per barrel
1658–64	4s–4$\frac{1}{2}$s per beer barrel
1664	3$\frac{1}{2}$s per cider barrel
1659	£5 for a cider press
1658	5$\frac{1}{2}$s per hogshead
1658	1$\frac{1}{2}$s per milking pail

Source: Stephen Innes, *Labor in a New Land: Economy and Society in Seventeenth-Century Springfield* (1983), 229–459.

TABLE 4.170 BARRELS AND OTHER CONTAINERS USED IN EXPORT TRADE, 1690–1760

Year	Tobacco[a] (Hogsheads)	Rice (Barrels)	Flax (Hogsheads)	Naval Stores (Barrels)
1760	84,557	67,290	21,226	9,157
1750	69,291	54,745	3,719	15,827
1740	41,305	96,280	10,408	14,390
1730	50,750	41,722	…	13,912
1720	43,150	14,410[b]	…	34,553
1710	31,180	3,560[b]	…	5,484
1700	47,300	875[b]	…	…
1690	25,280	…	…	…

[a] Weight of hogshead estimated at 1,000 lb., 1740–1760, 800 lb., 1700–1730, and 500 lb., 1690.
[b] Estimated at 450 lb. per barrel.
Source: Tables 4.42, 4.52, 4.70, 4.71, 4.104, 4.107.

Mining

Mining developed slowly in Anglo-America primarily because few English colonists had any practical experience at prospecting. Besides their difficulty in identifying significant ore deposits from outcroppings or excavations, the colonists possessed little knowledge of assaying the quality of rocks with metallic content, even though that science was well advanced in Europe by 1600. Initial efforts to find valuable minerals focused on gold, but even these attempts failed to locate the modest deposits of gold then existing in North Carolina and Georgia, and the discovery of other likely sites for mining resulted from accidents rather than deliberate prospecting.

Although iron smelting emerged as a major enterprise by 1730, this industry did not rely on mining for its ore. Not until 1750 were subterranean deposits of iron found in western Connecticut, and their contribution to colonial iron production was minor. Most forges and furnaces used brown limonite, or bog iron, which was dug from the numerous marshes or ponds near the Atlantic coast. Brown limonite was a mineral residue leached from iron-rich salts seeping through ground strata; it was a self-renewing resource that could replenish itself about every twenty years if the recovery process did not disturb the original patterns of soil and drainage.

Large copper reserves lay in the mountains just beyond the colonial frontier, but Dutch and English settlers began to stumble on small deposits in Massachusetts and New Jersey during the 1600s. The first major recovery efforts dated from 1709 when Connecticut chartered a company to exploit the copper veins at Simsbury (now East Granby). Connecticut copper was also excavated at Bristol, Cheshire, and Wallingford. About 1713 a slave discovered copper near the Hackensack marshes (now North Arlington) of New Jersey on the Schuyler estate. By 1721, the Schuyler mine's output had reached 22 tons, the greatest level of production known for any colonial copper operation. Other copper mines appeared near New Brunswick, New Jersey, and in two Maryland counties.

Only the copper industry made any extensive use of underground mining. A shaft in the Simsbury mine was 70 feet deep and some tunnels extended several hundred feet. The Schuyler mine reached down

TABLE 4.171 COPPER MINES OPERATED IN THE THIRTEEN COLONIES, 1660–1771

Year Opened	Location	Opened by	Operational Until
1660?	Delaware River Water Gap Pahaquarry, N.J.	Dutch	to 1664?
1709?	East Granby, Conn.	Simsbury Co.	to 1773
1712?	Wallingford, Conn.	…	to 1740?
1717	North Arlington, N.J.	Arent Schuyler	to 1770
1718	Woodbury, Conn.[a]	…	…
1724	York Co., Pa.	Sir William Keith	…
1728	Fairfax Co., Va.[a]	Robert Carter and Frying Pan Co.	to 1732?
1732	Gap Mine York Co., Pa.	Lewis Morris, William Allen, Thomas Penn	by 1755
1733	Prince George Co., Va.	Drury Stith and Cornelius Cargill	…
1735?	Soho Mine Belleville, N.J.	John Dod	to 1770?
1737	Rocky Hill Mine Griggstown, N.J.	John Stevens, William Allen, Thomas Penn	to 1770?
1748	New Brunswick, N.J.	Philip French	to 1770?
1760?	Amherst Co., Va.	…	by 1787
1760?	Buckingham Co., Va.	…	by 1787
1771?	Topsfield, Mass.	William Buntin	to 1772

[a] May have closed before significant production began.
Source: James A. Mulholland, *A History of Metals in Colonial America* (1981), 39–53.

100 feet. By eighteenth-century standards, American copper mines represented sophisticated achievements of engineering and technology. Because its depth led to continual problems with flooding, in 1755 the Schuyler mine became the first American industrial operation to operate an imported English steam engine, which pumped its tunnels dry.

Because it was difficult to find workers with the skills needed to smelt copper, and because such operations were expensive, most colonial copper was exported as raw ore. Probably no more than 10 tons was smelted for domestic consumption. Although copper was a primary compound of brass and bronze, the colonists could not produce these alloys without local sources of zinc (for brass) and tin (for bronze). Copper mining made the colonies marginally less dependent upon outside sources of the metal, but most copper goods used in early America were evidently imported as finished products manufactured in England.

Occupational Structure

Economic and social historians have expended little energy investigating the occupational structure of England's colonies. Although the majority of early Americans worked on farms, a large nonagricultural sector existed to provide essential products and services. No systematic studies exist to measure the division of colonial labor among various professions, nor have there been any attempts to chart shifts in occupational structure over time.

By the mid-eighteenth century, farmers accounted for perhaps four-fifths of male laborers. The proportion of farmers at former periods may not have been so high because the first decades of establishing settlements required a highly varied workforce to supply buildings, construction materials, numerous crafts, food, drink, essential repairs, transportation services, and professional skills. The first permanent settlement at Jamestown, for example, included relatively few agriculturalists in 1607, while most of the Pilgrims who founded Plymouth had little prior experience working the land in Europe. Because the earliest settlements were usually crippled by a shortage of labor and scarcity of essential products, many colonists would have found it more profitable to pursue nonagricultural pursuits than to work the land. Once an economic infrastructure existed to support a large population, however, competitive forces and a rising level of efficiency would have tended to reduce profit margins for this service sector so that the attractiveness of farming would have increased and the proportion of agriculturalists in society would have risen.

TABLE 4.172 OCCUPATIONAL STRUCTURE AT JAMESTOWN, VA., 1607–1609

Occupations	Arrivals in Spring 1607		Arrivals in Spring 1608		Arrivals in Spring 1609	
	Number	(%)	Number	(%)	Number	(%)
Council Members	6	(3.3%)	1	(.5%)	2	(1.5%)
Preacher	1	(.5%)	...	...	...	...
Gentlemen	46	(25.3%)	32	(16.7%)	26	(20.6%)
Carpenters	4	(2.2%)	...	...	...	...
Laborers	12	(6.6%)	21	(11.0%)	12	(9.5%)
Blacksmith	1	(.5%)	1	(.5%)	...	...
Bricklayer	1	(.5%)	...	...	...	...
Mason	1	(.5%)	...	...	...	...
Tailor	1	(.5%)	6	(3.1%)	...	...
Surgeon	2	(1.1%)	1	(.5%)	...	...
Barber	1	(.5%)	...	...	...	...
Sailor	1	(.5%)	...	...	...	...
Drummer	1	(.5%)	...	...	...	...
"Boys"	4	(2.2%)	...	...	2	(1.5%)
Apothecaries	...	...	2	(1.0%)	...	...
Gunsmith	...	...	1	(.5%)	...	...
Cooper	...	...	1	(.5%)	...	...
Goldsmith	...	...	1	(.5%)	...	...
Jeweler	...	...	1	(.5%)	...	...
Refiner	...	...	2	(1.0%)	...	...
Perfumer	...	...	1	(.5%)	...	...
Pipemaker	...	...	1	(.5%)	...	...
"divers others"	100	(54.9%)	120	(62.5%)	84	(67.7%)

Source: John Lankford, ed., *Captain John Smith's America: Selections From His Writings* (1967), 39–40, 57–58, 86–87.

TABLE 4.173 OCCUPATIONAL DISTRIBUTION OF HEADS OF HOUSEHOLDS IN ALL HALLOW'S PARISH, ANNE ARUNDEL CO., MD., 1660–1769

Decade	Farmers	Woodworkers[a]	Leatherworkers[b]	Tailors	Innkeepers	Shopkeepers	Others
1760–69	88.7%	1.4%	1.7%	.7%	.3%	3.1%	4.1%
1750–59	90.3%	2.2%	.4%	1.1%	.4%	3.3%	2.3%
1740–49	90.4%	.8%	1.2%	.8%	.4%	4.8%	1.6%
1730–39	84.2%	4.4%	1.7%	.4%	.9%	6.1%	2.3%
1720–29	88.6%	1.4%	.5%	...	1.0%	6.2%	2.3%
1710–19	84.0%	3.2%	.5%	1.6%	1.6%	7.0%	2.1%
1700–09	93.9%	1.7%	.6%	...	.6%	1.1%	2.1%
1690–99	94.9%	...	...	...	.7%	2.7%	1.7%
1680–89	91.7%	.8%	...	.8%	...	4.2%	2.5%
1660–79	89.0%	2.0%	...	2.0%	1.0%	4.0%	1.0%

[a] Carpenters, coopers, joiners, boatwrights, sawyers.
[b] Shoemakers, tanners, sadlers, hatters, furriers.
Source: Carville V. Earle, *The Evolution of a Tidewater Settlement System: All Hallow's Parish, Maryland, 1650–1783* (1975), 65–66.

TABLE 4.174 OCCUPATIONAL DISTRIBUTION IN TALBOT CO., MD., 1690–1759

Decade	Farmers	Craftsworkers
1750–59	90%	10%
1740–49	86%	14%
1730–39	81%	19%
1720–29	79%	21%
1710–19	80%	20%
1700–09	80%	20%
1690–99	98%	2%

Source: Jean B. Russo, "Self-Sufficiency and Local Exchange: Free Craftsmen in the Rural Chesapeake Economy," in Lois G. Carr, Philip D. Morgan, and Jean B. Russo, eds., *Colonial Chesapeake Society* (1988), 424.

TABLE 4.175 DISTRIBUTION OF CRAFTSWORKERS IN TALBOT CO., MD., 1690–1759

Craft Group	1740–1759	1720–1739	1690–1719
Carpenters	26%	28%	32%
Ship carpenters	6%	5%	6%
Coopers	4%	9%	10%
Sawyers	5%	6%	6%
Joiners	8%	7%	2%
Wheelwrights	3%	2%	3%
Misc. woodworkers	4%	2%	1%
Tailors	8%	6%	9%
Weavers	8%	7%	7%
Shoemakers	8%	11%	8%
Tanners	2%	2%	3%
Sadlers	1%	…	1%
Blacksmiths	9%	8%	5%
Misc. metalworkers	1%	1%	1%
Bricklayers–makers	5%	3%	3%
Plasters–glaziers	2%	1%	2%
Misc. crafts	…	2%	1%

Source: Jean B. Russo, "Self-Sufficiency and Local Exchange: Free Craftsmen in the Rural Chesapeake Economy," in Lois G. Carr, Philip D. Morgan, and Jean B. Russo, eds., *Colonial Chesapeake Society* (1988), 396–397.

TABLE 4.176 OCCUPATIONS OF PERSONS NAMED IN NEW JERSEY WILLS, 1670–1730

Occupation	Number	(%)
Farmers	519	(50.5%)
Carpenters	50	(4.8%)
Joiners, sawyers, misc. wrights	22	(2.1%)
Ropemakers	48	(4.7%)
Smiths	45	(4.4%)
Tailors	45	(4.4%)
Weavers	35	(3.4%)
Mariners	33	(3.2%)
Coopers	31	(3.0%)
Masons, bricklayers, brickmakers	24	(2.3%)
Innkeepers	23	(2.2%)
Shoemakers	14	(1.4%)
Tanners, curriers	12	(1.2%)
Potters, glaziers, turners	12	(1.2%)
Teachers	8	(.8%)
Sadlers	7	(.7%)
Hatters, feltmakers	5	(.5%)
Cooks, bakers	4	(.4%)
Butchers	4	(.4%)
Fullers, dyers	4	(.4%)
Millers	4	(.4%)
Glovers	3	(.3%)
Brewers	3	(.3%)
Vintners	2	(.2%)
Candlemakers	2	(.2%)

TABLE 4.176 (continued)

Occupation	Number	(%)
Barbers	2	(.2%)
Wigmaker	1	(.1%)
Servants	35	(3.4%)
Laborers	24	(2.3%)
Apprentices	7	(.7%)
Total	1,028	(100%)

Note: Merchants, lawyers, and doctors were unable to be calculated because of multiple listings for a few individuals.
Source: William A. Whitehead, et al., eds., *Archives of the State of New Jersey* (1880–1949), Ser. 1, XXIII, 659–660.

TABLE 4.177 OCCUPATIONS OF PERSONS WRITING WILLS IN NEW JERSEY, 1751–1770

County	Agriculture No.	Agriculture %	Crafts & Business No.	Crafts & Business %	Professional Classes No.	Professional Classes %	Government Officials No.	Government Officials %
Bergen	87	87.0%	11	11.0%	…	…	2	2.0%
Essex	218	74.1%	64	21.8%	8	2.7%	4	1.4%
Middlesex	198	78.5%	42	16.7%	6	2.4%	6	2.4%
Monmouth	207	85.9%	31	12.9%	2	.8%	1	.4%
Morris	110	85.1%	10	7.8%	3	2.3%	6	4.7%
Somerset	129	80.1%	19	11.8%	9	5.6%	4	2.5%
Sussex	55	88.7%	7	11.3%	…	…	…	…
Burlington	286	80.6%	63	17.7%	2	.6%	4	1.1%
Gloucester	217	86.8%	29	11.6%	2	.8%	2	.8%
Hunterdon	252	86.0%	36	13.3%	5	1.7%	…	…
Cumberland	136	85.0%	21	13.1%	3	1.9%	…	…
Salem	187	83.5%	34	15.2%	…	…	3	1.3%
Cape May	59	84.3%	8	11.4%	1	1.4%	2	2.9%
Totals	2,141	82.6%	375	14.5%	41	1.6%	34	1.3%

Source: Donald J. Mrozek, "Problems of Social History and Patterns of Inheritance in Pre-Revolutionary New Jersey, 1751–1770," *Journal of the Rutgers University Library,* XXXVI (1972), 13.

TABLE 4.178 OCCUPATIONS OF NEW YORK CITY TAXPAYERS, 1703

Occupation	Number	Percent
Widow	136	21.2%
Merchant	110	17.2%
Master	55	8.6%
Carpenter	41	6.4%
Shoemaker	38	5.9%
Mariner	31	4.8%
Gentleman	26	4.1%
Cooper	24	3.7%
Brickmaker	24	3.7%
Baker	24	3.7%
Shipwright	21	3.3%
Victualler	20	3.1%
Flour bolter	13	2.0%
Carman	13	2.0%
Blacksmith	12	1.9%
Tailor	10	1.6%
Butcher	9	1.4%
Doctor	8	1.2%
Silversmith	7	1.1%
Goldsmith	7	1.1%
Bellringer	7	1.1%
Yeoman	5	.8%

Source: Thomas J. Archdeacon, *New York City, 1664–1710: Conquest and Change* (1976), 52.

TABLE 4.179 CRAFTSWORKERS AS PERCENT OF NEW YORK'S MUNICIPAL CITIZENS, 1700–1776

Occupation	Number	(%) Enrolled as Citizens
Woodworkers	740	(17.0%)
Leatherworkers	536	(13.0%)
Metalworkers	262	(6.0%)
Millers and Bakers	201	(4.7%)
Shipbuilders	196	(4.8%)
Building trades	155	(3.5%)
Other occupations	2,103	(51.0%)

Source: Carl Bridenbaugh, *The Colonial Craftsman* (1961 ed.), 95.

TABLE 4.180 OCCUPATIONS LISTED IN BOSTON, MASS., INVENTORIES, 1685–1775

Occupation	Number	Percent
Government Officials	12	.4%
Professional Trades (30 doctors, 6 lawyers, 10 ministers, 12 teachers, 16 musicians or painters)	77	2.8%
Retailers (9 booksellers/binders, 14 chandlers, 17 grocers, 8 peddlers or hucksters)	48	1.7%
Retail Crafts (29 bakers, 15 butchers, 137 shopkeepers, 67 tailors, 7 tobacconists or snuffmakers)	255	9.2%
Building Trades (18 brickmen, 81 carpenters, 14 masons, 23 joiners, 9 glaziers, 8 painters)	153	5.5%
Blacksmiths, carters, innkeepers, porters	115	4.2%
Laborers, wigmakers, barbers, sawyers	65	2.3%
Textile and leather workers, shoemakers	123	4.4%
Brewers, millers, sugarboilers, bolters	50	1.8%
Shipwrights, ropemakers, sailmakers	116	4.2%
Metal crafts, clockmakers, gunsmiths	69	2.5%
Furniture makers, upholsterers	32	1.2%
Merchants	488	17.6%
Sea captains, pilots	153	5.5%
Common sailors	494	17.9%
Coopers	61	2.2%
Farmers, gardeners, yeomen	45	1.6%
Spinsters and widows	427	15.4%
Miscellaneous	57	2.0%

Source: Gary B. Nash, *The Urban Crucible: Social Change, Political Consciousness, and the Origins of the American Revolution* (1979), 387–391.

Wages and Income

Few subjects have greater potential to illuminate broads trends in colonial economic history than a reliable series of prevailing wage rates over time. Information regarding daily pay and yearly income would be of immense value for understanding changes in early America's standard of living, identifying periods when prospects for upward mobility were best, and charting the impact of short-term fluctuations in economic growth. A great variety of data exists on which tables of wages can be compiled, but few economic historians have exploited this material in any systematic fashion, except for selected communities and for relatively short periods. A history of incomes would enormously broaden the present ability to understand early American economic development.

A general consensus exists that wages were higher in Anglo-America, where labor was generally scarce, than in England, where workers were in less demand. This generalization was perhaps most accurate for the earliest decades of colonization and for frontier areas undergoing rapid development and less true for long-settled regions with large

The legal profession was small in early America, but its members probably enjoyed the highest per capita income of any occupational group, with the exception of rice planters. This photo shows the octagonal law office of attorney John Jones, at Salem, New Jersey. (Historic American Buildings Survey, Courtesy Library of Congress)

populations. A surplus of labor also developed in the largest seaports by the Revolutionary era, when many urban workers, in particular those with few skills, evidently found their standard of living squeezed by low pay. In general, however, wages were sufficiently high to allow landless families to accumulate savings for a mortgage and to enjoy a comfortable style of living by eighteenth-century standards.

TABLE 4.181 WAGE RATES FOR DAY LABOR IN VIRGINIA AND ENGLAND, 1600–1640

Year	Virginia Wages	English Wages
ca. 1600	...	30–50s per year[b]
1614	2s per day (laborers)	1s per day[b]
1621	2s per day[a] (laborers) 2s per day[a] (master tailors) 3s per day[a] (master craftsmen)[c] 5s per day[a] (master joiners) Servants of master craftsmen to earn 1/4 less than their masters	1s per day[b] ... ...
ca. 1640	2½s per day (10 lb. tobacco)[d]	1s per day[b]

[a] Increased by 1s if food unfurnished.
[b] Includes 6d per workday for victuals.
[c] Master bricklayers, carpenters, coopers, masons, shipwrights.
[d] Doubled if food unfurnished.
Source: Edmund B. Morgan, *American Slavery, American Freedom: The Ordeal of Colonial Virginia* (1975), 94, 106–107, 179. Richard B. Morris, *Government and Labor in Early America* (1965), 87.

TABLE 4.182 MAXIMUM DAILY WAGES SET BY MASSACHUSETTS BAY LEGISLATURE, 1633

Occupation	With Victuals	Without Victuals
Mowers, carpenters, sawyers, masons, bricklayers, thatchers, joiners, clapboard rivers, wheelwrights,	14d	24d
Master Tailors	12d	22d
Journeymen Tailors	8d	18d
"best sorte of [common] labourers"	8d	18d
common laborers	(wage set at town level, plus 10d for victuals)	

Source: Richard B. Morris, *Government and Labor in Early America* (1965), 59.

TABLE 4.183 MINIMUM WAGES AS FIXED BY LAW IN NEW HAVEN COLONY, 1640–1641

	1640		1641	
Jobs	Summer	Winter	Summer	Winter
Skilled workmen	30d	24d	24d	20d
Journeymen, skilled trades	24d	20d	20d	16d
Farmers and laborers	24d	18d	18d	14d
Sawing 100 boards	54d	…	44d	…
Sawing 100 planks	60d	…	48d	…
Sawing for slitwork	66d	…	54d	…
Sawing, top man, by day	30d	…	24d	…
Sawing, pitman, by day	24d	…	18d	…
Felling 18–24 ft. timber	2d per ft.	…	1½d per ft.	…
Felling over 24 in. timber	3d per ft.	…	2½d per ft.	…
Hewing-squaring timber	18d per tun	…	15d per tun	…
Hewing sills, beams, plates	1d per ft.	…	…	…
Mowing salt marsh, by acre	36d	…	42d	…
Mowing fresh marsh, by acre	30d	…	36d	…
Thatching	30d per day	…	…	…
Fencing with pales	24d per rod	…	18d per rod	…
Fencing, with five rails	24d per rod	…	18d per rod	…
Fencing with three rails	18d per rod	…	14d per rod	…
Lime work, by the bushel	9d	…	7d	…
Lime work, by the hogshead	60d	…	48d	…

Source: Richard B. Morris, *Government and Labor in Early America* (1965), 79–80.

TABLE 4.184 WAGES PAID BY DUTCH WEST INDIA CO. IN NEW NETHERLAND, 1645

Employee	Yearly Wage	
	Florins	(Sterling)
Director	F3,000	(£270)
Vice Director	F1,440	(£130)
Captain	F720	(£65)
Ensign	F540	(£50)
Sergeant	F300	(£27)
Corporal	F216	(£20)
Private	F156	(£14)
Clergyman	F1,440	(£130)
Chief Clerk	F720	(£65)
Schoolmaster	F360	(£33)
Doctor	F300	(£27)
Skipper	F300	(£27)
Gunsmith	F180	(£16)
Sailor	F156	(£14)

Note: Eleven florins (or guilders) equaled about £1 sterling.
Source: Edmund B. O'Callaghan, *History of New Netherland; or New York under the Dutch,* 2 vols. (1845), I, 351–352.

TABLE 4.185 ANNUAL WAGES PAID AT RENSSELAER-SWICK, NEW NETHERLAND, 1630–1644

Occupation	Lowest (Florins)	Highest (Florins)	Wage in Netherlands (Florins)
Farm servant	F80	F110	F84
Farm laborer	F30	F32	[no data]
Foreman	F140	F140	F100
Shoemaker	F40	F100	F65
Carpenter's boy	F40	F40	F25
Journeyman carpenter	F120	F120	F115
Master carpenter	F550	F550	F410
Cooper	F90	F168	F200
Servant	F25	F140	no data
Minister	F1,000	F1,200	F1,000

Source: Oliver A. Rink, *Holland on the Hudson: An Economic and Social History of Dutch New York* (1986), 153.

TABLE 4.186 DAILY AND MONTHLY WAGES OF MARYLAND FARM LABORERS, 1638–1676

Year	Monthly Wages (Including Room & Board)			Daily Wages (Including Two Meals)		
	In Tobacco	Value	Wages	In Tobacco	Value	Wages
1676	300 lb.	1.0d/lb.	25s	…	…	…
1670	175 lb.	1.5d/lb.	21s	…	…	…
1669	200 lb.	1.5d/lb.	25s	20 lb.	1.5d/lb.	2s,6d
1667	600 lb.	0.5d/lb.	25s	…	…	…
1662	266 lb.	1.2d/lb.	26s,8d	…	…	…
1660	225 lb.	1.0d/lb.	18s, 9d	…	…	…
1656	…	…	…	15 lb.	2.0d/lb.	2s,6d
1655	…	…	…	22.5 lb.	2.0d/lb.	3s,9d
1654	600 lb.	2.0d/lb.	100s	…	…	…
1652	600 lb.	2.0d/lb.	100s	…	…	…
1649	…	…	…	10 lb.	3.0d/lb.	2s,6d
1648	250 lb.	2.0d/lb.	41s,8d	15 lb.	2.0d/lb.	2s,6d
1647	170 lb.	1.5d/lb.	21s,3d	20 lb.	1.5d/lb.	2s,6d
1645	170 lb.	1.5d/lb.	21s,3d	…	…	…
1644	160 lb.	1.2d/lb.	16s	10 lb.	1.2d/lb.	1s
1642	100 lb.	0.6d/lb.	5s	15 lb.	0.6d/lb.	9d
1641	…	…	…	20 lb.	1.2d/lb.	2s
1638	…	…	8s,4d	…	…	…

Note: Wages were quoted in tobacco, at existing prices.
Source: Manfred Jonas, "Wages in Early Colonial Maryland," *Maryland Historical Magazine,* LI (1956), 34–35.

TABLE 4.187 WAGE RATES PROPOSED BY BILLS IN MASSACHUSETTS ASSEMBLY, 1670, 1672

Work Description	1670 Daily Wage	1672 Daily Wage
Laborers, for 10-hour day, without victuals		
Oct. 1 to Mar. 31	15d	same
Apr. 1 to Jun. 30	20d	same
Jul. 1 to Sep. 30	24d	same
For each task performed, without victuals		
mowing 1 acre salt marsh or grass	24d	same
reaping 1 acre of wheat	48d	60d
reaping 1 acre of rye	36d	same
mowing 1 acre of barley or oats	12d	same
cutting 1 acre of peas	36d	30d
cutting 1 cord of wood	15d	same
Craftsmen without victuals, Mar. 1 to Oct. 10 carpenters, masons, stonelayers	24d	same

Work Description	1670 Daily Wage	1672 Daily Wage
Cloth workers, for 12-hour day, without food		
master tailors and master weavers	20d	same
tailors and weavers with less than four years experience	12d	same
Shoemakers, coopers, smiths		
men's shoes size 11 or 12	60d	48d
women's shoes size 7 to 8	44d	36d
32-gallon barrel	32d	same
heavy iron work, per lb.	5d	4½d
light iron work, per lb.	6d	5½d
setting horseshoe of 7 nails	6d	5½d
removing horseshoe	2d	1½d
felling axe	42d	36d
broad axe	66d	54d
broad hoe	36d	30d

Note: Above wage rates not enacted into law.
Source: Richard B. Morris, *Government and Labor in Early America* (1965), 65–68.

TABLE 4.188   MARINER'S MONTHLY WAGES IN ENGLAND AND NEW ENGLAND, 1651–1700

Position	Peacetime (per Month)		Wartime (per Month)	
	New England	England	New England	England
Master	120s	120s	120s	120s
Chief mate	80s	78s	90s	90s
Sailor	35–55s	39s	60–75s	72s

Source: Terry L. Anderson, *The Economic Growth of Seventeenth-Century New England: A Measurement of Regional Income* (1975), 39.

TABLE 4.189   WAGES AND COMPENSATION IN MASSACHUSETTS, 1650–1709

Year	Seamen's Wages (Shillings/Month)	Seamen's Wages[a] plus Victuals (£ per Year)	Artisans' Wages[b] (£ per Year)
1700–09	25.55s	£25.55	£27.46
1690–99	24.89s	£24.89	£24.94
1680–89	24.20s	£24.20	£21.83
1670–79	23.52s	£23.52	£20.89
1660–69	22.84s	£22.84	£20.15
1650–59	22.19s	£22.16	£19.33

[a] Based on *English* seamen's wages.
[b] Carpenters, masons, and various craftsworkers.
Source: Terry L. Anderson, *The Economic Growth of Seventeenth-Century New England: A Measurement of Regional Income* (1975), 76.

TABLE 4.190   ANNUAL INCOME (IN £ STERLING) FROM TOBACCO, AND MARKET SHARE, AMONG FARM HOUSEHOLDS IN TALBOT CO., MD., ABOUT 1704

Type of Household	Number of Households	Average Workforce	Average Tobacco Produced	Average Value of Tobacco	Share of Total Output
Large slave owners	14	16.9	23,350 lb.	£116	15%
Small slave owners	131	4.2	6,300 lb.	£18	22%
Servant owners	334	2.3	3,500 lb.	£14	44%
Small landowners	111	2.0	3,000 lb.	£9	9%
Tenants	182	1.0	900 lb.[a]	£6[a]	10%
Average (totals)	772	2.5	3,750 lb.	£14	100%

[a] Tenants averaged 1,500 lb. tobacco, but paid 600 lb. (£4) in rent.
Source: Paul G. E. Clemens, *The Atlantic Economy and Colonial Maryland's Eastern Shore: From Tobacco to Grain* (1980), 87.

TABLE 4.191   DAILY WAGE RATES IN SOUTH CAROLINA, 1710

Occupation	Daily Wage
Tailor	5s
Shoemaker	2½s
Smith	7½s
Weaver	3s
Bricklayer	6s
Cooper	4s

Source: Jack P. Greene, ed., *Selling a New World: Two Colonial South Carolina Promotional Pamphlets* (1989), 65 [data by Thomas Nairn].

TABLE 4.192 WAGE RATES FOR UNSILLED LABOR IN SPRINGFIELD, MASS., 1638–1696

Task	Dates	Wage and Rate (Daily Except as Stated)
Ditching & Fencing	1665–1688	6d per rod (hedging)
	1673–1687	22d–24d (fencing & mending)
	1668–1673	28–29d (ditching & clearing brook)
	1665	24d (scouring ditch)
	1663	12d (ditching)
	1656–1670	8d–15d (ditching)
	1656	30d (ditching)
	1649–1682	24d–32d per rod (fencing)
Cowherding & Shepherding	1675–1692	6½s–15s (driving cattle to Boston)
	1683	12d (tending cattle)
	1675	25s (driving 4 cattle to Hartford)
	1675	22d (driving cattle from Hartford)
	1664	1d per sheep sheared
	1661–1682	24d–36d (rounding up mares)
	1661	14s (driving cattle to New London)
	1659	4s (driving sheep from Windsor)
	1656–1671	2s per day (shearing sheep)
	1656–1661	£5.2.6–£7.10.0 per year (tending sheep)
	1656	18d–20d per day (tending sheep)
	1656	£2.2.10 (driving cattle to Boston and returning with sheep)
Field Work	1696	£7 (specie) for six months
	1695–1696	6s per week
	1695–1696	10s per month, plus bed & board
	1695	23s (specie) per month in spring
	1692	£2.10.0 for making well
	1690	30s per month in spring
	1680–1684	15d–24d per day for winter work
	1680	7s, 2d per acre for breaking ground
	1673–1685	26s, 8d–50s per acre for stubbing, clearing, & plowing
	1672–1675	26s, 8d–30s per acre for bogging & clearing
	1671	40s per acre for clearing and plowing
	1670	£2.6.0 per month for reaping
	1670	£6.14.0 for stubbing, clearing, & plowing 2.5 acres
	1670	£14.17.0 for stubbing, clearing, & plowing 6 acres
	1660–1670	16s–30s per acre for clearing land
	1662–1665	7s–10s per week for summer work
	1662–1663	6s–7s per week, plus victuals, for summer work
	1661–1665	5s–8s per week for winter work
	1661	20d per day for bogging
	1658	2s per day for getting thatch
	1657–1665	2s per day for gardening
	1656–1659	1s plus victuals for field work
	1648–1675	20d–24d for carting dung & plowing
	1646–1661	8d–16d for youth's summer work
	1646–1649	22d–25d for reaping
	1646–1647	20d for haymaking
	1646	14d for weeding
	1645–1683	18d–30d for summer work
	1645–1668	16d for winter work
Mowing Reaping, & Threshing	1681–1684	3d per yard breaking & swingling flax
	1679	10s per week (mowing)
	1660–1677	16d–20d per day for fanning oats & winnowing wheat
	1672	£2.8.0 per month (harvest work)
	1669–1672	5½s–6s per acre for mowing, raking, carting, & ricking hay
	1659–1665	2½d per bu. of threshed oats
	1659–1665	5d–6d per bus. of threshed wheat
	1658	5s per acre (mowing)
	1655	20s–25s per acre for mowing marshland
	1653	2s per day for fanning & cleaning wheat
	1652	3½s per acre for mowing thick grass

Task	Dates	Wage and Rate (Daily Except as Stated)
	1652	18d per day for haymaking
	1646–1676	16d. per day for youth's reaping
	1645–1671	24d–30d per acre for mowing & reaping
Harrowing & Plowing	1680–1683	5s–8s, 3d per acre plowed
	1673–1675	16s, 8d–18s of new ground harrowed
	1672	7s. per acre of new ground plowed
	1669	15s per acre of plowing
	1661–1671	16d–18d per day for plowing
	1656	4s per day for harrowing
	1648	10s per acre of new ground plowed
	1645–1656	6s, 7d per acre plowed
Cutting Wood	1684	28d per day for getting posts & rails
	1679	30d per day getting logs
	1677	2½s per day for shaving shingles
	1675	4s per log (22 in. × 20 ft.) cut & taken to sawmill
	1675	3s per log (21 in. × 18 ft.) cut & taken to sawmill
	1668–1676	8d per cut log (18 in. × 12 to 25 ft.) and 2s for taking to sawmill
	1668	33d per 100 ft. of boards
	1665	4s per day for pit sawing
	1663	30d per day for felling timber
	1663	7s per 100 ft. for hewing rails
	1662	7s per 100 ft. for squaring logs
	1660	10d per rod for log rails
	1660	4s per 100 ft. of 6-ft. posts
	1660–1675	2½s–3s, 8d for hewing timber
	1660–1669	8s–12s per 100 ft. of 6-ft. rails
	1660	12s per 100 ft. of 11.5-ft rails
	1660	3d per foot for felling trees
	1660	8s per 100 5-ft. clapboards
	1659–1686	2s per 100 18-in. shingles
	1658–1665	24d–30d per day for hewing, sawing, & joining
	1658–1665	5s–6s per 100 clapboards
	1658–1663	4s–5s, 2d. per 100 3-ft. shingles
	1658	2s per day for general woodworking
	1657–1660	6s per 100 ft. of logs
	1655–1661	20d–30d per day for sawing
	1654–1661	6s–7s, 10d. per 100 ft. of planks
	1649	3s, 2d per 100 shingles
	1646	16d per day for cutting wood
	1645–1654	3⅔s–5½s per 100 ft. of boards
Female Service	1693–1695	£7–£7.10.0 per year
	1673–1692	£6 per year
	1679	20d per lb. for spinning yarn
	1673–1681	2s–3s per week
	1663	5d per lb. for spinning hemp
	1658–1662	4s per week for domestic work
	1655–1656	£2.5.0–£5 per year
	1653	£2.10.0 per year (without clothes)
	1645	£3.10.0 per year
	1645	3s for washing
	1645	6d per day
Male Service	1695–1697	£20 (£12 specie) per year for cutting & carting firewood, making fire, & tending cattle
	1667–1689	£9–£12 per year
	1665	£2.10.0, plus bed & food, per year for youth's service
	1658	£9, plus shoes & stockings, per year
	1655	£4 per year, clothing not provided
	1653	£2 per month for summer service
	1649–1654	12s–18s per month for winter service
	1646–1648	£8.10.0–£10 per year
	1638	£10.13.0 per year

Note: Wages given in local currency unless otherwise stated.
Source: Stephen Innes, *Labor in a New Land: Economy and Society in Seventeenth-Century Springfield* (1983), 229–459.

TABLE 4.193 AVERAGE WAGES AT PHILADELPHIA AND BOSTON, 1730–1775

Year	Boston Seamen (in £ Sterling) per Month	Philadelphia Seamen (in £ Pa. currency) per Month	Philadelphia Laborers (in £ Pa. currency) per Day
1730	...	£2.63	...
1731	£1.62	£2.63	2.50s
1732	£1.20	£3.00	...
1733	£1.21	£2.75	2.75s
1734	£1.10	...	2.50s
1735	...	£2.75	...
1736	£1.20	£2.50	...
1737	...	£2.63	2.50s
1738	...	...	...
1739	...	...	2.50s
1740	£1.20	...	...
1741	£1.62	...	...
1742	£1.70	...	...
1743	£1.53	...	...
1744	£1.65	£2.50	2.50s
1745	£1.70	...	...
1746	...	...	2.50s
1747	£2.50	...	3.00s
1748	...	...	...
1749	...	...	2.50s
1750	...	£3.00	3.00s
1751	£1.58	£2.96	3.50s
1752	£1.58	£2.80	3.41s
1753	£1.50	£2.69	3.40s
1754	£1.39	£2.50	3.25s
1755	£1.46	£2.75	3.23s
1756	£1.46	£3.50	3.50s
1757	£1.88	...	3.50s
1758	£1.75	...	3.42s
1759	£1.88	£4.50	3.50s
1760	£1.97	£5.00	4.47s
1761	£1.84	...	4.42s
1762	£2.00	£2.75	3.80s
1763	£1.65	£2.75	3.40s
1764	£1.78	£3.44	3.25s
1765	£1.55	£3.25	3.50s
1766	£1.69	£3.25	4.00s
1767	£1.84	£3.38	4.00s
1768	£1.80	£3.32	3.82s
1769	£1.50	...	3.19s
1770	£1.35	£3.12	3.38s
1771	£1.14	...	3.30s
1772	£1.20	...	3.12s
1773	£1.54	...	2.60s
1774	£1.51	...	3.00s
1775	£1.91	...	2.80s

Source: Gary B. Nash, *The Urban Crucible: Social Change, Political Consciousness, and the Origins of the Revolution* (1979), 392–393.

Currency and Money Supply

Every North American colony experienced some degree of economic hardship due to an inadequate supply of hard money that impeded commercial transactions and limited the amount of credit available to assist in capital formation. This currency shortage often left Anglo-Americans with insufficient money to carry on local commercial transactions, provide for external trade, and serve as a source of credit. Because Parliament forbade the export of sterling coins out of Great Britain where a cash shortage also existed, Americans had to rely on Spanish gold or silver as a circulating medium. Book debts and private promissory notes served as an alternative to cash for the mercantile community but not for the general public. In many isolated rural areas, bartering goods and services remained a reality of life well into the eighteenth century.

Colonists attempted to keep foreign coins circulating among themselves by overvaluing Spanish gold and silver relative to the rate at which British sterling could be exchanged for them in Europe. England officially recognized the necessity of this expedient in 1705 by setting the "proclamation rate" for lawful money in the provinces at a 33% premium over exchange rates in England so that goods costing £100 Spanish dollars at London would be considered worth £133 on the North American mainland. Americans thereafter calculated their monetary values according to this premium, or at higher rates, and foreign specie became known as proclamation money for the purpose of local business transactions.

A recurring shortage of hard money forced the colonists into experimenting with alternatives to specie. The Chesapeake's settlers designated tobacco as legal tender at fixed rates. Indian wampum also served as a convenient alternative to cash among whites in the northern provinces. Merchants and storekeepers extended an enormous volume of book credit to their cash-short customers.

The currency problem forced early Americans to experiment with the creation of paper money. England's colonies emerged as the Atlantic world's foremost innovators in techniques of issuing fiat money during the eighteenth century. Massachusetts became the earliest government to circulate paper money in 1690 when it printed promissory notes for financing military operations against the French. These early bills of credit amounted to a forced loan imposed on the citizens, who were promised repayment in specie with interest added at a future date. Pending redemption, these bills traded at whatever value the market determined was appropriate depending on the likelihood of prompt repayment.

TABLE 4.194 EQUIVALENT VALUES OF COLONIAL CURRENCIES WITH BRITISH STERLING, SPANISH DOLLARS, AND U.S. DOLLARS OF 1991

1713–1719						
Currency Values	Mass.	N.Y.	Pa.	Md.	Va.	S.C.
Amount of Local Money	£1.00	£1.00	£1.00	£1.00	£1.00	£1.00
Sterling Exchange Rate[a]	£1.73	£1.56	£1.33	£1.28	£1.12	£4.46
in Spanish Dollars[b]	$2.57	$2.85	$3.35	$3.47	$3.96	$1.00
in US Dollars (1991)	$43.58	$48.45	$56.89	$58.88	$67.30	$16.93

1725–1738						
Currency Values	Mass.	N.Y.	Pa.	Md.	Va.	S.C.
Amount of Local Money	£1.00	£1.00	£1.00	£1.00	£1.00	£1.00
Sterling Exchange Rate[a]	£3.62	£1.65	£1.57	£1.34	£1.20	£7.06
in Spanish Dollars[b]	$1.23	$2.69	$2.83	$3.33	$3.71	$0.63
in US Dollars (1991)	$26.59	$58.26	$61.23	$72.00	$80.25	$13.62

1766–1772						
Currency Values	Mass.	N.Y.	Pa.	Md.	Va.	S.C.
Amount of Local Money	£1.00	£1.00	£1.00	£1.00	£1.00	£1.00
Sterling Exchange Rate[a]	£1.31	£1.75	£1.62	£1.61	£1.24	£6.97
in Spanish Dollars[b]	$3.38	$2.54	$2.74	$2.76	$3.59	$0.64
in US Dollars (1991)	$56.66	$42.52	$45.99	$46.32	$60.19	$10.70

Note: Decimal figures in sterling represent percent of one pound, not shillings.
[a] Amount of local money needed to buy £1.00 sterling.
[b] A Spanish dollar was equal to a U.S. dollar's value in 1791
Source: John J. McCusker, "How Much Is That in Real Money?": A Historical Price Index for Use as a Deflator of Monetary Values in the Economy of the United States," *Proceedings of the American Antiquarian Society,* CI (1991–2), 333.

Every colonial government ultimately issued paper money prior to independence. (Virginia found tobacco such a convenient medium of exchange, however, that it did not print any paper bills until 1755.) Although many early issues became inflated and temporarily lost much of their value, the colonies soon discovered how to manage their artificial currencies responsibly. The most popular and successful technique was to issue bills of credit through a land bank, a course pioneered by Massachusetts in 1714.

Colonial governments erecting land banks declared a fixed amount of paper money as legal tender for payment of debts and taxes at a discount to sterling (usually valued at £155 proclamation to £100 sterling), and they then distributed the bills through special commissioners. The commissioners made loans to landowners who could pledge real estate as security. The debtors paid interest on the principal and liquidated the loan in annual installments over a number of years; during this period, the commissioners destroyed the treasury notes as the mortgages were repaid, except those returned as interest, which they used to fund the costs of running the government.

Most governments managed their paper money so efficiently that after some initial, modest depreciation of 10% to 15%, the bills held their value in relation to sterling. This system of "currency finance" provided an important source of credit that enabled an agricultural population to finance improvements that would expand farm output. By augmenting the money supply, this system also stimulated cash purchases and promoted commerce. Some colonies managed their interest-bearing loans so prudently that they financed much of the cost of governmental administration through them and were able to keep taxes much lower than they would otherwise have been. The colonial land banks were remarkably successful experiments in finance, especially in a country where commercial banks and other lending institutions had not yet become established. Most of them could be described in words similar to the characterization of Pennsylvania's land bank made by Gov. Thomas Pownall: "There never was a wiser or better measure, never once better calculated to serve the uses of an increasing country."

Because the colonies suffered from a shortage of hard currency that often complicated business transactions, many of them issued their own paper money, such as this 20-shillings note printed in 1759 by Pennsylvania. (Courtesy National Museum of American History, Smithsonian Institution)

TABLE 4.195 EXCHANGE RATES FOR COLONIAL CURRENCY AND BRITISH POUNDS STERLING (EXPRESSED AS COLONIAL EQUIVALENTS OF £100 STERLING), 1691–1775

Year	Massachusetts	New York	New Jersey	Pennsylvania	Maryland	Virginia	North Carolina	South Carolina	Georgia
1775	£117.45	£171.55	...	£161.12	...	£120.00	...	£758.67	£108.00
1774	£135.30	£180.62	£169.50	£169.46	...	£130.30	£175.00	£700.00	...
1773	£132.19	£177.71	...	£166.27	...	£129.75	...	£728.00	...
1772	£131.00	£173.27	...	£160.83	...	£123.59	£160.00	£679.00	£108.76
1771	£133.33	£178.43	...	£165.69	...	£123.60	...	£762.00	...
1770	£126.31	£165.90	...	£153.92	...	£118.00	...	£717.00	...
1769	£129.86	£172.47	...	£157.56	...	£121.97	...	...	...
1768	£133.33	£179.87	...	£166.62	...	£124.99	£180.00	£700.00	£108.93
1767	£133.33	£178.96	...	£166.02	...	£125.54	£172.96	£700.00	...
1766	£133.03	£177.18	£160.00	£162.96	...	£128.48	...	£707.00	...
1765	£133.54	£182.80	...	£169.90	£133.33	£160.36	£200.00	£709.33	£108.50
1764	£133.75	£184.85	£172.02	£172.86	£136.66	£160.73	£192.67	£717.97	...
1763	£136.00	£186.73	£169.83	£173.00	£140.00	£159.88	£200.00	£716.55	...
1762	£142.33	£189.76	£176.88	£176.26	£144.45	£152.40	£200.00	£700.00	...
1761	£140.10	£181.41	£171.25	£172.71	£148.48	£143.72	£200.00	£700.00	...
1760	£129.54	£167.20	£153.30	£158.61	£146.25	£141.43	£190.00	£700.00	...
1759	...	£168.39	£156.25	£153.52	£150.00	£139.97	£185.00	£700.00	...
1758	£128.34	£172.60	£161.25	£159.00	£150.00	£137.92	...	£700.00	...
1757	£133.33	£178.40	£166.10	£166.07	£145.00	£139.71	...	£700.19	...
1756	£133.33	£182.65	£165.92	£172.57	£170.00	£128.44	£179.80	£713.56	...
1755	£133.33	£180.13	£170.00	£168.79	...	£129.38	£160.00	£700.00	...
1754	£133.33	£179.72	£168.17	£168.35	£153.75	£127.55	£166.67	£700.00	...
1753	£130.00	£179.39	£167.50	£167.49	£151.75	£129.50	...	£700.00	...
1752	...	£175.92	£166.25	£166.85	£155.62	£129.92	...	£700.00	...
1751	£133.33	£181.50	£172.50	£169.86	£166.83	£128.42	...	£700.00	...
1750	£137.33	£179.33	£173.75	£170.60	£177.92	£125.94	£133.33	£702.28	...
1749	£1,033.33	£176.46	£170.00	£171.39	£184.58	£123.75	...	£725.36	...
1748	£912.50	£183.39	...	£174.12	£200.61	£132.29	£1,033.33	£762.50	...
1747	£925.00	£191.46	...	£183.78	£225.22	£135.01	...	£760.74	...
1746	£642.50	£185.83	£182.50	£179.86	£210.00	£131.87	£1,000.00	...	...

Year	Massachusetts	New York	New Jersey	Pennsyl-vania	Maryland	Virginia	North Carolina	South Carolina	Georgia
1745	£644.79	£183.33	...	£174.77	£200.00	£127.60	£1,000.00	£700.00	...
1744	£588.61	£175.42	...	£166.67	£166.67	£121.88	...	£700.00	...
1743	£550.70	£174.67	£160.00	£159.79	£285.13	£120.00	...	£700.00	...
1742	£550.28	£170.97	£150.00	£159.38	£275.00	£120.00	...	£698.96	...
1741	£548.44	£159.44	£142.50	£146.14	£238.17	£120.53	£1,000.00	£690.83	...
1740	£525.00	£166.25	£160.62	£165.45	£228.08	£119.17	£966.66	£795.95	...
1739	£500.00	£166.67	£168.33	£169.69	£212.34	£122.50	£1,000.00	£791.91	...
1738	£500.00	£165.00	...	£160.42	£225.00	£123.75	...	£775.00	...
1737	£516.67	£165.00	£170.00	£170.25	£250.00	£121.63	£866.67	£753.10	...
1736	£430.00	£165.00	...	£167.00	£230.00	£122.70	£700.00	£743.33	...
1735	£360.00	£165.00	...	£166.11	£140.00	£120.00	£720.00	£700.00	...
1734	£355.00	£165.00	...	£170.00	£160.00	£120.00	...	£700.00	...
1733	£350.00	£165.00	...	£166.94	...	£120.00	...	£700.00	...
1732	£339.51	£165.00	...	£160.90	...	£121.16	...	£700.00	...
1731	£334.31	£165.00	...	£153.28	...	£122.33	£650.00	£700.00	...
1730	£337.71	£166.88	...	£152.03	...	£119.92	...	£643.75	...
1729	£313.33	£165.00	...	£148.61	...	£118.75	£500.00	£700.00	...
1728	£298.82	£165.00	...	£150.62	...	£120.00	...	£700.00	...
1727	£291.98	£165.00	...	£149.58	...	£116.29	...	£700.00	...
1726	£290.98	£165.00	...	...	...	£114.34	...	£700.00	...
1725	£289.11	£165.00	...	£139.34	...	£117.50	...	£762.16	...
1724	£267.92	£165.00	...	£143.11	...	£116.44	£500.00	£650.00	...
1723	£241.81	£165.22	...	£140.37	...	£115.00	...	£675.00	...
1722	£229.79	...	...	£135.01	...	£115.00	£500.00	£580.00	...
1721	£225.98	£163.33	£155.00	£137.50	...	£115.00	...	£533.33	...
1720	£219.43	£162.92	...	£138.75	...	£115.00	...	£400.00	...
1719	£216.68	£154.17	£155.18	£135.42	...	£110.50	...	...	...
1718	£200.00	...	...	£132.22	...	...	...	£500.00	...
1717	£170.00	£160.00	...	£134.72	...	£105.50	...	£575.00	...
1716	£162.50	£157.78	£142.86	£133.52	...	...	...	...	...
1715	£160.33	£153.20	...	£130.36	...	...	£150.00	£300.00	...
1714	£153.33	£154.90	...	£132.50	...	£110.00	...	£200.00	...
1713	£150.00	£153.75	...	£130.36	...	...	...	£150.00	...
1712	£150.00	£155.62	...	£128.93	...	£110.00	...	£150.00	...
1711	£146.67	£151.12	...	...	...	£108.50	...	£150.00	...
1710	£155.00	£145.05	...	£128.16	...	...	...	£150.00	...
1709	£151.06	£150.00	...	£120.05	...	£107.62	...	...	...
1708	...	...	...	£153.96	...	...	...	£150.00	...
1707	...	...	...	£152.58	...	...	...	£150.00	...
1706	£150.00	...	...	£150.58	...	£115.00	...	...	...
1705	£135.00	...	...	£150.14	...	...	...	...	...
1704	£140.00	...	...	£150.00	...	...	...	...	...
1703	£140.00	£140.00	£166.67	£150.84	...	...	...	£150.00	...
1702	£130.00	£133.33	...	£150.72	...	...	...	...	...
1701	£136.50	£132.50	...	£147.92	...	...	...	...	...
1700	£139.43	£134.96	...	£155.00	...	...	...	£146.00	...
1699	£140.48	...	...	...	...	...	...	£111.75	...
1698	...	£130.00	...	£150.00	...	...	...	...	...
1697	£136.00	...	...	...	...	...	...	...	...
1696	£129.17	£130.00	...	£150.00	...	...	...	...	...
1695	£139.86	£130.00	...	...	...	...	...	...	...
1694	£133.66	£129.16	...	£135.86	...	...	...	...	...
1993	...	...	...	...	...	...	...	...	...
1992	...	...	...	...	...	...	...	...	...
1991	...	...	...	...	...	£110.00	...	...	...

Note: Numbers following decimals represent percents of a pound, and not shillings.
Source: John J. McCusker, *Money and Exchange in Europe and America, 1600–1775* (1978), 313–317.

TABLE 4.196   PAPER MONEY ISSUED AND OUTSTANDING IN THE THIRTEEN COLONIES, 1703–1775

Year	Massachusetts		New Hampshire		Rhode Island		Connecticut		New York		New Jersey	
	Issued	Outstanding	Issued	Outstanding	Issued	Outstanding	Issued	Outstanding	Issued	Outstanding	Issued	Outstanding
1775	...	...	£30,000	£30,000	£60,000	£60,000	£162,000	£162,000	£112,500	£292,500	...	£242,000
1774	...	£37,000	...	...	...	none	...	£12,000	...	£185,000	£100,000	£250,000
1773	...	...	...	...	...	none	£12,000	£12,000	...	£190,000	...	£155,000
1772	...	£84,600	...	...	...	none	...	£12,000	...	£190,000	...	£167,000
1771	...	£102,500	£2,000	£2,000	...	none	...	£22,000	£120,000	£195,000	...	£177,000

(continued)

TABLE 4.196   (continued)

Year	Massachusetts Issued	Massachusetts Outstanding	New Hampshire Issued	New Hampshire Outstanding	Rhode Island Issued	Rhode Island Outstanding	Connecticut Issued	Connecticut Outstanding	New York Issued	New York Outstanding	New Jersey Issued	New Jersey Outstanding
1770	...	£129,500	...	none	...	none	£10,000	£10,000	...	£80,000	...	£184,000
1769	...	£161,000	...	none	...	none	...	none	...	£85,000	...	£190,000
1768	...	£203,100	...	none	...	none	...	none	...	£85,000	...	£200,000
1767	...	£247,000	...	...	£2,000	none	...	£7,000	...	£110,000	...	£211,000
1766	...	£87,800	...	...	£1,000	...	...	£7,000	...	£130,000	...	£227,500
1765	...	£181,600	...	...	...	...	...	£7,000	...	£165,000	...	£233,000
1764	...	£175,500	...	£27,175	...	£13,000	£7,000	£17,000	...	£240,000	£25,000	£239,000
1763	...	...	...	...	...	...	£10,000	...	...	£287,163	£10,000	£240,000
1762	£60,000	...	£20,000	...	£13,000	...	£65,000	...	...	£330,807	£30,000	£246,531
1761	£70,000	...	£20,000	...	...	...	£45,000	...	...	£366,158	£25,000	£233,061
1760	...	...	£15,000	...	£27,000	...	£70,000	...	£60,000	£410,387	£45,000	£222,091
1759	...	...	£13,000	...	£20,000	...	£70,000	...	£100,000	£481,186	£50,000	£193,621
1758	...	...	£21,000	£212,200	£21,000	...	£30,000	...	£100,000	£307,198	£40,000	£155,152
1757	...	...	£20,000	...	...	...	...	...	...	£219,281	£40,000	£106,682
1756	...	...	£36,000	...	£14,000	...	...	...	£62,000	£230,773	£17,500	£68,212
1755	...	...	£40,000	...	£240,000	...	£62,000	...	£63,000	£179,076	£40,000	£52,242
1754	...	...	...	...	...	...	...	...	...	£126,081	...	£13,772
1753	...	...	...	...	...	...	...	...	...	£132,531	...	£15,302
1752	...	...	...	£113,800	...	...	...	...	...	£140,960	...	£22,850
1751	...	...	...	...	£25,000	...	...	£340,200	...	£148,214	...	£27,850
1750	...	...	...	...	...	...	...	...	...	£153,938	...	£32,850
1749	...	...	...	...	...	...	...	...	...	£163,016	...	£37,850
1748	£400,000	£2,135,300	...	£113,800	£30,000	£550,000	...	£281,000	...	£172,001	...	£43,350
1747	£348,000	...	...	...	£15,000	...	...	...	£28,000	£189,495	...	£50,850
1746	£662,000	...	£60,000	...	£11,000	...	£23,000	...	£53,000	...	£16,000	£57,350
1745	£1,040,000	...	£27,000	...	£9,000	...	£40,000	...	...	...	...	£50,000
1744	£344,000	£304,800	...	£29,900	£50,000	...	£19,000	£29,900	...	...	...	£52,500
1743	£85,000	...	£1,000	...	...	...	...	...	...	...	...	£55,000
1742	£117,000	...	£30,000	...	...	...	...	...	...	...	...	£57,500
1741	£120,000	...	...	...	£16,000	£340,000	...	...	...	...	...	£61,000
1740	£80,000	...	£2,000	...	£30,000	...	£49,000	...	...	£79,800	...	£62,000
1739	...	£243,000	...	£22,600	...	...	...	£22,600	...	[£10,000]	...	£60,000
1738	£26,000	...	...	...	£110,000	...	...	...	...	...	...	£60,000
1737	£81,000	...	£10,000	...	£30,000	...	...	...	£48,000	...	...	£60,000
1736	£48,000	...	...	...	...	...	...	...	...	...	...	£20,000
1735	£39,000	£309,400	...	£22,400	...	...	...	£22,400	...	...	...	£22,700
1734	£30,000	...	...	...	£2,000	...	...	...	£12,000	...	...	£25,400
1733	£79,000	...	...	...	£104,000	...	£30,000	...	...	...	£40,000	£28,460
1732	...	...	...	...	£60,000	...	...	...	...	...	...	£11,520
1731	£24,000	...	...	...	£60,000	...	...	...	...	...	...	£14,580
1730	£13,000	£311,300	£1,000	£26,800	...	...	...	£26,800	...	[£3,000]	£30,000	£17,640
1729	£20,000	...	[£2,000]	...	...	...	£6,000	...	...	...	...	£20,700
1728	£36,000	...	...	...	£48,000	£320,400	£4,000	...	...	...	...	£23,760
1727	£88,000	...	£2,000	...	...	...	£4,000	...	...	[£3,000]	[£25,000]	£27,820
1726	£25,000	...	£3,000	...	[£50,000]	...	...	...	...	...	...	£30,880
1725	£70,000	£350,700	£2,000	£26,600	...	...	...	£26,600	£7,000	...	...	£35,940
1724	£55,000	...	£2,000	...	...	...	£4,000	...	...	...	£40,000	£40,000
1723	£40,000	...	...	...	£2,000	...	...	...	£2,000	...	...	£970
1722	£45,000	...	[£10,000]	...	...	...	£4,000	...	...	...	...	(£2,450?)
1721	£17,000	...	...	...	£100,000	...	...	...	...	...	...	(£3,910?)
1720	£65,000	£229,500	...	£22,000	...	...	...	£22,000	...	...	...	(£5,370?)
1719	£15,000	...	...	...	...	...	£4,000	...	...	...	...	(£6,830?)
1718	£11,000	...	...	...	...	...	...	...	...	...	...	(£8,290?)
1717	£9,000	...	£15,000	...	£17,000	...	...	...	£17,000	...	...	(£9,750?)
1716	£111,000	...	£2,000	...	...	...	...	...	...	...	...	(£11,210?)
1715	£44,000	£170,000	£1,000	£8,200	£40,000	£51,000	...	£8,200	...	£36,300	£4,670	(£12,670?)
1714	£50,000	...	£1,000	...	...	...	...	...	£28,000	...	...	(£8,000?)
1713	£14,000	...	...	...	...	...	[£22,000]	...	...	...	...	(£8,000?)
1712	£25,000	...	[£2,000]	...	...	...	...	...	...	...	...	(£8,000?)
1711	£95,000	...	£4,000	...	£6,000	...	£10,000	...	£10,000	...	£5,000	£8,000
1710	£44,000	£89,000	£3,000	...	£7,000	£7,000	£5,000	...	...	£7,000	...	£3,000
1709	£25,000	...	...	...	...	...	£19,000	...	£13,000	...	£3,000	£3,000
1708	£32,000	...	...	...	...	...	...	...	...	...	...	...
1707	£32,000	...	...	...	...	...	...	...	...	...	...	...
1706	£44,000	...	...	...	...	...	...	...	...	...	...	...
1705	£18,000	£28,000	...	...	...	...	...	...	...	...	...	...
1704	£32,000	...	...	...	...	...	...	...	...	...	...	...
1703	£32,000	...	...	...	...	...	...	...	...	...	...	...

Year	Pennsylvania		Maryland		Virginia		North Carolina		South Carolina		Georgia	
	Issued	Outstanding	Issued	Outstanding	Issued	Outstanding	Issued	Outstanding	Issued	Outstanding	Issued	Outstanding
1775	£6,000	£316,600	£100,000	£295,000	...	£75,000	£25,000	£80,000	...	...	£10,000	£15,000
1774	£150,000	£220,500	...	...	...	...	...	...	...	£258,971	£800	...
1773	£11,000	£154,150	£130,125	...	[£36,834]	£55,000	...	...	...	£391,391	£4,299	£11,000
1772	£25,000	£174,643	...	...	...	£88,200	...	...	...	...	...	...
1771	£15,000	£184,500	...	...	£30,000	£105,000	£60,000	...	...	...	£3,355	...
1770	...	£204,500	...	...	...	...	...	£78,500	£70,000	£424,154	£106	...
1769	£30,000	£230,500	£112,500	...	£10,000	£130,000	...	...	[£106,500]	£497,654	...	...
1768	...	£234,450	...	...	...	£170,000	£20,000	£98,000	...	£482,000	£2,200	...
1767	£20,000	£263,900	...	£54,375	...	£205,000	...	£67,000	£60,000	£344,147	...	...
1766	...	£278,700	£64,875	£64,875	...	...	...	£67,880	...	£446,673	£1,815	...
1765	...	£302,400	...	£5,000	...	...	...	(£70,000?)	...	£472,378	£650	...
1764	£55,000	£328,000	...	£41,295	...	£230,000	...	£73,378	...	£585,246	...	£8,200
1763	...	£286,312	...	...	...	£302,000	...	(£79,000?)	...	£584,916	...	(£8,500?)
1762	...	£349,053	£1,000	...	£20,000	...	...	£85,322	£15,000	(£726,300?)	£540	(£8,900?)
1761	...	£438,104	...	...	...	...	£20,000	£95,335	...	£867,744	£180	(£8,400?)
1760	£100,000	£486,199	...	...	£52,000	...	£12,000	£75,806	£371,693	£863,827	£8,510	£8,237
1759	£100,000	£433,562	...	...	£62,000	...	...	£69,512	...	£521,369	£800	(£1,540?)
1758	£100,000	£329,774	...	...	£89,000	...	£11,000	£70,253	...	£595,567	...	(£2,490?)
1757	£100,000	£262,466	...	...	£180,000	...	£15,000	£68,255	£229,300	£542,837	£740	(£4,240?)
1756	£85,000	£147,510	£40,000	...	£35,000	£110,000	£4,000	£57,951	£50,000	£311,816	...	(£5,250?)
1755	[£15,000]	£81,000	...	...	£60,000	£35,000	...	£56,054	£33,600	£221,359	£7,000	£7,000
1754	...	£81,500	[£4,000]	...	...	...	£40,000	£57,951	...	£156,156	...	...
1753	...	£82,500	...	...	...	...	...	£18,289	...	£152,322	...	...
1752	...	£83,500	...	£60,000	...	...	...	£19,028	[£20,000]	(£153,000?)	...	...
1751	...	£84,000	...	...	...	...	...	£20,119	...	(£133,000?)	...	...
1750	...	£84,500	...	...	...	...	...	£20,647	...	(£133,000?)	...	...
1749	...	£85,000	...	...	...	...	...	£21,160	...	£133,000	...	...
1748	...	£85,000	...	£86,040	...	...	[£20,000]	£21,350	[£107,000]	...	...	...
1747	...	£85,000	...	£85,309	...	...	...	...	...	...	...	...
1746	£5,000	£85,000	[£6,000]	(£84,200?)	...	...	...	...	£210,000	...	...	...
1745	...	£80,000	...	£83,058	...	...	...	...	...	...	...	...
1744	[£10,000]	£80,000	£1,000	£82,252	...	...	...	...	...	...	...	...
1743	...	£80,000	...	(£82,252?)	...	...	...	...	...	...	...	...
1742	...	£80,000	...	£82,072	...	...	...	...	...	...	...	...
1741	...	£80,000	[£1,000]	£83,444	...	...	...	...	...	...	...	...
1740	...	£80,000	[£8,000]	£78,523	...	...	...	...	...	...	...	...
1739	[£11,110]	£80,000	...	£79,820	...	...	...	£52,500	...	£250,000	...	...
1738	...	£68,890	...	(£74,820?)	...	...	...	...	...	...	...	...
1737	...	£68,890	...	£69,856	...	...	...	...	...	...	...	...
1736	...	£68,890	[£1,000]	£57,864	...	...	...	...	£210,000	...	...	...
1735	...	£68,890	...	£56,495	...	...	[£53,000]	£52,500	...	...	...	...
1734	...	£68,890	...	(£60,000?)	...	...	...	...	...	...	...	...
1733	...	£68,890	£90,000	(£60,000?)	...	...	...	...	...	...	...	...
1732	...	£68,890	...	...	...	...	...	...	...	...	...	...
1731	...	£68,890	...	...	...	...	...	...	...	[£107,000]	...	...
1730	...	£68,890	...	...	...	...	...	£40,000	...	£106,500	...	...
1729	£30,000	£68,890	...	...	...	...	£40,000	...	£40,000	...	...	...
1728	...	£38,890	...	...	...	...	...	...	...	...	...	...
1727	...	£38,890	...	...	...	...	...	...	[£20,000]	...	...	...
1726	...	£38,890	...	...	...	...	...	...	...	...	...	...
1725	...	£38,915	...	...	...	...	...	...	...	...	...	...
1724	£30,000	£44,915	...	...	...	...	...	...	£63,000	£116,000	...	...
1723	£15,000	£15,000	...	...	...	...	...	...	...	(£117,000?)	...	...
1722	...	...	...	...	...	...	[£12,000]	...	...	(£119,000?)	...	...
1721	...	...	...	...	...	...	...	...	...	(£121,000?)	...	...
1720	...	...	...	...	...	...	...	£12,000	£34,000	(£123,000?)	...	...
1719	...	...	...	...	...	...	...	...	...	(£89,000?)	...	...
1718	...	...	...	...	...	...	...	...	...	(£89,000?)	...	...
1717	...	...	...	...	...	...	...	...	...	(£89,000?)	...	...
1716	...	...	...	...	...	...	...	...	£15,000	(£89,000?)	...	...
1715	...	...	...	...	...	...	[£24,000]	£24,000	£35,000	£74,000	...	...
1714	...	...	...	...	...	...	...	...	...	(£39,000?)	...	...
1713	...	...	...	...	...	...	£8,000	£12,000	...	...	...	...
1712	...	...	...	...	...	...	£4,000	£4,000	£52,000	...	...	...
1711	...	...	...	...	...	...	...	...	...	£7,000	...	...
1710	...	...	...	...	...	...	...	...	...	...	...	...
1709	...	...	...	...	...	...	...	...	...	...	...	...
1708	...	...	...	...	...	...	...	...	£8,000	...	...	...
1707	...	...	...	...	...	...	...	...	£8,000	...	...	...
1706	...	...	...	...	...	...	...	...	...	...	...	...
1705	...	...	...	...	...	...	...	...	...	...	...	...
1704	...	...	...	...	...	...	...	...	...	...	...	...
1703	...	...	...	...	...	...	...	...	£6,000	£6,000	...	...

Note: Reissues or exchanges of money outstanding are designated in brackets, i.e., [£30,000].
Source: Joseph A. Ernst, *Money and Politics in America, 1755–1775* (1973), 365–373. Leslie V. Brock, *The Currency of the American Colonies, 1770–1774* (1975), passim. Eric P. Newman, *The Early Paper Money of America* (1967). B. U. Ratchford, *American State Debts* (1941), 28.

International Trade

The thirteen colonies carried on a thriving oceanic trade, but most of the surviving statistical evidence concerns only their exports to and imports from the British Isles. Even this body of evidence is limited to data collected during the eighteenth century, when the royal customs service operated most efficiently. There is consequently little hard information on the exact dimensions of Anglo-American overseas commerce before 1697.

Northern and southern colonies developed different patterns of international trade. The southern colonies provided the bulk of goods shipped overseas from British North America. Tobacco and rice alone accounted for almost 40% of all products sold abroad from North America by the 1760s. All tobacco went to Great Britain, from which much was reexported to the continent of Europe, while most rice went to southern Europe. More than three-quarters of all goods shipped from southern ports were sent to Great Britain.

increased from 10% to 37%. Metal hardware, textiles, and other manufactured goods constituted the leading British products sold to Anglo-Americans. The colonists also bought a large volume of rum, molasses, and sugar from the Caribbean.

During the early eighteenth century, exports and imports between Britain and its mainland colonies were relatively even in value. By mid-century, however, colonial imports from Great Britain substantially outweighed exports to the mother country. This imbalance in trade was nevertheless offset by the heavy volume of North American exports to West Indian and southern European markets, which earned the thirteen colonies large surpluses in bills of exchange that could be used to cancel outstanding credit accounts with merchants in London, Bristol, and other British ports. Also offsetting about 75% of the trade deficit with Britain were substantial maritime earnings gained by New England's merchant marine through shipping cargoes, merchants' commissions, and insurance fees. The thirteen colonies consequently seem to have experienced no serious problems with trade deficits and managed to keep their international trade roughly in balance.

The thirteen colonies earned most of their circulating coins by exporting goods overseas. Because so much of their trade centered in the Spanish-dominated Caribbean, Spanish dollars, such as this 1737 eight-reales piece minted in Mexico, became the primary medium of business exchanges in Anglo-America. (Courtesy National Museum of American History, Smithsonian Institution)

Just slightly more than a third (36%) of all colonial exports originated in the northern colonies. The West Indies developed into the most lucrative market for northern products: they bought more than half of that region's exports, primarily fish, forestry products, and foodstuffs. Southern Europe also developed into a major market for northern commodities, especially for grains grown in the Hudson and Delaware valleys. New England produced just 17% of all exports shipped from British North America by the 1760s, but its merchant marine contributed enormously to colonial commerce by carrying the lion's share of northern goods to market.

The American colonies evolved into the most important market for British products during the eighteenth century. During the seven decades after 1700, the share of British domestic exports sent to the colonies

TABLE 4.197   SHIPS AND CARGO TONNAGE CLEARING COLONIAL PORTS, 1714–1768

Boston, Mass.						
	1768		1754		1714–1717[a]	
Destination	Ships	Tons	Ships	Tons	Ships	Tons
Outward Bound	612	33,695	447	26,669	416	20,927
Britain	67	6,428	26	2,510	48	3,985
Ireland	2	170	3	165	…	…
Europe	22	1,333	31	2,465	19	1,185
Africa	…	…	1	75	…	…
Caribbean	147	10,095	149	10,521	191	10,897
13 Colonies	281	11,451	156	7,052	117	3,583
Other	93[b]	4,218	81[c]	3,881	37[c]	1,139
Inward Bound	549	31,983	303	17,575	…	…
Britain	69	6,946	43	4,448	…	…
Ireland	3	220	2	110	…	…
Europe	22	1,871	37	2,763	…	…
Africa	…	…	…	…	…	…
Caribbean	160	10,811	71	4,432	…	…
13 Colonies	204	8,266	139	5,347	…	…
Other	91[b]	3,869	18[c]	790	…	…

New York, N.Y.								
	1768		1754		1734		1715–18[a]	
Destination	Ships	Tons	Ship	Tons	Ships	Tons	Ships	Tons
Outward Bound	480	23,566	322	13,322	184	6,374	215	7,464
Britain	56	5,130	31	2,085	8	645	21	1,461
Ireland	30	2,522	23	1,615	2	160	…	…
Europe	45	2,360	19	725	9	475	10	630
Africa	2	35	4	130	1	60	1	40
Caribbean	156	6,981	180	6,351	87	2,771	104	3,608
13 Colonies	125	3,754	51	2,076	70	1,959	68	1,406
Other	66[c]	2,784	18[c]	575	10[c]	388	11[c]	319
Inward Bound	462	21,847	266	10,921	213	7,442	…	…
Britain	79	7,158	28	2,475	18	1,350	…	…
Ireland	15	1,387	10	650	4	215	…	…
Europe	31	1,500	25	1,055	24	1,571	…	…
Africa	2	130	5	205	…	…	…	…
Caribbean	158	6,301	177	6,020	78	2,707	…	…
13 Colonies	139	3,952	23	931	71	1,366	…	…
Other	38[c]	1,419	16[c]	480	30[c]	911	…	…

Philadelphia, Pa.

Destination	1768 Ships	1768 Tons	1734 Ships	1733 Ships
Outward Bound	641	36,944	191	185
Britain	40	4,134	21	12
Ireland	38	3,482	16	17
Europe	88	7,255	22	20
Africa	...	...	...	...
Caribbean	206	12,019	74	87
13 Colonies	229	8,116	50	45
Other	40[c]	1,938	8[c]	4[c]
Inward Bound	528	34,970	210	190
Britain	60	6,924	24	26
Ireland	15	1,470	11	8
Europe	63	5,001	17	16
Africa	...	...	...	...
Caribbean	139	11,677	79	77
13 Colonies	218	7,978	68	58
Other	33[c]	1,920	12[d]	10[d]

Hampton, Va.

Destination	1768 Ships	1768 Tons	1752 Ships	1752 Tons	1733 Ships	1733 Tons	1727 Ships	1727 Tons
Outward Bound	246	15,776	156	8,008	82	3,769	104	4,577
Britain	33	5,252	20	2,285	11	1,110	22	2,046
Ireland	1	200	...	...	...	...	...	...
Europe	14	1,209	14	1,195	6	440	2	60
Africa	...	...	1	25	...	...	...	...
Caribbean	148	7,376	81	3,462	50	1,664	41	1,366
13 Colonies	37	1,369	31	806	10	415	20	622
Other	13[c]	370	9[e]	235	5[d]	140	19[d]	483
Inward Bound	254	19,673	169	10,557	87	4,816	94	4,023
Britain	55	8,411	37	4,912	19	2,285	18	1,785
Ireland	...	...	...	...	...	...	...	...

Hampton, Va.

Destination	1768 Ships	1768 Tons	1752 Ships	1752 Tons	1733 Ships	1733 Tons	1727 Ships	1727 Tons
Europe	9	1,065	10	1,015	4	440	2	130
Africa	...	...	2	140	1	25	...	...
Caribbean	134	8,152	78	3,580	50	1,769	37	1,273
13 Colonies	50	1,935	37	775	10	351	20	294
Other	6[e]	110	5[e]	135	7[e]	191	17[e]	541

Charles Town, S.C.

Destination	1768 Ships	1768 Tons	1735 Ships	1735 Tons	1731 Ships	1731 Tons
Outward Bound	429	31,551	247	14,530	198	12,366
Britain	121	15,873	88	7,919	94	8,424
Ireland	...	...	...	...	...	...
Europe	48	5,515	30	2,685	15	1,185
Africa	...	...	...	...	...	...
Caribbean	113	5,808	22	670	34	1,280
13 Colonies	83	2,852	65	2,644	31	1,059
Other	64[c]	1,503	42[c]	612	25[c]	438
Inward Bound	448	34,449	232	13,220	191	12,101
Britain	139	18,125	57	4,896	55	5,375
Ireland	11	1,010	4	320	1	74
Europe	18	2,023	38	3,130	10	870
Africa	...	...	9	885	9	755
Caribbean	129	8,238	42	2,039	55	3,501
13 Colonies	88	3,410	57	2,743	42	2,030
Other	63[c]	1,643	43[c]	777	30[c]	536

[a] Average of years
[b] Canada
[c] Canada, Bahamas, Bermuda
[d] Bermuda
[e] Bermuda, Bahamas

Source: Research of Lawrence A. Harper, published in Bureau of the Census, *Historical Statistics of the United States, Colonial Times to 1957* (1960), 759–760.

TABLE 4.198   TRADE OF THE THIRTEEN COLONIES WITH ENGLAND AND SCOTLAND, 1740–1775[a]

Year	New England	Middle Colonies	Virginia, Maryland	Carolinas & Georgia	Total
1775					
Imports	£85,114	£2,835	£1,921	£130,485	£220,355
Exports	£128,175	£372,942	£1,247,041	£708,904	£2,457,062
1774					
Imports	£576,651	£1,105,263	£690,066	£471,489	£2,843,469
Exports	£123,798	£153,091	£1,037,672	£532,355	£1,846,916
1773					
Imports	£543,165	£731,893	£589,427	£447,980	£2,312,465
Exports	£132,078	£115,202	£1,055,278	£584,625	£1,887,183
1772					
Imports	£844,422	£875,405	£1,015,570	£575,326	£3,310,723
Exports	£139,040	£111,910	£1,036,477	£512,984	£1,800,411
1771					
Imports	£1,435,837	£1,402,619	£1,223,726	£514,762	£4,576,944
Exports	£162,923	£147,551	£1,126,377	£509,453	£1,946,304
1770					
Imports	£416,694	£619,854	£997,157	£227,830	£2,261,535
Exports	£157,443	£130,062	£847,997	£362,239	£1,497,741
1769					
Imports	£223,694	£280,910	£714,943	£385,424	£1,604,971
Exports	£142,775	£141,494	£759,960	£487,284	£1,531,513
1768					
Imports	£430,807	£932,502	£669,523	£357,487	£2,390,319
Exports	£157,804	£153,480	£776,654	£568,644	£1,656,582

(continued)

TABLE 4.198 (continued)

Year	New England	Middle Colonies	Virginia, Maryland	Carolinas & Georgia	Total
1767					
Imports	£416,186	£807,100	£652,672	£292,152	£2,168,110
Exports	£147,516	£107,157	£769,990	£448,226	£1,472,889
1766					
Imports	£419,415	£667,085	£519,729	£375,770	£1,981,999
Exports	£157,542	£95,478	£796,033	£378,447	£1,427,500
1765					
Imports	£468,703	£756,366	£518,878	£375,978	£2,119,925
Exports	£175,573	£89,002	£879,074	£429,993	£1,573,642
1764					
Imports	£488,557	£962,597	£688,692	£334,813	£2,474,659
Exports	£97,261	£104,592	£860,756	£385,925	£1,448,534
1763					
Imports	£279,259	£552,323	£751,426	£309,932	£1,892,940
Exports	£79,097	£92,467	£986,391	£302,017	£1,459,972
1762					
Imports	£261,643	£516,808	£542,154	£226,516	£1,547,121
Exports	£51,136	£100,570	£717,301	£199,972	£1,068,979
1761					
Imports	£338,470	£497,411	£677,528	£283,189	£1,796,598
Exports	£51,852	£89,667	£744,345	£274,741	£1,160,605
1760					
Imports	£611,779	£1,200,660	£760,947	£224,392	£2,797,778
Exports	£39,808	£57,212	£859,038	£194,435	£1,150,493
1759					
Imports	£549,782	£1,147,361	£571,246	£237,608	£2,505,997
Exports	£26,740	£51,896	£527,290	£243,841	£849,767
1758					
Imports	£477,417	£626,852	£546,914	£196,939	£1,848,122
Exports	£30,275	£35,929	£744,167	£176,319	£986,690
1757					
Imports	£371,245	£632,552	£528,978	£219,367	£1,752,142
Exports	£32,069	£34,837	£611,360	£141,849	£820,115
1756					
Imports	£394,328	£458,763	£423,393	£187,359	£1,463,843
Exports	£61,777	£48,188	£473,004	£238,538	£821,507
1755					
Imports	£348,014	£298,552	£384,652	£191,865	£1,223,083
Exports	£65,776	£66,363	£659,180	£333,714	£1,125,033
1754					
Imports	£337,409	£373,889	£429,678	£156,616	£1,297,592
Exports	£73,593	£60,064	£729,086	£312,497	£1,175,240
1753					
Imports	£357,909	£529,822	£483,723	£239,032	£1,610,486
Exports	£89,714	£90,016	£836,901	£171,326	£1,187,957
1752					
Imports	£287,094	£398,560	£457,751	£159,812	£1,303,217
Exports	£80,288	£73,862	£745,195	£291,848	£1,191,193
1751					
Imports	£327,216	£443,489	£478,026	£148,642	£1,397,373
Exports	£69,689	£66,238	£650,696	£248,549	£1,035,172
1750					
Imports	£358,044	£487,287	£458,289	£136,659	£1,440,279
Exports	£51,660	£64,721	£663,989	£195,195	£975,565
1749					
Imports	£249,656	£507,397	£417,853	£170,299	£1,345,205
Exports	£44,628	£38,357	£603,900	£155,221	£842,106
1748					
Imports	£223,643	£218,702	£418,236	£161,486	£1,022,067
Exports	£32,451	£24,721	£641,006	£181,125	£879,303
1747					
Imports	£228,899	£228,332	£362,636	£97,362	£917,229
Exports	£47,316	£19,972	£590,138	£120,480	£777,907

Year	New England	Middle Colonies	Virginia, Maryland	Carolinas & Georgia	Total
1746					
Imports	£232,004	£160,818	£430,906	£107,152	£930,880
Exports	£41,089	£24,620	£506,029	£87,743	£659,481
1745					
Imports	£146,064	£110,895	£284,472	£91,029	£632,460
Exports	£39,927	£25,482	£520,720	£92,442	£678,571
1744					
Imports	£151,094	£184,934	£313,315	£81,194	£730,537
Exports	£52,667	£21,973	£496,287	£200,091	£771,018
1743					
Imports	£179,464	£214,827	£448,982	£116,460	£959,733
Exports	£64,800	£24,663	£674,021	£237,122	£1,000,606
1742					
Imports	£161,921	£245,520	£357,184	£144,081	£908,706
Exports	£55,154	£22,627	£522,955	£160,216	£760,952
1741					
Imports	£202,527	£232,175	£321,235	£208,506	£964,443
Exports	£64,030	£39,078	£658,468	£236,833	£998,409
1740					
Imports	£176,795	£176,464	£356,680	£185,533	£895,472
Exports	£74,690	£37,141	£390,032	£268,699	£770,562

Note: Data is in official sterling values as arbitrarily assigned by Customs Service, not market valuation of merchandise.

[a] Years of record end as of December 24.

Source: Jacob M. Price, "New Time Series for Scotland's and Britain's Trade with the Thirteen Colonies and States, 1740–1791," *William and Mary Quarterly,* XXXII (1975), 322–325.

TABLE 4.199 TRADE OF THE THIRTEEN COLONIES WITH ENGLAND, 1697–1739[a]

Year	New England	Middle Colonies	Virginia, Maryland	Carolinas & Georgia	Total
1739					
Imports	£220,378	£160,522	£217,200	£97,769	£695,869
Exports	£46,604	£26,593	£444,654	£236,425	£754,276
1738					
Imports	£203,233	£194,888	£258,860	£94,289	£751,270
Exports	£59,116	£28,146	£391,814	£141,136	£620,212
1737					
Imports	£223,923	£182,523	£211,301	£64,687	£682,434
Exports	£63,347	£32,031	£492,246	£187,758	£775,382
1736					
Imports	£222,158	£147,513	£204,794	£103,159	£677,624
Exports	£66,788	£38,730	£380,163	£214,083	£699,764
1735					
Imports	£189,125	£129,209	£220,381	£129,949	£668,664
Exports	£72,899	£36,074	£394,995	£148,358	£652,326
1734					
Imports	£146,460	£136,150	£172,086	£101,579	£556,275
Exports	£82,252	£35,524	£373,090	£120,484	£611,350
1733					
Imports	£184,570	£105,982	£186,177	£72,161	£548,890
Exports	£61,983	£26,402	£403,198	£178,048	£669,633
1732					
Imports	£216,600	£107,238	£148,289	£59,126	£531,253
Exports	£64,095	£17,935	£310,799	£126,207	£519,036
1731					
Imports	£183,467	£110,376	£171,278	£71,145	£536,266
Exports	£49,048	£33,542	£408,502	£159,771	£650,863
1730					
Imports	£208,196	£112,948	£150,931	£64,785	£536,860
Exports	£54,701	£19,322	£346,823	£151,739	£572,585
1729					
Imports	£161,102	£94,559	£108,931	£58,366	£422,958
Exports	£52,512	£23,267	£386,174	£113,329	£575,282
1728					
Imports	£194,590	£119,112	£171,092	£33,067	£517,861
Exports	£64,689	£36,371	£413,089	£91,175	£605,324

(continued)

TABLE 4.199   (continued)

Year	New England	Middle Colonies	Virginia, Maryland	Carolinas & Georgia	Total
1727					
Imports	£187,277	£99,431	£192,965	£23,254	£502,927
Exports	£75,052	£44,440	£421,588	£96,055	£637,135
1726					
Imports	£200,882	£122,500	£185,981	£43,934	£553,297
Exports	£63,816	£44,267	£324,767	£93,453	£526,303
1725					
Imports	£201,768	£112,859	£195,884	£39,182	£549,693
Exports	£72,021	£36,957	£214,730	£91,942	£415,650
1724					
Imports	£168,507	£93,344	£161,894	£37,839	£461,584
Exports	£69,585	£25,248	£277,344	£90,504	£462,681
1723					
Imports	£176,486	£69,005	£123,853	£42,246	£411,590
Exports	£59,337	£36,324	£287,997	£78,103	£461,761
1722					
Imports	£133,722	£83,875	£172,754	£34,374	£424,725
Exports	£47,955	£27,000	£283,091	£79,650	£437,696
1721					
Imports	£114,524	£72,302	£127,376	£17,703	£331,905
Exports	£50,483	£23,718	£357,812	£61,858	£493,871
1720					
Imports	£128,767	£61,928	£110,717	£18,290	£319,702
Exports	£49,206	£24,764	£331,482	£62,736	£468,188
1719					
Imports	£125,317	£83,423	£164,630	£19,630	£393,000
Exports	£54,452	£26,160	£332,069	£50,373	£463,054
1718					
Imports	£131,885	£85,682	£191,925	£15,841	£425,333
Exports	£61,591	£32,919	£316,576	£46,385	£457,471
1717					
Imports	£132,001	£66,645	£215,962	£25,058	£439,666
Exports	£58,898	£29,033	£296,884	£41,275	£426,090
1716					
Imports	£121,156	£74,015	£179,599	£27,272	£402,042
Exports	£69,595	£27,164	£281,343	£46,287	£424,389
1715					
Imports	£164,650	£71,811	£199,274	£16,631	£452,366
Exports	£66,555	£26,777	£174,756	£29,158	£297,246
1714					
Imports	£121,288	£59,570	£128,873	£23,712	£333,443
Exports	£51,541	£32,473	£280,470	£31,290	£395,774
1713					
Imports	£120,778	£63,507	£76,304	£23,967	£284,556
Exports	£49,904	£14,606	£206,263	£32,449	£303,222
1712					
Imports	£128,105	£26,988	£134,583	£20,015	£309,691
Exports	£24,699	£13,937	£297,941	£29,394	£365,971
1711					
Imports	£137,421	£48,264	£91,535	£20,406	£297,626
Exports	£26,415	£12,231	£273,181	£12,871	£324,698
1710					
Imports	£106,338	£40,069	£127,639	£19,613	£293,659
Exports	£31,112	£9,480	£188,429	£20,793	£249,814
1709					
Imports	£120,349	£40,458	£80,268	£28,521	£269,596
Exports	£29,559	£12,876	£261,668	£20,431	£324,534
1708					
Imports	£115,505	£33,621	£79,061	£11,996	£240,183
Exports	£49,635	£12,967	£213,493	£10,340	£286,435
1707					
Imports	£120,631	£44,220	£237,901	£10,492	£413,244
Exports	£38,793	£15,069	£207,625	£23,311	£284,798

Year	New England	Middle Colonies	Virginia, Maryland	Carolinas & Georgia	Total
1706					
Imports	£57,050	£42,625	£58,015	£4,001	£161,691
Exports	£22,210	£7,059	£149,152	£8,652	£187,073
1705					
Imports	£62,504	£35,108	£174,322	£19,788	£291,722
Exports	£22,793	£8,702	£116,768	£2,698	£150,961
1704					
Imports	£74,896	£34,113	£60,458	£6,621	£176,088
Exports	£30,823	£12,970	£264,112	£14,067	£321,972
1703					
Imports	£59,608	£27,461	£196,713	£12,428	£296,210
Exports	£33,539	£12,631	£144,928	£13,197	£204,295
1702					
Imports	£64,625	£39,333	£72,391	£10,460	£186,809
Exports	£37,026	£12,110	£274,782	£11,870	£335,788
1701					
Imports	£86,322	£43,913	£199,683	£13,908	£343,826
Exports	£32,656	£23,767	£235,738	£16,973	£309,134
1700					
Imports	£91,918	£67,939	£173,481	£11,003	£344,341
Exports	£41,486	£22,175	£317,302	£14,058	£395,021
1699					
Imports	£127,279	£59,856	£205,078	£11,401	£403,614
Exports	£26,660	£18,295	£198,115	£12,327	£255,397
1698					
Imports	£93,517	£35,983	£310,135	£18,462	£458,097
Exports	£31,254	£11,483	£174,053	£9,265	£226,055
1697					
Imports	£68,468	£7,576	£58,796	£5,289	£140,129
Exports	£26,282	£13,440	£227,756	£12,374	£279,852

Note: Data is in official sterling values as arbitrarily assigned by Customs Service, not market valuation of merchandise. Errors in original records have been corrected.
[a] Years of record end as of December 24, except 1697 and 1698, which end as of September 28.
Source: Bureau of the Census, *Historical Statistics of the United States, Colonial Times to 1957* (1960), 757.

TABLE 4.200   IRELAND'S DIRECT AND INDIRECT TRADE WITH THE THIRTEEN COLONIES, 1736–1776

Avg. of 4 years Ending	Exports to Colonies			Imports from Colonies							Balance
	Linen[a]	Provisions[b]	Total Exports	Flaxseed	Wood[c]	Wheat & flour	Rum[d]	Tobacco	Other goods[e]	Total Imports	
1736	£12,330	£10,410	£22,740	£4,410	£5,250	£2,630	£880	£30,150	£2,290	£45,610	(£22,870)
1740	£16,030	£8,290	£24,320	£13,880	£4,130	£4,010	£1,160	£22,430	£3,490	£49,100	(£24,780)
1744	£17,580	£12,660	£30,240	£15,810	£2,540	£20,340	£2,070	£26,560	£4,660	£71,980	(£41,740)
1748	£33,280	£11,490	£44,770	£14,140	£1,110	£3,050	£1,400	£29,750	£3,820	£53,270	(£8,500)
1752	£50,760	£12,640	£63,400	£13,160	£4,640	£1,330	£2,860	£33,410	£9,150	£64,550	(£1,150)
1756	£45,210	£14,110	£59,320	£30,660	£5,530	£4,910	£4,300	£30,290	£6,040	£81,730	(£22,410)
1760	£125,610	£49,590	£175,200	£30,910	£2,120	£11,390	£2,740	£37,870	£7,080	£92,110	£83,090
1764	£164,120	£39,130	£203,250	£32,760	£3,940	£230	£4,980	£43,750	£7,910	£93,570	£109,680
1768	£156,960	£21,140	£178,100	£40,090	£8,450	£25,690	£7,290	£39,400	£9,000	£129,920	£48,180
1772	£287,260	£23,020	£310,280	£50,020	£9,030	£42,080	£9,040	£43,410	£9,220	£162,800	£147,480
1776	£175,340	£23,880	£199,220	£54,300	£8,800	£18,690	£7,570	£41,660	£10,480	£141,500	£57,720

[a] Share of indirect component of total linen exports to British America landed in North America is estimated at 70% for 1733–56, 80% in the four years ending 1760, and 85% for 1761–76.
[b] North American share of provisions export is estimated at 10%, except for periods ending 1760 (25%) and 1764 (15%).
[c] Barrel staves, lumber, timber, and woodenware.
[d] Share of total rum imports landed from the North American mainland is estimated at 7%.
[e] Does not include colonial-built ships.
Source: Thomas M. Truxnes, *Irish-American Trade, 1660–1783* (1988), 52.

CHAPTER 5 Population Statistics

The governments of the thirteen colonies rarely attempted to make accurate counts of how many people occupied their boundaries. Their failure to conduct censuses at frequent intervals derived from two circumstances. The first was a superstitious fear that ill fortune would ensue from numbering a people, based on accounts in II Samuel 24:1–25 and I Chronicles 21:1–27 of how David brought a plague on the Israelites after having his officials count them. More significant, however, was the fact that European governments had yet to recognize the benefits of taking regular censuses. (Great Britain itself would not begin to count its population on a regular basis until 1801.) Colonial officials most commonly accumulated population data for the limited purposes of assessing their ability to raise taxes or troops, and such information did not require a complete enumeration of all inhabitants, only a militia muster or list of tithables.

No mainland colony carried out any censuses during the seventeenth century except Virginia (in 1624, 1625, 1634, and 1699) and New York (in 1698). After the Board of Trade's establishment in 1696, royal governors began to receive more frequent directives to determine the exact population within their jurisdiction. The thirteen colonies conducted forty-one censuses in the eighteenth century. Half

TABLE 5.1 ESTIMATED POPULATION OF THE THIRTEEN COLONIES, 1620–1760

Colony	1760 No.	1760 (%)	1750 No.	1750 (%)	1740 No.	1740 (%)	1730 No.	1730 (%)	1720 No.	1720 (%)	1710 No.	1710 (%)	1700 No.	1700 (%)	1690 No.	1690 (%)	1680 No.	1680 (%)
New Hampshire	39,093	(100%)	27,505	(100%)	23,256	(100%)	10,755	(100%)	9,375	(100%)	5,681	(100%)	4,958	(100%)	4,164	(100%)	2,047	(100%)
whites	38,493	(99%)	26,955	(98%)	22,756	(98%)	10,555	(98%)	9,205	(98%)	5,531	(97%)	4,828	(99%)	4,064	(98%)	1,972	(96%)
blacks	600	(1%)	550	(2%)	500	(2%)	200	(2%)	170	(2%)	150	(3%)	130	(1%)	100	(2%)	75	(4%)
Massachusetts[a]	220,600	(100%)	188,000	(100%)	151,613	(100%)	114,116	(100%)	91,008	(100%)	62,390	(100%)	55,941	(100%)	49,504	(100%)	39,752	(100%)
whites	217,734	(98%)	183,925	(98%)	148,578	(98%)	111,336	(98%)	88,858	(98%)	61,080	(98%)	55,141	(99%)	49,104	(99%)	39,582	(99%)
blacks	4,866	(2%)	4,075	(2%)	3,035	(2%)	2,780	(2%)	2,150	(2%)	1,310	(2%)	800	(1%)	400	(1%)	170	(1%)
Plymouth	...	...	...	...	...	...	...	...	...	...	...	...	...	...	7,424	(100%)	6,400	(100%)
whites	...	...	...	...	...	...	...	...	...	...	...	...	...	...	7,424	(100%)	6,400	(100%)
blacks	...	...	...	...	...	...	...	...	...	...	...	...	...	...	...	...	...	...
Rhode Island	45,471	(100%)	33,226	(100%)	25,255	(100%)	16,950	(100%)	11,680	(100%)	7,573	(100%)	5,894	(100%)	4,224	(100%)	3,017	(100%)
whites	42,003	(92%)	29,879	(90%)	22,847	(90%)	15,302	(90%)	11,137	(95%)	7,198	(95%)	5,594	(95%)	3,974	(94%)	2,842	(94%)
blacks	3,468	(8%)	3,347	(10%)	2,408	(10%)	1,648	(10%)	543	(5%)	375	(5%)	300	(5%)	250	(6%)	175	(6%)
Connecticut[b]	142,470	(100%)	111,280	(100%)	89,580	(100%)	75,530	(100%)	58,830	(100%)	39,450	(100%)	25,970	(100%)	21,645	(100%)	17,246	(100%)
whites	138,687	(97%)	108,270	(97%)	86,982	(97%)	74,040	(98%)	57,737	(98%)	38,700	(98%)	25,520	(98%)	21,445	(99%)	17,196	(100%)
blacks	3,783	(3%)	3,010	(3%)	2,598	(3%)	1,490	(2%)	1,093	(2%)	750	(2%)	450	(2%)	200	(1%)	50	...
New York	117,138	(100%)	76,696	(100%)	63,665	(100%)	48,594	(100%)	36,919	(100%)	21,625	(100%)	19,107	(100%)	13,909	(100%)	9,830	(100%)
whites	100,798	(86%)	65,682	(86%)	54,669	(86%)	41,638	(86%)	31,179	(84%)	18,814	(87%)	16,851	(88%)	12,239	(88%)	8,630	(88%)
blacks	16,340	(14%)	11,014	(14%)	8,996	(14%)	6,956	(14%)	5,740	(16%)	2,811	(13%)	2,256	(12%)	1,670	(12%)	1,200	(12%)
New Jersey	93,813	(100%)	71,393	(100%)	51,373	(100%)	37,510	(100%)	29,818	(100%)	19,872	(100%)	14,010	(100%)	8,000	(100%)	3,400	(100%)
whites	87,246	(93%)	66,039	(93%)	47,007	(92%)	34,502	(92%)	27,433	(92%)	18,540	(93%)	13,170	(94%)	7,550	(94%)	3,200	(94%)
blacks	6,567	(7%)	5,354	(7%)	4,366	(8%)	3,008	(8%)	2,385	(8%)	1,332	(7%)	840	(6%)	450	(6%)	200	(6%)
Pennsylvania	183,703	(100%)	119,666	(100%)	85,637	(100%)	51,707	(100%)	30,962	(100%)	24,450	(100%)	17,950	(100%)	11,450	(100%)	680	(100%)
whites	179,294	(98%)	116,794	(98%)	83,582	(98%)	50,466	(98%)	28,962	(94%)	22,875	(94%)	17,520	(98%)	11,180	(98%)	655	(96%)
blacks	4,409	(2%)	2,872	(2%)	2,055	(2%)	1,241	(2%)	2,000	(6%)	1,575	(6%)	430	(2%)	270	(2%)	25	(4%)
Delaware	33,250	(100%)	28,704	(100%)	19,870	(100%)	9,170	(100%)	5,385	(100%)	3,645	(100%)	2,470	(100%)	1,482	(100%)	1,005	(100%)
whites	31,517	(95%)	27,208	(95%)	18,835	(95%)	8,692	(95%)	4,685	(87%)	3,145	(86%)	2,335	(95%)	1,400	(94%)	950	(95%)
blacks	1,733	(5%)	1,496	(5%)	1,035	(5%)	478	(5%)	700	(13%)	500	(14%)	135	(5%)	82	(5%)	55	(5%)
Maryland	162,267	(100%)	141,073	(100%)	116,093	(100%)	91,113	(100%)	66,133	(100%)	42,741	(100%)	29,604	(100%)	24,024	(100%)	17,904	(100%)
whites	113,263	(70%)	97,623	(69%)	92,062	(79%)	73,893	(81%)	53,634	(81%)	34,796	(81%)	26,377	(89%)	21,862	(91%)	16,293	(91%)
blacks	49,004	(30%)	43,450	(31%)	24,031	(21%)	17,220	(19%)	12,499	(19%)	7,945	(19%)	3,227	(11%)	2,162	(9%)	1,611	(9%)
Virginia	339,726	(100%)	231,033	(100%)	180,440	(100%)	114,000	(100%)	87,757	(100%)	78,281	(100%)	58,560	(100%)	53,046	(100%)	43,596	(100%)
whites	199,156	(59%)	129,581	(56%)	120,440	(67%)	84,000	(74%)	61,198	(70%)	55,163	(70%)	42,170	(72%)	43,701	(82%)	40,596	(93%)
blacks	140,470	(41%)	101,452	(44%)	60,000	(33%)	30,000	(26%)	26,559	(30%)	23,118	(30%)	16,390	(28%)	9,345	(18%)	3,000	(7%)
North Carolina	110,442	(100%)	72,984	(100%)	51,760	(100%)	30,000	(100%)	21,270	(100%)	15,120	(100%)	10,720	(100%)	7,600	(100%)	5,430	(100%)
whites	76,888	(70%)	53,184	(73%)	40,760	(79%)	24,000	(80%)	18,270	(86%)	14,220	(94%)	10,305	(96%)	7,300	(96%)	5,220	(96%)
blacks	33,554	(30%)	19,800	(27%)	11,000	(21%)	6,000	(20%)	3,000	(14%)	900	(6%)	415	(4%)	300	(4%)	210	(4%)
South Carolina	94,074	(100%)	64,000	(100%)	45,000	(100%)	30,000	(100%)	17,048	(100%)	10,883	(100%)	5,704	(100%)	3,900	(100%)	1,200	(100%)
whites	36,740	(40%)	25,000	(39%)	15,000	(33%)	10,000	(33%)	5,048	(30%)	6,783	(62%)	3,260	(57%)	2,400	(62%)	1,000	(83%)
blacks	57,334	(60%)	39,000	(61%)	30,000	(67%)	20,000	(67%)	12,000	(70%)	4,100	(38%)	2,444	(43%)	1,500	(38%)	200	(17%)
Georgia	9,578	(100%)	5,200	(100%)	2,021	(100%)	...	...	...	...	...	...	...	...	...	...	...	...
whites	6,000	(63%)	4,200	(81%)	2,021	(100%)	...	...	...	...	...	...	...	...	...	...	...	...
blacks	3,578	(37%)	1,000	(19%)	...	...	...	...	...	...	...	...	...	...	...	...	...	...
Total	1,593,625	(100%)	1,170,760	(100%)	905,563	(100%)	629,445	(100%)	466,185	(100%)	331,711	(100%)	250,888	(100%)	210,372	(100%)	151,507	(100%)
whites	1,267,819	(80%)	934,340	(80%)	755,539	(83%)	538,424	(86%)	397,346	(85%)	286,845	(86%)	223,071	(89%)	193,643	(92%)	144,536	(95%)
blacks	325,806	(20%)	236,420	(20%)	150,024	(17%)	91,021	(14%)	68,839	(15%)	44,866	(14%)	27,817	(11%)	16,729	(8%)	6,971	(5%)

Colony	1670 No.	1670 (%)	1660 No.	1660 (%)	1650 No.	1650 (%)	1640 No.	1640 (%)	1630 No.	1630 (%)	1620 No.	1620 (%)
New Hampshire	1,805	(100%)	1,555	(100%)	1,305	(100%)	1,055	(100%)	500	(100%)	...	...
whites	1,740	(99%)	1,505	(97%)	1,265	(97%)	1,025	(99%)	500	(100%)	...	...
black	65	(1%)	50	(3%)	40	(3%)	30	(1%)	...	...	...	...
Massachusetts[a]	30,000	(100%)	20,082	(100%)	14,307	(100%)	8,932	(100%)	506	(100%)	...	...
whites	29,840	(99%)	19,660	(98%)	14,012	(98%)	8,782	(98%)	506	(100%)	...	...
blacks	160	(1%)	422	(2%)	295	(2%)	150	(2%)	...	...	...	...
Plymouth	5,333	(100%)	1,980	(100%)	1,566	(100%)	1,020	(100%)	390	(100%)	102	(100%)
whites	5,333	(100%)	1,980	(100%)	1,566	(100%)	1,020	(100%)	390	(100%)	102	(100%)
blacks	...	...	...	...	...	...	...	...	...	...	...	...
Rhode Island	2,155	(100%)	1,539	(100%)	785	(100%)	300	(100%)	...	...	...	...
whites	2,040	(95%)	1,474	(96%)	760	(97%)	...	...	...	...	...	...
blacks	115	(5%)	65	(4%)	25	(3%)	...	...	...	...	...	...
Connecticut[b]	12,603	(100%)	7,980	(100%)	4,139	(100%)	1,472	(100%)	...	...	...	...
whites	12,568	(100%)	7,955	(100%)	4,119	(100%)	1,457	(99%)	...	...	...	...
blacks	35	...	25	...	20	...	15	(1%)	...	...	...	...
New York	5,754	(100%)	4,936	(100%)	4,116	(100%)	1,930	(100%)	350	(100%)	...	...
whites	5,064	(88%)	4,336	(88%)	3,616	(88%)	1,698	(88%)	340	(97%)	...	...
blacks	690	(12%)	600	(12%)	500	(12%)	232	(12%)	10	(3%)	...	...
New Jersey	1,000	(100%)	...	...	...	...	...	...	...	...	...	...
whites	940	(94%)	...	...	...	...	...	...	...	...	...	...
blacks	60	(6%)	...	...	...	...	...	...	...	...	...	...
Pennsylvania	...	...	...	...	...	...	...	...	...	...	...	...
whites	...	...	...	...	...	...	...	...	...	...	...	...
blacks	...	...	...	...	...	...	...	...	...	...	...	...
Delware	700	(100%)	540	(100%)	185	(100%)	100	(100%)[c]	...	...	...	...
whites	660	(94%)	510	(94%)	170	(92%)	100	(100%)	...	...	...	...
blacks	40	(6%)	30	(6%)	15	(8%)	...	...	...	...	...	...
Maryland	13,226	(100%)	8,426	(100%)	4,504	(100%)	583	(100%)	...	...	...	...
whites	12,036	(91%)	7,668	(91%)	4,204	(93%)	563	(97%)	...	...	...	...
blacks	1,190	(9%)	758	(9%)	300	(7%)	20	(3%)	...	...	...	...
Virginia	35,309	(100%)	27,020	(100%)	18,731	(100%)	10,442	(100%)	2,500	(100%)	2,200	(100%)
whites	33,309	(94%)	26,070	(96%)	18,326	(98%)	10,292	(99%)	2,450	(98%)	2,180	(99%)
blacks	2,000	(6%)	950	(4%)	405	(2%)	150	(1%)	50	(2%)	20	(1%)
North Carolina	3,850	(100%)	1,000	(100%)	...	...	...	...	...	...	...	...
whites	3,700	(96%)	980	(98%)	...	...	...	...	...	...	...	...
blacks	150	(4%)	20	(2%)	...	...	...	...	...	...	...	...
South Carolina	200	(100%)	...	...	...	...	...	...	...	...	...	...
whites	170	(85%)	...	...	...	...	...	...	...	...	...	...
blacks	30	(15%)	...	...	...	...	...	...	...	...	...	...
Georgia	...	...	...	...	...	...	...	...	...	...	...	...
whites	...	...	...	...	...	...	...	...	...	...	...	...
blacks	...	...	...	...	...	...	...	...	...	...	...	...
Total	111,935	(100%)	75,058	(100%)	50,368	(100%)	26,734	(100%)	4,646	(100%)	2,302	(100%)
whites	107,400	(96%)	72,138	(96%)	48,768	(97%)	26,137	(98%)	4,586	(99%)	2,282	(99%)
blacks	4,535	(4%)	2,920	(4%)	1,600	(3%)	597	(2%)	60	(1%)	20	(1%)

[a] Includes Maine.
[b] Includes New Haven.
[c] Corrected from original.

Source: Research of Stella H. Sutherland in Bureau of the Census, *Historical Statistics of the United States: Colonial Times to 1957* (1960), 756.

of these enumerations came from just three provinces—New York, New Jersey, and Maryland. Virginia took its last census in 1703, while no counts at all were made by Pennsylvania, Delaware, North Carolina, and South Carolina.

The Board of Trade usually sent a general request for figures on a particular province's population, at which point the governor would give specific instructions on how to solicit information on the distribution of people according to race, sex, and age. Local officials, such as constables, town selectmen, or tax assessors, carried out the actual count. Although surviving evidence strongly indicates that conscientious efforts were made to achieve accurate figures by most census takers, every enumeration must have missed substantial numbers of people due to the dispersed nature of settlement and the high rate of geographic mobility. No studies have yet attempted to determine how precise these population statistics are, but it is unlikely that they are more reliable than the federal censuses of the late nineteenth century, which commonly missed a tenth or more of all U.S. residents.

By analyzing these censuses with taxpayer rolls and miscellaneous estimates of whites and blacks in various colonies, historians have calculated a reasonably accurate series of demographic statistics for the thirteen colonies. Their research has verified that these provinces increased their numbers with extreme rapidity. English and Dutch mainland colonies required only forty-three years before their inhabitants totaled 50,000; during the next quarter-century, they not only expanded to a quarter million but also for the first time became more numerous than the Indians living east of the Appalachians. During the period from 1700 to 1775, the thirteen colonies' population multiplied tenfold, to 2,500,000.

The colonies expanded at a rate of approximately 35% per decade in the eighteenth century. By comparison, the population of England and Wales generally increased at decennial rates varying from 5% to 8% in the same period. This disparity in growth quickly produced a major redistribution of population within England's empire. In 1670, almost two-thirds of the empire's inhabitants lived in England or Wales, compared to just 1% in the mainland colonies. A century later, however, slightly less than half of the empire's subjects resided in England or Wales, while 15% lived in the thirteen colonies. In only one century, the ratio of English and Welsh for every American had dropped from 50 to 1 in 1670 to approximately 3 to 1 on the eve of the Revolution.

The colonial population grew most rapidly in times of peace and frontier expansion in the eighteenth century. It multiplied at its highest rate in the 1720s in the aftermath of Queen Anne's War when settlers suddenly surged past the fall line to claim lands long ago vacated by Indians. Because the prospect of acquiring fertile lands at low prices stimulated both immigration and the importation of slaves, population kept rising at fast clip during the generation of peace that lasted through 1754. The last French and Indian War curtailed growth significantly for a decade after then, but British victory stimulated another major period of frontier settlement in the 1760s, when the colonial population rose at its second-greatest rate of the eighteenth century.

Frontier expansion steadily redistributed the colonial population. In 1650, 83% of Anglo-Americans lived in Virginia (37%), Massachusetts (29%), Maryland (9%), and Connecticut (8%), but by 1700, these provinces included just 71% of the total (25% in Massachusetts, 26% in Virginia, 11% in Maryland, and 9% in Connecticut). In 1760, these four colonies accounted for just 55% of all inhabitants (15% in Massachusetts, 9% in Connecticut, 21% in Virginia, and 10% in Maryland). The oldest regions grew at an increasingly slower rate as their inhabitants were siphoned off by the lure of inexpensive land in newly settled regions. By 1760, 27% of British Americans lived in the colonies that had grown most quickly due to either foreign immigration, Pennsylvania (14%), or to domestic in-migration, the Carolinas (13%).

Benjamin Franklin examined the dynamics by which the colonies expanded so rapidly in his 1751 essay *Observations Concerning the Increase of Mankind and the Peopling of Countries*. He correctly noted that despite heavy immigration from Europe and Africa, most American population increase derived from children born to the native-born inhabitants. Because young adults could afford to marry young (due to high wages arising from a labor scarcity and easy access to land), they began to raise families far earlier than did Europeans. A benign disease environment, in which the dispersed and well-nourished population suffered only minor losses to contagious maladies, kept mortality low among both infants and adults. Parents consequently raised an average of seven to eight children into adulthood, more than double the number in Europe. Natural increase approached the maximum limits of biological reproduction and accounted for two-thirds of the total increase in numbers. Anglo-Americans, in other words, were the first people in modern times to experience the phenomenon now termed a *population explosion* and did so without the benefit of modern medicine.

TABLE 5.2   POPULATION OF THE AMERICAN COLONIES AND BRITISH ISLES, 1650–1770

Year	England & Wales No.	(%)	Scotland No.	(%)	Ireland No.	(%)	West Indies[a] No.	(%)	Thirteen Colonies No.	(%)	Total No.	(%)
1770	7,052,000	(49%)	1,377,000	(9%)	3,542,000	(24%)	436,000	(3%)	2,148,000	(15%)	14,555,000	(100%)
1760	6,569,000	(50%)	1,302,000	(10%)	3,324,000	(25%)	392,000	(3%)	1,594,000	(12%)	13,181,000	(100%)
1750	6,140,000	(51%)	1,228,000	(10%)	3,160,000	(26%)	343,000	(3%)	1,171,000	(10%)	12,042,000	(100%)
1740	5,926,000	(52%)	1,185,000	(10%)	3,081,000	(27%)	296,000	(3%)	906,000	(8%)	11,394,000	(100%)
1730	5,947,000	(54%)	1,189,000	(11%)	3,022,000	(27%)	268,000	(2%)	629,000	(6%)	11,055,000	(100%)
1720	6,001,000	(55%)	1,200,000	(11%)	2,936,000	(27%)	221,000	(2%)	466,000	(4%)	10,824,000	(100%)
1710	5,981,000	(57%)	1,196,000	(12%)	2,741,000	(26%)	162,000	(2%)	332,000	(3%)	10,412,000	(100%)
1700	5,826,000	(59%)	1,165,000	(12%)	2,491,000	(25%)	129,000	(1%)	251,000	(3%)	9,862,000	(100%)
1690	5,739,000	(61%)	1,148,000	(12%)	2,242,000	(24%)	133,000	(1%)	210,000	(2%)	9,472,000	(100%)
1680	5,653,000	(62%)	1,131,000	(12%)	2,013,000	(22%)	107,000	(1%)	152,000	(2%)	9,056,000	(100%)
1670	5,566,000	(64%)	1,113,000	(13%)	1,793,000	(21%)	75,000	(1%)	112,000	(1%)	8,659,000	(100%)
1660	5,524,000	(66%)	1,105,000	(13%)	1,573,000	(19%)	56,000	(1%)	75,000	(1%)	8,333,000	(100%)
1650	5,482,000	(68%)	1,096,000	(14%)	1,353,000	(17%)	30,000	(0.4%)	50,000	(0.6%)	8,011,000	(100%)

[a] Includes Bermuda.

Source: Research of Stella H. Sutherland in Bureau of the Census, *Historical Statistics of the United States: Colonial Times to 1957* (1960), 756. Richard S. Dunn, *Sugar and Slaves: The Rise of the Planter Class in the English West Indies, 1624–1713* (1972), 312. John J. McCusker, *Rum and the American Revolution: The Rum Trade and the Balance of Payments of the Thirteen Continental Colonies*, 2 vols. (1989), II, 552, 692–704.

POPULATION DENSITY, 1650

This map shows the population density in 1650 (each dot represents 200 rural inhabitants). Total population was about 50,000, primarily clustered along Virginia's lower James River, New York's lower Hudson valley, the lower Connecticut valley, and the Massachusetts coastline. (Map drawn by Jeremy Eagle, based on information from *The Geographical Review*, XXX [1940], inset following p 464)

TABLE 5.3   RATES OF POPULATION GROWTH IN THE THIRTEEN COLONIES, BY DECADE, 1630–1770

Decade	Percentage of Increase in			Percent of Blacks in Total Population at Decade's End
	White Population	Black Population	Total Population	
1760–1770	33%	41%	37%	21%
1750–1760	36%	38%	33%	20%
1740–1750	24%	57%	36%	20%
1730–1740	41%	65%	36%	17%
1720–1730	36%	32%	38%	14%
1710–1720	38%	53%	33%	15%
1700–1710	29%	61%	30%	14%
1690–1700	15%	66%	19%	11%
1680–1690	34%	40%	39%	8%
1670–1680	35%	54%	35%	5%
1660–1670	49%	55%	49%	4%
1650–1660	48%	82%	49%	4%
1640–1650	87%	168%	88%	3%
1630–1640	450%	900%	475%	2%

Source: Jim Potter, "Demographic Development and Family Structure," in Jack P. Greene and J.R. Pole, eds., *Colonial British America: Essays in the History of the Early Modern Era* (1984), 137.

TABLE 5.4   PERCENT INCREASE IN POPULATION OF THE THIRTEEN COLONIES, BY DECADE, 1630–1770

Colony	1760–1770	1750–1760	1740–1750	1730–1740	1720–1730	1710–1720	1700–1710
New Hampshire	58%	23%	41%	83%	26%	27%	25%
Massachusetts[a]	27%	31%	14%	26%	36%	15%	14%
Plymouth	…	…	…	…	…	…	…
Rhode Island	25%	26%	46%	42%	54%	38%	33%
Connecticut[b]	23%	42%	43%	27%	38%	29%	29%
New England	**28%**	**33%**	**26%**	**31%**	**38%**	**20%**	**20%**
New York	64%	41%	27%	29%	36%	39%	37%
New Jersey	21%	38%	27%	41%	42%	30%	43%
Pennsylvania	25%	47%	50%	54%	35%	37%	75%
Delaware	7%	16%	44%	117%	70%	48%	48%
Middle Colonies	**34%**	**43%**	**38%**	**42%**	**37%**	**36%**	**53%**
Maryland	24%	18%	31%	28%	32%	44%	39%
Virginia	30%	26%	38%	31%	32%	33%	21%
North Carolina	100%	44%	60%	67%	130%	87%	40%
South Carolina	47%	40%	51%	50%	44%	60%	63%
Georgia	189%	80%	157%	…	…	…	…
South	**44%**	**29%**	**41%**	**36%**	**39%**	**41%**	**29%**

Colony	1690–1700	1680–1690	1670–1680	1660–1670	1650–1660	1640–1650	1630–1640
New Hampshire	19%	103%	13%	16%	19%	24%	111%
Massachusetts[a]	13%	25%	33%	49%	43%	57%	1,665%
Plymouth	…	16%	20%	169%	26%	54%	162%
Rhode Island	40%	40%	40%	40%	96%	162%	…
Connecticut[b]	20%	26%	37%	58%	93%	181%	…
New England	**22%**	**27%**	**32%**	**57%**	**45%**	**67%**	**662%**
New York	37%	41%	71%	17%	20%	113%	451%
New Jersey	75%	135%	240%	…	…	…	…
Pennsylvania	57%	1,584%	…	…	…	…	…
Delaware	67%	47%	44%	30%	192%	…	…
Middle Colonies	**51%**	**134%**	**100%**	**36%**	**27%**	**123%**	**451%**
Maryland	23%	34%	35%	57%	87%	673%	…
Virginia	10%	22%	23%	31%	44%	79%	318%
North Carolina	41%	40%	41%	285%	…	…	…
South Carolina	46%	225%	500%	…	…	…	…
Georgia	…	…	…	…	…	…	…
South	**31%**	**30%**	**30%**	**44%**	**57%**	**111%**	**341%**

[a] Includes Maine.
[b] Includes colony of New Haven.
Source: J[ames]. Potter, "The Growth of Population in America, 1700–1860," in D. V. Glass and D. E. C. Eversley, eds., *Population in History: Essays in Historical Demography* (1965), 639.

TABLE 5.5 DISTRIBUTION OF POPULATION WITHIN THE THIRTEEN COLONIES, 1640–1770

Colony	1770	1760	1750	1740	1730	1720	1710	1700	1690	1680	1670	1660	1650	1640
New Hampshire	3%	2%	3%	2%	2%	2%	2%	2%	2%	1%	2%	2%	3%	4%
Massachusetts[a]	14%	15%	15%	18%	19%	19%	22%	25%	24%	26%	27%	27%	29%	37%
Plymouth	...	...	...	...	...	...	...	...	3%	4%	5%	3%	3%	4%
Rhode Island	3%	3%	3%	3%	3%	2%	2%	2%	2%	2%	2%	2%	2%	1%
Connecticut[b]	8%	9%	8%	8%	8%	8%	9%	9%	10%	11%	11%	11%	8%	5%
New England	**28%**	**29%**	**29%**	**31%**	**32%**	**31%**	**35%**	**38%**	**41%**	**45%**	**46%**	**44%**	**45%**	**51%**
New York	8%	7%	7%	7%	7%	8%	7%	7%	7%	6%	5%	7%	8%	7%
New Jersey	5%	6%	5%	6%	6%	5%	6%	5%	4%	2%	1%	...	...	...
Pennsylvania	12%	14%	12%	11%	10%	10%	10%	7%	5%	c	c	c	...	...
Delaware	2%	2%	2%	2%	1%	1%	1%	1%	1%	1%	1%	1%	c	c
Middle Colonies	**26%**	**26%**	**24%**	**24%**	**23%**	**24%**	**23%**	**20%**	**17%**	**10%**	**7%**	**7%**	**9%**	**7%**
Maryland	9%	10%	11%	12%	13%	13%	12%	11%	11%	12%	12%	11%	9%	2%
Virginia	20%	21%	23%	22%	23%	24%	24%	26%	25%	29%	32%	36%	37%	39%
North Carolina	10%	7%	7%	6%	5%	3%	2%	2%	4%	3%	3%	1%	...	...
South Carolina	6%	6%	6%	5%	4%	4%	4%	3%	2%	1%	c	...	...	...
Georgia	1%	c	c	c	...	...	...	...	...	...	...	...	...	...
South	**46%**	**44%**	**47%**	**45%**	**45%**	**45%**	**42%**	**42%**	**42%**	**45%**	**47%**	**49%**	**46%**	**41%**

Note: Original data corrected to reflect addition of Delaware.
[a] Includes Maine.
[b] Includes colony of New Haven.
[c] Under 1%.
Source: J[ames]. Potter, "The Growth of Population in America, 1700–1860," in D. V. Glass and D. E. C. Eversley, eds., *Population in History: Essays in Historical Demography* (1965), 638.

Population of New England

During the decade after New England's first settlement in 1620, about 400 settlers came to inhabit Plymouth and approximately 1,400 other English established themselves in scattered fishing outposts from Cape Cod to southern Maine. The region's population rose sharply once the Massachusetts Bay Company initiated a large-scale Puritan migration in 1630. This flood of religious dissenters continued at a heavy pace until shortly after 1642 when the English Civil War reduced it to a trickle.

New England received so few immigrants after 1650 that its population growth derived primarily from natural increase for the rest of the colonial era. Natural increase occurred at a rate close to the biological maximum in large part because the sex ratio quickly became balanced because two-thirds of the first generation of Puritans arrived in family groups rather than as single male laborers. The low population density also made epidemics rare and kept infant mortality at minimal levels. The 38,800 English immigrants who arrived before 1670 consequently multiplied to 91,000 by 1700.

New England continued to grow almost exclusively from natural increase in the eighteenth century. Its rate of expansion nevertheless slowed considerably as rising population density promoted a swelling tide of out-migration to the Mid-Atlantic region. New England consequently experienced the lowest rate of growth within British North America, and it saw its share of the colonies' total population drop significantly from 39% in 1700 to 29% by 1760.

TABLE 5.6 COUNTS OF FREEMEN IN PLYMOUTH COLONY TOWNS, 1643–1690

Town	1643 Free-men[a]	1643 Able to Bear Arms[b]	1658 Free-men	1675 Free-men	1684 Free-men	1690 Militia
Plymouth	64	148	62	54	55	155
Duxbury	34	81	39	43	40	82
Scituate	31	105	46	50	62	173
Sandwich	12	69	8	11	15	100
Cohannet	15	...	...	...	...	...
Yarmouth	16	52	14	19	22	118
Barnstable	22	61	42	44	53	134
Marshfield	11	51	28	32	63	80
Rehoboth	4	...	16	40	52	166
Nawsett	10	...	...	...	...	...
Taunton	...	55	17	31	44	196
Eastham	...	...	21	34	35	119
Bridgewater	...	...	10	16	...	88
Dartmouth	...	...	...	6	...	96
Swansea	...	...	...	12	...	101
Middlebury	...	...	...	...	8	33
Bristol	...	...	...	...	...	108
Freetown	...	...	...	...	...	31
Little Compton	...	...	...	...	...	82
Others	...	...	...	...	7	...
Total	219	622	303	407	441	1,862

[a] Freemen were citizens with the right to vote.
[b] Men aged 16–60.
Source: Evarts B. Greene and Virginia D. Harrington, *American Population Before the Federal Census of 1790* (1932), 11–12, 21.

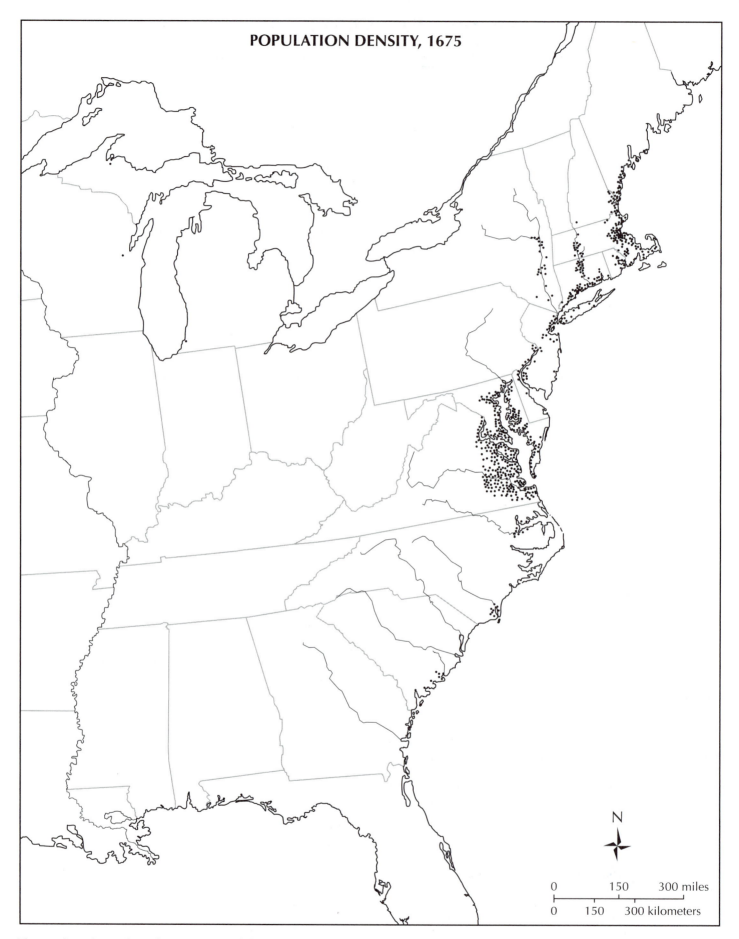

POPULATION DENSITY, 1675

0   150   300 miles

0   150   300 kilometers

This map shows the population density in 1675 (each dot represents 200 rural inhabitants). Total population was about 125,000. (Map drawn by Jeremy Eagle based on information from *The Geographical Review,* XXX [1940], inset following p. 464)

TABLE 5.7 CENSUS OF MASSACHUSETTS BAY MILITIA, 1690

County-Town	Population of Militia
Suffolk	
Boston	954
Roxberry	129
Dorchester	149
Braintree	139
Weymouth	116
Hingham	119
Dedham	111
Milton	78
Medfield	98
Hull	53
Muddy River	51
Wrentham	44
Mendham	52
Horse:	
Weymouth	56
Total	2,149
Middlesex One-Half	
Watertown	151
Cambridge	118
Cambridge Vill.	77
Charlestown	98
Charlestown	91
Redding	75
Oborne	142
Medfield	20
Malden	73
Horse: [1]	80
[2]	60
Total	985
Middlesex One-Half	
Groton	58
Malborough	68
Chelmsford	98
Dunstable	31
Billerica	105
Lancaster	58
Sherborne	63
Sudbury	103
Concord	162
Stow	29
Horse:	
Sudbury	104
Total	879
Essex One-Half	
Salem	129
Salem	115
Ipswich	129
Ipswich	175
Lynn	120
Marblehead	206
Beverly	137
Gloucester	77
Warham	70
Salem Village	82
Horse:	
Salem	40
Ipswich	71
Lynn	57
Beverly	37
Total	1,445

County-Town	Population of Militia
Essex One-Half	
Newberry	129
Newberry	116
Salsbury	112
Rowley	115
Haverhill	113
Topsfield	75
Andover	106
Amesbury	96
Bradford	48
Boxford	33
Horse:	
Newbury and Rowley	78
Haverhill } Salsbury }	45
Amesbury Andover Topsfield Bradford }	51
Total	1,112 [1,117]
Cornwall	
Newton and Sagadahoc	94
New Dartmouth	47
James Town and New Harbor	60
Total	201
Plymouth	
Plymouth	155
Bridgewater	88
Duxberry	82
Middleborough	33
Scituate	173
Marshfield	80
Total	606 [611]
Bristol	
Bristol	108
Freetown	31
Dartmouth	96
Rehoboth	166
Taunton	196
Swansey	101
Little Compton	82
Total	780
Hampshire	
Springfield	98
Hadley	62
Northampton	110
Hatfield	82
Deerfield	51
Northfield	34
Suffield	60
Westfield	56
Enfield	36
Horse:	
Springfield	65
Total	654
Barnstable	
Eastham	119
Yarmouth	118
Barnstable	134
Sandwich	100
Total	471
Total of all counties	9,292

Source: Evarts B. Greene and Virginia D. Harrington, *American Population Before the Federal Census of 1790* (1932), 19–21.

TABLE 5.8 PROVINCIAL CENSUS OF MASSACHUSETTS, 1764

Counties and Towns	Houses	Families	Whites				Negroes & Mulattoes		Indians		French Neutrals				Total
			Under 16 Male	Under 16 Female	Above 16 Male	Above 16 Female	Male	Female	Male	Female	Under 16 Male	Under 16 Female	Above 16 Male	Above 16 Female	
Suffolk county:															
Boston	1,676	2,069	4,109	4,010	2,941	3,612	510	301	21	16	...	...	...	...	15,520
Roxbury	212	212	291	324	371	421	47	33	...	...	1	3	1	1	1,493
Dorchester	204	245	292	284	343	404	23	14	...	...	...	...	...	...	1,360
Milton	124	141	215	222	214	245	31	16	...	...	2	1	1	1	948
Braintree	327	357	571	590	555	651	31	35	1	1	1	3	3	3	2,445
Weymouth	203	248	275	294	315	347	13	14	...	...	...	...	...	...	1,258
Hingham	375	426	594	539	555	702	38	39	...	...	7	11	9	12	2,506
Hull	31	33	31	27	39	57	9	7	...	...	...	...	...	...	170
Stoughton	265	424	593	555	567	580	9	17	9	10	...	...	...	...	2,340
Dedham	239	309	417	441	484	531	21	15	3	3	...	1	2	1	1,919
Medfield	113	121	111	126	176	211	3	1	2	4	1	2	1	1	639
Wrentham	293	347	464	463	514	551	18	12	1	...	4	1	1	1	2,030
Medway	123	138	165	178	215	210	10	7	1	...	1	1	2	3	793
Bellingham	72	82	119	111	116	108	8	...	...	...	...	...	...	...	462
Needham	129	168	209	226	246	250	8	6	...	...	...	...	...	...	945
Brookline	53	53	68	62	97	93	13	5	...	...	...	...	...	...	338
Chelsea	54	70	110	85	99	125	20	13	...	...	...	...	...	1	452
Walpole	100	106	188	177	207	209	2	2	...	...	...	1	3	3	792
Total	4,593	5,549	8,822	8,714	8,054	9,307	814	537	38	34	17	24	23	26	36,410
Essex county:															
Salem	509	923	884	985	1,050	1,335	117	56	...	...	8	3	13	18	4,469
Danvers	288	381	458	468	501	634	37	35	...	...	2	8	5	3	2,151
Ipswich	531	670	791	801	931	1,119	60	40	...	...	6	6	7	9	3,770
Newbury	401	489	622	605	819	872	21	17	...	...	1	1	1	1	2,960
Newburyport	357	546	613	566	739	837	35	29	...	...	15	11	14	23	2,882
Marblehead	519	935	1,189	1,031	1,199	1,435	71	29	...	...	...	...	...	...	4,954
Lynn	275	388	489	481	531	648	31	18	...	...	3	5	1	1	2,208
Andover	360	438	533	558	565	700	56	30	...	...	7	7	3	3	2,462
Beverly	307	404	495	482	472	635	37	42	1	...	...	...	2	5	2,171
Rowley	239	290	222	329	411	493	11	11	...	...	...	2	1	1	1,481
Salisbury	201	240	280	322	354	366	5	2	...	...	3	4	4	4	1,344
Haverhill	304	350	494	469	505	487	13	12	...	...	3	3	2	3	1,992
Glocester	404	677	865	841	887	1,061	57	52	...	...	1	1	4	3	3,772
Topsfield	105	130	160	141	183	219	12	4	...	...	...	...	...	...	719
Boxford	128	149	200	194	220	227	5	5	...	...	...	...	1	...	851
Almsbury	242	264	351	366	389	444	8	9	...	...	...	...	...	...	1,567
Bradford	173	192	257	238	281	384	9	6	...	...	2	2	1	1	1,181
Wenham	72	95	125	120	120	166	13	15	3	2	...	...	...	...	564
Middleton	83	97	125	121	140	160	14	21	...	...	...	...	...	...	581
Manchester	103	155	159	163	183	203	10	13	1	...	1	4	1	1	739
Methuen	158	158	250	194	247	239	2	...	...	1	...	...	...	...	933
Total	5,759	7,971	9,562	9,475	10,727	12,664	624	446	5	3	52	57	59	77	43,751

Counties and Towns	Houses	Families	Whites Under 16 years Male	Whites Under 16 years Female	Whites Above 16 years Male	Whites Above 16 years Female	Negroes & Mulattoes Male	Negroes & Mulattoes Female	Indians Male	Indians Female	French Neutrals Under 16 years Male	French Neutrals Under 16 years Female	French Neutrals Above 16 years Male	French Neutrals Above 16 years Female	Total
Middlesex county:															
Cambridge	237	257	311	286	374	510	47	43	…	…	2	2	4	3	1,582
Charlestown	289	375	369	392	486	648	84	52	…	…	2	2	6	7	2,048
Watertown	103	117	172	136	179	195	5	6	…	…	…	…	…	…	693
Woburn	228	287	365	314	373	424	20	19	…	…	…	…	…	…	1,515
Concord	244	265	335	389	381	432	15	12	…	…	…	…	…	…	1,564
Newton	174	222	304	316	322	348	10	7	…	1	…	…	…	…	1,308
Sudbury	263	316	422	416	436	471	15	12	1	…	…	…	…	…	1,773
Marlboro	183	213	307	255	348	356	10	11	…	…	…	…	…	…	1,287
Billerica	189	223	312	235	313	360	8	6	…	…	…	…	…	…	1,234
Framingham	205	234	325	302	306	347	14	11	…	…	1	1	2	4	1,313
Lexington	126	142	210	189	228	241	26	18	…	…	…	…	…	…	912
Chelmsford	133	176	224	227	246	304	7	4	…	…	…	…	…	…	1,012
Sherborn	106	113	172	140	156	187	4	8	2	1	…	2	1	…	673
Reading	224	296	335	339	400	422	25	9	…	…	…	1	3	3	1,537
Malden	144	174	206	210	230	289	27	21	…	…	4	3	1	1	992
Weston	105	126	195	175	196	184	10	8	…	…	…	…	…	…	768
Medford	104	147	161	150	207	223	29	18	…	2	…	…	…	…	790
Littleton	122	143	160	175	212	209	8	9	…	…	…	…	…	…	773
Hopkinston	135	154	242	274	223	271	9	7	…	1	…	…	…	…	1,027
Westford	143	169	231	217	233	269	5	7	…	…	…	…	…	…	962
Waltham	94	107	145	162	169	174	8	5	…	…	…	…	…	…	663
Wilmington	94	97	166	159	164	174	6	4	…	…	…	…	…	…	673
Groton	174	242	365	365	340	358	8	7	…	…	…	…	…	…	1,443
Shirley	41	72	122	102	90	110	4	2	…	…	…	…	…	…	430
Stow	121	135	196	191	194	204	6	3	…	…	…	…	…	…	794
Townsend	94	97	166	151	137	136	4	4	…	…	…	…	…	…	598
Stoneham	54	59	56	77	77	98	14	18	…	…	…	…	…	…	340
Natick	71	91	109	120	99	122	10	14	13	24	…	…	…	…	511
Dracut	…	…	…	…	…	…	…	…	…	…	…	…	…	…	…
Bedford	67	72	101	116	100	124	9	7	…	…	…	…	…	…	457
Lincoln	84	99	153	170	145	153	20	5	…	…	…	…	…	…	646
Tewksbury	103	147	191	198	184	203	2	3	…	…	…	…	…	…	781
Holliston	103	115	168	170	183	176	5	3	…	…	…	…	…	…	705
Acton	96	100	142	147	160	159	1	2	…	…	…	…	…	…	611
Dunstable	90	98	140	122	138	143	9	7	…	…	…	…	…	…	559
Pepperrell	117	130	193	200	189	172	1	3	…	…	…	…	…	…	758
Total	[4]14,860	[5]15,810	7,771	7,587	8,218	9,196	485	375	16	29	9	11	17	18	33,732
Hampshire county:															
Springfield	404	477	641	608	697	770	27	12	…	…	…	…	…	…	2,755
Northampton	188	203	314	285	341	334	5	6	…	…	…	…	…	…	1,285
Southampton	66	76	92	100	117	127	1	…	…	…	…	…	…	…	437
Southadley	133	142	193	213	202	209	…	…	…	…	…	…	…	…	817
Hadley	89	99	125	127	150	151	13	7	…	…	…	…	…	…	573
Amherst	96	104	167	160	150	162	5	1	…	…	…	…	…	…	645
Hatfield	126	132	192	177	204	209	14	7	…	…	2	4	2	4	815
Westfield	191	195	341	328	318	296	23	18	…	…	…	…	…	…	1,324

(continued)

TABLE 5.8 (continued)

Counties and Towns	Houses	Families	Whites Under 16 years Male	Female	Above 16 years Male	Female	Negroes & Mulattoes Male	Female	Indians Male	Female	French Neutrals Under 16 years Male	Female	Above 16 years Male	Female	Total
Deerfield	85	123	188	157	193	182	11	6	...	...	...	...	...	...	737
Greenfield	45	58	106	79	95	87	1	...	...	...	...	...	...	...	368
Montague	49	64	97	99	95	100	...	1	...	...	...	...	...	...	392
Northfield	60	60	105	97	103	104	3	3	...	...	...	...	...	...	415
Brimfield	121	130	198	161	207	203	2	2	...	...	...	...	...	...	773
South Brimfield	90	91	142	130	151	147	2	2	...	...	...	...	...	...	574
Monson	68	69	107	79	101	95	3	4	...	...	...	...	...	...	389
Pelham	57	57	87	87	84	111	2	...	...	...	...	...	...	...	371
New Salem	62	69	99	87	99	89	1	...	...	...	...	...	...	...	375
Blanford	68	68	116	90	99	99	1	1	...	...	...	...	...	...	406
Palmer	74	88	123	110	133	140	2	...	...	...	...	...	...	...	508
Granville	100	123	197	149	180	152	3	1	...	...	...	...	...	...	682
Belchertown	61	68	112	99	99	108	...	...	...	...	...	...	...	...	418
Colrain	45	48	76	65	74	82	...	...	...	...	...	...	...	...	297
Ware	74	76	127	122	109	126	...	1	...	...	...	...	...	...	¹545
Chesterfield	30	30	39	41	46	35	...	...	...	...	...	...	...	...	161
Bernardstown	38	40	56	68	54	53	...	...	...	...	...	...	...	...	231
Roxbury Canady, or Warwick	36	36	57	43	51	40	...	...	...	...	...	...	...	...	191
Shutesbury	56	59	76	98	82	73	1	...	...	...	...	...	...	...	330
Wilbraham	74	82	119	118	129	123	1	1	...	...	...	...	...	...	491
Sunderland	...	...	...	...	...	...	...	...	...	...	...	...	...	...	...
Greenwich	...	...	...	...	...	...	...	...	...	...	...	...	...	...	...
Huntstown	...	...	...	...	...	...	...	...	...	...	...	...	...	...	...
Total	2,586	2,867	4,292	3,977	¹4,423	4,407	121	73	...	...	2	4	2	4	17,305
Worcester county:															
Worcester	204	229	376	350	370	357	11	5	4	5	...	...	...	...	1,478
Lancaster	301	328	514	421	505	532	12	14	1	...	...	...	...	...	1,999
Sutton	294	370	558	497	510	555	6	11	...	...	...	...	...	...	2,137
Mendon	284	336	466	425	441	497	5	4	...	...	1	2	1	1	1,843
Brookfield	267	283	493	412	439	452	10	5	...	...	...	...	...	...	1,811
Shrewsbury	199	223	367	319	339	360	7	8	...	1	...	...	...	...	1,401
Uxbridge	186	211	283	308	305	304	6	7	...	...	...	...	...	...	1,213
Westboroughugh	163	181	278	218	277	324	4	5	...	3	...	...	...	...	1,110
Southborough	110	126	160	161	184	216	5	5	1	...	...	...	...	...	731
Rutland	166	182	275	244	281	273	9	8	...	...	...	...	...	...	1,090
Rutland district	118	118	187	192	177	159	10	9	...	...	...	...	...	...	734
Oxford	128	148	247	206	214	217	4	2	...	...	...	...	...	...	890
Charlton	114	124	191	164	195	188	1	...	1	...	1	...	1	...	741
Leicester	119	146	187	170	210	196	4	3	...	...	...	...	...	...	770
Spencer	100	111	174	173	160	152	2	3	...	...	...	...	...	...	664
New Braintree	94	98	152	146	152	141	2	1	...	...	...	...	...	...	594
Oakham	41	41	73	78	60	58	1	...	...	...	...	...	...	...	270
Lunenburg	145	175	220	136	237	221	5	2	...	...	...	...	...	5	821
Bolton	145	155	234	225	225	239	1	1	1	...	1	1	1	1	933
Sturbridge	136	136	212	240	218	219	3	1	2	1	1	...	1	...	899

Counties and Towns	Houses	Families	Whites Under 16 years Male	Whites Under 16 years Female	Whites Above 16 years Male	Whites Above 16 years Female	Negroes & Mulattoes Male	Negroes & Mulattoes Female	Indians Male	Indians Female	French Neutrals Under 16 years Male	French Neutrals Under 16 years Female	French Neutrals Above 16 years Male	French Neutrals Above 16 years Female	Total
Hardwick	153	161	259	256	239	251	3	...	1	1	...	...	...	...	1,010
Grafton	109	109	178	175	193	196	5	2	6	8	...	...	...	...	763
Upton	94	104	158	159	135	157	3	2	...	...	...	...	3	2	619
Leominster	104	107	186	199	173	180	2	3	...	...	...	...	...	...	743
Holden	62	75	161	116	109	107	1	1	...	...	...	...	...	...	495
Western	92	100	138	148	155	138	3	1	...	...	...	...	...	...	583
Douglass	90	97	142	139	111	129	5	...	...	...	...	...	...	...	521
Harvard	153	173	276	270	272	296	7	5	...	...	...	...	...	...	1,126
Dudley	...	...	...	...	...	...	...	...	...	...	...	...	...	...	...
Petersham	100	115	202	186	166	145	3	5	...	...	...	...	...	...	707
Templetown	65	64	95	84	88	81	...	...	...	...	...	...	...	...	348
Westminster	86	86	133	108	112	113	...	...	...	...	...	...	...	...	466
Athol	41	60	88	81	103	85	2	...	...	...	...	...	...	...	359
Princetown	57	55	82	65	72	65	...	...	...	...	...	...	...	...	284
Fitchburgh	43	43	70	66	61	60	1	1	...	...	...	...	...	...	259
Total	[1]4,563	5,070	7,815	7,137	7,488	7,663	138	114	15	19	4	7	7	5	30,412
Plymouth county:															
Plymouth	256	373	488	475	532	605	38	39	23	25	3	2	9	7	2,246
Bridgewater	571	630	964	932	910	1,042	45	49	8	15	8	9	3	5	3,990
Middleboro	498	577	855	841	804	880	17	15	8	18	...	...	...	...	3,438
Scituate	348	431	516	520	603	742	55	52	4	9	...	...	...	...	2,501
Rochester	272	326	470	442	485	520	12	10	10	27	1	2	3	3	1,985
Pembroke	210	283	315	290	357	425	14	8	7	21	5	2	1	1	1,446
Duxborg'	154	197	238	220	273	311	3	5	1	5	...	...	1	4	1,061
Marshfield	150	168	287	218	274	328	25	15	1	4	2	...	1	4	1,159
Plimpton	186	232	352	236	328	362	9	3	7	13	3	1	2	1	1,317
Kingston	110	131	194	162	196	196	6	5	...	...	4	...	5	6	774
Abington	174	217	323	308	300	311	11	10	...	...	...	...	...	...	1,263
Hallifax	85	97	122	130	127	166	6	5	...	1	...	...	...	...	557
Wareham	57	81	123	119	116	140	2	3	6	10	...	...	...	...	519
Hanover	...	...	...	...	...	...	...	...	...	...	...	...	...	...	...
Total	3,071	3,743	5,247	4,893	5,305	6,028	243	219	75	148	26	16	25	31	22,256
Barnstable county:															
Barnstable	325	361	474	432	524	622	36	20	6	7	6	6	3	2	2,138
Yarmouth	255	295	400	405	427	486	11	11	12	19	3	2	3	1	1,780
Sandwich	200	245	313	317	346	368	18	14	30	43	...	...	...	...	1,449
Harwich	235	283	398	386	420	454	12	11	35	56	...	...	...	...	1,772
Eastham	182	237	292	267	342	415	5	6	1	3	...	...	...	...	1,331
Wellfleet	129	157	243	217	216	227	9	5	3	8	...	...	...	...	928
Falmouth	145	182	266	266	266	234	19	12	35	27	...	...	...	...	1,125
Truro	107	134	225	230	241	222	3	3	...	1	...	...	...	...	925
Chatham	105	127	145	153	173	202	4	1	...	...	...	...	...	...	678
Mashpee	82	85	23	19	15	20	18	13	101	129	...	...	...	...	338
Total	1,765	[1]2,106	2,779	2,692	2,970	3,250	135	96	223	293	9	8	6	3	12,464
Bristol county:															
Taunton	397	493	651	617	678	734	26	29	1	8	...	...	...	...	2,744
Dartmouth	679	790	1,103	965	1,129	1,248	37	24	35	40	...	...	...	...	4,581

(continued)

TABLE 5.8 (continued)

Counties and Towns	Houses	Families	Whites Under 16 years Male	Whites Under 16 years Female	Whites Above 16 years Male	Whites Above 16 years Female	Negroes & Mulattoes Male	Negroes & Mulattoes Female	Indians Male	Indians Female	French Neutrals Under 16 years Male	French Neutrals Under 16 years Female	French Neutrals Above 16 years Male	French Neutrals Above 16 years Female	Total
Rehoboth	498	617	964	901	818	954	28	25	1	5	…	…	…	…	3,696
Swanzey	…	…	…	…	…	…	…	…	…	…	…	…	…	…	…
Attleboro'	266	301	461	419	422	422	13	2	…	…	…	…	…	…	1,739
Norton	295	343	477	447	460	528	19	11	…	…	…	…	…	…	1,942
Dighton	148	198	276	269	273	297	31	28	2	1	…	…	…	…	1,177
Easton	134	154	219	172	222	220	2	2	2	3	…	…	…	…	842
Raynham	100	109	170	146	181	184	3	3	…	…	1	1	2	3	694
Berkley	94	110	165	153	150	181	6	4	…	2	…	…	…	…	661
Freeton	…	…	…	…	…	…	…	…	…	…	…	…	…	…	…
Total	2,611	3,115	4,486	4,089	4,333	4,768	165	128	41	59	1	1	2	3	18,076
York county:															
York	272	397	496	486	568	671	36	20	…	…	6	5	4	6	2,298
Kittery	288	372	489	490	551	766	31	31	…	…	3	3	2	2	2,368
Berwick	222	364	664	552	567	547	20	24	…	…	…	…	…	…	2,374
Wells	219	251	427	382	363	357	21	13	…	…	3	1	1	1	1,569
Arundel	124	138	216	228	190	194	2	3	…	…	1	1	1	1	837
Biddeford	87	116	182	186	178	179	8	14	…	…	1	3	1	1	753
Pepperelboro	66	96	140	126	145	125	2	…	…	…	…	…	2	…	540
Narraganset No.1	…	…	…	…	…	…	…	…	…	…	…	…	…	…	…
Total	1,278	1,734	2,614	2,450	2,562	2,839	120	105	…	…	14	13	11	11	10,739
Cumberland county:															
Falmouth	160	585	969	918	964	875	30	14	…	…	2	7	…	4	3,783
North Yarm°	154	188	251	277	278	255	8	10	…	…	…	…	…	…	1,079
Scarborough	200	210	353	281	319	304	10	5	…	…	…	…	…	…	1,272
Harpswell	55	111	224	224	188	186	4	10	…	…	…	…	…	…	836
Brunswick	73	73	139	114	149	98	3	1	…	…	…	…	…	…	504
Gorham	…	…	…	…	…	…	…	…	…	…	…	…	…	…	…
Windham	…	…	…	…	…	…	…	…	…	…	…	…	…	…	…
Pearson town	…	…	…	…	…	…	…	…	…	…	…	…	…	…	…
Total	642	1,167	1,936	1,814	1,898	1,718	55	40	…	…	2	7	…	4	7,474
Lincoln county:															
Pownalboro'	161	175	210	223	225	232	6	3	…	…	…	…	…	…	899
Georgetown	180	184	388	325	317	287	8	4	…	…	…	…	…	…	1,329
Newcastle	69	69	127	117	100	109	1	…	…	…	…	…	…	…	454
Topsham	54	52	78	85	85	78	1	…	…	…	…	…	…	…	327
Woolwich	64	63	116	110	92	97	…	…	…	…	…	…	…	…	415
Bowdoinham	38	37	63	53	59	44	1	…	…	…	…	…	…	…	220
Total	566	580	982	913	878	847	17	7	…	…	…	…	…	…	3,644
Dukes county:															
Edgartown	128	150	234	209	233	248	12	8	37	49	…	…	…	…	1,030
Chilmark	90	114	152	156	159	179	9	8	72	116	…	…	…	…	851
Tisbury	110	100	165	166	226	233	4	5	15	24	…	…	…	…	838
Total	328	364	551	531	618	660	25	21	124	189	…	…	…	…	2,719

Counties and Towns	Houses	Families	Whites				Negroes & Mulattoes		Indians		French Neutrals				Total
			Under 16 years		Above 16 years						Under 16 years		Above 16 years		
			Male	Female	Male	Female	Male	Female	Male	Female	Male	Female	Male	Female	
Nantucket county:															
Sherburne	413	602	776	758	904	882	24	20	83	66	13	...	...	...	3,526
Berks county:															
Great Barrington	87	91	127	121	149	134	9	10	...	...	...	...	...	...	550
Sheffield	126	172	250	276	272	249	16	10	...	...	...	...	...	...	1,073
Sandisfield	66	69	126	93	105	81	2	2	...	...	...	...	...	...	409
Tyringham	51	55	95	85	77	66	2	...	...	...	...	...	...	...	325
Pittsfield	39	70	110	114	105	89	6	4	...	...	...	...	...	...	428
Egremont	...	...	...	...	...	...	...	...	...	...	...	...	...	...	...
Stockbridge	34	34	50	46	64	57	15	12	108	113	...	...	...	...	465
New Marlboro	...	...	...	...	...	...	...	...	...	...	...	...	...	...	...
No. 4	...	...	...	...	...	...	...	...	...	...	...	...	...	...	...
Total	403	491	758	735	772	676	50	38	108	113	133	128	141	167	3,250
Total for colony	31,707	43,483	52,859	50,588	53,752	59,501	2,824	2,067	728	953	133	128	141	167	223,841

SUMMARY OF WHITE, NEGRO, INDIAN, AND FRENCH NEUTRAL POPULATION OF MASSACHUSETTS, BY COUNTIES: CENSUS OF 1764

Counties	Houses	Families	Whites				Negroes & Mulattoes		Indians		French Neutrals				Total
			Under 16 years		Above 16 years						Under 16 years		Above 16 years		
			Male	Female	Male	Female	Male	Female	Male	Female	Male	Female	Male	Female	
Total for Massachusetts	31,707	43,483	52,859	50,588	53,752	59,501	2,824	2,067	728	953	133	128	141	167	223,841
Barnstable	1,765	2,286	2,779	2,692	2,970	3,250	135	96	223	293	9	8	6	3	12,464
Berks	403	491	758	735	772	676	50	38	108	113	...	1	2	3	3,250
Bristol	2,611	3,115	4,486	4,089	4,333	4,768	165	128	41	59	1	...	...	...	18,076
Dukes	328	364	551	531	618	660	25	21	124	189	...	...	...	...	2,719
Essex	5,759	7,971	9,562	9,475	10,727	12,664	624	446	5	3	52	57	59	77	43,751
Hampshire	2,586	2,867	4,292	3,977	4,363	4,407	121	73	...	...	2	4	2	4	17,245
Middlesex	5,618	11,425	7,771	7,587	8,218	9,196	485	375	16	29	9	11	17	18	33,732
Nantucket	413	602	776	758	904	882	24	20	83	66	13	...	...	...	3,526
Plymouth	3,071	3,743	5,247	4,893	5,305	6,028	243	219	75	148	26	16	25	31	22,256
Suffolk	4,593	5,549	8,822	8,714	8,054	9,307	814	537	38	34	17	24	23	26	36,410
Worcester	4,560	5,070	7,815	7,137	7,488	7,663	138	114	15	19	4	7	7	5	30,412
Total for Maine	2,486	3,481	5,532	5,177	5,338	5,404	192	152	...	...	16	20	11	15	21,857
Cumberland	642	1,167	1,936	1,814	1,898	1,718	55	40	...	...	2	7	...	4	7,474
Lincoln	566	580	982	913	878	847	17	7	...	...	...	...	...	...	3,644
York	1,278	1,734	2,614	2,450	2,562	2,839	120	105	...	...	14	13	11	11	10,739

[1] Corrected figures.
Source: Bureau of the Census, *A Century of Population Growth, 1790–1900* (1909), 158–162.

TABLE 5.9 CENSUS OF RHODE ISLAND MILITIA, 1690

Town	No. of Militia	Town	No. of Militia
Newport	104	Providence	175
...	85	Rochester	136
Portsmouth	105	Warwick	60
Jamestown	34	Forsham	56
		Deptford	37
Total	328	Total	464

Source: Evarts B. Greene and Virginia D. Harrington, *American Population Before the Federal Census of 1790* (1932), 64–65.

TABLE 5.10 CENSUS OF RHODE ISLAND POPULATION, 1708

Towns	Freemen	Militia[a]	White Servants	Black Servants	Total Number of Inhabitants
Newport	190	358	20	220	2,203
Providence	241	283	6	7	1,446
Portsmouth	98	104	8	40	628
Warwick	80	95	4	10	480
Westerly	95	100	5	20	570
New Shoreham	38	47	...	6	208
Kingstown	200	282	...	85	1,200
Jamestown	33	28	9	32	206
Greenwich	40	65	3	6	240
Total	1,015	1,362	55	426	7,181

[a] The militia included all males aged 16–60.
Source: J. R. Bartlett, ed., *Records of the Colony of Rhode Island and Providence Plantations in New England* (1856–1865), IV, 59.

TABLE 5.11 CENSUS OF RHODE ISLAND POPULATION, 1748

Towns	Whites	Negroes	Indians
Total	15,302	1,648	985
Newport	3,843	649	148
Providence	3,707	128	81
Portsmouth	643	100	70
Warwick	1,628	77	73
Westerly	1,620	56	250
North-Kingston	1,875	165	65
South-Kingston	965	333	225
East-Greenwich	1,149	40	34
Jamestown	222	80	19
New-Shoreham	250	20	20

Source: Bureau of the Census, *A Century of Population Growth, 1790–1900* (1909), 162.

TABLE 5.12 PERSONS SUBJECT TO TAXES IN NEW HAMPSHIRE, 1680

Town	No. of Persons Subject to Taxes
Bloody Point	24
Cocheco	66
Dover Neck	30
Exeter	66
Hampton	126
Portsmouth	133
Total	445

Source: Nathaniel Bouton, et al., eds., *Documents and Records Relating to the Province of New Hampshire* (1867–1943), I, 424–428.

TABLE 5.13 PROVINCIAL CENSUS OF NEW HAMPSHIRE, 1767

Name of the Towns	Unmarried Men from 16 to 60	Married Men from 16 to 60	Boys from 16 Years & under	Men 60 Years & above	Females Unmarried	Females Married	Male Slaves	Female Slaves	Widows	Total
Greenland	75	98	184	23	271	117	8	9	20	805
Rochester	86	142	257	26	280	166	3	2	22	984
Gosport	27	37	79	12	59	47	2	2	19	284
Winchester	35	64	107	10	132	74	1	1	4	428
Sandown	42	81	123	8	156	89	1	0	9	509
Somersworth	87	125	299	30	291	144	19	10	39	1,044
Chesterfield	30	56	107	4	104	60	0	0	4	365
Richmond	36	54	95	1	92	52	0	0	3	333
Hinsdale	18	23	36	2	50	24	0	1	4	158
Plymouth	31	31	62	0	72	31	...	...	...	227
Dunstable	32	69	151	10	169	78	2	2	7	520
Portsmouth	440	641	900	61	1,340	677	124	63	220	4,466
Hopkinton	37	75	141	4	132	75	0	0	9	473
New Durham	11	25	42	2	49	26	0	0	2	157
Dover	186	217	347	39	500	239	19	9	58	1,614
Parish of Madbury	54	95	162	29	220	119	1	2	13	695
Charlestown	31	44	86	4	114	48	1	0	6	334
Hampton	72	120	195	40	263	146	0	0	30	866
Candia	27	68	99	0	100	68	0	0	1	363
Londonderry	235	272	571	85	799	342	13	10	62	2,389
New Castle	50	83	146	21	167	98	11	8	22	606
Exeter	151	241	384	37	507	262	28	22	58	1,690
Walpole	24	52	104	1	72	52	0	0	3	308
Plainfield	10	20	36	...	26	20	...	...	...	112
Cornish	17	21	36	...	37	22	0	0	0	133
Alstead	15	25	30	...	35	25	0	0	0	130
Clarmont	13	27	50	...	40	27	0	0	0	157
Marlow	8	15	19	...	20	15	0	0	0	77
Newport	16	5	3	...	...	5	0	0	0	29
Hanover	11	26	16	...	13	26	...	...	...	92
Canaan	10	2	3	...	2	2	...	...	...	19
Lebanon	12	30	50	...	40	30	...	...	...	162

Name of the Towns	Unmarried Men from 16 to 60	Married Men from 16 to 60	Boys from 16 Years & under	Men 60 Years & above	Females Unmarried	Females Married	Male Slaves	Female Slaves	Widows	Total
Kingston	73	133	245	23	333	160	3	1	28	999
Swanzy	23	49	82	7	96	54	1	0	8	320
Westmoreland	28	71	112	3	103	71	0	0	3	391
Keene	51	66	84	4	149	68	0	0	8	430
Monadnock, No.4, Stoddarts To	14	20	25	…	14	20	…	…	…	93
Marlboro' No. 5	9	16	25	1	26	16	0	0	0	93
Gilsum	7	22	36	1	39	23	0	0	0	128
Croydon	16	9	7	…	10	9	…	…	…	51
Poplin	36	79	155	6	153	84	0	0	8	521
Newington	41	59	105	11	180	70	17	14	17	514
Dunbarton	25	39	70	6	80	45	2	0	4	271
Rye	46	109	159	16	223	126	11	7	39	736
Concord (formerly Rumford)	62	125	189	18	204	126	9	4	15	752
Kensington	62	107	166	28	250	118	…	…	24	755
Newtown	58	69	119	15	170	83	0	2	13	529
Newmarket	120	182	288	28	407	198	13	16	34	1,286
Boscawen	17	45	77	8	83	52	0	0	3	285
Stevenstown	18	36	55	0	62	36	1	0	2	210
Hillsboro'	3	16	27	0	3	15	0	0	0	64
New Boston	25	41	92	6	80	47	1	1	3	296
Barrington	66	161	272	18	292	170	4	0	18	1,001
Hawk	30	74	109	6	178	80	1	1	9	488
Nottingham West	49	75	155	16	176	92	1	1	18	583
Holles	81	117	223	12	227	127	1	1	20	809
Township No.1	20	47	80	1	79	47	0	0	4	278
Miles Slip, between Holles & No.1	4	12	15	1	24	12	0	0	0	68
Durham	104	166	272	38	386	192	21	11	42	1,232
Parish of Lee	63	147	198	19	269	143	3	1	18	861
Weare Town	8	50	80	2	78	50	0	0	0	268
Chester	116	168	289	31	357	190	3	1	34	1,189
Stratham	73	132	196	24	295	153	7	2	34	916
South Hampton	51	68	98	18	154	85	1	2	14	491
Wilton	27	62	100	3	92	63	0	0	3	350
Raymond	21	78	132	3	134	81	0	0	6	455
Bedford	30	43	93	13	117	51	6	3	6	362
Derryfield	9	31	59	7	81	38	0	0	5	230
Plastow	59	71	119	23	192	92	1	1	18	576
Atkinson	51	73	92	12	143	85	4	3	13	476
Nottingham	35	107	195	10	219	116	6	6	14	708
Epsom	15	40	71	5	66	40	0	0	2	239
Gilmanton	18	47	73	0	67	44	0	0	1	250
Pembroke	49	85	134	16	169	97	0	2	5	557
Bow	17	33	50	2	50	33	0	0	2	187
Litchfield	27	20	67	13	74	33	3	9	8	254
Pelham	37	81	154	18	158	81	0	1	13	543
Salem	63	138	239	16	204	155	2	2	28	847
Windham	19	50	117	15	120	66	1	3	11	402
Hampstead	48	96	162	10	197	105	1	0	25	644
North Hampton	28	93	142	18	189	96	0	1	16	583
East Kingston	50	58	100	20	127	81	3	0	12	451
Epping	99	205	378	21	464	214	6	3	20	1,410
Brentwood	86	142	271	22	345	163	1	1	33	1,064
Canterbury	42	82	138	11	140	83	3	0	4	503
Haverhill	21	32	43	1	43	29	2	1	0	172
Orford	12	14	18	1	18	12	0	0	0	75
Peterborough	33	64	113	13	149	68	1	0	2	443
Hampton Falls	127	188	313	33	457	208	3	3	49	1,381
Lynesborough	26	43	76	4	71	50	0	0	2	272
Monson	21	46	68	5	101	49	0	0	3	293
Amherst	63	135	200	17	270	147	6	2	18	858
Merrimac	31	65	98	8	121	65	2	1	9	400
Rindge	18	54	84	4	82	54	0	1	1	298
Total	4,510	7,670	12,924	1,160	15,992	8,467	384	249	1,364	52,720

Note: Arithmetic errors corrected from original.
Source: Nathaniel Bouton, et al., *Documents and Records Relating to the Province of New Hampshire* (1867–1943), VII, 168–170.

TABLE 5.14 CENSUS OF CONNECTICUT MILITIA IN 1690

County-Town	No. of Persons in Militia
New London County	
New London	243
Seabrooke	84
Preston	34
Norwich	106
Stonington	98
Killingsworth	46
Lyme	71
Total	682
New Haven County	
New Haven	246
Guilford	100
Derby	35
Wallingford	71
Milford	142
Branford	48
Total	642
Hartford County	
Hartford	128
Hartford	126
Wethersfield	191
Farmington	95
Windsor	110
Windsor	120
Middleton	130
Symsbury	61
Waterbury	43
Haddum	51
Subtotal	1,055
Hartford, horse	55
Total	1,110
Fairfield County	
Fairfield	96
Stratford	116
Danbury	22
Norwalk	80
Stamford	104
Woodbury	53
Greenwich	55
Fayrfield 2d	98
Total	624
Total militia:	3,058

Source: Evarts B. Greene and Virginia D. Harrington, *American Population Before the Federal Census of 1790* (1932), 51.

TABLE 5.15 CENSUS OF PERSONS SUBJECT TO TAXES IN CONNECTICUT, 1654–1709[a]

Towns	1654	1655	1669	1676	1677	1678	1679	1680	1681	1682	1683	1684
Brandford	...	...	8	48	45	49	53	60	63	51	50	50
Fairfield	94	90	44	152	157	177	171	177	184	172	181	184
Farmington	46	52	43	102	106	...[b]	95	95	96	97	101	96
Greenwich	...	...	...	36	40	38	39	33	52	48	55	50
Guilford	...	...	36	98	100	96	94	96	100	100	100	96
Haddum	...	...	7	29	29	32	36	40	37	40	36	43
Hartford	177	176	117	241	226	227	239	247	250	243	246	250
Killingworth	...	...	19	38	33	41	41	44	48	44	44	43
Lyme	...	...	...[b]	45	50	60	53	62	66	55	64	53
Middleton	31	32	...[b]	94	96	102	110	112	117	117	126	130
Milford	...	...	46	151	163	163	160	147	150	160	147	150
New Haven	...	...	91	237	214	294	265	268	240	238	248	268
New London	...	...	21	153	147	162	171	175	174	174	201	...
Norwalk	24	...[b]	33	65	68	70	78	82	85	92	92	88
Norwich	...	...	25	71	70	78	85	90	105	98	111	115
Preston	...	...	...	...	...	...	...	...	...	...	...	...
Rye	...	...	...[b]	32	38	44	48	49	50	50	47	...
Saybrook	53	...[b]	23	85	85	90	91	91	96	97	80	86
Stamford	...	...	8	81	90	88	105	105	110	94	90	97
Stonington	...	...	17	79	87	89	68	60	57	59	76	65
Stratford	74	65	64	78	84	100	99	94	101	102	122	120
Wallingford	...	...	...	43	48	49	51	50	52	55	52	61
Wethersfield	113	102	58	141	160	170	180	181	189	190	205	204
Windsor	165	152	113	204	219	216	220	216	218	233	240	240
Woodbury	...	...	...	...	...	...	...	...	...	...	62	62
Totals	777	669	773	2,303	2,355	2,435	2,552	2,574	2,640	2,609	2,776	2,551

Towns	1685	1686	1687	1689	1690	1691	1692	1693	1694	1695
Brandford	50	46	52	69	64	53	65	58	72	67
Derby	39	39	41	38	39	41	37	34	...	42
Fairfield	192	205	218	168	222	208	173	175	180	192
Farmington	100	108	111	81	93	109	104	106	109	112
Glassenbury	...	...	...	...	...	...	...	...	44	44
Greenwich	55	65	62	59	62	66	65	60	59	78
Guilford	100	107	104	110	108	120	120	115	120	120
Haddum	44	43	52	63	69	65	63	66	76	87
Hartford	255	269	273	298	307	253	274	267	275	285
Killingworth	42	36	43	45	...	43	45	46	48	53

(continued)

POPULATION DENSITY, 1700

This map shows the population density in 1700 (each dot represents 200 rural inhabitants). Total population was about 250,000. (Map drawn by Jeremy Eagle, based on information from *The Geographical Review*, XXX [1940], inset following p. 464)

TABLE 5.15 (continued)

Towns	1685	1686	1687	1689	1690	1691	1692	1693	1694	1695
Lyme	64	62	65	63	74	66	75	81	79	74
Middleton	130	130	130	124	120	110	110	120	120	120
Milford	158	160	160	155	170	144	160	155	171	157
New Haven	302	303	323	317	322	321	316	262	256	282
New London	164	189	156	172	182	190	180	182	203	216
Norwalk	77	85	93	55	93	88	90	65	85	74
Norwich	113	...	103	82	109	116	102	112	108	106
Preston	...	...	...	...	...	...	...	30	...	35
Rye	...	...	...	...	...	...	...	...	...	...
Saybrook	90	83	89	83	95	90	98	102	102	104
Simsbury	...	...	...	70	59	66	...	78	72	...
Stamford	99	104	102	113	111	109	108	80	112	90
Stonington	74	80	80	83	89	97	88	92	122	102
Stratford	134	110	140	110	127	124	130	130	130	...
Wallingford	63	69	72	73	76	76	80	83	60	95
Waterbury	...	...	...	...	37	43	43	46	43	...
Wethersfield	207	213	215	228	232	234	201	196	212	218
Windsor	260	270	278	259	279	285	290	290	319	300
Woodbury	74	64	91	53	46	52	52	61	61	62
Totals	2,886	2,840	3,053	2,971	3,185	3,169	3,069	3,092	3,238	3,115

Towns	1696	1697	1698	1699	1700	1701	1702	1703	1704	1705
Bedford	...	...	28	26	...	...	...	...	...	...
Brandford	69	76	73	80	80	80	86	80	84	82
Danbury	...	...	...	...	48	...	...	58	54	61
Derby	42	...	40	44	51	47	53	60	56	65
Fairfield	170	150	150	150	140	150	150	150	153	175
Farmington	115	112	114	116	115	115	118	120	124	127
Glassenbury	50	53	58	61	64	71	74	76	60	70
Greenwich	70	76	80	78	86	82	90	82	64	64
Groton	...	...	...	...	...	...	...	...	...	120
Guilford	125	125	130	136	136	137	150	140	150	160
Haddum	88	84	90	92	100	101	95	104	97	112
Hartford	285	302	293	300	307	307	310	302	305	313
Kenilworth	45	45	50	52	48	...	...	...	...	...
Killingworth	...	...	...	...	...	52	54	56	60	60
Lebanon	...	...	...	...	...	...	...	...	...	90
Lyme	99	86	72	93	111	123	117	115	120	110
Middleton	125	140	161	150	182	177	173	180	180	197
Milford	160	162	175	178	180	181	180	160	150	152
New Haven	290	300	310	315	330	332	350	355	360	276
New London	220	220	190	208	...	210	220	289	326	217
Norwalk	76	110	100	120	120	110	110	113	94	100
Norwich	110	130	117	125	117	122	111	120	120	163
Preston	42	42	58	61	62	68	69	78	70	69
Rye	...	...	56	60	...	...	...	...	...	...
Saybrook	112	113	132	134	124	126	134	126	97	109
Simsbury	70	70	76	90	83	67	70	92	93	76
Stamford	90	90	90	90	100	95	100	100	110	100
Stonington	86	103	96	108	128	136	147	138	135	119
Stratford	140	140	130	130	130	130	140	120	132	130
Wallingford	75	75	80	88	120	100	122	118	120	100
Waterbury	40	42	49	47	48	50	52	57	52	52
Wethersfield	213	220	212	218	240	252	257	262	239	200
Windham	...	...	...	...	...	59	50	63	62	56
Windsor	300	300	290	290	290	250	250	250	275	300
Woodbury	63	64	72	65	66	65	80	86	80	84
Totals	3,370	3,430	3,572	3,705	3,606	3,795	3,912	4,050	4,022	4,109

Towns	1706	1707	1708	1709
Brandford	83	90	104	80
Canterbury	...	...	...	35
Colchester	...	...	81	...
Danbury	...	62	63	57
Derby	57	53	50	49
Durham	...	...	...	47
Easthaven	...	44	43	40
Fairfield	170	171	160	...

Towns	1706	1707	1708	1709
Farmington	128	130	150	...
Glassenbury	78	82	83	61
Greenwich	60	84	70	64
Groton	117	125	140	105
Guilford	160	165	170	170
Haddum East	72	70	69	60
Haddum West	40	48	55	54
Hartford	290	310	300	230
Killingworth	63	70	63	...
Lebanon	105	135	140	112
Lyme	131	133	140	131
Mansfield	...	...	...	37
Middleton	202	180	172	190
Milford	171	170	180	170
New Haven	276	280	220	260
New London	134	226	249	188
Norwalk	110	130	115	100
Norwich	143	168	174	155
Plainfield	...	...	55	55
Preston	80	77	80	74
Saybrook	92	147	147	...
Simsbury	73	80	74	55
Stamford	110	100	110	110
Stonington	150	117	172	135
Stratford	135	140	134	...
Wallingford	120	130	132	122
Waterbury	55	49	50	43
Wethersfield	281	250	250	240
Windham	68	69	72	83
Windsor	300	315	315	297
Woodbury	90	80	86	79
Totals	4,144	4,480	4,668	3,688

a Figures corrected from original source.

Source: J. H. Trumbull and C. J. Hoadly, eds., *Public Records of the Colony of Connecticut* (1850–1890), I, 265, 279; II, 518–526, 290, 320; III, 17, 36, 66–67, 86–87, 106–107, 126, 156–157, 181, 215, 239, 296–298; IV, 9–10, 33, 56, 79, 106, 131, 149–150, 175, 222, 265, 297, 329, 360, 405, 441, 489–490, 521–522; V, 6–7, 31, 71, 115.

TABLE 5.16   CENSUS OF CONNECTICUT POPULATION, 1756

Counties and Towns	Whites	Negroes	Indians
Hartford county:			
Bolton	755	11	...
Colchester	2,228	84	...
East-Haddam	1,913	65	...
Enfield	1,050	...	...
Farmington	3,595	112	...
Glastenbury	1,091	24	...
Haddam	1,223	18	...
Hartford	2,926	101	...
Hebron	1,855	...	...
Middletown	5,446	218	...
Symsbury	2,222	23	...
Somers	900	...	...
Stafford	1,000	...	...
Suffield	1,414	24	...
Tolland	902	15	...
Wethersfield	2,374	109	...
Willington	650	...	...
Windsor	4,170	50	...
Total	35,714	854	...
New-Haven county:			
Branford	1,694	106	...
Derby	1,000	...	...
Durham	765	34	...
Guilford	2,263	59	...
Milford	1,633	...	...

Counties and Towns	Whites	Negroes	Indians
New-Haven	5,085	...	...
Wallingford	3,713	...	...
Waterbury	1,802	27	...
Total	17,955	226	...
New-London county:			
Groton	2,532	179	158
Lyme	2,762	100	94
Killingsworth	1,442	16	...
New-London	3,171	...	...
Norwich	5,317	223	...
Preston	1,940	78	...
Saybrook	1,898	33	...
Stonington	2,953	200	365
Total	22,015	829	617
Fairfield county:			
Danbury	1,509	18	...
Fairfield	4,195	260	...
Greenwich	2,021	...	...
New-Fairfield	713	...	...
New-Town	1,230	23	...
Norwalk	2,956	94	...
Reading	...	...	...
Ridgfield	1,069	46	...
Stanford	2,648	120	...
Strafford	3,508	150	...
Total	19,849	711	...
Windham county:			
Canterbury	1,240	20	...
Coventry	1,617	18	...
Pomphret	1,677	50	...
Killingly	2,100	...	...
Lebanon	3,171	103	...
Mansfield	1,598	16	...
Plainfield	1,751	49	...
Ashford	1,245	...	...
Voluntown	1,029	19	...
Union	500	...	...
Windham	2,406	40	...
Woodstock	1,336	30	...
Total	19,670	345	...
Litchfield county:			
Barkhemsted	18	...	...
Canaan	1,100	...	...
Colebrook	...	...	...
Cornwall	500	...	...
Goshen	610	...	...
Hartland	12	...	...
Harwinton	250	...	...
Kent	1,000	...	...
Litchfield	1,366	...	...
New-Hartford	260	...	...
New-Milford	1,121	16	...
Norfolk	84	...	...
Salisbury	1,100	...	...
Sharon	1,198	7	...
Torrington	250	...	...
Winchester	24	...	...
Woodbury	2,880	31	...
Total	11,773	54	...
Hartford county	35,714	854	...
New-Haven county	17,955	226	...
New-London county	22,015	829	617
Fairfield county	19,849	711	...
Windham county	19,670	345	...
Litchfield county	11,773	54	...
Total for colony	126,976	3,019	617

Source: J. H. Trumbull and C. J. Hoadly, eds., *Public Records of the Colony of Connecticut* (1850–1890), XIV, 492.

Population of the Middle Atlantic Colonies

The Dutch and Swedish colonies in the Middle Atlantic region grew slowly, and they contained barely 5,500 persons as of 1660. Not until England's conquest of New Netherland in 1664 did settlement begin to proceed rapidly. A large influx of Yankees poured into New York and New Jersey almost immediately, and a major migration of British Quakers started to arrive in the Delaware Valley during the 1680s. By 1700, the Mid-Atlantic's population stood at almost 54,000, tenfold more than its level forty years earlier.

The population of the Middle Atlantic colonies grew at a faster clip than any other area of Anglo-America once England acquired it. Although they possessed a sizable native-born population by the early eighteenth century, the Middle Atlantic colonies expanded less by natural increase than by in-migration from New England and Europe after 1700. Because these newcomers tended to arrive in family groups rather than as single men, they helped preserve a balanced sex ratio, which ensured that the middle colonies would experience a high ratio of births to general population.

Mainly because they were the principal entrepôt for an extremely heavy tide of immigration from northern Ireland and the Rhine valley—the largest sources of overseas immigration after 1710—the middle colonies experienced the highest rate of population growth in Anglo-America during the eighteenth century. The four Mid-Atlantic colonies expanded in approximately two generations from 54,000 in 1700 to 428,000 in 1760. The Mid-Atlantic region consequently increased its share of the colonies' total population from 19% in 1700 to 26% in 1760.

TABLE 5.17 CENSUS OF MILITIA IN NEW YORK, 1693

Counties	Militia
Albany City & County	359
Ulster & Dutchess	277
Orange	…
New York City & County	477
Richmond	104
Westchester	283
Suffolk	533
Kings	319
Queens	580
Total	2,932

Source: Edmund B. O'Callaghan, ed., *Documentary History of the State of New York* (1849–1851), I, 318–319.

TABLE 5.18 CENSUS OF NEW YORK POPULATION, 1698

Counties	Men	Women	Children	Negroes	Total
Albany	380	270	803	23	1,476
Dutchess and Ulster	248	111	869	156	1,384
Kings	308	332	1,081	296	2,017
New-York	1,019	1,057	2,161	700	4,937
Orange	29	31	140	19	219
Queens	1,465	1,350	551	199	3,565
Richmond	328	208	118	73	727
Suffolk	973	1,024	124	558	2,679
Westchester	316	294	307	146	1,063
Total	5,066	4,677	6,154	2,170	18,067

Source: Bureau of the Census, *A Century of Population Growth, 1790–1900* (1909), 170.

TABLE 5.19 CENSUS OF NEW YORK POPULATION, 1703

Counties	Males from 16 to 60	Females	Male Children	Female Children	Male Negroes	Female Negroes	Male Negro Children	Female Negro Children	All above 60	Total[1]
Albany	510	385	515	605	83	53	36	28	58	2,273
Kings	345	304	433	487	135	75	72	61	…	1,912
New-York	813	1,009	934	989	102	288	131	109	…	4,375
Orange	49	40	57	84	13	7	7	6	5	268
Queens	952	753	1,093	1,170	117	114	98	95	[2]	4,392
Richmond	176	140	42	49	60	32	4	1	…	504
Suffolk	787	756	818	797	60	52	38	38	[2]	3,346
Ulster	383	305	436	357	63	36	31	15	23	1,649
Westchester	472	469	382	386	74	45	50	29	39	1,946
Total	4,487	4,161	4,710	4,924	707	702	467	382	125	20,665

[1] In a subsequent communication to the Lords of Trade in 1712 (Colonial History of New-York, Vol. V, Page 339) the totals of the census of 1703 are quoted differently from those in the above table. There are no means for determining whether this difference arose from a subsequent correction of errors, or from mistakes in copying. As given in the latter, the totals were as follows: New York, 4,436; Kings, 1,915; Richmond, 503; Orange, 268; Westchester, 1,946; Queens, 4,392; Suffolk, 3,346; Albany, 2,273; Ulster and Dutchess, 1,669.
[2] Included in first column.
Source: Bureau of the Census, *A Century of Population Growth, 1790–1900* (1909), 170.

TABLE 5.20 CENSUS OF NEW YORK POPULATION, 1712

Counties	Whites						Slaves				Total
	Males under 16	Males between 16 and 60	Males over 60	Females under 16	Females 16 to 60	Females over 60	Males under 16	Males over 16	Females under 16	Females over 16	
Albany	753	688	54	651	676	49	98	155	83	122	3,329
Dutchess	120	89	11	98	97	1	6	12	4	7	445
Kings	…	…	…	…	…	…	…	…	…	…	1,925
New York	1,197	1,062	60	1,182	1,268	97	155	321	179	320	5,841
Orange	105	98	4	82	91	5	9	21	11	12	438
Richmond	…	…	…	…	…	…	…	…	…	…	1,279
Suffolk	1,092	929	114	1,044	926	64	26	116	32	70	4,413
Ulster	450	424	44	427	406	36	68	148	39	78	2,120
Westchester	672	560	75	577	539	62	72	127	62	72	2,818
Total	4,389	3,850	362	4,061	4,003	314	434	900	410	681	22,608

Source: Bureau of the Census, *A Century of Population Growth, 1790–1900* (1909), 181.

TABLE 5.21 CENSUS OF NEW YORK POPULATION, 1723

Name of the County	Whites					Negroes and Other Slaves					Total of Persons
	Men	Women	Male Children	Female Children	Total of White Persons	Men	Women	Male Children	Female Children	Total of Negroes & other Slaves	
New York	1,460	1,726	1,352	1,348	5,886	408	476	220	258	1,362	7,248
Richmond	335	320	305	291	1,251	101	63	49	42	255	1,506
Kings	490	476	414	394	1,774	171	123	83	67	444	2,218
Queens	1,568	1,599	1,530	1,371	6,068	393	294	228	208	1,123	7,191
Suffolk	1,441	1,348	1,321	1,156	5,266	357	367	197	54	975	6,241
West Chester	1,050	951	1,048	912	3,961	155	118	92	83	448	4,409
Orange	309	245	304	239	1,097	45	29	42	31	147	1,244
Dutchess	276	237	259	268	1,040	22	14	2	5	43	1,083
Ulster	642	453	563	699	2,357	227	126	119	94	556	2,923
Albany	1,512	1,408	1,404	1,369	5,693	307	200	146	155	808	6,501
Total	9,083	8,763	8,500	8,047	34,393	2,186	1,810	1,178	997	6,171	40,564

Source: Edmund B. O'Callaghan, ed., *Documentary History of the State of New York* (1849–1851), I, 693.

TABLE 5.22 CENSUS OF NEW YORK POPULATION, 1731[a]

Citys and Counties	Sheriffs	Whites Males above 10 Years Old	Whites Females above 10	Whites Males under 10	Whites Females under 10	Blacks Males above 10	Blacks Females under 10	Blacks Males under 10	Blacks Females under 10	The Amount in Each County
City and County of New York	Henry Beekman	2,628	2,250	1,143	1,024	599	607	186	185	8,622
City & County of Albany	Gosen Van Schick	2,481	1,255	2,352	1,212	568	185	346	174	8,573
Queens County	Thos Hicks	2,239	2,175	1,178	1,139	476	363	226	199	7,995
Suffolk County	David Corey 715 Indians	2,144	1,130	2,845	955	239	83	196	83	7,675
West Chester County	Gilbert Willet	1,879	1,701	1,054	707	269	96	176	151	6,033
Ulster County	John Wyncoop	990	914	577	515	321	196	124	91	3,728
Kings County	Domini Van Der Veer	629	518	243	268	205	146	65	76	2,150
Orange County	William Pullen	627	534	325	299	85	47	19	33	1,969
Richmond County	Charles Garritson	423	571	263	256	111	98	51	44	1,817
Dutchess County	William Squire	570	481	263	298	59	32	13	8	1,724
Total		14,610	11,529	10,243	6,673	2,932	1,853	1,402	1,044	50,286
		11,529	...	...	...	...	...	...	1,402	...
		10,243	...	...	...	...	...	...	1,853	...
		6,673	...	...	...	...	...	...	2,932	...
		43,055 Whites	...	...	...	...	...	...	7,231 Blacks	...

[a] Figures corrected from original source.
Source: Edmund B. O'Callaghan, ed., *Documentary History of the State of New York* (1849–1851), I, 694.

TABLE 5.23 CENSUS OF NEW YORK POPULATION, 1737[a]

Counties	Whites Males above 10 Years	White Females above 10 Years	Whites Males under 10 Years	White Females under 10 Years	Black Males above 10 Years	Black Females above 10 Years	Black Males under 10 Years	Black Females under 10 Years	Total of Each County	Total in 1731	Since Increased
New York	2,253	2,568	1,088	1,036	674	609	229	207	8,664	8,622	42
Albany	3,209	2,995	1,463	1,384	714	496	223	197	10,681	8,573	2,108
West Chester	2,110	1,890	950	944	304	254	153	140	6,745	6,033	712
Orange	860	753	501	433	125	95	38	35	2,840	1,969	871
Ulster	1,175	1,681	541	601	378	260	124	110	4,870	3,728	1,142
Dutchess	940	860	710	646	161	42	37	22	3,418	1,724	1,694
Richmond	488	497	289	266	132	112	52	53	1,889	1,817	72
Kings	654	631	235	264	210	169	84	101	2,348	2,150	198
Queens	2,407	2,290	1,395	1,656	460	370	254	227	9,059	7,995	1,064
Suffolk	2,297	2,353	1,175	1,008	393	307	203	187	7,923	7,675	248
Total	15,393	15,518	8,347	8,238	3,551	2,714	1,397	1,279	58,437	50,286	8,151

[a] Figures corrected from original source.
Source: Edmund B. O'Callaghan, ed., *Documentary History of the State of New York* (1849–1851), I, 694. Gary B. Nash, "The New York Census of 1737: A Critical Note on the Integration of Statistical and Literary Sources," *William and Mary Quarterly,* XXXVI (1979), 428–435.

TABLE 5.24 CENSUS OF NEW YORK POPULATION, 1746[a]

Cities and Counties	Males White under 16	Males White 16 & under 60	Males White above 60	Females White under 16	Females White 16 and Upwards	Males Black under 60	Males Black 16 & under 60	Males Black above 60	Females Black under 16	Females Black 16 Upwards	Total Number[b]
City & Co. of N.Y.	2,117	2,097	149	2,013	2,897	419	645	76	735	569	11,717
Kings County	350	435	71	366	464	140	167	32	154	152	2,331
Albany County	...	...	...	...	...	...	...	...	...	...	...
Queens County	1,946	1,826	233	2,077	1,914	365	466	61	391	361	9,640
Dutchess County	2,200	2,056	200	2,100	1,750	106	160	26	108	100	8,806
Suffolk County	1,887	1,835	226	1,891	2,016	329	393	52	315	310	9,254
Richmond County	445	376	35	421	414	92	88	13	95	94	2,073
Orange County	536	763	67	871	721	82	99	34	51	44	3,268
Westchester County	2,435	2,090	303	2,095	1,640	187	180	27	138	140	9,235
Ulster County	1,022	1,044	116	972	1,000	244	331	43	229	264	5,265
Total	12,938	12,522	1,400	12,806	12,816	1,964	2,529	364	2,216	2,034	61,589

[a] Figures corrected from original source.
[b] Total white was 52,482.
Source: Edmund B. O'Callaghan, ed., *Documentary History of the State of New York* (1849–1851), I, 695.

TABLE 5.25 CENSUS OF NEW YORK POPULATION, 1756[a]

Cities and Counties	Whites						Blacks					
	Males under 16	Males above 16 & under 60	Males 60 and Upwards	Females under 16	Females above 16	Total	Males under 16	Males above 16 & under 60	Males 60 and Upwards	Females under 16	Females above 16	Total
City and County of New York	2,260	2,308	174	2,359	3,667	10,768	468	604	68	443	695	2,278
City and County of Albany	3,474	3,795	456	3,234	3,846	14,805	658	786	76	496	403	2,419
Ulster County	1,655	1,687	156	1,489	1,618	6,605	328	437	49	326	360	1,500
Dutchess County	3,910	2,873	203	3,530	2,782	13,298	211	270	53	163	162	859
Orange County	1,213	1,088	74	1,083	998	4,456	103	116	24	93	94	430
Westchester County	3,153	2,908	1,039	2,440	2,379	11,919	296	418	77	267	280	1,338
Kings County	417	467	84	358	536	1,862	212	214	21	201	197	845
Queens County	1,960	2,147	253	1,892	2,365	8,617	581	563	55	500	470	2,169
Suffolk County	2,283	2,141	221	2,265	2,335	9,245	278	297	40	194	236	1,045
Richmond County	344	411	107	334	471	1,667	145	92	30	97	101	465
Total Whites						83,242	Total Blacks					13,348
Total	96,590											

[a] Figures corrected from original source.
Source: Edmund B. O'Callaghan, ed., *Documentary History of the State of New York* (1849–1851), I, 696.

TABLE 5.26 CENSUS OF NEW JERSEY POPULATION, 1726

Names of Counties	Whites					Negroes					Total of Both
	Males above 16	Females above 16	Males under 16	Females under 16	Total of Whites	Males above 16	Females above 16	Males under 16	Females under 16	Total of Negroes	
Middlesex	953	878	1,016	859	3,706	90	73	73	67	303	4,009
Essex	992	1,021	983	926	3,922	92	78	70	68	308	4,230
Monmouth	1,234	1,061	1,095	1,056	4,446	170	90	88	85	433	4,879
Somerset	582	502	403	405	1,892	126	96	87	70	379	2,271
Bergen	569	509	556	547	2,181	173	121	100	98	492	2,673
Burlington	1,080	983	965	844	3,872	86	63	53	55	257	4,129
Hunterdon	892	743	851	750	3,236	43	45	32	21	141	3,377
Glocester	608	462	526	529	2,125	32	21	24	27	104	2,229
Salem	1,060	861	1,015	891	3,827	52	38	35	25	150	3,977
Cape May	209	156	148	141	654	8	5	1	...	14	668
Total	8,179	7,176	7,558	6,948	29,861	872	630	563	516	2,581	32,442

Source: William A. Whitehead, et al., eds., *Archives of the State of New Jersey* (1880–1906), V, 164.

TABLE 5.27   CENSUS OF NEW JERSEY POPULATION, 1738[a]

Counties	Whites					Negroes & Other Slaves					Total of Both in Each County
	Males above 16	Females above 16	Males under 16	Females under 16	Total of Whites	Males above 16	Females above 16	Males under 16	Females under 16	Total of Slaves	
Middlesex	1,134	1,085	1,086	956	4,261	181	124	91	107	503	4,764
Essex	1,118	1,720	1,619	1,494	5,951	114	114	84	63	375	6,326
Bergen	939	822	820	708	3,289	256	203	187	160	806	4,095
Somersett	967	940	999	867	3,773	255	175	170	132	732	4,505
Monmouth	1,508	1,339	1,289	1,295	5,431	233	152	129	141	655	6,086
Burlington	1,487	1,222	1,190	996	4,895	134	87	58	64	343	5,238
Gloucester	930	757	782	676	3,145	42	24	32	24	122	3,267
Salem	1,669	1,391	1,313	1,327	5,700	57	56	40	31	184	5,884
Cape May	261	219	271	211	962	12	10	9	11	42	1,004
Hunterdon	1,618	1,230	1,270	1,170	5,288	75	53	49	42	219	5,507
Total	11,631	10,725	10,639	9,700	42,695	1,359[c]	998	849	775	3,981	46,676

[a] Figures corrected from original source.
Source: William A. Whitehead, et al., eds., *Archives of the State of New Jersey* (1880–1906), VI, 244.

TABLE 5.28   CENSUS OF NEW JERSEY POPULATION, 1745[a]

Counties	Males above 16 Years	Males under 16 Years	Females above 16 Years	Females under 16 Years	Quakers or Reputed Quakers	Slaves		Whole Number of Inhabitants	Increase since 1737–1738	Decrease since 1737–1738
						Males	Females			
Western Division										
Morris	1,109	1,190	957	1,087	22	57	36	4,436 ⎫	8,080	…
Hunterdon	2,302	2,182	2,117	2,090	240	244	216	9,151 ⎬		…
Burlington	1,786	1,528	1,605	1,454	3,237	233	197	6,803	1,565	…
Gloucester	913	786	797	808	1,436	121	81	3,506	239	…
Salem	1,716	1,746	1,603	1,595	1,090	90	97	6,847	963	…
Cape May	306	284	272	274	54	30	22	1,188	184	…
Total	8,132	7,716	7,351	7,308	6,079	775	649	31,931	11,031	…
Eastern Division										
Bergen	721	494	590	585	…	379	237	3,006	…	1,089
Essex	1,694	1,652	1,649	1,548	35	244	201	6,988	…	31
Middlesex	1,728	1,651	1,659	1,695	400	483	396	7,612	2,848	…
Monmouth	2,071	1,975	1,783	1,899	3,131	513	386	8,627	2,541	…
Somersett	740	765	672	719	91	194	149	3,239	…	…
Total	6,954	6,537	6,353	6,446	3,657	1,813	1,369	29,472	5,389	1,120
Total in both Divisions	15,086	14,253	13,704	13,754	9,736	2,588	2,018	61,403	16,420	…

[a] Figures corrected from original source.
Source: William A. Whitehead, et al., eds., *Archives of the State of New Jersey* (1880–1906), VI, 242–243.

TABLE 5.29   COUNT OF PERSONS SUBJECT TO TAXES IN PENNSYLVANIA, 1693–1760

Counties	1693	1720	1740	1749	1751	1760
Philadelphia	712	1,995	4,850	…	7,100	8,321
Bucks	…	…	…	…	3,012	3,148
Chester	…	…	3,007[a]	3,444[b]	3,951	4,761
Lancaster	…	205	2,560[c]	4,598	3,977	5,635
York	…	…	…	1,466	2,043	3,302
Cumberland	…	…	…	807	1,134	1,501
Berks	…	…	…	…	…	3,016
Northampton	…	…	…	…	…	1,989
Total	…	…	…	…	21,217	31,673

[a] From 1742.
[b] From 1747.
[c] From 1738.
Source: Evarts B. Greene and Virginia D. Harrington, *American Population Before the Federal Census of 1790* (1932), 117.

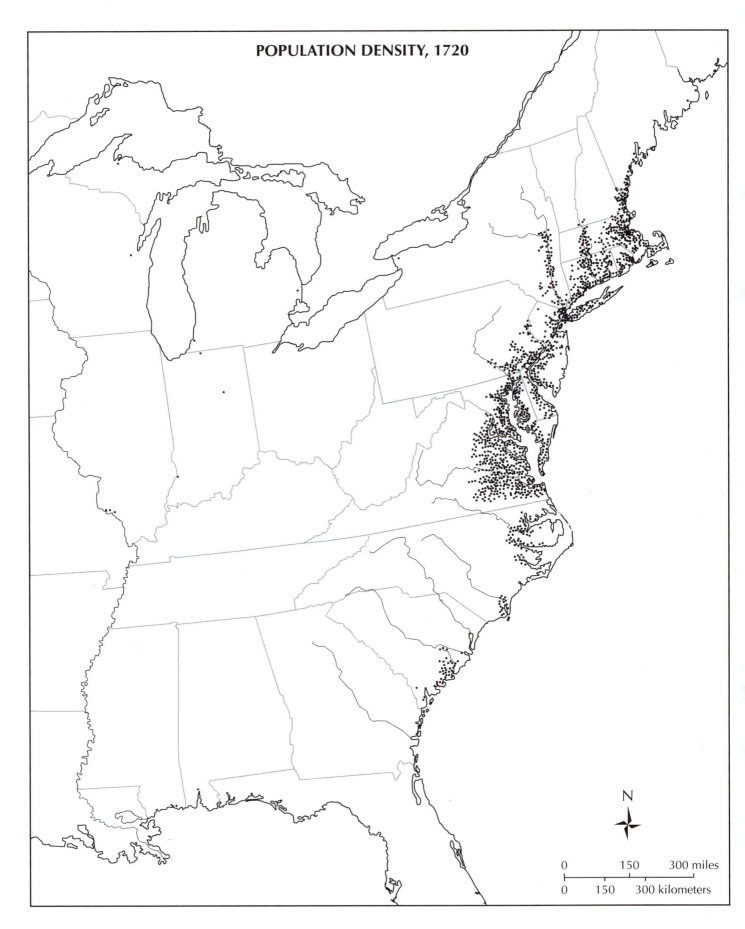

POPULATION DENSITY, 1720

This map shows the population density in 1720 (each dot represents 200 rural inhabitants). Total population was approaching a half-million. The Carolina Piedmont was still unoccupied; settlement of the Chesapeake Piedmont and Pennsylvania's Lancaster Plain had barely begun; and even much of east-central Massachusetts remained sparsely populated. (Map drawn by Jeremy Eagle, based on information from *The Geographical Review*, XXX [1940], inset following p. 464)

Population of the Southern Colonies

The population of Chesapeake Bay, the only part of the South settled until the 1650s, grew slowly from 1607 to 1630. The number of inhabitants first began to expand rapidly in the 1630s when the English increased fourfold, from 2,500 to 10,400. Despite receiving more than 110,000 immigrants in the seven decades after 1630, the Chesapeake contained just 69,000 white inhabitants in 1700. This low rate of increase arose from three factors: first, the low-lying tidewater's highly malignant disease environment, in which human germs easily contaminated stagnant water and in which swamps became breeding grounds for malaria-carrying mosquitoes; second, about 40–50% of indentured servants (who formed the bulk of immigrants) died before completing their contracts, and many of the survivors eventually left the region; and third, only a minority of residents could marry and raise children because females composed only a small percentage of all immigrants.

The dynamics of population growth changed dramatically after 1700 in the Chesapeake. By that time, the slow increase in households during the previous three generations had finally resulted in a roughly even division between white males and females. This situation permitted the Anglo-American population to multiply primarily by natural increase for the first time. Reproduction rates rose markedly once large numbers of white families from the malaria-ridden tidewater resettled in the healthier Piedmont where high levels of life expectancy and childhood survival enabled parents to raise almost double the number of offspring to adulthood than formerly.

Just as the South was acquiring a native-born society growing mainly by an excess of births over deaths rather than immigration, the region ceased to rely on European indentured servants and embarked on the large-scale importation of Africans. From 1710 to 1760, approximately 117,000 slaves landed in the Chesapeake and Carolinas. Their arrival nearly doubled the proportion of African Americans in the South from 21% in 1700 to 40% in 1760. Slave imports also enabled the South to increase its population at a far greater pace than New England, about a third faster than would have resulted had the South depended solely on natural increase and European immigrants for its growth. As a consequence, the South expanded at an exceptionally rapid rate in the eighteenth century, and its share of the thirteen colonies' population rose from 42% in 1700 to 45% in 1760. By 1770, almost half of the colonies' population, 48%, resided in the South.

TABLE 5.30   COUNT OF PERSONS SUBJECT TO TAXES IN MARYLAND, 1694–1697

Counties	1694	1695	1696	1697
Ann Arundel	1,539	1,525	1,564	1,564
Baltimore	468	871	495	483
Calvert	1,787	1,791	1,045	1,822
Cecil	...	496	669	671
Charles	895	...	991	731
Dorchester	661	1,509	628	628
Kent	447	618	515	680
Prince George	...	1,450	658	[514]
St. Mary's	1,006	1,014	1,049	1,005
Somerset	1,439	649	1,388	1,388
Talbot	1,505	467	1,379	1,544
Totals	9,747	10,390	10,381	11,030

Source: Evarts B. Greene and Virginia D. Harrington, *American Population Before the Federal Census of 1790* (1932), 127.

TABLE 5.31   CENSUS OF TAXED AND UNTAXED POPULATION IN MARYLAND, 1700

County	Taxables	Untaxed	Total	Ratio of Total to Taxables
St. Mary's	1277	2236	3513	2.75
Charles	(1122)	1686	(2808)	2.50
Calvert	1248	1569	2817	2.26
Prince George's	963	1395	2358	2.45
Anne Arundel	1809	2312	4121	2.28
Baltimore	(759)	(979)	(1738)	2.29
Cecil	870	(1134)	2004	2.30
Kent	707	1223	1930	2.73
Talbot	1846	3016	4862	2.63
Dorchester	868	1749	2617	3.01
Somerset	1680	3724	5404	3.22
Totals	(13,149)	(21,023)	(34,172)	2.60

Note: Figures in parentheses were corrected from original source.
Source: Russell R. Menard, "Five Maryland Censuses, 1700 to 1712: A Note on the Quality of the Quantities," *William and Mary Quarterly,* XXXVII (1980), 618.

TABLE 5.32   CENSUS OF POPULATION IN MARYLAND, 1704

County	Masters of Families	Free Women & Servants	Free Children Boys and Girls	Free Men and Servant Men	Servants Boys and Girls	Slaves Young and Old	Fit to Bear Arms	Total
St. Mary's	418	617	1065	938	151	(456)	1356	(3645)
Charles	408	485	931	390	197	578	(798)	2989
Calvert	309	560	942	619	243	938	928	3611
Prince George's	416	530	1166	464	92	(610)	880	(3278)
Anne Arundel	(765)	(858)	1418	503	145	(941)	(1268)	(4630)
Baltimore	364	418	632	(467)	74	(286)	(831)	(2241)
Cecil	407	489	716	430	95	(277)	837	(2414)
Kent	264	413	608	393	54	(223)	(657)	(1955)
Talbot	712	914	1207	822	115	(644)	1534	(4414)
Dorchester	305	512	814	418	64	(279)	723	(2392)
Somerset	804	1167	1436	642	83	(427)	(1446)	(4559)
Totals	5,172	(6,963)	10,935	(6,086)	1,313	(5,659)	(11,258)	(36,128)

Note: Figures in parentheses were corrected from original source.
Source: Russell R. Menard, "Five Maryland Censuses, 1700 to 1712: A Note on the Quality of the Quantities," *William and Mary Quarterly,* XXXVII (1980), 620.

TABLE 5.33 CENSUS OF POPULATION IN MARYLAND, 1710

County	Masters and Taxable Men	White Women	White Children	Negroes	Total
St. Mary's	1088	827	1538	668	4121
Charles	951	641	1199	638	3429
Calvert	708	560	1014	934	3216
Prince George's	845	637	1215	1297	3994
Anne Arundel	1014	793	1443	1528	4778
Baltimore	733	558	1098	438	2827
Cecil	497	406	856	197	1956
Kent	(783)	(529)	(897)	(399)	(2608)
Queen Anne	808	644	1241	374	3067
Talbot	1103	851	1681	470	4105
Dorchester	(749)	(678)	(1364)	(357)	(3148)
Somerset	1871	(1314)	2670	579	(6434)
Totals	(11,150)	(8,438)	(16,216)	(7,879)	(43,683)

Note: Figures in parentheses were corrected from original source.
Source: Russell R. Menard, "Five Maryland Censuses, 1700 to 1712: A Note on the Quality of the Quantities," *William and Mary Quarterly*, XXXVII (1980), 624.

TABLE 5.34 CENSUS OF POPULATION IN MARYLAND, 1755[a]

Taxable Persons 16 Years of Age

Name of the County	Whites Free Men.	Whites Servants Men, hired or indented	Whites Servants Men, convicts	Mulattoes Free Men	Mulattoes Free Women	Mulattoes Slaves Men	Mulattoes Slaves Women	Blacks Free Men	Blacks Free Women	Blacks Slaves Men	Blacks Slaves Women
Baltimore	2,630	595	472	36	21	25	16	2	2	1,144	833
Ann Arundell	1,534	438	184	16	22	25	11	8	4	1,472	1,060
Calvert	609	124	...	24	8	...	4	...	1	550	519
Prince George	1,515	255	73	17	21	37	43	3	3	1,278	151
Frederick	2,775	216	94	23	4	10	24	45	26	437	314
Charles	1,929	173	205	60	36	48	33	3	1	1,196	950
St. Mary's	1,561	194	29	16	17	38	27	16	5	822	761
Worcester	1,768	45	1	31	32	3	7	1	2	401	359
Somerset	1,348	31	1	23	16	15	15	4	3	637	571
Dorchester	1,950	172	7	9	7	9	22	7	3	624	514
Talbot	1,223	294	25	24	18	72	63	12	3	647	595
Queen Anne's	1,745	284	287	18	20	33	32	8	9	643	572
Kent	1,454	365	82	8	13	7	9	10	5	691	523
Cecil	1,345	390	47	2	12	120	86	...	2	286	216
Total	23,386	3,576	1,507	307	247	442	392	119	69	10,828	7,938

Persons Under 16 Years of Age

Name of the County	Whites Free Boys	Whites Free Girls	Whites Servants hired, or indented Boys	Whites Servants hired, or indented Girls	Whites Servants, convicts Boys	Whites Servants, convicts Girls	Mulattoes Free Boys	Mulattoes Free Girls	Mulattoes Slaves Boys	Mulattoes Slaves Girls
Baltimore	3,115	2,951	126	49	6	6	63	62	28	43
Ann Arundell	1,913	1,705	82	26	16	...	28	35	31	23
Calvert	861	745	48	28	...	...	30	31	15	17
Prince George	1,840	1,674	33	10	1	...	42	26	46	55
Frederick	3,246	3,105	80	56	9	1	22	23	19	19
Charles	1,681	1,799	228	41	16	7	69	57	52	51
St. Mary's	1,845	1,764	29	24	5	3	24	22	94	98
Worcester	2,067	2,083	28	12	...	...	28	29	7	8
Somerset	1,330	1,232	12	...	...	...	24	19	21	25
Dorchester	2,347	2,222	54	17	...	2	12	22	35	32
Talbot	1,322	1,197	57	9	...	...	20	19	74	81
Queen Anne's	2,037	1,864	82	44	9	...	31	24	57	58
Kent	1,527	1,423	134	76	4	1	16	19	9	20
Cecil	1,506	1,372	55	20	1	1	10	4	89	108
Total	26,637	25,136	1,048	412	67	21	419	392	577	638

[a] Figures corrected from original.
Source: The London *Gentleman's Magazine*, XXIV (1755), 261.

Persons Not Taxable

Whites					Mulattoes		Blacks	
Free			Servants, Women		Past Labor or Cripples		Past Labor or Cripples	
Clergy	Men, poor	Women	Hire or indented	Convicts	Free	Slaves	Free	Slaves
4	58	2,587	200	87	14	4	8	47
3	64	1,539	93	51	4	15	6	92
2	20	639	61	...	2	15	7	39
3	44	1,680	55	27	8	7	2	88
1	45	2,213	163	32	6	2	4	13
4	51	1,777	106	78	17	5	2	32
3	61	1,806	164	13	16	14	3	49
1	57	1,964	37	1	1	10	7	44
3	61	1,446	37	...	...	1	2	37
3	44	2,097	126	...	8	8	2	44
2	34	1,296	160	4	10	1	4	30
3	31	1,843	159	73	3	6	3	32
2	34	1,448	181	12	6	9	6	35
1	33	1,186	282	8	...	2	2	13
35	637	23,521	1,824	386	95	99	58	595

Blacks				Aggregate			
Free		Slaves					
Boys	Girls	Boys	Girls	Whites	Mulattoes	Blacks	Total
3	1	959	1,041	12,886	312	4,040	17,238
10	5	1,314	1,321	7,648	210	5,292	13,150
...	...	671	645	3,137	146	2,432	5,715
...	...	1,340	1,239	7,210	302	4,104	11,616
3	1	465	473	12,036	152	1,781	13,969
7	...	1,145	1,197	8,095	428	4,533	13,056
13	17	862	839	7,501	366	3,387	11,254
13	6	561	511	8,064	156	1,905	10,125
1	1	875	891	5,501	159	3,022	8,682
6	1	666	681	9,041	164	2,548	11,753
...	1	579	657	5,623	382	2,528	8,533
2	4	621	603	8,461	282	2,497	11,240
8	3	650	653	6,743	116	2,584	9,443
5	...	275	252	6,247	433	1,051	7,731
71	40	10,983	11,003	108,193	3,608	41,704	153,505

TABLE 5.35   CENSUS OF VIRGINIA POPULATION IN 1625

Settlement	White Male	White Female	White Total	Negro Male	Negro Female	Negro Total	Sum Total
Colledge Land	20	2	22	...	...	...	...
Neck of Land	25	19	44	...	...	...	...
W. and Sherley Hund	44	16	60	...	...	...	...
Jordan's Journey	36	19	55	...	...	...	...
Chaplain Choice and Truelove's Co.	13	4	17	...	...	...	...
Piersey's Hund.	40	9	49	4	3	7	...
Pasheayghs	35	8	43	...	...	...	...
The Maine	30	6	36	...	...	...	...
James City	122	53	175	3	6	9	...
Neck of Land	126	19	145	1	0	1	...
Hog Island	40	13	53	...	...	...	...
Martin's Hund.	20	7	27	...	...	...	...
Mulbury Island	25	5	30	...	...	...	...
Wariscoyack	8	...	8	1	1	2	...
Basses Choyse	16	3	19	...	...	...	...
Newportes Newes	20	...	20	...	...	...	...
Elizabeth City	198	59	257	2	1	3	...
Elizabeth City beyond Hampton Rd.	78	20	98	1	0	1	...
Eastern Shore	44	7	51	...	.	...	...
Total	940	269	1,209	12	11	23	1,232

Summary of Inhabitants, 1624–25

Place	Free	Servants	Children	Negroes	Total
Henrico	18	3	1	...	22
Charles City	119	84	26	7	236
James City	204	226	35	10	475
Elizabeth City	235	157	43 + 2 Inds.	6	443
Eastern Shore	32	17	2	...	51
Total	[608]	[487]	[109]	[23]	[1,227]

Total: 432 males, 176 females—free }
441 males, 46 females—servants } 1,095 emigrants }
107 children
11 males, 10 females, 2 children—Negroes

1,202 English
2 Indians
23 Negroes
1,227

Source: Evarts B. Greene and Virginia D. Harrington, *American Population Before the Federal Census of 1790* (1932), 144. See also, Irene W. D. Hecht, "The Virginia Muster of 1624/5 as a Source for Demographic History," *William and Mary Quarterly*, XXX (1973), 65–92.

TABLE 5.36   CENSUS OF VIRGINIA POPULATION, BY COUNTY, IN 1634

County	Population
Henrico	419
Charles City	511
James City	886
Warrick	811
Warrowerguyoake	522
Elizabeth City Co.	854
Charles River Co.	510
Accomacke Co.	396
Total	4,909

Source: Evarts B. Greene and Virginia D. Harrington, *American Population Before the Federal Census of 1790* (1932), 145.

TABLE 5.37   COUNTS OF PERSONS SUBJECT TO TAXES IN VIRGINIA, 1653–1699

Counties	1653	1682	1698	1699 Tithables	1699 Untithables
Accomack	...	583	866	854	1,814
Charles City	532	714	1,052	1,260	2,639
Elizabeth City	395	287	427	453	735
Essex	...	...	871	1,018	1,584
Gloucester	367	2,005	2,326	2,514	3,216
Henrico	...	471	699	724	1,498
Isle of Wight	673	735	732	781	1,985
James City	...	982	1,084	1,059	1,701
King and Queen	...	...	1,483	1,664	2,642
Lancaster	...	421	636	869	1,224
Middlesex	...	546	764	658	883
Nansemond	...	755	775	781	1,790
New Kent	...	1,802	1,056	1,116	2,056
Norfolk	...	694	674	684	1,572
Northampton	500	555	615	681	1,369
Northumberland	450	624	997	1,088	931
Princess Anne	...	...	646	620	1,351
Rappahanock	...	1,053	...	...	...
Richmond	...	...	1,036	1,262	1,278
Stafford	...	407	679	708	1,152
Surry	518	486	662	664	1,350
Warwick	...	306	463	474	888
Westmoreland	...	695	887	936	1,605
York	...	1,041	1,093	738	1,171
Total	[3,435]	15,162	20,523	21,606	36,434

Source: Evarts B. Greene and Virginia D. Harrington, *American Population Before the Federal Census of 1790* (1932), 145–146.

TABLE 5.38   MUSTER OF VIRGINIA MILITIA IN 1703

Counties	Com. and Noncom. Officers[a]	Horse	Dragoons	Foot
Henrico	53	79	171	124
Charles City	37	43	34	97
Prince George	46	58	81	144
Isle of Wight	71	150	40	305
Nansemond	58	123	105	200
Norfolk	28	60	37	193
Princess Ann	43	50	28	186
Elizabeth City	27	33	35	4 [sic]
Accomack	72	135	242	123
Northampton	37	60	90	118
Warwick	30	37	39	140
James City	81	83	50	286
New Kent	28	111	...	215
King William	50	62	80	172
King and Queen	79	104	120	225
Gloucester	116	146	...	625
Essex	68	105	40	204
Lancaster	56	66	91	137
Stafford	46	73	56	182
Richmond	59	171	46	349
Westmoreland	64	80	101	250
Northumberland	90	98	205	172
York	61	96	30	269
Middlesex	26	32	73	106
Surry	17	79	...	248
Total	1,343	2,134	1,794	5,074

[a] Of the 1,343 officers, approximately 370 would have been commissioned and 983 noncommissioned. See source below, p. 147.

Source: Evarts B. Greene and Virginia D. Harrington, *American Population Before the Federal Census of 1790* (1932), 148–149.

TABLE 5.39   COUNTS OF PERSONS SUBJECT TO TAXES IN VIRGINIA, 1703–1714

Counties	1703	1704	1705	1714
Accomack	1,061	1,061	1,061	1,055
Charles City	551	550	571	553
Elizabeth City	478	478	478	610
Essex	1,261	1,262	1,307	1,653
Gloucester	294	2,945	2,880	2,804
Henrico	1,018	1,020	1,020	1,335
James City	1,435	1,435	1,423	1,535
Isle of Wight	734	923	923	1,223
King William	884	884	936	1,226
King and Queen	1,545	1,546	1,574	1,814
Lancaster	909	909	909	1,019
Middlesex	807	807	824	926
Nansemond	1,117	1,017	1,017	1,250
New Kent	1,482	1,482	1,453	1,852
Norfolk	693	693	714	891
Northampton	716	728	728	831
Northumberland	1,188	1,180	1,180	1,272
Prince George	1,016	1,024	1,024	1,040
Princess Anne	728	728	728	921
Richmond	1,483	1,483	1,489	1,799

Counties	1703	1704	1705	1714
Stafford	892	892	892	1,069
Surry	844	855	895	1,320
Warwick	577	518	536	604
Westmoreland	1,229	1,229	1,229	1,543
York	1,279	1,279	1,262	1,395
Total	24,221	26,928	27,053	31,540

Source: Evarts B. Greene and Virginia D. Harrington, *American Population Before the Federal Census of 1790* (1932), 149–150.

TABLE 5.40   DISTRIBUTION OF PERSONS SUBJECT TO TAXES IN VIRGINIA, 1729–1773

Tax Districts	1773	1755	1749	1729
Tidewater	50%	60%	68%	92%
Piedmont	44%	35%	28%	8%
Shenandoah Valley	6%	5%	4%	…
Total Tithables	157,325	103,318	91,864	51,195

Source: Philip Morgan and Michael L. Nicholls, "Slaves in Piedmont Virginia, 1720–1790," *William and Mary Quarterly,* XLVI (1989), 215.

TABLE 5.41   COUNTS OF PERSONS SUBJECT TO TAXES IN VIRGINIA, 1722–1755

Counties	1722	1723	1724	1726	1729	1749	1755 Whites	1755 Blacks
Accomack	1,055	1,263	1,290	1,300	1,474	2,353	1,506	1,135
Albemarle	…	…	…	…	…	1,725	1,344	1,747
Amelia	…	…	…	…	…	2,383	1,251	1,652
Augusta	…	…	…	…	…	1,423	2,273	40
Brunswick	…	…	…	160	…	1,765	1,299	976
Bedford	…	…	…	…	…	…	357	143
Caroline	…	…	…	…	…	3,551	1,208	2,674
Charles City	918	922	1,088	1,082	1,081	1,506	537	1,058
Chesterfield	…	…	…	…	…	…	841	1,198
Culpepper	…	…	…	…	…	…	1,221	1,217
Cumberland	…	…	…	…	…	…	704	1,394
Dinwiddie	…	…	…	…	…	…	784	1,175
Elizabeth City	654	753	823	813	778	1,070	316	812
Essex	2,158	2,171	2,413	2,472	2,694	2,610	889	1,711
Fairfax	…	…	…	…	…	1,586	1,312	921
Frederick	…	…	…	…	…	1,581	2,173	340
Gloucester	3,109	3,260	3,451	3,421	3,473	4,307	1,137	3,284
Goochland	…	…	…	…	…	2,773	569	935
Halifax	…	…	…	…	…	…	629	141
Hampshire	…	…	…	…	…	…	558	12
Hanover	1,324	1,465	1,750	1,941	2,134	3,108	1,169	2,621
Henrico	1,842	1,922	2,227	2,453	2,767	2,979	529	898
Isle of Wight	1,715	1,686	1,849	1,844	2,075	3,244	810	966
James City	1,286	1,265	1,327	1,347	1,242	1,543	394	1,254
King George	915	1,016	1,130	1,300	1,275	1,744	720	1,068
King and Queen	2,337	2,482	2,670	2,685	2,850	2,899	944	2,103
King William	1,918	2,045	2,294	2,389	2,518	2,392	702	1,834
Lancaster	1,147	1,065	1,233	1,249	1,390	1,538	486	1,124
Louisa	…	…	…	…	…	1,519	655	1,452
Lunenburg	…	…	…	…	…	1,519	1,209	903
Middlesex	1,055	1,120	1,192	1,150	1,139	1,400	371	1,056
Nansemond	1,437	1,466	1,567	1,692	1,847	2,153	989	1,264
New Kent	1,190	1,216	1,296	1,348	1,364	1,610	465	1,209
Norfolk	1,094	1,127	906	1,188	1,245	2,190	1,132	1,408
Northampton	809	871	986	1,044	1,033	1,529	609	902
Northumberland	1,521	1,563	1,715	1,723	1,572	2,176	980	1,434
Orange	…	…	…	…	…	2,679	627	1,016

(continued)

TABLE 5.41 (continued)

Counties	1722	1723	1724	1726	1729	1749	1755 Whites	1755 Blacks
Princess Anne	954	1,000	1,185	1,046	1,147	1,559	840	880
Prince George	1,315	1,387	1,562	1,624	1,795	3,190	650	1,138
Prince William	...	...	...	...	...	2,222	1,384	1,414
Prince Edward	...	...	...	...	...	...	416	410
Richmond	1,020	1,394	1,551	1,450	1,839	1,837	761	1,036
Southampton	...	...	...	...	...	...	973	1,036
Spotsylvania	...	...	800	950	919	1,782	665	1,468
Stafford	1,503	1,554	1,747	1,800	2,060	1,811	889	1,126
Surry	1,701	1,712	1,924	2,049	2,190	3,367	587	1,006
Sussex	...	...	...	...	...	...	778	1,388
Warwick	581	631	692	701	675	818	181	665
Westmoreland	1,763	1,880	2,007	2,011	1,998	2,471	944	1,588
York	1,439	1,525	1,202	1,625	1,622	2,054	562	1,567
Total	37,760	39,761	43,877	45,857	48,196	85,966	43,329	59,999

Source: Evarts B. Greene and Virginia D. Harrington, *American Population Before the Federal Census of 1790* (1932), 150–151.

TABLE 5.42 COUNTS OF PERSONS SUBJECT TO TAXES IN NORTH CAROLINA, 1748–1759

Counties	1748	1749	1750	1751	1752	1753	1754	1755	1756	1757	1758	1759
Anson	...	...	516	588	965	702	600 [870]	854	450	364	178	350
Beaufort	832	1,000	1,009	866	866	1,200	1,241	1,311	1,302	1,211	1,285	1,252
Bertie	...	...	...	...	...	1,706	1,789	1,876	1,871	1,941	1,892	1,892
Bladen	800	705	903	988	949	899	684	661	664	933	1,064	1,010
Carteret	320	375	387	399	435	442	447	422	449	508	479	527
Chowan	...	...	...	...	...	1,400	1,456	1,536	1,592	1,287	1,413	1,420
Craven	1,278	1,374	1,214	1,435	1,543	1,629	1,644	1,836	1,836	1,967	2,049	2,090
Currituck	...	...	...	...	...	70–	707	717	721	705	706	811
Cumberland	...	...	...	...	...	...	323	377	371	612	348	394
Dobbs	...	...	...	...	...	...	...	...	...	...	...	1,054
Duplin	...	...	377	477	553	554	629	626	678	766	795	896
Edgecomb	...	...	...	...	...	2,103	2,190	2,410	2,414	2,222	2,050	1,331
Granville	870	922	1,0–8	991	969	1,004	1,200	1,318	1,304	1,655	1,852	2,097
Halifax	...	...	...	...	...	...	...	...	...	...	...	2,029
Hyde	396	429	414	412	400	409	415	424	425	485	488	520
Johnston	908	1,009	1,048	1,190	1,160	1,340	1,298	1,541	1,871	1,673	1,653	1,756
New Hanover	192	1,890	1,688	1,438	1,487	2,037	2,008	2,210	2,228	2,159	2,371	2,250
Northampton	...	...	...	...	...	1,753	1,805	1,875	1,933	1,963	1,955	2,210
Onslow	...	586	650	653	616	711	716	778	753	721	761	799
Orange	...	...	...	...	...	1,108	1,281	1,124	1,415	1,595	1,860	1,856
Pasquotank	...	...	...	...	...	1,180	1,200	1,223	1,250	1,332	1,229	1,247
Perquimans	...	...	...	...	...	1,028	1,117	1,136	1,023	1,173	1,240	1,198
Rowan	...	...	...	...	...	...	1,000	1,000	1,531	1,034	1,034	747
Tyrrell	...	...	...	...	...	700	710	710	827	788	634	649
Total	[5,596]	[8,290]	[9,214]	[9,437]	[9,943]	[22,605]	24,460	25,965	26,908	27,094	27,336	30,385

Source: Evarts B. Greene and Virginia D. Harrington, *American Population Before the Federal Census of 1790* (1932), 160–161.

TABLE 5.43 NUMBER OF MILITIA AND PERSONS TAXED IN NORTH CAROLINA, 1756

Counties	Militia	Taxables White	Taxables Black	Taxables Total	Horse
Anson	790	810	60	870	...
Beaufort	680	771	567	1,383	...
Bertie	902	...	...	1,876	44
Bladen	441	338	346	684	33
Carteret	230	...	...	400	...
Chowan	830	...	...	1,481	...
Craven	631	989	934	1,923	...
Cumberland	...	302	74	376	...
Currituck	390	470	150	620	...
Duplin	340	460	168	628	39
Edgecomb	1,317	1,674	1,091	2,765	...
Granville	734	835	470	1,305	...

Counties	Militia	Taxables White	Taxables Black	Taxables Total	Horse
Hyde	249	276	148	424	...
Johnson	894	1,242	397	1,639	...
New Hanover	508	396	1,420	1,816	33
Northampton	676	902	834	1,736	...
Onslow	308	448	247	695	...
Orange	490	...	...	1,113	...
Pasquotank	581	563	366	929	...
Perquimans	357	...	...	1,176	...
Rowan	996	1,116	54	1,176	...
Tyrell	438	477	335	722	...
Total	12,931	12,069	[7,661]	25,737	149

Source: W. L. Saunders, ed., *Colonial Records of North Carolina* (1886–1890), V, 575–576.

TABLE 5.44 COUNTS OF PERSONS SUBJECT TO TAXES IN NORTH CAROLINA, 1760–1765

Counties	1760	1761	1762	1763	1764	1765
Anson	600	776	776	776	745	644
Beaufort	1,2–2	712	716	742	751	740
Bertie	665	840	1,631	1,–66	1,641	1,426
Bladen	1,112	1,207	1,200	1,244	1,244	1,114
Brunswick	...	...	...	...	1,318	1,184
Bute	...	...	...	...	1,757	1,798
Carteret	503	528	541	541	594	657
Chowan	1,480	1,500	1,500	1,400	1,400	1,510
Craven	...	2,239	2,120	2,120	2,266	2,344
Currituck	6—	857	807	737	800	717
Cumberland	...	611	693	873	1,005	1,109
Dobbs	...	1,273	1,339	1,400	1,485	1,607
Duplin	...	1,029	1,055	1,085	1,085	881
Edgecombe	1,3—	1,663	1,666	1,566	1,480	1,557
Granville	2,009	2,877	2,828	3,128	1,362	1,479
Halifax	2,291	2,706	2,425	1,985	2,286	2,476
Hertford	1,324	1,488	1,392	1,384	1,496	1,552
Hyde	525	569	568	588	689	588
Johnston	817	973	982	1,282	1,282	1,298
Mecklenburg	...	...	...	791	1,071	1,217
New Hanover	2,003	2,670	2,790	2,356	1,747	1,805
Northampton	2,210	2,270	2,280	2,131	2,109	2,300
Onslow	780	873	877	890	1,050	1,017
Orange	1,928	2,627	2,427	2,669	3,028	3,064
Pasquotank	1,410	1,411	1,292	1,215	1,225	1,098
Perquimans	1,174	1,320	1,299	1,303	1,470	1,485
Pitt	...	987	995	1,093	1,061	1,062
Rowan	669	1,373	1,486	1,486	2,295	2,520
Tyrrell	624	840	748	618	834	816
Total	25,226	36,219	36,433	36,469	40,576	41,065

Source: Evarts B. Greene and Virginia D. Harrington, *American Population Before the Federal Census of 1790* (1932), 164–165.

TABLE 5.45 NORTH CAROLINIANS SUBJECT TO POLL TAX AND IN MILITIA, 1765–1767

Counties	1765			1766				1767		
	White	Black	Total	White	Black	Total	Militia	White	Black	Total
Anson	584	131	715	...	...	786	800	696	173	869
Beaufort	411	470	881	432	476	908	742	410	481	891
Bertie	636	877	1,513	...	...	1,745	1,634	...	...	1,829
Bladen	604	633	1,237	...	...	1,262	1,244	791	716	1,507
Brunswick	209	1,106	1,315	229	1,177	1,406	186	224	1,085	1,309
Bute	...	...	2,078	1,172	967	2,139	200	1,299	941	2,240
Carteret	411	931	1,342	460	269	729	541	470	290	760
Chowan	610	1,017	1,627	616	1,082	1,698	745	...	...	1,653
Craven	1,284	1,320	2,604	1,391	1,298	2,689	1,175	1,378	1,520	2,898
Cumberland	866	366	1,232	900	387	1,287	652	899	362	1,261
Currituck	...	...	796	...	...	875	709	...	...	889
Dobbs	1,176	609	1,785	1,211	643	1,854	954	1,268	706	1,974
Duplin	848	130	978	883	359	1,242	1,085	1,071	437	1,508
Edgecombe	...	...	1,739	...	...	2,066	1,207	...	...	2,260
Granville	974	701	1,675	926	809	1,735	2,882	1,022	906	1,928
Halifax	...	...	2,628	...	...	2,894	2,029	...	...	2,806
Hertford	...	...	1,567	...	...	1,667	1,393	...	...	1,690
Hyde	402	251	653	430	286	716	604	441	282	723
Johnston	984	458	1,442	1,003	511	1,514	899	1,129	567	1,696
Mecklenberg	...	...	1,352	...	...	1,461	791	...	...	2,163
New Hanover	529	1,476	2,005	507	1,531	2,038	446	511	1,492	2,003
Northampton	...	...	2,434	...	...	2,497	1,169	...	...	2,557
Onslow	678	451	1,129	...	...	1,192	978	716	500	1,216
Orange	2,825	579	3,404	3,324	649	3,973	2,699	3,573	729	4,302
Pasquotank	...	...	1,106	740	606	1,346	850	433	359	792
Perquimans	...	...	1,531	527	1,017	1,544	...	...	...	1,472
Pitt	750	429	1,179	798	470	1,268	741	775	448	1,223
Rowan	...	...	3,059	...	...	3,059	1,486	...	...	3,643
Tyrell	538	368	906	634	386	1,020	996	594	390	984
Total	15,319	12,303	45,912	16,183	12,923	48,610	29,837	17,700	12,384	51,046

Source: Evarts B. Greene and Virginia D. Harrington, *American Population Before the Federal Census of 1790* (1932), 165–167.

TABLE 5.46 POPULATION OF SOUTH CAROLINA PARISHES, 1720

Parishes	Taxable Acres	Tax-payers	Total White Population	Slaves	Total Population
St. Helena	51,817	30	150	42	192
St. Bartholomew's	30,559	47	235	144	379
St. George's	47,457	68	340	536	876
St. Paul's	187,976	201	1,005	1,634	2,639
St. Andrew's	197,169	210	1,050	2,493	3,543
St. James (Goose Creek)	153,268	107	535	2,027	2,562
St. Philip's (Charles Town)	64,265	283	1,415	1,390	2,805
St. John's (Berkeley)	181,375	97	485	1,439	1,924
St. Thomas & St. Dennis	74,580	113	565	942	1,507
Christ Church	57,580	107	535	637	1,172
St. James Santee	117,274	42	210	584	794
Total	1,163,319	1,305	6,525	11,828	18,393

Source: Peter H. Wood, *Black Majority: Negroes in Colonial South Carolina From 1670 Through the Stono Rebellion* (1975), 146–147.

TABLE 5.47 MUSTER OF SOUTH CAROLINA MILITIA, MAY 1757

Units	Men
3 Troops of Horse	115
Charles Town Infantry	912
Col. Izard's Regiment	829
Granville Regiment	449
Colleton County	732
Craven County	1,949
Welsh Tract	865
Berkeley County	563
Horse Creek on Savannah Riv.	109
New Windsor Township	67
Total Militia	6,590

Source: Evarts B. Greene and Virginia D. Harrington, *American Population Before the Federal Census of 1790* (1932), 176–177.

TABLE 5.48 REPORTED POPULATION OF GEORGIA, 1734–1765

Year	Whites	Blacks	Militia	Total Population
1765	6,800	4,500	...	11,300
1761	6,100	3,600	...	9,700
1760	6,000	3,578	895	9,578
1756	...	...	800	...
1755	...	...	756	6,500
1753	2,381	1,066	...	3,447
1751	1,700	420	...	2,720
1740	...	...	...	1,200
1737	...	...	700	...
1734	...	...	...	437[a]

[a] 259 in Savannah, 22 in Okegie, 3 in Highgate, 39 in Hamstead, 33 in Abercorn, 18 in Skidaw, 1 in Hutchinsons, 21 in Tybee, 5 at Cape Bluff, 4 in Westbrook, 28 in Thunderbold.

Source: Evarts B. Greene and Virginia D. Harrington, *American Population Before the Federal Census of 1790* (1932), 176–177.

Population Distribution by Age and Sex

The population of the thirteen colonies was distinguished by its youthful character. Because families reproduced at near the limit of biological possibility and infant mortality was quite low, early America literally teemed with children. The median age of eighteenth-century colonists was 16 (meaning that half of all persons were at or below that age). In contrast, by 1990, the median age of United States citizens had risen to 32, and only 23% of all persons were 16 or younger. In this aspect of its age structure, the thirteen colonies actually resembled the twentieth century's developing nations, where the median age of national populations is also typically about 16.

The elderly formed a much smaller part of the colonial population than among their descendants in 1990 when about 12% of Americans were over age 65. In the most unhealthy region of early America, the tidewater lowlands surrounding Chesapeake Bay, less than 1% of the population was that old in 1704. Although the average adult lived past 60 in the Mid-Atlantic colonies and in New England, persons over 65

TABLE 5.49 AGE DISTRIBUTION OF COLONIAL ANGLO-AMERICAN COMMUNITIES

Ages	Middlesex County, Va. 1668 Male	Middlesex County, Va. 1668 Female	Middlesex County, Va. 1704 Male	Middlesex County, Va. 1704 Female	Westchester Co., N.Y. 1698 Both	New England 1650–1700 Male	New England 1650–1700 Female	United States 1985 Male	United States 1985 Female
0–4	4.9%	5.0%	10.1%	10.5%	19.5%	8.9%	8.3%	3.9%	3.7%
5–9	3.0%	4.5%	8.0%	7.8%	16.6%	7.5%	6.7%	3.5%	3.3%
10–14	9.4%	2.9%	7.3%	7.5%	11.7%	6.3%	5.6%	3.9%	3.7%
15–19	15.1%	6.9%	7.9%	6.0%	6.2%	5.6%	4.9%	4.2%	4.0%
20–24	27.0%	3.2%	7.5%	5.1%	7.5%	4.8%	4.1%	4.7%	4.6%
25–29	6.5%	1.5%	5.0%	2.6%	4.4%	4.1%	3.4%	4.5%	4.5%
30–34	2.9%	1.0%	3.5%	2.0%	9.1%	3.4%	2.9%	4.0%	4.1%
35–39	2.4%	.7%	1.9%	1.0%	5.2%	2.9%	2.4%	3.4%	3.5%
40–44	1.9%	.1%	2.7%	.8%	4.9%	2.5%	2.0%	2.8%	2.9%
45–49	.9%	.1%	.9%	.3%	2.6%	2.1%	1.6%	2.3%	2.5%
50–54	...	...	1.0%	...	3.9%	1.7%	1.3%	2.3%	2.5%
55–59	...	...	.6%	...	2.6%	1.3%	1.0%	2.3%	2.6%
60–64	...	...	...	...	3.9%	1.0%	.8%	2.1%	2.5%
65–69	...	...	...	...	1.0%	.7%	.5%	3.0%	4.0%
70–74	...	...	...	...	.3%	.5%	.4%	[a]	[a]
75–79	...	...	...	...	.5%	.3%	.2%	1.7%	3.0%
80–84	...	...	...	...	...	.1%	.1%	[b]	[b]
85 +	...	...	...	...	...	.1%	...	[b]	[b]
Total	74.0%	25.9%	56.4%	43.6%	100%	53.8%	46.2%	48.6%	51.4%

[a] Included in data for 65–69.
[b] Included in data for 75–79.
Source: Darrett B. & Anita H. Rutman, *A Place in Time: Middlesex County, Virginia, 1650–1750* (1984), data for table, p. 76, given by authors in letter of October 2, 1994. Robert V. Wells, *The Population of the British Colonies in America Before 1776* (1975), 117. Terry L. Anderson, *The Economic Growth of New England: A Measurement of Regional Income* (1975), 65. Tom and Nancy Biracree, *Almanac of the American People* (1988), 4–5.

POPULATION DENSITY, 1740

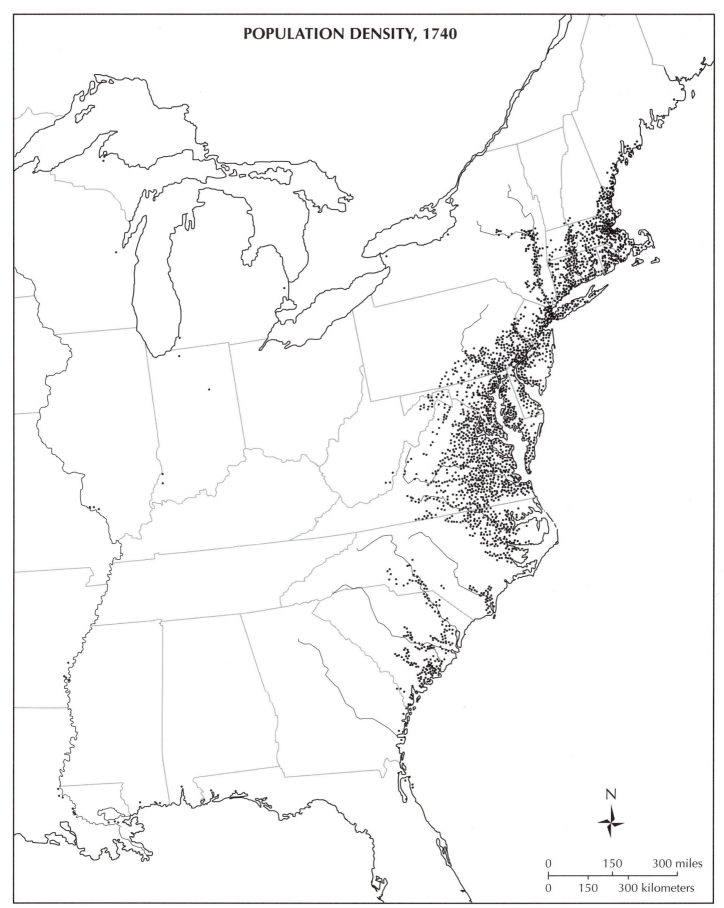

N

| 0 | 150 | 300 miles |

| 0 | 150 | 300 kilometers |

This map shows the population density in 1740 (each dot represents 200 rural inhabitants). Total population was about 900,000. Two decades of peace with the French, the Spanish, and the Indians had greatly stimulated frontier expansion during the previous two decades. (Map drawn by Jeremy Eagle, based on information from *The Geographical Review,* XXX [1940], inset following p. 464) composed a relatively small share of all inhabitants. In late seventeenth-century New England, only 3% of residents were 65 or more. Although social historians have undertaken few studies on this subject, limited evidence indicates that the proportion of elderly within colonial society increased from 1700 to the Revolution. The percentage of New York males age 61 or over, for example, rose from 4.2% in 1712 to 6.4% in 1756. By the Revolution, the share of elderly in the population was as large as possible in a society without mainstays of modern medicine such as antibiotics and indicated that colonial Americans were unusually healthy and well nourished.

The colonial population's sexual distribution began highly skewed toward men. For most of the 1600s, three males emigrated to the Chesapeake for every female, and even in New England, two males arrived for each female from 1620 to 1649. A relatively even sex ratio appeared early in New England, probably by the 1660s, as the first native-born generation grew to adulthood and immigration trickled to an end after 1650. Because a majority of southerners could not establish families for most of the 1600s because of the scarcity of women, an even sex ratio took much longer to emerge there. As late as 1704, for example, Maryland contained 154 adult men per 100 women, but by 1755 its population had become relatively balanced between the sexes, with 113 adult men per 100 women.

TABLE 5.50 CHARACTERISTICS OF MARYLAND'S SLAVE POPULATION, 1658–1710

Years	Number of Males per 100 Females	Percent of Population 15 & Under	Percent of Population Aged 16–50	Percent of Population Over 50
1721–1730	131	39.9%	49.5%	10.6%
1711–1720	146	32.4%	58.7%	8.9%
1701–1710	143	29.3%	63.1%	7.6%
1691–1700	131	33.9%	58.1%	8.0%
1681–1690	127	27.5%	61.9%	10.6%
1671–1680	112	25.9%	65.2%	8.9%
1658–1670	87	27.5%	58.8%	13.7%

Note: Data taken from inventories in counties of Calvert, Charles, Prince George's, and St. Mary's.
Source: Russell R. Menard, "The Maryland Slave Population, 1658–1730: A Demographic Profile of Blacks in Four Counties," *William and Mary Quarterly,* XXXII (1975), 32, 43.

TABLE 5.51 AGE DISTRIBUTION IN NEW YORK, 1698–1771

Years	Whites (%)			Blacks (%)			Children per Woman	
	Under 16	Above 16	Males over 60	Under 16	Above 16	Males over 60	Whites	Blacks
1698	38.7	61.3	…	…	…	…	1.32	…
1703	52.7	47.0	…	36.7	62.4	…	2.32	1.21
1712–14	49.1	50.9	4.2	35.3	64.7	…	1.88	1.30
1723	48.1	51.9	…	35.3	64.8	…	1.89	1.20
1746	49.1	51.0	5.2	45.9	54.1	7.8	2.01	2.06
1749	47.9	52.1	4.8	43.6	56.4	6.4	1.90	1.74
1756	47.6	52.4	6.4	45.4	56.1	6.5	1.89	1.89
1771	46.2	53.8	5.6	42.6	57.4	8.0	1.79	1.63

Source: Robert V. Wells, *The Population of the British Colonies in America Before 1776* (1975), 116.

TABLE 5.52 AGE DISTRIBUTION IN COLONIAL RHODE ISLAND, NEW JERSEY, AND MARYLAND

Year	Rhode Island		New Jersey		Maryland	
	Under 16	Over 16	Under 16	Over 16	Under 16	Over 16
1774 whites	46.0%	54.0%	…	…	…	…
blacks	…	…	…	…	…	…
1772[a] whites	…	…	49.3%	50.7%	…	…
blacks	…	…	44.6%	55.4%	…	…
1755 whites	49.4%	50.6%	…	…	49.3%	50.7%
blacks	45.9%	54.1%	…	…	53.2%	46.8%
1745 whites	…	…	49.3%	50.7%	…	…
1738 whites	…	…	47.6%	52.4%	…	…
blacks	…	…	40.8%	59.2%	…	…
1726 whites	…	…	48.6%	51.4%	…	…
blacks	…	…	41.8%	58.2%	…	…
1712 whites	…	…	…	…	46.7%	53.3%
1704 whites	…	…	…	…	40.2%	59.8%

[a] Western counties only.
Source: Robert V. Wells, *The Population of the British Colonies in America Before 1776* (1975), 102, 137, 152.

TABLE 5.53 NUMBER OF MALES PER 100 FEMALES IN COLONIAL RHODE ISLAND, NEW YORK, NEW JERSEY, AND MARYLAND

Year	Rhode Island		New York		New Jersey		Maryland	
	under 16	over 16	under 16	over 16	under 16	over 16	under 16	over 16
1774								
whites	103	91	…	…	…	…	…	…
blacks	…	…	…	…	…	…	…	…
1772[a]								
whites	…	…	…	…	102	110	…	…
blacks	…	…	…	…	113	133	…	…
1756								
whites	…	…	109	108	…	…	…	…
blacks	…	…	118	134	…	…	…	…
1755								
whites	97	103	…	…	…	…	109	113
blacks	106	101	…	…	…	…	100	135
1745								
whites	…	…	…	…	104	110	…	…
1738								
whites	…	…	…	…	110	108	…	…
blacks	…	…	…	…	110	136	…	…
1737								
whites	…	…	101	99	…	…	…	…
blacks	…	…	109	131	…	…	…	…
1726								
whites	…	…	…	…	109	114	…	…
blacks	…	…	…	…	109	138	…	…
1712								
whites	…	…	108	95	…	…	…	122
blacks	…	…	107	137	…	…	…	…
1704								
whites	…	…	…	…	…	…	…	154
blacks	…	…	…	…	…	…	…	…

[a] Western counties only.
Source: Robert V. Wells, *The Population of the British Colonies in America Before 1776* (1975), 103, 122, 139, 154.

Immigration and Slave Importations

Immigration proceeded so slowly during the first quarter-century of North American colonization that by 1630 fewer than 4,500 English lived on the continent. The first large wave of immigration came during the generation from 1630 to 1660 and has been termed the Great Migration. During those three decades, about 220,000 persons left England, a full 4% of that country's 5,500,000 inhabitants: 47,500 to the Chesapeake, 28,800 to New England, 113,600 to the Caribbean or Bermuda, and 30,000 to Ireland or Holland. The Great Migration bequeathed the American people their founding stock, including approximately two-fifths of all seventeenth-century arrivals in the Chesapeake and nearly all the Puritan founders of New England.

By raising the number of English on the North American mainland from 4,200 in 1630 to more than 70,000 by 1660, this sudden surge of humanity created a critical mass of Anglo-Saxons, far more numerous than could be expelled by their French and Spanish rivals for empire in North America and so ensured the ultimate success of British colonization. The Great Migration furthermore established a base of young families that raised large numbers of offspring to adulthood, and the high birthrate of the Great Migration's progeny thereafter became the principal means by which population multiplied. Although immigration continued to be heavy and brought 87,600 British to the Anglo-American colonies from 1660 to 1700—perhaps 90% of whom were indentured servants—its contribution to demographic growth steadily declined during those decades. The seventeenth century consequently marked the last period when the American population expanded chiefly by arrivals from overseas rather than by new offspring born to the native stock.

The most sigificant development in immigration after 1660 was a slow rise in the number of newcomers from countries other than England. Scots and Irish first started to appear in steadily larger numbers. So many Huguenots sought refuge from religious persecution in France, especially after Louis XIV revoked the Edict of Nantes in 1685, that by 1700 they constituted 13% of whites in South Carolina and 5% of whites in New York. (England's colonies also became more ethnically diverse in 1664 when they annexed New Netherland, which had previously been settled by perhaps 4,000 Dutch and 500 Swedish immigrants.) The latter seventeenth century furthermore witnessed the first large-scale importation of African slaves, whose numbers mushroomed by 850% from 1660 to 1700.

King William's War and Queen Anne's War discouraged Europeans from relocating in the colonies from 1691 to 1713, and not until 1720 did significant numbers start to come. Eighteenth-century immigration was primarily Celtic and Germanic. England and Wales furnished only 24% of Europeans who settled in the thirteen colonies, while Ireland provided 35%, Scotland 12%, and Germany 28%. Slightly more than 300,000 whites crossed the Atlantic to British North America by the Revolution—more than twice the number in the preceding century. The great entrepôt for this wave of humanity was Philadelphia, the Ellis Island of colonial America. Most immigrants made their homes in the Mid-Atlantic colonies, although from there a large minority also wound up in the Shenandoah valley and Carolina backcountry.

The eighteenth century also witnessed the highpoint of the mainland slave trade and the most rapid expansion of the African-American population. Slave imports remained at a relatively low level until the 1720s, when they first appear to have exceeded 20,000 in a decade. From 1720 to the Revolution, approximately 258,000 blacks were landed from Africa and the West Indies. During those five decades, the African-American population expanded 568% from 68,839 to 459,822 and increased its share of all colonial inhabitants from 15% to 20%. Unlike white society, the colonial black population multiplied primarily by additions from overseas during the half-century before 1775.

Although voluntary and involuntary migration brought a total of more than 500,000 whites and blacks to the thirteen colonies during the eighteenth century, this number accounted for far less of total population growth than is commonly believed. Demographers estimate that 25% of the rise in the number of white colonists derived from the influx of settlers from Europe. If about half the increase in African Americans resulted from slave importations, then this source provided about 10% of the overall colonial growth rate. It would appear that 40% of the cumulative expansion of population (taking account of the foreign born's descendants) resulted from the landing of immigrants or slaves. The addition of 500,000 Europeans and Africans enabled the thirteen colonies to double their numbers almost every 24 years and grow from 250,000 in 1700 to 1,998,000 in 1770. Without immigration and slave imports, the colonies would have required 30 years to double and would have held only 1,412,000 inhabitants by 1770.

TABLE 5.54 ESTIMATED BRITISH[a] IMMIGRATION TO THE NEW WORLD, 1607–1700

Years	To Virginia	To Maryland	To New England	To Delaware Valley	To[e] West Indies	Total
1607–1624	6,000	...	400[b]	...	...	6,400
1625–1633	3,000	...	2,500	...	6,000[b]	11,500
1634–1640	8,800[b]	700	17,500	...	11,300[b]	38,300
1641–1650	12,000	1,800	4,800	...	55,900	74,500
1651–1660	18,500	4,600	3,600	...	40,400	67,100
1661–1670	7,600[c]	12,200	10,000	...	29,500	59,300
1671–1680	7,400[d]	12,400	...	1,000[b]	23,700	44,500
1681–1700	18,200	10,800	...	8,000	45,600	82,600
1607–1700	81,500	42,500	38,800	9,000	212,400	384,200

[a] Prior to 1700, approximately 89% of British emigration was from England, 6% from Wales, 4% from Scotland, and 1% from Ireland. See *William and Mary Quarterly*, XLI (1984), 101, n. 31. Approximately 4,000 immigrants came to New Netherland before 1664, about 400 Swedes came to the Delaware Valley before 1655, and at least 1,500 French Huguenots came to the colonies from 1680 to 1700.
[b] Rough estimate, not available in cited source.
[c] Virginia awarded 18,369 headrights for white importees. See Wesley F. Craven, *White, Red, and Black: The Seventeenth-Century Virginian* (1977), 15.
[d] Virginia awarded 14,701 headrights for white importees. See Craven, ibid., 15–16.
[e] Not including Bermuda, to which 4,000 migrated during 1630–1660.
Source: Henry A. Gemery, "Emigration From the British Isles to the New World, 1630–1700: Inferences from Colonial Populations," *Research in Economic History*, V (1980), 215. Russell R. Menard, "British Migration to the Chesapeake Colonies in the Seventeenth Century," in Lois G. Carr, Philip D. Morgan, and Jean B. Russo, eds., *Colonial Chesapeake Society* (1988), 102–105. Robert C. Anderson, "On English Migration to Early New England," *Journal of Interdisciplinary History*, LIX (1986), 407. Richard T. Vann, "Quakerism: Made in America?" in Richard S. and Mary M. Dunn, eds., *The World of William Penn* (1986), 165.

TABLE 5.55 CHARACTERISTICS OF IMMIGRANTS TO NEW ENGLAND, 1620–1649

Sex	
Males	Females
67%	33%

Marital Status of Adults		
Status	Males	Females
Married	62%	88%
Widow/widower	1%	3%
Single	37%	9%

Age Distribution			
Age Range	Males	Females	Both Sexes
0–9	18.4%	25.3%	20.8%
10–19	24.3%	22.4%	23.6%
20–29	29.6%	23.7%	27.5%
30–39	16.0%	17.7%	16.6%
40–49	8.5%	7.3%	8.1%
50–59	2.7%	2.9%	2.8%
60+	0.6%	0.7%	0.7%

Source: Richard Archer, "New England Mosaic: A Demographic Analysis for the Seventeenth Century," *William and Mary Quarterly*, XLVII (1990), 480, 482.

TABLE 5.56 ESTIMATED IMMIGRATION TO THIRTEEN COLONIES, 1700–1775

Decade	Africans	Germans	Northern Irish	Southern Irish	Scots	English	Welsh	Other	Total
1700–09	9,000	100	600	800	200	400	300	100	11,500
1710–19	10,800	3,700	1,200	1,700	500	1,300	900	200	20,300
1720–29	9,900	2,300	2,100	3,000	800	2,200	1,500	200	22,000
1730–39	40,500	13,000	4,400	7,400	2,000	4,900	3,200	800	76,200
1740–49	58,500	16,600	9,200	9,100	3,100	7,500	4,900	1,100	110,000
1750–59	49,600	29,100	14,200	8,100	3,700	8,800	5,800	1,200	120,500
1760–69	82,300	14,500	21,200	8,500	10,000	11,900	7,800	1,600	157,800
1770–75	17,800	5,200	13,200	3,900	15,000	7,100	4,600	700	67,500
Total	278,400	84,500	66,100	42,500	35,300	44,100	29,000	5,900	585,800

Source: Aaron Fogleman, "Migrations to the Thirteen British North American Colonies, 1700–1775: New Estimates," *Journal of Interdisciplinary History*, XXII (1992), 698.

POPULATION DENSITY, 1760

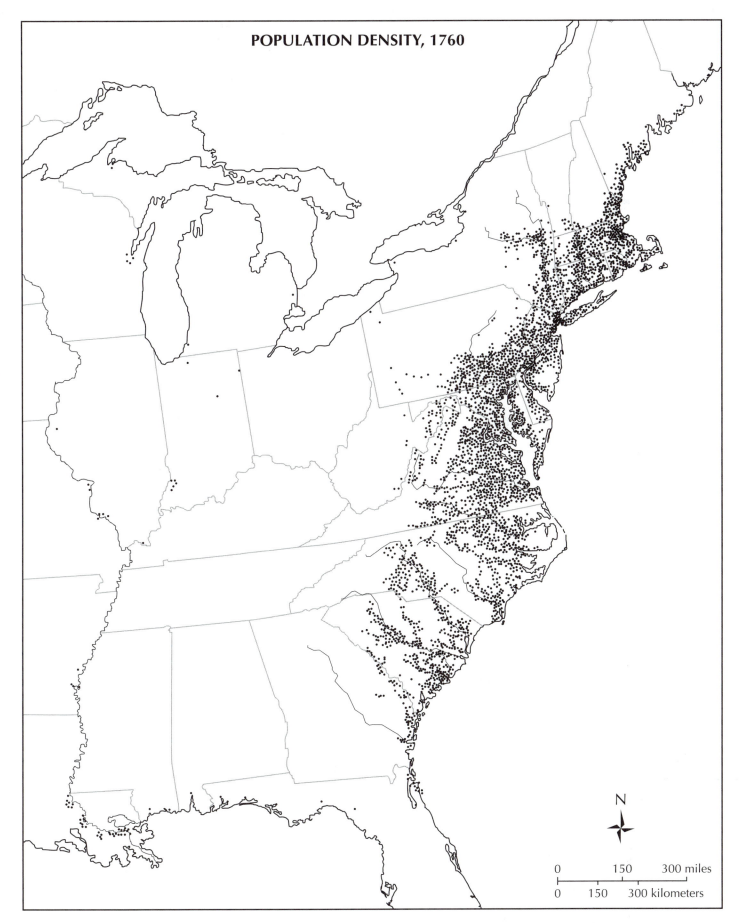

0   150   300 miles

0   150   300 kilometers

This map shows the population density in 1760 (each dot represents 200 rural inhabitants). Total population was approaching 1,200,000. Compare this figure with the map detailing population density as of 1760 in Chapter 1. (Map drawn by Jeremy Eagle, based on information from *The Geographical Review,* XXX [1940], inset following p. 464)

TABLE 5.57 DISTRIBUTION OF ENGLISH INDENTURED SERVANTS BY SEX, 1654–1759

Place of Origin	Years	Number	Male	Female
Bristol	1654–1686	8,173	76.9%	23.1%
London	1683–1686	608	69.2%	30.8%
Middlesex	1683–1684	655	80.7%	19.3%
Liverpool	1697–1707	1,039	72.0%	28.0%
London	1718–1759	3,013	94.5%	5.5%
London	1773–1775	3,359	90.6%	9.4%
Total		16,847	81.6%	18.4%

Source: David W. Galenson, *White Servitude in Colonial America An Economic Analysis* (1981), 24.

TABLE 5.58 OCCUPATIONAL DISTRIBUTION OF ENGLISH INDENTURED SERVANTS, 1654–1759

Occupations	2,675 from Bristol 1654–1660	655 from Middlesex 1683–1684	3,013 from London 1718–1759
Gentleman	1%	...	...
Farmer	30%	9%	11%
Laborer	9%	5%	6%
Food & drink	1%	2%	4%
Construction, wood, & metal work	6%	6%	18%[c]
Clothing & textiles	10%	8%	14%
Services[a]	2%	10%	10%
Unknown[b]	41%	60%	37%

[a] Includes learned professions, seamen, house servants, barbers.
[b] Most unknowns were probably unskilled laborers.
[c] 11% in construction, and 7% in metal and wood crafts.
Source: David W. Galenson, *White Servitude in Colonial America: An Economic Analysis* (1981), 35, 44, 52.

TABLE 5.59 DISTRIBUTION OF ENGLISH INDENTURED SERVANTS BY AGE, 1683–1776

Age	London 1683–1686 Men	Women	Middlesex 1683–1684 Men	Women	Liverpool 1697–1707 Men	Women	London 1718–1759 Men	Women	London 1773–1776 Men	Women
6–10	1%	...	...	...	2%	...	...	...	...	...
11–15	14%	7%	3%	3%	25%	7%	6%	3%	5%	2%
16–20	22%	42%	17%	26%	35%	45%	61%	78%	18%	25%
21–25	40%	42%	57%	61%	23%	34%	21%	12%	44%	48%
26–30	18%	8%	17%	9%	10%	11%	8%	4%	17%	18%
31–35	3%	...	5%	1%	3%	1%	3%	1%	7%	6%
36–40	2%	1%	1%	...	2%	2%	1%	...	6%	1%
41–45	...	...	...	...	...	...	...	...	2%	...
46–50	...	...	...	...	...	...	...	1%	1%	...
Median	22	21	22	21	19	20	19	19	23	21
Number	238	107	632	153	606	287	2,871	169	3,359	338

Source: David W. Galenson, *White Servitude in Colonial America: An Economic Analysis* (1981), 26, 30.

TABLE 5.60 SLAVES IMPORTED FROM OVERSEAS TO THE THIRTEEN COLONIES, 1700–1775

Years	New York	Pennsylvania[a]	Maryland	Virginia	South Carolina	Georgia	Total
1770–75	100	...	1,042	3,932	20,943	830	26,847
1760–69	240	1,032	3,381	9,709	20,810	3,380	38,552
1750–59	69	130	2,297	9,197	15,912	126	27,731
1740–49	141	72	3,815[d]	12,113	1,563[c]	...	17,704
1730–39	1,377	297	5,111[d]	16,226	20,464	...	43,475
1720–29	1,467	76	3,927[d]	12,466	8,817	...	26,753
1710–19	1,104	[b]	1,995[d]	6,333	2,746	...	12,178
1700–09	[b]	[b]	2,586	7,283	206	...	10,075
Total	4,498	1,607	24,154	77,259	91,461	4,336	203,315

Note: Only known imports are listed and actual total may have been 7,000 to 50,000 higher. See Philip D. Curtin, *The Atlantic Slave Trade: A Census* (1969), 137, which breaks down an estimated 255,100 slave arrivals by decade, but not by colony, and data by Fogelman in Table 5.56.
[a] Includes slaves landed in New Jersey or Delaware to avoid paying high import duty in 1760s.
[b] No data.
[c] Reduction caused by prohibitive import duty.
[d] Estimated at 31.5% of Virginia imports, based on ratio of 1700–09 and 1750–75.
Source: James G. Lydon, "New York and the Slave Trade, 1700–1774," *William and Mary Quarterly,* XXXV (1978), 382. Bureau of the Census, *Historical Statistics of the United States: Colonial Times to 1957* (1960), 769. Darold D. Wax, "Negro Imports Into Pennsylvania, 1720–1766," *Pennsylvania History,* XXXII (1965), 261–287. Darold D. Wax, "Black Immigrants: The Slave Trade in Colonial Maryland," *Maryland Historical Magazine,* LXXIII (1978), 35–37. Walter Minchinton et al., eds., *Virginia Slave-Trade Statistics, 1698–1775* (1984), xiii–xv, as updated by Philip D. Morgan and Michael L. Nicholls, "Slaves in Piedmont Virginia, 1720–1790," *William and Mary Quarterly,* XLVI (1989), 251. Peter H. Wood, *Black Majority: Negroes in Colonial South Carolina, From 1670 through the Stono Rebellion* (1974), 151. Daniel C. Littlefield, *Rice and Slaves: Ethnicity and the Slave Trade in Colonial South Carolina* (1981), 162. Julia Floyd Smith, *Slavery and Rice Culture in Low Country Georgia, 1750–1860* (1985), 94–95.

TABLE 5.61   ORIGINS OF AFRICANS IMPORTED TO THE THIRTEEN COLONIES

Port of Origin[a]	To York River, Va. 1718–1726	To York River, Va. 1728–1739	To Maryland 1750–1772	To South Carolina 1732–1775
Bight of Biafra	60%	44%	18%[b]	33%[e]
Angola-Congo	5%	41%	15%	30%
Gold Coast	13%	5%	13%	5%
Senegambia	4%	10%	43%[c]	20%
Madagascar	9%	...	...	...
Windward Coast	7%	...	11%[d]	10%
Sierra Leone	1%	...	...	...[f]
Number	8,400	5,818	4,386	907

[a] For Virginia and Maryland, origin refers to locale on African coast where cargoes were loaded for America and fails to identify actual home of slaves, many of whom were brought from interior districts by Africans for sale to Europeans. Data from South Carolina based on runaway advertisements, which state a person's homeland or ethnic identity.
[b] Termed [Gulf of] Guinea in source.
[c] Broken down as 26% Gambia, 13% Senegal, and 4% Senegambia.
[d] Includes some from Gold Coast.
[e] Termed [Gulf of] Guinea in source; also includes 10% designated from Niger Delta and 2% designated from Slave Coast (Benin-Togo).
[f] Counted with Windward Coast.
Source: Allan Kulikoff, *Tobacco and Slaves: The Development of Southern Cultures in the Chesapeake, 1680–1800* (1986), 322.
Darold D. Wax, "Black Immigrants: The Slave Trade in Colonial Maryland," *Maryland Historical Magazine*, LXXIII (1978), 36.
Daniel C. Littlefield, *Rice and Slaves: Ethnicity and the Slave Trade in Colonial South Carolina* (1981), 125.

CHAPTER 6 Diet and Health

Diet

The first Europeans who settled English North America arrived with the intention of raising and eating the same foods they had consumed in their homeland. Because domesticated livestock were initially in short supply and it often required a few seasons to discover how Old World crops grew best under New World conditions, the earliest colonists found themselves forced to rely heavily on American game and Indian vegetables. In a few extreme cases, like the calamitous Virginia winter of 1609–10, famished and desperate scavengers had to pick over "Doggs, Catts, ratts, Snakes, Toadstooles, horse hides, and what nott," according to one survivor's account. Such "starving times" were mercifully rare but only because more edible fare was widely available.

Europeans almost immediately exploited wild game and fish. Within six months of landing at Plymouth, the Pilgrims passed from a winter of excruciating malnutrition to a summer of plenty due to the abundance of local cod, bass, turkeys, and venison. In the Chesapeake, a study of seventeenth-century trash pits has concluded that a quarter to a third of all meat eaten came from wild species—including deer, turkeys, raccoons, opossums, turtles, and seafood—and that this source

provided up to 40% of animal flesh for some households. The same was certainly true for early New Englanders. Because the teeming wildlife population made hunting and fishing relatively easy, the first two generations of colonists could tap an alternative source of protein to compensate for their general scarcity of domesticated livestock.

Wild game supplemented the early European settlers' diet, but maize ("Indian corn") quickly became its mainstay. Having mutated into many hybrids by 1600, corn could produce good yields in a wide variety of climates; it could furthermore flourish both in regions too rainy for wheat and too dry for rice. Its husk furnished natural protection against insects and birds, and it served as an excellent fodder for animals. Corn generated 74% more calories per unit of soil than wheat, Europe's primary grain, but it also ripened into a nutritious source of carbohydrates, fat, and sugar more rapidly than any major staple. When eaten within fifteen minutes of beans, it combined with them to generate protein.

Maize immediately became the primary staple cultivated by Anglo-Americans. Southerners relied on it almost exclusively and grew little wheat or rye until the early eighteenth century. North of Chesapeake Bay, however, farmers relied on all three grains, but they commonly used a mixture of rye flour and ground corn for their home bread,

The vast majority of white colonists enjoyed a healthy and ample diet, but only a relatively small minority were fortunate enough to enjoy their meals in settings as well furnished as this kitchen (of a style befitting the upper class), which has been restored at York, Maine. (Historic American Buildings Survey, courtesy Library of Congress)

TABLE 6.1 BASIC WEEKLY DIETS OF AMERICANS, 1622–1761

Group/Organization	Date	Calories per Day	Weekly Allowances		
			Grains, Vegetables	Meat	Dairy/Liquor
British Army	1761	2,552–2,921	7 lb. flour, 3 pt. peas, $^1/_2$ lb. rice	7 lb. beef, or 4 lb. pork	$^3/_8$ lb. butter
Virginia Militia in Field	1757	2,600	7 lb. flour	7 lb. beef or pork	…
Acadians Sent to Maryland	1755	1,934	2 lb. bread, 5 lb. flour	1 lb. beef	…
English War Prisoners at Quebec	1747	1,934–2,278	7 lb. bread, 1 $^3/_4$ pt. peas[a]	1 $^5/_8$ lb. fish[b], or 3 $^1/_2$ lb. beef, or 1 $^3/_4$ lb. pork	1 $^4/_5$ gal. of beer, $^9/_{25}$ gal. of molasses
Rhode Island Armed Sloop	1744–46	3,951	7 lb. bread, 2 qt. peas or beans	4 lb. beef, 2 lb. pork	1 lb. butter, $^7/_{16}$ gal. of rum
Passengers to Georgia	1735	3,392	6 $^1/_8$ lb. bread, 2 lb. flour, 1 pt. peas	$^1/_2$ lb. fish, 3 $^1/_5$ lb. beef, 2 lb. pork	$^1/_{10}$ lb. butter, $^2/_5$ lb. suet or plums
Massachusetts Privateers	1700–48	4,748	7 lb. bread, 1 qt. peas, 1 pt. rice, 21 pt. of beer	3 lb. beef, 4 lb. pork	7 gal. beer
Massachusetts Militia In Post On March	1700–50	2,480 2,688	7 lb. bread, 3 $^1/_2$ pt. peas 7 lb. bread	4 $^2/_3$ lb. pork 7 lb. pork	$^1/_6$ gal. of molasses 7 gills of rum
Virginia Militia	1676	4,156	7 lb. biscuits	3 $^1/_2$ lb. beef, 3 $^1/_2$ lb. bacon	3 $^1/_2$ lb. cheese
Passengers to New England	1638	4,527[c]	7 lb. bread, 1 $^1/_2$ pt. peas, $^7/_{50}$ gal. of oatmeal	1 $^1/_2$ lb. fish, 4 $^7/_8$ lb. beef	$^3/_4$ lb. cheese, $^1/_4$ lb. butter, 7 gal. of beer
Children's Hospital at Norwich, England	1632	2,754	6 $^9/_{16}$ lb. bread	1 $^1/_8$ lb. beef	1 $^3/_8$ lb. cheese, 14 $^1/_2$ oz. butter, 2 $^3/_{16}$ gal. of beer, 3 pt. pottage
British Navy	1622	4,737–5,459	7 lb. biscuit	1 $^1/_2$ lb. fish, 4 lb. beef, 2 lb. pork or bacon	$^3/_4$ lb. cheese, $^3/_8$ lb. butter, 7 gal. beer

[a] With pork ration only.
[b] 10$^1/_2$ spoonfuls of oil and 21 spoonfuls of vinegar with fish.
[c] Does not include unknown portions of vinegar and mustard.
Source: Research of Austin White, printed in Bureau of the Census, *Historical Statistics of the United States: Colonial Times to 1957* (1960), 774.

which carried the sobriquet "Rye and Injun." Besides its dark color, rye-and-corn bread was distinguished from baked wheat (with its delicate surface) by a crust so hard it could be used to ladle dinner from a pot.

A significant shift in colonial diets occurred in the late seventeenth century when households began to rely more heavily on slaughtering domesticated animals for meat than hunting or fishing. Analysis of discarded bones from Chesapeake disposal pits has indicated that after 1660 wild game accounted for just 10% of a family's meat supply and that fish consumption had declined by almost half from before 1650. At the same time, livestock herds were increasing significantly as farmers learned how to raise cattle in a country whose natural grasses made poor fodder for grazing. In the South, where shorter and milder winters made it easier to keep cows year round, beef became the major meat dish by 1700. In New England, where cold and long winters made it expensive to feed cattle after autumn ended, pork dominated at the table because hogs could survive better by rooting for nuts and tubers.

Agriculture's seasonal rhythms created a distinct subsistence cycle during the first century of colonization. Because the last phase of the Little Ice Age created a wet, cold climate, crop yields were often low and winter fodder for cattle was generally scarce. Households consequently found it difficult to lay up enough food to last beyond the winter and into the time when the earliest crops ripened. During summer and fall, farmers enjoyed adequate corn and green vegetables, but they refrained from slaughtering any livestock because beef and pork frequently spoiled before they could be preserved with salt in warm weather. Wild game, fish, an occasional family chicken, and cheese provided alternative sources of protein during this time. During winter and spring, the family ate down its stocks of salted meat, flour or dried corn, and uncured cheese pounded before the cows went dry; its supply of greens frequently consisted of nothing more than dried peas, especially in New England. This shortage of fruit and vegetables gave

many colonists a debilitating brush with scurvy. Spring found many families scraping the bottoms of their provision barrels and being forced to rely once again on fishing or hunting before corn could begin to ripen.

Early American cuisine was filling but simple and monotonous. The standard fare was a "pottage" dish (meat stewed with cornmeal and vegetables), the origin of the traditional American one-pot dinner later nicknamed an "English meal" by northerners. A common variant began by boiling dried corn to softness over eight hours, and then adding preserved pork or meat that had been left sitting in water to drain its salt. To this base were added peas, beans, roots, greens, and perhaps apples or milk as its "sauce," which imparted variety of taste and soaked up more excess salt as they congealed into a thick mush over slow heat.

The ensuing hodgepodge could then be continuously replenished from the garden, root cellar, or with wild game to feed the family over a week or more, in which breakfast, lunch, and dinner were endlessly recycled. The colonial ancestor of the "English meal" represented an Anglo-American cousin to the central-European "hunter's stew." Outside of the upper class, which tilled herb gardens, no spices enhanced the meal aside from salt. To ensure that all the stomachs in large colonial families were full at meal's end, the pottage was eaten with bread baked in the hearth's coals from cornmeal, flour (rye or occasionally wheat), and milk.

The general state of American nutrition significantly improved after 1700 because of climatic conditions. Average annual temperatures rose quickly in the early eighteenth century and increased farm yields by lengthening the growing season, reducing the frequency of early frosts, and lessening the difficulty of subsisting livestock through the winter. Greater agricultural productivity made it possible, for the first time, for the vast bulk of households to preserve sufficient meat and grains for their needs from harvest to early summer when the next year's crops began to ripen. By eliminating the seasonal shortage in food stocks that traditionally had plagued families in early spring when their winter supplies approached exhaustion, the warming atmosphere enabled the vast majority of Anglo-Americans to stay well fed year round. Estate inventories indicate that even in New England, where the growing season was shortest, families were not only laying up enough meat, grains, and cider to get through winter and spring but also storing a far more adequate supply of perishables like vegetables, cheese, and butter than before.

Although few detailed accounts of diets survive from the colonial era, all indicate that the standard of living allowed the average person more than enough food to maintain personal health and strength. The majority of diets exceeded the recommended daily food allowance of 2,900 calories set by the National Research Council in 1968, and most did so by several hundred calories. By the mid-eighteenth century, New England widows seem to have enjoyed an average daily intake of 2,800 calories from grains and meat alone, without considering the produce of their gardens and dairies. Food available in such large quantities certainly sufficed to replenish calories expended by hard work and long exposure to outdoor elements.

Eighteenth-century Americans consumed ample amounts of food but may not have balanced their intake correctly among grains, meat, vegetables, fruit, and dairy products. Although most calories came from meat and grains on an annual basis, it is likely that gardens and root cellars provided most rural families with a regular supply of vegetables for at least nine or ten months out of twelve (at least among those types that decayed slowly, such as potatoes, cabbage, carrots, and turnips). Many families, even in New England, nevertheless succeeded by good management to have vegetables year long. Apple cider, which replaced beer as the beverage of choice after 1700, helped compensate for lack of fruit in winter among both adults and children. Because visitors or native observers rarely commented on diseases associated with deficiency of critical vitamins and minerals, such as rickets (vitamin D), goiter (iodine), or eye disorders (vitamin C), it would seem that most individuals experienced periods of extremely imbalanced diets only during short intervals, from which recovery was rapid.

Even without direct statistics on diet, data on average adult heights give some indication of the food supply's nutritional adequacy. A close correlation exists between children's physical growth and proper diet, and so a population's average height can give a strong indication of its general nutritional level. Muster rolls from the Seven Years' War allow a comparison between the typical stature of young, native-born males with foreign-born soldiers serving in colonial regiments. Americans born from 1720 to 1739 apparently consumed a healthy diet, for they were about 1 to 2 inches taller than troops born in Europe. The typical American male of this period grew to (or very near) 5 feet 8 inches, or as tall as the average for U.S. troops in World War II. Thanks to their diets, native-born Anglo-Americans stood taller than their distant cousins in Great Britain, where the population would not reach an equivalent height for another 150 years. There consequently seems to have been no significant rise in average adult stature among whites within the present United States from 1750 to 1950.

These figures on adult heights indicate an exceptionally high level of nutrition among the colonial population, especially regarding access to protein-rich red meat. (One study of farm life in seventeenth-century Maryland estimated that if a couple bought a pregnant cow and sow upon being married, they could begin to slaughter meat after two years, and their household could consume a half-pound per adult daily after five years.) Although science now links animal fats with circulatory disease and cancers of the lower organs, colonial cattle and hogs were exceptionally lean and probably represented much less of a threat, especially for a people who did vigorous outdoor work and reduced cholesterol levels in the bloodstream by drinking alcohol. Based on what is known of colonial diets, it would appear that they were fully adequate concerning caloric intake and probably provided a reasonable balance of vitamins, at least after agricultural yields improved after 1700. Based on a comparison of adult heights, early Americans ate better than contemporary Europeans, and they enjoyed a food supply that approached the nutritional level of diets consumed by their twentieth-century descendants.

TABLE 6.2   AVERAGE FOOD ALLOWANCES PROVIDED FOR NEW ENGLAND WIDOWS IN THEIR HUSBANDS' WILLS, 1654–1759

Food	1654–1698 Annual Amount bu.	1654–1698 Annual Amount lb.[a]	1654–1698 Daily[b] Caloric Intake	1705–1718 Annual Amount bu.	1705–1718 Annual Amount lb.[a]	1705–1718 Daily Caloric Intake[b]	1721–1739 Annual Amount bu.	1721–1739 Annual Amount lb.[a]	1721–1739 Daily Caloric Intake[b]	1740–1759 Annual Amount bu.	1740–1759 Annual Amount lb.[a]	1740–1759 Daily Caloric Intake[b]
Grains												
Indian corn	9.4	297.2	1,317	10.6	335.2	1,486	9.5	300.4	1,332	11.8	373.1	1,654
Rye	4.7	148.6	509	2.9	91.7	314	3.7	117.0	401	4.4	139.1	476
Wheat	4.3	136.0	596	1.6	50.6	222	1.6	50.6	222	1.4	44.3	194
Average Total[c]	18.4	581.8	2,422	15.1	477.5	2,022	14.8	468.0	1,955	17.6	556.5	2,324
Meat												
Salt pork	...	80.0	...	...	100.0	...	...	103.4	...	...	122.9	...
Salt beef	...	...	...	...	61.4	...	...	82.0	...	...	72.8	...
Average Total[c]	...	80.0	241	...	120.8	364	...	145.2	438	...	168.2	507
Total Daily Caloric Intake[d]	...	...	2,663	...	...	2,386	...	...	2,393	...	...	2,831

[a] Expressed as flour remaining after a miller received a toll of 15% for grinding. One bu. of grain yielded about 37.2 lb. of flour, based on yield of 17 to 21 barrels (of 196 lb. each) milled from 100 bu. of wheat (i.e., 6,000 lb. wheat yielded about 3,724 lb. flour before tolls). Greville Bathe and Dorothy Bathe, *Oliver Evans: A Chronicle of Early American Engineering* (1935), 28.
[b] 1 lb. wheat flour = 1,600 cal.; 1 lb. cornmeal = 1,618 cal.; 1 lb. ryemeal = 1,250 cal.; 1 lb. meat = 1,100 cal.
[c] Averages adjust for wills that do not provide both pork and beef, and includes other meats not identified in source.
[d] Source does not provide information on other allowances specified in the wills, but notes on pp. 57–59 that in period 1721–1739, the percent of widows receiving additional allotments was as follows: dairy products, 81.8%; vegetables, 51.5%; fruit, 57.8%.
Source: Sarah F. McMahon, "A Comfortable Subsistence: The Changing Composition of Diet in Rural New England, 1620–1840," *William and Mary Quarterly*, XLII (1985), 54, 56.

TABLE 6.3 ESTIMATED DIET, PER PERSON, OF FAMILY MEMBERS ON A PENNSYLVANIA FARM, 1740–1790

| Foodstuff | Annual Quantity Consumed | | | Daily Caloric Intake |
	Bu.	Lb.[a]	Bbl.	
Pork	...	101.8	...	307
Beef	...	51.3	...	155
Wheat[b]	13.2	417.4	...	1,830
Rye	5.4	170.7	...	585
Barley & malt[c]	3.8	120.2	...	...
Oats[d]	9.0	284.6	...	...
Cider	...	...	2.4[e]	...
Total	31.4	1,146	2.4	2,877

Note: Data is based primarily on food allowances specified for widows in farmers' wills from Lancaster and Chester counties.
[a] Expressed as flour remaining after a miller received a toll of 15% for grinding. One bu. of grain yielded about 37.2 lb. of flour, based on yield of 17 to 21 barrels (of 196 lb. each) milled from 100 bu. wheat (i.e., 6,000 lb. wheat yielded about 3,724 lb. flour before tolls). Greville Bathe and Dorothy Bathe, *Oliver Evans: A Chronicle of Early American Engineering* (1935), 28.
[b] When buckwheat was substituted for wheat, the annual quantity consumed was 4.8 bu. (151.8 lb.).
[c] For beer.
[d] Probably for fodder.
[e] Probably equal to 75.6 gal., or 1.66 pt. per day.
Source: James T. Lemon, *The Best Poor Man's Country: A Geographical Study of Early Southeastern Pennsylvania* (1972), 155.

TABLE 6.4 AVERAGE HEIGHTS OF COLONIAL SOLDIERS, AGE 24–35, BORN IN AMERICA AND EUROPE, WHO SERVED IN THE SEVEN YEARS' WAR, 1755–1763

| American Born | | European Born | |
Where Born	Inches Tall	Where Born	Inches Tall
New York or New Jersey	68.577	Ireland	67.439
Virginia	68.136	Scotland	67.221
New England or Nova Scotia[a]	68.101	England	66.846
North or South Carolina	67.778	Germany	66.488
Pennsylvania or Delaware	67.629	Other European than above	67.224
Resident of American city	67.067	Resident of foreign city	67.103
Born in American city	67.435	Born in European city	67.110
American-born laborer	66.971	European-born laborer	66.549
American-born artisan	66.964	European-born artisan	66.507
Nonwhite	66.512	European-born farmer or professional	66.770
American-born living outside his native colony	68.401	European-born resident of southern colonies	66.960

[a] Described in source as "Others born in America or Canada."
Source: Kenneth L. Sokoloff and Georgia C. Villaflor, "The Early Achievement of Modern Stature in America," *Social Science History,* VI (1982), 465.

Disease Environment and Epidemics

The medical history of Anglo-American colonization commenced with nearly two decades of unmitigated disaster in attempting to settle Virginia. The majority of settlers, who were overwhelmingly young men and women in the prime of their lives, died within three years of having arrived. Although food shortages and the Indian massacre of 1622 took a heavy toll, most loss of life resulted from typhoid, chronic dysentery, and salt poisoning.

Early Virginians were particularly susceptible to these killers because Jamestown and its surrounding communities lay precisely where the natural environment maximized human infection by the transmission of germs. Jamestown occupied that part of the James River where freshwater discharging downstream met the saltwater carried upstream by

tides. When the river's current was slow, as it was every summer, the salt tide would reach its maximum extent inland and contaminate the water with salinity levels six times higher than normal, at which point salt poisoning can occur. The overlapping forces of current and tide also tended to offset each other in this transition zone at midyear so that a large stretch of river became stagnant and polluted with germs from human waste that entered the water by runoff from shore.

Typhus and dysentery flourished in this environment every summer. The settlers were particularly vulnerable because the great majority lived almost directly on the riverbank and used the James as their main source of drinking water, rather than digging wells. As late as 1622, almost three-quarters of all Virginians still inhabited the river districts where the salt content was dangerously high and the summer season turned the James into a putrid, stagnant breeding pool for typhus and dysentery. In that region, the death rate seems to have hovered in most years at the epidemic rate of 28%. More than two-thirds of all deaths from 1618 to 1624, an interval that included a major Indian war, came from disease.

TABLE 6.5 MORTALITY RATES FROM DISEASE IN VIRGINIA, 1618–1624

| Period | Population | Disease Related Deaths | | Other Deaths | | % of Deaths from Disease |
		No.	%	No.	%	
Dec. 1618–Mar. 1620	1,514[a]	430	(28.3%)	197	(13.0%)	68.5%
Mar. 1620–Mar. 1621	1,938[b]	550	(28.3%)	545	(28.1%)	50.2%
Mar. 1621–Mar. 1622	2,423[c]	688	(28.3%)	495	(20.4%)	58.2%
Mar. 1622–Apr. 1623	1,935[d]	347	(17.9%)	347	(17.9%)	50.0%
Apr. 1623–Feb. 1624	1,646[e]	371	(22.5%)	[f]	...	100.0%
Total	...	2,538	...	1,332	...	65.6%

[a] Includes 914 immigrants.
[b] Includes 1,051 immigrants.
[c] Includes 1,580 immigrants.
[d] Includes 695 immigrants.
[e] Includes 405 immigrants.
[f] Overall death rate fell below the disease rate, so all deaths were assigned to disease.
Source: Carville V. Earle, "Environment, Disease, and Mortality in Early Virginia," in Thad W. Tate and David L. Ammerman, eds., *The Chesapeake in the Seventeenth Century: Essays on Anglo-American Society* (1979), 119.

Typhus, dysentery, and salt poisoning ceased taking such a terrible toll of Virginians as the population distributed itself inland, where wells provided drinking water, and upstream along the James River into the freshwater zone where tides did not penetrate. After 1650, however, the Chesapeake fell victim to a more virulent pathogen, malaria. The most lethal variants of malaria came to the New World from Africa in the veins of slaves and then entered the white population's bloodstreams by mosquito bites. Once established in a host human population, the disease was impossible to eradicate until the mosquitoes that carried the disease were exterminated by swamp drainage. Because colonial southerners had no knowledge of how the malady was transmitted, they could not strike at the root cause.

Malaria had a complex impact on public health in the southern tidewater. It was undoubtedly the primary reason why a person reaching age twenty-one in the Chesapeake could expect to live fifteen to twenty years less than a New Englander of the same age. Malaria nevertheless rarely killed its victims directly, especially because early Americans had access to cinchona bark, which contained quinine.

Malaria rather debilitated the body with recurring bouts of fever that robbed its victims of the strength needed to prevail over other illnesses, including many minor infections. Research indicates that for every death attributable to malaria itself, another five derive from its indirect causes. Pregnant women, or those who had recently given birth, were particularly vulnerable.

Population shifts within the South increasingly lowered the proportion of the population endangered by malaria. Because the disease was geographically limited to communities within about 4 miles of a swamp or marsh used by mosquitoes for breeding, malaria was almost entirely limited to the southern tidewater (although it also existed in some northern locales). As more individuals moved into the southern Piedmont, the part of the general public directly at risk shrank accordingly. The proportion of tidewater inhabitants at risk also decreased because of the changing racial composition of that area; African Americans had become a majority in most of its counties (except in North Carolina) by 1750. Although blacks were not immune to malaria, they could tolerate its attacks better and had a higher survival rate than whites, apparently because many inherited the "sickle cell" gene that is common among Africans and which offers some protection.

Outside of the southern tidewater, Anglo-Americans enjoyed an exceptionally benign disease environment that inhibited the spread of epidemics and allowed them to outlive their European cousins by a wide margin. This fortunate circumstance derived from the country's low population density, which minimized the chances of contracting or transmitting a fatal ailment. Poor roads furthermore kept a large part of the population locked in rural isolation for much of the winter, which was the season when lack of fresh food left individuals least able to fight off infection. Outside of winter, the typical household's diet was apparently more than adequate to provide the strength needed for warding off sickness and recovering from infections.

Public health emergencies consequently affected cities, where only a small fraction of Anglo-Americans dwelled, more than rural areas. Of thirty-four major smallpox outbreaks recorded from 1638 to 1763, more than half afflicted urban communities, with 38% occurring in the four largest cities of Boston, Philadelphia, New York, and Charles Town. Yellow fever was almost exclusively limited to cities. When epidemics spread through the countryside, they rarely covered an extensive area or infected a large percent of the dispersed inhabitants, except for diphtheria. By 1730, however, the chance of infectious diseases spreading through agricultural regions had significantly risen in the long-settled districts bordering the Atlantic coastline, especially in New England and the Delaware valley, where population densities were highest. Epidemics became more common in these areas, especially during the colonial wars, when large numbers of soldiers became exposed to various maladies on campaign and then returned home to spread these germs among their relatives or neighbors.

Smallpox, or variola, ranked as the most dangerous disease at large in North America. Because it had often been confused with syphilis in the fifteenth and sixteenth centuries, variola became known as the "small pox," while the venereal disease was termed the "great pox" or "French pox." Smallpox is characterized by the appearance of pus-filled eruptions on the skin after three or four days of high temperatures and rapid pulse. Exposure to the disease resulted in almost universal contagion among persons who had not acquired an immunity by having resisted a previous infection. Large-scale epidemics usually resulted after the disease had been absent from a locale for so long that a large percentage of inhabitants had no natural defense against its germs.

Smallpox most commonly traveled to the colonies on ships from large European ports, where it was endemic. Outbreaks were so common on vessels carrying immigrants that major cities mandated that their passengers be quarantined before being allowed to mix with their citizens. Quarantine also served as the primary course of action for halting the disease's spread once it was discovered.

As the colonial population grew, epidemics became a major threat, especially in cities. This pamphlet was written in response to the controversy over inoculation that developed from a smallpox epidemic in Boston during 1721, when almost 8% of the residents died. (Courtesy American Antiquarian Society)

Americans feared the disease with good reason, for no other malady had the capacity for infecting and killing a greater portion of people within a community. In 1721, 54% of Boston's inhabitants contracted smallpox, and 15% of all infections resulted in death. During less than three months in 1731, at least half of New York City's residents fell ill with smallpox and 7% died of it. Perhaps half the denizens of Charles Town, South Carolina, contracted the disease in 1738, and the sick experienced a mortality rate of 17.6%.

No cure existed then (or now) for the disease once contracted. It was nevertheless possible to introduce immunity to the disease by a procedure known as variolation, in which a healthy person was given a very small dose of the virus extracted from recently erupted pustules, which were far less potent than older pus and less likely to bring on the full range of symptoms. Variolation was nevertheless a dangerous option because it was typical for 2% to 3% of its recipients to die during the early 1700s, when European physicians first started to experiment with the procedure. This high risk of death made it unnecessarily risky for doctors to attempt an immunization of the general public, so

TABLE 6.6 EFFECTIVENESS OF SMALLPOX INOCULATION IN BOSTON, MASS., 1721–1752

Year	1752	1730	1721
City Population	15,684	13,500	10,700
Natural smallpox			
Cases	5,545	3,600	5,759
Deaths	539	500	842
Deaths per 1,000 cases	97	139	146
Inoculated smallpox			
Cases	2,124	400	287[a]
Deaths	30[b]	12	6
Deaths per 1,000 cases	14	30	21
Total smallpox (Boston residents only)			
Cases	7,669	4,000	5,889
Deaths	569	500	844
Deaths per 1,000 cases	74	125	143
Cases per 1,000 population	490	296	550
Deaths per 1,000 population	36	37	79
Percent of cases inoculated	28%	10%	2%
Persons who left town	1,843	…	…
Escaped disease in town	174	…	…
Had smallpox before	5,998	…	…

[a] Including 157 inoculated in neighboring towns.
[b] Including 4 deaths in neighboring towns.
Source: John B. Blake, *Public Health in the Town of Boston, 1630–1822* (1959), 244.

variolation was only used after smallpox had already become so widespread in a community that a majority of people without prior exposure were already in danger of being infected. With greater experience, however, physicians learned how to minimize the inherent danger of variolation, and after 1750 any competent doctor could keep mortality among the inoculated within a range of 0.5% to 1.5%.

Next to smallpox, the most lethal disease in early America was diphtheria, in which the throat swells and then becomes congested with a thick membrane over the larynx and trachea and, in extreme cases, causes death by suffocation. It is highly communicable and especially dangerous because infection could be spread by carriers who do not develop its symptoms. The disease chiefly strikes children below the age of puberty.

Minor outbreaks of diphtheria may have appeared in the colonies as early as 1659, but it was often confused with scarlet fever before 1730. The pathogen evidently mutated into its modern, highly virulent form in the 1730s and suddenly struck a population with no acquired immunity. Its first major attack occurred in 1737 at Kingston, New Hampshire, where every one of the first forty victims died. In Hampton Falls, New Hampshire, within a span of thirteen months, twenty families lost every one of their children, and 210 persons (95% of them children) perished out of a population of about 1,200, a death rate equal to smallpox. Haverhill, Massachusetts, suffered the loss of half of all its children under fifteen. Unlike other epidemics, which exhausted themselves in less than a year, diphtheria infested New England, spread to the Delaware valley, and by 1741 may have taken up to 20,000 lives, including a tenth of all children north of Maryland. Localized outbreaks continued through the colonial period, but by 1745 so many children had been exposed to the disease that the immune population was large enough to end the threat of another pandemic.

The colonial era's third-greatest pestilence was yellow fever, an infectious tropical malady brought to the West Indies from Africa. The disease produces fever followed by chills, yellows the skin, induces bloody vomiting, and kills a high percentage of its victims by liver and

TABLE 6.7 OUTBREAKS OF EPIDEMIC DISEASE IN COLONIAL AMERICA

Year	Disease	Location
1607–12	Typhus, Dysentery	Jamestown, Va.
1617–24	Typhus, Dysentery	James River Valley, Va.
1638	Smallpox	Massachusetts (few deaths)
1647	Influenza	Massachusetts, Connecticut (90 deaths)
1648–49	Smallpox & Whooping Cough	Massachusetts
1657	Measles	Boston, Mass. (few deaths)
1658	Typhoid Fever	New Amsterdam, New Netherland
1659	Diphtheria	Massachusetts
1659	Whooping Cough	Massachusetts
1660–61	Influenza	New England (few deaths)
1665	Influenza	New England (few deaths)
1666	Smallpox	New England (about 40 deaths)
1677–78	Smallpox	Boston, Mass. (more than 200 died)
1678–79	Influenza	New England (few deaths)
1687–88	Measles	Massachusetts
1688	Influenza	Virginia
1689	Diphtheria	New London, Conn. (many deaths)
1689–90	Smallpox	New England and New York (at least 320 deaths)
1693	Yellow Fever	Boston, Mass.
1693	Measles	Virginia
1696	Smallpox	Jamestown, Va.
1697–98	Smallpox	South Carolina (more than 200 deaths)
1699	Yellow Fever	Charles Town, S.C. (179 deaths)
1699	Yellow Fever	Philadelphia, Pa. (220 deaths)
1697–98	Influenza	New England (heavy mortality)
1699	Influenza	New England (heavy mortality)
1702	Smallpox	New York City
1702	Yellow Fever	New York City (570 deaths)
1702–03	Smallpox & Scarlet Fever	Boston, Mass. (about 300 deaths)
1707	Yellow Fever	Charles Town, S.C.
1710	Influenza	Connecticut (250 deaths)
1711–12	Smallpox	Charles Town, S.C.
1713–14	Measles	New England (at least 150 deaths)
1713–14	Measles	Mid-Atlantic colonies
1715–18	Smallpox	New York, New Jersey
1717	Measles	Virginia
1721	Smallpox	Boston, Mass. (844 deaths)
1724	Diphtheria or Scarlet Fever	Charles Town, S.C.
1727	Typhoid Fever	Norwich (40 deaths) and Woodbury, Conn.
1728	Yellow Fever	Charles Town, S.C.
1728	Influenza	South Carolina
1729	Measles	Boston, Mass. (15 deaths), New York City
1730	Smallpox	Boston, Mass. (about 500 deaths)
1731–32	Smallpox	New York (549 deaths in New York City, about 300 in rural areas)
1731–32	Smallpox	Pennsylvania, New Jersey
1732–34	Influenza	New England, mid-Atlantic colonies
1732	Yellow Fever	Charles Town, S.C.
1732	Dysentery	Salem, Mass.
1732	Smallpox	Wallingford, Conn. (14 deaths)
1732	Yellow Fever	New York City (70 deaths)
1734	Typhoid Fever	New Haven, Conn.
1734	Dysentery	Boston, Mass., and New London, Conn.
1735–41	Diphtheria	New England, New York, New Jersey (as many as 20,000 deaths)
1735–36	Scarlet Fever	Boston, Mass. (100 deaths)
1736	Scarlet Fever	Newport, R.I.
1736–37	Smallpox	Philadelphia, Pa.
1737	Typhoid Fever	Worcester Co., Mass.
1737	Smallpox	Charles Town, S.C. (311 deaths)
1737–38	Smallpox	Martha's Vineyard, Mass. (12 deaths)
1738	Whooping Cough	South Carolina
1738–39	Smallpox	New York City (1,550 cases)
1739	Yellow Fever	Charles Town, S.C.

(continued)

TABLE 6.7 (continued)

Year	Disease	Location
1739	Smallpox	Newport, R.I. (17 deaths)
1739	Measles	Massachusetts, Connecticut
1741	Yellow Fever	Philadelphia, Pa. (200 deaths)
1741	Typhoid Fever	Sutton, Mass. (19 deaths), and New London, Conn.
1742	Dysentery	New London, Conn.
1743	Yellow Fever	New York City (217 deaths)
1744–45	Diphtheria	Massachusetts, New Hampshire, New York
1745	Dysentery	Shrewsbury, Mass. (several deaths)
1745	Typhoid Fever	Stamford, Conn. (70 deaths)
1745	Yellow Fever	New York City
1745	Yellow Fever	Charles Town, S.C.
1746	Typhoid Fever	Albany, N.Y.
1746	Diphtheria	Pennsylvania, Delaware, New Jersey
1746	Typhoid Fever	Albany, N.Y.
1747	Smallpox	Harwich, Mass. (9 deaths)
1747	Smallpox	New York, New Jersey, Delaware, Maryland
1747	Typhoid Fever	New York City
1747	Yellow Fever	Charles Town, S.C.
1747–48	Diphtheria	Massachusetts
1747–48	Measles	Massachusetts, Connecticut, New York, Pennsylvania, South Carolina
1748	Smallpox	Williamsburg, Va.
1748	Yellow Fever	Charles Town, S.C.
1748–49	Influenza or Pneumonia	Atlantic seaboard
1749	Typhus and Dysentery	Connecticut (at least 150 deaths)
1749–50	Influenza or Pneumonia	Mid-Atlantic and southern colonies
1750–51	Diphtheria or Scarlet Fever	South Carolina
1750–55	Diptheria or Scarlet Fever	New England, New York
1751	Smallpox	Boston, Mass. (569 deaths)
1752	Smallpox	New York, New Jersey
1753	Smallpox	New London, Conn. (4 deaths)
1755	Mumps	Brookfield, Mass. (several deaths)
1755–56	Smallpox	New York
1756	Smallpox	Philadelphia, Pa.
1756	Dysentery	New England
1756–57	Smallpox	Annapolis, Md.
1759	Measles	Widespread in colonies
1759	Smallpox	New Jersey
1759	Whooping Cough	South Carolina
1760	Smallpox	Charles Town, S.C. (730 deaths)
1760–61	Smallpox	New England
1761	Influenza	Atlantic seaboard
1762	Yellow Fever	Philadelphia, Pa.
1762–63	Diphtheria	Massachusetts, Connecticut
1763	Typhus	Nantucket, Mass. (222 Indians died)
1763	Smallpox	South Carolina
1763	Diphtheria	Philadelphia, Pa.

Source: John Duffy, *Epidemics in Colonial America* (1972), passim.

kidney failure. Transmission of yellow fever necessitated a particular mosquito (*Stegomyia fasciata*) that was not native to North America; these insects sometimes stowed away on ships trading with the Caribbean islands and then carried infection to dockworkers on shore. Charles Town, Philadelphia, and New York bore the brunt of the ravaging illness, whose first appearance in North America dates from 1699 when it killed perhaps 7% of Charles Towners (including the chief justice and almost half the assembly's members) and 5% of Philadelphians. Three years later, it carried off about 10% of New Yorkers. Most other attacks resulted in mortality rates of 1% or 2%, however. Yellow fever last struck the colonies in 1763 and then did not recur for three decades.

The disease environment finally included many of today's commonplace illnesses, such as measles, mumps, and chicken pox. Although children can easily survive them with good care, these ailments produce violent reactions that can be fatal in adults. Because rural isolation prevented many colonists from contracting them as adolescents, outbreaks of these maladies posed great risk to adults. In 1729, for example, measles was the leading cause of death in Boston. Respiratory illnesses also posed great dangers, especially in winter when fresh food was unavailable. Flu killed more than 7% of Fairfield, Connecticut, residents in just three months of 1699, and pneumonia left 13% of Holliston, Massachusetts, inhabitants dead within six weeks during the winter of 1753–54. Such instances were nevertheless exceptions to the general rule that a low population density and adequate diet spared most Anglo-Americans from the scourge of disease, at least outside of the major port cities.

Life Expectancy and Mortality

Life expectancy and mortality rates varied greatly among different disease environments in colonial America. The least-healthy setting was the southern tidewater, where a lethal strain of malaria became entrenched after 1650. In the Chesapeake, half of all men who attained age twenty died before they reached fifty, while a typical twenty-year-old woman would probably die at forty. Life expectancy in seventeenth-century Virginia, where a man who survived adolescence would likely survive to forty-nine, was evidently lower than in England, where the same individual would die at fifty-two. Mortality was so high in Middlesex County, Virginia, that 48% of all persons born there before 1689 lost at least one parent by age nine and 61% of them by age thirteen, while 20% of children had neither father *nor* mother by age thirteen.

New Englanders found a disease environment that was far more benign than either the southern tidewater or England itself. Rural communities experienced few epidemics because of their low population densities and relative isolation from sources of contagion. One study of seventeenth-century Plymouth concluded that for persons who reached twenty-one, typical life spans would then extend to sixty-nine for men and sixty-two for women. Life expectancy was also found to be similar, although not so high for men, in Andover, Massachusetts, before 1700. Longevity in early New England was not only twelve to seventeen years greater than in old England; it furthermore compared favorably with the twentieth-century United States. In 1986, a typical white male American age twenty could expect to survive to be seventy-two, just three years older than a Plymouth man in the 1700s. The difference in life expectancy for women was broader, however, with modern white females surviving sixteen years longer than their Plymouth antecedants. Such data indicate a remarkable level of health and physical vigor among the earliest generations of New Englanders.

Life expectancy at birth, rather than at age twenty, nevertheless was far lower (forty-three for males and forty-two for females in seventeenth-century New England) than now (seventy-two for males and seventy-nine for females) due to high rates of infant and adolescent mortality. Whereas today infant mortality stands at about 1% of births, in the colonial era it was ten to twenty times greater. In the Chesapeake's malaria-ridden lowlands, two of every five children probably did not reach maturity. Infant and adolescent mortality was much lower, by at least half, in rural communities of the North, where 85% to 90% of children probably survived to twenty.

Life expectancy was high in colonial America, despite the medical profession's lack of knowledge about many elemental aspects of health care, such as how germs spread infection. Men who escaped childhood diseases like whooping cough or measles usually lived as long as Joseph Renalls, whose tombstone records that he survived into his sixty-ninth year. (Courtesy Library of Congress)

Mortality rates were relatively low for the great majority of Anglo-Americans living in the northern countryside and the southern Piedmont. Andover, Massachusetts, seems typical of such places, where isolation and an ample diet produced a healthy population that was largely spared from recurring bouts of contagious illness. Andover's mortality rate was 11.7 or less, per 1,000 persons, for most of the period from 1720 to 1774, or about 1% of all residents per year. Such a rate compares favorably with the twentieth-century United States, which had reduced annual mortality from 11.5 per thousand in 1921 to 8.5 in 1986, and even more so with eighteenth-century England, where yearly death rates appear to have ranged between 2.5% and 3.5% (two to three times higher than in Andover). Besides the malarial southern lowlands, colonial cities constituted the major exception to the general rule that most Anglo-Americans experienced a low level of mortality. Because of poor sanitation and constant exposure to communicable diseases, annual death rates in Boston and Philadelphia were almost three to four times higher than levels in the countryside. It would appear that mortality in these urban centers varied from 3.2% to 4.7% of all inhabitants over twelve months, a rate sufficient to kill off 33% to 40% of their populations every decade.

The general status of colonial health seems to have been quite high for the great majority of settlers outside the fetid and epidemic-prone cities. Most medical problems faced by the population were routine and not life threatening. Accidental death largely seems to have resulted from drowning or being kicked by draft animals, and they were evidently less of a factor in overall mortality than they have become in the twentieth century's complex, gadget-filled, high-speed society. Of eighty-nine patients treated at the Pennsylvania Hospital during 1754 and 1755, 60% were healed or had their symptoms relieved, while only 15% died or were declared incurable. The same hospital admitted 1,051 patients from 1753 to 1762, and it was able to restore full health to 60%. When treating the disorders most commonly encountered in the colonies (dropsy, scurvy, fevers, fluxes, and bodily injuries), the medical community was reasonably competent in curing its charges.

TABLE 6.8   LIFE EXPECTANCY IN COLONIAL AMERICA

Year of Age	Plymouth Colony, 1620–1691		Andover, Mass., 1670–1699		Andover, Mass., 1730–1759		Middlesex County, Va., b. 1650–1710		Charles Co., Md., b. 1600–1699		York County, Va., Eighteenth Century		Perquimans County, N.C., 1661–1699		Perquimans County, N.C., b. 1700–1739		United States 1986	
	Male Age at Death	Female Age at Death	Male Age at Death	Female Age at Death	Male Age at Death	Female Age at Death	Male Age at Death	Female Age at Death	Male Immigrants Age at Death	Male Natives Age at Death	Male[b] Age at Death	Female[b] Age at Death	Male Age at Death	Female Age at Death	Male Immigrants Age at Death	Male Natives Age at Death	Male[b] Age at Death	Female[b] Age at Death
0–1	…	…	…	…	…	…	…	…	…	…	…	…	…	…	…	…	72.0	78.8
15	…	…	…	…	…	…	…	39.9	…	…	…	…	…	…	…	…	58.0	64.7
20[a]	69.2	62.4	64.8	62.1	61.6	63.1	48.8	39.8	42.7	46.0	40.8	…	50.5	…	50.2	…	73.5	79.9
30	70.0	64.7	68.7	65.9	66.3	66.5	49.4	43.6	47.4	50.4	46.4	…	54.4	…	53.1	…	74.2	80.2
40	71.2	69.7	71.4	69.0	68.4	70.9	53.0	48.6	53.2	55.6	51.8	…	59.4	…	56.6	…	74.0	80.6
50	73.7	73.4	73.5	72.4	74.5	75.0	57.7	59.3	60.3	62.0	59.5	…	63.7	…	62.1	…	76.2	81.3
60	76.3	76.8	75.2	74.5	77.2	78.8	65.8	67.9	70.0	69.3	66.9	…	71.3	…	68.7	…	79.2	83.6
70	79.9	80.7	80.2	81.9	80.9	82.0	73.6	73.7	75.5	77.0	74.0	…	79.9	…	76.5	…	82.7	86.1
80	85.1	86.7	86.7	89.5	87.1	88.3	…	…	…	…	…	…	…	…	…	…	87.9	89.8

[a] Data for Plymouth given for age 21.

[b] Whites only.

Sources: John Demos, "Notes on Life in Plymouth Colony," William and Mary Quarterly, XXII (1965), 271. Darrett B. Rutman and Anita H. Rutman, "Of Agues and Fevers: Malaria in the Early Chesapeake," William and Mary Quarterly, XXXIII (1976), 48. Lorena S. Walsh and Russell R. Menard, "Death in the Chesapeake: Two Life Tables for Men in Early Colonial Maryland," Maryland Historical Magazine, LXIX (1974), 228. James M. Gallman, "Mortality Among White Males in Colonial North Carolina," Social Science History, IV (1980), 306. Department of Commerce, Statistical Abstract of the United States, 1989 (1989), 73.

TABLE 6.9   COMPARISON OF CRUDE DEATH RATES (PER 1,000 PERSONS) IN COLONIAL AMERICAN AND BRITISH COMMUNITIES WITH UNITED STATES IN 1986

Period	Andover, Mass.	Boston, Mass.	Philadelphia, Pa.	Nottingham, England	United States	
					Whites	Blacks
1720–24	11.1	46.8	…	37.2	…	…
1725–29	16.9	35.0	…	43.9	…	…
1730–34	9.6	38.8	…	44.4	…	…
1735–39	29.7	34.0	…	40.1	…	…
1740–44	11.7	34.6	39.9	48.3	…	…
1745–49	21.5	44.2	47.5	31.2	…	…
1750–54	15.1	40.2	47.2	34.3	…	…
1755–59	8.3	33.4	47.0	32.0	…	…
1760–64	13.5	32.2	45.3	31.2	…	…
1765–69	5.6	32.8	38.5	36.3	…	…
1770–74	3.8	34.2	36.3	38.5	…	…
1986	…	…	…	…	8.5	9.0

Sources: Billy G. Smith, "Death and Life in a Colonial Immigrant City: A Demographic Analysis of Philadelphia," Journal of Economic History, XXXVII (1977), 888. Department of Commerce, Statistical Abstract of the United States, 1989 (1989), 74, 76.

TABLE 6.10 PATIENTS ADMITTED TO THE PENNSYLVANIA HOSPITAL, PHILADELPHIA, APRIL 27, 1754–APRIL 26, 1755

Diseases	Admitted	Cured	Symptoms Relieved	Left Hospital Uncured[a]	Died	Incurable	Remained Under Care
Agues	2	2	...	...	...	1	...
Aneurysm	1	...	...	...	1	...	...
Asthma	1	...	...	...	...	...	...
Cancers	1	...	...	...	...	1	...
Consumption	1	...	...	...	1	...	...
Contusion	1	1	...	...	...	...	...
Cough, long-standing	2	2	...	...	...	...	...
Dropsy	10	3	...	1	3	3	2
Emphysema	1	1	...	...	...	...	...
Eyes diseased	1	1	...	...	...	...	...
Fevers	2	2	...	...	...	...	...
Fistulas	2	1	1	...	...	...	...
Flux, long-standing	5	3	...	...	1	...	1
Fracture	1	1	...	...	...	...	...
Hairlip	1	1	...	...	...	...	...
Hectick fevers	2	1	...	...	1	...	...
Hypochondriac melancholy	1	...	1	...	...	...	...
Lunacy	11	3	...	...	...	3	5
Palsy	1	...	1	1	...	3	...
Rupture	1	1	...	...	...	...	...
Rheumatism and sciatica	5	3	1	1	...	...	...
Scorbutic & scrophulous ulcers	22	16	...	...	1	...	5
Suppression of urine	1	1	...	...	...	...	...
Vertigo	1	1	...	...	...	...	...
Uterine disorders	1	...	...	...	1	...	...
Weakness, habitual	1	1	...	...	...	...	...
Wounded	2	1	...	...	...	...	1
White swelling	1	1	...	...	...	...	...
Ulcers with carious bones	7	...	1	...	...	...	6
Total	89	47	6	2	9	4	20

[a] Includes any discharged irregularly, such as taken out by friends.
Source: Francis R. Packard, *History of Medicine in the United States,* 2 vols. (1931), I, 207.

TABLE 6.11 PROFILE OF ACCIDENTAL DEATHS IN NEW JERSEY, 1730–1770

Type of Accident	Number of Accidents	Percent of Total Accidents	Number of Deaths	Percent of Total Deaths
Drowning	62	48.0%	150	67.0%
Land Transportation[a]	21	16.3%	21	9.4%
Shooting	11	8.5%	13	5.8%
Fire	9	7.0%	14	6.3%
Poisoning	7	5.4%	7	3.1%
Falling Objects	4	3.1%	4	1.8%
Falls	3	2.3%	3	1.3%
Explosions	3	2.3%	3	1.3%
Miscellaneous[b]	9	7.0%	9	4.0%
Total	129	100.0%	224	100.0%

[a] 11 thrown from cart or carriage, 6 thrown from horse, 4 killed or trampled by horse.
[b] 2 killed by lightning, 2 killed by wildcats, 1 laceration, 1 accidental hanging, 1 suffocation, 1 cave-in of wall, 1 child crushed between grindstones.
Source: Keith Krawczynski, "A Note on Accidental Death in New Jersey, 1730–1770," *New Jersey History,* CX (1992), 62.

CHAPTER 7 Religion

Of all the European overseas empires founded before 1750, only the thirteen North American colonies developed into a religiously pluralistic society. The emergence of religious diversity was one of the happy ironies of this historical period because it took root despite the fact that most early Americans believed neither that church and state should be separate nor that freedom of worship should be extended unconditionally. Although such views strike contemporary minds as bigoted or hypocritical, they were an inevitable legacy from the era of the colonies' founding, which occurred during the last great phase of Europe's wars of religion.

English Protestants confronted the powerful Catholic empires of France and Spain; they assumed that an individual's first loyalty was to his religion—to which he entrusted his soul—rather than to his native country. It likewise seemed prudent to distrust minority Protestant sects and see them as a seedbed for political subversion, especially in light of the Puritan-dominated revolution that beheaded Charles I in 1649. All major churches likewise felt genuinely obliged to extirpate blasphemy and heresy, to which they attached no legitimate right of conscience. For most of the colonial era, most Americans believed that freedom of religion could be legitimately denied to the unorthodox and to anyone whose faith compromised his or her political allegiance.

Church and State

The Virginia Company saw promoting religion as one of its principal responsibilities. It established the Church of England in 1609 and made attendance at its Sunday services mandatory the next year. Although the Anglican Church suffered from a shortage of ministers, rival denominations were slow to form congregations because they lacked legal recognition. It was not until after the Revolution, for example, that questions ceased to be raised about whether Baptist or Quaker marriages were fully legal in Virginia.

Maryland, settled in 1634 as a refuge for Catholics, became the first colony to promise freedom of religion to all orthodox Christians. This policy largely stemmed from its proprietor's need to forestall political unrest among Protestants, who quickly became numerous and rebelled against his authority in 1645. In 1649, to dampen further disaffection, Maryland's Catholic leaders promulgated the Toleration Act of 1649, which offered freedom of worship to all orthodox Christians believing in the Trinity, except blasphemers. This measure was the earliest American ordinance offering religious freedom to the broad majority of citizens, but it inspired no imitators among other colonies and was itself repealed in 1654. After Protestants finally ended Catholic rule in 1689, they prohibited Catholics from holding office—but not from holding their services—and forced Catholics and dissenting Protestants to pay Anglican tithes.

The New England colonies went furthest in linking church and state, although Plymouth's and New Hampshire's governments did little more than authorize tithes to support Congregational ministers. Connecticut and Massachusetts not only established the Congregational Church but also required that voters be formally admitted as members of its congregations until the colonies were forced to end this practice

Outside of New England, the leading established denomination was the Church of England. This painting portrays Anglicans gathering for Sunday services at Bruton Parish (built 1715) in Williamsburg, Virginia. (Courtesy Library of Congress)

TABLE 7.1 LOCATION OF MAJOR CHURCHES IN NORTH AMERICA, 1650

Colony	Anglican	Baptist	Congregational	Dutch Reformed	Lutheran	Presbyterian	Roman Catholic
New Hampshire	...	...	3	...	...	...	...
Massachusetts	...	...	39[a]	...	...	...	...
Maine	...	...	2	...	...	...	...
Connecticut	...	...	13	...	...	...	...
Rhode Island	...	2	2	...	...	...	...
New York	...	...	1	2	1	4	...
Pennsylvania	...	...	...	...	1	...	...
Maryland	4	...	1	...	...	...	5
Delaware	...	...	...	1	2	...	...
Virginia	26	...	...	...	...	...	...
Total number in all colonies	30	2	61	3	4	4	5
Number of colonies where found	2	1	6	2	3	1	1

Note: Church includes any regularly established place of worship, including places without resident clergy.
[a] 10 churches were in Plymouth.
Source: Edwin S. Gaustad, *Historical Atlas of Religion in America* (1962), 167.

by the British government. When Massachusetts codified its laws in 1641, it included many provisions taken from the Old Testament, and it gave the state authority to resolve intracongregational disputes. New Haven colony came closest to a theocracy by modeling its statutes and judicial practices so closely on Hebraic precedents that it neglected to establish jury trials because the Israelites never used them.

Rhode Island was the only New England colony with no significant connection between church and state. Its founder, Roger Williams, insisted that this arrangement was necessary to protect the church from the state's worldly and corrupting influence. What stands out about Rhode Island's tolerant example is nevertheless how much criticism it generated among its New England neighbors for failing to uphold orthodoxy. Even Rhode Island could not extinguish every connection between state and church, however, and in the eighteenth century, Jewish residents eventually lost their right to vote because they were non-Christians.

Besides Rhode Island, the only provinces to forebear from instituting an established religion were Pennsylvania, New Jersey, and Delaware. (New York established the Anglican Church but only in its four southernmost counties.) Having tasted persecution in England for his Quakerism, William Penn committed Pennsylvania to broad toleration for all believers in God, but he nevertheless required that the colony's officeholders not only believe in God but also be Christians. Pennsylvania's neighbors followed its example, largely because their populations were so religiously diverse that it made no practical sense to establish a single church.

Even in the nine colonies where established churches existed, they were a pale shadow of Europe's state churches. They could compel taxpayers to tithe but not—after the late seventeenth century—to attend their services. True power in each established Anglican parish or Congregational church furthermore lay not with the minister but with the laity who had invested him and could dismiss him at will. No bishops and virtually no other ecclesiastical structures existed within any denomination to reinforce the authority of pastors who faced challenges from their congregations. Even after churches belatedly began to organize synods and presbyteries in the early 1700s as a structure for uniting their congregations, local autonomy over religious affairs had become so deeply rooted that few laity were inclined to act deferentially, much less passively, toward clerical hierarchies.

Revivalism and the Great Awakening

In an area like the thirteen colonies with a tradition of lay independence on religious matters, any group of clergy who ignored their flocks' spiritual needs ran a grave risk of being rejected in favor of others who preached more meaningfully. During the early 1700s, such a situation slowly developed. The leadership of most religions fell to senior clerics whose rigorous training at Harvard, Yale, or European universities had taught them to preserve orthodoxy by defending their denomination's theological positions through highly learned but dry and tedious sermons; they judged candidates for the ministry primarily on scholarly knowledge rather than on spiritual commitment or any ability to inspire a congregation's members to recognize the need for moral regeneration in their own lives. By the 1720s, too many, if not most, Americans were under the charge of pedantic clergy who bored them with dull sermons, scolded them for their sins, and made Sunday services a stale, impersonal experience.

An additional problem existed among Presbyterians, the Dutch Reformed, and other groups dominated by foreign-born ministers. Most such individuals wanted to centralize authority within synods controlled by the clergy, and they opposed the idea of educating ministers in America rather than Europe. The Dutch and German Reformed hierarchies also opposed holding services in English, even though their flocks were becoming anglicized. They resisted the adaptation to American circumstances desired by their laity.

A widening rift gradually developed between the conservative, older hierarchies and a younger generation of clergy who saw that without change scholasticism and formalism would deprive religion of its meaning. Those ministers who strove for change sought to emphasize the spiritual experiences common to Christianity and to minimize the doctrinal differences separating churches. They also pioneered a direct, extemporaneous style of preaching that would prick the conscience, disgust listeners with sin's loathsomeness, and lead them into a personal decision to accept salvation through grace.

This new emphasis on stirring individual piety first appeared in the Refreshings, an interdenominational revival in central New Jersey led by Dutch Reformed minister Theodore Freylinghausen and Presbyterian William Tennent, who shared one another's pulpits and reaped a harvest of conversions for six years after 1726. In 1735, Congregationalist Jonathan Edwards led a well-publicized revival at Northampton, Massachusetts. Four years later, revivalism began to sweep across all the colonies in an outpouring of spiritual enthusiasm that lasted through the 1740s and was termed the Great Awakening.

Rev. George Whitefield, this era's great preacher, sparked the Great Awakening with his arrival from England in 1739. Whitefield drew huge outdoor crowds, estimated at more than 20,000, by ignoring theological subtleties, ministering to all denominations, and above all preaching in a vivid, dramatic, and heartfelt style—verging on religion as theatrical spectacle—that left enthralled listeners both emotionally uplifted and physically shaken by his message of repentence and salvation. Younger ministers imitated his methods, and soon the clergy was deeply split between New Lights (prorevival) and Old Lights (antirevival).

Among Congregationalists, the Great Awakening left most churches divided between New and Old Light factions that usually jostled for control until one side, usually the revivalists, seceded to form a separate congregation. Chafing under control by their Old Light hierarchy—one that criticized the revival as based on insincere religious experiences whipped up by ill-educated charlatans who manipulated their audience with frenzied preaching—New Light Presbyterians chose schism rather than submission and formed their own synod. Bitter animosity also divided the Dutch Reformed Church.

Ultimate victory went to the New Lights. When Presbyterians reunited, they did so under the revivalists' leadership. The antirevivalism of the Congregational and Anglican Churches crippled their growth in membership because so many dissidents joined evangelistic faiths. New Lights likewise came to dominate the Dutch Reformed Church. A major reason for these victories was that New Lights founded seminaries and trained a steady stream of ministers to preach their message, while the number of Old Light ministers remained steady or dropped.

The Great Awakening marked a major turning point in religious history. It decisively reinforced the laity's influence over church affairs, for it was the willingness of a majority of churchgoers to defy conservative church hierarchies that allowed the New Lights to prevail. The Awakening also diminished the theological distance between denominations as the revivalists purposely disregarded their divergent beliefs by preaching together, sharing each other's pulpits, and writing pamphlets to support one another. When Princeton, a Presbyterian college, needed a new president in 1757, it chose Jonathan Edwards, a Congregational minister. The Awakening finally shifted the balance of religious power in Anglo-America away from the established churches, both Congregational and Anglican, whose clergy were mainly Old Light, toward the largest revivalist denominations: the Presbyterians, the Baptists, and—after 1775—the Methodists.

Denominational Affiliation

Statistical information on church membership remains extremely poor for the colonial period. The only quantitative measures of relative size among denominations are counts of congregations organized at various dates. Using the broadest definition of a church—any religious organization meeting regularly for worship—the English and Dutch colonies contained 109 of them in 1650 (56% Congregational and 28% Anglican). The Reformed, or Calvinist, variety of Protestantism dominated the religious establishment and had founded about two-thirds of all churches by that date. The percent of Calvinists remained approximately the same in 1700, but the number of pulpits in either of the two established churches, Congregational or Anglican, declined from 84% to 69%.

As the Great Awakening was getting under way in the 1740s, Anglo-America remained a society in which 99% of all churches were Protestant and 69% were Calvinist. Half of all congregations were either Congregational (36%) or Presbyterian (14%). Lutheran and German Reformed societies equaled 12% of all churches, but because most of these were small, backcountry chapels without full-time min-

TABLE 7.2 EXPANSION OF CHURCHES IN BRITISH NORTH AMERICA, 1650–1750

Denomination	1650	1660	1700	1740	1750
Anglican	30	41	111	246	289
Baptist	2	4	33	96	132
Congregational	61	75	146	423	465
Dutch Reformed	3	13	26	78	79
German Reformed	…	…	…	51	90
Jewish	…	1	1	3	5
Lutheran	4	4	7	95	138
Presbyterian	4	5	28	160	233
Roman Catholic	5	12	22	27	30
Total	109	156	374	1,179	1,461

Note: Church includes any regularly established place of worship, including places without resident clergy.
Source: Edwin S. Gaustad, *Historical Atlas of Religion in America* (1962), 3, 4, 167.

This photo of the Old Tennent Presbyterian Church (built 1751) in Monmouth County, New Jersey, shows the typical interior layout of a colonial church. The ground level consists of enclosed boxes, where member families sat as a group during services. (The boxes were rented, with higher fees charged for the more prestigious ones nearer to the front.) Single persons, nonmembers, and nonwhites sat aboveground in the balcony, a portion of which is visible on the center-right side. (Historic American Buildings Survey, courtesy Library of Congress)

TABLE 7.3 LOCATION OF MAJOR CHURCHES IN NORTH AMERICA, 1750

Colony	Anglican	Baptist	Congregational	Reformed	Lutheran	Presbyterian	Roman Catholic	Jewish
New Hampshire	1	...	40	...	...	5	...	...
Massachusetts (incl. Maine)	17	16	247	...	1	13	...	...
Connecticut	19	12	155	...	...	1	...	...
Rhode Island	7	30	12	...	...	...	...	1
New York	20	4	5	59	26	35	1	1
New Jersey	18	14	2	28	19	51	2	...
Pennsylvania	19	29	...	71	73	56	11	1
Maryland	50	4	...	4	3	18	15	...
Delaware	14	2	...	...	3	27	1	...
Virginia	96	3	...	5	5	17	...	...
North Carolina	9	13	...	2	1	...	...	...
South Carolina	16	5	4	6	5	9	...	1
Georgia	3	...	...	...	2	1	...	1
Total number in all colonies	289	132	465	175	138	233	30	5
Number of colonies where found	13	11	7	7	9	11	5	5

Note: Church includes any regularly established place of worship, including places without resident clergy.
Source: Edwin S. Gaustad, *Historical Atlas of Religion in America* (1962), 167.

isters, their members likely composed just 5% of Christians. Anglican parishes composed 21% of all congregations, a decline of almost one-third from 1700. By 1740, the percent of churches belonging to the Anglican or Congregational establishment had declined significantly from 69% to 57% of all.

During the century after 1650, the number of churches rose 1,235%, from 109 to 1,456. This growth was nevertheless not sufficient to accommodate the white population's overall rise, which multiplied at a rate that was more rapid by almost half, 1,815%. The ratio of churches to total population as a consequence increased steadily from one congregation per 447 whites in 1650, to one per 598 in 1700, and one per 642 in 1750. Although some of this rise derived from greater population density in longer-settled areas, a more important factor would seem to have been that a substantial number of unaffiliated, frontier families were coming to live outside the boundaries of any religious society by 1750.

By 1750, significant differences existed between geographical regions and the ratio of churches to free population. The Mid-Atlantic colonies had more churches per inhabitants than any other section, one per 467 people, approximately the same rate as for all the colonies a century earlier. The ratio for New England, one congregation per 606 residents, was still lower than the average for all thirteen colonies in 1750. The South was the least churched region by far, with only one parish or congregation for every 1,046 whites. These figures indicate that by the mid-eighteenth century, only 56% of southerners held formal membership in a denomination, compared with 80% or more of northerners.

Reliable statistics on total church membership do not exist before the nineteenth century, but research has produced rough figures on the number of Anglo-Americans living in families that belonged to congregations. In 1700, about 80% of all whites seem to have been affiliated formally with a denomination. That figure fell slowly until it reached 75% in 1750, and then it dropped to 69% in 1765. It is most likely that this decline resulted from frontier expansion in the southern backcountry, where a shortage of clergy inhibited church building and left most people outside the scope of organized religion.

TABLE 7.4 RATIO OF CHURCHES TO WHITE POPULATION IN THE THIRTEEN COLONIES, 1750

Section	White Population	No. of Churches in Nine Denominations[a]	Ratio of Churches to Population[a]
New England	349,029	576	1/606
Middle	275,723	590	1/467
South	309,588	296	1/1046

[a] Nine denominations are represented: Anglican, Baptist, Congregational, Lutheran, Presbyterian, Dutch Reformed, French Reformed, German Reformed, and Catholic.
Source: Patricia U. Bonomi and Peter R. Eisenstadt, "Church Adherence in the Eighteenth-Century British Colonies," *William and Mary Quarterly*, XXXIX (1982), 273.

Denominational Development

Anglicans

The Virginia Company formed the first Anglican parish at Jamestown in 1607, and in 1619 the colony's legislature legally established the church by instituting tithes to support its clergy. In 1619, Virginia contained five ministers, or one per 440 persons, and in 1640 there were only twenty parishes (not all with resident clergy), or one per 750 laity; by 1660, the colony had just eleven ministers, one per 2,275 persons. For the rest of its history, the colonial Anglican church would be understaffed.

The "reformed," or Calvinist, clergy of the Church of England dominated the Chesapeake Anglican Church's early development far more than "high-churchmen." Of Virginia's first sixty-seven ministers who arrived by 1660, thirty-three were Puritans and twelve were high-church (the views of twenty-two cannot be ascertained). Anglican services in the Chesapeake consequently exhibited the simple tone of Calvinist worship, with the minister dressed in a black gown rather than vestments, little ornamentation within the church, and an emphasis on preaching rather than liturgy.

TABLE 7.5 PROPORTION OF CHURCH MEMBERS IN THE POPULATION OF THE THIRTEEN COLONIES, 1700–1785

Year	White Population	No. of Churches in Eight Denominations[a]	Ratio of Churches to Population[b]	Percent Church Adherents to Population at 80 Families per Church
1700	223,071	373	1/598	80
1720	397,346	646	1/615	78
1740	755,539	1176	1/642	74.7
1750	934,340	1462	1/639	75.1
1765	1,478,037	2110	1/700	69
1780	2,204,949	2731	1/807	59

[a] Eight denominations are represented: Anglican, Baptist, Congregational, Lutheran, Presbyterian, Dutch Reformed, German Reformed, and Catholic.
[b] The number of churchgoers assumes 80 families, of six members, per church.
Source: Patricia U. Bonomi and Peter R. Eisenstadt, "Church Adherence in the Eighteenth-Century British Colonies," *William and Mary Quarterly,* XXXIX (1982), 274.

Besides developing a ceremonial atmosphere that was decidedly low-church, colonial Anglicans placed parish affairs under the control of the laity, not the clergy. In place of bishops and ecclesiastical courts, which were not transplanted overseas, the dominant religious institution was the parish vestry. Vestrymen took their seats by parish election until 1662 when the members gained the right to fill their own vacancies and became a self-perpetuating body drawn from the local gentry. Vestries paid the minister, oversaw parish finances, and distributed "charity" (poor relief, or welfare). By renewing their ministers' appointments on a yearly basis, rather than installing them as permanent rectors as was done in Britain, the American gentry gained the power of dismissing pastors who displeased them, just as Puritan congregations could do in New England.

In 1690, all but one of the seventy-five Anglican parishes were in the South. Anglican worship first began in Massachusetts in 1686, in Pennsylvania in 1694, in New York in 1697, in New Jersey in 1702, and Connecticut in 1706. No colony besides Virginia established the faith legally until 1693 when New York authorized tithes to support Anglican ministers in New York City and three surrounding counties. The church became legally established in Maryland in 1702, South Carolina in 1706, North Carolina in 1711, and Georgia in 1758, even though dissenters predominated in all four provinces.

The Anglican Church grew substantially from 1700 to 1750 because of two British missionary organizations, the Society for the Promotion of Christian Knowledge (SPCK) and the Society for the Propagation of the Gospel in Foreign Parts (SPG). The SPCK (founded 1698) shipped Americans more than 100 libraries, with at least 100 books each. The SPG (founded 1701) financed ministers to evangelize dissenters; in 1730, it had fifty-eight missionaries preaching in every province but Virginia and Maryland, and by 1776 it had embarked 329 missionaries to the thirteen colonies.

By 1750, there were 289 Anglican parishes—with 40% outside the South—located in every colony, compared to seventy-five in 1690 existing in just five colonies. By 1750, the total membership of families worshiping in Anglican churches probably numbered about 140,000 persons—about 15% of the free population—including 50%–55% of southern whites. Because most Anglican priests lacked sympathy with the Great Awakening and spurned revivalistic techniques, the church lost many converts to Presbyterian and Baptist itinerant preachers in the 1750s and 1760s.

Baptists

The earliest Baptist congregation in Anglo-America was organized under the temporary leadership of the Puritan Roger Williams. Far more significant as a leader of early Baptists was John Clarke, who founded a second church at Newport about 1644. Newport, Rhode Island, became a center for the sect, with a "Six-Principle" church (which baptized with the laying on of hands) forming in 1654 and a Seventh-Day church starting in 1671. Other than requiring adult baptism for those who experienced spiritual redemption, the early Baptists held a wide variety of views, including belief in both predestination and free will. Each congregation was autonomous.

The earliest Baptist church in the Middle Atlantic region formed near Bristol, Pennsylvania, in 1684. Baptists organized their first southern congregation in South Carolina in 1696. By 1700, there were thirty-three Baptist congregations, about 9% of all colonial churches. In 1707, three Baptist churches in Pennsylvania and six in New Jersey founded the Philadelphia Association, which was the only such organization until 1751 when another was formed in South Carolina. The Philadelphia Association became the major influence on the sect's development; it ordained clergymen, encouraged missionary activity, and formulated a confession of faith that cast the church's theology in Calvinist terms.

The Great Awakening brought rapid growth to the Baptists, who were strongly prorevivalist and sent out many itinerant preachers, both lay and clergy, to win converts. It was due to the Great Awakening that the Baptists evolved from a minor sect into one of the country's three largest religions by the early nineteenth century. Baptist churches increased by 38% during the 1740s, from ninety-six to 132. The denomination found many converts among New Light Congregationalists in New England by 1750, and it won a wide following in Virginia and the Carolinas after 1760. In 1764, the denomination received a charter for Rhode Island College, which was the origin of Brown University.

Catholicism

The history of Roman Catholicism in early Anglo-America largely concerns the development of Maryland, a proprietary colony founded by a Catholic, Cecil Calvert, Second Baron Baltimore. The first parish was established in 1634 at St. Mary's, where a Jesuit priest celebrated the first mass on March 25. Because England's Catholic population was just 2%, the proprietors had difficulty peopling the colony with their coreligionists, and Protestants were either a majority, or close to a majority, within a dozen years.

During a state of heightened religious tensions created by the Puritan-led English Civil War, Protestants briefly displaced the Calvert government from 1645 to 1647. To alleviate Protestant anxieties that they would be forced to accept Catholicism, the proprietary party in the legislature passed the Toleration Act of 1649 guaranteeing all Trinitarian Christians freedom of worship. Another Protestant coup in 1654 led to a minor civil war, the execution of four Catholics, the expulsion of all priests overseas, and the Toleration Act's repeal.

After the Calverts regained their proprietorship in 1656, the Catholic minority grew steadily smaller, until it stood at less than one-quarter of all whites by the late 1680s. In 1689, a Protestant revolt ended proprietary authority and resulted in Maryland becoming a royal colony in 1691. The Calverts would not regain Maryland until 1715, by which time the Fourth Baron Baltimore had joined the Church of England. From 1689 to 1702, the Protestant legislature denied Catholics the right to vote, barred them from holding office or practicing law, legally established the Anglican Church, expelled priests, prohibited public worship by Catholics, and tried to stop Catholic planters from importing indentured servants of their own faith from Ireland.

By 1708, Catholics composed about 10% of all Maryland whites, and their population slowly declined relative to Protestants over the next half-century. During the eighteenth century, restrictions on Catholic behavior gradually eased and an atmosphere of limited toleration emerged. Wealthy Catholics were left undisturbed for maintaining chaplains who said mass for the entire neighboring community in their private chapels. Jesuits openly operated commercial farms that supported schools for educating young Catholics, of whom many of the brightest studied at European seminaries to become priests.

Officials ceased barring Catholics from practicing law after 1700. The landed aristocracy included a disproportionate number of fabulously wealthy Catholic families, notably the Carrolls, Dulanys, and Bennetts. By 1766, Catholics at Newtown were able to build their own church and worship without interference.

Outside of Maryland, a significant Catholic population took root only in Pennsylvania, where the first mass was celebrated at Philadelphia in 1708. The first resident priest, a Jesuit, settled in Philadelphia in 1729 and began to organize St. Joseph's Parish, the first Catholic church allowed to worship publicly in eighteenth-century Anglo-America. Philadelphia acquired a second functioning parish, St. Mary's, in 1763. By 1750, two Jesuits had established a circuit of ten chapels in the Pennsylvania hinterland to minister to a dispersed German Catholic population, which evidently equaled about 3% of the colony's whites. As the colonial period ended, the total number of practicing Catholics in the colonies probably equaled just 1% of all whites in 1760, or about 13,000.

Congregationalism

The Pilgrims founded the earliest Congregational church in 1620 at Plymouth. The founders of Massachusetts, Connecticut, and New Haven declared Congregationalism their established religion in the 1630s, as did New Hampshire later. Congregationalism originated in Puritanism, which sought to reform the Church of England along Calvinistic lines by giving the laity greater influence over their congregations, opposing the control of church affairs by bishops, restricting the sacraments to baptism and communion, substituting the highly ceremonial Anglican liturgy with worship centered around preaching, and using the ministry to guide members through their preparation for spiritual rebirth. The distinguishing feature of Congregationalism was that each church was organized by and composed of "visible saints,"—the elect capable of testifying to having received saving grace—who created an autonomous religious body and installed a minister of their own choosing.

While laymen and clergy might organize ad hoc consociations or synods to examine problems of a religious nature, no official hierarchy of clergymen existed in early Congregationalism. In 1648, a synod of ministers led by John Cotton drafted the Cambridge, Massachusetts, Platform, which outlined the basic elements of New England Puritanism and served as an ecclesiastical constitution. The Cambridge Platform limited the autonomy of congregations by authorizing both state officials and specially summoned synods to discipline wayward ministers or churches for theological errors or disorderly behavior, but it denied civil officials any right to pronounce on questions of doctrine.

During the first generation of New England's settlement, a large majority of adults had qualified as full church members by giving public testimony to their congregation about their own spiritual redemption. Once accepted as a visible saint, he or she was entitled to have his or her own children baptized. After 1650, a large—and growing—proportion of young adults in New England's second generation failed to qualify as saints because they could not testify to having been born again, and they were denied the right of having their own children baptized. Had this situation gone on, a majority of churchgoers might have abandoned Congregationalism for another religion with more lenient standards for infant baptism. A synod met in 1662 that permitted any child to be baptized so long as either parent was baptized, even if neither was saved. This compromise ended the danger of a schism within the church over infant baptism that might have left Congregationalism a minority religion in New England.

The Puritan, a monumental statue sculpted by Augustus Saint Gaudens for display in Springfield, Massachusetts, conveys a powerful sense of the religious certainty and strength of character exhibited by so many of the "visible saints" who established Congregationalism in New England. (Courtesy Saint-Gaudens National Historic Site, Cornish, New Hampshire)

The only attempt to create an ecclesiastical structure for Congregationalism occured in Connecticut. In 1708, a synod of ministers adopted the Saybrook Platform, which organized every county's churches into consociations of clergy and laymen that had the power to hear disputes from each congregation and discipline erring parties. Decisions of the consociation could not be appealed. The Saybrook Platform created a religious expedient resembling a cross between Congregationalism and Presbyterianism.

Although there were more Congregational churches in 1750 than any other religion (465, versus 289 for Anglicans), 98% were in New England. By then, about two-thirds of New Englanders worshiped in that faith. The Great Awakening badly split Congregationalists into revivalist and conservative camps. Disaffected New Lights seceded from numerous churches and formed "separate congregations," which then stirred political controversy by seeking exemption from paying tithes to their former ministers; many others simply left the faith and became Baptists. After 1750, Congregationalism healed its wounds slowly, and its membership grew far more slowly than prorevivalist denominations such as the Baptists and Presbyterians.

Dutch Reformed

The first Dutch Reformed church was founded at New Amsterdam in 1628. New Netherland had just two churches (a second was established at Albany in 1642) until 1654 when five others were created. By the time of the English conquest in 1664, there were nine churches and four chapels functioning as out-stations of other congregations. The English conquest ended the Dutch Reformed legal establishment, but its members were left free to worship as they wished and maintain church discipline as before.

During the early eighteenth century, the Dutch Reformed Church split deeply between pietistic and orthodox wings. The orthodox hierarchy, which dominated the sophisticated and wealthy churches of New York City, upheld high standards of theological scholarship, opened the sacraments to all people baptized, and preferred a highly ceremonial and formal liturgy for worship. The pietists, who primarily lived in semi-isolated rural communities, disparaged doctrinal exactness and clerical education as much less important than the state of a minister's soul; limited communion to the faithful who could make a full confession of faith attesting to the work of saving grace on their souls; and sought religious meaning in ecstatic, spontaneous worship.

During the 1720s, Rev. Theodore Freylinghausen, charismatic pastor of four central New Jersey churches, became the preeminent pietistic leader after using revivalistic techniques to stimulate conversions during a period of religious enthusiasm known as the Refreshings. He emphasized personal piety over mere good works and warned that without spiritual redemption, an upright life was meaningless. He modified liturgical ceremonies to suit the spiritual mood of his parishoners and had so little patience with doctrinal differences that he shared pulpits with Presbyterians.

During the Great Awakening, Freylinghausen's faction won the support of most Dutch Reformed laity in the countryside, while the orthodox party dominated New York City's congregations. The pietists then petitioned the Classis of Amsterdam, the Dutch clerical body with direct responsibility for North America, to authorize the formation of a colonial coetus (presbytery); this would permit the American ministers to resolve internal disputes locally rather than appealing them to the Classis, whose members were largely orthodox in sentiment. Although the Classis agreed and a local coetus was instituted in 1747, the conservatives refused to participate and formed the Conferentie party, which fought to increase the dependence of the American congregations on the Classis of Amsterdam and to oppose pietistic plans to ordain ministers trained at an American seminary and allow services to be conducted in English. By 1766, when the pietists succeeded in chartering Queens College (now Rutgers), they stood as the dominant force in the Dutch Reformed Church, but the fellowship remained badly divided between themselves and their Conferentie antagonists.

German Reformed

The first German Reformed church was not founded until 1710 in New York. The church's subsequent growth resulted from a heavy migration of Germans and Swiss from the Rhine valley to the colonies, in particular to Pennsylvania, Maryland, and New York, of whom perhaps one-third were Reformed. By 1740, there were fifty-one German Reformed congregations, but they were woefully short of clergy. It was reported in the next year that in the Mid-Atlantic colonies there were only four competent ordained ministers to care for the area's 15,000 German Reformed settlers.

Because reformed religion was basically similar among the Dutch and Germans, German Reformed congregations accepted the Dutch Reformed Classis of Amsterdam as their ecclesiastical superior. The Classis provided spiritual guidance, certified ministers as orthodox, and served as a final authority for resolving intracongregational disputes. There was nevertheless little cooperation between German and Dutch churches in the colonies because few members of the two ethnic groups lived in close proximity. In 1747, the two communions took a significant step toward self-differentiation by establishing a separate coetus for the Germans of the Delaware valley and the Dutch of New York and New Jersey, although both remained under the authority of the Amsterdam Classis.

German Reformed settlers experienced their own revival during the 1740s, just as English-speaking colonists did. Because Reformed preachers emphasized personal religious experience over theological dogma or liturgy, they won a receptive audience among the numerous, small independent sects and unchurched families who comprised up to a third of the German population. The church consequently enjoyed a period of sharp expansion during the Great Awakening; it added forty-nine congregations from 1740 to 1750, just two shy of all those that had been previously founded. After its most notable leader, Rev. Michael Schlatter, doubled the number of ordained German Reformed clergy by inducing six pietistic ministers to emigrate to America in 1752, the denomination continued growing strongly over the next two decades.

Judaism

The earliest known Jewish colonist in Anglo-America, Elias Legardo, arrived at Virginia on the ship *Abigail* in 1621. Like Legardo, most Jewish immigrants came as individuals rather than in groups and so tended to blend in with the majority Christian population. Because the Dutch tolerated Judaism, a regular stream of transient Jewish colonists seem to have passed in and out of New Netherland since its founding by the Dutch West India Company. The earliest Jewish community to develop on mainland North America appeared in September 1654 when twenty-three refugees (mostly Sephardim) landed at New Amsterdam from Recife, Brazil; they had abandoned Recife after the Portuguese recaptured it following a long occupation by the Dutch West India Company.

In February 1655, the Dutch West India Company overruled Gov. Peter Stuyvesant, who wished to embark the refugees from Recife on a ship to Holland, and directed that they be permitted to remain and take up businesses. By 1657, the company had forced Stuyvesant to grant them status as burghers, which included the right to bear arms as militiamen, become merchants, buy land, and lay out their own cemetery, but it withheld the privilege of worshiping publicly, although they could do so privately in their homes.

Although New York City's Jewish population fluctuated greatly in the decades after 1654, a kosher butcher became available after 1660, and the sabbath was apparently observed during much of the late 1600s. By 1695, a rented building was temporarily serving as a synagogue for congregation Shearith Israel (Remnant of Israel). By 1722, New York City contained thirty-one Jewish families, about 2.8% of all whites, and a few other Jewish families lived on rural estates on Long Island, Westchester County, and Orange County. In April 1730, worship began in the first synagogue built in Anglo-America. New York's Jewish community included several prosperous merchants, provided minor civic officeholders, and evidently voted.

Four other synagogues were founded in the British colonies by 1750. Jews totaled about 3.2% of all persons who settled in Georgia from 1733 to 1741, and by 1735 they had established a congregation in Savannah named Mikve Israel (Hope of Israel), which dissolved in the 1740s without having built a synagogue. In 1749, Congregation Beth Shalom (House of Peace) was formed by the Charles Town community, which soon included nearly fifty families. There were probably 300 Jews in Philadelphia, or 1% of the city, in 1747 upon the forming of Congregation Mikve Israel, which built its first synagogue in 1771. The Jewish presence in Newport, Rhode Island, dated from 1678, but a formal congregation (at first Nephuse Israel, or Scattered of Israel, and Yeshuat Israel, or Salvation of Israel, after 1769) was not formed until 1756 and Touro Synagogue—the only colonial synagogue still standing—was not completed until 1763.

For the entire colonial period, no ordained rabbis served the congregations of North America. Although most congregations included both Sephardim and Ashkenazim, the Sephardic liturgy was used. Kosher butchers, Hebrew teachers, and mohelim (ritual circumcisers) were also in short supply. The freedom to own land, vote in most provinces, pursue trades without legal disabilities, and mix socially with Christians also tended to lessen the sense of separate identity felt

The oldest, surviving place of worship for Judaism in the United States is Touro Synagogue (completed 1763) in Newport, Rhode Island. This photograph shows its beautifully designed interior, which is still used as a place of worship. (Historic American Buildings Survey, courtesy Library of Congress)

by Jews elsewhere, with the result that American Jews often ignored many points of Hebrew law and seem not to have actively discouraged marriages with Christians. Given these practical problems in maintaining customs and orthodoxy, it is all the more remarkable that the small Jewish community succeeded in preserving its traditions and identity through the colonial era.

Lutheranism

Swedish colonists founded the first Lutheran church at Wilmington, Delaware, in 1638. A small German Lutheran chapel was instituted at New Amsterdam in 1648 but did not become permanent. When New Netherland annexed New Sweden in 1655, Gov. Peter Stuyvesant tried to suppress Lutheranism and jailed both Swedish laity and clergy who participated in public worship. Although the Swedes received toleration when England conquered New Netherland in 1664, they also went long periods when their national church failed to provide ministers for them. Colonial Lutheranism came close to dying out by 1700 when there were just seven churches in the Delaware and Hudson valleys.

The church's subsequent growth resulted from large-scale immigration after 1720 of Germans and Swiss from the Rhine valley, of whom perhaps a third were Lutheran. Most settled in the Delaware valley. By 1740, there were ninety-five congregations, but they were woefully short of clergy. It was reported in the next year that only three effective ordained ministers resided in the Mid-Atlantic colonies to care for its 16,000 Lutherans.

Colonial Lutheranism deemphasized liturgy and dogma in favor of pietism, which was characterized by an intense concern for spiritual redemption and holiness in one's daily life. During the Great Awaken-

ing, this perspective enabled them not only to renew their own members' spiritual commitment but also to evangelize successfully among the many independent sects and unchurched families who comprised up to a third of the German population. The church accordingly grew significantly during the Great Awakening; from 1740 to 1750, it added forty-two congregations, almost half as many as existed in 1740. Under Rev. Henry Melchior Muhlenberg, their most important leader, Lutherans began to build an ecclesiastical structure for an autonomous American church, and by 1748, they succeeded in establishing a "ministerium," or annual assembly of pastors and laity. During the next quarter century to 1775, the faith grew steadily and doubled its congregations from 138 to 228.

Presbyterianism

The roots of colonial Presbyterianism lay in both Puritanism and Scottish Presbyterianism. A significant minority of Puritans believed that congregations should not be autonomous but organized into local associations of laity and clergy called presbyteries, which collectively made up the highest authoritative bodies, the synods. Beginning in 1640, with formation of the Southampton, New York, congregation, Puritans founded several churches on eastern Long Island whose members desired a presbyterian hierarchy but, in the absense of one, were forced to function as ordinary Congregational churches. They later affiliated with Delaware valley Presbyterians, whose religious tradition was largely Scottish.

The church grew slowly to 1700, when it included just twenty-eight congregations, nearly all former Puritan churches in New York and New Jersey that preferred Presbyterianism to Congregationalism. The most vigorous center of Presbyterian growth was thereafter the Delaware valley, to which most Scotch-Irish immigrants came. In 1706, three American-raised and four European-born ministers founded the earliest presbytery at Philadelphia, and a decade later, a synod was created from three presbyteries in Pennsylvania, Delaware, and New York.

During the 1720s, Rev. William Tennent of New Brunswick emerged as an early pioneer of revival techniques during a period of heightened religious activity in central New Jersey termed the Refreshings. When Tennent founded his "Log College" at Neshaminy, Pennsylvania, in 1735 to produce an American-trained ministry, he found himself opposed by the Synod of Philadelphia's orthodox leaders; they were largely Scots or Ulstermen and believed that only college graduates from Europe merited ordination, even though too few emigrated for the church's needs.

When the Great Awakening arrived, William Tennent, his son Gilbert, and "Log College" graduates enthusiastically embraced the revival, which the "Old-Side" Philadelphia Synod opposed. Schism resulted in 1741 when the Synod expelled Tennent and his "New-Side" followers, who formed the rival Synod of New York in 1745. The New Side meanwhile in 1746 transferred their Log College to New Jersey—where it later became Princeton University—and produced a steady stream of ministers to take over vacant congregations. By 1758, the New Side Synod of New York numbered seventy-three ministers, a gain of fifty-one since its founding in 1745, but the Old-Side Synod of Philadelphia, which was dependent on importing foreign clergy, had only twenty-three ministers, three less than in 1745.

The rival synods reunited in 1758, and the New Side ministers emerged as the driving force within the church. It was the Great Awakening that transformed Presbyterianism from a religion of the second rank to one of the three leading denominations in America. By sending out a large number of Log College graduates and other itinerants, the New Side won large numbers of converts and deserved most of the credit for the doubling of Presbyterian churches from 160 in 1740 to 233 in 1750. The church continued its rapid growth for the next quarter-century and by 1775 was exceeded in numbers only by the Congregationalists.

Quakerism

George Fox founded the Society of Friends in England about 1647. Called Quakers because they trembled in the Lord's presence, they premised their beliefs on the Inner Light, a source of moral insight promoted by divine assistance. The main purpose of Quaker meetings was to await and discuss inspirations provided by the Inner Light. The Society of Friends also eliminated all formal sacraments, had no trained or ordained clergy, refused to show deference to any rank of society, insisted on absolute separation of church and state, and would neither swear oaths nor perform military service. They periodically suffered rigorous persecution in England and Ireland for these beliefs from 1660 to 1685.

The first American Quakers appeared in New England during the 1650s. They were left unmolested in only Rhode Island and experienced harsh repression in Massachusetts, which executed Mary Dyer and three others during 1659–61. In 1661, the first American Yearly Meeting was established in Newport, Rhode Island. Local centers of Quakerism also developed at early dates on Long Island, New York; Maryland; and North Carolina.

In 1674, Quakers organized the proprietary colony of West Jersey, which became a major center of population for the sect. In 1681, Charles II awarded the Quaker William Penn, who as his father's heir was owed an enormous debt by the king, a charter to govern Pennsylvania (which included Delaware until 1704) as a proprietary colony. Penn refused to establish the Society of Friends legally and offered freedom of worship to all faiths.

Pennsylvania and West Jersey became the major center of Quakerism. A major schism occurred in the 1690s when William Keith tried to introduce scriptural limitations on the Inner Light's authority. The controversy left the Friends badly divided, and many members left the fold, including Keith, who became an Anglican priest and led many Quakers into that faith. Pennsylvania and West Jersey ceased to have Quaker majorities sometime after 1710, when the migration of British Friends fell sharply, and the immigration of other European Protestants eventually left Quakers a small minority. By 1770, the Philadelphia Yearly Meeting—which included Pennsylvania, New Jersey, and Delaware—included about 100 meetinghouses and 30,000 members, or less than a tenth of all whites. There may have been an additional 16,000 Friends in New England and another 11,000 in the South, so the total number of Quakers may have equaled 3% of all whites.

Quakers gathered for worship in unpretentious buildings that reflected their disdain for ostentatious displays. This simple meetinghouse for the Society of Friends was built during the mid-eighteenth century in Kennett Square, Pennsylvania. (Record Group 12 [Photographic Unit, Department of Highways] Courtesy Pennsylvania State Archives)

CHAPTER 8 Government

Imperial Administration

During the early seventeenth century, the English government encouraged its own citizens to establish settlements in North America but took no active role in colonization itself. Because neither the crown nor Parliament imposed a centralized system of administration to regulate Anglo-American affairs, the settlers gained the opportunity to create a great variety of political arrangements to rule themselves. The colonists were furthermore able to escape close control from London for most of their history; they enjoyed such an enormous amount of local autonomy that they were virtually self-governing.

The first permanent English colonies began as offshoots of business corporations whose charters allowed their officers to exercise political power over the civil societies they created overseas. Both Virginia and Massachusetts originated in this fashion, and Plymouth was settled by virtue of a business contract drawn up between the Pilgrims and London merchants. The first Virginians were not technically citizens of a colony but company employees. Not until 1618 would Virginians obtain the right of making their own laws, and not until 1632 would counties be established to administer local government. Having no legal right from a royal charter to govern themselves, the Pilgrims created their own authority by the Mayflower Compact (1620), which served as Plymouth's social contract until its annexation by Massachusetts.

Three separate forms of constitutional authority served as the basis for political power in British North America, where the provinces were divided among charter colonies, proprietary colonies, and royal colonies. (Two colonies, Plymouth and New Haven, never obtained any explicit legal authorization and were eventually annexed by their neighbors.) Although all three types had coexisted since the 1630s, the British government gradually managed to bring most proprietary and charter colonies under its own control as royal provinces by 1763.

The oldest type of colony was the charter colony, whose authority derived from a royal patent granting a corporation or trustees exclusive powers of governance, free from involvement by the crown, over a land grant from the king. In the case of the Virginia and Massachusetts charters, which were both given to business corporations, the only governmental institutions required to be established were regular meetings for company officers and stockholders in England. Virginia's

This photograph shows a reconstruction of one of the most imposing settings at which justice was dispensed during the colonial era, Virginia's General Court at Williamsburg. (Courtesy Library of Congress)

charter remained valid until 1624. Massachusetts fended off royal efforts to revoke its charter by taking the document to America but finally lost it and came under direct royal control in 1684. Connecticut and Rhode Island received charters in the 1660s, which allowed them to elect their own governors, and Georgia temporarily enjoyed that status under a corporation of trustees from 1732 to 1752.

The greatest number of colonies began as proprietary grants, in which the Crown granted extensive political powers to an individual or group in return for their efforts to settle the area with British subjects. These colonies were modeled on precedents from medieval history when certain English lords along the violent Scottish border received sweeping authority to maintain order and repel invasions. Proprietorship was hereditary but was not a title of nobility. The crown benefited by this arrangement because the cost of developing its overseas dominions was borne by private, rather than governmental, expense. The proprietors stood to profit greatly if they could attract large numbers of newcomers who would buy land from them and pay annual real estate fees called quitrents. Although proprietary charters enjoined their holders to obtain the consent of their settlers for all laws made, the proprietor himself was given the right to design the legislature's structure, specify which citizens were eligible to sit in it, and appoint the governor, the governor's council, executive officials, and judges. Because of political conflicts between the proprietors and the citizens, most such ventures became royal colonies, and by 1776 only Maryland, Pennsylvania, and Delaware held proprietary status.

Royal colonies were those governed directly by the crown through its own appointed governor, who appointed his council (except in Massachusetts), militia officers, and judges. Royal administration was fatally flawed, however, by the governors' dependence on their assemblies to pay their salaries and fund the budget. The "power of the purse" enabled the assemblies repeatedly to win concessions and compromises from their governors, who rarely could count on strong support from the imperial bureaucracy in London after they assumed their duties in America. Beginning with Virginia in 1625, the crown gradually assumed control of various colonies whose chartered corporations or proprietors could no longer maintain their authority; by the Revolution, eight of the thirteen colonies had royal governments.

The common thread uniting the colonies within the English Empire was the monarchy. It was the crown that had vested each province with its title to the soil and its legal authority. Because Parliament had no right to interfere with how kings and queens disposed of their personal estate, which included the North American colonies, it passed little legislation concerning the provinces except trade regulations and did not attempt to raise taxes upon Americans until the 1760s. For its own part, the crown's chief roles in governance lay in giving final approval to all legislative statutes and naming governors for royal colonies.

By 1696, the basic structure of imperial administration had taken form in London. Specific responsibility for oversight of American affairs lay with the Board of Trade. The board issued commissions for royal governors, drafted guidelines for their conduct in office, and collected information on colonial affairs. For most of its existence, the board performed its duties in a routine manner and showed little initiative. From 1748 to 1761, however, the Board of Trade's president, Lord Halifax, usually handled correspondence with American officials and acted as de facto secretary for colonial business.

Colonial affairs at the cabinet level were handled by the secretary for the Northern Department from 1702 to 1717 and by the secretary for the Southern Department thereafter until 1768, when a separate secretaryship for the American Department was created. These officials provided personal advice to the monarch at meetings of the Privy Council on policies concerning particular colonies or America in general.

The crown performed all official business concerning Anglo-America at meetings of the Privy Council, or cabinet. It was largely on the Privy Council's advice that kings appointed royal governors, issued proclamations, and settled disputes appealed from the colonial courts.

TABLE 8.1 CONSTITUTIONAL STATUS OF BRITISH NORTH AMERICAN COLONIES

Colony	Chartered or Acquired	Type of Colony	Became a Royal Colony
Virginia	Apr. 20, 1606	Charter	May 13, 1625[a]
Maryland	Jun. 30, 1632	Proprietary	[b]
Plymouth	Dec. 26, 1620	Private[c]	Oct. 17, 1691[d]
Massachusetts	Mar. 14, 1629	Charter	Jun. 21, 1684
Connecticut	May 3, 1662[e]	Charter	…
New Haven	Nov. 6, 1643	Private[c]	[f]
Rhode Island	Jul. 18, 1663[g]	Charter	…
New Hampshire	Sep. 18, 1680[h]	Royal	…
South Carolina	Apr. 3, 1663	Proprietary	May 29, 1721
North Carolina	Apr. 3, 1663	Proprietary	Jul. 25, 1729
New York	Mar. 12, 1664	Proprietary	Feb. 6, 1685
East Jersey	Jul. 4, 1664[i]	Proprietary	Apr. 15, 1702[j]
West Jersey	Jul. 4, 1664[i]	Proprietary	Apr. 15, 1702[j]
Pennsylvania	Mar. 14, 1681	Proprietary	[k]
Delaware	Mar. 14, 1681	Proprietary	…
Georgia	Jun. 20, 1732	Charter	Jul. 4, 1752
East Florida	Feb. 10, 1763	Royal	…
West Florida	Feb. 10, 1763	Royal	…

[a] Date of royal proclamation; last charter revoked May 24, 1624.
[b] Under temporary royal control from 1689 to 1715.
[c] Never received royal recognition of its existence.
[d] Annexed to Massachusetts.
[e] Settled by English in Sep. 1633.
[f] Annexed to Connecticut in 1662.
[g] Settled by English in Jun. 1636.
[h] Settled by English in Spring 1623.
[i] As Nova Caesaria; divided into East and West Jersey in 1674.
[j] Consolidated into New Jersey.
[k] Under royal control, 1692–1694.
Source: Richard B. Morris, ed., *Encyclopedia of American History* (rev. ed., 1961), 25–56, passim.

The council's most significant responsibility lay in recommending when the monarch should exercise his prerogative to disallow laws passed by colonial legislatures. When governors yielded to pressure from the assemblies to sign bills prohibited by their instructions, as they often did, it was the relevant secretary of state's task to identify the offending statutes to the king. From 1696 to 1776, the Board of Trade reviewed 8,563 acts submitted by the mainland American provinces and had 469 (5%) of them disallowed entirely or in part.

The earliest Anglo-American diplomats were agents paid by the provincial legislatures to represent their interests at the royal court or lobby in their behalf before Parliament. Because the colonies had always governed themselves with relatively little interference from imperial authorities, they underestimated the potential importance of such agents. The assemblies not only failed to provide salaries appropriate for men of high caliber but also staffed the positions primarily with British citizens rather than Americans. Some British agents had family members or business associates in America, but most lacked any personal stake in the colonies' welfare and were reluctant to uphold American interests vigorously during the years of crisis before 1776.

Although some colonists of exceptional ability, such as Arthur Lee of Virginia and Benjamin Franklin of Pennsylvania, served as agents in the 1770s, they were not enough to lobby effectively against the British government's objectionable measures. After independence, these former agents served as the nucleus for America's embryonic foreign service. Arthur Lee and Benjamin Franklin served on the joint commission that negotiated treaties of alliance and trade with France, and Franklin became first minister to France.

Overseas Englishmen enjoyed a wide degree of latitude in political affairs, but they also had to be self-reliant out of necessity. The British government appropriated no significant financial aid to any of the colonies except to help found Georgia in 1732; it provided no significant military forces to aid in defending Anglo-Americans until the Seven Years' War began in 1756. By permitting the provinces great discretion in managing their own internal affairs and forcing them to fend for themselves against enemies such as the French, the Spanish, and the Indians, Great Britain inadvertently helped set the stage for American independence, for the colonists slowly learned through hard experience how to govern and defend themselves.

TABLE 8.2 COLONIAL AGENTS TO THE BRITISH GOVERNMENT

Connecticut

Dates Served	Agent	Birth/Death	Occupation
1661–1663	John Winthrop, Jr.	1606–1676	governor of Conn.
1750–1759	Richard Partridge	1681–1759	merchant (for assembly)
1758–1761	Jared Ingersoll	1722–1781	attorney
1760–1770	Thomas Life	ca. 1720–1777	barrister (deputy agent)
1760–1764	Richard Jackson	ca. 1721–1787	barrister and M.P.
1764–1765	Jared Ingersoll	1722–1781	attorney
1765–1770	Richard Jackson	ca. 1721–1787	barrister and M.P.
1766–1771	William S. Johnson	1727–1819	attorney and educator
1771–1775	Thomas Life	ca. 1720–1777	barrister

Delaware

Dates Served	Agent	Birth/Death	Occupation
1760–1765	David Barclay, Jr.	1728–1809	merchant and banker
1765–1770	Dennys De Berdt	1694–1770	merchant

Georgia

Dates Served	Agent	Birth/Death	Occupation
1753–1763	Benjamin Martyn	1699–1763	civil servant
1756	Alexander Kellet	…	(special agent for assembly)
1757	William Little	…	Georgia clerk (agent to Board of Trade only)
1762–1765	William Knox	1732–1810	civil servant
1763–1765	Charles Garth	ca. 1734–1784	barrister and M.P.
1768–1774	Benjamin Franklin	1706–1790	American philosophe

Maryland

[Maryland had no regular agent after 1746 because the proprietors opposed such appointments. The Assembly temporarily named South Carolina's agent Charles Garth in 1765 but failed to appropriate funds for his salary; Garth ended his services in 1766.]

Massachusetts

Dates Served	Agent	Birth/Death	Occupation
1641	Rev. Hugh Peter	1598–1660	Puritan minister
1641	Rev. Thomas Weld	…	Puritan minister
1641	William Hibbens	…	…
1646	Edward Winslow	1595–1655	governor of Plymouth
1662	Simon Bradstreet	1603–1697	governor of Massachusetts
1662	Rev. John Norton	…	…
1676	John Richards	…	…
1682–1683	Joseph Dudley	1647–1720	Massachusetts politician
1682–1683	John Richards	…	…
1688–1691	Rev. Increase Mather	1639–1723	Puritan minister
1688–1691	Sir Henry Ashurst	…	…
1690–1691	Elisha Cooke	…	…
1690–1691	Thomas Oakes	…	…
1745–1762	William Bollan	ca. 1710–1782	attorney
1762–1765	Jasper Mauduit	1697–1772	manufacturer, merchant
1765–1766	Richard Jackson	ca. 1721–1787	barrister and M.P.

Massachusetts

Dates Served	Agent	Birth/Death	Occupation
1765–1770	Dennys De Berdt	1694–1770	merchant
1770–1774	Benjamin Franklin	1706–1790	printer and philosophe
1774–1775	Arthur Lee	1740–1792	lawyer
1768–1775	[Council] William Bollan	ca. 1710–1782	attorney

New Hampshire

Dates Served	Agent	Birth/Death	Occupation
1734–1767	John Thomlinson	?–1767	merchant
1763–1767	John Thomlinson, Jr.	1731–1767	attorney and M.P.
1766–1774	Barlow Trecothick	ca. 1718–1775	merchant and M.P.
1774–1775	Paul Wentworth	?–1793	stockbroker

New Jersey

Dates Served	Agent	Birth/Death	Occupation
1724–1725	Peter La Heupe	…	…
1728–1759	Richard Partridge	1681–1759	merchant (for assembly)
1735–1755	Ferdinand John Paris (representing only the Council and the eastern proprietors)	…	…
1759–1766	Joseph Sherwood	ca. 1708–1773	attorney
1766–1769	Henry Wilmot	1709–1794	solicitor
1769–1774	Benjamin Franklin	1706–1790	father of N.J. gov., printer, philosophe,
1775	Dennis De Berdt, Jr.	ca. 1742–1817	merchant

New York

Dates Served	Agent	Birth/Death	Occupation
1702–1704	John Thrale	…	…
1705–1709	William Sloper	…	…
1715–1716	John Campante	…	…
1716–1720	Ambrose Philips	…	…
1721–1725	George Bampfield	…	…
1724–1730	Peter La Heupe	…	…
1731	Richard Partridge	1681–1759	merchant and career agent
1748–1770	Robert Charles	ca. 1706–1770	civil servant
1771–1775	Edmund Burke	1729–1797	M.P.

North Carolina

Dates Served	Agent	Birth/Death	Occupation
1748–1759	James Abercromby	1707–1775	barrister and M.P. (for the colony 1748–1757 and for its assembly 1757–1760)
1759–1764	[for the Council] Samuel Smith	…	attorney and merchant
1761–1765	Peter Cuchet Jouvencal	?–1786	civil servant, clerk
1768–1773	Henry Eustace McColloh	ca. 1739–ca. 1788	…
1774–1775	Thomas Barker	1733–1787	attorney and merchant

Pennsylvania

Dates Served	Agent	Birth/Death	Occupation
1740–1759	Richard Partridge	1681–1759	merchant (for assembly)
1751–1761	Robert Charles	ca. 1706–1770	civil servant (assistant agent from 1751 to 1754)
1757–1762 1764–1775	Benjamin Franklin	1706–1790	printer and philosophe
1762–1764	John Sargent	1715–1791	merchant, banker, and M.P.
1762–1764	David Barclay, Jr.	1728–1809	merchant and banker
1763–1769	Richard Jackson	ca. 1721–1787	barrister and M.P.

(continued)

TABLE 8.2   (continued)

Rhode Island

Dates Served	Agent	Birth/Death	Occupation
1651	Roger Williams	ca. 1603–1683	Puritan minister
1651	Dr. John Clark	1609–1676	…
1660	Dr. John Clark	1609–1676	…
1670	Dr. John Clark	1609–1676	…
1670	Capt. John Greene, of Warwick, R.I.	…	…
1699	Capt. Joseph Sheffield	…	…
1699–1700	Johleel Brenton	…	…
1708	William Wharton	…	…
1715–1759	Richard Partridge	1681–1759	merchant
1759–1773	Joseph Sherwood	ca. 1708–1773	attorney
1771–1772	Henry Marchant	1741–1796	lawyer

South Carolina

Dates Served	Agent	Birth/Death	Occupation
1754–1756	Charles Pinckney	1699–1758	S.C. politician
1757–1760	James Wright	1716–1785	attorney (later gov. of Ga.)
1762–1775	Charles Garth	ca. 1734–1784	barrister and M.P.

Virginia

Dates Served	Agent	Birth/Death	Occupation
1754–1774	James Abercromby	1707–1775	barrister and M.P. (for the colony 1754–1759 and for its council 1759–1774)
1759–1770	[Assembly] Edward Montagu	ca. 1720–1798	barrister

Source: Micheal G. Kammen, *A Rope of Sand: The Colonial Agents, British Politics, and the American Revolution* (1968), 323–326.

The Legislatures

The assemblies served as the principal means by which a tradition of representative government gained permanence in Anglo-America. The earliest British American assembly convened at Jamestown, Virginia, in 1619, twelve years after the colony's founding. The Virginia Company created this governing body primarily as an incentive to enlist the inhabitants' active support for its policies. The assembly's primary duties were to endorse decisions passed by the company headquarters in London and to enact necessary regulations, which lacked legal force

Members of the governor's council functioned as an upper house in colonial legislatures. This photograph shows a reconstruction of the chamber where royal councillors convened at Williamsburg, Virginia. (Courtesy Library of Congress)

unless approved by the corporate headquarters. When Virginia became a royal colony in 1624, the crown governed exclusively through its governor and his appointed councillors until 1628 when it again began to summon assemblies to pass taxes and other necessary laws.

Representative government developed in New England under the auspices of the Massachusetts Bay Company. The company's charter of 1629 authorized a corporate headquarters to manage the colony's affairs, but it did not guarantee the settlers themselves any participatory rights. When the company removed its charter to America in 1630 to lessen the likelihood of its being annulled by a royal judge, it became possible to transform the commercial bureaucracy into a civil government. In 1631, the General Court, as the company government was termed, declared any adult male who was a full church member to be a freeman—the equivalent of a shareholder—and thus entitled to attend its meetings. In 1634, because of the impracticality of having hundreds of freeman attend the assembly, the General Court restructured itself to permit two delegates from each town to attend its annual meeting, which was chaired by the governor and his appointed assistants.

Legislative institutions of a truly republican character only appeared in Virginia and Massachusetts several years after each was founded. In both instances, representative government emerged as part of the administrative apparatus of a business enterprise, and managed to endure after its commercial creator disappeared. In neither province was the government's structure consciously modeled after Parliament, which was composed of the crown, a hereditary House of Lords, and an elective House of Commons. The popularly chosen representatives in both colonies at first sat not as a separate chamber but with the governor and his appointed council. Both legislatures did not become bicameral until the early 1640s.

The experiences of most other colonies in establishing assemblies generally followed the pattern described above. Rarely did the first sitting of a colony's legislature occur within two years of its first settlement, and in five colonies (Virginia, Plymouth, Rhode Island, New York, and Georgia) a decade or more elapsed between their founding and the first assembly's meeting. Elected representatives initially met in joint sessions with the governor and his council rather than as a separate house. Most provinces required at least two decades for their legislatures to start to function, develop continuity, and take permanent form as bicameral bodies. All assemblies apportioned their members equally among various units of local government (towns in New England, parishes in South Carolina, and counties elsewhere), rather than on the basis of population.

During the colonies' first century of representative government, the lower houses, or assemblies, suffered from careless record-keeping, poor internal organization, inadequate mastery over parliamentary procedure, and poor leadership. The Pennsylvania Assembly once lost all its records from October 1701 to April 1704. By 1700, Massachusetts was the only province that had attempted to compile its laws, and no colony published its journal. Assembly sessions proceeded at an awkward, inefficient pace, and lawmaking was often characterized by both laxness and ineptitude that left innumerable statutes either ineffective or unenforceable.

After 1720, the assemblies began to transform themselves into more professional and proficient institutions. A major reason for this development was the rise of a new generation of speakers who were more motivated, politically experienced, and strong willed. These men frequently held long tenures, during which they insisted on detailed, accurate record-keeping, created a viable system of standing committees, ensured that the most competent members received important committee assignments, and managed debates more professionally. By the mid-

TABLE 8.3   ORIGINS OF REPRESENTATIVE GOVERNMENT IN ENGLISH NORTH AMERICA

Colony	English Settlement First Established	First Assembly	No. of Deputies	Became Bicameral
Virginia	1607	Jul. 30, 1619	22	ca. 1642[a]
Bermuda	1612	Aug. 1, 1620	16	unicameral
Mass. Bay	1628	May 14, 1634	24	1644
Maryland	1634	[1635?] Jan. 25, 1638	24	1650
Connecticut	1636	May 1, 1637	12	1698
Plymouth	1620	Mar. 5, 1639	17	unicameral
New Haven	1638	Jun. 1639	4	unicameral
Barbados	1627	1639	22	1639
St. Kitts	1624	ca. 1642	24	ca.1672
Antigua	1632	ca. 1644	...	ca.1682
Rhode Island	1637	May 19, 1647	24	1696
Montserrat	1632	post-1654	...	1696
Nevis	1628	ca. 1658	...	post-1672
Jamaica	1655	Jan. 20, 1664	20	1664
N. Carolina	1663	1665	12	1691
S. Carolina	1670	Jul. 1671	20	1691
E. Jersey	1664	May 26, 1668	10	1672
W. Jersey	1675	Nov. 21, 1681	34	1696
N. Hampshire	1633	Mar. 16, 1680	11	1692
Pennsylvania	1682	Dec. 4, 1682	42	unicameral
New York	1664	Oct. 17, 1683	18	1691

[a] Altered from source to reflect new research.

Source: Michael Kammen, *Deputyes & Libertyes: The Origins of Representative Government in Colonial America* (1969), 11–22.

TABLE 8.4   AVERAGE NUMBER OF PETITIONS RECEIVED PER YEAR BY COLONIAL ASSEMBLIES, 1715–1765

Colony	1715–1720	1750–1755	1760–1765
Virginia	28.5	60.0	88.8
Massachusetts	95.2	212.0	257.0
New York	13.8	13.8	12.2
Pennsylvania	18.0	26.6	25.5
Rhode Island	2.2	58.1	100.3
South Carolina	10.8	17.6	9.6
Maryland	17.8	16.3	28.0
Connecticut	39.0	90.25	130.3
New Hampshire	...	47.0	62.0
New Jersey	13.6	18.5	43.1
Average for ten colonies	26.5	56.0	75.7

Source: Alison G. Olson, "Eighteenth-Century Colonial Legislatures and their Constituents," *Journal of American History,* LXXIX (1992), 557.

TABLE 8.5   AVERAGE NUMBER OF LAWS ENACTED PER YEAR BY COLONIAL ASSEMBLIES, 1730–1765

Colony	1730–1735	1740–1745	1760–1765
Virginia	31.3	31.6	37.8
Pennsylvania	4.3	5	12.1
Massachusetts	17.1	23.1	31.5
New York	13.3	25.5	27.0
Rhode Island	11.3	23.0	10.4
New Jersey	6.2	5.0	18.5
Maryland	22.6	18.2	24.8
North Carolina	...	11.5	26.2
Connecticut	15.0	10.8	8.0
South Carolina	13.8	16.0	12.0

Source: Alison G. Olson, "Eighteenth-Century Colonial Legislatures and their Constituents," *Journal of American History,* LXXIX (1992), 563.

Colonial legislatures saw themselves as little Parliaments. This reconstruction of Virginia's House of Burgesses expresses that sense of identification literally because the chamber is modeled (on a small scale) directly after the layout of the English House of Commons. (Courtesy Library of Congress)

eighteenth century, virtually every colony published its assembly journal and ensured that the county courts received copies of the latest statutes.

These reforms enabled the legislators to serve their constituents more effectively and encouraged citizens to seek their assistance through petitions. During the half-century from 1715 to 1765, the volume of constituent requests sent to the assemblies multiplied rapidly. In Virginia, New Jersey, and Connecticut, the number more than tripled between the years 1715–20 and 1760–65, and it almost did so in Massachusetts as well. The citizens of New York, Pennsylvania, South Carolina, and Maryland used petitions to a far less degree. Overall, however, the average volume of petitions written annually to assemblies roughly tripled from the period 1715–20 to 1760–65.

Expanded recourse to petitioning was of enormous importance because after 1750 the greatest portion of any assembly's workload generally came from this source. Up to three-fifths of assembly journal entries might concern issues raised by constituents. In Pennsylvania, 52% of all laws passed from 1717 to 1775 originated from petitions, while in Virginia the number of laws written to answer petitions ranged from 44% to 50% from 1710 to 1770. In New Jersey, the number of statutes arising from petitions rose from 14% during 1703–21 to 43% during 1750–64.

Most assemblies consequently increased their legislative output in the period from 1730 to 1765. The average number of laws enacted annually tripled in Pennsylvania and almost doubled in Massachusetts. Many of these were nevertheless "private bills" that did not represent substantive issues of concern to the citizens at large. Because the scope of government was kept purposefully limited to minimize the tax burden, and because the courts utilized Britain's criminal and civil code, the assemblies were able to avoid writing large numbers of laws. In the early 1760s, for example, Pennsylvania was able to limit its legislative output to a yearly average of twelve laws. When Virginia printed an updated compendium of its statute book in 1749, it listed only sixty-seven public acts then in force. From 1748 to 1776, the New Jersey legislature added only eighty-four public laws to its statute book, or an average of about three per year.

As the assemblies became more efficient and useful to their constituents, they started to take the initiative to reverse the balance of legislative power longstanding since the early 1600s when lower houses generally contented themselves with ratifying measures initiated by the governor or his appointed council in the manner of a rubber stamp. During the late seventeenth century, the lower houses of assembly started to assert their own authority as a means of checking potential threats to local autonomy posed by their governors and royal appointees, whose first loyalties were to either the crown or an absentee proprietor.

Under an increasingly strong-willed set of speakers, the lower houses shifted the balance of constitutional power away from the governor and his councillors by refusing to permit any external meddling in their own internal proceedings, by gaining firm control over both taxes and the budget, and by refusing to vote permanent, independent salaries or other incomes to executive officers. Despite a considerable range of gubernatorial powers (including the right to veto bills, summon or dismiss an assembly at will, call elections with little advance notice, and appoint his council, which functioned as the legislature's upper house), a determined assembly always had the advantage because the governor was dependent on local revenues for the provincial budget, which paid his salary, and because he was rarely given effective backing by the Board of Trade or Privy Council. By the early eighteenth century, the assemblies had succeeded in winning the initiative in legislative proceedings and establishing themselves as the dominant force in government.

Candidates and Elections

In most colonies, the only election in which voters could participate was for a candidate to sit in the legislature's lower house. Only in

TABLE 8.6 PROPERTY QUALIFICATIONS FOR VOTERS AND ASSEMBLY CANDIDATES, 1763

Colony	Property Required to Vote	Property Required of Assembly Candidates
New Hampshire	Estate valued at £50	Land valued at £300
Massachusetts	Land worth £2 annual rent or any property worth £40	Same as for voters
Rhode Island	Land worth £2 annual rent or valued at £40	Same as for voters
Connecticut	Land worth £2 annual rent or livestock valued at £40	Same as for voters
New York	Landed estate valued at £40	Same as for voters
New Jersey	Landed estate valued at £50	1,000 acres or land and other property worth £500
Pennsylvania	50 acres or any property valued at £50	Same as for voters
Delaware	50 acres or any property valued at £40	Same as for voters
Maryland	50 acres or any property worth £40	Same as for voters
Virginia	25 acres with house on it, or 100 acres of unimproved land	Same as for voters
North Carolina	50 acres	100 acres
South Carolina	50 acres or land worth £2 annual rent	500 acres or property valued at £500
Georgia	50 acres	500 acres

Source: Robert J. Dinkin, *Voting in Provincial America: A Study of Elections in the Thirteen Colonies, 1689–1776* (1977), 51–52.

Connecticut and Rhode Island were governors and members of the upper house also chosen by ballot. While New England towns and certain townships in Pennsylvania and New Jersey elected minor officials, local government was usually staffed by justices of the peace, a sheriff, and a clerk who gained their posts by appointment from the governor.

Candidates qualified for election primarily by meeting their colony's property qualifications. In most colonies, any voter could run for office, but five of the thirteen colonies required their assemblymen to possess a significant amount of wealth. Georgia and South Carolina both allowed anyone to vote who owned 50 acres but specified that assemblymen possess 500 acres. In New Jersey, where the typical farmer probably owned 80 acres by 1760 and had a total estate worth about £400 proclamation, representatives needed either 1,000 acres or a combination of land and personal property worth £500 proclamation.

Even in provinces where any voter could run for office, most candidates came from the local economic elite. This result was inevitable at a time legislators received no salary for their duties, only a modest living allowance. By the mid-eighteenth century, public service placed a heavy burden on the time and resources of assemblymen. Assembly sessions lasted at least one month, often two, and sometimes three, during which members could not pursue their occupations. Their compensation for living expenses furthermore was usually set a minimum levels, and it often failed to cover their full costs. A man of average means would have found it virtually impossible to afford the personal sacrifices of time and money, especially if called to the assembly at planting time or harvest time when even wealthy individuals remained on their estates to supervise their servants or slaves personally.

So onerous was public service in some colonies that numerous individuals tried to avoid the honor after being elected. In South Carolina, the percent of elected representatives who failed to take their seats in the house ranged from 17% to 37% in the years 1721–70. So many South Carolina assemblymen stayed home in 1747 and 1749 that the legislature could not legally meet because it lacked a quorum. In 1742, it was noted by the governor of Massachusetts, where incorpo-

TABLE 8.7 BACKGROUND CHARACTERISTICS OF COLONIAL LEGISLATORS, ABOUT 1763

Characteristic	South Carolina Lower House	South Carolina Upper House	Maryland Lower House	Maryland Upper House	New York Lower House	New York Upper House
Occupation						
Merchant	12%	13%	2%	0	28%	31%
Merchant/planter	10%	0	0	18%	7%	44%
Lawyer	2%	7%	6%	5%	4%	13%
Lawyer/planter	10%	0	8%	27%	11%	6%
Planter	49%	73%	57%	46%	…	…
Large landowner	…	…	…	…	18%	6%
Doctor	…	…	0	4%	…	…
Other nonfarm	6%	7%	4%	0	4%	0
Large farmer	…	…	2%	0	…	…
Farmer	2%	0	16%	0	25%	0
Unknown	9%	0	5%	0	3%	0
Economic Status						
Wealthy[a]	68%	80%	37%	91%	43%	94%
Well-to-do[b]	20%	20%	39%	9%	50%	6%
Moderate[c]	0	0	19%	0	7%	0
Unknown	12%	0	5%	0	0	0
Social Origin						
Prominent old family	47%	80%	30%	82%	36%	75%
Old family	18%	0	56%	5%	57%	0
New resident	14%	20%	15%	13%	7%	25%
Unknown	21%	0	0	0	0	0

[a] Defined as owning property worth £5,000 (Proclamation) or more, or wealthiest 2% of population.
[b] Defined as owning property worth £2,000 (Proclamation) or more, but less than £5,000, or wealthiest 8%–10% of population.
[c] Defined as owning property worth less than £2,000 (Proclamation).
Source: Jackson T. Main, *The Upper House in Revolutionary America, 1763–1788* (1967), 269, 276, 272.

rated towns were allowed to elect two delegates—provided the town paid their expenses—that the great majority sent only one representative to economize on expenses. In 1762, of 168 towns in Massachusetts, sixty-four elected no assemblymen and only four of the other 104 opted to send all delegates to which they were entitled.

Under such circumstances, it was inevitable that the assemblies would be drawn primarily from the economic and social elite, whose members were the only significant group with the surplus wealth and leisure time to afford the sacrifices of public life. About 1760, the typical member of Virginia's House of Burgesses owned 1,800 acres and forty slaves. Of the representatives elected to New Jersey's colonial assembly after 1737, 44% ranked among the province's wealthiest 2%, and another 27% stood among the richest 5%. Membership in the assemblies also became progressively more interrelated as dynastic groups like the First Families of Virginia sent succeeding generations into public service. In New Jersey, for example, 53% of all colonial assemblymen elected since 1703 were either the sons, sons-in-law, or grandsons of men who had sat in either house of the legislature before their own election.

The increasingly elitist character of representation also stemmed from the rising ratio of constituents to assemblymen. In no colony did the lower house's size expand proportionally with the white population's tenfold increase from 1700 to 1775. In Pennsylvania, the number of adult white males per assemblyman rose from 134 in 1700 to 336 in 1730, and it would later reach 1,301 by 1770. Whereas a large majority of electors probably had some prior acquaintance or knowledge of the candidates in 1700, after 1750 it was increasingly rare for voters to be part of election districts small enough to ensure they would have experienced some personal interaction with candidates before an election. As a result, the social gap between voters and officeholders widened even further as the century progressed.

Nowhere in Anglo-America did universal male suffrage exist, nor was it ever proposed to that every adult man should be able to vote. A few taxpaying Christian Indians enjoyed the franchise in New England, but free blacks were excluded from voting everywhere, either by law or custom. Property qualifications varied greatly among the provinces. In most of New England and South Carolina, electors could qualify by meeting the test set by England's Parliament since 1430: ownership of any land that would rent for 40 shillings (£2) a year. The most common alternatives were to require possession of 50 acres or any property (including tools, livestock, and furniture) worth £40 or £50. Six colonies limited suffrage to landowners.

To qualify as an elector, a man needed a relatively small amount of property. Ownership of £40 to £50 of personal goods amounted to little more than the tools, animals, and household furnishings that most married farmers and artisans would accumulate by age thirty if not before then. In the six colonies where voters must be landholders, which was fulfilled by negotiating a mortgage, a larger segment of society was excluded because many men did not accumulate the large sums then required as a down payment on a farm until their mid or late thirties.

Current scholarship indicates that property qualifications excluded a large minority of adult males. In colonies where land ownership determined the franchise, nonvoters largely included indentured servants, single sons still residing at home, and young men just beginning married life, but these groups sometimes approached half of all men over age twenty-one and probably averaged 40% of all adult white males. When voters could qualify with personal property worth £40 or £50, disfranchisement was much lower, perhaps 20% to 30% of adult white males. The main effect of property qualifications was to delay most men from obtaining the suffrage but not to deny it from them permanently. Perhaps half of all Anglo-American men age twenty-one to thirty lacked the vote at any given moment, but it would seem that well over 90% of all men over forty would be enfranchised by the same guidelines.

Election procedures kept voter turnout far below the number of qualified electors. Aside from Massachusetts, Connecticut, Rhode Island, and Pennsylvania, which all held annual elections, the colonies made no provision for balloting on a regular schedule. Governors could issue the writs at any time, and sheriffs were required to give

TABLE 8.8 SIZE OF ASSEMBLIES AND RATIO OF REPRESENTATIVES TO ADULT WHITE MALES, 1700 AND 1730

Colony	1700 Number of Members[a]	1700 Members per Adult White Males	1730 Number of Members[a]	1730 Members per Adult White Males	Percent Change from 1700 to 1730
New Hampshire	13	1:74	17	1:124	67%
Massachusetts	80	1:137	91	1:244	78%
Rhode Island	26	1:43	30	1:102	137%
Connecticut	47	1:108	79	1:187	73%
New York	20	1:168	26	1:320	90%
New Jersey	23	1:114	24	1:287	151%
Pennsylvania	26	1:134	30	1:336	150%
Delaware	18	1:25	18	1:96	284%
Maryland	46	1:114	50	1:295	158%
Virginia	44	1:191	58	1:289	51%
North Carolina	22	1:94	31	1:154	63%
South Carolina	30	1:21	38	1:52	147%

[a] Figures show members of lower house only.
Source: Jack P. Greene, "Legislative Turnover in British America, 1696–1775," *William and Mary Quarterly,* XXXVIII (1981), 461.

TABLE 8.9 ESTIMATED PERCENTAGE OF ADULT WHITE MALES KNOWN TO HAVE VOTED IN COLONIAL ELECTIONS

New Hampshire[a]

Town	1745	1755	1762
Dover	40%	...	...
Dunstable-Hollis	...	...	70%
Durham	...	45%	...
Londonderry-Windham	...	...	67%

Massachusetts[c]

	1674	1676	1677	1679	1682	1683	1684	1685	1686
Colonywide	39%	33%	33%	28%	24%	26%	25%	25%	26%

	1696	1698	1699	1703	1704	1709	1711	1715	1716	1717	1718	1719	1721	1722	1723	1724	1725	1726	1727	1728	1729
Boston	10.2%	25.0%	23.3%	31.1%	13.7%	12.6%	10.4%	14.9%	21.1%	15.7%	13.2%	24.6%	13.0%	10.7%	13.9%	10.2%	15.7%	9.4%	9.1%	10.8%	8.1%

	1730	1731	1732	1733	1734	1735	1736	1737	1738	1739	1740	1741	1742	1743
Boston	21.9%	19.1%	25.8%	23.0%	22.6%	19.0%	9.8%	8.8%	18.9%	26.2%	18.3%	22.2%	23.6%	20.2%
Salem	...	...	...	...	...	23.6%	...	...	29.4%	15.1%	21.1%	38.6%	24.1%	...

	1744	1745	1746	1747	1748	1749	1750	1751	1752	1753	1754	1755	1756	1757
Boston	23.9%	15.3%	19.9%	20.2%	32.4%	30.7%	24.3%	20.8%	14.2%	20.0%	27.1%	22.1%	23.9%	23.7%
Lynn	...	...	...	...	...	...	31.7%	32.4%	37.2%	20.9%	24.4%	...	26.1%	...

	1758	1759	1760	1761	1762	1763
Boston	16.6%	21.0%	44.7%	15.0%	28.2%	48.9%

Rhode Island[b]

	1758	1760	1762	1763
Colonywide	44.5%	44.4%	46.8%	47.3%

Connecticut[b]

	1723	1740	1748	1755
Colonywide	20.0%	24.5%	23.0%	20.5%

New York[a]

County	1698	1699	1733	1737	1739	1745	1748	1761
Albany Co.	...	...	...	...	35.3%	...	...	...
New York	...	80.0%	...	55.4%	41.8%	10.7%	...	56.1%
Queens Co.	54.5%	...	...	48.6%	48.4%	...	50.1%	34.6%
Richmond Co.	...	...	...	...	...	...	...	38.5%
Ulster Co.	...	...	...	...	...	...	14.2%	...
Westchester Co.	...	...	32.9%	...	...	...	...	14.0%

New Jersey[a]

County	1738	1739	1754	1761
Hunterdon Co.	14.4%	...	...	...
Burlington Co.	...	35.2%	...	...
Middlesex Co.	...	...	37.1%	...
Cape May Co.	...	...	...	35.0%

Pennsylvania[a]

County	1727	1728	1730	1732	1734	1735
Philadelphia	...	...	...	...	...	...
Philadelphia Co.	27.7%	32.8%	19.4%	26.2%	22.2%	28.3%

County	1736	1737	1738	1739	1740	1741	1742	1743	1749	1750	1751	1752	1754	1755	1756	1757	1758	1761
Bucks Co.	...	...	26.0%	19.1%	22.5%	...	...	...	...	...	...	...	...	...	...	...	...	...
Chester Co.	...	28.6%	36.7%	31.8%	...	...	32.0%	...	...	...	...	...	...	...	...	13.8%	...	...
Lancaster Co.	...	31.5%	39.8%	...	33.7%	36.9%	44.8%	...	31.9%	...	...	...	...	...	...	22.7%	6.8%	...
Philadelphia	...	14.7%	...	...	...	...	...	...	...	...	36.5%	...	...	...	...	...	...	...
Philadelphia Co.	17.6%	21.2%	29.3%	11.9%	37.6%	22.8%	34.2%	18.8%	...	29.1%	20.7%	13.1%	29.2%	16.3%	23.0%	10.0%	19.7%	11.1%
York Co.	...	...	...	...	...	...	...	...	...	...	...	......		45.5%	38.4%	...	...	[???]

(continued)

TABLE 8.9 (continued)

County	1748[a]	1752[a]	1755[a]	1758[a]
Virginia[a]				
Accomac Co.	48.7%	42.6%	47.8%	49.6%
Amelia	...	...	...	49.6%
Brunswick Co.	45.7%	...	...	...
Elizabeth City Co.	...	...	...	44.7%
Essex Co.	52.6%	44.4%	53.4%	53.5%
Fairfax Co.	41.7%	...	35.7%	...
Frederick	...	...	18.9%	24.4%
Henrico Co.	...	58.2%	...	...
King George Co.	...	33.9%	45.0%	...
Lancaster Co.	57.8%	49.9%	39.2%	59.7%
Northumberland	...	...	...	44.8%
Prince Edward Co.	...	...	26.6%	44.9%
Prince George Co.	...	...	...	55.3%
Richmond	...	44.7%	36.6%	40.1%
Spotsylvania Co.	46.4%	35.1%	41.8%	...
Westmoreland	52.5%	57.5%	47.7%	...
Average Percent	48.8%	45.4%	37.4%	43.4%

South Carolina[a]	1736		1742	
Charles Town (St. Philip's)	40%		30%	

[a] For assembly.
[b] For governor.
[c] 1674–1686 are nominations or elections for Upper House of Legislature (Assistants), and rest are assembly elections.
Sources: Robert J. Dinkin, *Voting in Provincial America: A Study of Elections in the Thirteen Colonies, 1689–1776* (1977), 148, 149, 156, 158, 159, 162, 174, 176. Thomas L. Purvis, *Proprietors, Patronage, and Paper Money: Legislative Politics in New Jersey, 1703–1776* (1986), 101. Theodore H. Lewis and Linda M. Webb, "Voting for the Massachusetts Council of Assistants, 1674–1686: A Statistical Note," *William and Mary Quarterly,* XXX (1973), 632–33.

TABLE 8.10   ELECTORAL TURNOVER IN COLONIAL ASSEMBLY ELECTIONS, 1679–1762

Percentage of New Members

Year	N.H.	Mass.	Conn.[a]	R.I.	N.Y.	N.J.	Penn.	Del.	Md.	Va.	N.C.	S.C.	Ga.
1762	54%	28%	41%–42%	51%	...	...	19%	6%	43%	...	38%–32%	48%–23%	...
1761	...	34%	43%–48%	60%	44%	29%	25%	33%	...	39%	35%	40%	24%
1760	...	34%	41%–39%	53%	...	...	25%	28%	...	...	60%	46%	53%
1759	...	37%	63%–43%	53%	63%	...	11%	28%	...	...	...	...	...
1758	38%	46%	56%–41%	63%	...	...	19%	39%	29%	47%	...	...	...
1757	...	43%	54%–45%	36%–60%[a]	...	...	22%	6%	47%	...	...	58%	58%
1756	...	52%	78%–63%	71%	...	...	42%	33%	...	38%	...	...	...
1755	67%	45%	66%–52%	41%	...	...	17%	17%	...	...	...	...	...
1754	...	40%	57%–50%	53%	...	54%	6%	17%	38%	...	58%	68%	...
1753	...	42%	46%–55%	51%	...	...	14%	22%	...	...	11%	...	...
1752	11%	45%	47%–35%	46%	15%	...	26%	28%	...	49%	...	...	...
1751	...	60%	47%–49%	55%	...	46%	22%	28%	41%	...	...	73%	...
1750	...	53%	42%–48%	64%	26%	...	25%	6%	...	...	...	...	...
1749	...	46%	37%–45%	65%	...	29%	40%	17%	39%	...	...	50%–70%[a]	...
1748	28%	34%	36%–46%	60%	26%	...	13%	22%	...	40%	...	47%	...
1747	70%–50%	43%	29%–61%	70%	...	...	13%	22%	...	...	31%	59%	...
1746	...	39%	40%–40%	63%	...	8%	20%	28%	17%	...	62%	70%	...
1745	...	43%	41%–42%	78%	19%	42%	17%	0	28%	...	...	84%	...
1744	...	47%	41%–47%	68%	...	25%	7%	0	...	...	32%	...	...
1743	...	39%	29%–31%	52%	26%	42%	13%	17%	...	...	41%	...	...
1742	35%	56%	47%–37%	56%	...	...	0	72%	28%	59%	...	74%	...
1741	...	58%	49%–59%	68%	...	...	13%	11%	...	...	100%	...	...
1740	21%	49%	53%–44%	56%	...	38%	13%	0	...	...	49%	...	...
1739	...	53%	40%–47%	61%	37%	...	37%	17%	16%	...	46%	55%	...
1738	...	48%	45%–41%	60%	...	46%	33%	0	42%	...	...	...	...
1737	32%	52%	42%–42%	46%	48%	...	23%	11%	...	...	...	...	...
1736	26%	33%	46%–41%	56%	...	...	13%	22%	...	70%	69%	66%	...
1735	32%	43%	44%–49%	60%	...	...	27%	28%	30%	...	50%	...	...
1734	37%–16%[a]	49%	48%–38%	80%	...	...	30%	17%	...	...	33%	...	...
1733	...	43%	45%–40%	47%	...	...	27%	17%	...	...	56%–11%[a]	50%	...

Percentage of New Members

Year	N.H.	Mass.	Conn.[a]	R.I.	N.Y.	N.J.	Penn.	Del.	Md.	Va.	N.C.	S.C.	Ga.
1732	41%	44%	49%–39%	47%	...	...	30%	50%	44%	...	...	...	...
1731	35%	38%	38%–51%	60%	...	...	33%	0	...	...	52%	42%	...
1730	6%	44%	51%–54%	56%	...	42%	37%	67%	...	...	...	49%	...
1729	...	40%	42%–39%	57%	...	...	35%	...	...	...	100%	34%–44%[a]	...
1728	13%	50%	52%–46%	70%	19%	...	19%	...	44%	...	...	69%–37%–44%[a]	...
1727	...	53%	56%–51%	54%	15%	64%	31%	...	...	55%	50%	...	...
1726	...	60%	37%–57%	37%–54%–50%[a]	46%	...	35%	...	...	...	...	...	...
1725	...	57%	51%–48%	58%–43%	...	...	31%	...	43%	...	68%	58%	...
1724	...	50%	50%–45%	69%–46%	...	...	19%	...	...	...	...	...	...
1723	...	67%	49%–54%	46%	...	...	62%	...	...	44%	60%	...	...
1722	...	53%	38%–47%	68%–42%	...	75%	31%	...	74%	...	63%	...	...
1721	...	61%	58%–51%	68%–48%	...	...	54%	...	...	...	...	56%	...
1720	...	62%	49%–51%	76%–78%	...	...	35%	...	...	38%	...	71%	...
1719	...	61%	55%–53%	62%	...	...	54%	...	...	52%	...	...	...
1718	...	60%	51%–45%	62%–100%–65%[a]	...	...	58%	...	...	35%	...	...	...
1717	...	55%	50%–46%	68%–76%	...	...	77%	...	...	...	...	54%	...
1716	...	58%	44%–47%	80%–74%	38%	79%	69%	...	46%	...	...	66%	...
1715	...	50%	50%–41%	76%–90%	26%	...	58%	...	54%	69%	86%	...	...
1714	...	...	42%–46%	79%–76%	...	...	46%	...	...	...	...	...	...
1713	...	...	56%–42%	75%	27%	...	65%	...	...	...	...	70%	...
1712	...	...	68%–58%	75%	...	...	69%	...	60%	29%	...	...	...
1711	...	...	54%–65%	82%	14%	...	58%	...	...	...	83%–86%[a]	67%	...
1710	...	...	69%–64%	92%	41%	54%	100%	...	...	71%	...	65%	...
1709	...	...	53%–66%	79%–80%[a]	46%	58%–63%	27%	...	...	...	82%	...	...
1708	...	...	45%–50%	72%–77%	14%	...	31%	...	57%–18%[a]	...	...	79%	...
1707	...	...	46%–45%	61%–62%–76%	...	65%	19%	...	...	...	...	70%–20%[a]	...
1706	...	...	...	85%–65%	...	...	81%	...	...	...	...	80%	...
1705	...	...	67%–52%	69%–75%–73%	23%	...	62%	...	...	53%	...	...	...
1704	...	...	47%–55%	70%–92%	...	...	62%	...	76%	...	...	...	...
1703	...	...	56%–53%	89%	...	...	...	...	...	...	58%	43%	...
1702	...	...	52%–39%	77%	72%	46%	...	...	...	...	...	70%	...
1701	...	...	55%–40%	73%	35%	...	...	...	46%	...	...	...	...
1700	...	...	60%–49%	46%	...	...	...	...	...	57%	...	47%	...
1699	...	...	64%–57%	67%	37%	...	...	...	...	39%	...	...	...
1698	...	...	44%–39%	...	69%	...	...	...	48%	48%	...	53%	...
1697	...	...	50%–55%	...	...	...	...	...	...	...	...	...	...
1696	...	...	65%–59%	...	...	...	...	...	...	44%	...	79%	...
1695	...	...	60%–38%	...	58%	...	...	...	...	57%	...	...	...
1694	...	...	48%–50%	...	37%	...	...	...	63%	...	...	85%	...
1693	...	...	58%–50%	...	49%	...	...	...	...	58%	...	...	...
1692	...	...	63%–38%	...	...	...	...	...	68%	80%	...	...	...
1691	...	...	32%–49%	75%–25%[a]	22%	...	...	...	...	45%	...	...	...
1690	...	...	56%–60%	82%	...	...	...	...	...	...	...	...	...
1689	...	...	46%	...	...	...	...	...	48%	...	...	...	...
1688	...	...	...	...	...	...	...	...	...	56%	...	...	...
1687	...	...	...	...	...	...	...	...	...	...	...	...	...
1686	...	...	...	...	...	...	...	...	86%	67%	...	...	...
1685	...	...	...	...	...	...	...	...	...	...	...	...	...
1684	...	...	...	...	...	...	...	...	...	60%	...	...	...
1683	...	...	...	...	...	...	...	...	...	...	...	...	...
1682	...	...	...	...	...	...	...	...	...	...	...	...	...
1681	...	...	...	...	...	...	...	...	...	...	...	...	...
1680	...	...	...	...	...	...	...	...	...	...	...	...	...
1679	...	...	...	...	...	...	...	...	...	...	50%	...	...

Note: Turnover is calculated by the formula:

$$\% \text{ replacements} = \frac{(\text{number new members}) - (\text{number new seats})}{(\text{number seats}) - (\text{number new seats})}$$

[a] Multiple elections in one year.

Sources: Data compiled by Jack P. Greene for "Legislative Turnover in British America, 1696–1775," *William and Mary Quarterly*, XXXVIII (1981), 442–461, but not printed in that source. Martin H. Quitt, *The Virginia House of Burgesses, 1660–1706: The Social, Educational, and Economic Bases of Political Power* (1989), 184.

only a few weeks' notice to the freeholders, who were informed by announcements posted at commonly frequented sites. An additional deterrent to widespread participation was that the county courthouse generally served as the only polling place; in practical terms, this fact meant that outlying voters had to travel long distances and that some would have to bear the expense of overnight lodging. These circumstances made it inevitable that numerous freeholders would be left uninformed of elections and that many more would be discouraged from voting by the personal inconvenience and minor expenses of traveling many miles at awkward times.

Voter turnout consequently remained low. It was extremely rare for more than half of all adult white males to cast ballots, although a few contests had participation rates from upward of 67% to 80%. The usual level of turnout ranged from 25% to 40% of adult white males.

The British government expected its mainland provinces to defend themselves under normal circumstances and garrisoned relatively few troops in the thirteen colonies until after the Seven Years' War commenced. These barracks were built at Trenton, New Jersey, as quarters for a regiment (about 600 troops) in 1759. Officers occupied the two-story house on the right, while enlisted personnel were crammed into the less-commodious bays forming a square horseshoe to the left. (Historic American Buildings Survey, courtesy Library of Congress)

Given that 25% to 40% of free males over twenty-one could not qualify as electors, such a level of turnout would indicate that, on average, from 40% to 53% of qualified voters went to the polls.

Colonial elections usually resulted in a large percentage of new assemblymen being seated. Delaware had the lowest average turnover rate, about 20%, while Rhode Island had the highest, with more than 60% of representatives being freshly chosen in a typical election. Elections in the colonies produced far more change than in Britain; turnover in the House of Commons alternated between 27% and 35%. During the eighteenth century, however, colonial elections became less volatile, and by the 1760s turnover in many provinces approximated that of the British House of Commons. As the colonial period ended, only in Rhode Island did elections routinely send a majority of newcomers to the assembly.

The reason for the high level of turnover in early America does not seem to have been a high level of partisan competition but rather a tendency for most representatives to retire voluntarily after two or three terms. In large part, legislators seem to have left public office after relatively short tenures because of the inconvenience to their private lives and because of financial affairs caused by attending legislative sessions. Early America was consequently a period in which politicians actually shouldered a public burden that offered little financial or personal award—save recognition for one's abilities—rather than pursue public office as a remunerative career.

CHAPTER 9 The Colonies

U.S. citizens customarily refer to their country as having originated from thirteen colonies, but a total of nineteen colonies had actually been founded within the boundaries of the United States as of its independence in 1776. New Sweden occupied the Delaware valley until its annexation in 1655 by New Netherland, which in turn was absorbed into England's empire in 1664. Plymouth, New Haven, East Jersey, and West Jersey were short-lived Anglo-American provinces that had all disappeared by 1702. This chapter furnishes summaries of the early histories of these provinces.

Connecticut

Connecticut's original pre-Columbian inhabitants included the Algonquian-speaking Western Niantic, Nipmuc, and Wappinger Indians. After 1500, these peoples came into conflict with a people they called Pequot (meaning "Destroyers"), who invaded their territory from the Hudson Valley. The Connecticut River gave the area its name, a Mohican word meaning "the long river."

European settlement began in 1633 when Dutch fur merchants from New Netherland placed a trading post at modern Hartford in June. English Puritans founded towns at Windsor and Wethersfield in September of that year. In 1637, Rev. Thomas Hooker brought his Puritan congregation from Cambridge, Massachusetts, to settle at Hartford, which the Dutch then abandoned.

Tensions with the Pequot escalated following the death of nine English mariners in early 1634. These tensions resulted in Massachusetts sending a punitive expedition to punish that tribe in August 1636; two Indian villages were burned. Connecticut militia joined with the Pequot's Indian enemies in a war that killed probably 40% of the 2,000 Pequot by autumn of 1637 (compared to less than fifty of the colony's 800 whites), established Puritan military superiority over New England's Indians for the next generation, and opened Connecticut to rapid colonization.

Hartford, Windsor, and Wethersfield agreed on January 24, 1639, to govern themselves by the Fundamental Orders of Connecticut. This frame of government established a legislature and court system. By 1662, fifteen other towns founded in the Connecticut valley had adopted the Fundamental Orders, which were never confirmed by a royal charter. Congregationalism received legal protection as the colony's established church, but church membership was not a condition for voters (who only had to meet a property requirement). The southwestern territory of modern Connecticut meanwhile organized itself as the colony of New Haven in 1643.

After the Stuart dynasty resumed the English throne in 1660, Charles II vested Connecticut with the right of self-government by a charter dated May 3, 1662. The charter also gave the new government jurisdiction over New Haven's towns, which were then annexed. Connecticut briefly lost its rights to self-government when it was placed under the authority of the autocratic Dominion of New England in 1687, but it resumed its charter privileges in 1689.

By 1700, Connecticut included 26,000 inhabitants, including 450 slaves. Connecticut received few immigrants during the eighteenth century, but a healthy climate and a high birthrate enabled the population to double approximately every thirty years. The ensuing growth placed great pressure on agricultural resources, and the land available for farming dropped from 404 acres per family about 1705, to 241 acres about 1735, and 131 acres about 1765. Because Connecticut failed to develop any large towns capable of absorbing the many young adults who found it difficult to afford their own farms as land became increasingly scarce in rural communities, Connecticut's population experienced a significant out-migration to neighboring New York after 1750. By 1760, the colony had 142,470 residents, of whom 97% were white, and ranked as the fifth most-populous colony (behind Virginia, Massachusetts, Pennsylvania, and Maryland).

Governors
1639—John Haynes
1640—Edward Hopkins
1642—George Wyllys
1643—John Haynes
1644—Edward Hopkins
1645—John Haynes
1646—Edward Hopkins
1647—John Haynes
1648—Edward Hopkins
1649—John Haynes
1650—Edward Hopkins
1651—John Haynes
1652—Edward Hopkins
1653—John Haynes
1654—Edward Hopkins
1655—Thomas Welles
1656—John Webster
1657—John Winthrop, Jr.
1658—Thomas Welles
1659—John Winthrop, Jr.
1676—William Leete
1683—Robert Treat
1687—Sir Edmund Andros
    absentee governor of the Dominion of New England at Boston
1689—Robert Treat
1698—Fitz John Winthrop
1707—Gurdon Saltonstall
1724—Joseph Talcott
1741—Jonathan Law
1750—Roger Walcott
1754—Thomas Fitch
1766—William Pitkin

Chief Justices
1711—Gurdon Saltonstall
1712—Nathan Gould
1713—William Pitkin
1714—Nathan Gould
1723—Peter Burr
1725—Jonathan Law
1741—Roger Wolcott
1750—Thomas Fitch
1754—William Pitkin
1766—Jonathan Trumbull

Speakers of the Lower House of Assembly
1699—John Chester
1700—Thomas Hart
1701—Peter Burr
1702—John Elliot
1706—Thomas Hart
1707—Samuel Eels

1709—John Elliot
1710—Joseph Talcott
1711—John Sherman
1713—Richard Bushnell
1714—John Hooker
1715—Richard Bushnell
1716—Jonathan Law
1717—Richard Bushnell
1717—James Wadsworth
1718—John Hooker
1719—Richard Bushnell
1721—Hezekiah Brainerd
1723—William Clark
1724—John Burr
1725—James Rogers
1727—Thomas Kimberley
1728—Roger Newton
1729—Thomas Kimberley
1730—Roger Newton
1732—William Pitkin
1733—Roger Newton
1736—Samuel Hill
1737—Ebenezer Silliman
1739—Jonathan Trumbull
1740—Elisha Williams
1742—Andrew Burr
1745—Samuel Hill
1747—Thomas Welles
1752—Jonathan Trumbull
1753—Elisha Williams
1754—Jonathan Trumbull
1755—Shubael Conant
1756—Joseph Fowler
1757—Shubael Conant
1760—Jabez Huntington
1764—Abraham Davenport

Delaware

In April 1631, the Dutch made the first European settlement in Delaware (near Lewes) at Swanendael, which was destroyed by the local Algonquian-speaking Indians a year later. In March 1638, the first Swedes landed near Lewes and claimed the area as part of New Sweden; they placed their capital at Ft. Christina (near Wilmington). They competed for control of the local fur trade with New Netherland, which annexed the colony (then about 350 persons) on September 26, 1655.

England acquired Delaware by its conquest of New Netherland in 1664. William Penn received Delaware in 1681 as part of his proprietary colony of Pennsylvania. Representatives from Delaware played a major role in blocking supporters of William Penn from controlling the Pennsylvania legislature, so in 1701 the proprietor allowed the region to become a self-governing entity with its own legislature, which first met on November 22, 1704. The governor of Pennsylvania officiated as chief executive of Delaware, which became properly known as the Three Lower Counties on the Delaware.

As an appendage of Pennsylvania, Delaware had no established church. Its southern counties attracted many former residents of the Chesapeake, who made the area a minor extension of the tobacco belt, while its northernmost county received a large share of the Scotch-Irish immigration that flowed through Philadelphia during the eighteenth century. The colony's primary economic activity was raising grain and livestock for overseas export. Because much of the soil in Delaware's two southern counties was poor, it remained thinly inhabited and consistently ranked as the smallest colony in population during the eighteenth century (excepting only Georgia, which was not settled until 1733). In 1760, it contained 33,205 residents, of whom 5% were slaves.

Governors

Pennsylvania's chief executive presided over this proprietary colony's government after the "Three Lower Counties on the Delaware" ceased to be represented in Pennsylvania's assembly.

Chief Justices

Pennsylvania's Superior Court heard cases from Delaware.

Speakers of the Lower House of Assembly
1704—William Rodney
1715—Jasper Yeates
1719—Joseph England
1721—John French
1729—Andrew Hamilton
1730—Henry Brooke
1733—Andrew Hamilton
1738—David French
1741—Thomas Noxon
1742—Jehu Curtis
1743—Ryves Holt
1753—Benjamin Chew
1758—Jacob Kollock
1760—John Dickinson
1761—Jacob Kollock
1766—John Vining

East Jersey

On July 4, 1664, in anticipation of New Netherland's conquest by an English amphibious task force, Charles II granted the territory between the Delaware River and Atlantic to two court favorites, John Lord Berkeley and Sir George Carteret. After Berkeley sold his proprietary rights in 1674, East Jersey passed to Carteret, whose heirs sold it for £3,400 on February 2, 1681, to twelve proprietors, who admitted twelve more partners by 1682. Most were Scots, and twenty of the twenty-four were Quakers, including William Penn. Control gradually passed to non-Quakers, who wished to profit by land speculation, establishing estates, and commerce.

When acquired by England in 1664, East Jersey's white population consisted of thirty-three adult men and their families residing opposite Manhattan Island at the Dutch outpost of Bergen. The colony immediately attracted an influx of English Puritans and Quakers from eastern Long Island and New England, who founded Elizabeth, Newark, Piscataway, Woodbridge, Middletown, and Shrewsbury by 1666. The Scottish proprietors stimulated immigration by their fellow country people and established Perth Amboy as their capital in 1683.

The English settlers repeatedly frustrated their Scottish overlords' attempts to collect quitrents and concentrate political power firmly in proprietary hands. The proprietors stirred widespread resentment by challenging the validity of the settlers' land titles, until widespread rioting convulsed the colony from 1698 to 1701 and left constituted authority in a shambles. The proprietors surrendered political control of East Jersey to the crown on April 15, 1702, but they retained all rights to unpatented lands for themselves and influenced the English government to adopt policies that enhanced their own political power under the new royal government.

East Jersey's proprietary government began to exercise local authority with the arrival of Gov. Philip Carteret at Elizabeth in the summer of 1665, as portrayed here by Howard Pyle. (Courtesy Library of Congress)

Proprietors

Sir George Carteret's heirs conveyed East Jersey on February 2, 1681, to twelve proprietors. The twelve proprietors took on an equal number of partners in 1682 (finalized on March 14, 1683) and divided ownership into 24 equal shares.

The Twelve Proprietors

1. William Penn
   gentleman of Worminghurst, Sussex
2. Robert West
   lawyer of Middle Temple
3. Thomas Rudyard
   lawyer of London
4. Samuel Groom
   lawyer of Stepney, Middlesex
5. Thomas Hart
   merchant of Enfield, Middlesex
6. Richard Mew
   baker and merchant of Stepney, Middlesex
7. Thomas Wilcox
   goldsmith of London
8. Ambrose Rigge
   gentleman of Gratton Place, Surrey
9. John Heywood
   upholsterer of London
10. Hugh Hartshorne
    upholsterer of London
11. Clement Plumstead
    draper of London
12. Thomas Cooper
    merchant-tailor of London

The Twenty-four Proprietors

1. William Penn
2. Robert Barclay
   of Scotland
3. Robert West
4. Edward Byllinge
   gentleman and brewer of London
5. Thomas Rudyard
6. Robert Turner
   draper-merchant of Dublin
7. Samuel Groom
8. James Brain
   merchant of London
9. Thomas Hart
10. Arent Sonmans
    merchant of Wallingford, Scotland
11. Richard Mew
12. William Gibson
    haberdasher of London
13. Gawen Lawrie
    merchant of London
14. David Barclay
    of Scotland
15. Ambrose Rigge
16. Thomas Barker
    merchant of London
17. John Heywood
18. Thomas Warne
    merchant of Dublin
19. Hugh Hartshorne
20. James Drummond
    Earl of Perth
21. Clement Plumstead
22. Robert Gordon
    merchant of Cluny, Scotland
23. Thomas Cooper
24. John Drummond
    of Lundin, Viscount Melfort

Governors

1665—Philip Carteret
1682—Robert Barclay
   absentee governor to 1690
1682—Thomas Rudyard
   Deputy Governor
1683—Gawen Lawrie
   Deputy Governor
1686—Lord Neil Campbell
   Deputy Governor

1687—Andrew Hamilton
  Deputy Governor
1690—John Tatham
1691—Joseph Dudley
  (from 1692 to 1702 East and West Jersey shared the same governor)
1692—Andrew Hamilton of East Jersey
1698—Jeremiah Basse of West Jersey
1699—Andrew Hamilton of East Jersey

Speakers of the Lower House of Assembly
1680—John Bowne
1685—Richard Hartshorne
1693—William Lawrence
1694—John Harriman
1695—Richard Hartshorne
1698—Samuel Dennis
1699—John Harriman

Georgia

Georgia originated as a colonization project aimed at securing South Carolina's frontier against Spanish Florida, giving employment to imprisoned debtors and poor families in England, providing Britain's garment industry with silk—for which there was a great demand—and offering a refuge for various groups of Protestants who suffered religious persecution on the European continent. On June 20, 1732, George II issued a charter to twenty trustees, who were responsible for overseeing the colony for twenty-one years. On February 12, 1733, James Oglethorpe formally began settlement by founding Savannah.

The colony languished under the trustees' supervision because their policies often retarded development. By placing a cap on the amount of land an individual could acquire and forbidding the introduction of slavery, the trustees deterred Anglo-Americans in nearby southern colonies from relocating their plantations to Georgia. Their requirement that all Georgians plant orchards for silk cultivation was likewise impractical because the local variety of mulberry leaves was unsuitable for worms to produce silk. Only when these policies were abandoned in the 1740s did the province begin to expand.

Georgia was a major battleground in the War of Jenkins' Ear. After Governor Oglethorpe's settlers invaded Florida and besieged St. Augustine in 1740, the Spaniards determined to exterminate the colony. Spanish troops invaded Georgia in 1742, but Oglethorpe's troops (outnumbered by two to one) repulsed them at the Battle of Bloody Swamp on St. Simon's Island. Georgia forces again attacked St. Augustine unsuccessfully in 1743, after which fighting lapsed into small-scale raids through 1748.

The crown ended Georgia's charter status and made it a royal colony on July 4, 1752. After the legalization of slavery in 1750, Georgia became a major center of rice production and it grew significantly by attracting large numbers of new arrivals from the Carolinas. Its population almost doubled during the 1750s, from 5,200 (81% white) to 9,578 (63% white), but it still ranked as the smallest colony in 1760.

Governors
1732—James E. Oglethorpe
1743—William Stephens
  Acting Governor
1751—Henry Parker
  Acting Governor
1754—John Reynolds
1757—Henry Ellis
1760—James Wright

1771—James Habersham
  President of Council

Speakers of the Lower House of Assembly
1755—David Douglas
1757—William Little
1757—David Montaight
1760—Grey Elliott
1761—Lewis Johnson
1764—Alexander Wylly

Maryland

Maryland's original inhabitants included both Algonquian speakers—such as the Piscataway, Conoy, Nanticoke, and Delaware (Lenni Lenape)—and Iroquoian stocks—such as the Erie and Susquehanna. In 1631, the first English settlement was made on Kent Island by William Claiborne and 100 former residents of Virginia. On June 30, 1632, James I granted Maryland as a proprietary colony to the second Lord Baltimore, Cecilius Calvert, as a refuge for English Catholics.

On March 25, 1634, Gov. Leonard Calvert landed with 200 colonists, who later founded St. Mary's. The Calverts intended that the colony's basic social institution be the manor, from which Catholic landlords could hold their own baronial courts, have political privileges, and support private chaplains who would function as the manors' de facto parish priests. The Calverts nevertheless experienced much difficulty in recruiting immigrants among their fellow Catholics (who then equaled barely 2% of the English people), and Protestants formed a high percentage of Maryland's inhabitants from the very beginning.

After being arrested in 1644 for voicing support for Parliament in the English Civil War, Capt. Richard Ingle led a revolt against Gov. Leonard Calvert, whose loyalty lay with the king. Ingle captured St. Mary's in 1645, drove Calvert into Virginia, and looted Calvert's backers. Until Calvert regained control with aid from Virginia officials in 1647, the population fell by perhaps 50% to less than 300. To appease the Protestant majority, Maryland guaranteed freedom of worship to all Christians by the Toleration Act of 1649. Protestants nevertheless overthrew the proprietary government again in 1654, and then defeated an attempt to oust themselves at the battle of the Severn River the next year. Parliament restored the colony to Lord Baltimore in 1656. Discontent with the Calverts' rule flared up in short-lived uprisings in 1676 and 1681 and later overthrew proprietary authority in Coode's Revolt of 1689. The crown governed Maryland as a proprietary colony from 1691 to 1715 when it restored the government to the fourth Lord Baltimore, who was an Anglican.

Tobacco was the main agricultural staple. Indentured servants initially formed the bulk of the labor force, but after Maryland passed the first Anglo-American statute defining slavery in 1661, African bondsmen gradually replaced white servants as the main source of unfree labor. The population grew from 8,400 (91% white) in 1660 to 29,600 (89% white) in 1700. The colony's only Indian hostilities were a brief spate of raids by Susquehanna Indians in 1675 and attacks by France's Indian allies in the Seven Years' War.

After the treaty of Lancaster with the Iroquois in 1744, settlement expanded into the Piedmont beyond Baltimore, where grains were the predominant crop. A long-standing boundary dispute with Pennsylvania was resolved in the five years after 1763, when the Mason-Dixon Line was surveyed to the Monongahela River. By 1760, Maryland had 162,300 inhabitants (70% white) and ranked as the fourth-largest colony.

Cary Carson's painting of St. Mary's depicts how Maryland's first capital probably appeared for the first several years after it was founded. (Courtesy St. Mary's City Commission)

Proprietors

Barons of Baltimore and Lords Proprietary

George Calvert (1579–1632) created first Lord Baltimore in February 1625 and petitioned the king for a proprietary grant.

Cecelius Calvert (1605–75) second Lord Baltimore and Lord Proprietor of Maryland.

Charles Calvert (1637–1715) third Lord Baltimore

Benedict Leonard Calvert (1679–1715) fourth Lord Baltimore

Charles Calvert (1699–1751) fifth Lord Baltimore

Frederick Calvert (1732–71) sixth Lord Baltimore

Henry Harford (1759–1834) was bequeathed the Maryland proprietorship in Frederick Calvert's will but could not take the title when the sixth Lord Baltimore died on September 4, 1771, because he was an illegitimate son. Harford renounced his Maryland claims in return for a monetary grant from Parliament after the Revolution.

Governors

During 1652 and 1654–57, Parliamentary Commissioners acted collectively as Maryland's executive authority.

1634—Leonard Calvert
1643—Giles Brent
    Acting Governor
1644—Leonard Calvert

1645—Richard Ingle
1646—Edward Hill
1646—Leonard Calvert
1647—Thomas Greene
1649—William Stone
1649—Thomas Greene (acting)
1650—Thomas Hatton (acting)
1652—William Stone
1657—Josias Fendall
1657—Luke Barber (acting)
1660—Philip Calvert
1661—Charles Calvert
1676—Jesse Wharton
1676—Thomas Notley
1679—Charles Calvert
1684—Benedict Calvert
    absentee governor, power delegated to a council of seven deputies
1688—William Joseph
    President of Council
1689—John Coode
1690—Nehemiah Blakiston
1692—Sir Lionel Copley
1693—Sir Thomas Lawrence
1693—Sir Edmund Andros
1693—Nicholas Greenberry
    President of Council

1694—Sir Edmund Andros
1694—Sir Thomas Lawrence
    President of Council
1694—Sir Francis Nicholson
1698—Nathaniel Blakiston
1702—Thomas Tench
    President of Council
1704—John Seymour
1709—Edward Lloyd
    President of Council
1714—John Hart
1720—Thomas Brooke
    President of Council
1720—Charles Calvert
1727—Benedict Leonard Calvert
1731—Samuel Ogle
1732—Charles Calvert, Proprietor
1733—Samuel Ogle
1742—Thomas Bladen
1747—Samuel Ogle
1752—Benjamin Tasker
1753—Horatio Sharpe
1769—Robert Eden

Speakers of the Lower House of Assembly

1650—James Coxe
1654—Richard Preston
1657—Richard Ewen
1661—Richard Preston
1663—Robert Slye
1666—Thomas Notley
1669—Thomas Manning
1671—Thomas Taylor
1671—Thomas Notley
1677—Philemon Lloyd
1692—Kenelm Cheseldyne
1694—Robert Smith
1698—Thomas Smithson
1704—William Dent
1704—Thomas Smith
1708—Thomas Smithson
1708—Robert Bradley
1712—Robert Ungle
1716—Mathew Tilghman Ward
1719—Robert Ungle
1727—John Mackall
1735—Daniel Dulany
1736—James Harris
1738—John Mackall
1740—Philip Hammond
1742—Edward Sprigg
1749—Philip Hammond
1754—Henry Hooper
1757—Alexander Williamson
1757—Henry Hooper
1765—Robert Lloyd

Massachusetts Bay

Massachusetts Bay's original pre-Columbian inhabitants included the Algonquian-speaking Mahican, Nipmuc, Pennacook, Pocumtuck, and Massachuset, who gave their name to the colony. In 1616, European sailors transmitted an unknown but deadly plague that killed perhaps every third Indian north of Narragansett Bay. This disaster depopulated most of the Massachusetts coast and created a vacuum that could be rapidly filled by English settlers, beginning with the founding of Plymouth colony in 1620.

On March 14, 1629, Charles I granted the Massachusetts Bay Company all land between the Charles and Merrimack Rivers as a charter colony. A large migration of Puritans began in June 1630 when Gov. John Winthrop landed with 700 colonists at Salem (settled the year before by an advance party), but soon after the population became concentrated around Boston. Immigration to Massachusetts Bay proceeded rapidly during the 1630s (although many newcomers quickly "hived out" to settle in neighboring colonies), but it virtually ceased with the outbreak of England's Civil War in 1645 and never resumed to any significant degree during the colonial era. The colony protected Congregationalism as its established church and required voters to have been formally admitted by their parishes. The colony had 14,300 residents by 1650. It escaped serious Indian hostilities until 1675 when it was engulfed by King Philip's War, in which half of its towns were attacked.

Massachusetts Bay chartered Harvard College in 1636, established North America's earliest printing press in 1639, and became the first civil society anywhere in the world to mandate compulsory primary education in 1647 through its Old Deluder Act. Most families operated farms, but thin soil and a short growing season severely curtailed agriculture's profitability. The economy early on diversified by creating a large fishing fleet. Massachusetts emerged as the mainstay of the American merchant marine by the 1690s, and Boston remained the colonies' largest city until it was surpassed by Philadelphia in the 1750s.

Massachusetts annexed the settlements in Maine on May 31, 1652, and organized them as York County. It extended its jurisdiction over New Hampshire's towns in the 1640s, but English authorities detached New Hampshire as a separate royal colony in 1680. On June 21, 1684, England's Chancery Court transformed Massachusetts Bay into a royal colony by voiding its 1629 charter. Congregationalism retained its established status, but voting thereafter depended on meeting a property requirement and not church membership. In May 1686, Charles II placed the colony under the administration of the Dominion of New England, which was overthrown (in the name of William III) by a bloodless uprising at Boston in April 1689. On October 17, 1691, William III issued Massachusetts Bay a new, liberal charter as a royal colony and annexed Plymouth to it.

In 1700, Massachusetts was the second-largest colony, with 56,000 people, of whom almost 99% were English or Welsh in background. It provided the largest number of colonial troops furnished in the French and Indian Wars from the 1690s to 1763. During the eighteenth century, overseas commerce and fishing established themselves as the economy's most dynamic components, while agriculture declined to the point where the colony had to import approximately a tenth of the foodstuffs needed to feed its population by the early 1760s. In 1760, it still ranked as the second-largest colony (behind Virginia), with approximately a quarter million inhabitants, of whom 98% were white and a tenth lived in Maine.

Governors

1629—John Endecott
1630—John Winthrop
1634—Thomas Dudley
1635—John Haynes
1636—Sir Henry Vane
1637—John Winthrop
1640—Thomas Dudley
1641—Richard Bellingham
1642—John Winthrop
1644—John Endecott
1645—Thomas Dudley
1646—John Winthrop

1649—John Endecott
1650—Thomas Dudley
1651—John Endecott
1654—Richard Bellingham
1655—John Endecott
1665—Richard Bellingham
1672—John Leverett
1679—Simon Bradstreet
1686—Joseph Dudley
1687—Sir Edmund Andros
1689—Simon Bradstreet
1691—Sir William Phips
1694—William Stoughton
    Lieutenant Governor
1699—Richard Coote, Earl of Bellomont
1700—William Stoughton
    Lieutenant Governor
1701—The Council
1702—Joseph Dudley
1715—William Tailer
    Lieutenant Governor
1716—Samuel Shute
1722—William Dummer
    Lieutenant Governor
1727—William Burnet
1729—William Dummer
    Lieutenant Governor
1730—Jonathan Belcher
1741—William Shirley
1757—Thomas Pownall
1760—Thomas Hutchinson
    Lieutenant Governor
1760—Sir Francis Bernard
1769—Thomas Hutchinson

Chief Justices

1692—William Stoughton
1701—Waitstill Winthrop
1702—Isaac Addington
1708—Waitstill Winthrop
1718—Samuel Sewall
1729—Benjamin Lynde
1745—Paul Dudley
1753—Stephen Sewall
1761—Thomas Hutchinson
1769—Benjamin Lynde

Speakers of the Lower House of Assembly

1644—William Hawthorne
1645—George Cook
1646—William Hawthorne
1646—Robert Bridges
1647—Joseph Hill
1647—Richard Russell
1648—William Hawthorne
1648—Richard Russell
1649—Daniel Denison
1650—William Hawthorne
1651—Daniel Gookin
1651—Daniel Denison
1653—Humphrey Atherton
1654—Richard Russell
1655—Edward Johnson
1656—Richard Russell
1657—William Hawthorne

1658—Richard Russell
1659—Thomas Savage
1661—William Hawthorne
1662—Thomas Clarke
1663—John Leverett
1665—Thomas Clarke
1666—Richard Waldron
1669—Thomas Clarke
1671—Thomas Savage
1672—Thomas Clarke
1673—Richard Waldron
1674—Josh. Hubbard
1674—Richard Waldron
1676—Peter Bulkley
1677—Thomas Savage
1679—Richard Waldron
1680—John Richards
1680—Daniel Fisher
1683—Elisha Cooke
1684—John Wayt
1685—Isaac Addington
1686—John Saffin
1692—William Bond
1694—Nehemiah Jewett
1695—William Bond
1696—Penn Townsend
1698—Nathaniel Byfield
1699—James Converse
1700—John Leverett
1701—Nehemiah Jewett
1702—James Converse
1705—Thomas Oakes
1707—John Burrill
1708—Thomas Oliver
1709—John Clark
1711—John Burrill
1720—Elisha Cooke
1720—Timothy Lindall
1721—John Clarke
1724—William Dudley
1729—John Quincy
1739—Paul Dudley
1740—John Quincy
1741—William Fairfield
1741—John Hobson
1742—Thomas Cushing
1746—Thomas Hutchinson
1749—Joseph Dwight
1750—Thomas Hubbard
1760—James Otis
1763—Timothy Ruggles

New Hampshire

New Hampshire's original pre-Columbian inhabitants included the Algonquian-speaking Abnaki and Pennacook, whose numbers were greatly thinned by a massive but unknown epidemic transmitted by European sailors in 1616. Because this plague depopulated much of the New Hampshire coast, English settlement proceeded with minimal Indian opposition. David Thompson founded the first European community at Rye on the Piscataqua River estuary in spring of 1623. Four towns had been established at Portsmouth, Exeter, Dover, and Hampton by 1638, but they remained ununited by any central authority until Massachusetts annexed the territory in that year. By 1650,

New Hampshire contained 1,300 residents. On September 18, 1680, English authorities detatched it from Massachusetts Bay as a separate royal colony. The colony created a de facto established church by authorizing Congregational parishes to collect tithes, but church-state links were otherwise weak.

Approximately 5,000 whites lived in New Hampshire by 1700. Lumbering was its most important economic activity. Its frontier sustained major damage in King Philip's War, and it suffered even greater losses in King William's War, when one of every eight residents was either killed or captured. New Hampshire also endured a steady succession of raiding parties in the later French and Indian Wars, but their impact was far less disruptive. The population rose to 23,000 by 1740. In 1760, New Hampshire had 39,100 residents, of whom 99% were white, and ranked as the third smallest colony, ahead of Delaware and Georgia.

Governors

From 1680 to 1741, the governorship of Massachusetts and New Hampshire were consolidated. New Hampshire's lieutenant governor or chief councillor often acted as the province's chief magistrate.

1680—John Cutt
President of Council
1681—Richard Waldron
President of Council
1682—Edward Cranfield
Lieutenant Governor
1685—Walter Barefotte
Deputy Governor
1686—Gov. Joseph Dudley
1687—Gov. Sir Edmund Andros
1689—Gov. Simon Bradstreet
1692—John Usher
Lieutenant Governor
1697—William Partridge
Lieutenant Governor
1698—Samuel Allen
1699—William Partridge
Lieutenant Governor
1702—John Usher
Lieutenant Governor
1715—George Vaughan
Lieutenant Governor
1717—John Wentworth
Lieutenant Governor
1731—Daniel Dunbar
Lieutenant Governor
1741—Benning Wentworth
1767—John Wentworth

Chief Justices

New Hampshire's governor and council reserved the right to sit as a final court of appeal on civil and criminal matters.

Speakers of the Lower House of Assembly

1692—Richard Martin
1693—John Gilman
1693—John Pickering
1694—George Jaffrey
1696—John Plaisted
1697—John Pickering
1698—Henry Dow
1698—John Pickering
1699—Samuel Penhallow
1702—John Pickering

1703—Daniel Tilton
1703—John Pickering
1709—Mark Hunking
1710—Richard Gerrish
1717—John Plaisted
1717—Thomas Packer
1719—Joshua Peirce
1722—Peter Weare
1727—Nathaniel Weare
1728—Andrew Wiggin
1745—Nathaniel Rogers
1745—Ebenezer Stevens
1749—Richard Waldron
1752—Meshech Weare
1755—Henry Sherburne
1766—Peter Gilman

New Haven

The colony of New Haven emerged in the wake of Connecticut's victory in the Pequot War, which opened up southwestern New England to English settlement. The colony primarily owed its existence to Rev. John Davenport who led a large number of Puritans from St. Stephen's Parish in London to the Quinnipiac River, where they founded a "New Haven" for orthodox Calvinists in the summer of 1637. On November 6, 1643, the four towns of New Haven, Stamford, Guilford, and Milford formed the territory lying between New Netherland and Connecticut into a legislative government to which each could send two representatives. New Haven grew to include the neighboring communities of Branford, Fairfield, Greenwich, and Medford in later years, plus Southold on Long Island.

Davenport influenced New Haven to establish a commonwealth where power lay firmly in the saints' hands and the Congregational Church was legally established. The colony was not a theocracy because clergy could not hold public office, but unlike Connecticut, it limited voting to males who were full-fledged church members. The Mosaic Law, rather than English Common Law, served as the chief underpinning for its criminal code. Davenport inspired the citizens to rely on Biblical jurisprudence to such an extent that juries were dispensed with because Hebrew courts had never used them.

New Haven never acquired a royal charter to legitimate its existence. After the restoration of the Stuart monarchy to England in 1660, the colony entered no petition for the crown to recognize its legality. Connecticut, however, secured a royal patent that annexed the New Haven communities to itself on May 3, 1662. When the Hartford government demanded that New Haven's towns accept its jurisdiction, all but three towns did so by the end of 1662. Branford, Milford, and New Haven continued to resist the Hartford government's authority until January 7, 1665, when the colony finally became defunct. New Haven's legacy endured in one respect, however, for Connecticut's legislature followed the custom of convening alternately at Hartford and New Haven until 1873.

Governors

1639—Theophilus Eaton
1658—Francis Newman
1660—William Leete

New Jersey

In the spring of 1643, the first European settlement was made at Ft. Nye Elfborg on the Delaware River as a trading outpost of New Sweden. The Dutch established communities opposite Manhattan

Island as early as 1641, but Indian opposition prevented continuous occupation by Dutch farmers until the late 1650s. New Jersey's history as an English possession began in September 1664 when an Anglo-American amphibious expedition conquered the territory as part of New Netherland. Available for settlement were almost 8,000 square miles of virtually uninhabited wilderness. The Indian population seems not to have exceeded 6,000 Delaware (Lenni Lenape) and may have been no more than 2,400. A handful of Swedes lived along the lower Delaware River, and the largest European community contained only thirty-three adult Dutch men and their families at Bergen, opposite Manhattan.

English settlement began with the purchase of the Elizabeth area by settlers from eastern Long Island in October 1664. Charles II gave New Jersey (officially Nova Caesaria, after an island in the English Channel) to John Lord Berkeley and Sir George Carteret, two court favorites, as a proprietary colony, which was later divided into East and West Jersey. Disputed land titles and widespread opposition to the proprietors, who were badly divided among themselves, led to the consolidation of East and West Jersey into the royal colony of New Jersey on April 26, 1702.

New Jersey's population stood at approximately 14,000 in 1702. It attracted large numbers of new settlers from New York and New England, plus a steady flow of immigrants from the British Isles and Germany. The inhabitants supported themselves mainly by sending grain, livestock, and cut lumber for the West Indies and other external markets. Slaves became an important element of the colony's labor structure, and they equaled about 7% of the inhabitants by 1750. The province's leading urban centers were Burlington and Perth Amboy, which alternated as meeting sites for the legislature, but they never grew beyond minor centers for conducting the intercoastal trade, each inhabited by only a few hundred people. The colony experienced no violence with Indians while under English administration until the 1750s when French-allied warriors raided the northwest frontier during the Seven Years' War. By 1760, New Jersey's population had increased more than sixfold since 1700, and it ranked as the ninth among the thirteen colonies with 93,800 inhabitants.

Governors

1703—Edward Hyde,
   Viscount Cornbury
1708—John Lovelace
1709—Richard Ingoldesby
   Lieutenant Governor
1710—Robert Hunter
1720—William Burnet
1728—John Montgomerie
1731—Lewis Morris
   President of Council
1732—William Cosby
1736—John Anderson
   President of Council
1736—John Hamilton
   President of Council
1738—Lewis Morris
1746—John Hamilton
   President of Council
1746—John Reading
   President of Council
1747—Jonathan Belcher
1757—John Reading
   President of Council
1758—Sir Francis Bernard
1760—Thomas Boone

1761—Josiah Hardy
1763—William Franklin

Chief Justices

1704—Roger Mompesson
1709—Thomas Gordon
1709—Roger Mompesson
1711—David Jameson
1723—William Trent
1724—Robert Lettice Hooper
1727—Thomas Farmar
1729—Robert Lettice Hooper
1739—Robert Hunter Morris
1757—William Aynsley
1759—Nathaniel Jones (never
   took office)
1761—Robert Hunter Morris
1764—Charles Reade (acting)
1764—Frederick Smyth

Speakers of the Lower House of Assembly

1703—Thomas Gardiner
1704—Peter Fretwell
1707—Samuel Jennings
1708—Thomas Gordon
1709—John Kay
1716—Daniel Coxe (expelled)
1716—John Kinsey
1722—John Johnstone
1723—William Trent
1725—John Johnstone
1730—John Kinsey, Jr.
1738—Joseph Bonnell
1740—Andrew Johnstone
1744—Samuel Nevill
1746—Robert Lawrence
1747—Samuel Nevill
1751—Charles Read
1754—Robert Lawrence
1759—Samuel Nevill
1763—Robert Ogden

New Netherland

Dutch merchants had sponsored explorations of the Mid-Atlantic region, such as Henry Hudson's voyage that located Hudson River, and had built a temporary trading post opposite modern Albany in 1614. The first permanent settlement was not made until summer 1624 when the Dutch West India Company built outposts at New York Bay, Albany, and on the Delaware River (Ft. Nassau) near modern Gloucester, New Jersey. On May 4, 1626, Peter Minuit founded New Amsterdam on Manhattan Island.

The company claimed modern Delaware, Pennsylvania, New Jersey, and all land west of the Connecticut River. Because it lacked the resources to exploit this vast territory, New Sweden's settlers trespassed on Dutch claims in the Delaware valley and English Puritans eventually pressured the company to abandon a stockade it used as an Indian trading post at modern Hartford, Connecticut. The English established a firm hold on Connecticut, but Peter Stuyvesant led an expedition that forcibly brought New Sweden under Dutch control in 1655.

The fur trade was New Netherland's economic mainstay, but the West India Company also tried to develop the colony as a supplier of foodstuffs for Dutch outposts in the Caribbean. On June 7, 1629, the company offered to compensate anyone transporting fifty adult immi-

The first major impetus to settling present-day New York came after Henry Hudson discovered the river that bears his name and determined that it allowed oceangoing vessels to travel far into the continent's interior. (Courtesy Library of Congress)

grants with an estate fronting 16 miles along a navigable river. These patroons (grantees) would be free from taxes for eight years and possess authority to preside over private courts on their estates. Of the three patroonships settled—Swaanendael in Delaware, Pavonia in New Jersey, and Rensselaerwyck near Albany—only the last was not abandoned and survived to be part of New York's later system of landed manors.

Relations between the Dutch and the neighboring Algonquian tribes were exceptionally bad. In Kiefft's War of 1643–44, Indians devastated nearly all the outlying settlements beyond New Amsterdam before assistance from the English Puritan towns on eastern Long Island enabled the Dutch to prevail. In the Peach War of 1655, 500 warriors looted New Amsterdam and then destroyed all settlements on Staten Island and New Jersey. The intermittent Esopus Wars disrupted life in the lower Hudson valley from 1659 to 1664.

The Dutch West India Company experienced such difficulty in attracting settlers to the colony that it was forced to recruit labor from a wide variety of nationalities. Barely half of all immigrants to New Netherland were Dutch, while a quarter were German, a seventh were either Walloons (from modern Belgium) or French Huguenots, one in fourteen were Scandanavians, and many of the rest were English. The population grew slowly and by 1660 probably numbered just 5,500, of whom 600 lived along the Delaware.

In 1664, England inaugurated the Second Anglo-Dutch War to conquer New Netherland. In September, Peter Stuyvesant surrendered New Amsterdam without resistance to a task force of four frigates, 300 redcoats, and 2,000 Yankee militia. English forces peacefully occupied Fort Orange (Albany) on September 20, and they took Ft. Casimir, Delaware, by storm on October 10. The Dutch residents received generous terms of surrender, including freedom of religion and confirmation of their property rights, and few exercised their option of leaving when the colony became the province of New York.

Governors

In New Netherland, the chief executive was the director.

1623—Adriaen Joris
1624—Cornelis Jacobsen May
1625—William Verhulst
1626—Peter Minuit
1633—Wouter van Twiller
1638—William Kieft
1647—Peter Stuyvesant

New Sweden

In 1637, Willem Usselinx and Peter Minuit, two businessmen previously engaged in the Dutch West India Company's New Netherland colony, played a leading role in convincing the Swedish monarch to grant a charter authorizing the New Sweden (or New South) Company—which had been initially organized in 1633—to establish a colony in the Delaware River valley for conducting the fur trade and producing valuable commodities like tobacco. Minuit landed with the earliest settlers near Lewes, Delaware, in March 1638 and then built Ft. Christina near modern Wilmington. Many of the early immigrants were actually Finns, and the Lutheran church was the established church.

New Sweden languished without strong leadership after Minuit died at sea in June 1638. By 1642, it had established Ft. Nye Elfborg as a trading post in southern New Jersey. Geographic expansion accelerated after 1643 with the arrival of Johan Björnsson Printz, a governor who was surprisingly energetic despite being seriously overweight (he tipped the scales at more than 400 pounds and was nicknamed "Big Tub" by the Indians). Printz placed Pennsylvania's first permanent European community at Tinicum, 9 miles south of the Schuykill River, in 1643, and in 1647 he constructed Fort New Krisholm near the Schuykill's mouth.

New Sweden maintained amicable relations with local Indians but not with the rival Dutch. Because New Netherland claimed the Delaware valley, the Dutch countered Printz's actions by placing Ft. Beversrede at the site of modern Philadelphia in 1648 and constructing Ft. Casimir at modern Newcastle in 1651. The Swedes twice burned Ft. Beversrede, and Printz's successor, Johan Classon Rising, captured Ft. Casimir in 1654. New Sweden's existence came to an end on September 26, 1655, when Gov. Peter Stuyvesant completed a military conquest of the colony and annexed the territory (then holding 350 inhabitants) to New Netherland.

Governors

1638—Peter Minuit
1640—Jost van Bogardt
   Acting Governor
1640—Peter Hollander
1643—Johan Printz
1653—John Papegoga
   Acting Governor
1653—Johan Rising

New York

New York's pre-Columbian inhabitants included the Five Nations of the Iroquois (Cayuga, Mohawk, Oneida, Onondaga, and Seneca), Mahicans, and many small nations of Algonquian-speaking Indians in the lower Hudson valley. Giovanni da Verrazano became the first recorded European to see New York Harbor in 1524; Henry Hudson discovered the river bearing his name in 1609; the Dutch made the earliest European settlement at Albany in 1614; and the West India Company later colonized the area as New Netherland. The fur trade immediately emerged as the central economic activity with Albany as its hub and created close ties between the Dutch and the Iroquois, who collectively competed for control of this commerce with the French and their Algonquian allies.

On March 12, 1664, Charles II gave his brother James, duke of York, title to New York as its proprietor. Colonel Richard Nicolls ended Dutch authority on September 7, 1664, by accepting the surrender of New Amsterdam. Without a shot being fired, England had acquired a territory containing about 5,000 inhabitants and the best water-borne route for exploiting the fur trade to be found within Anglo-America. The Netherlands reoccupied the colony during the Third Anglo-Dutch War in 1673 but returned possession to England in 1674. When the duke of York was proclaimed James II on February 6, 1685, New York became a royal colony. New York was annexed to the Dominion of New England in 1688, but it was released from external rule by a bloodless coup called Leisler's Rebellion in 1689.

New York first became a major theater of military operations when King William's War erupted in 1689. The destruction of Schenectady during that conflict in 1690 ranks as the greatest loss of life in any massacre during the intercolonial wars. New York remained a major battleground during all of the French and Indian Wars that continued from then until 1763.

New York contained 19,000 colonists in 1700. Foodstuffs produced in the fertile Hudson valley gradually replaced furs as the most valuable export. Population grew slowly because Indian resistance blocked settlement in most of the colony's interior, and the monopolization of large tracts on the lower Hudson River by a small landlord class prevented much of the best land from being occupied unless a family was resigned to renting a farm all their life. New Yorkers incorporated slavery into their economy to a greater degree than any other northern colonists did, and slaves composed nearly a seventh of the population by the mid-eighteenth century. By 1760, New York remained a modest-size province of 117,000 inhabitants that ranked sixth among the thirteen colonies in size (with New York City standing just third among urban areas).

Governors

1664—Col. Richard Nicolls
1667—Francis Lovelace
1673—Anthony Colve
    Director-General during the Dutch reconquest to 1674
1674—Edmund Andros
1682—Thomas Dongan
1687—Sir Edmund Andros
    absentee governor of the Dominion of New England at Boston
1687—Col. Francis Nicholson
    Lieutenant Governor
1689—Jacob Leisler
1691—Henry Sloughter
1692—Richard Ingoldesby
    Acting Governor
1692—Benjamin Fletcher
1698—Richard Coote,
    Earl of Bellomont

1701—John Nanfan
    Lieutenant Governor
1702—Edward Hyde,
    Viscount Cornbury
1708—John Lovelace
1709—Peter Schuyler
    President of Council
1709—Gerardus Beekman
    President of Council
1710—Richard Ingoldesby
    Lieutenant Governor
1710—Robert Hunter
1719—Peter Schuyler
    President of Council
1720—William Burnet
1728—John Montgomerie
1731—Rip Van Dam
    President of Council
1732—William Cosby
1736—George Clarke
    Lieutenant Governor
1737—Lord De La Warr
    resigned governorship before exercising any authority of office
1743—George Clinton
1753—Sir Danvers Osborne
1753—James DeLancey
    Lieutenant Governor
1755—Sir Charles Hardy
1757—James DeLancey
    Lieutenant Governor
1760—Cadwallader Colden
    Lieutenant Governor
1761—Gen. Robert Monckton
1761—Cadwallader Colden
    Lieutenant Governor
1762—Gen. Robert Monckton
1763—Cadwallader Colden
    Lieutenant Governor

Chief Justices

1691—Joseph Dudley
1692—William Smith
1700—Stephen Van Cortlandt
1701—Abraham De Peyster
1701—William Atwood
1702—William Smith
1703—John Bridges
1704—Roger Mompesson
1715—Lewis Morris
1733—James Delancey
1761—Benjamin Pratt
1763—Daniel Horsmanden

Speakers of the Lower House of Assembly

1691—James Graham
1693—Henry Pierson
1695—James Graham
1698—Philip French
1699—James Graham
1699—Abraham Gouverneur
1702—William Nicoll
1718—Robert Livingston
1725—Adolph Philipse
1737—Lewis Morris

1739—Adolph Philipse
1745—David Jones
1759—William Nicoll
1768—Philip Livingston

North Carolina

North Carolina's native Indian peoples included a wide range of groups speaking Algonquian and Siouan languages, but the two largest nations, the Cherokee and Tuscarora, came from Iroquoian stock. After receiving a patent from Elizabeth I to plant England's first colony in North America, Sir Walter Raleigh chose the vicinity of Albemarle Sound for its site. Raleigh placed 117 colonists on Roanoke Island in 1587, but the Spanish Armada's impending invasion of England prevented him from resupplying the outpost until 1590. When a relief party finally reached the island, it discovered the community to have been been abandoned and could not locate any survivors. Approximately seventy years were to pass before the English again occupied North Carolina.

At least as early as 1657, settlers had moved to Albemarle Sound in modern North Carolina from Virginia. North Carolina's official history began as part of the proprietary colony of Carolina, which Charles II awarded to seven English aristocrats and the governor of Virginia in 1663. Through Virginia's governor, the proprietors encouraged the relocation of families to Albemarle Sound, and they also succeeded in stimulating the migration of several hundred English islanders from the Caribbean to Cape Fear between 1663 and 1668. Separate legislatures were initially established to provide self-government for the enclaves at Albemarle and Cape Fear. The proprietors experienced great difficulty in winning political cooperation from North Carolinians, who consistently blocked the proprietors' initiatives through their assemblies. These disputes led to North Carolina being made a royal colony on July 25, 1729.

North Carolina society closely resembled that of Virginia. All but a few families occupied small farms and lived an isolated existence growing tobacco for a cash crop, which had to be carried to Virginia for export because navigation in the North Carolina banks was so treacherous. A thriving lumber-and-naval-stores industry flourished around Cape Fear. The county was government's basic unit. Few parishes had resident ministers because sentiment among Anglican priests was so adverse to accepting pulpits there that the typical cleric was said to be more willing to serve as vicar to a bear garden than bishop of Carolina.

In 1711, when the colonial population stood at 15,100, war with the Tuscarora erupted. North Carolinians did not achieve victory in this conflict until 1713 and then only with substantial aid from South Carolina and several allied Indian nations. Because the war crushed the Tuscarora so decisively (20% were killed or enslaved; the survivors joined their Iroquois kin in New York and in 1722 became the sixth nation in the Iroquois League), it ended resistance to white frontier expansion in North Carolina for almost a half-century. North Carolina escaped involvement in the French and Indian Wars until the Seven Years' War when the Cherokee attacked its western settlements in 1760.

The province grew gradually until its interior counties were opened for settlement in the 1740s. Large numbers of settlers then arrived from colonies to the north. Newcomers from the Chesapeake brought an increasing number of slaves into the colony, and the percentage of blacks rose from 4% in 1700 to 30% in 1760. By 1760, North Carolina had 110,400 residents and ranked as the seventh-largest colony.

Governors

As Albemarle District
1663—William Drummond
1667—Samuel Stephens
1670—Peter Carteret

1673—John Jenkins
President of Council
1676—Thomas Eastchurch
1677—Thomas Miller
Deputy Governor
1677—John Culpeper (usurper)
1678—Seth Sothel
1679—John Harvey
Deputy Governor
1679—John Jenkins
President of Council
1682—Seth Sothel

As "Carolina North and East of Cape Fear"
1689—Philip Ludwell
1691—Thomas Jarvis
1694—Thomas Harvey
1699—Henderson Walker
President of Council
1704—Robert Daniel
1705—Thomas Cary
1706—William Glover
President of Council
1708—Thomas Cary
President of Council
1711—Edward Hyde

As Proprietary North Carolina
1712—Edward Hyde
1712—Thomas Pollock
President of Council
1714—Charles Eden
1722—Thomas Pollock
President of Council
1722—William Reed
President of Council
1724—George Burrington
1725—Richard Everard

As Royal North Carolina
1731—George Burrington
1734—Gabriel Johnston
1752—Nathaniel Rice
President of Council
1753—Matthew Rowan
President of Council
1754—Arthur Dobbs
1765—William Tryon
1771—James Hasell
President of Council

Chief Justices
1722—Christopher Gale
1724—Thomas Pollock
1724—Christopher Gale
1731—William Smith
1732—John Palin
1732—William Little
1733—Daniel Hamner
1734—William Smith
1743—John Montgomery
1749—Eleazer Allen
1749—Enoch Hall
1750—James Hassell
1755—Peter Henley
1758—Charles Berry
1761—Martin Howard

Speakers of the Lower House of Assembly

1697—John Porter
1708—Edward Moseley
1711—William Swann
1712—Thomas Snowden
1715—Edward Moseley
1724—Thomas Swann
1725—Maurice Moore
1726—John Baptista Ashe
1731—Edward Moseley
1734—William Downing
1739—John Hodgson
1742—Samuel Swann, Sr.
1754—John Campbell
1756—Samuel Swann, Sr.
1762—John Ashe
1766—John Harvey, Jr.

Pennsylvania

Pennsylvania's original pre-Columbian inhabitants included Indians speaking both Algonquian (Delaware [Lenni Lenape], Shawnee) and Iroquoian (Erie, Honniasont, Seneca, Susquehanna, and Wenrohronon) languages. The Delaware and Susquehanna were the largest groups occupying the Delaware River watershed where Europeans first settled. The broad estuary of Delaware Bay was not recognized as the gateway to Pennsylvania's hinterland until its mapping by Henry Hudson in 1609.

In the spring of 1643, Swedes made the first permanent white settlement in Pennsylvania at Tinicum, 9 miles below the mouth of the Schuykill River. New Sweden and New Netherland actively competed for control of the local fur trade at rival stockades (Swedish Fort New Krisholm and Dutch Ft. Beversrede), which were built facing one another across the mouth of the Schuykill in 1647 and 1648. After several years of minor violence, New Netherland's militia invaded the Delaware valley and annexed New Sweden's colonists into the Dutch Atlantic commercial empire in 1655.

England acquired the territory through its conquest of New Netherland in 1664. On March 14, 1681, Charles II awarded William Penn a charter for a proprietary colony, including Pennsylvania and Delaware, to serve as a refuge for Britain's persecuted Quakers. The first ship of Quakers landed in December 1681, and Penn arrived as governor in October 1682. On June 23, 1683, Penn and the Delaware Indians concluded a treaty of friendship that laid the basis for seven decades of peaceful frontier expansion. Because representatives from Delaware took a key role in blocking Penn's supporters from controlling the assembly, a separate legislature began to meet for Delaware in 1704, but Pennsylvania's governor performed the duties of that colony's chief executive.

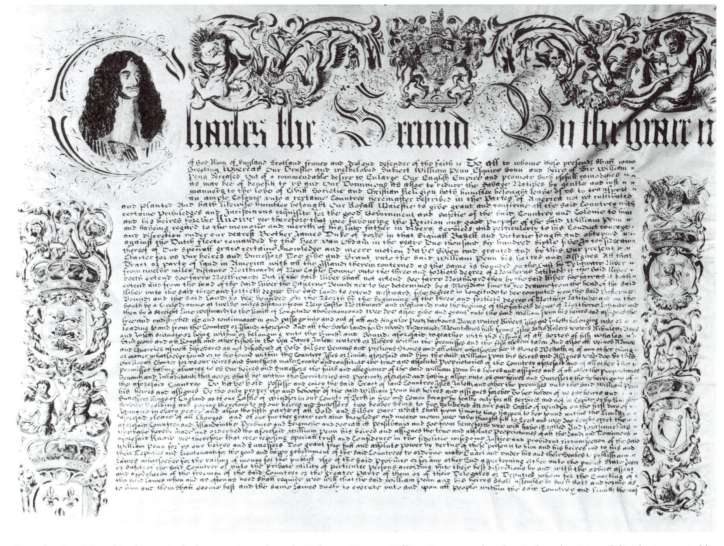

Pennsylvania originated in the grant of a large territory along the Delaware River to William Penn as a refuge for Quakers, by virtue of this charter granted by Charles II. (Record Group 12 [Photographic Unit, Department of Highways] Courtesy Pennsylvania State Archives)

By 1700, Pennsylvania included 18,000 inhabitants, of whom 98% were white and 90% were English or Welsh in background. Although the colony's climate was equally as suited to a plantation-based agricultural system as was Maryland, and although slavery had become well established in neighboring New Jersey and New York by the early 1700s, Pennsylvania relied more heavily on white indentured servants than slaves. Small family farms dominated the social landscape of its hinterland rather than plantations or baronial estates of landlords renting to tenants.

Pennsylvania grew rapidly after 1720 due to heavy immigration by Germans, Swiss, and Scotch-Irish. After a half-century of this foreign influx, Pennsylvania was the only one of the thirteen colonies in which the English and Welsh stock were a minority of whites. It became a leading exporter of foodstuffs to the West Indies and southern Europe, and the great volume of this trade swelled Philadelphia's size until it emerged as the largest city in Anglo-America during the 1760s.

The colonists were spared involvement in the French and Indian Wars until the Seven Years' War was sparked by an engagement at Ft. Necessity, 60 miles south of the forks of the Ohio, in 1754. Indian raids engulfed the colony until British and colonial troops expelled French forces from the Ohio's headwaters in 1758 and then founded the first English settlement beyond the Appalachian crest at Pittsburgh. By 1760, Pennsylvania with 183,700 residents ranked as the third-largest province (behind Virginia and Massachusetts).

Proprietors

First Generation
William Penn (1644–1718) received proprietorship on March 14, 1681.

Second Generation
John Penn (died 1746) inherited half of the proprietorship as eldest son on July 30, 1718, but bequeathed his share to his brother Thomas Penn in 1746.

Thomas Penn (1702–75) inherited a quarter of the proprietorship at his father's death and half upon his brother John's death.

Richard Penn (1706–71) inherited a quarter of the proprietorship at his father's death.

Third Generation
Children of Thomas Penn (died March 21, 1775) who survived infancy: Juliana, John, Granville, and Sophia Margaretta.

Children of Richard Penn (died 1771): John Penn (1729–95), who was Lieutenant Governor 1763–71 and 1773–76; Richard Penn (1735–1811), who was Lieutenant Governor 1771–76.

Governors

Aside from William Penn and Benjamin Fletcher, none of the colony's resident chief executives held full rank as governor.

1681—William Markham
  Deputy Governor
1682—William Penn
1684—Thomas Lloyd
  President of Council
1688—John Blackwell
  Deputy Governor
1690—Thomas Lloyd
  President of Council and Deputy Governor
1693—Benjamin Fletcher
  (royal governor)
1693—William Markham
  Lieutenant Governor
1699—William Penn
1701—Andrew Hamilton
  Deputy Governor

1703—Edward Shippen
  President of Council
1704—John Evans
  Deputy Governor
1709—Charles Gookin
  Deputy Governor
1726—William Keith
  Deputy Governor
1726—Patrick Gordon
  Deputy Governor
1736—James Logan
  President of Council
1738—George Thomas
  Deputy Governor
1747—Anthony Palmer
  President of Council
1748—James Hamilton
  Deputy Governor
1754—Robert Hunter Morris
  Deputy Governor
1756—William Denny
  Deputy Governor
1759—James Hamilton
  Deputy Governor
1763—John Penn
  Deputy Governor

Chief Justices
1684—Nicholas More
1701—John Guest
1706—Roger Mompesson
1708—Joseph Growden
1717—David Lloyd
1731—James Logan
1739—Jeremiah Langhorne
1743—John Kinsey
1750—William Allen

Speakers of the Lower House of Assembly
1685—John White
1689—Arthur Cooke
1690—Joseph Growden
1694—David Lloyd
1695—Edward Shippen
1696—John Simcock
1697—John Blunston
1698—Phineas Pemberton
1699—John Blunston
1700—Joseph Growden
1703—David Lloyd
1705—Joseph Growden
1706—David Lloyd
1709—Joseph Growden
1710—Richard Hill
1712—Isaac Norris
1713—Joseph Growden
1714—David Lloyd
1715—Joseph Growden
1716—Richard Hill
1717—William Trent
1718—Jonathan Dickinson
1719—William Trent
1720—Isaac Norris
1721—Jeremiah Langhorne

1722—Joseph Growden
1723—David Lloyd
1724—William Biles
1725—David Lloyd
1729—Andrew Hamilton
1733—Jeremiah Langhorne
1739—John Kinsey
1750—Isaac Norris, Jr.
1764—Joseph Fox

Plymouth

Plymouth Colony occupied the area south of Boston Bay between Cape Cod and Rhode Island. The region's original pre-Columbian inhabitants included the Algonquian-speaking Nauset, Pocasset, Sakonnet, and Wampanoag. These Indians lost perhaps half their numbers from 1616 to 1618 during an unknown epidemic contracted from European sailors navigating in local waters.

English settlement originated with the Pilgrims, a group that began among a congregation of Puritan exiles living at Leyden, Holland. Under William Brewster, they obtained financing from London merchants to found a community in Virginia. In September 1620, the *Mayflower* left Plymouth, England, with 102 Pilgrims, of whom thirty-five were from Leyden and sixty-one had been recruited in London or Southampton. The party made landfall in November far north of Virginia, at Cape Cod, and its forty-one adult men signed the Mayflower Compact on November 21 to create a civil government.

The Pilgrims disembarked at Plymouth harbor on December 26 but were so unprepared for the rigors of a New England winter that by spring, half the group had died of malnutrition, exposure, or disease. In 1621, they learned from local Indians—including Squanto, a Wampanoag who spoke English—how to grow corn and survive in the wilderness. The survivors held New England's first Thanksgiving the next November to celebrate their first successful harvest. Systematically cheated by their London creditors, they did not pay off their debts and establish clear title to the land until 1644. Plymouth created a de facto established church by requiring tithes for Congregational parishes, but the state otherwise avoided involvement in ecclesiastical affairs.

In 1675, King Philip's War began in Plymouth (at Swansea) by tensions created by the colony's efforts to extend the jurisdiction of English courts over the Wampanoag. Plymouth sustained Indian attacks on eight of its towns and provided 15% of the English forces. The Wampanoag and their allies were decimated and lost any ability to deter further white expansion.

Plymouth and the Massachusetts Bay Company agreed on a mutually acceptable boundary in the early 1630s, but it never received a charter from the crown establishing its legal status. When Massachusetts Bay obtained its second royal charter in 1691, it received authority to annex Plymouth. At the time when it ceased to exist, the colony's population numbered about 7,400 persons living in the present counties of Bristol, Barnstable, and Plymouth.

Governors

1620—John Carver
1621—William Bradford
1633—Edward Winslow
1634—Thomas Prence
1635—William Bradford
1636—Edward Winslow
1637—William Bradford
1638—Thomas Prence
1639—William Bradford
1644—Edward Winslow
1645—William Bradford
1657—Thomas Prence
1673—Josiah Winslow
1680—Thomas Hinckley

Rhode Island

The first European to view what is the modern state of Rhode Island was Giovanni da Verrazano, who compared Block Island in 1524 to the Greek isle of Rhodes, after which the state became known. A mild climate, numerous waterfowl, and abundant seafood enabled the small area of early seventeenth-century Narragansett Bay to support a relatively large Algonquian-speaking population, mostly Narraganset, Eastern Niantic, and Nipmuck. These groups escaped contagion in the great European epidemic that destroyed at least a third of New England's Indians from 1616 to 1618, and they may have numbered 10,000 when white settlement began. In June 1636, Roger Williams left Massachusetts to escape a sentence of banishment to England, wintered with the Narraganset, and bought land at modern Providence, which became the earliest white settlement. Other religious dissidents, uneasy with the Bay colony's orthodox Congregationalism, founded towns at Narragansett, Pawtuxet, Pocasset, Newport, and Warwick by 1643.

To protect local land titles against the claims of neighboring colonies, Williams personally petitioned Parliament (then in revolt against the Crown) to recognize these towns as a charter colony on March 24, 1644. Rhode Island was the only part of New England that refused to create a state-supported church. It became a haven for Antinomians, Quakers, and Baptists, besides attracting a small Jewish enclave as early as 1658 at Newport. After England's monarchy was restored in 1660, Williams succeeded in winning a royal charter from Charles II on July 18, 1663, that reconfirmed the privileges enjoyed since 1644.

During King Philip's War, the colony's only Indian conflict, six of its towns were attacked. The struggle's turning point occurred in Rhode Island in November and December 1675 when the English overran the main Narraganset stronghold and defeated their warriors in the Great Swamp Fight. The Indian remnant that survived the conflict either drifted away or remained as a steadily declining minority. By 1700, Rhode Island had 6,000 people, including 300 slaves (both blacks and Indians). The eighteenth-century economy's most important activities were livestock raising, distilling, and overseas commerce. A strong rivalry emerged between Newport and Providence for primacy as a maritime center. Rhode Island finally clarified its exact boundary with Connecticut in 1727 and succeeded in establishing its claim to Bristol and other towns on Narragansett Bay's eastern coast by 1747 when its territory reached 1,500 square miles (including 28% water or tidal beach). By 1760, the colony's population stood at 45,500, of whom 8% were nonwhite, and ranked as the fourth-smallest province.

Governors

1663—Benedict Arnold
1666—William Brenton
1669—Benedict Arnold
1672—Nicholas Eaton
1674—William Coddington
1676—Walter Clarke
1677—Benedict Arnold
1678—William Coddington
1678—John Cranston
1680—Peleg Stanford
1683—William Coddington, Jr.
1685—Henry Bull

1686—Walter Clarke
1687—Sir Edmund Andros
   absentee governor of the Dominion of New England at its capital, Boston
1689—John Coggeshal
   Deputy Governor
1690—Henry Bull
1690—John Easton
1695—Caleb Carr
1696—Walter Clarke
1698—Samuel Cranston
1727—Joseph Jenckes
1732—William Wanton
1734—John Wanton
1740—Richard Ward
1743—William Greene
1745—Gideon Wanton
1746—William Greene
1747—Gideon Wanton
1748—William Greene
1755—Stephen Hopkins
1757—William Greene
1758—Stephen Hopkins
1762—Samuel Ward
1763—Stephen Hopkins

Chief Justices

1747—Gideon Cornell
1749—Joshua Babcock
1751—Stephen Hopkins
1755—Francis Willett
1755—Stephen Hopkins
1756—John Gardner
1761—Samuel Ward
1762—Jeremiah Niles
1763—Joshua Babcock
1764—John Cole

Speakers of the Lower House of Assembly

1696 (Oct.)—Jonathan Holmes
1698 (Oct.)—Joseph Jenckes, Jr.
1699 (Feb.)—Benjamin Newberry
1700 (Apr.)—Jonathan Holmes
1703 (May)—Jonathan Sprague
1703 (Oct.)—Benjamin Barton
1704 (May)—Edward Greenman
1704 (Oct.)—John Dexter
1705 (May)—William Wanton
1706 (May)—Benjamin Arnold
1707 (Feb.)—John Wanton
1707 (May)—Joseph Jenckes
1707 (May)—James Greene
1707 (Oct.)—Richard Arnold
1708 (May)—Joseph Jenckes
1708 (Oct.)—William Wanton
1709 (May)—Simon Smith
1709 (Oct.)—Abraham Anthony
1710 (May)—John Wanton
1710 (Oct.)—William Wanton
1711 (Nov.)—James Greene
1712 (Feb.)—John Spencer
1712 (May)—Ebenezer Slocum
1713 (May)—John Wanton
1713 (Oct.)—Thomas Fry

1714 (Oct.)—Randall Holden
1715 (May)—William Wanton
1715 (Oct.)—William Hopkins
1716 (May)—John Cranston
1716 (Oct.)—William Wanton
1717 (Oct.)—Thomas Fry
1718 (May)—William Wanton
1718 (Oct.)—Nathaniel Sheffield
1719 (May)—William Wanton
1722 (May)—Thomas Fry
1722 (Oct.)—William Coddington
1723 (Feb.)—William Wanton
1724 (May)—William Coddington
1724 (May)—Thomas Fry
1724 (Oct.)—William Coddington
1725 (Oct.)—Thomas Fry
1726 (May)—William Coddington
1726 (Oct.)—Jeremiah Gould
1727 (Aug.)—Thomas Fry
1727 (Oct.)—Job Greene
1728 (Apr.)—Henry Bull
1728 (Oct.)—Joseph Whipple
1729 (Feb.)—John Spencer
1729 (May)—Samuel Clarke
1729 (Oct.)—Thomas Fry
1730 (May)—Samuel Clarke
1731 (Oct.)—Jeremiah Gould
1732 (May)—Samuel Clarke
1732 (Oct.)—George Hazard
1733 (May)—Jeremiah Gould
1733 (Jun.)—George Hazard
1733 (Jul.)—Jeremiah Gould
1733 (Oct.)—Samuel Clarke
1734 (Apr.)—Henry Bull
1734 (May)—William Greene
1734 (Oct.)—Samuel Clarke
1735 (Oct.)—William Robinson
1736 (May)—Francis Willett
1736 (Oct.)—Samuel Clarke
1737 (May)—Francis Willett
1738 (May)—Daniel Abbott
1738 (May)—Thomas Spenser
1738 (Oct.)—Stephen Hopkins
1739 (May)—Francis Willett
1739 (Jul.)—William Greene
1739 (Oct.)—Stephen Hopkins
1740 (May)—Samuel Clarke
1741 (May)—Stephen Hopkins
1741 (Jun.)—Joseph Whipple
1741 (Aug.)—Stephen Hopkins
1741 (Oct.)—William Robinson
1742 (Oct.)—Stephen Hopkins
1743 (May)—John Potter
1743 (Oct.)—Joseph Stafford
1744 (May)—Stephen Hopkins
1744 (Oct.)—Peter Bours
1746 (Oct.)—Jeremiah Niles
1747 (May)—Samuel Wickham
1747 (Oct.)—Daniel Jenckes
1748 (Oct.)—Thomas Cranston
1749 (May)—Stephen Hopkins
1749 (Aug.)—Joshua Babcock
1750 (May)—Thomas Cranston
1757 (May)—Benjamin Wickham
1757 (Oct.)—Peter Bours

1759 (May)—Joshua Babcock
1759 (Oct.)—Job Randall
1760 (May)—Thomas Cranston
1762 (May)—Daniel Ayault, Jr.
1762 (Oct.)—Philip Greene
1763 (May)—John Dexter

South Carolina

The first European attempt to settle South Carolina occurred in 1562 when French Huguenots occupied Port Royal, which was abandoned two years later. English interest in occupying the region, which was claimed by Spain, did not materialize until Charles II granted all of Carolina as a proprietary colony to eight individuals in 1663. The proprietors were unable to outfit an expedition until 1670, when the earliest English outpost was planted 25 miles inland on the Ashley River, "in the very chops of the Spanish," as one nervous settler described it. The Spanish sent an armed fleet to evict the trespassers, but a tropical storm dispersed the ships before they could attack.

South Carolina developed slowly, and by 1672 it contained just 200 English. By 1680, when Charles Town was founded, the settlers barely numbered 1,200. The most important influence on the colony's development were the numerous settlers from the English Caribbean islands, especially Barbados. These individuals immediately began to lay the basis for a slave society and modeled race relations on patterns already worked out in the West Indies, especially upon the Barbados slave code.

The first generation of colonists primarily engaged in grazing cattle and various forestry industries. Rice production dominated the economy after 1690, and its introduction enormously stimulated demand for slaves to perform the uncomfortable tasks of cultivating the submerged fields. Slaves became a majority by 1720 and composed about 70% of the population for most of the 1700s.

The proprietors' plans to develop South Carolina engendered only resistance from the colonists, who persuaded the crown to make it a royal colony on May 29, 1721. As the most exposed British colony, South Carolina faced continual threats to its survival in the early 1700s. Charles Town barely escaped capture during Queen Anne's War in 1706 when a hurricane scattered a combined French-Spanish fleet poised for the attack. During the Yamasee War, the Indians' offensive was not repulsed in 1715 until it had reached within 12 miles of Charles Town, and victory over the Yamasee was only achieved by arming hundreds of slaves and enlisting other Indians as allies. South Carolina was also the scene of the colonial era's bloodiest slave revolt in 1739 when twenty whites and more than 100 blacks died near Stono Creek.

The colony entered a new phase of growth after the Stono Creek rebellion. The widespread adoption of indigo cultivation helped diversify agriculture. Settlers from northern colonies and Europe rapidly settled the Piedmont, where grains and livestock grazing predominated. By 1760, South Carolina had 94,000 inhabitants, and ranked as the eighth-largest colony.

Proprietors

Sir Anthony Ashley Cooper, Earl of Shaftesbury (succeeded by Anthony Ashley Cooper II, and then by Maurice Ashley)

John, Lord Berkeley (succeeded by Joseph Blake)

Gov. Sir William Berkeley of Virginia (succeeded by John Archdale and John Danson)

Sir George Carteret (succeeded by John, Lord Carteret, who later became Lord Granville)

Sir John Colleton (succeeded by Sir John Colleton and William Thornborough)

William, Earl of Craven (succeeded by William, Lord Craven)

Edward Hyde, Earl of Clarendon (succeeded by Soth Sothell, and then by Thomas Amy and Nicholas Trott)

Christopher Monck, Duke of Albemarle (succeeded by John Grenville, Earl of Bath)

Governors

As Proprietary South Carolina
1669—William Sayle
1670—Joseph West
    President of Council
1672—John Yeamans
1674—Joseph West
1682—Joseph Morton
1684—Richard Kyrle
1684—Robert Quary
    President of Council
1685—Joseph West
1685—Joseph Morton
    President of Council
1686—James Colleton
1690—Seth Sothel
1691—Philip Ludwell
1693—Thomas Smith
1694—Joseph Blake
    President of Council
1694—John Archdale
1696—Joseph Blake
1700—James Moore
    President of Council
1702—Nathaniel Johnson
1706—Edward Tynte
1709—Robert Gibbes
    President of Council
1712—Charles Craven
1716—Robert Daniel
    Deputy Governor
1717—Robert Johnson
1719—James Moore, Jr.
    Elected by convention

As Royal South Carolina
1721—Francis Nicholson
1725—Arthur Middleton
    President of Council
1730—Robert Johnson
1735—Thomas Broughton
    Lieutenant Governor
1737—William Bull, Sr.
    President of Council
1738—James Glen
1756—William Henry Lyttelton
1760—William Bull, Jr.
    Lieutenant Governor
1761—Thomas Boone
1764—William Bull, Jr.
    Lieutenant Governor

Chief Justices
1698—Edmund Bohun
1700—James Moore
1702—Nicholas Trott
1709—Robert Gibbes
1713—Nicholas Trott
1719—Richard Allein
1722—Charles Hill

1724—Thomas Hepworth
1727—Richard Allein
1730—Robert Wright
1739—Benjamin Whitaker
1750—James Graeme
1752—Charles Pinckney
1753—Peter Leigh
1759—James Michie
1761—William Simpson
1762—Charles Shinner
1767—Rawlins Lowndes (acting)

Speakers of the Lower House of Assembly

1692—Jonathan Amory
1694—Ralph Izard, Sr.
1696—Jonathan Amory
1700—Job Howes
1702—Edward Bourne
1703—Job Howes
1706—William Rhett
1707—Thomas Cary
1707—Thomas Smith
1708—James Risbee
1711—William Rhett
1716—Thomas Broughton
1717—George Logan
1720—Thomas Hepworth
1721—James Moore
1724—Thomas Hepworth
1725—Thomas Broughton
1727—John Fenwick
1728—William Dry
1730—John Lloyd
1731—William Donning
1731—John Lloyd
1732—Robert Hume
1733—Paul Jenys
1736—Charles Pinckney
1740—William Bull., Jr.
1742—Benjamin Whitaker
1744—William Bull, Jr.
1747—Henry Middleton
1748—William Bull, Jr.
1749—Andrew Rutledge
1752—James Michie
1754—Henry Middleton
1755—Benjamin Smith
1763—Rawlins Lowndes
1765—Peter Manigault

Virginia

Virginia's most important body of native inhabitants was the Powhatan Confederacy, a league of some thirty-two Algonquian-speaking bands and their villages (with perhaps 9,000 inhabitants) along Chesapeake Bay that had been founded by Powhatan's father and then strengthened in the late sixteenth century by Powhatan. On April 20, 1606, James I granted a patent to the Virginia Company to colonize North America's entire southern mainland. The company founded the the first permanent English community at Jamestown on May 24, 1607. Except for a brief period of orderly development under John Smith, Virginia drifted chaotically through its earliest years and almost disintegrated during the "starving time" of 1609–10 when about 80% of the colony perished from malnutrition and disease. Gross misman-

agement and crushing overhead expenses finally pushed the company into bankruptcy in 1624, and James II proclaimed it a royal colony on May 13, 1625.

After Powhatan's death in 1618, his brother Opechancanough led the Powhatan in a massive offensive that nearly destroyed Virginia. Three hundred and forty-seven of the 1,200 colonists were killed on Good Friday of 1622. Trapped in stockades with insufficient food, another 500 died during the next nine months before reinforcements from England turned the tide against the Indians. A second Powhatan War killed 500 of the 8,000 Virginians but left the Indians defeated so decisively that they no longer posed a threat to English expansion after 1645.

John Rolfe's successful experiments in curing a marketable brand of local tobacco resulted in that crop becoming the colony's most valuable export by 1619, but overproduction eventually spawned a long agricultural depression from 1660 to 1715. To satisfy the need for laborers, the assembly offered a headright of fifty acres for each white indentured servant or slave brought to the colony. In spite of tobacco's marginal profitability, Virginia always ranked as the largest colony, and its population rose from 18,700 in 1650 to 58,600 in 1700. The colony progressively shifted its reliance on indentured servants in favor of slaves, whose share of the population rose from 6% in 1670, to 28% in 1700, and 41% in 1760.

Settlement spread rapidly beyond the fall line into the Piedmont after 1720. In the 1740s, whites began to migrate to the Shenandoah River, whose valley became a center of livestock and grain production by German and Scotch-Irish pioneers. By 1760, Virginia's population had risen to 339,700 and constituted 21% of all inhabitants in the thirteen colonies.

Governor

As Private Virginia Governed by the Virginia Company
Dates of service represent the periods of residence in Virginia.

1607—Edward Maria Wingfield
President of Council
1607—Captain John Ratcliffe
President of Council
1608—Captain John Smith
President of Council
1609—Captain George Percy
President of Council
1610—Sir Thomas Gates
Lieutenant Deputy Governor
1610—Thomas Lord De La Warr
Governor and Captain General
1611—Captain George Percy
Deputy Governor
1611—Sir Thomas Dale
High Marshal
1611—Sir Thomas Gates
Acting Governor
1614—Sir Thomas Dale
Acting Governor
1616—Captain George Yeardley
Lieutenant Governor
1617—Captain Samuel Argall
Lieutenant Governor
1619—Captain Nathanial Powell
President of Council
1619—Sir George Yeardley
Governor and Captain General
1621—Sir Francis Wyatt
Governor and Captain General

Eighteenth-century Virginia faced the first serious challenge to its security during the Seven Years' War, when French-allied Indians raided its frontiers. Jackson Walker's painting depicts one engagement during that conflict, when twenty militia from Hampshire County under Capt. Jeremiah Smith routed a much larger war party of fifty Indians at the head of the Capon River in the spring of 1756. (Courtesy National Guard Bureau)

As Royal Virginia

The dates of service represent periods of residence in Virginia. Virginia's governors rarely presided personally over the government after the accession of Lord George Hamilton in 1704 but instead deputized individuals to perform their duties.

1626—Gov. Sir George Yeardley
1627—Captain Francis West
    President of Council
1629—Dr. John Pott
    President of Council
1630—Gov. Sir John Harvey
1635—Capt. John West
    Deputy Governor
1637—Gov. Sir John Harvey
1639—Gov. Sir Francis Wyatt
1642—Gov. Sir William Berkeley
1644—Richard Kemp
    Deputy Governor
1645—Gov. Sir William Berkeley
1652—Richard Bennett (acting)
1655—Edward Digges
    President of Council
1658—Capt. Samuel Mathews
    President of Council
1660—Gov. Sir William Berkeley

1661—Francis Moryson
    President of Council
1662—Gov. Sir William Berkeley
1677—Herbert Jeffries
    Lieutenant Governor
1678—Sir Henry Chichley
    Deputy Governor
1682—Gov. Thomas Lord Culpeper
1683—Col. Nicholas Spencer
    President of Council
1684—Nathaniel Bacon, Sr.
1684—Gov. Francis Lord Howard
1688—Nathaniel Bacon, Sr.
    President of Council
1690—Francis Nicholson
    Lieutenant Governor
1692—Gov. Sir Edmund Andros
1693—Ralph Wormeley
    President of Council
1693—Gov. Sir Edmund Andros
1698—Francis Nicholson
    Lieutenant Governor
1700—William Byrd
    President of Council
1701—Francis Nicholson
    Lieutenant Governor

1703—William Byrd
    President of Council
1703—Francis Nicholson
    Lieutenant Governor
1704—William Byrd
    President of Council
1704—[Gov. Lord George Hamilton,
    absentee governor to 1737]
1705—Francis Nicholson
    Lieutenant Governor
1705—Col. Edward Nott
    Lieutenant Governor
1706—Edmund Jennings
    President of Council
1710—Alexander Spotswood
    Lieutenant Governor
1722—Hugh Drysdale
    Lieutenant Governor
1726—Robert Carter
    President of Council
1727—William Gooch
    Lieutenant Governor
1734—[William Anne Keppel,
    absentee governor to 1754]
1740—Rev. James Blair
    President of Council
1741—William Gooch
    Lieutenant Governor
1749—Thomas Lee
    President of Council
1750—Lewis Burwell
    President of Council
1751—Robert Dinwiddie
    Lieutenant Governor
1756—[John Campbell, Lord Loudoun
    absentee governor to 1757]
1758—John Blair
    President of Council
1758—Francis Fauquier
    Lieutenant Governor
1759—[Sir Jeffery Amherst
    absentee governor to 1768]

Chief Justices

Prior to 1683, appeals were taken to the Assembly or the Governor in Council. Afterwards, appeals from county courts were heard by the General Court, in which the governor presided over his Council.

Speakers of the Lower House of Assembly

1642—Thomas Stegg
1644—Edward Hill, Sr.
1645—Edmund Scarborough
1646—Ambrose Harmer
1648—Thomas Harwood
1652—Edward Major
1652—Thomas Dew
1653—William Whitby
1654—Edward Hill, Sr.
1655—Francis Moryson
1657—John Smith
1658—Edward Hill, Sr.
1659—Theodorick Bland
1660—Henry Sloane
1661—Robert Wynne
1676—Augustine Warner

1676—Thomas Godwin
1677—Augustine Warner
1677—William Travers
1679—Mathew Kemp
1680—Thomas Ballard
1684—Edward Hill, Jr.
1686—Arthur Allen
1691—Thomas Milner
1695—Philip Ludwell, Jr.
1696—Robert Carter
1698—William Randolph
1700—Peter Beverley
1705—Benjamin Harrison
1710—Peter Beverley
1715—Daniel McCarty, Sr.
1720—John Holloway
1734—Sir John Randolph
1738—John Robinson
1766—Peyton Randolph

West Jersey

On July 4, 1664, in expectation that an amphibious task force would place New Netherland under English control, Charles II granted the territory between the Delaware River and the Atlantic Ocean to two court favorites, John Lord Berkeley and Sir George Carteret. Berkeley sold his rights in 1674 for £1,000 to a Quaker partnership that ultimately expanded to 120 investors, including William Penn. John Fenwick, who held the right to claim a tenth of all lands, founded the first English settlement in the Delaware valley at Salem, New Jersey, in November 1675. The other proprietors stimulated a modest migration of perhaps 2,000 British Quakers to West Jersey by 1682.

About half the proprietors established residence in West Jersey, where they dominated elections but increasingly fought among themselves. Factional divisions within the proprietors' ranks frustrated the formation of a cohesive government, especially after 1685 when certain shares controlling the appointment of West Jersey's governor passed out of Quaker hands. Partisan conflict then sharply increased between the assembly and governor until the proprietors petitioned the crown to assume responsibility for governing the province. The proprietors surrendered their power of government to the monarchy on April 15, 1702, but they kept all property rights to unpatented lands in the royal colony.

Governors

1680—Edward Byllinge
    absentee governor to 1687
1679—Samuel Jennings
    Deputy Governor
1684—Thomas Olive
    Lieutenant Governor
1685—John Skene
    Lieutenant Governor
1687—Daniel Coxe
    absentee governor to 1690
1690—Edward Hunloke
    Deputy Governor (from 1692 to 1702 East and West Jersey shared the same governor)
1692—Andrew Hamilton of East Jersey
1698—Jeremiah Basse of West Jersey
1699—Andrew Hamilton of East Jersey

Speakers of the Lower House of Assembly

1696—Francis Davenport
1697—Samuel Jennings

Proprietors

The proprietorship of West Jersey derived from the sale of John Lord Berkeley's half-share of New Jersey to John Fenwick and Edward Byllinge in 1674. Disagreement between Byllinge and Fenwick resulted in a Quaker trusteeship being formed for West Jersey the next year from which emerged a joint-stock company that offered 100 shares for sale. The following list identifies the earliest stockholders and their respective shares to about 1685.

Shares	Stockholders
1 sh.	William Abott
$^1/_2$ sh.	Hector Allen, mariner of Prestonpans, Scotland
$^1/_{10}$ sh.	Thomas Atherton, shoemaker of Dublin
$^{13}/_{14}$ sh.	Benjamin Bartlet, gentleman of Westminster (later of W. Jer.)
5 sh.	Benjamin Bartlet, merchant of London
$^1/_{20}$ sh.	William Bate, carpenter of Co. Wicklow, Ireland (later of W. Jer.)
$^1/_8$ sh.	Henry Beale, maltster of Bradly, Staffordshire
2 sh.	George Beer, financier of Edmonton, Middlesex
$^1/_6$ sh.	Nicholas Bell
1 sh.	John Bellers, merchant of London
1 sh.	William Biddle, shoemaker of London (later of W. Jer.)
$^6/_7$ sh.	John Braman
1 sh.	Thomas Budd, merchant of Ash, Somerset (later of W. Jer.)
$^1/_7$ sh.	John Bull, draper and hosier of London
$^1/_8$ sh.	Thomas Bull (later of W. Jer. & Pa.)
$^1/_{16}$ sh.	Thomas Cary, silkman of London
1 sh.	John Clark, brewer of London
$^1/_4$ sh.	William Clark, merchant of Dublin (later of W. Jer. & Pa.)
$^1/_6$ sh.	Richard Clayton, owned estate in Furness, Westmoreland and was a travelling minister
$^1/_5$ sh.	Isaac Cocks, merchant and tailor of London
$^1/_2$ sh.	Samuel Coles, haberdasher of London (later of W. Jer.)
$^4/_7$ sh.	Francis Collins, bricklayer of Stepney, Middlesex (later of W. Jer.)
1 sh.	John Cook, brazier (of London?)
1 sh.	Dr. Daniel Coxe, gentleman of London
$^1/_{16}$ sh.	Samuel Cradock, fishmonger of London
$^1/_8$ sh.	John Cripps, woolcomber of London (later of W. Jer.)
$^4/_{25}$ sh.	Thomas Crouch, merchant-maltster of Amersham, Bucks
$^1/_7$ sh.	Thomas Davis, merchant of Ratcliff, Middlesex
$^1/_{14}$ sh.	John Dennis, joiner of Cork, Ireland (later of W. Jer.)
$^1/_7$ sh.	Samuel Dennis, merchant of Cork, Ireland
$^1/_8$ sh.	Thomas Doll, comber, of London? (later of W. Jer.)
$^1/_5$ sh.	Thomas Dorman
$^1/_8$ sh.	William Drewitt, of Circester, Gloucestershire?
$^4/_{25}$ sh.	Thomas Farr, tailor of Amersham, Buckinghamshire
10 sh.	John Fenwick, gentleman of Binfield, Berkshire (later of W. Jer.)
$^1/_7$ sh.	Elizabeth Forster of London, who married Henry Gouldney
$^1/_{10}$ sh.?	Mathias Foster, merchant of Dublin
$^1/_3$ sh.	James Frazer
$^1/_7$ sh.	Abraham Godowne, broadweaver of Stepney, Middlesex
1 sh.	John Goodchild and others
$^1/_4$ sh.	Samuel Groom, Jr., mariner of London (later of W. Jer.)
1 sh.	William Haige, merchant of London (later of E. Jer.)
$^2/_7$ sh.	Elizabeth Harris of London, travelling evangelist (later of Maryland)
$^1/_6$ sh.	Peter Hayles
1 sh.	Joseph Helby
2 sh.	Joseph Helmsley, yeoman of Great Kelke, Yorkshire (later of W. Jer.)
$^4/_{25}$ sh.	Thomas Hester, bricklayer of St. Martin's in London (later of W. Jer.)
5 sh.	John Hind, draper of Cornhill in London
3 sh.	Thomas Hooten, chandler of London (later of W. Jer.)
$^1/_{10}$ sh.	Richard Hunter, tanner of Dublin (later of W. Jer.)
2 sh.	George Hutcheson, distiller of Sheffield (later of W. Jer.)
2 sh.	Thomas Hutchinson, tanner of Beverley, Yorkshire (later of W. Jer.)
3 sh.	Nicholas Johnson (of Lincolnshire?)
1 sh.	William Kemp, Sr., of Chelsea, Middlesex
$^1/_8$ sh.	William Kent, cheesemonger of London
1 sh.	John Kinsey, Sr., gentleman of Great Hadam, Hertford (later of W. Jer.)
$^1/_{16}$ sh.	Richard Lawrence, gentleman of London (later of W. Jer.)
2 sh.	Gawen Lawrie, merchant of London and Hereford (later of E. Jer.)
$^1/_3$ sh.	Nicholas Lax (of London?)
$^1/_{16}$ sh.	Gilbert Mace, weaver of London
$1^1/_2$ sh.	Humphrey Madge

Shares	Stockholders
$^1/_3$ sh.	Henry March
$^6/_{25}$ sh.	Isaac Martin, grocer of London
$^1/_6$ sh.	Thomas Martin, mealman of Stepney, Middlesex
$^1/_8$ sh.	Richard Mathews, merchant of London
$^3/_8$ sh.	Thomas Mathews, carpenter of London (later of W. Jer.)
$^{19}/_{42}$ sh.	Richard Mew, merchant and baker of Stepney, Middlesex (son in W. Jer.)
$^1/_5$ sh.	Charles Milson
$^1/_7$ sh.	Apollo Morris
1 sh.	Edward Neltrup (or Nelthorp)
$^2/_7$ sh.	Samuel Norris of London
$^1/_3$ sh.	William Ogle, gentleman (of London?)
1 sh.	Thomas Olive, haberdasher of Wellingborough, Northamptonsh (later of W. Jer.)
$^1/_5$ sh.	John Pauley of London
$^1/_8$ sh.	William Peachee, haberdasher of London (later of W. Jer.)
$^1/_{16}$ sh.	Edward Peare, shipwright of London
2 sh.	Thomas Pearson, yeoman of Bonwick, Yorkshire
1 sh.	John Penford, gentleman of Kirby-Muxloe, Leicestershire (later of W. Jer., but soon after returned to England)
1 sh.	William Perkins of Leicestershire (later of W. Jer., but died soon after arrival)
$^1/_4$ sh.	John Reading, merchant of London (later of W. Jer.)
$^1/_2$ sh.	John Ridges, skinner of London
$^1/_4$ sh.?	Roger Roberts, innholder of Dublin
1 sh.	Andrew Robinson, merchant of Clonmel, Ireland (recently of London, later of W. Jer.)
1 sh.	John Rogers (later of W. Jer.)
$^1/_3$ sh.	William Royden, brewer & merchant of Christ Church, Surry and of London
$2^1/_2$ sh.	Thomas Rudyard, lawyer of London (later of E. Jer.) [1 sh. held by Rudyard as a trustee.]
2 sh.	Thomas Sadler, gentleman of Lincoln's Inn
$^1/_4$ sh.	Robert Scholey (later of W. Jer.)
1 sh.	John Scot of London
$^1/_{10}$ sh.	Anthony Sharp, merchant of Dublin
$^1/_5$ sh.	Joseph Sleigh, tanner of Dublin
1 sh.	John Smith (later of Delaware in America)
1 sh.	Jonah Smith, merchant of London
1 sh.	Josiah Smith, merchant of London
$^1/_8$ sh.	Richard Smith of Nailsworth, Gloucester?
2 sh.	Arent Sonmans, merchant of Wallingford, East Lothian, Scotland
2 sh.	Robert Squibb, Jr.
$^1/_8$ sh.	Henry Stacy, merchant of Stepney, Middlesex (later of W. Jer.)
2 sh.	Mahlon Stacy, tanner of Hansworth, Yorkshire (later of W. Jer.)
$^3/_{25}$ sh.	Thomas Stanton, maltster of Upton, Berkshire
$^1/_{10}$ sh.	Thomas Starkey, gentleman of Abby-Lace, Co. Queens, Ire
$^1/_{14}$ sh.	William Steel, merchant of Cork, Ireland
$^1/_4$ sh.	Robert Tailor
$^1/_{20}$ sh.	Thomas Thackary, stuffweaver of Dublin (later of W. Jer.)
$^2/_7$ sh.	Josiah Thomas
$^1/_6$ sh.	Percival Towle, baker of London (later of W. Jer.)
$^1/_2$ sh.	Morris Trent, merchant of Leith, Scotland
$^1/_2$ sh.	Robert Turner, linen draper & merchant of Dublin (later of W. Jer. & Pa.)
1 sh.	Daniel Wait, bodicemaker of Westminster
$^1/_{16}$ sh.	Joseph Webster, weaver of London
1 sh.	William Welch, merchant of London
$^1/_3$ sh.	Henry West
3 sh.	Thomas Williams of London
1 sh.	Daniel Wills, doctor of Northamptonshire (later of W. Jer.)
$1^4/_{25}$ sh.	John Willis, yeoman of Wantage, Berksh. (son of W. Jer.)
$^1/_5$ sh.	Thomas Wilson
$^1/_5$ sh.	Robert Zane, sergemaker of Dublin (later of W. Jer.)

CHAPTER 10 The Cities

Five major cities emerged in the thirteen colonies prior to 1763: Boston, Charles Town, New York, Newport, and Philadelphia. These five were the only communities whose populations exceeded 5,000 in 1760. (Baltimore, which would have 5,934 residents in 1776, had remained a small village of 200 people as late as 1752.) All except Newport would continue to grow and develop into major centers of commerce and industry during the nineteenth century.

Although the economy of British America was predominantly agricultural, the cities contained a larger part of its population than has often been appreciated. From 1630 to 1710, approximately one of every twelve colonists usually lived in cities, even though no urban community except Boston ever had more than 6,000 residents during that time. After 1720, the five largest cities' share of overall population steadily fell, until reaching less than 5% in 1760. A major reason for this decline seems to have been the rise of lesser urban areas—such as Gloucester, Massachusetts; Lancaster, Pennsylvania; Hampton, Virginia; Baltimore, Maryland; and Savannah, Georgia—that siphoned off a significant share of the largest seaports' commerce.

Once Anglo-American cities had passed their half-century marks, several compared favorably to British cities in many respects. By 1740, Boston, New York, and Philadelphia possessed populations that rivaled

TABLE 10.1 URBAN POPULATION OF THE THIRTEEN COLONIES, 1630–1760

Year	Urban Residents	% of Total Population
1760	72,881	4.6%
1742	53,382	5.9%
1730	42,262	6.7%
1720	36,300	7.8%
1710	27,000	8.1%
1700	21,300	8.5%
1690	18,600	8.8%
1680	10,900	7.2%
1660	6,100	8.1%
1650	3,300	6.5%
1640	1,696	6.3%
1630	450	9.7%

Sources: Carl Bridenbaugh, *Cities in the Wilderness: The First Century of Urban Life in America, 1625–1742* (1938), 6, 143, 303, and *Cities in Revolt: Urban Life in America, 1743–1776* (1955), 5. For Boston in 1630, Darrett B. Rutman, *Winthrop's Boston: A Portrait of a Puritan Town, 1630–1649* (1965), 29.

the size of many British provincial ports such as Glasgow, Hull, and Norwich. By 1760, Philadelphia and New York both ranked among the ten largest cities in the British empire. Because most British cities were demographically stagnant, the rapid growth rates of American seaports left them poised to overtake the former in a few decades or less. Americans furthermore had frequently made more progress in improving their urban infrastructures than had been accomplished in the old country. Boston's drainage system, Philadelphia's night lamps, and Boston's paved streets were better than most such systems in British cities. Visitors from Britain almost uniformly expressed amazement at the level of development found in the largest American seaports. "I had no idea of finding a place in America," wrote a pleasantly surprised naval officer on reaching New York in 1756, "consisting of near 2,000 houses, elegantly built of brick, raised on an eminence and streets paved and spacious, furnished with commodious keys and warehouses, and employing some hundreds of vessels in foreign trade

and fisheries—but such is this city that very few in England can rival it in its show." By the 1750s, American cities had come of age.

Boston, Massachusetts

Founded: 1630 (incorporated 1800)
Population in 1760: 15,631
Colonial Rank by Population: third
Elevation: sea level to 330 feet
Average Temperatures (1743–59): January, 29.5°F; April, 45.7°F; July, 64.4°F; October, 45.5°F; annual average, 46.2°F
Average Annual Precipitation: unknown for period
Type of Government: town meeting, chaired by an elected moderator, with decisions made by majority vote of the citizens in attendance

Modern Boston's terrain bears little resemblance to its original geographic setting because massive landfill projects created the foundation for a major metropolis in the nineteenth century by pushing back the bay's waters. Boston initially sat on a tadpole-shaped peninsula named Shawmut, connected to the mainland by a narrow sliver of a causeway. Marshes covered much of the ground, but it attracted settlers because it was well watered with springs and immediately ready for cultivation because trees were scarce.

Shawmut's first settler was Rev. William Blackston, a Puritan minister who arrived about 1625 and built a solitary home at the base of three hills that led many English to call the peninsula Tramount ("the tri-mountains"). After large-scale colonization began in 1630 with the arrival of 700 settlers on the Massachusetts Bay Company's "great fleet," Blackston persuaded many prominent leaders to join him, and Shawmut became the colony's de facto capital when Gov. John Winthrop built his home there. By September, when Tramount had 150 occupants, it received the official name of Boston to commemorate the city where the great fleet's wayfarers had heard their last sermon in old England.

For more than a decade, early Boston remained primarily an agricultural community. (The irregular pattern of the city's streets serve as an enduring reminder of how its transportation system originated as a network of country lanes linking farmsteads to a shared pasture, which has survived as Boston Common.) In 1634, the village established a market to be held on "lecture day" (Thursday) when outlying residents came to town to hear a midweek sermon. Boston's rise as a commercial center developed after the English Civil War, which severely disrupted the colony's economy and forced Massachusetts Bay to build up its own merchant marine.

Boston emerged as a maritime hub because it was conveniently located for most of the colony's population, which was centered along the Charles River, and because its peninsular waterline allowed generous space for erecting wharves and storehouses. The city gradually drew to itself the lion's share of New England's traffic, starting with the coastal carrying trade. By 1649—when it contained 315 houses, 481 families, and 14% of the population in Massachusetts Bay—Boston had became the primary supplier of foodstuffs, lumber, dried fish, and other provisions for the rapidly growing population of the English Caribbean islands. "Boston may be esteemed the mart town of the West Indies," said a representative of the Board of Trade in 1676, but he should have added that the city's ships could be found in every port known to English mariners by that date. Boston would remain Anglo-America's largest harbor for a century after 1650.

Municipal government evolved after it proved impractical to manage the community's affairs as an extension of the local Congregational church, as they evidently were through late 1633. During the next year,

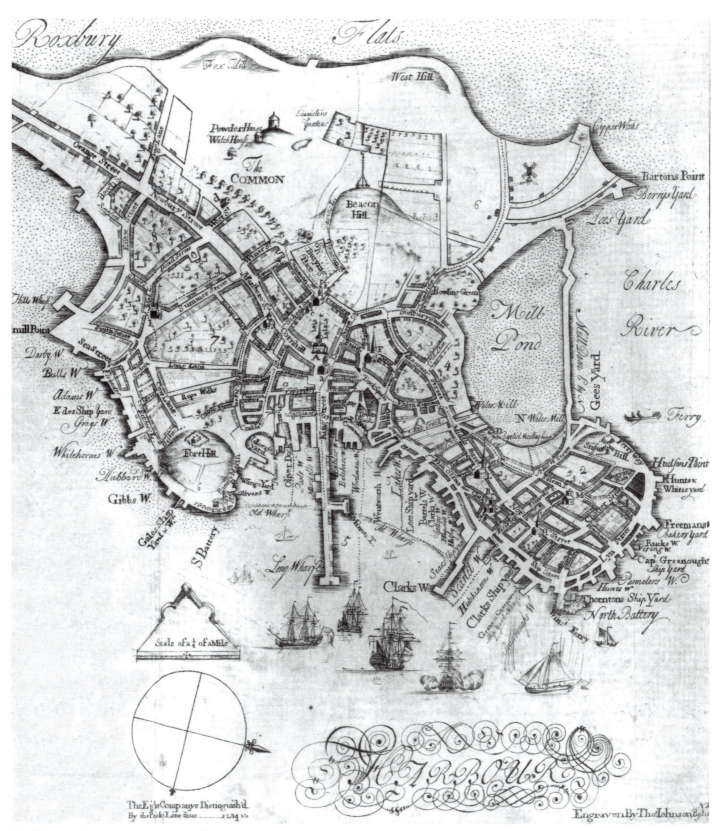

This 1728 map shows Boston when it was still the largest city in the thirteen colonies. Even so, the map reveals that much of the land available for urban expansion remained either part of the Common or was being used for agricultural purposes. (Courtesy Geography and Maps Division, Library of Congress)

the town established a town meeting to give all voters a voice in its affairs and began to rely on an executive committee (later termed *selectmen*) for general administration. Like other American cities, Boston preferred civic involvement and self-help over the creation of an urban bureaucracy; it required so many unpaid appointees to carry out the town's duties that by 1700, every tenth adult male had to hold some post each

year. The citizens petitioned the legislature for a charter four times from 1650 to 1677 without success and stayed unincorporated until 1800.

With rapid growth and higher population density came increasing problems with sanitation. The city hired its first street cleaner, whom it termed a "scavenger," 1662 to remove rotting animal carcasses and other "matters of offensive natuer." Although an ordinance required that all animal entrails and other garbage be dumped off the draw-bridge into Mill Creek—where they accumulated and generated an overpowering stench—so many householders furtively evaded its provisions that the number of scavengers had to be increased to four by 1684. (Boston at least tried to keep its public thoroughfares clean, unlike Bristol—England's second-largest city—which made no such provision during the six decades prior to 1700.)

Boston also promoted public hygiene by becoming the first colonial city to pave its major passageways, an improvement that allowed rainfall to flush away the contents of chamber pots and animal waste that scavengers left behind. The city began to make annual appropriations in 1704 for covering 24 feet in the middle of streets and 8 feet in lanes, while homeowners took responsibility for paving the part abutting their own property. After 1713, the selectmen had streets graded for proper drainage and added a crown down the middle and side gutters for most freshly paved thoroughfares. To prevent the expense of

TABLE 10.2 POPULATION OF BOSTON, MASS., 1630–1760

Year	Population	% Increase
1760	15,631	(4.6%)[a]
1742	16,382	26.0%
1730	13,000	8.3%
1720	12,000	33.3%
1710	9,000	34.3%
1700	6,700	11.7%
1690	6,000	33.3%
1680	4,500	50.0%
1660	3,000	50.0%
1650	2,000	66.7%
1640	1,200	700.0%
1630	150	...

[a] decrease

Sources: Carl Bridenbaugh, *Cities in the Wilderness: The First Century of Urban Life in America, 1625–1742* (1938), 6, 143, 303, and *Cities in Revolt: Urban Life in America, 1743–1776* (1955), 5. Gary B. Nash, *The Urban Crucible: The Northern Seaports and the Origins of the American Revolution* (1986), 1, 9. For Boston in 1630, Darrett B. Rutman, *Winthrop's Boston: A Portrait of a Puritan Town, 1630–1649* (1965), 29.

unnecessary repairs, ordinances were passed regulating the maximum loads permitted for carts. By 1720, Boston's street system was not only the best in the colonies but also superior to most in England.

The city's most advanced civic improvement was the introduction of subterranean drainage, especially because few European cities utilized this technology. Francis Thrasher built the first drain in 1704 to carry waste water from his basement down the street, and his neighbors soon connected their homes to his line. Private initiative led to the construction of 420 sections of underground sewers connected to house drains from 1708 to 1720.

Fire posed the greatest danger to Bostonians because, as a minister noted in 1663, "the houses were for the most part . . . close together on each side of the streets as in London." Ten great conflagrations struck (1658, 1676, 1679, 1682, 1690, 1691, 1711, 1747, 1753, and 1760), and their collective destruction was so great that only one house constructed in the seventeenth century still survives: the "Paul Revere" home (1676). The fire of 1747 even destroyed the town hall and city market. Because it was so difficult to extinguish a raging fire, the usual manner of halting a blaze was to tear down a building in flames or to create a firebreak, which was sometimes accomplished by blowing up exposed buildings with gunpowder.

After the fire of 1679 destroyed 150 dwellings, the town ordered that all subsequent structures be made of brick or stone, but by 1692, two-thirds of Boston's housing stock remained in wood. Fires had at least one redeeming feature: they permitted the selectmen to resurvey

the streets so they could be widened or rerouted for greater efficiency. After the fire of 1676 swept away fifty homes, the selectmen ordered a mechanical fire engine from England. When this machine arrived in 1679, Boston could claim to own the most modern fire-fighting equipment then existing. (Paris would not acquire its first fire engine for another twenty years.)

Population growth brought increased danger of disease as people increasingly crowded together on the small peninsula. Smallpox infected half the city's 12,000 inhabitants in 1720 and carried off 650, or one in every twenty, and returned in 1730 to kill another 500. The city probably lost every tenth child to diphtheria from 1735 to 1737. In 1736, burials exceeded births, and many families were reported leaving the city to resettle in less disease-ridden ports.

Poverty assumed an unsettling presence, increasingly among widows and orphans of soldiers who died in the intercolonial wars with the French. It has been estimated that up to 30% of the city's adult women were widows by 1742. Revenue assessors removed every sixth taxpayer from the rolls for poverty from 1735 to 1741. To reduce the cost of poor relief, Boston officials "warned out" (or declared ineligible for poor relief) an increasing number of non-natives deemed incapable of self-support. Although the number of persons warned out rose from 25 per year before 1742 to 222 annually in 1755, poor relief was being paid to about one in seven adults in 1757, in large part because the early campaigns of the Seven Years' War created so many widows.

Boston's primacy in Anglo-American trade steadily eroded in the half-century after 1700 by competition from Philadelphia and New York. The number of ships clearing harbor outbound in 1754, 447, only slightly exceeded the average of 416 departures recorded during the period 1714–17. After growing 25% since 1720, population in 1742 peaked near 16,382, of whom 8.5% were slaves. Boston thereafter stagnated and slipped to the rank of third-largest seaport, behind Philadelphia and New York, in the 1750s.

Moderators of Boston

Boston had no mayor until 1822. Voters made civic decisions at town meetings and elected selectmen to handle administrative business. Beginning on June 13, 1659, however, Boston citizens chose a moderator to preside over town meetings. The following individuals served as moderator.

1659—William Davis
1661—Thomas Savage
1664—John Leverett
1665—Thomas Savage
1682—Thomas Brattle
1684—William Gerrish
1689—Theophilus Frary
1695—John Walley
1696—Henry Deering
1697—Penn Townsend
1698—Samuel Sewall
1699—Penn Townsend
1700—Nathaniel Byfield
1728—Elisha Cooke
1738—Thomas Cushing
1747—James Allen
1748—Thomas Hutchinson
1749—James Allen
1754—Thomas Hubbard
1756—John Phillips
1760—Thomas Hubbard
1761—John Phillips
1762—Thomas Hubbard
1763—James Otis

This 1704 map of Charles Town shows the extent to which it remained a fortified city, protected by a series of bastians and two lines of defensive perimeters. (Courtesy Geography and Maps Division, Library of Congress)

References.

A	Granville Bastion	H	Draw Bridge in the Line	P	English Church	1	Pasquero Garretts House	9	Starling House
B	Craven Do.	I	Johnson's covered half Moon	Q	French Do.	2	Landsacks Do.	10	M. Boone Do.
C	Carleset Do.	K	Draw Bridge in „ „	R	Indpendent Do.	3	Jno. Crosskeys Do.	11	Tradd Do.
D	Colleton Do.	L	Palisades	S	Ana Baptist	4	Chaliers Do.	12	Langdon Smith Do.
E	Ashley Do.	M	Lt. Col. Rhetts Bridge	T	Quaker Meeting House	5	Geo Logan	13	Col. Rhett Do.
F	Blake Do.	N	Kea. L. Smiths Do.	V	Court of Guard	6	Pursett Do.	14	Ben. Spanking Do.
G	Half Moon	O	Ministers House	W	First Rice Patch	7	Elliott Do.	15	Lindery Do.

Charles Town, South Carolina

Founded: 1680 (unincorporated until 1783)

Population in 1760: ca. 8,000

Colonial Rank by Population: fourth

Elevation: sea level to 330 feet

Average Temperatures (1760–78): January, 49.3°F; April, 65.2°F; July, 80.2°F; October, 65.3°F; annual average, 65.5°F

Average Annual Precipitation (1738–59): 45.11 inches

Type of Government: With no established municipal government, public order was kept by justices of the peace and special commissioners appointed by legislature to ensure compliance with laws.

The proprietors of Carolina founded "old Charles Town," named after Charles II, in 1670 at Albemarle Point, 25 miles inland on the Ashley River. The village was shifted to the confluence of the Ashley and Cooper Rivers in 1680 and became "new Charles Town." The location's excellent harbor behind Sullivan's Island, which offered a base for defensive fortifications, would enable to city to become a major mercantile center. "The Town which two years since had but 3 or 4 houses," wrote a resident named Thomas Newe in 1682, "hath now about a hundred houses, all of which are wholly built of wood, tho there is excellent Brick."

Charles Town was the only Anglo-American community besides Philadelphia to survey its streets before the first buildings were constructed. The streets consequently ran straight, if in a slightly trapazoidal shape. Because there was no city government, the streets remained without names until descriptive titles began to be applied in 1698, and all landmark thoroughfares of the walled city seem not to have received their modern designations until about 1720. Because the colony lay in constant danger of invasion by Spanish forces, Charles Town originated as a fortified city, and few homes stood outside the defensive perimeter until after 1717.

The proprietors and later the South Carolina legislature failed to incorporate Charles Town as a legal entity. (A charter creating an open corporation like New York's passed the legislature in 1722, but it was disallowed by the crown after complaints surfaced from various interest groups in the colony.) The seaport lacked municipal government per se, and it possessed no more authority than any other locality, namely the right to elect parish firemasters, workhouse commissioners and measurers (during 1737–38), and overseers of the highways after 1742. Law and order rested on justices of the peace and a sheriff, whom the governor named. Anglican vestries carried out poor relief and many miscellaneous social services. Whenever the legislature passed laws requiring implementation by local authorities, it designated special "commissioners" to put the measure into existence. Despite this political vacuum, or perhaps because of it, the city managed to function and prosper quite well.

Charles Town initially served as the terminus for the southern deerskin trade. It began to rise as a major harbor that could rival the northern seaports in the early eighteenth century when South Carolina started to export large amounts of rice. Because virtually all the South Carolina economy's mercantile and urban functions were concentrated at Charles Town, the city seems to have included at least 20% of the colony's population from its founding to 1720.

For most of its first half-century, Charles Town was an exposed frontier outpost in danger of being snuffed out by England's enemies. In 1706, French and Spanish privateers coordinated two attacks on the city, but their landing parties were decisively defeated, and a large Spanish invasion fleet failed to take the city only because a hurricane dispersed it at sea. In 1715, Yamasee and Creek Indians threw back the Carolina frontier, drove hundreds of refugees into Charles Town, and attacked plantations within 12 miles of the city before being repulsed.

The city's greatest enemy turned out not to be military forces but the force of nature. A tropical storm struck the city in 1713 and wrecked twenty-three ships sitting in port. A severe gale lashed the community in 1728, smashed twenty-three vessels, and damaged all piers, many warehouses, and other harbor facilities. The great hurricane of 1752 brought more devastation than any other natural disaster in the colonial era. Within two hours of slamming into the seaport at 9:00 A.M., it drove all ships ashore, washed away all docks and their warehouses, demolished 500 houses, and blew off uncountable roofs. The destruction was so vast that by 1760 Charles Town impressed visitors as a newly built city.

The Carolina city also imported a regular succession of dangerous maladies and miscellaneous shipboard fevers through its busy harbor. Slave cargoes from Africa transmitted yellow fever at least once in nearly every decade after 1699, when the first outbreak killed 179 people, equal to 9% of the city's denizens. Smallpox struck almost as regularly after 1697, when a tenth of the population perished in an epidemic that lingered for more than a year. Smallpox thereafter ranked as the greatest killer in Charles Town's history: it took 311 lives in 1737 (5% of the city) and 730 in 1760 (9% of the city).

Fire was another calamity that plagued the town. The first major conflagration occurred on February 24, 1698, and destroyed about fifty homes and warehouses. A severe blaze broke out a year later, and an uncontrollable fire left most of the community in ashes in 1700. Charles Town responded by appointing fire commissioners, stockpiling fire-fighting equipment, and becoming the second Anglo-American city to import a water-pumping engine from England in 1713. After a severe blaze gutted most of the city in 1731 and a rash of small fires soon after vexed the citizens, the legislature passed a law strengthening the fire commissioners' authority and requiring all householders to own buckets and a ladder.

These precautions proved futile during the holocaust of November 1740 when frantic efforts to create successive fire breaks by blowing up homes with gunpowder failed to keep the flames from wiping out the city's trading district and consuming 334 homes. Only one person perished, fortunately, but losses totaled £200,000 sterling. The legislature responded by forbidding the construction of any new buildings not made of brick or stone and requiring the total elimination of wooden structures within five years. The fire commissioners steadily improved their preparedness for emergencies by purchasing new water pumpers and drilling the engine crews every three months. Such measures enabled the city to avoid another major fire until 1771 when the merchant's exchange burned and caused £7,000 in losses.

Despite the shocks of hurricanes and fires, Charles Town grew rapidly as the colony's planters swelled the port with bountiful exports of rice and indigo. The town expanded beyond its fortified walls through the 1720s and by 1739 had more than doubled its land area over the preceding two decades. Many of its new buildings were summer homes erected by planters who were eager to flee the oppressive heat and humidity of their inland estates for Charles Town's refreshing sea breezes.

Charles Town emerged as the premier Anglo-American center of gaming and conviviality. Its citizens (primarily the men) created more private associations for the enjoyment of leisure time than did any of the other four major seaports. These societies included the Whisk Club, Beef-Steak Club, Smoking Club, Laughing Club, the Medlers, the Fort Jolly Volunteers, and the Brooms, who regularly held "a special sweep." For those who needed relatively little excuse to join with like-minded gentlemen for conversation and cards over rum, there were the Monday-Night Club, Fryday-Night Club, and (one suspects) clubs for the week's other five nights.

The general range of activities embraced by these clubs' members was summarized by the pseudonymous essayist "Margery Distaff" in a letter published by the *South Carolina Gazette* in the 1760s. "There is not one night in the week," she insisted, "in which they [the men] are not engaged in some club or other at the tavern, where they injure their fortunes by GAMING in various ways, and impair their healths by the intemperate use of spiritous liquors, and keeping late hours, or rather spending whole nights, sometimes, in these disgraceful and ruinous practices." Distaff's opinion was echoed by visitors to the Carolinas. "Cards, dice, the bottle and horses engross prodigious portions of time and attention," wrote Josiah Quincy of Charles Town's gentry, whom he described as "mostly men of the turf and gamesters."

TABLE 10.3 POPULATION OF CHARLES TOWN, S.C., 1680–1760

Year	Population	% Increase
1760	8,000	17.6%
1742	6,800	51.1%
1730	4,500	28.8%
1720	3,500	16.6%
1710	3,000	50.0%
1700	2,000	81.8%
1690	1,100	22.2%
1685	900	28.6%
1680	700	…

Sources: Carl Bridenbaugh, *Cities in the Wilderness: The First Century of Urban Life in America, 1625–1742* (1938), 6,143, 303, and *Cities in Revolt: Urban Life in America, 1743–1776* (1955), 5.

Charles Town's strongest period of growth came in the three decades after 1730. The number of vessels clearing port outbound grew by 117%, from 198 in 1731 to 429 in 1768, while cargo tonnage rose 155%. The population had been approximately half black since 1709, and it remained so through the colonial period. By 1742, Charles Town had surpassed Newport, Rhode Island, in population and ranked as the fourth-largest Anglo-America city.

Mayors of Charles Town

Charles Town had no municipal government and hence no mayors until incorporated in 1783.

New York, New York

Founded: 1625 (incorporated 1653)
Population in 1760: ca. 18,000
Colonial Rank by Population: second
Elevation: sea level to 410 feet
Average Temperatures: unknown for period
Average Annual Precipitation: unknown for period
Type of Government: a chartered open corporation, in which voters of each ward annually elected an alderman and a councilman, but the city council chose the mayor

Dutch West India Company officials in New Netherland founded New Amsterdam in July 1625 when they transferred a settlement on

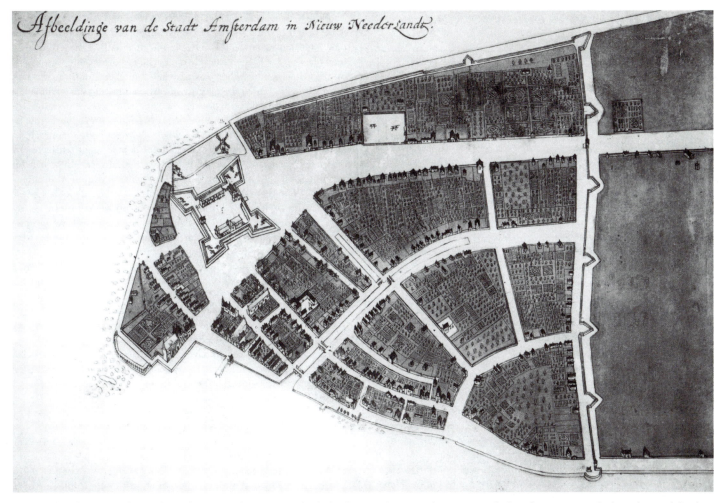

Afbeeldinge van de Stadt Amsterdam in Nieuw Neederlandt.

This map by Johannes Vingboons shows the extent of New Amsterdam's development by 1665. The western end of Manhattan contained a large fort, and development had not yet expanded north of modern Wall Street. The wall from which Wall Street took its name appears quite clearly as the city's northern boundary. (Courtesy Geography and Maps Division, Library of Congress)

Governor's Island to lower Manhattan Island, a site chosen by their engineer Cryn Fredericksen. The village contained 270 persons in 1628. By 1637, the company had built five large stone houses for use as shops and two windmills for grinding grain. The first market for agricultural produce and other wares opened in 1648, but New Netherland was so small that a single day of business per week (Saturday) sufficed to meet the population's food needs until 1662 when the market's schedule expanded to include Tuesday.

Although chosen for settlement because of its superior harbor, New Amsterdam lacked a proper wharf for more than two decades. The West India Company finally constructed a small pier with a crane in 1649. The port continued to languish as a trading center because its merchants operated few ships of their own and depended on the Dutch merchant marine to carry exports and imports.

New Amsterdam quickly became the most polyglot community in North America. A French Jesuit noted in 1643 that the town's denizens, who included Jews and even Muslims as well as Christians, spoke eighteen different languages. The citizens were a worldly lot, whatever their backgrounds, for they supported seventeen taverns but only one church. The town had grown to 1,000 residents and 120 houses by 1656.

The Dutch entrepôt lived under constant threat of armed attack. The town served as New Netherland's last line of defense in 1643 during Kiefft's War, when Indians destroyed all outlying hamlets and drove the survivors to take refuge there. Just before daybreak on September 15, 1655, 500 armed Algonquians landed at New Amsterdam, beat down house doors, rustled late-sleepers from their beds, ransacked homes for plunder under the pretext of searching

for Canadian Indians, and left after a brief exchange of fire with the militia.

The greatest threat to New Amsterdam came from England, which wanted to eliminate its use as a way station for Dutch ships that violated the Navigation Laws by smuggling goods to Anglo-American customers. On September 7, 1664, the city surrendered without resistance to an English task force of four frigates, 300 redcoats, and 2,000 Connecticut militia. On August 8, 1673, during the Third Anglo-Dutch War, eight Dutch men-of-war bombarded the English garrison into submission and restored authority to the Netherlands. England reasserted control on November 10, 1674, and renamed the city New York.

The Dutch West India Company failed to permit any self-rule for New Amsterdam until 1653, when it created govenment by a burgomeister (mayor) and schepens (magistrates), who were transformed into the mayor and common council by a charter given by English governor Thomas Dongan in 1685. The mayor, the common council, and the aldermen constituted an open corporation in which citizens of each ward voted annually for an alderman and a councilman. The mayor, the recorder, and the aldermen also sat as a Mayor's Court, an institution modeled after most English boroughs that adjudicated over a wide range of civil cases. The council appointed the mayor and the recorder. In 1731, the city received an amended charter that extended its boundaries, conferred a valuable monopoly over ferries, and allowed voters to elect assessors and tax collectors.

New York was a compact town of approximately 1 square mile, and consequently disease played havoc with public health. Contagion most commonly arrived with ill sailors who spread infection on shore

TABLE 10.4 POPULATION OF NEW YORK, N.Y., 1630–1760

Year	Population	% Increase
1760	18,000	63.6%
1742	11,000	27.6%
1730	8,622	23.2%
1720	7,000	22.8%
1710	5,700	14.0%
1700	5,000	28.2%
1690	3,900	21.9%
1680	3,200	33.3%
1660	2,400	140.0%
1650	1,000	150.0%
1640	400	33.3%
1630	300	…

Sources: Carl Bridenbaugh, *Cities in the Wilderness: The First Century of Urban Life in America, 1625–1742* (1938), 6, 143, 303, and *Cities in Revolt: Urban Life in America, 1743–1776* (1955), 5.

before symptoms of their sickness appeared. Epidemics rarely plagued New York in the 1600s while its population was relatively low, but they produced a major catastrophe almost every generation after its size reached 5,000 in 1700. The first great disaster came in 1702 when yellow fever carried away 570 persons, more than a tenth of all residents. The next major pestilence arrived in 1731, when one in every sixteen denizens (549) succumbed to smallpox. Smallpox returned in 1738 and infected approximately every seventh inhabitant (1,550 cases) before subsiding in 1739. Four years later, yellow fever hit again and left 217 dead (about 2% of the city). Less dramatic outbreaks of miscellaneous "shipboard fevers" struck regularly each decade.

New York succeeded in escaping serious damage from fires. Such emergencies as did erupt generally resembled the fire of 1714, when a blaze consumed three houses before the tearing down of nearby buildings checked its progress. The city's good fortune stemmed partly from the fact that brick or stone formed most of its housing stock and partly from wise preventive measures. Beginning in 1697, an alderman and one assistant became responsible for ensuring that two inspectors verified each week that all chimneys in their ward were serviceable. This precaution virtually eliminated the discharge of flaming cinders from dirty and clogged flues. The city also bought its first water-pumping engines in 1730, established fire-fighting companies in all six wards during the 1740s, and compensated their unpaid members with an exemption from all civic burdens, including jury duty.

By the 1690s, when the city's population approached 5,000, sizable numbers regularly walked or rode at night across town in complete darkness. The city ordered every seven households to share the expense of placing a candle or lantern in one of their windows for the convenience of passersby. By 1750, private taxpayers had begun to set out glass lamps outside their homes, and in 1761, the city placed more than 100 oil-burning lights at strategic locations and hired lamplighters for them. The city had instituted London's system of hanging 10-feet high lamps every 50 feet along the street by the 1760s. The lamps were such a novelty, however, that they posed a tempting target for destruction by boys with slingshots and even adult vandals. In 1766, for example, four drunken British officers smashed thirty-four lights along the "Broad Way" and then became embroiled in a fistfight with four watchmen who tried to stop their fun.

New York developed a significant African-American population well before the other major seaports. Most nonwhites were slaves, but the nucleus of a free black community emerged in 1644 when Gov. Willem Kieft freed eleven slaves and their wives who had served the West India Company for nineteen years. In 1664, New Amsterdam's population was 20% black. The proportion of blacks in New York had declined to 14% by 1703 but rose to 21% by 1746.

New York became the only seaport to experience a slave revolt, on April 6, 1712, when a score of bondsmen burned a building and killed nine whites attracted to the blaze. In the aftermath of this event, thirteen blacks were hanged, three were burned to death, one was broken on the wheel, and another was suspended in chains until he starved, but six others cheated the executioner by committing suicide in jail.

Slavery continued to poison the city with racial anxieties for another generation. A sense of the prevailing atmosphere can be glimpsed from the events of 1735 when a coroner's jury exonerated a master who whipped his slave to death for being caught truant on the streets after curfew, when the sheriff burned alive a black man for attempted assault on a white woman, and when a white family almost perished after their slaves slipped ratsbane into their chocolate. Each race felt threatened by the other—and each with good reason.

These tensions culminated in a huge witch hunt in 1741, when a rash of unsolved burglaries and arson led whites to assume blacks were responsible. When a dissolute white servant girl began to spread tales of a conspiracy among blacks to kill their masters, panic struck. A reign of terror ensued as hundreds of slaves and free blacks were caught up in a brutal dragnet and subjected to fearful interrogations. After extorting sixty-seven confessions (largely through torture), the authorities hanged eighteen slaves, burned thirteen others to death, and also hanged four whites who socialized with blacks as accomplices in the conspiracy.

No plot seems in fact to have existed in 1741, however. The trials and executions evidently generated among whites such apprehension of living together with a large racial minority that New Yorkers began gradually to lessen their reliance on slavery. The proportion of African Americans among New York's population consequently dropped by almost a third during the next three decades, to 14% in 1771.

Poverty remained rare in New York through the early 1760s. The city contained on its poor list in 1713 only thirteen persons out of a population approximating 6,000; it did not even need to build a poorhouse until 1736, and even then it housed just forty people. It had to support relatively few poor through the late 1750s; these were largely the disabled, the aged, or abandoned children.

The major reason why public assistance posed such a minor problem was that New York grew at a healthy rate during the eighteenth century. The number of ships clearing harbor outbound increased by 50%, from an average of 215 during 1715–18 to 322 in 1754, while tonnage carried almost doubled from 7,464 to 13,322 tons. The number of houses more than doubled from 1,140 in 1743 to 2,600 in 1760, plus 250 warehouses, distilleries, and sugar refineries lining the docks. During the 1750s, New York surpassed Boston in size and by 1760 ranked as the second-largest seaport, with 18,000 inhabitants.

Mayors of New York

1665—Thomas Willett
1666—Thomas Delavall
1667—Thomas Willett
1668—Cornelius Steenwyck
1671—Thomas Delavall
1672—Matthias Nicolls
1673—John Lawrence
1675—William Dervall
1676—Nicholas De Meyer
1677—Stephanus Van Cortlandt
1678—Thomas Delavall
1679—Francis Rombouts
1680—William Dyre
1682—Cornelius Steenwyck
1684—Gabriel Minvielle
1685—Nicholas Bayard
1686—Stephanus Van Cortlandt
1689—Peter Delanoy
1691—John Lawrence

1692—Abraham De Peyster
1694—Charles Lodwick
1695—William Merritt
1698—Johannes DePeyster
1699—David Provoost
1700—Isaac De Reimer
1701—Thomas Noell
1702—Philip French
1703—William Peartree
1707—Ebenezer Wilson
1710—Jacobus Van Cortlandt
1711—Caleb Heathcote
1714—John Johnstone
1719—Jacobus Van Cortlandt
1720—Robert Walters
1725—Johannes Jansen
1726—Robert Lurting
1735—Paul Richard
1739—John Cruger
1744—Stephen Bayard
1747—Edward Holland
1757—John Cruger, Jr.
1766—Whitehead Hicks

Newport, Rhode Island

Founded: 1639 (unincorporated through 1763)
Population in 1760: ca. 7,500
Colonial Rank by Population: fifth
Elevation: sea level to 200 feet.
Average Temperatures: unknown for period
Average Annual Precipitation: unknown for period
Type of Government: town meeting, chaired by an elected moderator,
   with decisions made by majority vote of the citizens in attendance.

In 1639, William Coddington and thirteen other men bought Aquidneck Island in Narragansett Bay from local Indians and established an agricultural settlement approximately 70 miles from Boston and 180 from New Amsterdam. They had left Massachusetts out of disagreement with its prevailing Congregational orthodoxy and decided to remain in Rhode Island rather than traveling to Delaware as planned, after meeting with Roger Williams and learning that Aquidneck could be purchased. Their settlement included ninety-six persons within a year.

Although originating as an agricultural village, the community began to develop into a town almost immediately. In 1639, two ambitious citizens built the first wharf, and many individuals soon started to acquire small vessels and to market the island's livestock via the coastal trade. The town expanded into carrying provisions to the West Indies, and by the late seventeenth century virtually all of Rhode Island's imports and exports passed through it.

In 1675, Aquidneck Island reportedly contained 400 homes, of which perhaps 260 stood within the village proper. The urban community's population rose sharply from 700 in 1660 to 2,500 in 1680, when it ranked as the third-largest Anglo-American city after Boston and New York. Once Philadelphia was founded, it consistently held the place of fourth-largest seaport until the mid-1700s.

Newport was the least compact of all colonial seaports. It tended to spread out along the water line following the road to Portsmouth. It developed into a village of scattered houses facing the two main streets. The earliest homes had large yards and did not sit directly on streets, although the city's later growth did not permit residents to continue this luxury long after 1700. Beginning with a vote by the town meeting in 1679, Newport was the first American community to name its streets in an orderly and methodical manner.

TABLE 10.5 POPULATION OF NEWPORT, R.I., 1640–1760

Year	Population	% Increase
1760	7,500	21.0%
1742	6,200	33.6%
1730	4,640	22.1%
1720	3,800	35.7%
1710	2,800	7.7%
1700	2,600	…
1690	2,600	4.0%
1680	2,500	257.1%
1660	700	133.3%
1650	300	212.5%
1640	96	…

Sources: Carl Bridenbaugh, *Cities in the Wilderness: The First Century of Urban Life in America, 1625–1742* (1938), 6, 143, 303, and *Cities in Revolt: Urban Life in America, 1743–1776* (1955), 5.

Newport also had the largest percentage of its buildings built of wood rather than brick or stone. Had homes not been dispersed in the town's center, this heavy reliance on wood structures would inevitably have sparked many devastating fires. The first large fire nevertheless did not break out until November 4, 1730, when flames incinerated six warehouses and two houses. Newport fortunately had formed a volunteer fire club and purchased a fire engine in 1726, so it was prepared for this emergency. The town might have sustained severe losses from numerous accidental blazes, such as when several black youngsters in a playful mood exploded a keg of gunpowder in their master's home in 1743, but the town maintained its three pumping engines well and kept their nine-man crews proficiently trained and highly motivated. The unusually large number of eighteenth-century buildings still standing in Newport is a testimony to the effectiveness of the city's early efforts at fire prevention.

Having begun as an agricultural village, Newport experienced difficulty eliminating the vestiges of its rural background. A formal market for farm produce did not need to be established until 1672 because neighbors simply swapped goods among themselves. The most irritating legacy of its farming heritage concerned stray livestock that wandered through the village at will. The town meeting resolved in 1639 that hogs must be confined on their owners' property, but the ordnance lacked teeth and was forgotten in the face of public indifference. In 1663, the General Assembly ordered towns to keep swine in a community pound, but Newport did not build the necessary pen for another two decades.

Newport's economy added an extra dimension after 1730 by developing into early America's only prominent health spa and vacation resort. Its mild climate, pleasant scenery, and urban amenities attracted a substantial number of wealthy patrons. South Carolinians were especially numerous, and many rice planters left their estates in the hands of overseers to stay all summer and relax with their fellow southerners who flocked to the town.

Newport's growth slowed to a standstill in the 1750s when virtually no new homes were built. In 1760, its real estate consisted of 888 dwellings, 439 warehouses, and six windmills. Its inhabitants numbered about 7,500 and stood fifth among seaports, a ranking it had held since being surpassed in population by Charles Town about 1740.

Philadelphia, Pennsylvania

Founded: 1682 (incorporated 1691)
Population in 1760: 23,750
Colonial Rank by Population: first
Elevation: sea level to 440 feet

The distinctive appearance of an eighteenth-century colonial city still survives in Philadelphia's Elfreth's Alley, near Independence Hall National Historic Site. (Historic American Buildings Survey, Library of Congress)

Average Temperatures (1758–77): January, 32.1°F; April, 51.0°F; July, 74.1°F; October, 54.6°F; annual average, 52.7°F

Average Annual Precipitation (1738–63): 41.73 inch.

Type of Government: a chartered close corporation in which aldermen and councilmen were initially appointed by the proprietor for life and thereafter chose the mayor and their own replacements

William Penn directed that his proprietary's capital city be situated where the Schuykill River flowed into the Delaware. Penn made a wise choice because the city's wharves would be situated within easy reach of a steadily expanding agricultural hinterland that would produce ever-larger surpluses of foodstuffs for export. Because the Delaware's broad channel allowed the most capacious seagoing ships to reach Philadelphia, despite its location 100 miles from the Atlantic, the city truly constituted an ocean port and would rise to prosperity through overseas commerce.

Thomas Holme surveyed boundaries for the "city of brotherly love" in 1682 before colonists arrived. Nine broad avenues ran east and west from the Delaware to the Schuykill, and twenty-one streets crossed them at right angles. Philadelphia's original land area equaled 2 square miles. When settlers landed later that year, they found that the easiest means of building shelter was to burrow cave dwellings into the steep riverbanks. Some of these subterranean homes proved so comfortable that city officials had to order their occupants to abandon them in April 1687.

Early Philadelphia grew more rapidly than any other colonial city. About 150 houses and cottages had appeared by December 1683, not counting cave dwellings, and 357 were built in 1684. The population skyrocketed from zero to 2,000 from 1682 to 1685 and overtook New York as the second-largest seaport in the late 1740s.

Philadelphia first gained autonomy in 1684, when it officially became a borough. Penn granted a charter incorporating it as a town in 1691. Citizens elected minor officers like coroners and tax assessors, but the government functioned as a closed corporation, in which William Penn awarded lifetime tenure to the first aldermen and councilmen, who then appointed their own successors. The council selected a new mayor each year.

Public health suffered greatly because of various seaborne diseases contracted from the crews of merchant vessels or newly landed immigrants. The city's worst epidemic occurred in 1699 when yellow fever brought from the Caribbean caused 220 deaths, a tenth of the total population. The city's most important effort to limit the incidence of epidemic disease came in 1719 when it appointed health officers empowered to inspect incoming ships and quarantine crewmen or passengers with infectious distempers. Philadelphia never again lost as many residents to illness as in 1699, although yellow fever took another 200 lives in 1741 (2% of the population). It nevertheless endured four major outbreaks of smallpox (1730, 1732, 1736, and 1756), a recurrence of yellow fever (1762), and diphtheria (1763).

Philadelphia fortunately suffered less from many problems that bedeviled other large cities. It could leave many of its streets unpaved until the 1750s without undue distress because the local soil had a high content of sand and consequently allowed for rapid drainage and drying. Because the majority of its housing stock was brick or stone, the city suffered no massive conflagrations; once it organized three firefighting companies, dating from 1736 to 1742, and bought a water pumper in 1739, blazes rarely spread from the building in which they originated. So little poverty existed in Philadelphia's early decades that its poor rolls included just three men, four widows, and seven children in 1709. Not until 1752, when the Philadelphia Hospital for the Sick Poor was founded, did a large class of dependent and indigent persons (largely widows and orphans) begin to overtax the city's resources.

Philadelphia's unlighted streets had resulted in so many mishaps on dark nights by 1749 that a voluntary association formed to hang lanterns over their own doors and hire a lamplighter to tend them. The public-spirited experiment proved so popular that in 1750 a board of six wardens was established to plan and erect a comprehensive network of whale-oil lamps throughout the city. The system was first illuminated in September 1751, and from then on Philadelphians enjoyed a system of nocturnal lighting equal to—if not superior—to any city in the British Empire.

Philadelphia outpaced all other colonial cities in its pursuit of learning. The mainspring behind its cultural activities was usually Benjamin Franklin, who promoted numerous projects for self-improvement and civic betterment. Franklin organized the city's earliest association for the discussion of current topics relating to philosophi-

TABLE 10.6 POPULATION OF PHILADELPHIA, PA., 1680–1760

Year	Population	% Increase
1760	23,750	69.6%
1750	14,000	55.5%
1740	9,000	12.5%
1734	8,000	23.1%
1730	…	…
1720	…	…
1710	6,500	30.0%
1700	5,000	138.0%
1690	2,100	5.0%
1685	2,000	…

Sources: Carl Bridenbaugh, *Cities in the Wilderness: The First Century of Urban Life in America, 1625–1742* (1938), 6, 143, 303, and *Cities in Revolt: Urban Life in America, 1743–1776* (1955), 5. Gary B. Nash, *The Urban Crucible: The Northern Seaports and the Origins of the American Revolution* (1986 ed.), 1, 9–10, 33, 110.

cal issues or current issues, the Junto, in 1727. It was the Junto's members who founded the town's first subscription library in 1731. By 1747, two competing libraries had appeared. Franklin's library company assembled a public display of various scientific instruments and artifacts that evolved during the 1740s into the earliest American museum. In 1744, Franklin and others invited amateur scientists to join an organization devoted to promoting the acquisition of useful knowledge, and they founded the American Philosophical Society, which still remains in existence. By 1755, geographer Lewis Evans spoke for all knowledgeable Americans when he remarked that Philadelphia "far excells in the Progress of Letters, mechanic Arts, and the public Spirit of the Inhabitants."

The city's growth began to accelerate rapidly after 1734, and during the next seventeen years its population increased 75%. Fueling this expansion were the opening of new export markets in southern Europe, particularly the Portuguese Empire and Mediterranean nations. The number of ships clearing harbor outbound increased 266% between 1733 and 1768 from 185 to 678. The city's population also swelled because it was the major entry point for German and Irish immigrants; it also acquired a significant number of black slaves, who equaled 10% of all inhabitants by 1740. The number of dwelling houses rose by more than half between 1743 and 1753 (from 1,500 to 2,300) and then by another 30% in the seven years from then to 1760 (to 2,969). Philadelphia surpassed Boston in size during the 1750s, and by 1760 it ranked as the largest seaport, with approximately 24,000 residents.

Mayors of Philadelphia

1691—Humphrey Morrey
1701—Edward Shippen
1703—Anthony Morris
1704—Griffith Jones
1705—Joseph Wilcox
1706—Nathan Stanbury
1707—Thomas Masters
1709—Richard Hill
1710—William Carter
1711—Samuel Preston
1712—Jonathan Dickinson
1713—George Roch

1714—Richard Hill
1717—Jonathan Dickinson
1719—William Fishbourn
1722—James Logan
1723—Clement Plumsted
1724—Isaac Norris
1725—William Hudson
1726—Charles Read
1728—Thomas Lawrence
1729—Thomas Griffiths
1731—Samuel Hasell
1733—Thomas Griffiths
1734—Thomas Lawrence
1735—William Allen
1736—Clement Plumsted
1737—Thomas Griffiths
1738—Anthony Morris
1739—Edward Roberts
1740—Samuel Hasell
1741—Clement Plumsted
1742—William Till
1743—Benjamin Shoemaker
1744—Edward Shippen
1745—James Hamilton
1746—William Atwood
1748—Charles Willing
1749—Thomas Lawrence
1750—William Plumsted
1751—Robert Strettell
1752—Benjamin Shoemaker
1753—Thomas Lawrence
1754—Charles Willing
1755—William Plumsted
1756—Atwood Shute
1758—Thomas Lawrence
1759—John Stamper
1760—Benjamin Shoemaker
1761—Jacob Duche
1762—Henry Harrison
1763—Thomas Willing

CHAPTER 11 Prominent and Representative Americans

The colonial era was so lengthy that it would be impossible to provide biographies with sufficient detail of all the notable men and praiseworthy women whose accomplishments fell within the years 1607–1763 in a single chapter. That period presented unprecedented opportunities and harrowing perils to people in all ranks of society. This chapter constitutes a gallery of eight legendary and lesser-known celebrities whose lives illustrate how the hazards of creating a new society could bring out the best and worst aspects of human nature.

Tom Bell

Thomas Bell, the colonial era's most notorious confidence man, was born on February 18, 1713, in Boston, Massachusetts. His father was a prosperous shipowner who sent his son to Boston's best Latin school. Harvard admitted Thomas at age seventeen in 1730 and ranked him twenty-first out of thirty-four boys, a position based entirely on its evaluation of his parents' social status.

Young Master Thomas showed himself equal to the challenge of a rigorous educational program. He conquered Latin and Greek conjugations with no apparent difficulty, and he stayed in good academic standing so long as he applied himself. No reason existed why he could not have been a lawyer, doctor, clergyman, or surveyor.

Young Master Thomas began to give telltale signs of impending trouble early at Harvard, however. Records survive that show him to have been reproved in his freshman year for "Saucy behaviour" to an upperclassman. His debts started to rise sharply to satisfy his appetite for expensive clothes, rich foods, and fine wines. His earliest recorded fraud occurred during his second year when he forged a charge for two bottles of wine on a fellow student's account at the buttery. The president announced after evening prayers on February 8, 1733, that Thomas Bell had not only been discovered in several thefts but also in "the most notorious, complicated lying" and had fallen into "a Scandalous neglect of his college Exercises." Declaring him "a disgrace to the Society," Harvard expelled Bell ten days before his twenty-first birthday.

The quondam scholar followed in his father's footsteps and went to sea, but the uncomfortable confines of a ship held no allure for a refined scapegrace with a taste for high living. He soon realized that his education presented opportunities for making quick money by the "pranks" of a strolling rogue. Because he knew the classical languages, possessed a facile tongue, and had acquired a wealth of knowledge suitable for polite conversation with gentleman, he was uniquely qualified to fleece the wealthy as a swindling imposter.

Anglo-Americans (like too many of their modern descendants) accepted the enduring myth that criminal behavior was a problem associated with the lower classes, not the social elite. The colonists had their share of frauds, but they stereotyped them in common with John Hill, an unsophisticated vagrant who tricked gullible Yankees into handing over their hard-earned money by showing a parchment attesting that he had been captured by sadistic Turks who cut out his tongue—at least until a dubious parson at Abington, Massachusetts, throttled the supposed Christian martyr's throat and forced his tongue into the open in 1733. Bell would base his criminal career on the naive predisposition of polite society to assume that a well-bred "gentleman" would never abuse the trust of his hosts or other gentlemen who befriended him.

Tom Bell, as he became known, could successfully impersonate many wealthy New Englanders because he had picked up numerous anecdotes about them or their families from his well-born classmates

at Harvard. He gained the confidence of his victims by passing himself off as a close relative or business associate of prominent merchants or landlords, who always lived at a distance. After a spell of agreeable company and good conversation, he would explain his temporary embarrassment at being short of funds and arrange to borrow cash on the credit of his wealthy sponsors. He obviously had a shrewd eye for identifying idealistic individuals who sincerely believed that a gentleman proved himself worthy of that title by showing liberality with his fortune when confronted with a deserving person in need of help. An alternative strategy was simply to gain access to a newly found patron's home and then to rifle its hiding places for secreted cash.

Bell's earliest frauds involved assuming the identities of prominent New England families such as the Winthrops, Hutchinsons, and Winslows. He expanded his repertoire to include characters from New York's great mercantile houses, such as the Livingstons, Van Dams, Wendells, and De Lanceys, and eventually mastered the art of impersonating such members of the southern gentry as the Virginia Fairfaxes and South Carolina Middletons. The *Boston Evening Post* saluted Tom Bell's phenomenal success in duping wealthy targets when it declared on September 10, 1739, "if he has play'd Half of the Pranks, that are imputed to him, we may venture to pronounce that the ENGLISH ROGUE was a meer Idiot, compar'd to him."

Some of Bell's pranks had social consequences serious enough to leave communities at loggerheads for months. The worst such incident occurred at Speightstown, Barbados, in July 1739 while the sharper was traveling as Gilbert Burnet, shipwrecked son of Massachusetts Bay's governor and grandson of famous historian Bishop Burnet. A wealthy Jewish merchant named Lopez befriended Bell and invited him to his son's wedding, where his guest feigned a disabling headache and asked to rest in the family chambers. Mr. Lopez's son fortunately suspected that the guest was a humbug, went to verify that the family's valuables remained secure after Bell returned to the banquet, and pummeled or otherwise manhandled the guest after finding that money was indeed missing, but young Lopez could not force him to reveal where he had stashed it.

Facing charges of theft, "Burnet" implored his fellow Christians to protect a bishop's grandson from Jewish slanders and blows. A Gentile mob responded by destroying the Speightstown synagogue and driving its congregation to Bridgetown for safety. The rioters later justified their actions in a manifesto claiming that Jews "do now daily attack, assault, and beat the Christians," but the only such incident was Bell's rough seizure for burglary. The responsibility for sparking the earliest anti-Semitic riot in the New World thus belongs to an ex-Harvard miscreant.

After leaving the West Indies, Bell turned up "on the pad" in central New Jersey, where a local squire unexpectedly addressed him as Rev. John Rowland, a Presbyterian revivalist known as "Hell-Fire" Rowland from that vicinity who was temporarily preaching in Pennsylvania. Bell bore a remarkable resemblance to the minister and quickly assumed his identity; he then arranged to give a Sunday sermon at Hopewell's Presbyterian church, whose clergyman (who happened to be a former classmate from Harvard) had been called away—provided a certain rich farmer gave him a bed.

As they neared the meeting house on a Sunday morning in July 1741, Bell exclaimed that he had left his notes behind and galloped back to retrieve them at his host's farm, where he stole £90 from a desk and then fled the area. Unfortunate Rev. Rowland found himself arrested for theft upon returning to New Jersey and had to defend himself before the local bench and the colony's superior court before his name was cleared. The Rowland case sorely deepened Presbyterian divisions over the Great Awakening because even after Rowland's acquittal, many conservative clergy refused to accept his innocence and used the charges wrongly to discredit revivalism.

Benjamin Franklin proclaimed Tom Bell public enemy number one, in effect, by placing a special notice of his activities and description in the *Pennsylvania Gazette* on February 10, 1743. Bell had become such an infamous intercolonial scoundral by that time that the *South Carolina Gazette* carried news of his escape from Philadelphia's jail on July 16, 1743, and warned its readers that "the notorious Tom Bell, may (in his present Travels) possibly make his Appearance here." Less than a year and a half after this notice, the *Gazette* announced on February 11, 1745, that "the famous Tom Bell, alias Burnet, alias Rowland, alias Fairfax, alias Wentworth, alias Livingston, alias Rip Van Dam, &c. &c. &c., is arrived among us . . . . His is a slim Fellow, thin visaged, appears like a Gentleman, talks of all Persons of Note as if intimately acquainted with them, and changes his Name and Cloathes very often."

The legal system proved almost entirely incapable of stopping Bell for more than short periods. He committed hundreds of frauds and burglaries but seems to have been whipped just three times in his heyday from 1735 to 1750: at New York in 1738, at Barbados in 1739, and at Boston in 1744. His career might have ended had he been branded with an "R"—for rogue—on each cheek as a Barbados court decreed in 1739, but the governor remitted that punishment at the "assiduous Intercession" of local ladies (perhaps an indication that he stole more in bedrooms than mere money). He was such an expert lock-pick that he invariably skipped jail before he could be tried.

Bell reached the height of his notoriety in 1749 when he received a death sentence from a Boston court. He somehow escaped the noose and decided to lay low as a teacher in Virginia with his wife. By that time, any charlatan who conned his or her mark—the colonies contained female rogues as well—was invariably described in terms like "a Touch on TOM BELL." Tom Bell was the first native-born American whose reputation became widely known throughout all the colonies for more than a transitory period and who attained legendary standing. (Only George Whitefield [see his biography], who resided intermittently in the colonies, won equal recognition as a traveling celebrity.)

Bell eventually returned to the sea. He became chief mate of a sloop sailing out of Jamaica under Captain Yarr. In 1771, Bell and Yarr overhauled a Spanish schooner, robbed it of 14,000 silver dollars, and tried to eliminate all witnesses by setting their own crewmen and the Spaniards adrift without water or provisions. The sailors survived, however, and their testimony convicted the two officers of piracy. Tom Bell was hanged at Kingston, Jamaica, on April 21, 1771.

Hannah Emerson Duston

The French and Indian Wars severely tested the fortitude of civilians whose homes lay within reach of raiding parties from Canada. Anglo-American women shared no less in these dangers than their men and often performed courageous services. During Queen Anne's War, for example, when Esther Jones was left as the sole occupant of a fortified house while its residents went to church at nearby Dover, New Hampshire, a band of Indians broke off their stealthy approach to storm her building after she bluffed them into retreating by shouting out to imaginary militia within, "Here they are! Come on! Come on!" When women at Oyster River came under attack in a fortified home while their husbands were working in distant fields, they disguised themselves in male clothing, fired from the loopholes, and drove off the enemy. Of all the exploits performed by women during the intercolonial wars with the French, however, the ordeal of Hannah Duston remains in a class by itself.

Hannah Emerson was born on December 23, 1657, in Haverhill, Massachusetts. As the oldest of her parents' fifteen children, she learned much of the responsibility and resourcefulness she would later

Hannah Emerson Duston's memory is commemorated in Haverhill, Massachusetts, by this statue. (Photo by Susan Cloutier, courtesy Haverhill Historical Society)

show when her community became a battleground. At age twenty, she married Thomas Duston, a local bricklayer and farmer. The Dustons lived in a cottage about 2 miles from Haverhill's meeting house, where Hannah delivered twelve children by age thirty-nine and had already seen three of them die in infancy.

During the course of King William's War, which commenced in 1689, New England's frontier steadily contracted under the weight of French and Indian attacks from Canada. Haverhill, which stood on the Merrimack River's north bank just south of New Hampshire, was a village exposed to enemy attack by early 1697. Hannah delivered her twelfth child, Martha Duston, on March 9 of that year and was joined at her home by a neighbor, Mary Neff, who came to help manage the household while she regained her strength.

On March 15, 1697, Thomas Duston went to work the farm with his seven children and left his wife and newborn daughter under Neff's care. Later that day, he spied Indians approaching, ordered his children to run toward a neighbor's home, and headed on horseback to bring Hannah to safety. Before he could reach his wife, however, he discovered that Indians had surrounded his house and rescue was impossible; he then raced back to his children (the youngest of whom was a toddler of two) and held another group of warriors at bay with his musket until all reached safety.

The Indians dragged Hannah Duston so quickly from her home that she left wearing only one shoe, even though winter had not yet ended. Upon reaching the wood line, a warrior grabbed little Martha Duston from her mother's arms, swung the baby by her ankles toward a tree, and crushed her skull. Having made the point that anyone who threatened to delay their evasion of the Haverhill militia would be killed unhesitatingly, twenty Indians roughly hurried Hannah, Neff, and several other local captives toward Canada.

Hannah Duston marched relentlessly for days as she endured exposure to the elements (during a winter reputed to be one of the century's most frigid), exhaustion compounded by a recent childbirth, and stark trauma at having seen the bloody, twitching body of her murdered baby discarded unceremoniously on the frozen ground. At some point, as she regained emotional control, an overwhelming desire for revenge started consuming her. She was first able to assess her situation at an island in the Merrimack River (near modern Concord, New Hampshire), where she and Neff were left in an isolated shelter with the family of the warrior who had captured them, along with Samuel Lennardson, an English boy captured earlier who had learned to speak Pennacook.

The women learned from Lennardson that upon reaching their captor's village, they would be stripped and beaten while forced to run the gauntlet—and then tied to poles and tormented while their fate was decided. Hannah determined to go no farther. She persuaded Lennardson to flatter one of the two Indian warriors and ask how to strike a death blow to the head and remove a scalp. With this information, she awaited the best moment to flee the twelve Indians holding her and to avenge her baby girl's murder.

Having lain awake all evening to ensure that her captors were asleep, Hannah nudged Lennardson a few hours before dawn on March 30, 1697. She and the lad found two hatchets and then simultaneously plunged them into the skulls of the two Indian men laying on the ground. Hannah then began to tomahawk the men's families, which included three women and seven children, and remorselessly killed all of them herself except a woman and child who ran away after being awakened by glancing blows. She then grimly scalped her victims.

Haverhill's astonished residents welcomed the former prisoners back a few days later when they landed in a canoe. The legislature soon after voted a bounty of £25 to Hannah. Lennardson and Mary Neff each received £12.10.

In 1698, the Dustons had their last child, a girl named Lydia who took her butchered sister's place. Hannah survived her husband by four years and died at age seventy-nine in early 1736. Haverhill honored her memory in 1879 with a statue that portrayed her brandishing a tomahawk. Hannah Duston's legacy is complex. Her determination, endurance, and courage exemplify the hardiness of pioneer women, but her slaughter of six sleeping children poses dark questions about how fearfully frontier warfare brutalized early Americans.

John Godfrey

Memory of John Godfrey vanished almost entirely over the three centuries since his death until he was rediscovered by historian John Demos, but he was notorious among his neighbors in Essex County, Massachusetts, as a suspected disciple of the devil. His life remains particularly fascinating because allegations of witchcraft in New England overwhelmingly concerned women—who were generally accused by other females—not men, unless they were husbands of witches. He furthermore managed to frustrate two attempts to convict him for sorcery in court, even though he was highly unpopular and widely suspected of occult arts.

Godfrey was born in England about 1620, and he evidently left London for Massachusetts in March 1634 as a young lad traveling alone. He worked as a cattle herdsman all his life, never married, and left a moderate estate of 100 acres and a few oxen in Haverhill. He led an unsettled career, shuffling every few years among several Essex County towns, and so became infamous to many people of that locale.

A complaint described him in 1659 as "John Godfrey, resident of Andover or elsewhere at his pleasure." Another lawsuit characterized him in 1668 as "an evil-looked fellow ... and if he came before a judge, his looks [alone] would hang him."

The first association of Godfrey with Satan took place in 1640. After he described entering into a mysterious oral contract to herd cattle with a man who did not reveal his name, Godfrey was told by a neighbor that he was either a "mad fellow" to make such a strange agreement or had entered a "covenant with the devil." The roving herdsman won two suits for slander in 1642 and 1649, but it was unknown whether either calumny concerned calling him a sorcerer.

Godfrey rarely appeared in court from 1650 to 1657. He evidently accumulated a modest sum of money in those years and began to lend it out at interest; he later initiated many lawsuits against debtors. During the eighteen years from 1658 to his death, not a year passed without his being involved in at least one lawsuit—and frequently several. Godfrey participated in so many court actions either as plaintiff or defendant—at least 132 by the best count, which is not complete—that historian Charles Upham declared of him, "he had more lawsuits, it is probable, than any other man in the colony." After Godfrey lodged his first suit for debt recovery in 1658, his neighbors came to revile him as "a great usurer," although his loans were often for small or trivial sums.

Godfrey found himself accused of witchcraft in 1658 by twenty-four witnesses from six different towns (including four men he was suing for debt). After Godfrey became highly angry that a Haverhill selectman refused to propose him as herdsman for the town's cattle, one complaint stated, cattle belonging to the selectman and his son-in-law began to vanish mysteriously. Another deposition related how Godfrey warned a person who would not hire him to tend two oxen that "One of them oxen should never come home alive anymore," and that one ox indeed became lost and was found dead. Former neighbors testified that he spoke about the power of witches to cause death by staring hard at any creature.

The depositions offered no more than circumstantial or ambiguous evidence of witchcraft, but they nevertheless conveyed a disturbing picture of the defendant. It was obvious that he often provoked arguments, turned abusive on short notice, and made people feel uneasy or even threatened. Many of his neighbors saw him as greedy, abrasive, impolite, and uncouth, and at least some of them felt genuine apprehension for their own well-being. The bachelor herdsman moved so often between towns that a personal bond of community never developed between himself and his neighbors.

The General Court at Boston, where all capital cases had to be tried, found Godfrey innocent of witchcraft. He then sued his accusers for slander. An Essex County jury decided the suit in his favor, although it added ominously that "by the testimonies he is rendered suspicious."

Relations between Godfrey and his neighbors became even more contentious after this episode. He filed thirty-four lawsuits and was a defendant in thirteen cases from 1660 to 1664. He won about 60% of his suits as a plaintiff, while losing less than one-third of cases initiated against him.

Godfrey's neighbors continued to hold suspicions that he was a sorcerer. They insisted that a calf died inexplicably after being petted and called a "poor rogue" by him. Witnesses could describe how he claimed the ability to "unwitch" cattle and seemed capable of using this power to restore health to disturbed herds. A family spread the tale that after it argued with Godfrey over the care of its cows, he took the shape of a great crow and caused their son to have a serious fall from his horse. Testimony was offered by a farmer jailed for a debt to Godfrey that the "usurer" magically appeared in his cell to torment him late one night and then vanished into thin air. Several individuals swore that they could prove he had been seen in two spots miles from each other simultaneously.

These allegations led Godfrey to stand trial a second time for witchcraft at Boston in 1666. "He has made himself suspiciously guilty of witchcraft," the jury stated, "but not legally guilty according to law and evidence we have received." The court duly noted that the jury had declared him "not to have the fear of God in his heart," however, and ordered him to pay all the costs of his own trial, even though he was exonerated.

Godfrey had beaten the hangman for the second time, despite overwhelming sentiment in Essex County that he was a "witching rogue." He faced death again in 1669 when a local jury convicted him of causing a woman's death by setting fire to her home, but a higher court threw out the verdict (possibly due to prejudice among the jurors against him). In his last years, he accumulated a dismal succession of fines for drunkenness, cursing in public, and sabbath breaking. He died of unknown causes sometime during the summer of 1675 at Boston.

Pocahantas

Pocahantas was born about 1595 or 1596 in the lower James River valley of Virginia. Her actual name was Matoaka (or Matoaba) meaning "playful child" or perhaps "little mischief." Her father, Powhatan, greatly strengthened the Powhatan Confederacy (founded by his father), the most powerful confederation of Indians inhabiting Chesapeake Bay when the Virginia Company founded Jamestown in 1607.

She first emerged as an intermediary between the English and Powhatan Confederacy in late December 1607 by interceding with her father to forebear from ordering two warriors to beat out the brains of Capt. John Smith (see his biography). Although Smith reported that her pleas saved him from being killed just as the death blows were poised to fall, most historians now suspect that he misunderstood his actual predicament. It seems more likely that Smith's "rescue" actually constituted an orchestrated ceremony of reconciliation between Smith and his captor Powhatan. The purpose evidently was to let Smith know that thenceforth his life would not be in danger and to create a sense of

This portrait of Pocahantas in European dress was painted less than a year before her death while she was traveling in England with her husband John Rolfe. (Courtesy Library of Congress)

goodwill toward Powhatan's clan because of his daughter's action. Smith's part was to demonstrate his gratitude by establishing good relations, and perhaps an alliance, between the two peoples. Smith's melodramatic deliverance consequently should be understood as Powhatan and Pocahantas cooperating in a strategem that combined elements of high drama, psychology, diplomacy, and a rather rough-and-tumble sense of Indian humor.

Authors of romantic fiction later concocted legends of romantic interest between Pocahantas and Smith. These accounts lack any basis in historical evidence. Pocahantas was a girl of about eleven years old when she met Smith. Neither Smith nor other English sources ever suggested any strong emotional attraction beyond mutual respect and ordinary friendship.

Powhatan's daughter became a familiar figure at Jamestown during casual trips to the outpost over the next few years. On a few of these visits she acted as her father's envoy and in 1609 even warned of impending hostility after relations had worsened. During these early years, she functioned as a personal link between the colonists and her father's confederacy, in effect, an adolescent ambassador who could play an adult role because of her royal pedigree. Her effectiveness as an emissary undoubtedly derived in part because her youthful, outgoing personality fascinated and charmed the English. She conveyed a sense of trustfulness by her innocent and spontaneous behavior, such as occasions at Jamestown when she gave full rein to her impulse to spring cartwheels "all the Fort over" while "naked" (that is, without a shirt to cover her girl's bosom).

She married a respected Indian named Kocoum at about age fourteen and had relatively little interaction with the English over the next four years. Capt. Samuel Argall, an English ship captain, found her visiting Indians along the Potomac in spring 1613 and learned that she wished to see Jamestown again. Argall lured her aboard his vessel, but for the purpose of using her as a pawn to force concessions from Powhatan's confederacy, which had become increasingly hostile toward the colonists.

Pocahantas went to Jamestown officially as an honored guest but in reality was a comfortably maintained hostage while the colony negotiated to improve relations with her father. She may have been a willing accomplice in this de facto kidnapping because she seemed eager to expand her command of English and learn more of white culture over the next year, and she enjoyed great personal freedom. She met John Rolfe, the individual most responsible for perfecting a marketable variety of local tobacco, in mid-1613.

Rolfe was a widower about ten years older than she, and he found himself striving with "the unbridled desire of carnall affection," as he wrote in 1614, for this pagan woman. She began to take steps to remove a major impediment for their marriage by receiving religious instruction from Rev. Alexander Whitaker, who housed her for a long period. She converted to Christianity in less than a year and took the baptismal name Rebecca.

Rolfe's request that the governor allow the first Indian-English marriage in early America stirred a minor controversy but not over the issue of race. The local Algonquians certainly had a darker complexion—tawny it was generally described—than Europeans, but their other physical features seemed familiar; the colonists did not characterize them as a distinct race but rather as a very dusky variety of the same branch of humanity as themselves. What concerned the English in both the colony and the old country was that Rolfe was a commoner, but Pocahantas was a king's daughter and therefore royalty. Many therefore demurred that Rolfe was her inferior, and it was below *her* social status to marry him.

John Rolfe nevertheless won the governor's permission to wed the princess once she abandoned paganism, and Pocahantas obtained her father's reluctant approval. The marriage was undoubtedly inevitable, however, because Virginia Company officials recognized that converting a member of the preeminent Indian dynasty and engineering a marriage with diplomatic advantages would be of enormous political benefit to them in England. The views of her Indian husband Kocoum have not survived. "Rebecca" married Rolfe about April 5, 1614. The marriage played a major role in improving relations with the Powhatan, who showed a conciliatory attitude and agreed to a new treaty of friendship in 1614.

Pocahantas evidently wished to remain with the settlers of her own free will after her stay as a pampered hostage. As Lady Rebecca Rolfe, she sailed with her husband and a retinue of Indians to England, arrived there in June 1616, and renewed acquaintances with John Smith. The Virginia Company needed good publicity and transformed her into the first American touring celebrity, for which they paid her the large sum of £4 weekly to tantalize London society's curiosity. She attended Ben Jonson's masque *The Vision of Delight* and received an audience with James I and his queen, who had also demurred that she married beneath her noble station to a commoner. For most of their sojourn, the Rolfes lived in the Thames River village of Brentford to escape London's foul air.

Pocahantas found Europe exciting and unsuccessfully tried to have her family stay beyond nine months. Rolfe nevertheless made preprations to leave on the ship of Samuel Argall, who had inveigled her into being a hostage. While awaiting fair weather at Gravesend with her only son Thomas, she died of unknown causes and was buried at St. George parish on March 21, 1617.

Having played a central role in the founding of England's first permanent outpost in the New World, an especially significant accomplishment given her sex and youth, Pocahantas emerged as the first inhabitant of the present-day United States—white or Indian—to achieve the status of an international celebrity. Her historical legacy has become progressively ambiguous over the nearly four centuries since her death. She has assumed almost mythic proportions among whites, who have instinctively viewed her from the perspective of what Prof. Richard R. Johnson has termed "the search for a usable Indian," namely as a symbol of how Native Americans presumably should have accepted and cooperated with European colonists. Native Americans would prefer she be admired as a spirited individualist who demonstrated a vast capacity for initiative, daring, and open-mindedness while attempting to bridge the chasm between an alien culture and her own background.

Robert Rogers

Robert Rogers was born in Methuen, Massachusetts, and grew to manhood on the frontier near Concord, New Hampshire. He foolishly became involved in 1754 (in a very minor capacity) with a ring that passed counterfeit money. His chance to escape prosecution came with the outbreak of the Seven Years' War, when he recruited a company of Hampshire men in 1755 and took rank as captain. He soon earned a reputation as a skilled woodsman and aggressive fighter, and he gained appointment to command an independent company raised "to range the woods" and harass the French in March 1756. Rogers raised nine such companies in 1757, and by the time he took rank as major in 1758, they had become known as Rogers's Rangers.

The Rogers style of fighting first showed itself during a scout against the French in September 1755. Rogers paddled with four men deep behind enemy lines on Lake George and located two major camps with 4,000 French troops, who had their own patrols and Indian spies criss-crossing the territory as well. While waiting for night to head home, Rogers glimpsed a canoe with ten Indians and French skirting the shore where his party was hiding. Rather than let the craft pass by so he could return safely in darkness, Rogers had his men open fire, with deadly effect, and then gave chase in their own boat. The gunshots at once attracted three more enemy canoes, however, and Rogers had to flee back under pursuit.

In their intercolonial wars with the British, the French had long been used to having the luxury of secure rear areas, but they now found themselves challenged in the heart of their own territory. The most daring *coup de main* devised by Rogers occurred on October 22, 1756, when he lay waiting outside Ft. Carillon (Ticonderoga) to take a Frenchman for interrogation. Impatient at having been given no opportunity to spring an ambush, he focused his attention on a soldier standing guard on a road within close range of the stockade ramparts. He organized five men into a file and marched them toward the fort's gate in broad daylight. When challenged for identification, Rogers answered in French that they were *amis* (friends), and indeed the rangers' clothing resembled the dress of Canadian coureurs de bois. The sentinal only realized something was amiss at the last moment and asked *"Qui êtes vous?"* (Who are you?) as the Rangers were almost upon him, to which their commander whispered *"Je suis Rogers"* (I am Rogers) as his formation briskly turned about-face and whisked the astonished guard toward the woods at the fast pace.

The Rangers' missions entailed great personal risk from both the enemy and the elements. Rogers led one of his most grueling patrols in March 1759 when he took a large force to reconnoiter Ft. Carillon and seize prisoners for intelligence. French and Indians pursued his withdrawal so relentlessly that the Rangers marched and skirmished for twenty-one straight hours without rest. Only four Rangers were shot, but the weather was so frigid that two-thirds of them limped in with frostbitten feet, as did Rogers.

Given his penchant for risk taking and the nature of his service behind enemy lines, Rogers bit off more than he could chew on several occasions. His first major battle ensued while patrolling with seventy-three men around Ft. Carillon on January 21, 1756. Several sleighs of French escaped from an ambush near the fort to unleash 300 Canadians and Indians in hot pursuit. The Rangers were overtaken on a ridge, which they held against a foe four times their number in combat that was often hand to hand. The fighting lasted long after midnight until the firing ceased, when Rogers passed the word, "Every man for himself," and his surrounded men began quietly to slip down snowy slopes through the enemy perimeter. Only fifty of seventy-four men at the battle reached British lines, including Rogers, who had been wounded twice.

The Rangers again triggered a pitched battle with superior forces on February 13, 1758. Rogers and 181 men cut down about fifty Indians traversing Lake George, only to discover they were just the advance guard for a French column numbering 400. After one Ranger company was wiped out by a French fusillade, the others fought tree to tree through the woods but found themselves pinned down by an overwhelming force. One company under Rogers fired a volley, crashed through the enemy lines, and scattered, every man for himself. Another surrounded company capitulated on promise of quarter and was immediately butchered by Indians. Only fifty-four survivors of the 181 Rangers returned to British lines, and many of them were wounded.

The most celebrated exploit of Major Rogers was to destroy the Abnaki village at St. François, Quebec, which was a staging ground for Indian raids on New England. Rogers had to cross 150 miles of wilderness, much of it a marshy bog. For half that distance he was chased by 400 French and Indians (more than twice his own number) who had discovered the boats that had carried him up Lake Champlain before he struck off overland. His Rangers stormed the village on October 6, 1759, killed dozens of Abnaki, burned their huts and food caches, and rescued five female prisoners from New England. Rogers split his Rangers into small units that might better evade the enemy, who were hot on his heels and eager for revenge. Before the last starving Rangers straggled back to New Hampshire, 30% of the 180 who assaulted St. François had been killed or captured.

Rogers left the Rangers after the last French army in Canada surrendered in 1760; he then took a captain's commission in the British army. He accepted the surrender of all major French posts in the Great

Lakes region during 1760, and he commanded a company in the Cherokee War in 1761. He participated in the relief of Ft. Detroit during Pontiac's War and was wounded at that siege.

Like many military heroes, his talents did not lend themselves to success in peacetime. He accumulated huge debts, lost his post as commander of Ft. Michilimackinac in 1767, and failed to convince the British government to finance an expedition under himself to discover a northwest passage along the rivers of North America. Rogers remained bold and vigorous, even as he fell prey to alcoholism. The *London Evening Post* reported on October 1, 1771, for instance, that although without weapons, the former ranger captured an armed highwayman who attempted to rob his coach near Gravesend. Robert Rogers went to England an exile in 1780 after becoming a Tory during the Revolution. He received half-pay for his military services, died on May 18, 1795, and was buried at the Elephant and Castle in Southwick, Surrey.

John Smith

John Smith was baptized at Willoughby, Lincolnshire, on January 9, 1579. He received a grammar school education and became apprenticed to a merchant at Lynn. He left England to fight as a mercenary and served with Austrian imperial forces against the Turks. His memoirs recounted his adventures after being captured in Transylvania, including a dramatic interlude with a pasha's wife who purchased him for reasons seemingly associated with his muscular physique. After being transferred to her brother's keeping, Smith escaped by killing his new master and eventually drifted back to England.

The Virginia Company of London retained Smith as an officer for its expedition to found Jamestown and named him to the first governor's original council. The ex-mercenary possessed daring, decisiveness, and invaluable organizational ability, but he was also prone to be impatient, overbearing, and pugnacious. After the expedition left London in 1606, Smith's rough-hewn personality led to frequent arguments with leaders whom he deemed incompetent—as most of them proved to be; after repeatedly challenging authority and instigating one too many brawls, he was locked below decks in irons and deprived of his seat on the governing council for mutiny.

To make life easier for themselves, Jamestown's leaders kept Smith at arm's length by sending him out on long journeys to explore the local area. Starvation loomed by early autumn because the poorly led settlers had failed to raise crops. Smith undertook the mission of obtaining corn from the Indians, who openly scorned the English as famished beggars beneath their contempt. Unwilling to let the colony disintegrate, Smith recognized that unless he made calculated shows of strength, the Indians would not only refuse to provide food to the colonists but also be tempted to attack and destroy the colony, which had dwindled to little more than three dozen men by December 1608.

Smith kept Jamestown's dwindling population fed the same way he had learned to forage with the Austrian army on campaign in the Balkans—by seizing food from town graineries. After a nearby village refused his entreaty to share their surplus corn through "trade and courtesy," Smith unleashed a terrifying demonstration of his matchlocks' firepower. When seventy warriors regrouped and counterattacked, he drove them off with just six men. Through cajoling or outright plundering, Smith acquired the food necessary for Jamestown to subsist until supply ships could return from London with provisions and reinforcements.

While on one such mission in December 1607, 200 Pamunkey under Opechancanough ambushed a party of himself, two colonists, and two Indian guides. Both of Smith's English companions perished, but he managed to slay two of his attackers before being overwhelmed by sheer numbers and captured. Smith seems to have known instinctively that Indians admired courage; he earned their grudging respect

This statue in Jamestown, Virginia, conveys a vivid sense of the strength of character, daring, and decisiveness that led John Smith to emerge as the first Anglo-American figure of truly heroic proportions in U.S. history. (Courtesy Library of Congress)

by stoically ignoring his wounds, treating their threats cavalierly, and using a compass to make them believe he could conjure magic.

Opechancanough dragged Smith to his brother Powhatan, who led the dominant Indian confederacy of Chesapeake Bay, 200 consolidated Algonquian villages with 9,000 Indians. Powhatan received the Englishman with "exceeding great courtesie." After three weeks at this court, several Indians suddenly seized Smith as if to dash his brains out while Powhatan looked on, only for the sentence to be remitted when the captain's head was shielded from the blows by Pocahontas, who pleaded with her father to release Smith in what was probably an elaborately staged reconciliation ceremony (see her biography).

Powhatan then declared his goodwill toward Smith, exchanged a large tract of land for a grindstone and two cannons, had him escorted back to Jamestown, and kept the colonists supplied with corn until their relief ships arrived. Smith received no reward for this accomplishment, and he was even accused of negligence because two colonists under his command had been slain. Pres. John Ratcliffe and the council allowed him no significant role in supervising the settlement but rather kept him away from Jamestown by directing him to map Chesapeake Bay in 1608. Smith mapped the shoreline so accurately that his work remained unsurpassed for a century; he also named the bay's largest island after himself.

Smith returned from exploring the bay to find that the settlers had become obsessed with the discovery of fool's gold and again had neglected to raise crops needed for the winter. Smith organized another foraging party that acquired a boatload of provisions. The council elected him president in place of the ineffectual Ratcliffe on September 10, 1608.

Smith brought order to the colony by reorganizing it as a military garrison with strict discipline. For the first time in Jamestown's precarious history, buildings were erected on schedule, seed sown, livestock tended, and shamming slackers were forced to do honest labor by the threat of banishment to the wilderness. Smith also dispersed the colonists away from Jamestown's unhealthy location during the winter despite great opposition from the council, because infection by contagious disease greatly increased mortality. This action substantially decreased the death toll because although half of Jamestown's 100 occupants died before summer, only a dozen of the 100 others who settled at other locales perished. By mid-1609, Smith had ensured the colony's short-term success by keeping it fed and forcing its workers to be productive.

The Virginia Company issued a new charter in 1609 that left Smith no real authority as the council's president. Smith watched the colony divide into ungovernable factions during that summer, suffered a serious wound from a gunpowder explosion, and finally left for England in October 1609. Without his strong leadership and good sense, Jamestown drifted into chaos and experienced its infamous starving time when more than 80% of the settlers perished.

Smith never returned to Virginia, but he provided an invaluable historical source by publishing his map of Chesapeake Bay, with written commentary on the country in 1612, plus a full account of his career in that colony in 1624. He made an important voyage of exploration along the coast of New England—a name he coined for the area in place of its former title, Norumbega—and helped stimulate settlement there by publicizing its maritime and forestry resources. He died on June 21, 1631, in London, England.

Smith was an almost shameless self-promoter, but he was also a lusty man of action who was eager to take charge in times of crisis. He played a vital role in saving Jamestown from internal collapse at its most vulnerable moment—as a once skeptical historical profession now grudgingly acknowledges—despite his tendency to embellish many episodes and villify his enemies. This magnificent bragadoccio, with all his excesses and flaws, established the standard by which later generations of frontiersmen would be judged, and ranks as the first great heroic figure in Anglo-American history,

Edward Teach (Blackbeard)

Blackbeard's true identity remains disputed, despite his notoriety as a pirate. Official documents most commonly identify him as Edward Teach, but his name also appeared as Thatch, Tache, or Tash. Writer Daniel Defoe asserted that he was baptized as Edmund Drummond. His birth probably occurred about 1685 in Bristol, England, which was a notorious spawning ground for buccaneers.

Edward Teach enlisted during Queen Anne's War as a crewman on a British privateer engaged in seeking French or Spanish prizes. Privateering formed an entirely legal aspect of early modern warfare and served the purpose of sapping an enemy's strength by destroying its commerce; it might also be profitable because crews received a share of the booty as their pay. During the long span of King William's and Queen Anne's Wars, which raged with scarcely a break from 1689 to 1713, the excitement of the chase and lure of fortune intoxicated

This painting of Blackbeard's death captures the desperate combat at close quarters that took place during Edward Teach's death struggle with Lieutenant Maynard. (Howard Pyle Collection, Delaware Art Museum, Wilmington, Delaware)

thousands of privateer veterans who found themselves unable to abandon the freebooters' life when peace resumed and thereafter sailed against all flags as pirates.

His years as a privateersman earned Teach a reputation for fighting spirit—a "courageous brute," according to Daniel Defoe, with the potential to be a hero in a good cause. He drifted to the Bahamas and joined the pirate crew of Benjamin Hornigold's *Ranger* in 1715. After the *Ranger* captured a rich French sloop, the *Concorde,* off St. Vincent in 1716, Hornigold made Teach captain of the prize, which was renamed *Queen Anne's Revenge* and outfitted at Nassau with an unusually heavy armament of forty guns.

Teach assumed an independent command in 1717 and soon plundered a British ship, the *Great Allan,* which he burned after marooning its crew. A British frigate, the thirty-gun *Scarborough,* assumed the mission of running down the *Great Allan's* attackers and in due time located *Queen Anne's Revenge.* Most pirates fled when faced with a royal warship, but Teach maneuvered against his adversary, raked its decks with accurate broadsides, and forced it to retreat after several hours of combat. The battle was one of the few in which pirates bested an armed warship. The exploit made Teach so feared that no merchant vessel seems to have afterward resisted a demand to yield from *Queen Anne's Revenge.*

Victory over the *Scarborough* transformed Teach into the British navy's most-wanted man. To make naval officers think twice about taking on his ship again, Teach created the personna of Blackbeard. He accentuated the awe-inspiring aspects of his physique, which was tall and powerful, by creating a truly fearsome presence centered around his beard. His face sprouted a thick crop of hair almost up to his eyes, and by letting it grow long and bushy he seems to have transformed his demeanor into something resembling a wolf-man. He twined his beard into many small tails tied with colored ribbons. Teach appeared for battle armed to the teeth, with an unsheathed cutlass and several daggers dangling from his waist and three pairs of pistols tucked in a bandolier worn across his chest. He finally created an image of the devil incarnate by draping the points of his tricornered hat with lighted gunner's matches (braided hemp cords that burned an inch every five minutes after being soaked in a solution of lime and saltpeter) so that a thin cloud of sulfurous smoke surrounded his head.

Blackbeard alternated between violent extremes of free-wheeling comaraderie and maniacal abuse when in command of his crew. Having invited some trusted mates to drink with him in his cabin, he secretly drew two cocked pistols under the table, fired, and shot one of his oldest companions in the knee. He justified his action to the crew by explaining that "if he did not now and then kill one of them, they would forget who he is." If he was brutal to his crew, he was sadistic with the victims of his captures, one of whom was forced to eat his own ears.

The diabolical captain reveled in proving his powers of endurance. "[L]et us make a hell of our own," he once challenged his listeners on ship, "and try how long we can bear it." He and the boldest crewmen shut themselves below deck and set afire pitch and other foul-smelling materials until the hold filled with smoke. After all the rest had fled choking and stumbling to the fresh air, Teach emerged grinning through his coughs. "The next time we shall play at gallows and see who can swing longest without being throttled," he suggested but found no takers among his men.

The British navy eventually made the Caribbean too hot even for Blackbeard, and the *Queen Anne's Revenge* headed to North Carolina for sanctuary. A large segment of every colony's population willingly connived with pirates to fence their stolen goods and provision their ships, but nowhere were buccaneers more welcome than North Carolina. Not only did the colony's languishing economy ensure a welcome for buccaneers with pieces of eight at any shop or tavern, but Gov. Charles Eden and the collector of customs, Tobias Knight, also exchanged favors for bribes.

In January 1718, Governor Eden obligingly extended the king's pardon to Blackbeard's crew, which then disposed of their booty to the merchants of Bath after Knight certified it as legal cargo. Teach thereafter used Bath, North Carolina, as a safe base for his voyages of plunder. After making repairs and stocking provisions, Teach's *Queen Anne's Revenge* despoiled the West Indian sea lanes and became the flagship in a freebooting flotilla of four large vessels and several tenders manned by 400 pirates. In May, Blackbeard's ships captured eight merchant ships off Charles Town, South Carolina, bottled up the harbor, and did not leave until the government provided them with £300 worth of medicine to relieve an epidemic of syphilis afflicting the "jolly rogers."

Blackbeard returned to Bath and "surrendered" to Governor Eden, who obligingly extended the king's mercy for any and all past crimes, including his blockade of Charles Town. Collector Knight meanwhile certified his loot as legitimate trade goods. Teach then set off for another voyage of plunder, during which the following undated fragments from his log may have been penned.

> such a Day—Rum all out—Our Company somewhat sober:—
> A damn'd Confusion among us!—Rogues a plotting;—great
> Talk of Separation—So I look'd Sharp for a Prize ... took one,
> with a great deal of Liquor on Board, so kept the Company hot,
> damned hot, then all Things went well again.

Blackbeard dissolved his flotilla after this expedition and returned to North Carolina with forty crewmen on the sloop *Adventure* to refit his vessel on Ocracoke Island off Cape Hatteras.

Virginians and South Carolinians understandably did not share their North Carolina neighbors' indulgent attitude toward Teach's depredations. In a short career of just two years, Teach had taken at least forty rich prizes, including many off the mainland coast. Gov. Alexander Spotswood of Virginia financed an attack on Ocracoke Island by a force of two sloops and sixty sailors under Lt. Joseph Maynard of the royal navy. On November 21, 1718, Maynard located his prey, who had not only ignored a warning by North Carolina's collector of customs to flee but also spent that night getting drunk. Blackbeard had seventeen men present, almost evenly split between whites and blacks.

Maynard attacked the next day but immediately saw his supporting vessel disabled by the pirates' guns; he then lost two-thirds of his own sailors to murderous cannonades from the *Adventure*. The lieutenant and his survivors took cover until Blackbeard led a boarding party, when they counterattacked. It had been two years since the pirates' last sea battle, and most fought sluggishly because of their hangovers—except for their captain. Blackbeard received a ball from Maynard's pistol, but he fell upon the lieutenant with such force that he snapped his adversary's naval sword like a twig with his pirate's cutlass. Teach fought on like a wild bull until four more bullets and twenty sword wounds cut through his body. With their captain dead, the pirates surrendered. Maynard's men cut off Blackbeard's head, threw his body overboard, and hung his head from the rigging as grisly testimony to their victory over the most fearful pirate to menace the North American mainland.

George Whitefield

George Whitefield (pronounced Whit-field) was born on December 16, 1714, in Gloucester, England, at the Bell Inn kept by his father, who died when the boy was two. Whitefield had several clergymen among his recent ancestors, but he had no intention of joining the ministry when he entered Oxford's Pembroke College in 1732. He occasionally succumbed to rakish temptations, but a search for spiritual regeneration dominated his college career until he experienced the rebirth of saving grace in 1735. The bishop of Gloucester was so struck with his zeal that he made Whitefield a deacon in June 1736 when he was still twenty-one, despite a diocesan rule stipulating that no one receive ordination before age twenty-three.

His powerful preaching style made Whitefield a leading and controversial figure in the Methodist movement while he was a deacon. His voice was so moving that England's great actor, David Garrick, once quipped that he would give 100 guineas, "if I could only say 'Oh!' like Mr. Whitefield." Others remarked that he could make listeners faint by pronouncing *Mesopotamia*. England's premier man of letters, Samuel Johnson, remarked that Whitefield was so charismatic that he could have attracted throngs even if he preached from trees clad only in a nightcap.

The Nature and Necessity of Our New Birth in Christ Jesus, in Order to Salvation, Whitefield's first pamphlet, proved so popular after its publication in August 1737 that it went through three editions in twelve months. Thousands flocked to hear him wherever he preached from Bristol to London. The bulk of established clergy nevertheless resented his success and poor comparison their own sermons made to his. Whitefield found himself unwelcome in the Church of England's pulpits because rectors complained that the masses who clogged pews and choirs to hear him jammed out their regular parishioners and that by collecting large sums for his own charities (schools for the poor, missions among Indians, and an orphanage at Savannah), he reduced their own income the next Sunday service. Within a few years, Whitefield consequently found most of England's established churches closed to him.

The first great evangelist in American history was the English clergyman George Whitefield, here shown in a contemporary painting exercising his remarkable powers of persuasion. (Courtesy Library of Congress)

John Wesley became acquainted with Whitefield through his brother Charles, who had known the young evangelist at Oxford. Whitefield made his first trip to America in 1738 to join John Wesley at his parish in Savannah, but ironically he set sail before he could receive a letter from Wesley advising him to stay in England due to Georgia's unsettled condition. Whitefield stayed in Georgia for four months and laid the foundation for an orphanage that would be funded largely through his preaching.

Deacon Whitefield returned to England, where he was consecrated as an Anglican priest in January 1739. Because few rectors would allow him to give sermons in their churches, he pioneered a new style of evangelization by preaching to a multitude of working-class people at Kingswood Hill, near Bristol, on February 17, 1739. Open-field preaching would thenceforth be a trademark of Methodism. He embarked again for America after being named to succeed Wesley at Savannah, but he landed at Philadelphia in November 1739.

Rather than head directly for Savannah, Whitefield began the most spectacular tour ever conducted by an itinerant minister in the thirteen colonies. As in England, he found himself barred from all but a few of the established pulpits, so he preached in the fields. Benjamin Franklin was fascinated by him and thought he clearly ranked as the most influential public figure among the broad mass of people, notwithstanding, as Franklin noted, "his common abuse of them, by assuring them they were naturally *half beasts and half devils.*"

Benjamin Franklin described Whitefield as one of the greatest orators of all times; he conducted calculations at one of the evangelist's mass assemblies that convinced him that Whitefield's voice was powerful enough to be heard clearly by as many as 30,000 people. (Several sources independently reported that the Englishman had successfully preached to crowds as large as 25,000, a number greater than any colonial city's population.) He also managed to preach as many as forty hours per week without losing his voice.

Whitefield evoked dramatic responses from audiences, and he once wrote that "the groans and outcries of the wounded were such that my voice could not be heard." He could hold thousands in rapt silence as he described the imminence of punishment by a wrathful God, then make them shudder, moan, and cry out in agony for their sins, and finally bring relief with a forgiving deity's promise of redemption for lost humankind. Conservative critics decried his techniques as "enthusiasm" divorced from sound theological scholarship, and they insisted that his followers experienced hysteria rather than true soul searching. Whitefield responded that his opponents were spiritually dead and incapable of stirring the seeds of salvation within their congregations. Most Anglo-Americans sided with Whitefield as he blazed a trail of scorched souls between Boston and Savannah from 1739 to 1741. This trip sparked the Great Awakening, the country's first major religious revival.

The twenty-four-year-old English prelate touched an especially wide audience because he appealed to impulses that would now be termed ecumenical. He preached in his Episcopal robes and became known as the Church of England's "dissenting priest." He was especially popular among Presbyterians, Congregationalists, and Baptists, who thought the Great Awakening would be a means of reforming the Church of England along true Calvinist lines.

The "dissenting priest" gave America its first taste of theater under the banner of religion. He consequently popularized a style of proselytizing that has become the dominant way of sparking conversions through the present. Whitefield's itinerant mission, which touched perhaps 200,000 persons from New Hampshire to Georgia, furthermore marked the first time Americans in all sections of the land shared a common cultural experience through personal interaction with a single individual. Whitefield was consequently the first celebrity whose actions linked a broad range of American society from north to south.

Whitefield returned to England from the colonies in January 1741. He made five other sweeps of the colonies during 1744–48, 1751, 1754–55, 1763–64, and 1769–70. He died on his last American tour at Newburyport, Massachusetts, on September 30, 1770, when he succumbed to a lung infection.

CHAPTER 12 Education

An otherwise obscure widow from seventeenth-century York County, Virginia, named Susan English wrote a will that hints strongly at education's status among the early colonists. English left each of her offspring a heifer and ordered that all its male calves be used to finance the child's schooling. Such arrangements were not unusual, but what makes this document special is that Sarah English could not sign her own will and marked it with an X. Even illiterate Anglo-Americans recognized the value of learning.

Education assumed an important station in the colonies because the settlers feared that cultural standards would wither under wilderness conditions and threaten their children with a "reversion to savagery." "We in this country," wrote Jonathan Mitchell of Massachusetts about 1663, "being far removed from the cultivated parts of the world, had need to use utmost care and diligence to keep up learning and all helps to education among us, lest degeneracy, barbarism, ignorance and irreligion do by degrees break in upon us." Because of this heightened consciousness that education was critical in preserving their society from cultural retrogression, the colonists (especially those in the North) took decisive steps to preserve literacy among their children and make it possible for young men to earn college degrees without going to Europe.

Pre-Collegiate Education

The Virginia Company made early efforts to sponsor schools in its colony for both whites and Indians, but its efforts produced no results prior to Virginia being proclaimed a royal colony in 1625. The Indian War of 1622–24 scotched plans to educate Native Americans. Because its settlers scattered widely over the landscape in search of the best locations for growing tobacco, Virginia seems to have lacked any formal classroom instruction for its children during its first three decades, although some private tutors certainly taught there.

Benjamin Syms endowed Virginia's first school in 1635 when he donated 200 acres and eight cattle to finance hiring a teacher to instruct

Local schools in early, rural America were all one-room structures. This schoolhouse at Valley Forge, Pennsylvania, was superior to the great majority because of its stone construction. (Record Group 12 [Photographic Unit, Department of Highways] Courtesy Pennsylvania State Archives)

children living near Elizabeth City, but classes evidently did not commence until after 1643. By 1671, Virginia seems to have contained just two schools with masters qualified to teach classical languages (the primary requirement for college and most learned professions), although English reading and writing lessons must have been available in other neighborhoods through "dame schools" operated by women who charged modest fees for their services. Neither Virginia nor any other southern colonies established a system of community-sponsored schools. Educational opportunities primarily expanded through the philanthropy of wealthy planters who established legacies to finance the salaries of grammar school masters who could teach Latin and Greek to advanced scholars besides imparting literacy and basic numeracy. By 1689, however, Virginia, whose population probably included more than 12,000 free children between the ages of five and sixteen, evidently contained just eight such public schools.

Education received far more community support north of Maryland. In the Mid-Atlantic region, where organized religion set down deeper roots than in the South, churches assumed the burden for schooling, and a system of parochial instruction emerged. This pattern first emerged in New Netherland, where no clear line of authority over schooling existed initially between the Dutch Reformed Church and West India Company, but that responsibility fell by default to the former after England despoiled the company of its colony in 1664. Anglican, Presbyterian, and Quaker congregations likewise provided for their children's secular education. Because the Mid-Atlantic colonies contained many small villages with relatively high population densities, a relatively large number of juveniles there enjoyed access to classes, and the population became more literate than was possible in the dispersed agricultural settlements of the South.

Nowhere did local circumstances favor the creation of schools more than early New England. Unlike other areas whose earliest immigrants mainly consisted of unmarried male laborers, the first generation of Puritans included numerous families with school-age offspring. The great majority of children found it easy to attend classes, once established, because most families outside of Plymouth initially settled in small villages where a majority of inhabitants lived within a half-mile of the meetinghouse. Religious idealism stimulated a high degree of concern over education because Puritans strongly believed that Christians should be able to study the Bible in their own home and read it to their children.

Boston established the first New England grammar school in 1635, five years after that settlement's founding. During the 1630s, seven of the twenty-two towns in the Massachusetts Bay Colony had established schools, but some of these institutions lapsed after a few years. Most of the earliest schools originated from a decision of their town meeting to fund a teacher's salary, either by taxes or rents from a specified tract of common land. The remaining communities obtained their schools because either a schoolmaster was charging students tuition to attend classes in his home or several families had pooled their resources by subscription to hire a teacher.

Although Massachusetts Bay had made more progress to provide access to schooling in the 1630s than any other colonies would do in their early histories, most of its towns nevertheless left education as the private domain of households or congregations. In 1642, the legislature complained of "the great neglect in many parents & masters in training up their children in learning" and passed a statute allowing the courts to fine family heads who neglected to ensure that adolescents (including any apprentices under their care) could "read & understand the principles of religion and the capital lawes of the country." Every occidental society professed a high regard for literacy, but Massachusetts was unique in holding parents legally responsible for their youngsters' ability to read.

The 1642 education law ignored the practical problem that numerous parents, including many who were literate themselves, lacked the skills needed to impart reading and writing to juveniles. The law did not mandate the founding of schools, but its goal of universal literacy could not be met unless they existed in all major communities. The legislature rectified this situation on November 11, 1647, when it enacted a statute mandating the first system of universal education established anywhere. This measure became known as the Old Deluder Act because its preamble summarized the religious motives underlying its passage as follows: "It being one cheife project of the ould deluder, Satan, to keepe men from the knowledge of the Scriptures." The Old Deluder Act required every town of fifty householders to make provision for maintaining a teacher who would give lessons in English at a petty school. It ordered each town of 100 families establish a grammar school to offer mastery over the classical languages to prepare boys for college. The law left towns free to make whatever financial arrangements best suited their circumstances, whether they be taxes, rents, tuition, subscriptions, or land grants, but experience eventually led to almost universal reliance on assessing taxpayers for the cost.

The 1647 act did not immediately produce a colonywide system of free education. Although grammar schools existed in all eight Massachusetts towns holding over 100 families by 1657, only a third of towns with fifty families fulfilled their obligation to create a petty school. Towns complying with the law shared no common interpretation as to who could attend a "public school." (As in England, the term *public school* simply meant a place for instructing students outside their homes—usually by a teacher who charged tuition—as opposed to private lessons from a tutor hired to teach members of a single family; the expression still retains that special meaning in Great Britain.) When the residents of Roxbury, Massachusetts, founded their "free" school in 1645, they permitted open entrance only to children of those families who pledged a yearly contribution for the teacher's salary, and they required tuition to admit offspring whose parents did not donate to this subscription fund. In many places, the poorest children attended gratis as a public service. A few communities admitted all adolescents to learn without charge, and eventually their example became nearly universal in New England.

The Old Deluder Act never received full compliance among towns in Massachusetts. Many communities of more than 100 families evaded their obligation to support grammar schools, and by 1765 no Latin schools existed in almost two-thirds of the towns responsible for maintaining them. The courts nevertheless succeeded in compelling nearly all towns with fifty households to finance petty schools so that access to reading and writing in English became nearly universal in all but very small villages and frontier settlements.

The Old Deluder Act's influence extended throughout nearly all of New England. Connecticut adopted it almost word for word in 1650. Plymouth recommended that all its towns form petty schools in 1658 and directed the founding of grammar schools in all towns with more than fifty households in 1677. New Hampshire adopted a similar measure in 1689. Rhode Island never instituted such a measure, but nearly all its communities voluntarily supported petty schools. New England thus became the first significant society—anywhere in the world—to establish a nearly universal system of state-supported, free primary education. The remaining Anglo-American colonies unfortunately failed to follow New England's example. As early as 1689, for example, Massachusetts had three times as many grammar schools as Virginia did, although its population was smaller; this disparity in educational opportunities increased during the 1700s.

Everywhere in early America, including New England, a drastic shortage of teachers impeded educational opportunities. About a quarter of Harvard's seventeenth-century graduates taught for a year or two while waiting for a congregation to call them as a minister, but barely 3% of people holding college degrees had lifelong careers in education, usually as masters at the better grammar schools. Dedham, Massachusetts, for instance, possessed just one teacher for its 220 school-age children in 1700, and even sixty-five years later, when it had 4 instructors, there were still 120 potential students per each of them. The lack of teachers reached acute levels in the port cities (except it seems for Boston). From 1700 to 1744, the number of children age five to fifteen per each teacher averaged 308 in Philadelphia and 357 in New York,

TABLE 12.1 EDUCATIONAL INSTITUTIONS IN COLONIAL AMERICA, 1650 AND 1689

Year	1650			1689		
Colony	Va.	N.Y.[a]	Mass.	Va.	N.Y.	Mass.
Population	18,731	4,116	14,037	52,101	13,501	48,529
Households	3,122	686	2,339	7,232	2,250	8,088
White Children[b]	3,750	1,400	4,700	12,000	4,450	16,000
Churches	27	8	43	52	34	88
Grammar Schools	2[c]	7[d]	11	8	11[d]	23
Colleges	0	0	1	0	0	1
Presses	0	0	1	0	1	2

[a] New Netherland.
[b] Estimated (5 to 15).
[c] Corrected from source.
[d] Most of these schools probably operated as petty schools but had a master who knew Latin.
Source: Lawrence A. Cremin, *American Education: The Colonial Experience, 1607–1783* (1970), 238, 241, 243.

TABLE 12.2 NUMBER OF TEACHERS PER SCHOOL-AGE CHILDREN IN COLONIAL AMERICAN COMMUNITIES, 1650 AND 1689

	Dedham, Mass.	Elizabeth City, Va.	
	1700	1700	
Population	750	1,200	
Households	111	170	
Children[b]	220	300[c]	
Teachers	1	2	
Children per Teacher	220	150	
	New York		
	1700–04[a]	1730–35[a]	1745–49[a]
Population	4,587	9,600	11,852
Households	829	1,684	2,079
Children[b]	1,241	2,388	2,799
Teachers	5	7	10
Children per Teacher	248	332	286
	Philadelphia		
	1700–04[a]	1730–34[a]	1745–49[a]
Population	2,132	5,728	9,991
Households	374	1,005	1,753
Children[b]	581	1,425	2,359
Teachers	3	6	8
Children per Teacher	194	230	281

[a] Five-year average.
[b] Estimated (5 to 15).
[c] Whites only.
Source: Lawrence A. Cremin, *American Education: The Colonial Experience, 1607–1783* (1970), 526, 534, 539.

although the ratio of potential students to instructors improved to 255 in New York and 175 in New York during 1745–74.

Petty schools seem to have followed a simple curriculum based on learning tools that one scholar could study individually at his or her bench seat while others waited in line to recite their own lessons at the master's desk. The youngest children learned the alphabet from hornbooks that often infused their text with moral lessons, such as these classic lines used in New England schools.

A In *Adam's* fall,
we sinned all.

B Thy life to mend,
this *Book* attend.

C The *Cat* doth play
and after slay.

D A *Dog* will bite
a thief at night.

E An *Eagle's* flight
is out of sight.

F The idle *Fool*
is whipt at school.

G As runs the [hour] *Glass*
man's life doth pass.

H My book and *Heart*
shall never part.

J *Job* feels the rod
yet blesses God.

K Our *King* the good
no man of blood.

L The *Lion* bold
the *Lamb* doth hold.

M The *Moon* gives light
in time of night.

N *Nightingales* sing
in time of spring.

O The Royal *Oak* it was the tree
that sav'd His Royal Majestie.

P *Peter* denies
his Lord and cries.

Q *Queen* Esther courts
in royal state
to save the Jews
from dismal fate.

R *Rachel* doth mourn
for her first born.

S *Samuel* annoits
whom God appoints.

T *Time* cuts down all
both great and small.

U *Uriah's* beauteous wife
made David seek his life.

W *Whales* in the sea
God's voice obey.

X *Xerxes* the great did die
and so must you and I.

Y *Youth* forward slips
death soonest nips.

Z *Zacheus* he did climb the tree
his Lord to see.

A child would master the alphabet and work out the principles of syllabication at his or her own speed rather than as part of a class progressing in unison. If his or her school were well supplied with academic works, the scholar would then progress to a primer composed for the most elemental learning level. Many schools lacked such elementary materials or possessed insufficient copies, however, and forced neophyte readers to begin immediately upon a rather formidable catechism or Psalter (book of the Psalms). Instruction simultaneously covered basic arithmetic, writing, and basic composition. Because numerous teachers were divinity graduates awaiting a call to the ministry, they did not teach religion so as to avoid infringing on the local clergyman's religious authority.

Classes operated on a twelve-month basis with separate summer and winter sessions. Offspring too young for important farmwork often attended the summer term, while their older brothers and sisters usually took lessons in the winter. No laws mandated when children had to begin school, how much of the year they must spend being taught, or when they might quit. Students routinely withdrew from class in midterm based on changing family circumstances and might not return for a year or more. Most students in the North attended petty schools in spurts of four or five months over three to six years before their education ended and they resumed working full time for their parents.

Few towns could afford to operate a grammar school separate from the petty school, so a single master supervised the curricula of both under the same roof. Scholars faced a daunting regimen if they expected to meet the standards for Harvard or Yale. Once a boy had spent twelve to twenty-four months mastering basic literacy and numeracy, he could begin pre-collegiate studies, usually at about age seven. One such institution, New Haven's Hopkins Grammar School, defined its mission as the education of "hopeful youth in the Latin tongue, and other learned languages so far as to prepare such youths for the college and public service of the country in church and commonwealth." Most such "hopeful youth" pursued a challenging succession of readings from the classical languages. The scholars not only became proficient in Latin syntax and grammar but also achieved a high degree of oratorical fluency. The better schools in large cities also introduced them to Greek, and sometimes to Hebrew. Rhetoric and logic received much emphasis. The students gained a smattering of mathematics, perhaps through elemental trigonometry useful in navigation and surveying, geography, and astronomy. Habits of piety and civility were also inculcated as part of a gentleman's training. After six or seven years of this regimen, which entailed up to nine hours of class hours per day, the scholars were ready to enter college at age fourteen or fifteen.

Collegiate Education

The earliest plans for a colonial college concerned an institution for teaching Indians rather than whites. In 1621, the Virginia Company revived an earlier proposal, for which some funds had already been donated, to found a college for training a small elite of Native Americans in the more sophisticated aspects of civility and Christianity. The company reserved 10,000 acres at modern Richmond as an endowment to cover its educational expenses, and it sent 100 tenants to begin to generate income to finance its construction, but the devastating Indian massacre of Good Friday 1622 snuffed out support for this project.

New England was the only section of Anglo-America to which a significant number of university-educated emigrants came. Scholars have identified 130 former Cambridge and Oxford students (of whom ninety earned bachelor's degrees) who arrived in that region during the 1630s. Ministers composed ninety-eight of the 130 college-trained personnel. By 1640, there were seventy college graduates per each

Virtually all college students lived in dormitories or rented rooms while pursuing their studies. This painting of Harvard undergraduates in 1679 hints at the sense of comaraderie that could develop from several years of living together, during which that distinctive type known as the "Harvard Man" would come to be formed. (Howard Pyle Collection, courtesy Delaware Art Museum, Wilmington, Delaware)

10,000 colonists in New England, a ratio exceeding that of contemporary England and higher than the proportion of college graduates alive within the U.S. population until 1910.

New England nevertheless had a difficult time retaining highly educated European gentlemen, and at least forty-three of its first 130 college men returned to England and died there. After the first decade of settlement, moreover, the flow of Cambridge and Oxford graduates shriveled to a trickle and threatened New England with a serious shortage of qualified persons fit to serve as ministers.

Recognizing the need for a local seminary to provide a steady, reliable supply of competent clergy, the Massachusetts legislature chartered a "Schoale or Colledge" and funded its initial expenses with a £400 grant on October 28, 1636, after which the institution was to be self-supporting. On November 15, 1637, the government fixed the campus at Cambridge (then Newtown). The school received the name Harvard on March 13, 1639, to honor its first benefactor, John Harvard, who left his library of 400 volumes and half of his estate (just over £700) as an endowment.

Through an oversight, the college's 1636 charter did not specifically grant the right to convey baccalaureate degrees, and so this power had to be granted explicitly by statute in 1650. On September 23, 1642, Harvard graduated its first class of nine bachelors, who gave a public display of their learning through an oral exam conducted in Latin covering topics in grammar, rhetoric, logic, ethics, metaphysics, and physics. The scholars trained at this wilderness outpost soon won respect for their erudition, and Oxford first officially recognized a Harvard graduate as possessing a valid bachelor's degree in 1648. Harvard's graduating classes averaged about eight per year during the seventeenth century, and twenty-eight from 1701 to 1775. Harvard matriculated 2,562 graduates by the Revolution, or 54% of all bachelor degrees awarded until then in the British colonies.

Harvard remained the only Anglo-American college for more than a half-century. Virginia's assembly considered establishing a college in 1661, as did Maryland in 1671, but neither project came to fruition. Virginia eventually chartered the colonies' second college, William and Mary, at Williamsburg on February 8, 1693. The institution required a lengthy gestation period before classes began, in large part because the first president spent more than half the college's income on his own princely salary of £150. In 1705, a student's carelessness sparked a fire that consumed the campus's wooden buildings. A chronic shortage of senior faculty left the administration unable to offer classes higher than the grammar school level until after 1726, when the House of Burgesses voted the funds needed to create a baccalaureate curriculum.

Even after maturing into a full college, William and Mary never achieved its full potential as the South's leading center of learning. By 1750, perhaps only 100 students had entered its halls as bachelor-degree candidates, but none had matriculated. Its first commencement may not have occurred until 1753, although vague contemporary accounts exist of a baccalaureate graduation ceremony in 1700. The careers of most William and Mary scholars resembled Thomas Jefferson's. Jefferson attended lectures given by the college's two professors and president (who was almost dismissed for habitual drunkenness at that time) for two years and a month before returning home without a degree. By 1775, William and Mary had conferred diplomas on just four young men since its founding.

By 1690, Harvard had produced 180 clergymen since 1642, and yet New England still had a shortage of Congregational ministers. To rectify this situation, a "Collegiate School within his Maj'ties Colony of Connecticut" received its charter on October 16, 1701. Killingworth was the school's initial location, but New Haven soon became the campus. In 1718, it received the name Yale in honor of benefactor Elihu Yale. The college awarded its first baccalaureate degree in 1702, just a year after its founding. By 1775, it had matriculated 1,382 bachelors of arts, or 29% of all degrees earned in Anglo-America before the Revolution.

A fourth institution of higher learning evolved from the "Log College" at Neshaminy, Pennsylvania, established in 1735 as a seminary for training Presbyterian ministers, who were in short supply within the Mid-Atlantic colonies. To carry on the Log College's work within a formal collegiate setting, Presbyterians obtained a charter on October 22, 1746, for the College of New Jersey. The school opened in May 1747 at Elizabeth Town (now Elizabeth), soon moved to Newark, and in 1756 relocated to Nassau Hall (the largest nonmilitary structure in British America when completed) at Princeton, which formally became its name when it became a university in 1896. The college's first class of six bachelors graduated in 1748. From then until 1775, it produced 462 bachelors of arts, 9.7% of all baccalaureate degrees given in British America before the Revolution.

To counteract the growing influence of Dissenters from the Church of England after the revivals of the Great Awakening, Anglican laymen petitioned New York's assembly for a college charter. The legislature responded with a charter for King's College on October 13, 1754, but insisted that it not be officially organized as an Anglican institution. Although ostensibly nonsectarian, King's College nevertheless had an Anglican president and a majority of that faith among its board of trustees and early faculty. King's College held its first commencement in 1758 and graduated 111 students through 1775. It largely suspended academic activities during the Revolution and reopened in 1784 as Columbia.

Believed to have been inspired by the work of Sir Christopher Wren when it was built in the early eighteenth century, the Wren Building served for many years as the College of William and Mary's sole structure to house all classrooms, faculty offices, and dormitory quarters. (Courtesy Library of Congress)

The last college founded before 1763 was the "College, Academy, and Charitable School of Philadelphia," chartered on June 16, 1755. This institution originated in a grammar school established in 1751 by leading Pennsylvanians, including Benjamin Franklin. The College of Philadelphia was officially a nonsectarian school, but it soon fell under de facto Anglican control. It awarded its earliest baccalaureate degrees in 1757, and it graduated 164 bachelors of arts or medicine by 1775. The College of Philadelphia was later renamed the University of Pennsylvania in 1791.

All the colleges founded prior to 1760 were private rather than state-supported institutions; they supported themselves through tuition and income from an endowment (usually rents), not by legislative subsidies. All except William and Mary and the College of Philadelphia owed their origin to religious motivation. Even in the case of William and Mary, its first president was the minister then serving as the Bishop of London's commissary (local representative) in Virginia, and Anglican clergymen conducted virtually all instruction until the 1760s.

It is not surprising that most graduates entered the ministry given the religious foundation underlying early American higher education. Of all 320 Harvard graduates matriculating by 1689 whose occupations have been identified, 56% entered the clergy, compared to just 13% who held high political office, 8% who practiced medicine, and 4% who became teachers. The Enlightenment's secularizing influence gradually lessened the attraction of the pulpit as a career after 1700. Of the seventy-one young men earning degrees from Harvard, Yale, and the College of New Jersey in 1760, for example, only 32% devoted their lives to the ministry.

Anglo-American colleges immediately diverged from their English counterparts regarding the roles of faculty and president. At Oxford and Cambridge, where universities had matured from ancient communities of scholarship and teaching, the faculty controlled all administrative affairs by collective vote and delegated limited responsibility to its appointed administrators. Colonial colleges appeared almost overnight, without faculties, and their immediate success depended heavily on the energy and ingenuity of their early presidents. Strong-willed presidents such as Harvard's Henry Dunster and William and Mary's James Blair chose their own faculties, designed the curriculum, and centralized college governance in the hands of themselves and the corporation trustees. Their example set the mold for American higher education's internal structure and minimized the chance for faculties to create an autonomous base of power vis-à-vis the administration.

Also contributing to the institutional weakness of colonial faculties was their small size. Harvard opened with a single instructor assisted by two ushers; it evidently never had more than three faculty members simultaneously teaching during its first seventy years; yet it managed to produce more than 450 bachelors of arts during that period. Yale's president, who was also minister of a local congregation, taught all classes

TABLE 12.3 OCCUPATIONS OF GRADUATES OF HARVARD, YALE, AND THE COLLEGE OF NEW JERSEY, 1700–1770

Occupations	Harvard					Yale				College of New Jersey		
	1700	1725	1750	1760	1770	1725	1750	1760	1770	1750	1760	1770
Number of graduates	15	47	19	27	34	9	16	33	19	6	11	22
Ministers	7	17	7	6	9	4	3	13	8	2	4	10
Physicians	1	6	1	3	4	0	4	5	1	2	1	1
Lawyers	0	1	1	4	7	0	2	4	2	0	0	3
Teachers	2	3	1	0	1	0	0	0	0	0	0	2
Merchants	1	5	1	2	2	2	2	1	3	0	2	0
Farmers	0	4	1	2	1	0	0	3	0	0	0	0
Public servants	1	3	1	1	1	1	0	0	0	0	0	1
Minister-teachers	0	1	0	0	0	0	0	1	0	0	1	0
Physician-merchants	0	0	0	0	0	0	1	0	0	0	0	0
Minister-lawyers	0	0	0	1	0	1	0	0	0	0	0	0
Teacher-merchants	0	1	0	0	0	0	0	0	0	0	0	0
Minister-farmers	0	0	0	0	1	0	0	0	0	0	1	0
Minister–public servants	0	1	0	0	1	0	0	0	0	0	1	1
Teacher-farmers	0	0	0	1	1	0	0	0	0	0	0	0
Minister-physicians	0	1	0	0	0	0	0	0	0	0	0	0
Other	3	4	6	7	6	1	4	6	5	2	1	4

Source: Lawrence A. Cremin, *American Education: The Colonial Experience, 1607–1783* (1970), 554.

until the first commencement, after which an assistant aided him; not until 1723 did the staff expand to include the rector and two tutors. In 1700, William and Mary's staff consisted of its president (who taught), a professor of humanities, and an usher. During the first fifteen years that King's College operated, its faculty (including the president) never exceeded three. The total number of active professors in all the colonies stood at just ten in 1750 but had doubled by 1760 as two new colleges emerged and the older institutions expanded in size.

The number of degrees earned in Anglo-America continually rose at a rate doubling approximately every quarter-century, as the figures in Table 12.4 demonstrate. It is rather sobering to consider that a few colonies isolated on the edge of a howling wilderness could produce 3,355 bachelors of arts with a educational system that never numbered more than two dozen full-time professors until the early 1760s. Harvard and Yale awarded 99% of all degrees conferred by 1750, but their share of the total slipped to about two-thirds by the 1760s.

By the 1660s, Harvard was graduating classes that averaged about seven per year. In 1670, the ratio of living degree holders from American colleges to the general population reached its peak of 14.0 per 10,000 persons (30.8 per 10,000 in New England alone). The proportion of college-educated individuals gradually declined until 1690, when it reached 10.1 per 10,000 (24.7 per 10,000 in New England); it again rose to its former high 14.0 per 10,000 (42.9 per 10,000 in

New England) by 1740 but then sustained another long-term decline until reaching 11.8 per 10,000 in 1760. Because college was blocked to blacks, these figures nevertheless underestimate the educational attainments of whites. For the thirteen colonies as a group, the ratio of bachelors of arts per 10,000 whites rose from 12.8 in 1700 to 16.5 in 1740 and then fell slightly to 15.0 by 1760.

Colonial colleges followed the custom of European universities, where young men normally studied for the bachelor of arts between the ages of fifteen and nineteen. The baccalaureate course of instruction usually lasted four years in Europe and early America, although

TABLE 12.4 NUMBER OF DEGREES, 1642–1763

Interval	Number of Colleges	Number of Degrees	Percent of All Degrees
1642–1650	1	45	1.3%
1651–1675	1	167	5.0%
1676–1700	1	234	7.0%
1700–1725	2	616	18.4%
1726–1750	3	1,217	36.3%
1751–1763	6	1,076	32.0%
Total	6	3,355	100.0%

Source: Walter Crosby Eells, *Baccalaureate Degrees Conferred by American Colleges in the Seventeenth and Eighteenth centuries,* U.S. Office of Education Circular No. 528 (May 1958), 33–36.

TABLE 12.5 BACCALAUREATE DEGREES AWARDED BY ANGLO-AMERICAN COLLEGES AND NUMBER OF BACHELOR-DEGREE GRADUATES ALIVE BY YEAR, 1642–1776

Year	No. of Institutions	No. of Degrees	Cumulative No. of Graduates	No. Living	No. of Living Graduates per 10,000 Population
1642	1	9	9	9	…
1643	1	4	13	13	…
1644	1	0	13	13	…
1645	1	7	20	20	…
1646	1	4	24	23	…
1647	1	7	31	30	…
1648	1	0	31	30	…
1649	1	5	36	35	…
1650	1	9	45	43	8.3
1651	1	10	55	53	…
1652	1	1	56	54	…
1653	1	17	73	71	…
1654	1	1	74	72	…
1655	1	2	76	72	…
1656	1	8	84	80	…
1657	1	7	91	84	…
1658	1	7	98	91	…
1659	1	10	108	101	…
1660	1	8	116	108	12.7
1661	1	12	128	119	…
1662	1	6	134	124	…
1663	1	6	140	129	…
1664	1	7	147	135	…

Year	No. of Institutions	No. of Degrees	Cumulative No. of Graduates	No. Living	No. of Living Graduates per 10,000 Population
1665	1	8	155	142	...
1666	1	4	159	144	...
1667	1	7	166	151	...
1668	1	5	171	150	...
1669	1	10	181	158	...
1670	1	4	185	160	14.0
1671	1	11	196	169	...
1672	1	0	196	167	...
1673	1	4	200	171	...
1674	1	3	203	172	...
1675	1	9	212	180	...
1676	1	3	215	180	...
1677	1	6	221	183	...
1678	1	4	225	181	...
1679	1	4	229	180	...
1680	1	5	234	182	11.7
1681	1	9	243	186	...
1682	1	0	243	180	...
1683	1	3	246	179	...
1684	1	9	255	181	...
1685	1	14	269	191	...
1686	1	7	276	196	...
1687	1	11	287	203	...
1688	1	0	287	199	...
1689	1	14	301	199	...
1690	1	22	323	215	10.1
1691	1	8	331	216	...
1692	1	6	337	215	...
1693	1	15	352	226	...
1694	1	8	360	230	...
1695	1	22	382	249	...
1696	1	9	391	251	...
1697	1	14	405	254	...
1698	1	14	419	267	...
1699	1	12	431	276	...
1700	1	15	446	285	10.4
1701	1	19	465	298	...
1702	2	14	479	308	...
1703	2	15	494	316	...
1704	2	7	501	316	...
1705	2	16	517	326	...
1706	2	10	527	333	...
1707	2	22	549	348	...
1708	2	16	565	359	...
1709	2	19	584	373	...
1710	2	16	600	384	10.7
1711	2	15	615	391	...
1712	2	19	634	404	...
1713	2	8	642	401	...
1714	2	20	662	414	...
1715	2	21	683	428	...
1716	2	11	694	434	...
1717	2	22	716	444	...
1718	2	32	748	470	...
1719	2	27	775	487	...
1720	2	31	806	509	10.7
1721	2	51	857	549	...
1722	2	39	896	579	...
1723	2	54	950	616	...
1724	2	58	1,008	664	...
1725	2	54	1,062	703	...
1726	2	54	1,116	747	...
1727	2	47	1,163	779	...
1728	2	54	1,217	824	...
1729	2	40	1,257	849	...
1730	2	54	1,311	893	13.6
1731	2	47	1,358	924	...
1732	2	50	1,408	958	...
1733	2	54	1,462	1,002	...
1734	2	41	1,503	1,039	...
1735	2	62	1,565	1,089	...

Year	No. of Institutions	No. of Degrees	Cumulative No. of Graduates	No. Living	No. of Living Graduates per 10,000 Population
1736	2	46	1,611	1,117	...
1737	2	58	1,669	1,164	...
1738	2	48	1,717	1,197	...
1739	2	42	1,759	1,222	...
1740	2	43	1,802	1,245	14.0
1741	2	45	1,847	1,275	...
1742	2	41	1,888	1,295	...
1743	2	55	1,943	1,336	...
1744	2	45	1,988	1,366	...
1745	2	51	2,039	1,391	...
1746	2	24	2,063	1,384	...
1747	2	56	2,119	1,406	...
1748	3	66	2,185	1,445	...
1749	3	52	2,237	1,468	...
1750	3	42	2,279	1,487	12.3
1751	3	67	2,346	1,526	...
1752	3	50	2,396	1,545	...
1753	4	49	2,445	1,558	...
1754	4	55	2,500	1,578	...
1755	4	59	2,559	1,601	...
1756	4	69	2,628	1,633	...
1757	5	94	2,722	1,700	...
1758	6	99	2,821	1,768	...
1759	6	115	2,936	1,861	...
1760	6	85	3,021	1,904	11.8
1761	6	98	3,119	1,972	...
1762	6	125	3,244	2,054	...
1763	6	111	3,355	2,140	...
1764	6	90	3,445	2,192	...
1765	6	144	3,589	2,290	...
1766	6	131	3,720	2,369	...
1767	6	85	3,805	2,408	...
1768	6	106	3,911	2,470	...
1769	7	107	4,018	2,534	...
1770	7	102	4,120	2,595	11.8
1771	8	133	4,251	2,667	...
1772	8	117	4,366	2,740	...
1773	8	126	4,492	2,806	...
1774	9	127	4,619	2,879	12.2
1775	9	150	4,769	2,961	...
1776	9	138	4,906	3,023	...

Note: The population figures on which the source based its ratio of living graduates per 10,000 population are higher than those used in Table 5.1, which is based on the latest data.

Source: Walter Crosby Eells, *Baccalaureate Degrees Conferred by American Colleges in the Seventeenth and Eighteenth Centuries,* U.S. Office of Education Circular No. 528 (May 1958), 33–36.

Harvard compressed it to three years for a brief time before 1655 and William and Mary decreed two years sufficient for a bachelor's degree in 1727. The average Anglo-American scholar graduated when 20.8 years old. John Trumbull of Connecticut satisfied Yale's entrance examinations when just seven years and five months old but delayed his entry until 1763 when he turned thirteen. The oldest graduate of any colonial institution was John Phelps, who entered Yale when thirty-nine and matriculated at forty-three in 1759.

The college curriculum assumed that students would already be fluent in Latin and be familiar with Greek grammar. The program of studies revolved around three academic exercises: the lecture, declamation, and disputation—all in classical languages. Lectures served as oral textbooks, with faculty delineating a great author's ideas or demonstrating systematic thought at its most precise to examine a

TABLE 12.6   THE TIMES AND ORDER OF STUDIES AT HARVARD IN 1642

First Year

Day	8 A.M.	9 A.M.	10 A.M.	1 P.M.	2 P.M.	3 P.M.	4 P.M.
Monday and Tuesday	Logic; physics	...	...	...	Disputations	...	...
Wednesday	Greek etymology and syntax	...	...	...	Greek grammar, from literature	...	...
Thursday	Hebrew grammar	...	...	...	Hebrew Bible readings	...	...
Friday	Rhetoric	Declamations	Rhetoric	...	R h e t o r i c		
Saturday	Catechetical divinity	Commonplaces	...	History; nature of plants	...	...	...

Second Year

Day	8 A.M.	9 A.M.	10 A.M.	1 P.M.	2 P.M.	3 P.M.	4 P.M.
Monday and Tuesday	...	Ethics; politics	...	...	...	Disputations	...
Wednesday	...	Greek prosody and dialects	...	...	...	Greek poetry	...
Thursday	...	"Chaldee" grammar	...	...	...	Practice in Chaldee; Ezra and Daniel	...
Friday	Rhetoric	Declamations	Rhetoric	...	R h e t o r i c		
Saturday	Catechetical divinity	Commonplaces	...	History; nature of plants	...	...	...

Third Year

Day	8 A.M.	9 A.M.	10 A.M.	1 P.M.	2 P.M.	3 P.M.	4 P.M.
Monday and Tuesday	...	...	Arithmetic; geometry; astronomy	...	...	...	Disputations
Wednesday	...	T h e o r y o f G r e e k [s t y l e]		...	Exercise in Greek style, both in prose and verse		...
Thursday	...	...	Syriac grammar	...	...	...	Practice in Syriac: New Testament
Friday	Rhetoric	Declamations	Rhetoric	...	R h e t o r i c		...
Saturday	Catechetical divinity	Commonplaces	...	History; nature of plants	...	...	...

Source: Lawrence J. Cremin, *American Education: The Colonial Experience, 1607–1783* (1970), 214.

problem in disciplines such as logic or ethics. Students used lectures as a model for their own declamations in which they exhibited their skill at rhetoric by eloquent phraseology and their accumulated knowledge by parading a small army of allusions from ancient literature. The disputation pitted two or more scholars in a debate over a proposition introduced by a moderator. The object was to rebut accusations that one's thesis was illogical or unfounded in fact and to explose flaws in opposing arguments with oratical flourish, clever puns, or apt axioms from classical savants. In 1642, Harvard adopted a modified version of Cambridge's curriculum shown in Table 12.6.

Early American colleges modeled their progression of studies on England's university curriculum, which originated in medieval times. The first year concentrated on Latin, Greek, and rhetoric. Besides more Latin, Greek, and rhetoric, the second year generally included geography, mathematics, and philosophy's first principles. The third year deemphasized classical languages in favor of mathematics and philosophy (both natural and moral). The fourth year combined variations of the above, plus the president's special lectures on topics such as history, law, philosophy, criticism, and composition.

During the eighteenth century, science and moral philosophy received more emphasis, and classical languages less. French and a few other modern languages began to find their way into the curriculum. Colleges also began to deviate from the tutorial system, in which a tutor taught all subjects to a group of students during their years of attendance, in place of naming professors to teach specific disciplines. The eighteenth century also witnessed a slow decline in the popularity of Latin disputations in favor of debates in English on current topics like politics.

William Smith (1727–1803), whom Benjamin Franklin enticed to become the College of Philadelphia's provost, devised the period's most progressive curriculum in 1756. He limited Latin and Greek to a third of the program, allowed another third for science and mathematics, and allocated the remaining time for logic, ethics, metaphysics, and rhetoric. He also recommended that students read works by important current authors. Smith's three-year plan of study, with suggested readings, was as follows in Table 12.7.

Innovations such as Smith's nevertheless represented reform at slow pace. It was the classical curriculum, as inherited from the

TABLE 12.7   WILLIAM SMITH'S PLAN OF STUDY

		First Year		
Term	Lecture I	Lecture II	Lecture III	Private Hours
First Term	Latin and English exercises	Arithmetic Decimal arithmetic Algebra	Homer, *Iliad* Juvenal	*The Spectator, The Rambler,* and monthly magazines for the improvement of style and knowledge of life
Second Term	...	Fractions and extracting roots Simple and quadratic equations Euclid, *Elements,* demonstrated by Edmund Stone (Books I–VI)	Pindar Cicero Livy	Isaac Barrow, *Geometrical Lectures* Ignace Gaston Pardies, *Short, but Yet Plain Elements of Geometry and Plain Trigonometry* Colin Maclaurin, *A Treatise of Algebra* John Ward, *The Young Mathematician's Guide* John Keill, *The Elements of Plain and Spherical Trigonometry*
Third Term	Logic with metaphysics William Duncan, *The Elements of Logick* Jean Le Clerc, *Logica,* or Jean Pierre de Crousaz, *A New Treatise of the Art of Thinking*	Euclid, *Elements,* demonstrated by Edmund Stone (Books I–VI) Logarithmical arithmetic Henry Wilson, *Trigonometry Improved* Henry Sherwin, ed., *Mathematical Tables*	Thucydides or Euripides Dionysius Periegetes, *Geography,* translated by E. Wells	Isaac Watts, *Logick, Philosophical Essays on Various Subjects,* and *Brief Scheme of Ontology* John Locke, *An Essay Concerning Human Understanding* Francis Hutcheson, *Metaphysicae synopsis* Bernardus Varenius, *A Compleat System of General Geography,* corrected by Peter Shaw William King, *An Essay on the Origin of Evil,* with notes by E. Law
Throughout	Occasional disputation	...	Occasional declamation	...

		Second Year		
	Lecture I	Lecture II	Lecture III	Private Hours
First Term	Logic, etc., reviewed Surveying and dialing Navigation	Plane and spherical trigonometry	"Rhetoric," in Robert Dodsley, *The Preceptor* Longinus	Gerhard Johannes Vossius, *Elements rhetorica* René Le Bossu, *Traité du Poème Épique* Dominique Bouhours, *The Art of Criticism* John Dryden, *Select Essays on the Belles Lettres* Joseph Spence, *An Essay on Pope's Odyssey* Joseph Trapp, *Lectures on Poetry* Dionysius of Halicarnassus, *De structura orationis liber*
Second Term	Conic sections Fluxions	Euclid, *Elements,* demonstrated by Edmund Stone (Books XI–XII) Architecture with fortification	Horace, *Art of Poetry* Aristotle, *Art of Poetry* Quintilian	Demetrius Phalereus, *De elocutione, sive dictione rhetorica* Famianus Strada, *Prolusiones academicae oratoriae, historicae, poeticae, etc.* Archibald Patoun, *A Complete Treatise of Practical Navigation* David Gregory, *A Treatise of Practical Geometry* Charles Bisset, *The Theory and Construction of Fortification* Thomas Simpson, *Elements of Plane Geometry*
Third Term	David Fordyce, *The Elements of Moral Philosophy* (Fordyce well understood will be an excellent introduction to the larger ethic writers.)	John Rowning, *A Compendious System of Natural Philosophy* ("The Properties of Bodies," "The Mechanic Powers," "Hydrostatics," and "Pneumatics") (Rowning's *System* may be supplemented by the larger works recommended for private study.)	Cicero, *Pro Milone* Demosthenes, *Pro Ctesiphon* (During the application of the rules to these famous orations, imitations of them are to be attempted on the models of perfect eloquence.)	Colin Maclaurin, *A Treatise on Fluxions* William Emerson, *The Doctrine of Fluxions* Andrea Palladio, *Architecture,* translated by Isaac Ware Richard Helsham, *A Course of Lectures in Natural Philosophy* Willem Jakob Gravesande, *Mathematical Elements of Natural Philosophy* Roger Cotes, *Hydrostatical and Pneumatical Lectures* Desaguliers, J. T. Pieter van Musschenbroek, *Elements physicae* John Keill, *An Introduction to Natural Philosophy* Benjamin Martin, *Philosophia Britannica* Isaac Newton, *The Mathematical Principles of Natural Philosophy* Colin Maclaurin, *An Account of Sir Isaac Newton's Philosophical Discoveries* Jacques Rohault, *Natural Philosophy,* with notes by S. Clarke
Throughout	Occasional disputation	Occasional declamation	...	...

		Third Year		
	Lecture I	Lecture II	Lecture III	Private Hours
First Term	Francis Hutcheson, *A Short Introduction to Moral Philosophy* Jean Jacques Burlamaqui, *The Principles of Natural Law* Introduction to civil history	John Rowning, *A Compendious System of Natural Philosophy* ("Light," "Colours," and "Optics") (Anonymous Jesuit), *Perspective Practical* John Keill, *An Introduction to the True Astronomy*	Epictetus, *Enchiridion* Cicero, *De officiis* and *Tusculanae quaestiones* Xenophon, *Memorabilia* Denys Petau, *Rationarium temporum*	Samuel von Pufendorf, *Law of Nature and Nations,* with notes by Jean Barbeyrac Richard Cumberland, *A Treatise of the Laws of Nature* John Selden, *Of the Judicature in Parliaments* Montesquieu, *The Spirit of Laws* Algernon Sidney, *Discourses Concerning Government* James Harrington Seneca Francis Hutcheson, *A System of Moral Philosophy* John Locke, *Two Treatises of Government*
Second Term	Introduction to laws and government Introduction to trade and commerce	Natural history of vegetables Natural history of animals	Plato, *Laws* Hugo Grotius, *De jure belli ac pacis*	Richard Hooker, *Of the Lawes of Ecclesiastical Politie* Joseph Justus Scaliger, *Opus novum de emendatione temporum* Robert Dodsley, *The Preceptor* Jean Le Clerc, *Compendium historiae universalis*

(continued)

TABLE 12.7   (continued)

Third Year				
Term	Lecture I	Lecture II	Lecture III	Private Hours
Third Term	Review of the whole Examination for degree of B.A.	Hermann Boerhaave, *A New Method of Chemistry,* with notes by Peter Shaw Natural history of fossils Natural history of agriculture	Composition and declamation on moral and physical subjects Philosophy acts held	David Gregory, *The Elements of Astronomy* John Fortescue, *A Learned Commendation of the Politique Lawes of Englande* Nathaniel Bacon, *An Historical and Political Discourse of the Laws & Government of England* Francis Bacon, *Works* John Locke, *Several Papers Relating to Money, Interest and Trade of England* Charles Davenant, *Discourse on the Publik Revenues, and on the Trade of England* Joshua Gee, *The Trade and Navigation of Great-Britain Considered* John Ray, *The Wisdom of God Manifested in the Works of Creation* William Derham, *Physico-Theology* N. A. Pluche, *Spectacle de la Nature* Guillaume Rondelet, *Libri de piscibus marinis* Bernard Nieuwentijt, *The Religious Philosopher* Holy Bible
During All Three Years				
	Lecture I	Lecture II	Lecture III	Private Hours
		Study of the French language at leisure hours, if desired		Holy Bible to be read daily

Source: Lawrence J. Cremin, *Amererican Education: The Colonial Experience, 1607–1783* (1970), 382–83.

Middle Ages via the example of seventeenth-century Cambridge, that remained the core of colonial higher education. The six colleges founded by 1763 changed far more by the accretion of new knowledge or approaches spawned by the Enlightenment than by breaking with past traditions. Old traditions died hard, but at least new and practical subjects were not rejected once their value was seen.

Literacy and Libraries

England began to establish its overseas colonies at a time when few of its own people could read and still fewer could write. According to the best current estimate, about 30% of adult English males could write their own name as of 1641–44, and perhaps 10%—or less—of English women had also mastered this skill. Access to schooling varied significantly by locale, with illiteracy generally reaching levels of 75% in the north and southwest of England, 66% in the southeast and within the Thames River basin, and less than half of people raised in London and other major cities. The same pattern of illiteracy prevailed in seventeenth-century France.

The educational attainments of New England's first generation of Puritans diverged notably from those of the countrypeople they left behind. As of 1660, probate records indicate that the proportion of New Englanders who could sign their names stood at 61% of men (twice the rate as in their homeland) and 31% of women (three times female literacy rates in England). These testators comprised the first generation of Puritan settlers, who had sprung largely from more affluent individuals able to afford the cost of transporting their families to America, an expense beyond the means of tenants and unskilled laborers who composed the majority of England's unlettered masses. The Puritan exodus disproportionately drew on middle-class yeomen and village craftsworkers, groups that were far more literate than the average English person of the 1600s.

New England was unique among the English colonies in attracting settlers who were unusually learned by European standards. This founding stock almost immediately took active steps, such as passing the Old Deluder Act, to create a local school system that would ensure that their children received sufficient instruction to read the Bible and keep a tradesman's business accounts. Literacy among Yankees consequently made steady gains during the colonial era. The number of adult men able to sign their own wills rose from 61% in 1660, to 69% by 1710, 84% by 1760, and approached 90% by 1790. By the end of the eighteenth century, New England was poised to become the modern world's first society—on either side of the Atlantic—to achieve universal male literacy.

Indentured servants furnished the main source of settlers for the southern colonies, and their educational backgrounds were more typical of English society than New England's Puritans. Of 758 servants who left Middlesex, England, for the New World during 1683 and 1684, only 40.5% of men and 10.8% of women could sign their own indenture papers. The most careful study of literacy yet completed on seventeenth-century Virginia determined that 53.3% of Middlesex County's former servants were illiterate and that 61.6% of unskilled laborers also could not write or read.

Although literacy among adult males in England rose sharply from about 30% around 1640 to approximately 50% by 1750, it still lagged behind the thirteen colonies. Among the middle-class farmers of Middlesex County, Virginia (who included many owners of one or two slaves), approximately 60% were literate by the mid-eighteenth century, as were about 27% of the county's white women. Current studies indicate that literacy in the Chesapeake peaked at about 60% to 70% for males and 30% for women during the late 1700s. High levels of literacy in the thirteen colonies resulted not only from improved access to schooling for American children but also from the immigration of groups that were better educated than Europeans in general. Among German immigrants, for instance, 71% of adult males could sign their names. One study of English indentured servants bound for America from 1718 to 1759 revealed that 68.8% of males and 34.9% of females were literate. For the Mid-Atlantic region, current research indicates that 65% to 70% of white men could write by 1750, and undoubtedly a greater number could read. Even members of low-paying occupations with little social status, like mariners, were surprisingly literate. Of seventy-six sailors enlisted at New York in early 1756 as the crew for a royal warship on Lake Ontario, for example, 63% could sign their names.

One result of widespread literacy was the proliferation of book ownership across a broad range of social classes. Based on a major

TABLE 12.8 OWNERSHIP OF BOOKS AT TIME OF DEATH AMONG ANGLO-AMERICAN OCCUPATIONAL GROUPS IN 1760s

Groups	% Owning Books
Lawyers	100%
Ministers	94%
Doctors	94%
Esquires	85%
Merchants	70%
Farmers	68%
Artisans	58%
Shopkeepers	51%
Innkeepers	50%
Ships' Captains	50%
Misc. nonfarm	48%
Mariners	33%

Note: Data based on 1,800 inventories from Massachusetts, Virginia., and South Carolina.
Source: Jackson T. Main, *The Social Structure of Revolutionary America* (1965), 257.

Many country gentlemen kept and expanded private libraries, from which they often lent books to their relatives and neighbors. Most holdings were small, however, and their owners—like this Virginia planter portrayed by Howard Pyle—undoubtedly read and reread each volume several times during their lifetime because of the general scarcity of books. (*Harper's Magazine,* January 1896)

study of inventories probated in Massachusetts, Virginia, and South Carolina, colonial America was a remarkably well-read society. More than two-thirds of farmers, almost three-fifths of craftsworkers, and even a third of seamen possessed printed materials. Even among rather penurious decedants who left less than £50 in property, almost half left at least one item for reading, most often a Bible and commonly some devotional writings plus some old almanacs.

Farmers and craftsworkers might own a few well-thumbed books, but only learned wealthy planters, sophisticated merchants, and learned ministers accumulated substantial libraries. In the early seventeenth century, a modest collection like John Harvard's of Massachusetts, which totaled 400 volumes divided among 329 titles at his death in 1638, ranked as a major body of knowledge. By 1720, the 4,000 books and pamphlets owned by Boston's Rev. Cotton Mather constituted Anglo-America's greatest library. Among the renowned libraries of the 1740s were the 2,000 books owned by James Logan of Philadelphia and the 3,600 texts arranged along twenty-three black-walnut cases of William Byrd's Charles City County, Virginia, plantation.

Most college libraries, all of which were private collections belonging to private corporations, grew modestly in the colonial

TABLE 12.9 SUBJECT ANALYSIS OF PRIVATE LIBRARIES IN COLONIAL VIRGINIA

Name, County	Year	Total Titles	Philosophy	Classical	History	Religion	Science	Literature	Doubtful
Seventeenth Century									
John Carter, Lancaster	1690	64	18%	18%	4%	32%	20%	7%	1%
Thomas Cocke, Princess Anne	1697	33	23%	1%	…	30%	23%	2%	…
Mathew Hubard, York	1667	34	6%	8%	4%	40%	25%	12%	5%
Arthur Spicer, Richmond	1600	114	62%	3%	5%	26%	2%	2%	…
Sarah Willoughby, Lower Norfolk	1673	49	6%	20%	10%	40%	15%	5%	4%
Eighteenth Century									
Edmund Berkeley	1718	102	25%	12%	15%	28%	15%	3%	7%
Robert Carter, Westmoreland	1772	659	20%	30%	12%	10%	10%	15%	5%
William Dunlop, Prince William	1740	110	7%	25%	12%	13%	9%	30%	4%
William Fleming, Montgomery	1787	209	12%	10%	10%	15%	30%	20%	3%
John Herbert, Chesterfield	1760	157	30%	20%	10%	5%	10%	20%	5%
Richard Lee, Westmoreland	1715	301	15%	35%	5%	15%	5%	15%	10%
Daniel McCarty, Westmoreland	1724	109	50%	15%	3%	15%	8%	2%	7%
John Waller, Spotsylvania	1755	128	13%	4%	25%	17%	17%	24%	…
Ralph Wormeley, Middlesex	1763	383	20%	12%	17%	21%	17%	5%	8%

Source: George K. Smart, "Private Libraries in Colonial Virginia," *American Literature,* X (1938), 33.

TABLE 12.10   TOPICAL DISTRIBUTION OF BOOKS IN HARVARD COLLEGE LIBRARY, 1723

Subject	Number of Titles	Percentage of Titles
Theology	1726	58
Literature	277	9
Science	232	8
Philosophy	219	7
History	202	7
Law	57	2
Geography	49	2
Government	49	2
Biography	23	1
Arts	9 }	
Commerce	2 }	4
Other	116 }	

Source: Lawrence A. Cremin, *American Education: The Colonial Experience, 1607–1783* (1970), 397.

period. The typical college funded acquisitions at a painfully slow rate of thirty to forty titles a year, so none had holdings that exceeded a thousand imprints (including many pamphlets) by 1763 except Harvard and Yale. The greatest collection of all was Harvard's, which numbered 3,500 volumes (covering 2,961 titles by 1723 and probably included at least 4,700 in 1763).

Robert Keyne, a wealthy merchant, sponsored the earliest effort to create a public library in 1657 by leaving a bequest through his will for funding a public collection for use by city officials and some others. The first genuine Anglo-American lending libraries originated through efforts of the Society for the Propagation of Christian Knowledge (SPCK), an organization founded by Rev. Thomas Bray and other Anglicans for the encouragement of the return of colonial dissenters to the Church of England's fold. The SPCK contributed funds for endowing Anglican parishes with parochial libraries, which would elevate the clergy's intellectual qualifications and uplift the laity spiritually. A shipment of 1,095 volumes to Annapolis, Maryland, resulted in the founding at that city of early America's first lending library, which opened to the public in 1696. These "Bray libraries" not only offered the Bible, the Book of Common Prayer, and other religious tracts but also made available works on philosophy, ethics, metaphysics, rhetoric, science, mathematics, medicine, law, history, politics, classical grammars, prose, poetry, and drama. By 1700, the colonies contained more than thirty such institutions in locations ranging from major cities like Charles Town, South Carolina, to small hamlets like Burlington, New Jersey.

As an alternative to tax-supported libraries (of which none existed in the colonial period), Anglo-Americans began to organize subscription libraries, which had originated in Britain. These organizations raised money to buy books by charging members an entry fee and annual dues, and they operated from one of the officers' homes at least one afternoon a week. In 1731, Benjamin Franklin was instrumental in founding the earliest such "book society," the Library Company of Philadelphia, which he later termed the "mother of all the North American subscription libraries." Although officially limited to dues-paying members, many of these "book clubs" permitted others to read for free in the few hours when the collection was open to lend and receive publications. By 1762, at least nineteen subscription libraries had appeared in the colonies, of which sixteen were in New England. Privately organized societies would serve as the primary means of providing widespread access to books for the public until 1803 when the country's first tax-supported library was founded in New York City.

CHAPTER 13 Arts and Letters

Publishing and Literature

Anglo-American publishing commenced in 1638 when Rev. Jose Glover emigrated from England to Massachusetts with a printing press and his apprentice, Stephen Day, a locksmith by trade. Glover died at sea, but his widow established the press at Cambridge and retained Day and his son Matthew to operate it for her. The Glover-Day printery continued until 1649 when it became the property of Samuel Green, whose descendants composed the first family of early American publishing and operated presses for almost two centuries in Massachusetts, Connecticut, Virginia, and Maryland.

The colonies' first imprint rolled off Stephen and Matthew Day's Cambridge press in early 1639; it was a half-sheet broadside of 222 words titled "The Oath of a Freeman," which prescribed the pledge taken when an adult received the right to vote. Later that year, the Days produced *An Almanac Calculated for New England by Mr. Peirce, Mariner,* a work of uncertain length; no copy has survived. The third work typeset at Cambridge ranks as the first bound book (rather than a pamphlet) of North American manufacture, the *Whole Book of Psalmes* (1640), an original translation from Hebrew by Richard Mather, John Eliot, and Thomas Weld and better known as the *Bay Psalm Book.* The *Bay Psalm Book* was a respectable entry into book publishing: it totaled 294 pages, had a first printing of 1,700 copies, and is the earliest imprint to have survived from colonial times to the present.

Cambridge remained the sole preserve of colonial publishing until 1675, when John Foster, a Harvard graduate, brought a press into operation at Boston. An amateur engraver who carved his own wood-cuts, Foster produced the earliest American books featuring illustrations and maps. When the Greens moved their Cambridge press to Boston in 1692, the latter city became the de facto center of American publishing and maintained that distinction until the 1760s when Philadelphia surpassed it. By 1714, Boston possessed three print shops, which satisfied the demand generated by all of New England. New England's demand for printed material inevitably outgrew Boston's capacity to meet it, however, and it became economically feasible to establish presses in Connecticut by 1709, Rhode Island by 1727, and New Hampshire by 1756.

The first press outside New England was founded in 1685 by William Bradford at Philadelphia, which also became the site of the first North American paper mill in 1690. After printing pamphlets critical of Pennsylvania's ruling faction, Bradford found himself in jail for a technical violation of the British Parliament's law for licensing printers; in 1693, he left Pennsylvania—which was thereafter without a publisher for more than two decades—and established the first press in New York, where the governor named him royal printer. New York City later emerged as a major publishing center in the decade after 1760 when the number of its presses rose from four to seven. Philadelphia meanwhile had overtaken Boston as the greatest producer of printed materials by 1750 when the former contained eight presses.

William Nuthead, an Englishman, founded a press at Jamestown, Virginia, in 1682, but the House of Burgesses closed his shop the next year after he reprinted its journals without obtaining formal permission. He then relocated his press to St. Mary's, Maryland, where it continued until his death in 1795 when his widow Dinah—who could

This painting of apprentices setting type and working the press gives a sense of how small were the offices at which colonial printers turned out newspapers and books. (Courtesy Library of Congress)

TABLE 13.1   ESTABLISHMENT OF EARLY PRINTING PRESSES IN THE THIRTEEN COLONIES

Year	City
1639	Cambridge, Mass.
1675	Boston, Mass.
1682	Jamestown, Va.
1685	Annapolis, Md.
1686	Philadelphia, Pa.
1693	New York, N.Y.
1709	New London, Conn.
1723	Perth Amboy, N.J.
1727	Burlington, N.J.
1727	Newport, R.I.
1730	Williamsburg, Va.
1732	Charles Town, S.C.
1738	Germantown, Pa.
1745	Ephrata, Pa.
1747	Lancaster, Pa.
1751	New Bern, N.C.
1754	New Haven, Conn.
1755	Woodbridge, N.J.
1756	Portsmouth, N.H.
1761	Wilmington, Del.
1762	Savannah, Ga.
1762	Providence, R.I.
1763	Bethlehem, Pa.
1764	Hartford, Conn.

Sources: Arthur B. Berthold, *American Colonial Printing as Determined by Contemporary Cultural Forces* (1934), 85. John Tebbel, *A History of Book Publishing in the United States, I, The Creation of an Industry, 1630–1865* (1972), 41–42.

not sign her name but knew the alphabet well enough to set type— succeeded him, became the country's first female printer, and moved operations to Annapolis. Nuthead soon abandoned the business, however, as did her successor Thomas Reading, and printing did not revive on a permanent basis in the South until 1726 when William Parks opened a press at Annapolis, followed by another at Williamsburg in 1730. Four printers went into competition at Charles Town, South Carolina, from 1731 to 1733, but the only one to succeed was Benjamin Franklin's protégé Lewis Timothy, whose family and descendants continued as publishers for almost seventy-five years. Printing was established in North Carolina at New Bern by James Davis in 1749 and in Georgia at Savannah by James Johnston in 1763.

The total number of print shops increased steadily during the colonial era from four in 1690 to seven in 1710, fourteen in 1730, twenty-one in 1755, and thirty-four in 1763. Boston, Philadelphia, and New York City dominated this industry, and even as late as 1760, about three of every five printers resided in one of those cities. Many of the smallest and most rural provinces, including New Hampshire, New Jersey, and North Carolina, ceased depending on printers from neigh-

TABLE 13.2   REGIONAL DISTRIBUTION OF IMPRINTS, 1639–1763

Region	Years of Printing	Total Output	Percent of Total	Imprints per Year
New England	125	5,360	61.2%	42.9
Mid-Atlantic	79	3,149	35.9%	39.9
The South	38	251	2.9%	6.1

Source: Arthur B. Berthold, *American Colonial Printing as Determined by Contemporary Cultural Forces* (1934), 29.

boring colonies in the 1750s and acquired their own presses. By the 1770s, a permanent press existed in every one of the thirteen colonies.

Regional presses varied greatly according to their respective output. New England printers turned out just more than three-fifths of all colonial imprints during the period ending 1763. Publishers in the Mid-Atlantic colonies had an annual rate of production somewhat less than that in New England, and they accounted for slightly more than a third of all imprints. Just 3% of all published material came from southern presses, which collectively averaged just six items per year.

The number of items produced by Anglo-America's press rose exponentially over time. During the first half-century of colonial printing, the country's print shops (which never numbered more than four) are known to have turned out 462 imprints, but their output rose 143% to 1,124 during the next quarter-century from 1689 to 1713. Output doubled to 2,427 during the years 1714–38 and then doubled again during the next quarter-century. The 4,747 works published from 1739 to 1763 constituted 54% of all imprints made to that time.

The great majority of items that rolled off colonial presses were quite short, with most of them probably under twenty-four pages. Excluding the years before 1700, which accounted for only 10% of all publications, it was extremely rare for more than a quarter of any year's imprints to qualify as a book-length publication under the modern standard set by UNESCO, namely a bound volume of printed matter equaling fifty pages or more. Works of 150 pages or more were especially rare and only composed 10% or more of any given year's production on seven occasions during the seventy-five years from 1688 to 1763.

Because it is only possible to catalogue imprints for which some evidence of their manufacture has survived, their exact number remains unknown. On the basis of comparing printers' account books with surviving publications and other eighteenth-century sources, historians have estimated that the ratio of total imprints to known publications is approximately 4.7 to 1. If correct, then the full scale of colonial printing is much more extensive than the 8,760 works identified by bibliographers and would actually stand at approximately 41,000 separate pieces.

A small but increasingly significant production of foreign-language material (excluding text books) had emerged in Anglo-America by the 1760s. The earliest non-English imprint was a Dutch religious text of 126 pages by Justus Falckner, *Grondlycke Onderricht Van Sekere Hoofd-stricken . . . . ,* typeset by William Bradford at New York in 1708. The first German publication was a devotional pamphlet by Conrad Beissel, *Das Buechlein Vom Sabbath,* put out by Andrew Bradford at Philadelphia in 1728. For the period ending 1763, 3% of all colonial imprints appeared in a foreign language, of which 88% were German.

A few categories of reading material provided the economic mainstay of Anglo-America's publishing industry. The largest branch included government documents, mostly laws and proclamations, which composed nearly a fifth of all imprints before 1763. Government contracts were not especially lucrative because colonial assemblies were tight with their purse strings, but they ensured a regular source of income through the temporary lulls in business that beset all printers. They were particularly important because so many projects, such as statute books or legislative journals, required up to several hundred pages and generated large press runs. Government imprints were most crucial to the financial success of printers in the South where they formed 52% of all published material, compared to 21% in the Mid-Atlantic region, and 17% in New England.

The next-largest subdivision of publishing was sermons, which came in a great variety—including Sabbath services, days of thanksgiving or fasting, elections, militia training days, and marriages. Sermons represented almost 16% of the total output of colonial presses. Their

TABLE 13.3 OUTPUT OF PRINTERS IN THE THIRTEEN COLONIES, 1639–1763

Year	Number of Print Shops	Total Imprints[a]	German and Dutch Imprints[b]	Percent Equaling 50–149 Pages	Percent with 150 Pages or More
1763	34	343	23	8%	8%
1762	30	356	20	9%	7%
1761	28	347	12	6%	4%
1760	25	346	11	11%	5%
1759	26	321	8	8%	3%
1758	24	297	7	11%	5%
1757	23	324	7	9%	3%
1756	23	283	14	7%	2%
1755	21	349	18	8%	3%
1754	22	263	11	6%	6%
1753	20	231	8	10%	5%
1752	20	185	10	9%	9%
1751	19	219	11	9%	4%
1750	18	222	6	10%	6%
1749	18	188	15	14%	8%
1748	20	271	23	12%	3%
1747	20	224	13	11%	5%
1746	18	202	6	5%	4%
1745	18	239	10	8%	5%
1744	18	242	9	12%	12%
1743	18	247	14	12%	5%
1742	17	266	23	12%	8%
1741	15	257	4	16%	6%
1740	15	244	8	14%	3%
1739	15	164	3	9%	3%
1738	14	143	3	17%	5%
1737	13	128	1	15%	5%
1736	13	151	2	12%	5%
1735	14	140	…	16%	3%
1734	15	149	…	10%	…
1733	15	146	…	8%	3%
1732	15	154	2	8%	5%
1731	13	138	1	12%	6%
1730	14	167	7	10%	5%
1729	13	153	3	12%	10%
1728	11	174	1	14%	8%
1727	11	172	…	16%	4%
1726	10	125	3	15%	10%
1725	8	146	1	12%	3%
1724	8	122	…	15%	4%
1723	8	112	…	12%	8%
1722	8	116	…	6%	8%
1721	7	140	2	11%	9%
1720	7	127	1	11%	8%
1719	7	91	…	15%	7%
1718	6	88	…	18%	10%
1717	5	94	…	30%	5%
1716	4	84	…	19%	9%
1715	4	107	…	26%	8%
1714	4	87	…	8%	7%
1713	3	96	…	18%	8%
1712	3	76	…	27%	1%
1711	3	61	…	10%	10%
1710	4	72	…	25%	5%
1709	4	84	…	11%	6%
1708	3	56	1	12%	7%
1707	3	70	…	14%	8%
1706	4	59	…	19%	3%
1705	4	61	…	18%	11%
1704	4	63	…	11%	6%
1703	4	61	…	13%	3%
1702	4	77	…	16%	8%
1701	4	74	…	15%	5%
1700	4	77	…	17%	4%
1699	4	68	…	13%	6%
1698	3	48	…	15%	6%
1697	3	44	…	23%	2%
1696	3	41	…	15%	2%
1695	4	31	…	6%	10%
1694	3	32	…	31%	…
1693	5	61	…	18%	3%
1692	4	53	…	13%	…
1691	5	49	…	18%	2%
1690	4	59	…	14%	10%
1689	4	76	…	3%	5%
1688	4	35	…	14%	9%
1687	4	22	…	23%	9%
1686	4	32	…	6%	12%
1685	4	24	…	17%	12%
1684	2	27	…	7%	22%
1683	2	20	…	25%	…
1682	3	33	…	15%	9%
1681	2	15	…	…	7%
1680	2	21	…	14%	…
1679	2	22	…	14%	…
1678	2	23	…	4%	4%
1677	2	17	…	12%	…
1676	2	26	…	8%	4%
1675	2	19	…	5%	5%
1674	2	20	…	15%	…
1673	2	13	…	23%	8%
1672	2	10	…	10%	20%
1671	2	6	…	17%	…
1670	2	13	…	8%	8%
1669	2	12	…	8%	17%
1668	2	21	…	5%	…
1667	2	7	…	…	…
1666	2	7	…	29%	14%
1665	2	11	…	9%	9%
1664	2	13	…	23%	15%
1663	2	12	…	17%	17%
1662	2	1	…	100%	…
1661	2	4	…	50%	…
1660	2	7	…	14%	14%
1659	1	4	…	25%	…
1658	1	6	…	50%	…
1657	1	5	…	20%	…
1656	1	4	…	…	…
1655	1	4	…	…	…
1654	1	3	…	…	…
1653	1	3	…	…	…
1652	1	1	…	…	…
1651	1	2	…	…	…
1650	1	3	…	…	…
1649	1	4	…	25%	…
1648	1	3	…	…	…
1647	1	2	…	…	…
1646	1	3	…	…	…
1645	1	2	…	…	…
1644	1	2	…	…	…
1643	1	3	…	…	…
1642	1	3	…	…	…
1641	1	1	…	…	…
1640	1	2	…	50%	…
1639	1	2	…	…	…

[a] An imprint is a separately typecast publication. Multivolume works and each year's entire run of a newspaper count as one imprint.
[b] Of total, 283 were German and 39 were Dutch.

Sources: Charles Evans, *American Bibliography: A Chronological Dictionary of All Books, Pamphlets, and Periodicals Printed in the United States ... 1630 ... to 1820,* 12 vols (1903–34), I–III. Roger P. Bristol, *Supplement to Charles Evans' American Bibliography* (1970). Karl R. Arndt and Reimer C. Eck, "The First Century of German Language Printing in the United States of America," *Publications of the Pennsylvania German Society,* XXI (1989). John Tebbel, *A History of Book Publishing in the United States, I, The Creation of an Industry, 1630–1865* (1972), passim.

popularity peaked during 1714–38, when they outnumbered all other varieties of publication (including government documents) and constituted 19% of all imprints.

The almanac trade made up the third-largest component of publishing and accounted for every tenth imprint. Almanacs had become particularly profitable by the 1760s when the most popular titles, Benjamin Franklin's *Poor Richard's Almanac* and the Ames family's *Astronomical Diary and Almanac,* both had press runs of 10,000 copies. Although full of climatic information of practical use to the numerous farming population, almanacs achieved their greatest success when they strove for the broadest possible audience.

In his *Autobiography,* Benjamin Franklin described the main philosophy promoting *Poor Richard's* widespread circulation:

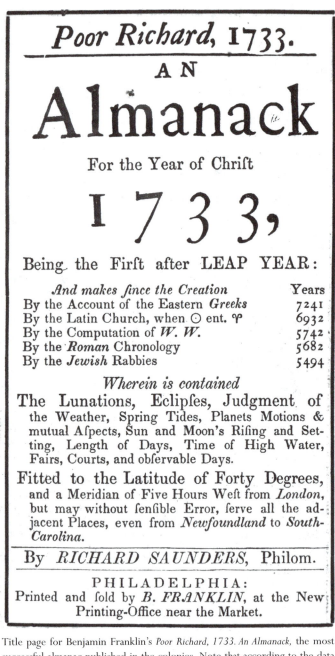

Title page for Benjamin Franklin's *Poor Richard, 1733. An Almanack,* the most successful almanac published in the colonies. Note that according to the data on its cover, the best scholarly sources then available estimated the earth to have been created no more than 7,241 years before 1733. (Courtesy Library of Congress)

I consider'd it as a proper vehicle for conveying instruction among the common people, who bought scarcely any other books; I therefore filled all the little spaces that occurr'd between the remarkable days in the calendar with proverbial sentences, chiefly such as inculcated industry and frugality, as the means of procuring wealth, and thereby securing virtue; it being more difficult for a man in want, to act always honestly, as, to use here one of those proverbs, it is hard for an empty sack to stand upright.

A compendium of *Poor Richard's* proverbs proved so popular when published in 1758 that it was excerpted by most colonial papers, reprinted widely in England, and translated twice into French. In this fashion, the eighteenth-century almanac became a powerful force that molded early America's folk culture and established the commonsense values prized ever since then, such as he "that goes a-borrowing goes a-sorrowing."

Theological subjects furnished the subject of three of every seven colonial imprints. This situation resulted in large part from the fact that the clergy attracted more college graduates than any other profession. From 1730 to 1750, for instance, the most prolific authors were all ministers, including George Whitefield (sixty-one titles), Gilbert Tennent (fifty-two titles), Benjamin Colman (thirty-three titles), Charles Chauncey (twenty-six titles), Jonathan Dickinson (twenty-three titles), and Jonathan Edwards (twenty-three titles); collectively, they wrote 242 titles representing 7.2% of all that period's imprints. During that same time, 10% of all publications came from the pens of just fifteen ministers (the preceding six, plus Nathaniel Appleton, Mather Byles, William Cooper, Thomas Foxcroft, Cotton Mather, Thomas Prince, Joseph Sewall, Josiah Smith, and Solomon Williams).

The most widely read religious work, the Bible (whether in whole or in part), represented less than 3% of all theological imprints. The first American bible ironically appeared not in English but in John Eliot's translation of the Algonquian Massachuset dialect as *Mamusse Wunneetupanatamwe Up-Biblum God Naneeswe Nukkone Testament Kah Wonk Wusku Testament* (Boston, 1663), better known as the *Up-Biblum God.* The earliest American edition of the complete scriptures in a European language appeared in German, not English, when Christopher Sauer of Philadelphia printed Martin Luther's translation in 1743. English publishers dominated the colonial market for bibles with such inexpensive exports that it was not until after independence that John Aitken printed the first American edition at Philadelphia in 1782. Anglo-American presses nevertheless produced numerous editions of scriptural segments, including the *Bay Psalm Book* (1640), the first major commercial success of publishing in the thirteen colonies.

A few ministers stumbled into commercial success with warnings to avoid eternal punishment through repentence. This genre attained a popularity in English North America, especially in New England, that was unsurpassed anywhere else in the world. Rev. Michael Wigglesworth authored the first best-seller of this type in 1662 with his epic poem of perdition, *The Day of Doom,* which allowed the righteous to savor their own sanctification and anticipate watching their unregenerate neighbors be cast into eternal misery by a stern God at the last judgment. Wigglesworth composed this work of eighty pages in a jog-trot verse that lacked literary sophistication but served the practical purpose of being easy for children to memorize for schoolroom recitation. Many generations of impressionable young Yankees passed through this ritual of adolescence. The ballad's first edition of 1,800 sold out in a year, and because no surviving copies remain of the first three editions, it seems to have been literally "read to pieces." Its popularity was sufficient to have warranted the printing of a new edition every decade until the Revolution.

Wigglesworth followed up this success with another best-seller written in the same vein, *Meat out of the Eater; or Meditations Concerning the Necessity, End, and Usefulness of Afflictions unto God's Children; All Tend-*

TABLE 13.4   SUBJECT MATTER OF IMPRINTS PUBLISHED IN THIRTEEN COLONIES

Subject	1639–1663	1664–1688	1689–1713	1714–1738	1739–1763	Total	Percent
Theology	…	44	167	283	338	832	9.5%
Bible and Parts	13	6	2	9	55	85	1.0%
Controversy	4	20	92	142	342	600	6.8%
Doctrine	6	18	45	69	185	323	3.7%
Sermons	6	34	130	460	751	1,381	15.8%
Supernaturalism	…	5	17	5	14	41	.5%
Philosophy	…	1	1	6	28	36	.4%
Science	…	4	4	16	25	49	.5%
Medical Science	…	1	1	36	35	73	.8%
Education	2	2	4	1	31	40	.5%
Catechisms and Primers	10	10	14	12	24	70	.8%
Textbooks	…	2	12	29	64	107	1.2%
Varia	6	18	6	15	83	128	1.4%
Social Science	…	23	92	133	132	380	4.3%
Economics	…	2	3	38	56	99	1.1%
Political Science	3	17	66	185	295	566	6.5%
Law and Proclamations	8	75	133	426	967	1,709	19.5%
Applied Science and Arts	…	…	…	1	7	8	.1%
Military Science	…	…	4	4	23	31	.3%
Agriculture	…	…	2	5	15	22	.2%
Domestic Science	…	…	…	…	8	8	.1%
Literature	…	5	7	20	51	83	1.0%
Almanacs	19	42	91	226	483	861	10.1%
Biography	…	6	27	74	117	224	2.5%
Drama	…	…	…	1	47	48	.5%
Narratives	…	12	15	56	143	226	2.6%
Verse	2	14	16	52	201	284	3.2%
History	…	…	10	15	34	59	.7%
Colonies	…	13	51	79	137	280	3.2%
Indians	3	5	10	12	19	49	.5%
Bibliology	…	1	3	17	37	58	.7%
Total	82	380	1,124	2,427	4,747	8,760	100.0%
Percentages	1.0	4.5	13.0	27.5	54.0	100.0	100.0%

Source: Arthur B. Berthold, *American Colonial Printing as Determined by Contemporary Forces* (1970), 86.

ing to Prepare Them for, and Comfort Them Under the Cross,* which spawned five editions through 1721. The example of Wigglesworth inspired imitation by other clergy. *Dooms-Day; or, the Great Day of the Lord Drawing Nigh* by Andrew Jones had appeared in its ninth edition 1684. Despite the influence of the Enlightenment in promoting a less-harrowing understanding of Christianity, this genre remained popular well into the eighteenth century, as evidenced by the publication in 1732 of Israel Loring's pamphlets, *Serious Thoughts on the Miseries of Hell* and *The Map of Misery; or the Poor Man's Pocket-Book: Being a Perpetual Almanack of Spiritual Meditations.*

Religious themes permeated the general culture so thoroughly that many authors gave nontheological topics a spiritual twist to increase their popularity. Mary Rowlandson's 1682 account of her capture and ransom during King Philip's War established a long-standing convention that Indian captivity narratives should serve as allegories for spiritual redemption. A miscreant's grisly autobiography could be made into respectable reading material by treating its debauched villain's life as a moral lesson, as in *A Warning Piece to All Clergymen; Being an Impartial Account of the Life, Character, Behaviour and Last Dying Words of Peter Vine, Who Was Executed … 1743, for a Rape and Murder.* John Oliver similarly described his 1694 childbearing manual in otherworldly terms as *A Present for Teeming Women, or, Scriptural Directions for Women with Child, How to Prepare for the Houre of Travel.*

TABLE 13.5   BEST-SELLERS AUTHORED IN THE THIRTEEN COLONIES

First Printing	Editions to 1763	Author	Title
1640	27	…	*Bay Psalm Book*
1662	5 to 1717 (10 by 1760?)	Michael Wigglesworth	*The Day of Doom; or, a Poetical Description of the Great and Last Judgement*
1670	10 by 1760	Michael Wigglesworth	*Meat out of the Eater; or Meditations Concerning the Necessity, End, and Usefulness of Afflictions unto God's Children*
1682	…	Mary Rowlandson	*Narrative of the Captivity and Restoration of Mrs. Mary Rowlandson*
1683	…	Benjamin Harris	*The New England Primer* (total sales estimated at 6 to 8 million)
1699	…	Jonathan Dickinson	*God's Protecting Providence Man's Surest Help in the Times of Greatest Difficulty*
1707	…	John Williams	*The Redeemed Captive*
1725	40 to 1764	Nathaniel Ames	*Astronomical Diary and Almanack*
1732	26 to 1757	Benjamin Franklin	*Poor Richard's Almanack*

Sources: Charles Evans, *American Bibliography: A Chronological Dictionary of All Books, Pamphlets, and Periodicals Printed in the United States … 1630 … to 1820,* 12 vols (1903–34), I–III. Richard B. Morris, ed., *Encyclopedia of American History* (1961), 593.

Two-thirds of all colonial imprints fell under the categories of theology, government documents, and almanacs. The largest remaining category included drama, poetry, and prose fiction, which composed 4.7% of all colonial publications. Belles lettres formed such a small portion of printed works in large part because British publishers regularly met most of the demand for these items by exporting their surplus stock to be auctioned in major cities—sometimes in lots of 2,000—or peddled through the country. Eighteenth-century Boston averaged about ten book auctions yearly.

For the same reason, colonial presses ran off few works of philosophy, economics, or any of the emerging social sciences. Natural and medical science were likewise rare. Political science and history fared better, however, and composed more than 10% of all colonial imprints, with two-thirds being the former.

Anglo-Americans produced no novels, few plays, and little poetry before 1763. Anne Bradstreet, a Massachusetts farmer's wife, wrote what many consider to be the best poetry that found its way into print, but the colonial press was so limited when she finished her first volume, *The Tenth Muse Lately Sprung Up in America,* that she had its premier edition published at London in 1650. Not until 1678 was an American edition manufactured. Edward Taylor, a Westfield, Massachusetts, minister, composed the best colonial poetry, but his treasures remained undiscovered until the twentieth century. Such plays as existed generally represented satires aimed at one's political enemies, such as *Androborus, A Biographical Farce in Three Acts* (ca. 1715) by New York governor Robert Hunter about his predecessor Sir Edmund Andros, and Col. Robert Munford's *The Candidates; or, the Humours of a Virginia Election* (ca. 1765). No play written by a native-born American was even performed in America until Philadelphians produced Thomas Godfrey's *The Prince of Parthia* in 1767.

Beyond the polite world of scholarly and serious writing lay a realm of less-refined literature aimed at popular tastes. Such materials included both accounts of American events and reprints of British pamphlets. A staple variety of the popular press was the criminal biography or autobiography, usually dictated before the subject ascended the gallows. Typical pamphlets of this type included *A Short and Plain, but Faithful Narrative of the Wicked Life of Philip Kennison, Who Was Executed at Cambridge on the 25th of September 1738; Written by Himself* (Boston, 1738) and *The Declaration and Confession of Jeffrey, A Negro, Who Was Executed at Worcester, Oct. 17, 1745, for the Murder of Mrs. Tabitha Sandford, at Mendon* (Boston, 1745).

The audience for this variety of entertainment frequently seems to have found colonial crimes too mundane for their tastes. To meet this demand, American printers pirated lurid tales involving murder, betrayal, and—frequently—sex among English aristocrats. Among such potboilers were *The Virgin's Advice ... Shewing How a Knight's Daughter in Oxfordshire was Courted by a Gentleman, Who ... Got Her With Child, And Afterwards Murder'd Her; Also How a Damask Rose-Bush Grew Over Her Grave Which Flourished Winter and Summer, Till Being Touch'd by Him It Immediately Wither'd; Upon Which He Confess'd the Murder* (Newport, 1730) and *The Bristol Tragedy, Being an Exact and Impartial Narrative of the Horrid and Dreadful Murder of Sir John Dinely Goodere, Bar[onet]., Perpetuated by his Brother Samuel Goodere Esq[uire], Commander of the Ruby Man-of-War and Executed by Matthew Mahoney, an Irish Papist, and Charles White, an Irishman, in January Last* (Boston, 1741).

A broad variety of other ephemera catered to readers with similar tastes. For those seeking accounts of strange lands there were books like *The Traveller, Part 1, Containing, A Journal of Three Thousand Miles, Through the Mainland of South America; by Mr. Thomas Gage, an Englishman and a Missionary Friar in New Spain, Twelve Years* (Woodbridge, N.J., 1758). For those with a penchant for keeping up with the latest quack medicine, there were pamphlets like *A Treatise Proving That Most of the Disorders Incident to the Fair Sex Are Owing to Flatuencies Not Seasonably Vented* (Boston, 1748). For the gullible tenth of adults willing to believe anything associated with the supernatural, there were booklets like *The Yorkshire Wonder; ... a Full and True Account of one Mr. John Ford, A Pious Divine of the Church of England, Shewing How He Fell and Lay in a Trance, ... Being Four Days and Four Nights; Likewise When Great Preparations Were Made for his Burial, And Just as They Were Going to Lay his Body in the Dust, They Found Him Not to be Dead But Alive ... And in the Space of Six Hours He Revived; Then He Declared the Wonderful Things He had Seen and Heard in the Other World ...* (New York, 1747).

The popular press of the colonies consequently included elements familiar to devotees of today's tabloid journals. Therein could be found purported accounts of after-death experiences, pseudoscientific reports of improbable medical advances, and stories of strange peoples in foreign lands. The large literature surrounding condemned criminals and their sensational crimes likewise bears strong resemblance to modern pulp magazines that are devoted to summarizing the most grisly and shocking cases from police files. Despite the predominance of theological subjects among colonial imprints, it would seem that a large audience existed with a taste for the lurid, the exotic, the sensational, and the mysterious to provide escape from the humdrum regularity of everyday life.

Journalism

No newspapers existed in the Anglo-American colonies for the first eighty-three years of their existence. It is scarcely surprising that this trade developed so slowly in the provinces because journalism was a novel craft unknown in England as late as the sixteenth century. Regular publication of current events did not commence in England until 1622 when a London printer started to issue news booklets that reported the latest happenings from the European continent. Not until 1641 was an English news booklet published whose purpose was to cover domestic affairs. The modern newspaper format, in sheet form with multiple columns of reading material, first appeared in 1665 as the *Oxford Gazette* (later the *London Gazette*), which was the royal court's official organ. The first American production of a newspaper occurred on February 9, 1684, when a Boston press reprinted an issue of the *London Gazette.*

In 1690, when Benjamin Harris founded the first American news periodical at Boston, *Public Occurrences,* only two other papers existed in the English empire (the *London Gazette* and *Dublin's News-Letter*). Harris concluded that England was an "uneasy ... place for honest men" after editing a London paper that had been quashed in 1681 for criticizing royal policies, and he emigrated to Massachusetts to escape a heavy fine and a session in the public pillory. His Boston venture was to be issued monthly on three 6 × 9 1/2-inch sheets, printed in two columns without headlines. The governor of Massachusetts suppressed *Public Occurrences* after one issue because Harris had ignored a British law requiring editors to obtain a license for their papers. After Parliament allowed this statute to expire in 1694, Harris returned to England and founded the London *Post.*

Colonial journals consciously patterned themselves after British newspapers, which proliferated rapidly in the early 1700s. British papers almost immediately solicited advertisements to increase profits. They also experimented with eye-catching typographical techniques, such as headlines in capital letters, the pointing-finger device to catch attention, and woodcut pictures. British editors furthermore coined the standard repertoire of newspaper titles—the Post, Gazette, Intelligencer, Mercury, and Courant—all of which would be copied by American publishers.

Boston, the largest North American city until about 1760, was the cradle of colonial journalism, as it had been for the printing industry. When John Campbell established the *Boston News-Letter* in 1704, newspaper production in the English empire was limited to London, Edinburgh, and Dublin. Campbell was Boston's postmaster and as such, he enjoyed the "franking" privilege of distributing his publication free by mail. The *Boston News-Letter* appeared weekly as a single sheet, 8 × 12¾ inches, printed in two columns on both sides; it was dull and uninteresting to the eye because it did not employ headlines and utilized only one variety of type. Campbell used no headlines and wrote no editorials, although he often expressed his private views by appending brief moralizing comments to stories or anecdotes; he charged two pence a copy or twelve shillings for a year's subscription. During its first year, the *Boston News-Letter* had 300 paid subscribers; its printed output rose from 10,200 copies in 1704 to 15,600 copies in 1710.

The *Boston News-Letter's* mock-up techniques were typical of early American journalism. The primary interest of colonial audiences lay in European affairs, and so the first page was reserved for coverage of foreign events. When John Campbell expanded the paper from three to four pages in 1719, he did so in order to double the amount of overseas news. North American news was deemphasized during peacetime because it seemed dull compared to court gossip from European capitals. The *Boston News-Letter* devoted relatively little coverage to events in its own city because its subscribers usually knew what transpired among their neighbors before each week's issue could be produced.

America's first permanent news journal emerged at a time when sales of papers alone could not provide an adequate income. To be viable financially, a paper needed to be an adjunct activity of a postmastership, book seller, stationer, or general printer and would often be actively engaged in soliciting government contracts or acting as a sales agent for indentured servants or slaves. Profitability also depended on limiting overhead by keeping staff to the bare minimum. John Campbell, for instance, not only served as the *Boston News-Letter's* editor but also gathered information, wrote copy, solicited advertising, and—as postmaster—distributed each issue. (Campbell's typesetting was done by a local printer who required three hours to run off an edition of 300 copies.)

As a rising population made colonial journalism more profitable after 1725, the profession remained unspecialized. Because no papers appeared more frequently than once a week, it required just one competent person to collect news, acquire advertising, and write the entire issue. When production fell behind schedule, the editor's spouse and children could furnish temporary and rather knowledgeable assistance. Most editors operated their own press and needed to hire only one or two printer's apprentices, who also served as delivery boys for local customers. Because editors relied on word-of-mouth for local news and simply reprinted foreign news wholesale from British papers, they employed no hometown, national, nor overseas correspondents at any time in the eighteenth century.

Anglo-America's second regularly published paper emerged shortly after the governor of Massachusetts dismissed John Campbell as Boston's postmaster in 1719 and named William Brooker to succeed him. Brooker also decided to combine superintending the mail with journalism and arranged for James Franklin to print the *Boston Gazette*. The *Gazette's* founding made Boston the first competitive market between rival newspapers, although neither differed substantially from the other in style, format, or focus. When James Franklin lost his contract for producing the *Gazette* to another Boston printer in 1721, he founded the city's third journal, the *New-England Courant*.

Franklin broke new ground in American journalism by creating a publication designed to entertain readers who had been fed a dull diet of stodgy news and to stimulate debate on controversial subjects. "The Publisher desires his Friends might favour him from Time to Time," he wrote on August 7, 1721, "with some short Pieces[:] Serious, Sarcastic, Ludicrous or in other ways amusing." Imitating lively English journals like the *Spectator* and *Tatler*, he printed essays challenging orthodox thinking written anonymously by malcontents who frequented Richard Hall's Tavern and were known as the "Hell-Fire Club." He also accepted satirical columns composed under the pseudonym "Silence Dogood" by his half-brother Benjamin. The *New-England Courant* criticized Boston's preeminent clergyman, Rev. Cotton Mather, lampooned Harvard College as a bastion of conservatism catering to ill-mannered children of the rich, fanned the fires of a hyperemotional debate over inoculation during a smallpox epidemic, and accused the government of failing to protect local waters from pirates. When the government jailed James Franklin for contempt in 1723, seventeen-year-old Benjamin edited the paper until a grand jury failed to uphold an indictment of contempt against his brother. Franklin's *Courant* was a seminal influence in early American journalism: It provided the first example of a newspaper dedicated to expressing controversial views opposed by the powers that be, and it popularized the personal, familiar style of essay writing pioneered by English writers such as Joseph Addison and Daniel Defoe.

Andrew Bradford founded Philadelphia's first paper, *The American Weekly Mercury*, in 1719. The *Mercury* endured for three decades, during which it served as the principal organ of discontent against Pennsylvania's Quaker-dominated government. In 1728, a second Philadelphia paper emerged bearing as its title *The Universal Instructor in All Arts and Sciences and Pennsylvania Gazette*. After a short editorship under Samuel Keimer, who filled the columns with pieces lifted from an English encyclopedia, it was bought by Benjamin Franklin and became the simple *Pennsylvania Gazette*. The *Gazette* continued the journalistic tradition set by the *New-England Courant* by emphasizing original and witty articles that entertained and educated readers in science, literature, philosophy, and politics.

William Bradford, father of Philadelphia's first journalist, established New York's first paper, the *New-York Gazette*, in 1726. Eight years later, when John Peter Zenger founded that city's second paper, the *New-York Weekly Journal*, Philadelphia and New York each had two competing papers, while Boston had four. In each of these three metropolises, successful papers had not been founded until the population had risen to approximately 7,000, and a second paper had not appeared until the population rose another 50%. Financial success seems to have required a minimum of 300 paying customers, for, when Benjamin Franklin launched the German-language *Philadelphische Zeitung* in 1732, the paper died on its second edition for lack of that many subscribers.

The press began to expand among the southern colonies in 1728 when the *Maryland Gazette* appeared at Annapolis. Benjamin Franklin helped finance the establishment of the *South-Carolina Gazette* at Charles Town by Thomas Whitemarsh, one of his former apprentices, in 1732. William Parks, the *Maryland Gazette's* owner, founded the *Virginia Gazette* at Williamsburg in 1736.

A small foreign-language press existed in Pennsylvania. In 1739, Christopher Sauer founded the *Hoch-Deutsch [High-Dutch] Pennsylvanische Gesette* at Germantown. Other successful German-language papers were established at Philadelphia in 1750 and Lancaster in 1752.

Forty newspapers had been established in seven of the thirteen colonies by 1750, but two-thirds (twenty-seven) had gone out of business by then. The failure of one paper nevertheless invariably led to the opening of another because each abandoned press quickly passed into the hands of some entrepreneur (most often a former printer's apprentice) who was eager to start his own journal. A resident paper existed in every colony by 1764, except for Delaware, which remained without one until the 1780s. After having grown slowly during most of the eighteenth century, the number of papers more than doubled between 1761 and 1775, from sixteen to thirty-six.

Just as colonial newspapers mushroomed in the shadow of England's fledgling press, so too did Anglo-American magazines originate as imitations of English periodicals. The first publication designated as such was the *Gentleman's Magazine* of London, founded in 1731. Its editor, Edward Cave, intended the term *magazine* to be understood as a literary storehouse brimming with a variety of reading material. Cave's publication and the *London Magazine* (1732) created the modern conception of what a magazine should be: a bound pamphlet, issued at regular intervals, that

TABLE 13.6 NEWSPAPERS PUBLISHED IN THE THIRTEEN COLONIES, 1690–1775

Year	Mass.	Pa.	N.Y.	Conn.	R.I.	Md.	Va.	S.C.	N.C.	Ga.	Total
1775	8	7	3	4	2	2	3	3	2	1	36
1774	8	6	3	4	2	2	3	3	2	1	34
1773	7	6	4	4	2	2	2	3	2	1	33
1772	7	6	4	3	2	1	2	3	2	1	31
1771	7	6	4	3	2	1	2	3	2	1	31
1770	7	5	4	3	2	1	2	3	2	1	30
1769	7	6	4	3	2	1	2	3	2	1	31
1768	7	5	4	4	2	1	2	3	1	1	30
1767	5	5	4	4	2	1	2	3	...	1	27
1766	4	4	4	3	2	1	2	3	1	1	25
1765	4	4	3	3	2	1	1	3	2	1	24
1764	4	4	3	3	2	1	1	2	1	1	22
1763	4	4	4	3	2	1	1	1	...	1	21
1762	4	4	4	2	2	1	1	1	...	...	19
1761	4	3	3	2	1	1	1	1	...	...	16
1760	4	3	3	2	1	1	1	1	...	...	16
1759	4	3	3	2	1	1	1	2	1	...	18
1758	4	3	2	2	1	1	1	1	1	...	16
1757	4	4	2	1	...	1	1	1	1	...	15
1756	3	4	2	1	...	1	1	1	1	...	14
1755	3	4	4	1	...	1	1	1	1	...	16
1754	4	3	2	...	...	1	1	1	1	...	13
1753	4	4	4	...	...	1	1	1	1	...	16
1752	4	5	4	...	...	1	1	1	1	...	17
1751	4	3	3	...	...	1	1	1	1	...	14
1750	4	3	3	...	...	1	...	1	...	...	12
1749	5	3	3	...	...	1	...	1	...	...	13
1748	5	3	3	...	...	1	...	1	...	...	13
1747	4	3	4	...	...	1	...	1	...	...	13
1746	4	5	3	...	...	1	1	1	...	...	15
1745	4	4	3	...	...	1	1	1	...	...	14
1744	4	4	4	...	...	...	1	1	...	...	14
1743	4	4	3	...	...	...	1	1	...	...	13
1742	4	4	2	...	...	...	1	1	...	...	12
1741	5	3	2	...	...	...	1	1	...	...	12
1740	5	3	2	...	...	...	1	1	...	...	12
1739	5	3	2	...	...	...	1	1	...	...	12
1738	5	2	2	...	...	...	1	1	...	...	11
1737	5	2	2	...	...	...	1	1	...	...	11
1736	5	2	2	...	...	...	1	1	...	...	11
1735	6	2	2	...	...	...	...	1	...	...	11
1734	4	2	2	...	...	1	...	1	...	...	10
1733	4	2	2	...	1	1	...	1	...	...	11
1732	4	3	1	...	1	1	...	1	...	...	11
1731	4	2	1	...	...	1	...	...	...	...	8
1730	3	2	1	...	...	1	...	...	...	...	7
1729	4	2	1	...	...	1	...	...	...	...	8
1728	4	2	1	...	...	1	...	...	...	...	8
1727	3	1	1	...	...	...	...	...	...	...	5
1726	3	1	1	...	...	...	...	...	...	...	5
1725	3	1	...	...	...	...	...	...	...	...	4
1724	3	1	...	...	...	...	...	...	...	...	4
1723	3	1	...	...	...	...	...	...	...	...	4
1722	3	1	...	...	...	...	...	...	...	...	4
1721	3	1	...	...	...	...	...	...	...	...	4
1720	2	1	...	...	...	...	...	...	...	...	3
1719	2	1	...	...	...	...	...	...	...	...	3
1718	1	...	...	...	...	...	...	...	...	...	1
1717	1	...	...	...	...	...	...	...	...	...	1
1716	1	...	...	...	...	...	...	...	...	...	1
1715	1	...	...	...	...	...	...	...	...	...	1
1714	1	...	...	...	...	...	...	...	...	...	1
1713	1	...	...	...	...	...	...	...	...	...	1
1712	1	...	...	...	...	...	...	...	...	...	1
1711	1	...	...	...	...	...	...	...	...	...	1
1710	1	...	...	...	...	...	...	...	...	...	1
1709	1	...	...	...	...	...	...	...	...	...	1
1708	1	...	...	...	...	...	...	...	...	...	1

Year	Mass.	Pa.	N.Y.	Conn.	R.I.	Md.	Va.	S.C.	N.C.	Ga.	Total
1707	1	...	...	...	...	...	...	...	...	...	1
1706	1	...	...	...	...	...	...	...	...	...	1
1705	1	...	...	...	...	...	...	...	...	...	1
1704	1	...	...	...	...	...	...	...	...	...	1
1703	...	...	...	...	...	...	...	...	...	...	0
1702	...	...	...	...	...	...	...	...	...	...	0
1701	...	...	...	...	...	...	...	...	...	...	0
1700	...	...	...	...	...	...	...	...	...	...	0
1699	...	...	...	...	...	...	...	...	...	...	0
1698	...	...	...	...	...	...	...	...	...	...	0
1697	...	...	...	...	...	...	...	...	...	...	0
1696	...	...	...	...	...	...	...	...	...	...	0
1695	...	...	...	...	...	...	...	...	...	...	0
1694	...	...	...	...	...	...	...	...	...	...	0
1693	...	...	...	...	...	...	...	...	...	...	0
1692	...	...	...	...	...	...	...	...	...	...	0
1691	...	...	...	...	...	...	...	...	...	...	0
1690	1	...	...	...	...	...	...	...	...	...	1

Note: Figures refer to all newspapers published during any part of a year, even if they were discontinued by December 31.
Source: Edward C. Lathem, *Chronological Tables of American Newspapers, 1690–1820* (1972), 2–9.

provides an eclectic mixture of written materials for the readers' entertainment and self-improvement.

William Bradford, editor of Philadelphia's first newspaper, brought out the earliest colonial periodical, the thirty-four page *American Magazine, or Monthly View,* on February 13, 1741 (dated January), a decade after London's first magazine had appeared. Three days later, Benjamin Franklin offered for sale the colonies' second periodical, his seventy-five page *General Magazine, and Historical Chronicle, for All the British Plantations in America.* Both editors primarily intended to focus on contemporary political issues. Bradford's journal printed little else, with almost half the pages occupied by long excerpts from the legislative journals of Pennsylvania, New Jersey, and Maryland. Franklin's publication devoted about a third of its space to proceedings in Parliament or colonial assemblies, and it also heavily emphasized controversies over the religious revival termed the Great Awakening and debates over issuing paper money by provincial governments. In both journals, the relatively few specimens of belles lettres were pirated from London magazines. The *American Magazine* lasted just three issues, while the *General Magazine* survived for six.

Subsequent magazines bore a very close resemblance to Bradford's and Franklin's rival works. Most held approximately sixty-four pages, the usual length of their basic model, London's *Gentlemen's Magazine.* Aside from the cover's logo, there were few or no illustrations. The usual price per issue was a shilling in local money (about eight pence sterling), a high price necessitated by the almost complete absence of advertising. Colonial magazines printed few items by colonial authors but instead extracted three-fourths or more of their contents from British magazines, papers, pamphlets, or books.

The personal essay, written in the style popularized by Joseph Addison, served as the grist for American magazines. Fortunately for American readers, their editors could pirate from the British press a large and eclectic choice of essays concerning philosophy, social life, religion, manners, and the latest fashions. Poetry was a standard feature, but prose fiction occupied relatively little space. Character sketches and biographies were common. The most popular subjects for informational articles were politics, international affairs, and warfare.

Of the sixteen colonial magazines founded before 1776, nine folded in less than a year, often within a few months. The most sophisticated journals were William Bradford's *American Magazine and Monthly*

TABLE 13.7 MAGAZINES PUBLISHED IN THE THIRTEEN COLONIES

Title	Where Printed	First Issue	Last Issue
American Magazine, or Monthly View	Philadelphia	Jan. 1741	Mar. 1741
General Magazine and Historical Chronicle	Philadelphia	Jan. 1741	Jun. 1741
Boston Weekly Magazine	Boston	Mar. 2, 1743	Mar. 16, 1743
Christian History	Boston	Mar. 5, 1743	Feb. 23, 1745
American Magazine and Historical Chronicle	Boston	Sep. 1743	Dec. 1746
Independent Reflector	New York	Nov. 30, 1752	Nov. 22, 1753
Occasional Reverberator	New York	Sep. 7, 1753	Oct. 5, 1753
Instructor	New York	Mar. 6, 1755	May 8, 1755
John Englishman	New York	Apr. 9, 1755	Jul. 5, 1755
American Magazine and Monthly Chronicle	Philadelphia	Oct. 1757	Oct. 1758
New American Magazine	Woodbridge, N.J.	Jan. 1758	Mar. 1760
New-England Magazine	Boston	Aug. 1758	1758
American Magazine or General Repository	Philadelphia	Jan. 1769	Sep. 1769
Censor	Boston	Nov. 23, 1771	1771
Royal American Magazine	Boston	Jan. 1774	Mar. 1775
Pennsylvania Magazine	Philadelphia	Jan. 1775	Jul. 1776

Source: Frank L. Mott, *A History of American Magazines, 1741–1850* (1957), 787–88.

Chronicle (1743–46), which compared favorably with *Gentleman's* or the *London Magazine,* the *New American Magazine* (1758–60) of Speaker of the New Jersey House Samuel Nevill, who had formerly edited London's *Evening Post,* and Isaiah Thomas's *Royal American Magazine* (1774–75), which was the first colonial journal to use illustrations liberally, most notably those of Paul Revere. The longest run for any provincial publication was the forty months enjoyed by Boston's *American Magazine and Historical Chronicle* in the mid-1740s. It would seem, in general, that the colonies were not yet ready to support such periodicals, especially because their natural constituency, the upper class, could afford to import London or Edinburgh magazines of superior quality to the typical Anglo-American publication.

Painting

Painting was a luxury slow to cross the Atlantic during the first century of colonization. While it is true that John White, governor of the doomed colony of Roanoke, completed a striking series of water colors during his own brief sojourn in the New World during the 1580s, he saw his work as part of a scientific description of the land's vegetation and inhabitants, not as art for the sake of itself. The earliest settlers had little time for aesthetic pursuits during their first decades of hewing out a tenuous fingerhold on the North American mainland. "The plowman that raiseth grain," opined a practical, early New Englander, "is more serviceable to mankind than the painter who draws only to please the eye." So negligible was the amount of art produced during the seventeenth century that fewer than 500 paintings have survived from the thirteen colonies that can be positively dated prior to 1700.

The cultural atmosphere also discouraged painting in those regions of the Atlantic coast where Calvinists predominated. Sacred art had functioned as an inspiration and financial mainstay of great European painters for centuries in Catholic Europe, but it engendered open hostility among the English and Dutch Reformed settlers in the northern provinces. In both England and the Netherlands, the Protestant Reformation had generated a bitter reaction against the devotional religious paintings of medieval Catholicism. Puritans, Dutch Reformed, and even most Anglicans preferred their churches to be kept bare and simple so that ornate decoration would not distract worshipers from soul-searching spirituality. While religious art flourished in New Spain and to a lesser extent in New France, it provided no outlet for the creativity of early painters in New Netherland or Anglo-America.

Pious impulses nevertheless did stimulate one unique art form among the Puritans: the mortuary painting. Funerals of prominent individuals served as a form of gruesome diversion for ordinary citizens because of the ostentation and pomp displayed by their survivors at the wake, memorial service, and procession to the grave. Funeral processions of wealthy persons customarily included mortuary paintings of the deceased that were carried by specially designated mourners and perhaps attached to mourning cloths hung in the meeting house.

Self-portrait by Boston artist Thomas Smith. Smith was one of several painters specializing in funeral art, and he portrayed himself with his hand on a skull. (Courtesy Worcester Museum of Art)

Because mortuary art was necessarily done in such great haste that it rarely attained a level of true craftsmanship, it was often discarded, so few examples have been preserved in collections. Such paintings nevertheless seem to have conformed to the same conventions characteristic of gravestone iconography, with winged skulls, hourglasses, and the familiar figure of the grim reaper, beside strutting peacocks (a symbol of resurrection), symbols of the deceased's profession, and a coat-of-arms if appropriate. (Symbols of death sometimes intruded into live portraiture, as when Boston painter Thomas Smith portrayed himself with one of his palms resting on a bare skull.) Sufficient demand existed for funereal pictures to permit a few New England artists to specialize in this macabre genre. One such specialist was Thomas Child (1655–1706) of Boston, who was so well known for this trade that when he died, the noted diarist, Judge Samuel Sewall, penned this ironic epitaph:

Tom Child has often painted death
But never to the life before.
Doing it now, he's out of breath;
He paints it once, and then no more.

Opportunities for painters seem to have expanded considerably after 1660, especially in New England because of the growing prosperity of the colonies' largest city, Boston. Having acquired some affluence and enjoying the luxury to think about the future, family elders started to show a desire to have their likenesses preserved for their descendants. Stiff portraits of stern patriarchs began to appear in many American parlors by the late seventeenth century. Some colonials had themselves painted in Europe during visits to England or the Netherlands, but only indigenous craftsworkers could meet the rising demand for portraits.

Boston, a city of about 6,000 around 1690, probably had five to ten active painters in residence about that time so that the level of artistic activity went far beyond what would be expected from the popular stereotype of the dour Puritan. For a couple of decades, Boston possessed a remarkably competent coterie of portrait makers, who unfortunately signed few of their works and now remain anonymous. This Boston circle did not produce great art, but it did leave behind some creations that demonstrated originality, delicate detail, and mastery of contrasting colors with one another that rise above mundane portraiture. These unknown limners mostly painted their subjects in the formal, elegant, two-dimensional style typical of Tudor England, which had become archaic among fashionable circles at Restoration London's royal court by the 1670s. The best of Boston's late-seventeenth-century artists nevertheless showed a talent for revealing individuality through their subjects' faces, which usually appear honest to the point of being unflattering and impart a mysterious quaintness and charm precisely because their dated style was somewhat behind the times.

During the eighteenth century, prosperity allowed greater numbers of ambitious families to rise to the status of landed gentry or urban grandees, and these *arrivistes* multiplied the demand for portraits not just of men but also of women and children. The early painters typically demonstrated more talent (perhaps based on more practice) in capturing the features of adult men than women—who often appear somewhat masculine, at least to modern eyes—and also had less success in depicting children. In most cases, however, the subjects themselves apparently cared less that their physiques would be accurately rendered than that a memorial would be left behind expressing their high social status through such flourishes as showing them with expensive clothing and wigs, a background identifying them as extensive landowners or prosperous merchants, and perhaps a coat of arms so that they would appear to posterity as courtly aristocrats.

Despite the growing demand for portraits, few colonial artists became wealthy during the early eighteenth century. These limners often had to make ends meet by painting crests on carriages, signs for

A 1740 portrait of Madelena Douw Gansevoort (*The Girl with the Red Shoes*) by an unknown artist. This picture exemplifies the Patroon School of painting, America's first authentic school of art, with its flattened perspective, bright colors, and composition that is both harmonious and understated. (Courtesy Henry Francis du Pont Winterthur Museum)

taverns and tradesmen's shops, and even houses. Many were itinerants who padded along the roads on a wearying quest for fresh commissions. Opportunities for artists seem to have been least favorable in the South, where it was considered stylish for planters to have their portraits done in England, often sight unseen, based on written descriptions of their face and physique.

As in all times, mediocre artists outnumbered the genuinely talented ones, but a singular flash of genius flared unexpectedly during the early eighteenth century in New York. The first authentic school of American art, which is still little appreciated, emerged during the 1720s in the Hudson Valley under the patronage of wealthy Dutch merchants and landowners. Art historians have identified these craftspeople, most of whose names have been lost, as the Patroon Painters.

New York's prosperous upper class cultivated a group of perhaps a half-dozen limners who—at their best—developed an overall unity of style despite individual differences. Unlike New England artists, who worked on modest-size canvases, the Patroon School often created three-quarter and full-length images of their subjects; this technique enabled them to work on an expansive scale. "Energy, movement, rhythm, these were their attributes," wrote James T. Flexner, who elaborated that "long lines, straight or curved, held the pictures together, often crossing near the center; such portraits represent a considerable deviation from recognized European models, and in [early] America are almost unique."

The Patroon Painters were not truly accomplished artists according to the standards of contemporary Amsterdam or Paris, however. None of them ever completely mastered the technique of depicting a thoroughly accurate representation of the face. They all showed weakness in dealing with perspective and proportion in some degree. They lacked the skill to create gradual shadings of direct or reflected light, they portrayed movement in a static fashion, and they had little finesse in subtle coloring techniques.

They succeeded at producing evocative and strong portraits precisely because they recognized these limitations and found a means of expression suited to their own talents. Rather than attempt to replicate the subtle colorations of Baroque artists, the Patroon Painters relied on a few tints of bold intensity, broadly applied and juxtaposed to create a sense of heightened contrast. The contours of their lines are rarely graceful, but they convey a sense of forceful, yet orderly, design and inner vitality. Rather than try to attain a lifelike image that was beyond their representational abilities, they simplified and flattened the contours of the body and clothing to emphasize the most important lines, especially of the face, so that the subject's essential features stand out in a spare, seemingly literal, two-dimensional relief that might seem vaguely modern to late-twentieth-century viewers, as in *The Girl with the Red Shoes* (Madelena Douw Gansevoort). At their best, the Patroon Painters' canvases inspire a sense of fascination through their directness, insight to the subject, and resplendent colors.

No other indigenous school of art evolved anywhere else in the colonies to complement these first "Hudson Valley" painters. Mid-eighteenth-century American art was instead dominated by a conscious effort to replicate contemporary European fashions in vogue at the major royal courts, especially to imitate the work of Augustan England's preeminent painter, Sir Godfrey Kneller. Portraiture continued to be the mainstay of American artists, and approximately 800 portraits of American origin survive from the period 1700–50.

Among the most notable eighteenth-century painters were a small group of immigrants who had learned their craft in Europe but could not find sufficient patronage there. Justus Englehardt Kuhn (?–1717), a native of Germany, was the earliest documented portraitist in the South; he flourished on Maryland's western shore where he completed many highly competent pictures of that province's gentry. Jeremiah Theus (1716–74) dominated the art scene in Charles Town, South Carolina, for nearly four decades after he came there from Switzerland in 1735. Gustavus Hesselius (1682–1755) left Sweden and arrived at

Robert Feke was considered by many to be the most accomplished American-born painter practicing in the colonies before 1763. This self-portrait (about 1741–45) is not his best work, but it shows his ability to capture individual character in his portraits with graceful lines and lifelike images. (Courtesy Museum of Fine Arts, Boston)

Wilmington, Delaware, in 1712; after a long career as an itinerant painter in that province, Maryland, and Pennsylvania, he died in Maryland, where his son John succeeded him as fashionable artist. John Smibert (1688–1751), a Scot who apprenticed as a painter in London under Sir Godfrey Kneller, came to Newport, Rhode Island, in 1729, relocated later to Boston, and thereafter ranked as New England's leading artist until 1748, when his eyesight began to fail. Other immigrants who demonstrated a high degree of technical proficiency were the Englishmen Charles Bridges (1670–1747), John Wollaston (fl. 1742–75), and William Williams (1727–91), who practiced their craft in the South.

Charles Town, South Carolina, furnished the setting in which British America's first two female artists emerged. Henrietta Dering Johnston (ca. 1675–1729) was born in Ireland and came to Charles Town in 1708 as a clergyman's wife. Johnston ranks as the first known woman artist to work in the thirteen colonies and also as their earliest pastelist. Scholars have catalogued at least thirty of her portraits produced in America that have survived to the present. Mary Roberts (?–1761) was the wife of Charles Town engraver Bishop Roberts; she was one of the first colonial miniaturists and the first female to work in that field, apparently as early as the 1740s, but only three of her autographed miniatures (signed as MR) are known to exist today.

The thirteen colonies produced one outstanding native son in the field of painting prior to 1760, Robert Feke (ca. 1707–51). A native of Oyster Bay, Long Island, Feke developed into a self-taught prodigy at Newport, Rhode Island, during the 1740s; he also painted at various times in Boston and Philadelphia. He enlivened his canvases with a keen sense of color, a raw energy, graceful lines, and a striking ability to create exceptionally lifelike images, particularly of the face. His career reached its zenith in 1748 when many of Boston's elite families commissioned him to do their portraits. His best works show enormous technical skill that seems to capture his subject's character and individuality with a riveting directness and penetrating insight, in particular the self-portrait he completed about 1745. Robert Feke's brief career represented a minor milestone in the history of early American art: he was the first identifiably native-born, Anglo-American to achieve true virtuosity, for, as James T. Flexner has observed, "His pictures were the most finished creations of the early Colonial style."

Music

Practical considerations determined which musical devices initially appeared in North America, so the first tunes heard in early Virginia were marching airs tapped out on drums. The earliest mention of music in New England likewise occurred in 1627, when Isaac de Rasieres, a visiting Dutchman, noted that the Pilgrims at Plymouth "assemble by beat of drum, each with his firelock or musket, in front of the captain's door." Besides drums and fifes, trumpets also served the practical purpose of calling citizens to militia musters or other public activities, such as in Windsor, Connecticut, whose selectmen ordered a platform constructed atop its meetinghouse "to sound a trumpet or a drum to give warning" according to the town minutes of 1638.

Drums, fifes, and trumpets nevertheless could furnish little appropriate entertainment for weddings, christenings, or harvest celebrations, so a wider range of musical instruments quickly made their way to Anglo-America. Although New Hampshire had been settled barely a decade by the summer of 1633, it appears according to inventories taken at that time that a total of forty-one oboes and recorders lay stored among the inventories of merchants in the adjoining communities of Newitchwanicke and Piscataquog by that early date. Another merchant's bill from Roxbury, Massachusetts, (dated March 17, 1635) included charge for four dozen Jew's harps, which apparently were intended for bartering furs from the Indians. Musicologists have located references to fiddles, violas, treble violins, base violins, and guitars among inventories probated in Massachusetts courthouses during the 1660s and 1670s.

Religious scruples cast music in an ambiguous light among most early Calvinists during the seventeenth century. Puritans acknowledged that music ranked among the legitimate pleasures crafted by the Lord for humanity's enjoyment and that it served an important role in holy worship, but they saw it as having little value when employed for secular purposes. Rev. Leonard Hoar, one of Harvard's early presidents, summarized their attitude in a letter responding to a request from his nephew Josiah Flint, who was then studying for the ministry in Massachusetts, that he send him a fiddle from London.

"Musick I had almost forgot," wrote Reverend Hoar on March 27, 1661. "I suspect you seek it both to[o] soon and to[o] much. This be assured of, that if you be not excellent at it, It's worth nothing at all. And if you be excellent, it will take up so much of your mind and time that you will be worth little else; And when all that excellence is attained, your acquest will prove little or nothing of real profit to you unless you intend to take upon you the trade of fiddling."

Flint's uncle consequently declined to send him the fiddle he so eagerly sought because practicing on it would distract him from his true calling as a minister. Reverend Hoar nevertheless saw no contradiction in developing musical talents among devout Congregational females—"for whom tis more proper and they also have more leisure to looke after it." He consequently purchased several instruments in London for Josiah Flint's sisters, who thus emerged as ironic beneficiaries of that period's double standard toward the social roles of men and women.

Puritans viewed music as an inherently innocent amusement but one that had a small place in their grand scheme of things. Its true value lay not in being enjoyed for its own sake but as a means of praising the Creator through pious hymns at divine worship according to the Biblical injunction "to sing praise unto the Lord, with the words of David." The primary musical experience for most Puritans, as well as the majority of other colonial Calvinists, consisted of bleating out the psalms, all 150 of them, in both formal worship and private family devotions.

Several English translations of David's poems provided Protestants with metrical versions of appropriate for singing, and many editions of the King James Bible had such psalters stitched into them as an appendix. Even among those early settlers who were literate, however, relatively few possessed the skill of deciphering musical notation. The only significant exception to this general situation consisted of the Pilgrims, many of whom were "very expert in music" on landing at Plymouth Colony according to Gov. Edward Winslow.

Hymn singing among Plymouth congregations evidently conformed to customary practices used by Church of England parishes, namely for a church official (usually the clerk) to lead the tune and text as the members followed along either from their psalters or by memory. About 1682, Plymouth congregations abandoned this practice because too few worshipers still retained the skill of reading musical notes or could remember the varied metrical styles used in all 150 psalms. Plymouth churches then copied the example of their neighbors in Massachusetts Bay, where ecclesiastical singing depended on virtually no reference to printed materials but rather functioned according to a system termed "lining out."

Lining out evidently had become well established in the Bay Colony as early as 1647 when Rev. John Cotton described it in his pamphlet *Singing of Psalmes A Gospel-Ordinance* as the only expedient by which persons "who want either books or skill to reade, may know what is to be sung, and joyne with the rest in the dutie of singing." The practice of lining out consisted of a precentor, who was typically a church elder, singing a psalm line by line, with pauses in between each that allowed the congregation to repeat the stanza in his meter and melody. This method interrupted the flow of the text and ruined musical continuity. Precentors often had little sense of pitch or rhythm, so tunes were corrupted and embellished until no two congregations sang the same psalm alike.

Contributing to this lack of regularity was the first work of music published in North America, *The Whole Book of Psalmes Faithfully Translated into English Metre,* popularly known as the *Bay Psalm Book,* 1,700 copies of which were printed at Cambridge, Massachusetts, in 1640. This work was published without tunes scored as bars of music—probably because the Cambridge press did not possess any typeface for such engraving—so that each congregation was left to choose its own mode of psalmody according to the whims of its precentor. Almost every church in New England ultimately adopted this psalter, which also came into widespread use as far south as New Jersey.

The *Bay Psalm Book* emerged as early America's first best-seller and went through at least twenty-seven editions by 1773. Its 1698 edition constitutes the first book illustrated with musical notation to roll off a colonial press. (This 1698 Boston edition nevertheless may have been a reprint of the *Bay Psalm Book* that some bibliographers believe was published in England by London book dealer Richard Chiswell.) The first American music textbook appeared in 1721 when Rev. John Tufts of Newbury, Massachusetts, published *A Very Plain and Easy Introduction to the Whole Art of Singing Psalm Tunes,* containing twenty-eight tunes in three-part harmony that were presented with notes on the staff represented by letters of the alphabet and timing indicated by one or more dots alongside each letter; this innovative work went through eleven editions by 1744. In the same year that Tufts's instruction book appeared, Rev. Thomas Walter of Roxbury also published *The Grounds and Rules of Musick Explained; Or An Introduction to the Art of Singing*, in which he outlined a set of "Rules for Tuning [th]e Voice."

By the time Tufts and Walter authored these pioneering works in 1721, musical literacy had virtually become a forgotten art in the colonies. In the single most-important setting where early Americans produced music, their churches, singing was little more than a confused cacophony. Reverend Walter described the typical psalmody of New England congregations in the following words.

> Tunes are now miserably tortured, and twisted, and quavered, in some Churches, into an horrid Medley of confused and discordant Noises; much time is taken up in shaking out these Turns and Quavers, and besides no two men in the Congregation quavering alike, or together, which sounds in the Ears of a Good Judge like five hundred tunes roared out in the Same Time.

Out of this situation arose the first significant musical controversy in America. Many educated clergy and cultivated lay persons recoiled at the discordance routinely characteristic of hymn singing as an entire congregation would waver a complete tone above or below a note, with each member providing an idiosyncratic interpretation. Such individual freedom (with everyone bellowing out his or her personal variation, highly embellished, with no two in unison) nevertheless represented a multigeneration oral culture that was evolving into a genuine folk tradition. Despite its manifold imperfections, the "old way" of singing had become very popular among a wide segment of the churchgoing population, who venerated lining out as an ancient ritual and appreciated that its lack of structure afforded an outlet for their personality.

Rev. Thomas Symmes, a Harvard graduate of 1698 who appended the title *Philomusicus* (Lover of Music) after his name, emerged as the most prominent opponent to lining out and other traditional forms of sacred music. Symmes fired the first shot of New England's "singing war" by issuing *The Reasonableness of Regular Singing, or Singing by Note* at Boston in 1720, when he denounced the abysmal state of psalmody in Congregational churches and argued forcefully for the necessity of learning to sing music in formal unison. Symmes provoked the "old way" of singing's conservative defenders into mad rage by referring to them as "Anti-Regular Singers," which he then impishly abbreviated as "A.R.S.es." Although many—perhaps most—church members supported the old way of singing by rote rather than note, ministers such as Symmes, Tufts, and Walter soon convinced most clergy that "regular music" would contribute to a far more spiritually edifying atmosphere at Sunday worship.

In order to develop the necessary level of musical literacy, Reverend Symmes had advocated the establishment of singing schools in each town. Such institutions were not unknown in Anglo-America, with the first such organization having appeared at one of Maryland's Anglican parishes in 1699, but they were still very much of a novelty. Bostonians could take advantage of formal hymn instruction as early as 1714, and singing schools began to spring up in larger market towns during the 1720s. Singing schools typically organized adolescents, rather than adults, and trained them in music reading and other choral techniques for two or three nights weekly; they operated under the guidance of local masters in musicology or, on occasion, under itinerant voice teachers.

Singing schools had became widespread and influential by 1760 among Congregationalists and Anglicans. Churches increasingly gave their members a more prominent role in the Sunday liturgy by reserving the gallery's first seats for the best singers and then appointing a chorister to lead them through a more polished rendition of the psalms than the general congregation could accomplish. It was from these practices that the church choir came to evolve during the 1750s and 1760s, even though this institution was originally foreign to the

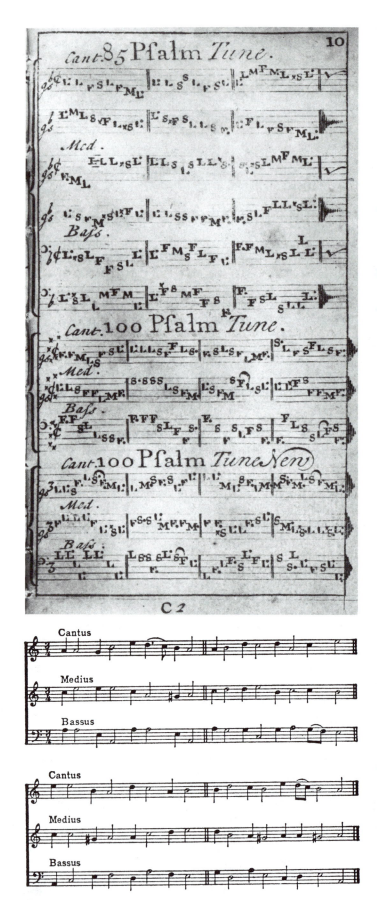

The sheet of music on the top comes from John Tufts *An Introduction to The Singing of Psalm Tunes* (1721) and shows the style of notation he devised for teaching how to read music. The sheet on the bottom shows how the 100th Psalm would be transcribed in modern notation. (Courtesy American Antiquarian Society)

Calvinist tradition with which the overwhelming majority of early Americans were affiliated.

Sacred music also became more sophisticated during the eighteenth century as organs slowly began to proliferate among congregations. Philadelphia's Gloria Dei (Swedish) Lutheran Church acquired the colonies' first organ in 1703. Thomas Brattle imported the first organ in New England to Boston in 1711, but after the local Congregationalists declined to accept it as a gift, he willed it to Anglican King's Chapel in 1713. (This instrument was later sold to Newburyport in 1756 and then in 1836 to St. John's Church at Portsmouth, New Hampshire, where it still can be found in usable condition.) Organs had to be imported from Britain until 1746, when Edward Bromfield built the first American organ in Boston.

Secular music began to emerge as a significant form of popular entertainment during the eighteenth century. Edward Enstone, who had been imported from England by King's Chapel to play the organ donated by Thomas Brattle, set up a multifaceted musical business at Boston shortly after arriving in 1713. Enstone ran the following advertisement in the *Boston News-Letter* on April 16, 1716.

> This is to give notice that there is lately sent over from London, a choice Collection of Musickal Instruments, consisting of Flageolets [recorders], Flutes, Haut-Boys [oboes], Bass-Viols, Violins, Bows, Strings, Reeds for Haut-Boys, Books of Instruction for all these Instruments, Books of ruled Paper. To be Sold at the Dancing Schoole of Mr. Enstone in Sudbury Street near the Orange Tree, Boston.

> NOTE. Any person may have all Instruments of Musick mended, or Virginalls [harpsichords] and Spinnets [small keyboards] Strung and Tuned at a reasonable Rate, and likewise may be taught to Play on any of these Instruments above mention'd; dancing taught by a true and easier method than has been heretofore.

Amateur musicians had clearly become sufficiently numerous by the early 1700s to provide an income for instrument sellers like Enstone. Amateur performers most often acquired their instrumental skills from tutors in order to cultivate the refinement expected of young men and women from the gentry; they rarely played outside their own homes or the households of close friends, but they nevertheless stimulated a growing appreciation of the Baroque style then blossoming in Europe. From this source, there developed a rising demand for public performances of chamber or vocal pieces.

The earliest-known public-paid concert occurred on December 30, 1731, at a large gathering room in a private home at Boston. This event, the first for which a newspaper advertisement has survived, was hardly unique, however, for notice of concerts featuring vocal and instrumental performances can be found in newspapers from Charles Town, South Carolina, barely a few months later in July 1732. Among the early virtuosos then active at Charles Town (and later at New York and Newport, Rhode Island) was Karl Theodore Pachelbel, son of Johann Pachelbel, the German composer of the now-famous "Canon in D Minor." The first recorded operatic performance featured the ballad-opera *Flora, or Hob in the Well* at Charles Town on February 8, 1735. Early concerts resembled this program for a Charles Town benefit of October 16, 1765.

Act I

French Horn Concerto
2d Concerto of [John] Stanley
Solo on the Violincello
5th Concerto of Stanley
Bassoon Concerto
Song
Overture from Handel's Opera *Scipio*

Act II

French Horn Concerto
Concerto on the Harpsichord
Trio
Bassoon Concerto
Song French Horn Concerto by Hasse

Large-scale ensembles also appeared in the colonies during the early eighteenth century. The first was the Collegium Musicum organized by the Moravian German congregation at Bethlehem, Pennsylvania, which ranks as the first chamber orchestra within the present bounds of the United States; by 1748, it contained eight pieces in its string section, four in the brass, and two flutes. This group primarily played religious music, but it also performed the earliest pieces by Johann Sebastian Bach and Franz Joseph Haydn heard in the colonies; it also accompanied the first American debut of parts of the score for Handel's *Messiah* at Bethlehem in 1760 (just nineteen years after its premier at Dublin).

A slow expansion in the scope of musical entertainment also can be seen during the mid-eighteenth century. The first use of an orchestra to accompany an opera took place in 1752, when *The Beggar's Opera* was staged at Upper Marlboro, Maryland. Gilbert Deblois opened the first true concert hall two years later in 1754 at Boston. A series of open-air summer concerts ran successfully at Raneleigh Gardens in New York for four years after 1759.

The colonial era's final musical highlight occurred in 1762, when citizens of Charles Town founded the St. Cecelia Society, the oldest, secular music organization in North America. It was formed of "gentlemen performers," whose numbers were supplemented by professional musicians engaged by the season. The group consisted of 120 members a decade later and gave regular cycles of concerts until it disbanded in 1912.

By the St. Cecelia Society's inception, organized music was starting to acquire a respectable place in American life. Singing schools and organized choirs were transforming sacred music from a crude, collective chant to an art form that brought a new sense of sweetness and grace to public worship. Public concerts and a rising level of interest in Baroque compositions were meanwhile exposing a significant number of colonists from many walks of life to chamber works and vocal pieces by European masters such as Handel, Bach, and Haydn.

CHAPTER 14 Science and Technology

Early American science emerged in the shadow of Europe's scientific revolution, which developed slowly from the late sixteenth century through the publication of Isaac Newton's *Principia Mathematica* in 1687. The scientific revolution reshaped attitudes about investigating natural phenomena, but it produced little more than a slow, incremental rise in the total stock of scientific knowledge until well after 1800. Aside from mathematics and astronomy, the modern disciplines of physics, botany, zoology, and entomology had not yet emerged as discrete areas of study and were considered to be related aspects of "natural philosophy."

Universities continued to base their curricula almost exclusively around the classical humanities (aside from specialized study for medical degrees) and offered almost no instruction in the various fields of natural philosophy. This lack of institutional support for scientific research affected Europeans no less than their overseas colonists. Anglo-Americans suffered relatively little disadvantage vis-à-vis Europeans in their ability to pursue scientific inquiries, except in regards to the time-consuming and tenuous nature of trans-Atlantic communication with like-minded scholars. Scientific progress emerged essentially through experimentation by amateurs able to support themselves as doctors, apothecaries, civil servants, or professors.

The primary deterrent to scientific activity in the colonies was their small population, which placed a practical limit on the number of people with sufficient wealth and leisure to study "natural history" in a rigorous fashion. The primary stimulus for increasing scientific knowledge came from organizations such as England's Royal Society, which was chartered in 1662 to promote "Experimental Learning." The American Philosophical Society, founded at Philadelphia in 1743, served the same function.

Scientists of the early modern era worked toward two broad objectives: the collection of data regarding natural phenomena and the classification of that data according to logical systems of nomenclature or theorizing. Europeans viewed one of the most important tasks in natural philosophy to be the delineation of the New World's flora and fauna. It was hoped that colonials would play an integral role in this process, and England's Royal Society included an American among its charter members. Most Americans who contributed to this process collected data for European scientists who could synthesize their information but played a key role nevertheless by their increasingly accurate and sophisticated observations. By the last generation prior to the American Revolution, Anglo-Americans had started to organize, synthesize, and theorize about data from recorded observations or experimentation and consequently had begun to contribute original scientific ideas of their own.

Astronomy

The New World held great promise as a base for astronomical observations. Sightings in America would greatly refine the accuracy of the period's crude maps by giving cartographers more-precise data on the exact latitude and longitude of known locations. Colonial notations of celestial objects would also enable scientists to reevaluate contemporary estimates of the Earth's distance to other planets and points in the solar system.

John Winthrop, Jr. (1606–76), governor of Connecticut, was America's first astronomer. His reputation ranked high among English scholars, and he shared the honor of being a charter member of the Royal Society. Designated as "chief correspondent of the Royal Society in the West," he returned to Connecticut in 1663 with the first tele-

scope owned in the Western Hemisphere. The instrument measured $3^1/_2$ feet long and had several attachments.

At Hartford, Connecticut, Winthrop made the earliest systematic astronomical observations by any colonial European. In 1664, he recorded the passage of a comet that probably had not been visible across the Atlantic, but he then seems to have been frustrated in honoring the Royal Society's request to observe a lunar eclipse, probably due to bad weather conditions. He reported having discovered a fifth satellite orbiting Jupiter on August 6, 1664, and this news stirred considerable debate among scientists for several years. Although Jupiter does indeed have a fifth moon, astronomers now discount that the Connecticut governor actually saw it and officially date its first true sighting as 1892.

Weakening eyes motivated Winthrop to donate his telescope to Harvard in 1672 when he was sixty-six years old. Harvard was well suited to appreciate its potential as a tool for investigating "experimental philosophy." One of its tutors, Alexander Nowell, had already authored a paper on comets, and its faculty evidently accepted Copernicus's model of the solar system as centered around the Sun rather than the Earth. This position Galileo had been forced to recant under threat of death as recently as 1633 in Rome.

Thomas Brattle (1658–1713) assumed Winthrop's place as Anglo-America's foremost astronomer. Brattle was a Harvard graduate (master of science, 1676) and a merchant whose almanac in 1678 demonstrated an advanced knowledge of astronomy. His observations on "Newton's comet" of 1680 became the first American research to influence international science on a significant matter after they appeared in his almanac the next year and were sent to the Royal Society. The society deemed his data sufficiently important to forward to the Greenwich observatory's royal astronomer, who then shared the findings with Isaac Newton. Newton found Brattle's tracking of the comet to be one of several key pieces of evidence for his argument that orbiting satellites followed an elliptical rather than a circular path, and he used his work to validate Kepler's laws of motion and to hypothesize the concept of universal gravitation in his magnum opus, *Principia Mathematica*.

When Halley's comet reappeared on schedule in 1682, Increase Mather (1639–1723), who would shortly become Harvard's president, and his two sons took readings and wrote about the phenomenon. While still an undergraduate, Increase Mather's son Nathaniel brought New Englanders up to date with the latest astronomical discoveries by authoring a survey of the field's scholarship in *The Boston Ephemeris, an Almanac for MDCLXXXIII [1683]*. As clergymen, the Mathers noted that comets sometimes accompanied events of divine intervention in human affairs, but as scientists they also taught their Puritan readers that comets had perfectly natural causes and operated according to fixed laws of motion.

Harvard meanwhile slowly expanded its stock of astronomical instruments from 1680 to 1700. Its major acquisitions included a brass quadrant with telescopic sights that had been owned by Edmond Halley; a second, more powerful, telescope of $4^1/_2$ feet, with four magnification glasses; and a universal ring dial for calibrating clocks accurately. Thomas Brattle used Halley's quadrant to record the progress of the solar eclipse of June 12, 1694, an event that enabled him to calculate Boston's longitude within fifteen minutes of its exact value—a remarkable feat given the imprecision of his tools.

Brattle's later accomplishments included detailed observations on a solar eclipse of 1703 and lunar eclipses in 1700, 1703, and 1707. He completed another highly important undertaking on April 5, 1707, when he assessed the variation of a compass's magnetic needle at Boston to be 9 degrees west of north. This finding was the first precise measure of magnetic variation in the Western Hemisphere; it also determined that the needle had shifted to a position consistent with readings 200 years prior and so helped establish that magnetic variation occurs on a periodic basis.

New England's most prominent astronomer after Brattle was Thomas Robie (1689–1729), a holder of a master of arts degree from Harvard and a physician. Starting in 1708, he published a series of almanacs entitled *An Ephemeris of the Coelestial Motions ...* , in which he often printed essays educating his readers on science, such as "an account of the Solar System, according to Copernicus and the modern Astronomers," with Sir Isaac Newton's calculations. Robie corresponded with several English scientists and the Royal Society accumulated many of his reports. His research led to the purchase or donation of much scientific equipment for Harvard's observatory. The papers he sent abroad included data on the aurora borealis in 1719; measurements of the halo surrounding the solar eclipse of November 27, 1722; a transit of Mercury over the Sun on October 29, 1723; and meteorological diaries. He left Boston to practice medicine at Salem in 1723, became a fellow of the Royal Society in 1725, and died prematurely four years later.

The southern colonies yielded little astronomical information, and none of it involved the use of telescopes. Richard Brooke informed the Royal Society of having witnessed three concentric rings around the Sun on May 3, 1749, in Maryland. Richard Lewis of Annapolis sent the first report from America of having seen sunspots (on October 22, 1730) with the naked eye.

The Mid-Atlantic region likewise produced few astronomers prior to the Revolutionary era. A flurry of activity followed the arrival of William Burnet, a Fellow of the Royal Society, as joint governor of New York and New Jersey in 1720. He sent the society a report on a solar eclipse viewed from the fort at New York City in 1722. In 1724, he dispatched information on four eclipses of Jupiter's first moon—which occurred on August 9, August 25, and September 10 of 1723, and June 26, 1724—along with calculations derived from this data on the latitude and longitude of New York City. The pursuit of science nevertheless proceeded slowly in New York, and Boston remained the center of Anglo-American astronomy.

John Winthrop IV (1714–79), a great grandnephew of John Winthrop, Jr., was the colonial era's last great astronomer. A master of arts from Harvard (1735), he became professor of mathematics and natural philosophy at Harvard at age twenty-three and ultimately emerged as the first faculty member of his college to devote his nonteaching schedule full-time to productive research. He ranked as the greatest American scientist of the mid-eighteenth century, and he was inducted as a fellow by the Royal Society in 1765.

The bulk of Winthrop's career entailed making celestial observations, but his work also demonstrated competence as a theoretical scientist. A paper on gravitation and gravitational balance in the universe that he authored in 1760 was his best endeavor in this area; it suggested the possibility of estimating the density and volume of comets by observations and reasoning. Although routinely done by modern cosmetologists, this approach had never been previously articulated and was highly visionary. The Royal Society published a revised version of the argument in its *Philosophical Transactions* of 1767.

Winthrop's earliest scientific investigations concerned the sunspots that he first viewed with his naked eye on a hazy April 19, 1739. He resumed his observations the next daybreak through an 8-foot telescope at Harvard. Although the professor's sketches of the spots were too inexact for calculating their latitude on the Sun's surface, he correctly noted the association between sunspots and aurora-borealis activity. The professor did not formally hypothesize a relation between the two, but he anticipated later scientists of the mid-nineteenth century who were to document that a causal connection existed.

In 1740, Winthrop trained his 24-foot telescope on the transit of Mercury over the Sun on April 21, an event not visible in Europe. This observation marked the first occasion reported to the Royal Society in which Mercury's transit had been traced in its descending phase. He made similar recordings in 1743 when he measured another transit of Mercury on October 25. His readings were not only exceptionally sophisticated for a scientist who was not yet thirty years old but also enabled him to establish an accurate longitude of Cambridge, Massachusetts, relative to Greenwich, England, so that his future research could be correlated with data from the Royal Observatory.

Winthrop provided highly detailed reports on other significant crossings within the solar system and of meteors. His most important observation traced the transit of Venus across the Sun on June 6, 1761. This event created an eclipse by passing between the Earth and the Sun and so gave scientists a chance to ascertain this planet's exact parallax angle with the Sun; using a technique devised by Edmond Halley, astronomers had a rare chance—occurring just four times every 243 years—to make the first simultaneous determination of the exact distance of their own planet and Venus from the Sun. Winthrop recognized that observations from St. Johns, Newfoundland, would be far more valuable than from Cambridge because only from the former was the transit's egress visible in the Western Hemisphere. He organized Harvard's first scientific expedition and convinced the Massachusetts Assembly to finance its expenses.

On the day of the transit, Winthrop coordinated a highly complex set of readings of altitudes and azimuths taken from both refracting and reflecting telescopes, a quadrant, and a finely calibrated clock timed to coincide with daybreak at Greenwich, England. Winthrop's data appeared not only in the Royal Society's *Philosophical Transactions* but was also declared to be taken "with great care, and as much exactness as the low situation of the sun [in northen latitudes] at that time would permit." The Harvard expedition succeeded in providing the only data from North America. Winthrop's party suffered from the disadvantage of having less-accurate equipment than other groups dispatched from Europe plus the lack of predetermined latitudinal-longitudinal data for St. Johns, but its estimate for the solar parallax, 8.25″, was 93.75% precise within the current estimate of 8.80″. Harvard's survey of the 1761 transit of Venus marked the apogee of early American astronomical achievement.

Botany and Zoology

New England excelled, almost to the exclusion of every other region of Anglo-America, in the advancement of astronomy, but it contributed little to knowledge of natural history. The Royal Society solicited "curiosities" but received relatively little from its Yankee correspondents. The largest consignment of such miscellanea arrived in 1670 through the efforts of John Winthrop, Jr., who sent four chests containing fifty specimens, such as local vegetables, a starfish, a flying fish, fossils, shells, soil samples, stones, minerals, types of wood, nuts, and insects.

John Josselyn (1608–75), an Englishman with some medical training who lived in the region from 1663 to 1671, authored the most important account of its flora and fauna in his *New-England's Rarities Discovered: In Birds, Beasts, Fishes, Serpents, and Plants of the Country; Together With the Physical and Chyrurgical Remedies wherewith the Natives constantly use to Cure their Distempers, Wounds and Sores ...* (London, 1672). Josselyn's work resembled a traveler's account more than a scientific study, however. The book's most-thorough section listed 163 plants and vegetables growing in the region, including twenty-two varieties transplanted from Great Britain, but its treatment of animals, birds, and fish lacked comprehensiveness. Despite his work's flaws, Josselyn produced the only catalogue of New England's wildlife completed until 1785.

In the seventeenth century, Virginia was the primary scene of research by naturalists. Rev. John Clayton (1657–1725), a minister well versed in many scientific pursuits, went to Virginia in 1684 intending to examine carefully the natural environment. Clayton had the potential to make noteworthy observations, for his property included a small library, various chemical instruments and glasses, microscopes, lens-grinding tools, a barometer, and thermometer. These books and equipment nevertheless failed to arrive because they traveled on a separate vessel that was lost at sea. Badly discouraged, Clayton observed avidly but took few notes before his return to England in 1686. He answered the Royal Society's request to write a scientific description of Virginia by composing six letters from 1688 to 1693. The minister devoted little space to marine life, entomology, or botany, but his letters on "beasts" and birds constituted a modest beginning for zoology in the South.

Clayton's pioneering efforts paled in comparison to research into botany and entomology by his contemporary John Bannister (1650–92), however. Bannister evidently secured funding from wealthy English patrons of science to compile a catalogue of Virginia's natural environment. He arrived in 1678 and existed on increasingly slender finances until 1688 when he married a widow and became a planter of independent means in Charles City County. Bannister helped organize the College of William and Mary and enjoyed a steadily rising reputation until his premature death in 1692, when a hunter along the Roanoke River mistook the botanist for a deer and shot him.

Bannister had completed enough fieldwork by 1689 that he could envision an outline for a natural history of the Old Dominion. He had prepared some of his research for publication by 1692, but most of his work had to be reviewed, catalogued, and edited. Sir Hans Sloan, founder of the British Museum (where his collection now resides), acquired and preserved most of his papers, but other, less-competent conservators allowed careless damage to his specimens, drawings, and writings. Because the Royal Society could not immediately afford to print Bannister's work in comprehensive fashion, many naturalists and other authors simply appropriated his findings and published them piecemeal. Recognition of Bannister as a botanist consequently lagged his actual achievements until more modern times.

Bannister ranks as the first great American botanist. He not only listed more than 340 plants as native to Virginia (two-thirds of which were new species) but also produced dried specimens from his herbarium and careful descriptions of them, including eighty illustrations that have survived. He identified more than 100 insects (fifty-two unique to Virginia), twenty mollusks, and a variety of fossils and stones. Although his catalogue of mammals and birds was far inferior to Clayton's, zoology lay outside his primary interest. Bannister's work stands as the first systematic study of North American flora.

Just as Bannister had followed John Clayton as Virginia's leading naturalist, through an appropriately fitting coincidence his own successor proved to be another John Clayton (1694–1773), a distant English cousin of the earlier Chesapeake scientist by that name. The second John Clayton arrived in Virginia about 1720, established a plantation, and became clerk of the Gloucester Country court. Clayton developed a correspondence with several leading European naturalists, to whom he sent a large volume of local seeds and pressed plants. He prepared an updated catalogue of Virginia's plants, fruits, and trees during the 1730s and forwarded it to the Dutch scientist John Gronovius. Gronovius and Carl Linnaeus, who was then in the Netherlands, collaborated to reorganize Clayton's lists more accurately.

Gronovius skirted the limits of plagiarization by publishing this reworked catalogue as *Flora Virginica* (1739) neither with Clayton's permission, nor even crediting him on the title page as its actual compiler. He nevertheless identified Clayton's efforts in the prefatory section, although this acknowledgment subtly denigrated Clayton's accomplishment by confusing readers about the full extent of his contributions vis-à-vis Gronovius. Clayton's scientific idealism prevailed

over Gronovius's appalling behavior, and he furnished the Dutch naturalist with additional materials that Gronovius printed as a second part of *Flora Virginica* in 1743.

Clayton carried on his observations and became a self-taught master of the Linnaean system. His plantation and duties as county clerk deterred him from taking long expeditions, but in 1748 he undertook a botanizing expedition to the Shenandoah valley, where settlement had just recently begun. On several occasions, he identified errors in classification that Linnaeus then corrected. Linnaeus respected Clayton considerably and named the American spring beauty flower as the *Claytonia* in his honor.

Clayton contacted both Gronovius and an English scientist about updating *Flora Virginica* with specially made illustrations, additional specimens, and a more precise Linnaean classification of species and genera. His English correspondent took the revisions and had printer's plates made of the pictures, but before he could find a publisher, a son of Gronovius brought out a new edition in 1762 without informing Clayton in advance. The 1762 Dutch imprint lacked illustrations and numerous alterations based on fieldwork in the Shenandoah Valley; it furthermore was indifferently edited and far inferior to the manuscript available in England. No further versions of *Flora Virginica* appeared before most of his research notes and specimens perished during the Revolution. Although ranked among the New World's leading naturalists, Clayton's dependence on incompetent foreign editors kept the reading public from seeing the fruits of his research at its very best.

Most American naturalists performed the valuable work of description and classification, but James Logan (1674–1751) undertook actual experimentation in physiological botany. He was a wealthy Philadelphia landowner who amassed Pennsylvania's largest library, including many scientific volumes. Logan investigated the process of fertilizing seeds. Botanists already acknowledged the sexual nature of plants, and two Americans, Paul Dudley (1675–1751) and Cotton Mather (1663–1728), had previously written about plant hybridization. The exact process of fructification remained ill-defined, however. In 1734 and 1735, Logan sent the Royal Society reports of his experiments on the pollination of maize. His work was the first detailed account of to explain the function of various plant organs in Indian corn's germination, and it suggested that impregnation proceeded by complex processes in other plants. The society printed his results in 1736, and scientific opinion was so overwhelmingly favorable that the great Swedish botanist Carl Linnaeus named a genus of plant after him. Logan unfortunately did no more research after suffering a stroke in 1740.

Dr. John Mitchell (ca. 1690–1768) pursued one of the most fruitful careers of any naturalists while residing at Urbana, Virginia, from 1735 to 1746. Besides botany and zoology, his interests spanned meteorology, cartography, electricity, and medicine. His report of 1741 to the Royal Society dissecting the anatomy of male and female opossums ranks as one of the most precise zoological papers by any Anglo-American prior to 1763.

Mitchell spent most of the time he was not engaged in his medical practice in his herbarium and laboratory. He also conducted a large correspondence with prominent naturalists in western Europe. He cultivated an enormous array of flora with the goals of identifying unknown plants, improving botanical classification, and deriving new cures from vegetation. The extensiveness of his research is indicated by his shipment of 560 plant specimens to a member of the Royal Society in March 1742. When the society published his updated catalogue of Bannister's listing of Virginia flora in 1748, he was credited with discovering ten new genera of plants.

His most important contribution to botany lay in taxonomy, however. Mitchell ranked the foremost colonial pioneer in applying the Linnaean system and vocabulary of classifying the natural world to

American wildlife. He nevertheless did not entirely agree with the Swedish scientist's techniques, and Mitchell's catalogue included a prefatory essay on the difficulties of classifying species by this means, in particular to its unnecessary complexity. (Mitchell asserted, for example, that it would greatly simplify organizing types of plants or creatures if any two types in which a male of one and a female of another are able to procreate prolific offspring were categorized as being of one species, despite any other superficial difference.) Linnaeus respected Mitchell despite such criticisms and gave the partridgeberry its name *Mitchella repens* in his honor.

When Mitchell returned to Britain in 1746, he embarked with a massive collection of more than 1,000 specimens. A Spanish privateer captured his ship and confiscated both it and the cargo for auction. The doctor managed to locate his plants and have them sent to England, but improper treatment had ruined most of them. After his election as a fellow of the Royal Society in 1748, he remained in Britain and contributed little to American botany.

The Carolinas produced one major naturalist, Dr. Alexander Garden (1730–91), a Scot who established a medical practice at Charles Town in 1752. He became an avid botanist who corresponded with all the leading European naturalists and forwarded large collections of dried plants and seeds to them. Garden twice identified errors in Carl Linnaeus's system of classifying plants, and he forced the great Swede to admit his mistake by redesignating the items (by misidentifying the genus of a shrub as gentian rather than vervain and by mislabeling the sago palm as a fern rather than of the cycad family). Appropriate recognition of his achievements came in 1760 when Linnaeus approved a Royal Society proposal to name the Cape jasmine as the *Gardenia*.

Garden began to provide significant zoological specimens after 1760. Linnaeus, not only incorporated many of them into the twelfth edition of his *Natural Systems* (1766–68), but he created an entirely new class of amphibia (*Serenidae*) based on the doctor's analysis of the mud iguana. Garden tried to stay neutral in the Revolution but became tainted with Toryism and moved to London in 1783.

Cadwallader Colden (1688–1776) won a brief measure of international fame as a botanist rivaling Garden's renown. Colden was a prominent officeholder who owned a large estate near New York City. He avidly collected plant specimens from 1742 to 1755, forwarded them to such leading European naturalists as John Gronovius and Carl Linnaeus, and compiled the first catalogue of New York flora according to the Linnaean system. Linnaeus named a plant (the *Coldenia*) for him in 1747, and he gave a conspicuous place to Colden as a major source of information for North American vegetation in his *Species Plantarum* (1753).

Of all the pre-Revolutionary botanists, none was perhaps more sincerely devoted to unlocking nature's secrets than John Bartram (1699–1777). This modest Quaker was born in Pennsylvania and began life as an ordinary farmer with little education. He came under the spell of science during a rest break from plowing when he picked a flower at random, became absorbed by its complexity, and felt an irresistible urge to learn about plants. He scoured the forests seeking their wonders with a missionary's zeal for the next half-century until nature itself became his religion and his Quaker meeting house was forced to expel him for espousing Deism.

Patrons in nearby Philadelphia such as James Logan and Benjamin Franklin lent Bartram scientific books and even tutored him in Latin, which he never fully mastered. Possibly inspired by Logan's example about 1728, Bartram started a botanical garden that grew to cover 5 acres and was esteemed as the best in Anglo-America. English naturalists freed Bartram from complete dependence on his farm by paying him to undertake fieldwork as early as 1738 and also sent him many exotic plants from around the world to cultivate in his farm. Bartram soon began to collect specimens for zoologists and entomologists as

well, and his first publication (1735) described the dissection of a rattlesnake; he also contributed to cartography by tracing the Schuykill River to its source in 1736.

Bartram's expeditions ranged from Lake Ontario to the Florida panhandle. In 1738 alone, he probably covered about 1,100 miles traveling from Pennsylvania to the Virginia tidewater and then through the backcountry. George III named him royal botanist in 1765 but set his stipend at just L50. Bartram became Europe's most important field agent and sent more specimens overseas for study than any other colonist did. Britain's Royal Society never inducted him, but the Swedish Royal Academy of Science elected him a member in 1769, and the Edinburgh Society of Arts awarded him a gold medal in 1772. Although lacking in much elementary scientific knowledge, Bartram's passion for collecting samples gave him claim to be, in the authoritative words of Carl Linnaeus, "the greatest natural botanist in the world."

Cartography

The mapping of North America proceeded far more slowly than that of South America. This lack of progress largely resulted from the disappointing reports of early navigators such as England's John Cabot and France's Giovanni da Verrazano who described the northern coast as sparsely inhabited and the aborigines as possessing few riches. Europeans primarily hoped to exploit the wealth and labor of native societies, but North America offered little prospects for plundering on the scale practiced by Spain in Mexico and Peru.

The New World's exploration consequently advanced most rapidly along the lands bordering the Gulf of Mexico, the Caribbean Sea, and South America's eastern coast. The great accomplishment of sixteenth-century seafarers was to demonstrate that North America was a continuous landmass rather than an extended archipelago. Sebastian Cabot succeeded in delineating North America as a true continent in his Antwerp map of 1544, but other cartographers had their doubts. As late as 1582, Englishman Michael Lok produced a map (admittedly of very poor workmanship) that portrayed New England—then called Norumbega—as an island, as well as showing Canada and the Mid-Atlantic region to be a small continent linked to Florida by an isthmus.

So little was learned of the coast from the Savannah to the Piscataqua Rivers in the 1500s that not until 1609 was Hudson River discovered. Progress in charting the Atlantic shoreline came gradually after the first English settlements appeared. John White, governor of Sir Walter Raleigh's Roanoke colony, drafted the first detailed map of English America in 1585 when he completed a remarkably accurate outline of Albemarle and Pamlico sounds. John Smith, a Virginia adventurer, ranks as one of the most important colonial mapmakers for having produced fairly close depictions of Chesapeake Bay (reconnoitered 1607–08 and printed 1612) and New England (1614) in rather short time frames. Smith's maps remained the most accurate renderings of those areas for more than six decades. By 1620, primarily through the efforts of Henry Hudson, John White, and John Smith, Europeans could obtain maps for the first time that gave a good approximation of North America's Atlantic coast.

Mapmaking was more properly an exercise in exploration than cartography until the late seventeenth century. The earliest charts did little more than present headlands and other terrain features in their order of appearance to a passing vessel; they almost never took sightings of latitude and longitude on shore to correlate such landmarks to an exact geographic coordinate. Colonial cartography first began to approximate the rigorous standards of a precise discipline in 1673 with the London printing of Augustine Herman's map of Maryland and Virginia. A surveyor originally from Prague, Herman spent ten years refining this map's features for Lord Baltimore, and he received a

One of the earliest efforts at Anglo-American cartography, John White's map of the Albemarle Sound region in 1585 was also notable for its precision and graceful design. When compared with modern charts, this first attempt at outlining the North Carolina coast appears remarkably accurate. Note how White showed that the largest English ships had to stay east of the Outer Banks and that only shallops, pinnaces, and other small vessels could safely navigate the treacherous coastline. (Courtesy Library of Congress)

manor of 20,000 acres as his reward. Herman not only produced the first colonial map whose proportions and outline approached modern standards for accuracy but also fixed an accurate baseline for the northern boundary claimed by Maryland at the fortieth degree of north latitude.

A milestone of another sort occurred in 1677 with the publication of William Hubbard's *A Narrative of the Troubles with the Indians in New*

England (Boston). Hubbard embellished his book with John Foster's "A Map of New-England." Foster gave a poor depiction of the region's coastline—far inferior to John Smith's work of 1614—and even arranged the orientation awkwardly on an east-west axis rather than north-south. Despite its crudeness, this illustration was the first map drawn, engraved, and printed in the English colonies rather than in Europe.

Henry Popple produced the first large-scale printed map of North America at London in 1733. Popple's work appeared in atlas format, with the artwork comprising twenty separate sheets. A one-sheet reduction of the grand map was provided on the first page to orient the reader. Popple had few truly accurate maps to work from except Herman's of Chesapeake Bay, however, and his project went to press with many errors in projection and proportion, even though his outline of the Atlantic coast was reasonably correct.

The first truly significant colonial cartographer since Augustine Herman was Lewis Evans of Philadelphia. Beginning with a detailed survey of Bucks County, Pennsylvania, in 1737, he steadily became the leading authority on Mid-Atlantic geography. In 1749, he published his masterpiece, "A Map of Pensilvania, New-Jersey, New-York, and the Three Delaware Counties." The Evans map stood as a landmark of cartography for two reasons: First, it was the most detailed map published of any large area within Anglo-America to that time; second, Evans used his surveying skills to make astronomical observations that fixed positions on the ground at their exact latitude, with his prime meridian passing through Pennsylvania's state house at its correct parallel. This map consequently set new standards of precision and usefulness for American cartographers. A revision issued in 1755, which showed the Ohio Valley, went through eighteen editions by 1814.

Another major advance in Anglo-American cartography came from the efforts of Joshua Fisher, a native of Lewes, Delaware, who was deputy surveyor-general of his province. Fisher spent almost twenty years preparing a chart of Delaware Bay. His work not only rendered creeks, headland, sandbars, shoals, and ship channels in minute detail—with all their names—but also noted the depth of soundings in feet and fathoms. Fisher's chart set new standards for accuracy in depicting coastal hazards for shipping; it went through ten editions from its first printing at Philadelphia in 1756 until 1800, including versions published at London and Paris.

The high point of colonial cartography was the publication of John Mitchell's "A Map of the British and French Dominions in North America, with the Roads, Distances, Limits, and Extent of the Settlements" in 1755. Dr. Mitchell had won international acclaim for the botanical research he conducted in Virginia from 1735 to 1746. The doctor worked from original surveys, drafts, and charts at the Board of Trade's London office and produced a geographic counterargument against French pretensions in the Ohio Valley and modern New Brunswick.

Although Mitchell's endeavor had a partisan purpose, it showed such a concern for detail and precision in every line—including the incorporation of latitudinal determinations taken from exact quadrant sightings—that it did not purposefully distort geographic reality to make its argument for Britain's territorial claims. A member of the Royal Society described it as the "most perfect of any before published and is universally approved." Mitchell's map appeared in twenty-one editions (in four different languages) from 1755 to 1781. The Mitchell map provided the basis for U.S. boundaries drawn by the Treaty of Paris (1783), Webster-Ashburton Treaty (1842), and Quebec boundary accord (1871), besides domestic controversies such as the adjudication of state borders between Wisconsin and Michigan (1926) and between Delaware and New Jersey (1932). Given its authoritative reputation among diplomats and jurists, one can only agree with Lawrence Martin, former geographer for the State Department, who wrote in 1933 that Mitchell produced "the most important map in American history."

John Mitchell's 1755 map of North America is considered to be the most significant map drafted in early Anglo-America. It was the primary source used to determine the boundaries of the United States at the Treaty of Paris in 1783; it was furthermore used repeatedly by negotiators to resolve boundary disputes throughout the next century and was consulted for that purpose even as recently as 1932. (Courtesy Geography and Maps Division, Library of Congress)

Mathematics and Physics

Mathematics remained in great neglect through most of the colonial era. The first chair in mathematics (a joint position with natural philosophy) was not appointed until 1717 at William and Mary. Harvard created the second such position in 1727. Not until after the appointment of John Winthrop as Harvard's Hollis Professor of Mathematics and Natural Philosophy at Harvard in 1738, did any college offer instruction in integral and differential calculus (known then as fluxions).

Cadwallader Colden became the earliest Anglo-American to trigger an international debate on physics: In 1745 he published *An Explication of the First Causes of Action in Matter; And of the Cause of Gravitation* at New York (printed at London in 1751 as *The Principles of Action in Matter*). He attempted no less than explaining gravity itself, a problem that had confounded Sir Isaac Newton, who simply described its properties. "No more audacious claim to intellectual eminence," wrote historian Brooke Hindle of his ideas, "was ever made in colonial America." Colden theorized that gravity's force originated from an etherlike substance that contracted around objects, while motion resulted from a force exerted by light particles.

Members of the Royal Society not only considered Colden's work seriously but also made French and German translations to circulate on the European continent, where it attracted much attention. Colden's peers judged him harshly. The American was woefully ignorant of current scholarship, did not understand basic Newtonian concepts like inertia, and left his readers hopelessly confused. The issue unfortunately tarnished Colden's reputation, which was highly regarded among botanists, and led one European to speculate that he was "a Little touched in his pericranium."

The greatest scientific renown won by any Anglo-American fell to Benjamin Franklin for his research on electricity. After having his first discussion about its properties with a visiting Scottish lecturer in 1743, Franklin read voraciously on that topic and replicated European experiments that collected static electricity by rubbing glass. Franklin began his own original experiments in 1747. He refined earlier observations about electricity's bipolar nature into the modern understanding of positive and negative charges. He also described the similarity of electricity to magnetism in exerting force at distances.

Franklin's research led him to conclude that lightning, which was then a scientific mystery, was electrical in nature. Through his English connections, he published a letter (written in 1749) in 1751 at London in which he suggested an experiment to conduct lightning from the sky through a pointed rod to prove its electric nature. A French translation stirred much interest and led three French scientists to complete the experiment successfully in May 1752 before Franklin

The most highly praised scientific research conducted by any colonial American was Benjamin Franklin's pioneering work on the nature of electricity. Franklin is shown here during one of his famous experiments, with his son as assistant (right). (Courtesy Library of Congress)

himself had attempted it. The French gave Franklin credit for conceptualizing the theoretical basis for the test, however, and he soon became famous among European scientists.

A month after the French verified his hypothesis, Franklin undertook his legendary experiment of drawing lightning to the ground with an airborne key hoisted by a kite during a thunderstorm. He then used the electricity to charge a pail, produce combustion with spirits, and for other experiments. (The high element of risk in this undertaking was dramatically revealed in late 1753 when Professor George Wilhelm Richman died of electrocution trying to replicate the kite experiment in St. Petersburg, Russia.)

International acclaim immediately showered on Franklin because of the fundamental nature of his discovery and its practical application in protecting buildings and ships with lightning rods. The Royal Society awarded him its highest honor, the Copley Medal, in 1753 and then not only admitted him as a member in 1756 but also waived all fees or dues for the rest of his life. Franklin continued his observations of electrical phenomena, and by the late 1750s he was universally considered by knowledgeable Europeans as the world's leading authority on all aspects of that subject. Franklin attained such fame in Europe that Europeans printed eleven editions of the book describing his electrical experiments—five in English, three in French, and one each in German, Italian, and Latin. (No American edition was published, ironically, until 1941.)

Benjamin Franklin deserves to be considered the premier Anglo-American scientist for his research on electricity. Despite having little formal education, he displayed a firm mastery of the scientific method, a keen insight, and a striking ability to describe his careful conclusions in clear, precise language. He started to work in a relatively new field but rapidly absorbed the existing scholarship and quickly became far more sophisticated than his European contemporaries in the topic of electricity. He made original discoveries and delineated sound principles for interpreting, correlating, and predicting electrical behavior. He began to research a misunderstood and little-known subject, and after barely a decade of experimentation, he left it an organized discipline that reinforced the Newtonian paradigm of natural laws. Benjamin Franklin's accomplishments in physics marked the first instance when natural genius brought international acclaim to an American scientist.

Inventions

Early Americans did not lack ingenuity, but they improvised more than they innovated. By modifying technology inherited from Europe, the colonists produced several items that their descendants now consider distinctively American. By the 1750s, Pennsylvanians had transformed the standard European freight vehicle into the Conestoga wagon, an enormously reinforced and enlarged farm wagon with a specially rigged cloth awning to protect goods from the elements. The Pennsylvania (later Kentucky) rifle evolved from the German "jaeger," a heavy, clumsy firearm that gunsmiths streamlined into a weapon far superior to its predecessor for wilderness use. By 1742, Benjamin Franklin had adapted the small, portable, iron chamber used for heating rooms by some German immigrants into the ventilated Franklin (or Pennsylvania) stove, which could heat homes with a fraction of the wood wasted by open-hearth fireplaces. The most original product perfected in early America was the flatboat, which Jacob Yoder of Pennsylvania designed around 1750 as a practical means of shooting over rapids and riffles with large cargoes when many small rivers swelled with water during the rains of spring and autumn.

The earliest true invention of American origin was a navigational instrument. By November 1730, Thomas Godfrey of Philadelphia perfected the octant, a new device for measuring angles of the Sun or stars at sea. His octant proved far superior to the backstaff and various quadrants then in use, which failed to provide distinct readings under various circumstances. James Logan promised to present the implement to the Royal Society, of which he was a regular correspondent, but failed to do so until 1732. In the interval, the society learned that an Englishman working for the Royal Navy had independently and simultaneously developed an apparatus that operated identically according to Godfrey's principle, John Hadley's reflecting quadrant. Hadley won an exclusive patent granting full rights to the invention's commercial uses from 1734 to 1745. Godfrey managed to have a New York crafts worker manufacture and sell the octant under that name, but Hadley's quadrant dominated the market and compromised Godfrey's claim to be the first notable Anglo-American inventor.

The second significant colonial invention was also a direction-finding tool. In 1735, Robert Houghton, a Boston pump maker, obtained a patent for his theodolate, the first surveying instrument produced in the British colonies. No theodolate remains in existence, but it evidently functioned as an improved surveying compass (possibly made of wood) that allowed for horizontal angles to be read more accurately.

One innovation of fundamental importance originated in colonial America: the lightning rod. Benjamin Franklin conceptualized the rod as an experimental means of verifying lightning's electrical properties in 1749 and then immediately recognized its potential for protecting buildings and ships from fire. He published a simple description of the implement under the heading, "How to secure Houses, &c. from Lightning" in *Poor Richard's Almanac* for 1753. Grounding rods came into such common usage by 1759 that Andrew Burnaby, an English traveler, related that in a short time it had become rare to hear of buildings being destroyed by lightning. Franklin's rod took longer to emerge as a fixture of British life because electrical storms occurred less often there than in the colonies, but before the eighteenth century ended, the lightning rod had become the first American invention in common use among Europeans.

Scientific Societies

Of all the disadvantages facing early American scientists, perhaps the most serious was the isolation in which most conducted their work. The great majority lacked the intellectual stimulation and reinforcement of spirit that comes from interacting with peers of scholarly attainments. Scientific societies were so rare in early America that colonial naturalists and astronomers most often established mutual contacts by correspondence with England's Royal Society or naturalists on the European continent.

Anglo-America's earliest scientific association originated at Boston in 1683 as the Philosophical Society. Its members met every two weeks for "a Conference upon Improvements in Philosophy and Additions to the Stores of Natural History." The group probably included Increase Mather, later president of Harvard, his sons Cotton and Nathaniel, astronomer Thomas Brattle, and a dozen less-famous individuals. No records of their activities survive, except for some letters about a double rainbow sent to a professor at the University of Leiden, and the group ceased meeting in 1688.

Benjamin Franklin played the leading role in founding the only other formally established scientific community in the colonies. On May 14, 1743, he drafted proposals to create a Philadelphia equivalent of London's Royal Society, The American Philosophical Society, which would "improve the knowledge of natural things, and all useful Arts, Manufactures, Mechanick practices, Engynes and Inventions by Experiments." The group adopted by-laws, chose officers, discussed papers on natural phenomena, and laid plans to publish a regular series of scientific reports. The organization's novelty soon wore off, however, and interest waned among the members, whom Franklin described in 1745 as "very idle gentlemen." The association somehow survived a long, moribund period from 1744 to 1768, during which it met seldom if at all (no minutes survive). Franklin and seventeen others revived the body on

January 19, 1768, and amalgamated with a like-minded group that had recently formed; they assumed the title of "The American Philosophical Society, held at Philadelphia, for promoting useful knowledge" on December 20, 1768. Since then, it has ranked as the oldest and most-distinguished American philanthropic organization.

No association did more to encourage scientific activity in the colonies or to recognize outstanding research by Americans than England's Royal Society. Its charter members of 1662 included Gov. John Winthrop of Connecticut, and every generation of its fellows actively engaged Anglo-Americans in learned correspondence and enthusiastically printed colonial research in its *Philosophical Transactions*. The society ultimately admitted fifty-five Americans as fellows (including thirty-six from the thirteen mainland colonies) prior to 1800 and awarded its highest honor, the Copley Medal, to Benjamin Franklin.

TABLE 14.1 COLONIAL FELLOWS OF THE ROYAL SOCIETY OF LONDON TO 1800

Name	Life Span	Location	Date of Election	Date of Formal Admission
Barham, Henry	c. 1650–1726	Jamaica	Nov. 14, 1717	Nov. 21, 1717
Boylston, Zabdiel	1680–1766	Massachusetts	Jul. 7, 1726	Jul. 7, 1726
Brattle, William,	1662–1717	Massachusetts	Mar. 11, 1713/14	Declined as "unqualified"
Burnet, Gov. William	1688–1729	New York, New Jersey, Massachusetts	Feb. 13, 1705/06	Feb. 27, 1705/06
Butt, Dr. John Martin	d. 1769	Jamaica	Feb. 26, 1767	Mar. 18, 1767
Byrd, William, II,	1674–1744	Virginia	Apr. 29, 1696	Apr. 29, 1696
Calvert, Gov. Benedict Leonard	1700–32	Maryland	Mar. 25, 1731	no record
Calvert, Gov. Charles, fifth Lord Baltimore	1699–1751	Maryland	Dec. 9, 1731	Jan. 27, 1731/32
Campbell, Colin	d. 1752	Jamaica	Dec. 10, 1730	Nov. 7, 1734
Cuming (Cumming, Comyns), Sir Alexander	c. 1690–1775	South Carolina	Jun. 30, 1720	Jul. 7, 1720[a]
Douglas, John	d. 1743	Antigua	Nov. 30, 1720	Dec. 8, 1720
Douglas, Gov. Walter	fl. 1695–1716	Leeward Islands	Nov. 30, 1711	no record
Dudley, Paul	1675–1751	Massachusetts	Nov. 2, 1721	no record
Ellis, Gov. Henry	1721–1806	Georgia, Nova Scotia, etc.	Feb. 8, 1749/50	Feb. 22, 1749/50
Fauquier, Lt. Gov. Francis	c. 1704–68	Virginia	Feb. 15, 1753	no record
Franklin, Benjamin	1706–90	Pennsylvania	Apr. 29, 1756	Nov. 24, 1757
Fuller, Dr. Rose	d. 1777	Jamaica	Apr. 20, 1732	May 4, 1732
Garden, Dr. Alexander	1730–91	South Carolina	Jun. 10, 1773	May 15, 1783
Glenie, Lt. John	1750–1817	Canada	Mar. 18, 1779	no record
Gray, John	fl. 1730	Cartagena	Mar. 16, 1731/32	Mar. 22, 1732/33
Greg (Gregg), John	fl. 1765	South Carolina, Dominica	Jul. 9, 1772	Feb. 10, 1785
Houstoun, Dr. William	1695–1733	Georgia	Jan. 18, 1732/33	no record
Hoy, Dr. Thomas	1659–c. 1725	Jamaica	Dec. 1, 1707	no record
Hughes, Rev. Griffith	c. 1707–50	Barbados	Jun. 9, 1748	no record
Hunter, Gov. Robert	d. 1734	New York	May 4, 1709	no record
Kuckhan (Kukhan), Tesser Samuel	d. 1776	Jamaica	Jun. 4, 1772	no record
Lashley, Dr. Thomas	d. 1807	Barbados	Nov. 24, 1768	Nov. 25, 1784
Lee, Dr. Arthur	1740–92	Virginia	May 29, 1766	Nov. 10, 1768[b]
Lettsom, Dr. John Coakley	1744–1815	Virgin Islands	Nov. 18, 1773	Nov. 18, 1773

Name	Life Span	Location	Date of Election	Date of Formal Admission
Leverett, John, President, Harvard College	1662–1724	Massachusetts	Mar. 11, 1713/14	no record
Livius, Peter	1727–95	New Hampshire, Canada	Apr. 29, 1773	Jul. 1, 1773
Lloyd, Philemon	fl. 1725	Maryland	Nov. 9, 1727	no record
Macfarlane, Alexander	d. 1755	Jamaica	Feb. 19, 1746/47	no record
Mather, Dr. Cotton,	1663–1728	Massachusetts	Jul. 27, 1713	no record
Mathew, Gov. William	d. 1751?	Leeward Islands	Mar. 10, 1719/20	Mar. 10, 1719/20
Mitchell, Dr. John	1690?–1768	Virginia	Dec. 15, 1748	Dec. 22, 1748
Morgan, Dr. John,	1735–89	Pennsylvania	Mar. 7, 1765	no record
Morris, Gov. Robert Hunter	c. 1700–64	New York, New Jersey, Pennsylvania	Jun. 12, 1755	Feb. 15, 1759
Nicholson, Gov. Francis	1655–1728	Virginia, South Carolina, etc.	Dec. 4, 1706	Dec. 4, 1706
Oglethorpe, James Edward	1696–1785	Georgia	Nov. 9, 1749	Nov. 16, 1749[c]
Penn, William	1644–1718	Pennsylvania	Nov. 9, 1681	no record
Pownall, Gov. Thomas	1722–1805	New Jersey, Massachusetts, South Carolina	Apr. 9, 1772	May 7, 1772[d]
Riz, David	fl. 1765	Jamaica	Jun. 5, 1766	Jun. 19, 1766[e]
Robie (Roby), Dr. Thomas	1689–1729	Massachusetts	Apr. 15, 1725	no record
Taylor, John (later Bart.)	d. 1786	Jamaica	May 9, 1776	Jun. 20, 1776
Tennant, Dr. John	fl. 1750–70	New York	Jun. 13, 1765	Jun. 20, 1765
Thompson, Benjamin (later Sir Benjamin, Count von Rumford)	1753–1814	New Hampshire	Apr. 22, 1779	May 6, 1779
Wales, William	1734?–98	Hudson's Bay	Nov. 6, 1776	no record
Winthrop, John,	1606–76	Connecticut	original Fellow, Jan. 1, 1661/62; confirmed under second charter, May 20, 1663	
Winthrop, John	1681–1747	Connecticut	Apr. 4, 1734	Apr. 25, 1734
Winthrop, Prof. John	1714–79	Massachusetts	Feb. 20, 1766	no record
Wright, Dr. William	1735–1819	Jamaica, Barbados	Mar. 12, 1778	Feb. 3, 1780
Yale, Elihu	1649–1721	Massachusetts, East Indies, Connecticut	Nov. 30, 1717	no record

Note: James Bowdoin (1726–90) of Massachusetts was elected Fellow of the Royal Society on the foreign list, April 3, 1788, and David Rittenhouse (1732–96) of Pennsylvania also was elected on the foreign list, April 16, 1795. These men, the first citizens of the United States of America to be so honored, were also the last North Americans to be elected to the society in the eighteenth century.
[a] Ejected June 9, 1757, for nonpayment of dues.
[b] Fellowship terminated by president and council on January 17, 1788.
[c] Ejected June 9, 1757, for nonpayment of dues.
[d] Withdrew August 14, 1789.
[e] Ejected May 1, 1783, for nonpayment of fees.
Source: Raymond P. Stearns, *Science in the British Colonies of America* (1970), 708–711.

CHAPTER 15 Architecture

The development of colonial architecture proceeded in four over-lapping stages, during which increasingly complex and sturdy styles successively appeared. Temporary, makeshift structures overwhelmingly predominated during the initial phase of European occupancy. These earliest windbreaks or huts lasted no longer than the time it took for their inhabitants to replace them with cottagelike dwellings that were only slightly more substantial: small, framed buildings that lacked solid foundations but might still stand for several decades before ground moisture left their rotting corner posts crumbling under the roof's weight. Colonial homes eventually became equal in quality to European folk housing during their next cycle of improvement, in which the majority of families came to live in fully carpentered, framed habitations erected on stone or brick foundations. The final sequence in early American architecture's maturation flowered during the mid-eighteenth century with the rise of the grand house as increasing numbers of the upper class began to construct mansions built of masonry that were patterned on the English gentry's country seats.

Primitive Dwellings

The earliest colonial dwellings employed a variety of primitive modes of building. Virtually all these styles utilized techniques long known in Europe and did not derive from any adaptation to frontier conditions or contact with aboriginal cultures. Even occasional references to "English wigwams" did not indicate a borrowing from Native American architectural types, for in sparsely populated, relatively inaccessible districts of Yorkshire and Cumberland, a tradition had survived from medieval times of using conical huts of sod and branches as habitations for shepherds or families headed by marginal day laborers like charcoal burners and bark peelers.

Another style of primitive housing utilized in both early New England and Pennsylvania entailed digging three sides of a room into a riverbank or some sharply rising elevation, extending the chamber with wood walls to the front, and covering the dugout with a sod roof. In flatter terrain, settlers desperate for immediate shelter put up dwellings that were literally roofs without walls. Such buildings were essentially identical to the modern construction type known as the A-frame, in which two steeply pitched sides meet at an angle high above the ground to create a triangular front and back.

According to Edmund Plowden in 1650, New England colonists found their first protection from a climate of notoriously fierce winters in little more than huts that could be patched together for about ten shillings "in the first 15. days whilst the[ir] ship at anchor is unlading and bound to diet and lodge the passenger." Most of the first settlers evidently managed to shelter their families in cabins of sawed timber that were rickety and cheaply fashioned. Puncheon buildings were the most common type of these lumber hovels. A puncheon

A conjectural painting of how the cave dwellings bored into the Delaware River's banks might have appeared during Philadelphia's early days of the 1680s. (Howard Pyle Collection, Delaware Art Museum, Wilmington, Delaware)

house's distinguishing characteristic consisted of upright planks (or sometimes unplaned tree trunks) nailed to stand vertically, like palisades, against supporting cross poles laid at right angles. Such "pallisadoed" homes had a dirt floor, lacked a foundation, and cohered by joints so clumsy that a strong wind might blow off the roof or tumble the entire structure over.

Even the best of puncheon houses were exceptionally cramped, wet, and drafty. Families nevertheless often endured three or four years of extreme privation within their walls because little of their labor and cash could be spared from the pressing task of bringing a farm into operation from scratch. Even when they were able to afford the time and expense of improving their lodgings, few colonists could do more than trade their impermanent puncheon homes for anything more than a waterproof, but small and inexpensive, dwelling capable of standing until their incomes could afford a truly comfortable structure.

Cottages

These replacement homes constituted the second stage in the development of early American architecture. Puncheon houses and other primitive shelters gave way to humble, framed structures of sawed wood or half-timbered houses that derived their name because the diagonally braced frame could be seen in between walls of wattle and daub (long twigs intertwined to form a framework base for thick-caked mud). Because few skilled woodworkers crossed the Atlantic, the frame was held together with a minimum of carpentry skills. (Only two types of joints were commonly used: a lap joint, in which a notched beam rested on top a brace, and a mortice-and-tenon joint, in which a beam was notched so that a trimmed corner post could be slipped within it and then locked together with a wooden pin.) Such buildings represented little more than what was known in rural England as a cottage, a domicile for farm laborers or other folk of modest means.

Early American cottages generally stood just one story high and contained a single room at the ground level. Most of them also had an aboveground loft for storage and extra sleeping room. Windows were rare, and it was not unusual for cottages lodging single laborers not to have any at all; oiled paper was used in place of glass, so wooden shutters were needed to keep out the elements during inclement weather. The chimney usually consisted of wattle and daub (often with oak boards nailed over the flue to keep it from deteriorating during rainstorms) or logs covered with clay because there were few individuals skilled in laying stone, so the chimney was a fire hazard. Because the colonists retained the custom of roofing cottages with thatch during much of the early seventeenth century, these homes were highly combustible.

The size of such cottages was normally quite small. Based on excavations at Martin's Hundred, the average dwelling provided for a single laborer near Jamestown, Virginia, about 1625 was 14 feet long and 12 feet wide (168 square feet), barely more than a hut. William Rix, a Massachusetts Bay weaver, paid a joiner the significant sum of £21 in 1640 to provide him and his family with a framed home measuring just 16 feet long and 14 feet wide (224 square feet). Houses so small could not comfortably be divided into more than one room on the ground floor.

Despite their lack of amenities, cottages represented a genuine improvement over puncheon houses. Most seem to have had clapboard walls and as such enjoyed greater protection from wind and rain (as also did the less-substantial ones with wattle and daub). A majority were constructed without a ground sill on which to lay elevated floorboards, but many nevertheless contained plank floors, which were rough and uneven but still helped keep the interior somewhat dry. In a few of the better ones that had been inhabited for a while, the walls might be plastered with white lime.

The distinguishing feature of this second-generation housing type, however, was its lack of a waterproof foundation. In the absence of a stone or brick base, early colonial cottages derived their stability from timbers set deep in holes, to which the frame's beams and braces were attached. This earth-fast technique (termed *post in the ground* or *bastard frame* by early Americans) provided the necessary stability to withstand fierce storms but only for so many years. Posts set in the earth and other elements of the frame exposed to the ground could not be prevented from rotting within a dozen years. For that reason, not a single hole-set, framed cottage has survived from the colonial era to the present. Their owners did not expect them to last indefinitely, however, and viewed them only as a cheap expedient suitable for several years of tolerable living until they could afford to have a more substantial, permanent residence constructed.

One simple technique nevertheless enabled seventeenth-century settlers to prolong the usefulness of their earth-fast buildings for the length of an average adult's lifespan. Long-term structural soundness could be achieved by setting a frame above the ground on top of thick, wooden blocks embedded in the soil so that the sills and frame escaped deterioration from moisture. The corner blocks themselves would rot, of course, but their life could be prolonged by choosing wood that stood up well in spite of damp conditions. Red cedar, chestnut, and sassafras proved very durable, but black locust became the wood of choice for knowledgeable carpenters to use for underpinning blocks. Even after decay had caused a corner to sag over a decrepit block, it was relatively easy to restore the house's soundness by raising the foundation through leverage, replacing the decayed block, and substituting another. Through a combination of using decay-resistant wood and periodically replacing foundation blocks, it was possible to extend the life of an earth-fast, framed building resting on hole-set blocks up to a half-century. If such a cottage could be enlarged to accommodate a family's growing need for space, this course of action offered an inexpensive alternative to building a larger house on a base of stone or brick.

Houses

The transition to the third phase of colonial architecture's evolution developed once the first generation of settlers found themselves able to afford the construction of fully carpentered, framed buildings with waterproof foundations. This development occurred initially in New England where an extensive rebuilding of the housing stock seems

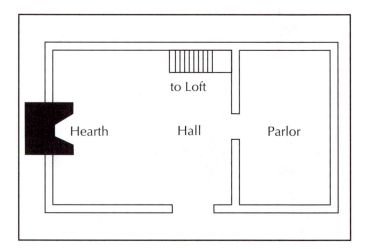

Floor plan of a hall-and-parlor house—the ground floor was usually supplemented by a loft for sleeping and storage under the roof. (Drawn by Jeremy Eagle)

Photograph of the Peter Lutkins home, a hall-and-parlor house built in 1760 on a 22-acre farm near Paramus, New Jersey. This one-and-a-half-story building was typical of the homes occupied by most American colonists south of New England. It was exceptionally small by modern standards, measuring just 16.75 feet by 15.75 feet in its original dimensions (a lean-to kitchen was later added) so that total living space on the ground floor was just 263.8 square feet. Contrast this dwelling for a middle-class family with the Cornelius Low house on page 283. (Historical American Buildings Survey, courtesy Library of Congress)

to have begun in the 1650s and led to a rapid upgrading of the quality of homes in the region. The Chesapeake colonies, however, continued to rely on highly impermanent, post-in-the-ground dwellings until the 1690s when improved, earth-fast structures raised on wood blocks had emerged as the standard form of house construction. Not until after 1710 did fully framed houses with brick piers or full-stone foundations emerge as a common variety of folk housing for middle-class, southern landowners.

It was consequently not until after 1650 in New England and after 1710 in the Chesapeake that large numbers of professionally carpentered, wooden buildings began to appear that could withstand the elements to endure for three centuries or more. Fewer than a half-dozen standing structures can be authenticated as having been erected in Virginia and Maryland by 1700 (and none date from before 1650), whereas in Massachusetts, a colony in which fully framed, dry-foundation-based homes became the norm much earlier, seventy-one dwellings can be positively identified as constructed before 1700 (ten of which originated before 1660).

Fully framed homes with masonry foundations marked an improvement over their predecessors not only in sturdiness but also in size. A new standard emerged for what constituted a commodious home. Impermanent, post-in-the-hole structures rarely measured more than 16 feet wide by 20 feet long (320 square feet), utilized a highly dangerous wattle and daub chimney, and made due with a rather leaky, weatherboarded roof. Fully framed and dry-based homes more likely had a width of 16 feet and a length ranging from 24 to 30 feet (384 to 480 square feet), which allowed for easy division into two ground floors; they moreover tended to have a stone or brick chimney 7 feet across (sometimes with an oven built in), a shingled roof, stairs leading to the loft (rather than a ladder), and raised floorboards (rather than planks resting on the ground).

Adequate ground space came to be seen as 500 to 550 square feet (approximately 18 feet wide by 28 to 30 feet long) for an average family during the early eighteenth century. Because homes of this size could not be subdivided into more than two ground rooms, extra

rooms were tacked on by lean-to sheds built along the rear or side walls for a pantry or buttery, a more comfortable kitchen, or quarters for a hired hand. Aside from small attached rooms, which were most common in New England, houses usually contained just one-and-a-half stories with two ground-floor rooms: a hall (an all-purpose dining and family room with the hearth as its center) and an "inner room" or parlor (the parents' bedroom, which normally occupied about one-third of the ground level).

Early American architectural styles basically resembled contemporary English housing, but noticeable differences began to appear by the mid-seventeenth century, primarily in regard to construction materials. The first generation of colonists retained the English preference for roofs of thatch, even though a shortage of good hay forced them to rely on inferior substitutes like marsh reeds or field grass. Thatch continued as the most common roofing for inexpensive homes in many areas of Britain until the late eighteenth century (and can still be found in use there, although mainly as a novelty) but failed to persist in Anglo-America beyond the 1670s, by which time shingles had superseded it.

Half-timbered homes of wattle and daub likewise failed to endure as part of the architectural landscape long past 1650. The settlers quickly abandoned wattle-and-daub construction for wooden boarding, which generally consisted of clapboards laid in parallel sections of 10 to 12 feet in length across a wall. Based on the accounts left by foreign visitors, clapboard exteriors had become almost ubiquitous in Anglo-America by the mid-seventeenth century. "Such are almost all the English houses in the country," wrote the Dutchman Jasper Dankaerts in 1680.

Early American architecture also diverged from contemporary British housing styles in failing to make any extensive use of "long houses," which commonly sheltered tenants on rural manors. Long houses originated as an economical way for a landlord to build quarters for several tenant families; they sheltered two or more households in multiple, full-size units with common framing, each standing a single story (often just 12 feet by 18 feet, or 216 square feet) under a loft, in the same fashion as modern duplex houses. Although economical for the landlord, these structures kept their inhabitants in uncomfortably close proximity with neighbors and had a very limited capacity for expanding the living space by adding sheds or lean-tos onto side walls. This style of family barracks evidently appeared briefly in early Virginia as housing for servants on tobacco plantations but then died out in preference to individual domestic units.

Subtle regional differences slowly came to distinguish folk housing in the North and the South. Southerners long adhered to the medieval custom of pitching roofs at a steep angle so that the loft's residents had more room to move about comfortably upright; New Englanders often built their roofs at angles of from 45 to 50 degrees. Gambrel roofs (a roof with two slopes on each of two sides, the lower steeper than the higher) were also more common in the North—among both the Dutch and New Englanders—than in the South. Northerners invariably located their hearth centrally within the home where it could radiate heat more efficiently, while southern houses usually built fireplaces abutting a side wall. This difference in placing hearths furthermore meant that interior space was used far differently in each region so that few southern homes were divided into more than two ground-floor rooms, while most northern dwellings contained three first-story rooms; more than a few held up to five.

Log Cabins

Colonial housewrights modified European building styles but remained essentially conservative in their choice of structural designs, materials, and techniques. This traditional impulse predisposed virtually all the arrivals during the seventeenth century to ignore the advantages of log cabin construction, which was entirely unknown in western Europe

Photograph of an eighteenth-century, two-story log cabin in the vicinity of Bernville, North Heidelberg Township, of Berks County, Pennsylvania. The structure is two-and-a-half stories, has a two-bay front, is one bay deep, and provides a total of less than 900 square feet of living space on its two floors. Its square logs dovetail at the corners so that at a later date the owner might hide its humble origins with shingles or plaster. (Historical American Buildings Survey, courtesy Library of Congress)

outside of Scandinavia. The American log cabin's pedigree stretches back to Sweden, where it was a common form of dwelling, especially in Swedish-governed Finland. Although little direct architectural evidence exists to document the log cabin's introduction to the Swedes and Finns who colonized the Delaware valley after 1638, literary sources provide important confirmation for this conclusion. In 1749, Swedish-born pastor Peter Kalm, for example, wrote that a ninety-one-year-old Scandinavian settler asserted that the first houses in the Delaware valley were round logs chinked with clay. A contemporary account from 1643 furthermore described dwellings at New Sweden's Ft. Gothenburg as "made of hemlock beams, laid one upon the other."

The original log cabins resembled other early American folk dwellings in their simplicity. They typically contained one ground-floor room that measured about 16 feet by 18 feet (288 square feet). A variety of notches, chosen according to the owner's judgment, held the logs in place, and mud daubing sealed the walls. To prevent decay, the bark was stripped off the wood. The fireplace hearth lay outside the structure, and the typical chimney consisted of sticks lined with mud. This construction technique did not require a carpenter's expertise because no extra framework was needed to prop up the walls, and the shingled roof could be nailed to pole rafters upheld by a basic A-frame design. The natural insulation of thick wood gave log cabins the additional advantage of being warm in winter and cool in summer.

Commerce between New Sweden and its English neighbors exposed both to each other's architectural styles. Some Swedes adopted the framed, clapboard houses, but few English built log cabins for themselves. Mention of a handful of log cabins can be found in legal documents from Virginia and Maryland as early as 1655, but such notices were extremely rare during the next seven decades. None of the early records from New England suggests that its population saw any utility in fashioning homes from horizontal tree trunks.

The log cabin eventually came into its own after 1720 during the settlement of southeastern Pennsylvania. The early settlers, who were a mix of German, Scots-Irish, and English families, responded to a severe shortage of housewrights and the high cost of sawed lumber by making use of inexpensive indigenous materials—the trees and rocks they cleared from fields intended for farming—and they copied the construction techniques practiced by Swedes living nearby along the Delaware River. From southeast Pennsylvania, log building spread throughout that colony as settlers pushed toward the Ohio and also south into western Maryland, Virginia's Shenandoah Valley, and the Carolina backcountry. The log cabin consequently became the initial home of choice for pioneers in the backwoods, but even by the colonial period's end, it remained a regional folk style that probably gave shelter to less than a tenth of white Americans.

Stone-Enders

Although the great majority of colonists living in long-settled districts along the Atlantic remained highly traditional in their architectural tastes, they managed to produce some distinctively American styles by modifying standard English dwellings. An early example was the stone-ender. Stone-enders originated in Rhode Island and have long been particularly associated with that locale. This housing type took its name from the massive exterior chimney that covered part or all of one wall. The chimney usually faced northward to deflect the prevailing cold winds. Stone-enders became almost unique to Rhode Island because only that colony possessed an abundance of lime endowed with both the cohesive strength required for mortaring and the durability necessary to resist corrosion from rain. By surrounding the entire chimney with stone, except for a small portion of the roof touching the flue's exterior, this structure minimized the chances of accidental fires and won a reputation for rarely burning down.

Garrison Houses

The garrison house was another Yankee variation on an English prototype. It expanded the two-room home, with its half-story loft, upward into a full second story. This structure's unique shape came from extending the second-story floor forward (and occasionally backward as well) so that it projected beyond the first floor's front wall like the overhang of a frontier blockhouse. Although legend attributes this design as intended to give defenders the opportunity to fire weapons down on Indians who were attempting to storm the main entrance, few garrison houses actually seem to have been intentionally constructed for this purpose. It appears more likely that the purpose of the jettied upstairs was to extend the living area available on the second floor and, if so, may have been inspired by the many two-story homes similarly constructed in London, Amsterdam, and Paris so that their second story jutted above the street to create additional floor space in crowded urban settings.

This stone-ender, the Thomas Clemence House, was built in 1679 at Johnston, Rhode Island. This structure also exhibits the classic, extended-slope roof characteristic of saltbox architecture. (Historical American Buildings Survey, courtesy Library of Congress)

This photograph shows the McIntire garrison house with its telltale second-story overhang, built by 1692 at York, Maine. (Historical American Buildings Survey, courtesy Library of Congress)

Saltbox Houses

The most common manner of modifying colonial homes was by attaching a single-story shed across the building's rear and covering it with an extension of the loft roof. This technique proved to be the most practical manner of gaining more space for storage, sleeping quarters, or a full-sized kitchen organized around an additional hearth. In the Chesapeake, such buildings were described as having a "catslide" roof because cats would have difficulty climbing up its long, steep incline. In New England, the same construction style became popularly known as "saltbox" houses because their shape resembled a common form of salt dispenser. The catslide home never became com-

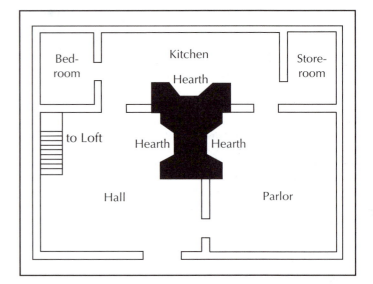

As this floor plan shows, the saltbox house constituted an expansion of the basic hall-and-parlor style, in which such additions as a storeroom, a kitchen, or an extra bedroom might be appended to the rear wall and be covered by extending the roof. Besides providing more space, these adjoining cubicles helped keep the building warmer in winter by insulating the core of the family area around the fireplace. (Drawn by Jeremy Eagle.)

mon in the South, but saltboxes emerged as a major type of folk housing in New England.

Cape Cod Houses

The Cape Cod originated as a single-room English cottage, but it underwent several modifications that gave it a distinctive New England look. Carpenters in the old Plymouth colony reduced the steep pitch

Photograph of a "half–Cape Cod," dated at about 1731, the Rowell House at Wellfleet in Barnstable County, Massachusetts. This structure conformed to the general floor plan typical of a hall-and-parlor house. The side addition was not part of the original building. (Historical American Buildings Survey, courtesy Library of Congress)

inherited from traditional medieval roofing to an angle of about 45 degrees, and they left virtually no overhang above the walls because the Atlantic's fierce ocean winds could tear an exposed roof off its rafters. Ceiling heights were low by colonial standards and often reached just 7 feet. A preference for covering outside walls with cedar shingles rather than clapboards also gave this home a distinctive look by the late 1600s.

The Cape Cod home evolved further during the early eighteenth century as an alternative to enlarging farmhouses by adding lean-tos at the rear in saltbox fashion; its design instead facilitated the expansion of living space lengthwise. Many Cape Cod dwellings originated as partially built structures that could be extended as a growing family needed more room for storage and beds. The smallest Cape Cod structure was a one-room cottage about 24 feet square, termed a *half-house*. By extending the walls and roof another 8 feet beyond the chimney, which would normally be improved by adding another hearth, the owner could create a so-called three-quarter house, with one large room (the original bay) and a smaller one that could expand the kitchen area or form a more spacious bedroom for the parents. A full Cape Cod, or "double-house" in traditional parlance, resulted from elongating the small room by another 8 feet to create a dwelling 40 feet long with two equal bays straddling the chimney, which now occupied the building's center. Few families could manage to finance the complete progression from a half-house to a double-house, however, and those that could afford a three-quarter structure considered themselves fortunate.

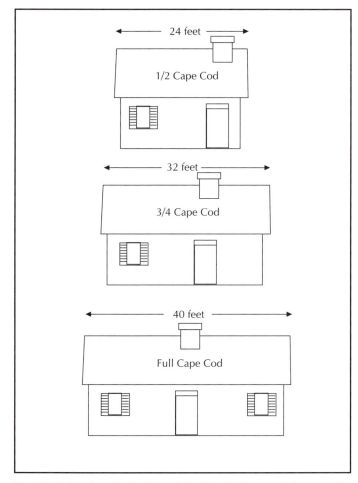

New Englanders ingeniously designed the Cape Cod to permit its expansion lengthways if its homeowner managed to save enough money to afford the modifications. Adding a half-bay room to one side of the chimney created a three-quarter Cape Cod, while a building with two full-size bays on each side of the chimney was termed a *full Cape Cod*. (Drawn by Jeremy Eagle.)

The colonial housing stock improved steadily in the decades after 1700. Much of the progress took place piecemeal, as households made minor changes that added value to their homes. This rebuilding of seventeenth-century architecture entailed not only increasing living space through additional rooms and stories but also substituting a brick or stone chimney for one made of logs or wattle and daub, replacing shuttered oilskin windows with glass cased in lead frames, providing access to the loft by a staircase instead of a ladder, and allowing additional light and ventilation for the loft by dormers cut into the roof.

The early American housing stock nevertheless still remained modest in scale as the eighteenth century matured. Middle-class homeowners contented themselves with structures whose ground levels held just 500 to 550 square feet. The upper class, whether rural gentry or urban merchants, occupied homes that were only somewhat larger and decidedly unpretentious. As late as 1720, most of the Chesapeake's larger slaveowning planters evidently lived in one-and-a-half-story, clapboard-sided houses with two large ground rooms measuring about 20 feet by 40 feet (just 800 square feet of floor space on the ground level).

Grand Houses

The last important development in colonial architecture's evolution took place during the eighteenth century's early decades with the sudden proliferation of grand houses built according to the latest European style. Such homes were nonexistent in the previous century, when prosperous landowners preferred to use their capital for buying servants, slaves, or real estate rather than for building expensive mansions. William Fitzhugh, who founded one of Virginia's first families, expressed the prevailing sentiment when he warned a correspondent in 1687 against contracting to build "a great or English framed house" on arriving in his own colony because "labor is so intolerably dear & workmen so Idle & negligent that the building of a good house to you there will seem insupportable."

Even in the few instances when seventeenth-century Americans had built imposing homes, the structures possessed little style and less grace. Greenspring, the first great American house, was built by Virginia's governor Sir William Berkeley near Jamestown soon after 1642. It inspired contemporaries with a sense of awe at its massive front of 97 feet 5 inches (the longest frontage of any domestic building erected before the mid-1700s, although its width was just 24 feet 9 inches), but it followed a conventional floor plan for a larger-than-average English farmhouse with three adjoining rooms. Bacon's Castle (built 1655 in Surrey County), one of the most widely admired county seats in Virginia, stood two full stories and occupied 700 square feet on its ground floor; despite a magnificent exterior design incorporating Flemish-style gables with Jacobean steps and cusps, however, its basic design followed the ordinary pattern of a hall-and-parlor home (with central passageway) to which enclosed front and back porches had been attached so that its outline resembled a cruciform-shaped parish church. The earliest American great houses depended on mass for their visual impact rather than on graceful or imaginative lines.

More than any other event, it was Alexander Spotswood's completion of the Governor's Palace at Williamsburg, Virginia, in 1714 that signaled the emergence of the grand house as the dominant presence in colonial architecture. This structure, which required eight years to complete, set a new standard for the mansion in America, less for its size than for the elegance of its style. Unlike previous grand homes, it lay a full two rooms deep as well as two rooms wide; it featured a fully developed front hall for receiving visitors of state and a grand staircase to the second-story rooms. The building's overall plan, marked by careful attention to creating a sense of mathematical unity (capped by its twin chimneys and four-sided, hipped roof), conveyed an aura of balance and refinement. The Governor's Palace allowed viewers to glimpse the vision of Andrea Palladio, the sixteenth-century Italian

The Joseph Gilpin house, near Chadd's Ford, Delaware County, Pennsylvania, shows how the scale of building expanded for upper-class families during the eighteenth century. The framed, hall-and-parlor building on the right was built about 1695, but its family prospered unusually well and added the two-story fieldstone structure in 1745. (A side view of this home is shown on page 53.) However, most Americans continued to raise large families in modest hall-and-parlor houses throughout the 1700s like this farmstead's original structure. (Historical American Buildings Survey, courtesy Library of Congress)

whose emphasis on Greco-Roman classical forms had become the principal influence on western Europe's architecture by reviving an appreciation of symmetry, proportion, and hierarchy.

Williamsburg's Governor's Palace stimulated the first families of Virginia into competing with one another by displaying their wealth through expensive improvements to their homes. Robert Beverley, the earliest historian of the Old Dominion, wrote in 1722 that the planters "of late ... have made their [house] stories much higher than formerly, and their windows larger, and sashed [windows] with crystal glass, adorning their apartments with rich furniture." More than a dozen great mansions began construction during the 1710s and 1720s, followed by a second building boom that saw work begin on more than two dozen in the quarter-century after 1750. Virginia set the pace for the South in seeding the landscape with great houses, although it was closely followed by South Carolina's landed aristocracy. In the North, meanwhile, the most notable neo-Palladian mansions were constructed as homes for prosperous merchants in large seaports; houses of this style did not become common in New England's rural districts until after 1750, and then they generally appeared far less imposing because so many were fashioned out of wood rather than stone or brick.

The Palladian-inspired style eventually would be termed *Georgian* in the British Empire because it became popular during the reigns of the first two Hanoverian kings, George I and George II. The trademarks of classic Georgian architecture included features organized around the principles of formality, simplicity, and harmonious relationships, such as a brick facade with door and windows symmetrically arranged, dual chimneys balancing one another, a hipped (four-sided) roof, and understated ornamentation. As the Georgian style matured, however, it

Left: Reconstruction of the Governor's Palace at Williamsburg whose example greatly stimulated the building of great houses among the Virginia gentry. (Historical American Buildings Survey, courtesy Library of Congress)

This Georgian mansion, the Cornelius Low House, was built with 350 tons of sandstone in 1741 by a wealthy merchant at Raritan Landing, New Jersey. Said to be the costliest residence in eastern New Jersey on completion, it featured eight fireplaces embellished with Delft tile, elaborate paneling, elegantly sculpted pilasters, and a massive open staircase. The Low House is now maintained for the public by the Middlesex County Cultural & Heritage Commission. (Photo by Jim Padilla, courtesy Middlesex County Cultural & Heritage Commission)

entered a more flamboyant and imposing phase in the 1760s, especially in the seaports where many wealthy merchants had large fortunes to lavish on their dwellings. Homes grew larger through added ceiling heights, chimneys became wider and higher, doorways were bordered with ornately carved entryways, and increased decoration was provided by wooden cornice work trimming the roof's base and inlaid quoins of brick or stone accenting the building's four corners.

With their immediately recognizable crisp, clean lines, Georgian buildings gave a new sense of unity to the architectural landscape of early America. Regional styles of folk housing remained not only vibrant but also virtually universal among the common people, of course: Saltboxes

and Cape Cods formed the most typical form of domestic housing in New England, a basic hall-and-parlor type prevailed within the territory from New Jersey through Georgia, and the log cabin was well established in frontier districts. The sudden rise in popularity of Georgian housing among the elite nevertheless marked a decisive shift in orienting American architecture toward greater sophistication. The colonial human-made landscape, which had long resembled little more than a provincial backwater oblivious to the cosmopolitan tastes of western Europe, could finally boast of private and public buildings that mirrored the most current fashions in England, France, and the Netherlands.

CHAPTER 16 Holidays and Calendars

Holidays

Days of rest and recreation were one element of western European culture that fared poorly in the transplantation of people to the New World. Seventeenth-century Europeans lived in a social world rich with occasions for ritual observances and neighborhood celebrations, especially in regard to the holy days of the Christian liturgical calendar. Because of Calvinist hostility toward traditional holidays associated with the Catholic Church, and in no small part because low population density greatly limited the opportunity for large communal gatherings to take place, only a small part of the grand stock of Europe's folk festivals and seasonal customs survived to take root in the thirteen colonies.

Sabbath

The only day of rest universally observed in the colonies was the Lord's Day. For the Dutch, it was a leisurely time for reviving one's strength and spirits after a hard week of work. Their taverns stayed open and friends enjoyed sports or other relaxations with one another according to the opportunities given by the weather.

Sundays tended to be taken more seriously by English colonists. In 1611, Virginia forbade any "gaming" on the Sabbath, even in the privacy of one's home, and required the inhabitants not merely to attend divine service in the morning but also to return in the afternoon to hear a sermon. The code also prescribed draconian punishments for missing Sunday services more than once: two absences merited a flogging, and a third could result in death.

Virginians nevertheless matured into a highly secular people by the eighteenth century, by which time the government had long ceased enforcing church attendance. Only a minority came to weekly service on a regular basis, in large part because so many parishes covered an exceptionally wide area, making travel to church a substantial hardship for most of the congregation. For those Virginians who did make it to church, Sunday seems to have been viewed as a day for socializing and conviviality. "I observe it is a general custom on Sundays here, with Gentlemen" observed a plantation tutor from New Jersey in the late colonial period, "to invite one another home to dine after Church." Although they could not repair to grog shops, as Dutch colonists might, Virginians nevertheless still managed to enjoy some amenities associated with the term *Continental Sunday,* as they partook of a good meal, indulged in pleasant conversation over a pipe of tobacco, and sampled the contents of their hosts' wine cellar.

New Englanders, however, made a point of observing the Sabbath strenuously. Seventeenth-century New England seems to have been the only community in the Christian world that followed the example of the ancient Hebrews in considering the Lord's Day to start at sundown on Saturday. John Winthrop, first governor of Massachusetts Bay, sometimes noted beginning his Sabbath as early as midafternoon on Saturday.

Early Puritans forbade virtually all nonessential, secular activities on Sunday. Their courts fined careless or unwary people for such minor infractions as smoking tobacco, playing quoits (a game for tossing rings of rope over a peg, as with horseshoes), and even picking strawberries. A couple in New London, Connecticut, found themselves indicted in 1670 for "sitting together on the Lord's Day under an apple tree." While Ebenezer Taylor patiently waited to be pulled from a 40-foot dry well into which he had fallen late Saturday afternoon at Yarmouth, Massachusetts, a group of his neighbors actually debated among themselves whether extricating him would break the Sabbath!

Christmas

Strict Calvinists strove mightily to end popular observances of Christmas customs, which they viewed as not only unscriptural but also irredeemably intertwined with practices inherited from the pagan past. When several Plymouth settlers decided to celebrate Christmas Day in 1621 by playing games like pitching the bar and stool-ball, Gov. William Bradford stopped them immediately and Christmas effectively disappeared from the Cape Cod region from then until the nineteenth century. Massachusetts Bay enacted a five shilling fine for anyone frivolous enough to celebrate the birth of Christ with games or reveling. By the eighteenth century, New England seems to have been the only place in the Christian world where Christmas (December 25) was no longer observed either publicly or privately.

Outside of New England, Christmas continued in the colonies, although it was everywhere highly abbreviated from the manner of its full observance in Europe, where each week from Advent (four Sundays before Christmas) to Epiphany (January 6) was sprinkled with several feast days that provided excuses for banquets, parties, family reunions, gift giving, and all sorts of rituals such as wassailing. Southerners retained the custom of celebrating Christmas, and they also kept some of the European understanding of the holiday as an extended period of mirthmaking when individuals renewed ties with family and friends through social visiting and attending balls. Virginians threw themselves into Christmas with such great gusto in the late colonial period that a tutor on a Westmoreland County plantation reported not only hearing guns being fired all through the countryside to celebrate Christmas Eve but also that early on the next day he "was waked this morning by Guns fired all round the House." In certain parts of the southern backcountry, settlers also preserved the old custom of commemorating Epiphany as "Old Christmas" with bonfires and the shooting of guns.

The Puritans' zeal for honoring Sunday was matched by an intense hostility toward the Catholic church's liturgical cycle of saints' and feast days. The Puritans' abolished observance of all such feast days, including the tradition for craftspeople such as shoemakers to take off work and celebrate the feast of their patron, St. Crispian. (Quakers also vehemently opposed the custom of Christian feast days, in part because they opposed the cult of saints and also because they insisted that aside from Sunday, God had not intended for any day to be considered more sacred than another.)

Feast Days and Other Religious Holidays

Although celebration of traditional Christian feast days (other than Christmas) withered away in America, the names of many holy days remained part of public consciousness because they assumed a secular function. It was long traditional for the courts to hold their four annual "quarter sessions" on the old feasts of Christmas, "Lady Day" (the Annunciation, March 25), St. John the Baptist (commonly called "Midsummer's Day," June 24), and Michaelmas (September 29). Rent payments and interest on debts were also commonly due as of these dates.

In general, the first several generations of colonists discarded nearly all the rituals and folk customs that enlivened the year's seasonal passage in western Europe. The courtship practices of St. Valentine's Day (February 14) disappeared almost entirely until they were revived in the early nineteenth century. May Day (May 1, the feast of St. Philip and St. James) ceased to be an occasion for a spring festival of dancing and cider drinking. The rites of harvest home (feast of the Assumption, August 15), in which servants paraded around their masters' homes bearing horns as fertility symbols, briefly sprouted in the Chesapeake and then died out. Gradually the colonists ceased following the centuries-old folk customs associated with particular days, such as cooking pancakes (a convenient way of using up eggs plus butter, two foods forbidden during the Lenten Fast) or playing football on Shrove Tuesday (the Tuesday before Ash Wednesday, often the second Tuesday in February), lighting bonfires on St. George's Day (April 23), eating goose on Michaelmas, cockfighting on Hock Tuesday (the second Tuesday after Easter), and rush bearing—refurbishing the floor of the local church—on St. Swithin's Day (July 15).

Occasionally an ancient folk custom endured and passed into American life. The best-known example concerns Candlemas (the feast of the candles), which had long been assumed to have special significance for determining whether spring would come early, as this traditional rhyme explained.

> If Candlemas Day be fair and bright,
> Winter will have another fright;
> But if it be dark with clouds and rain,
> Winter is gone and will not come again.

The feast of candles fell on February 2, which still holds a superstitious fascination for Americans but is now known as Groundhog Day.

Secular Holidays

Only in New England did a distinctive cycle of festivals arise as secular holidays to substitute for the customary observance of religious feast days. Election Day took on the dimensions of a public holiday, even though its purpose was to choose members for the legislature. Held every year on an April Wednesday, it assumed the character of a spring festival. Besides offering men a chance to socialize, it developed its own rituals, including the delivery of a sermon and a special meal with "election cake" and "election beer."

Commencement Day honored Harvard's graduating class during a summer weekend, usually in July. Besides the commencement ceremonies, the event constituted a yearly reunion for the college's alumni, including innumerable ministers and magistrates, who poured into Boston for the event. It naturally attracted a swarm of peddlers and throngs of ordinary citizens so that Boston Common turned into something of an impromptu urban fair for an unofficial midsummer's holiday.

The Protestant celebration of Guy Fawkes Day took root in New England and lasted until the Revolution. This day commemorated the failure of Catholic conspirators to blow up Parliament and murder James I in 1606. Traditionally celebrated with bonfires on November 5 (as it still is in England), it became exceptionally raucous in Boston, where it was also known as Pope's Day. Mobs from the North End and

In New England, militia days came to resemble election days and commencement days by taking on the air of unofficial excuses to celebrate as if they were holidays with socializing, sports, and merrymaking once the muster and training had been completed. This painting shows the Eastern Regiment of Massachusetts going through its first drill at Salem in 1637. (Courtesy National Guard Bureau)

South End competed with one another to see which side of town could burn the most magnificent effigy of the pope. On one occasion, a group filled its dummy with dozens of cats so that, as it burned, the onlookers could be treated to what sounded like the pope hissing in agony.

Thanksgiving

Although Virginians proclaimed the first day of Thanksgiving in Anglo-America in 1614, the transmission of this celebration to the present derives from New England. The earliest such event was a harvest festival held by the Pilgrims sometime in October 1621. Massachusetts Bay held its first Thanksgiving Day on February 22, 1631, in gratitude for the timely arrival of several provision ships that forestalled a food crisis. Massachusetts declared at least twenty-two days of Thanksgiving during its first fifty years of existence and then began to hold them on a regular basis after it prevailed in King Philip's War of 1675–76.

The favored day for such celebrations was a Thursday, a customary sermon day in many Puritan towns, and the event became a postharvest ritual, with November being the most convenient month to schedule it. Thanksgiving days followed a day of fasting and featured a sermon at the meetinghouse, after which families returned to their homes for a plentiful repast. Thanksgivings were not optional holidays by any means because the laws to regulate Sabbath-keeping extended over them and adults could be fined for performing work. By the end of the colonial era, the day was both a communal ritual and a family celebration and as such was uniquely suited to evolve into the most American of holidays.

Calendars

At the time when Christopher Columbus made his exploratory voyages across the Atlantic, all western Europeans still relied on the calendar authorized by Roman emperor Julius Caesar in 46 B.C. This Julian calendar started the year with the vernal equinox (the first day of spring) and so rather arbitrarily set March 25 as its official "new year's day." March consequently ranked as the first month of each year (even though twenty-four of its days were still counted as part of the preceding year), and February as the twelfth (for which reason, leap years always add a day to that month rather than December). Because the Latin roots for seven, eight, nine, and ten served as prefixes for September, October, November, and December, the Julian calendar influenced later Europeans to employ the following shorthand abbreviations for these months

September	7ber
October	8ber
November	9ber
December	10ber

Caesar relied on the Greek authority Sosigenes when he declared that the year's length would be considered as 365 days and six hours. Sosigenes had in fact overstated the true year's actual length by eleven minutes and fourteen seconds so that the Julian calendar gained a day about every 128 years. By the fourth century A.D., scholars realized that Julian chronology was inaccurate, but no consensus arose regarding a solution for over twelve centuries.

By 1582, the cumulative error had grown to ten days, and a religious controversy was created by making it increasingly difficult for pious Christians to observe important feasts like Christmas and Easter within their proper seasons. Pope Gregory XIII rectified this problem with his papal bull of February 24, 1582, which promulgated the Gregorian calendar. To restore the vernal equinox to a more precise moment in solar time, Gregory decreed that ten days would be stricken from that year's total so that the day after October 4 would be reckoned as

TABLE 16.1   NUMERICAL SEQUENCE OF MONTHS ACCORDING TO THE JULIAN (O.S.) AND GREGORIAN (N.S.) CALENDARS

Month	Rank in O.S.	Rank in N.S.
January	11	1
February	12	2
March	1	3
April	2	4
May	3	5
June	4	6
July	5	7
August	6	8
September	7	9
October	8	10
November	9	11
December	10	12

October 15. He also changed the official start of each year from March 25 to January 1.

Because the Protestant Reformation had already polarized Europe's Christians into warring factions, Pope Gregory's bull did not meet with universal acceptance. Spain, Italy, France, and Holland adopted the New Style (N.S.), as the Gregorian calendar was termed, in 1582, as did the Catholic provinces of Germany in 1584. Switzerland, the Scandinavian countries, and Germany's Protestant districts adhered to Old Style (O.S.) dating until the last decade of the seventeenth century.

By 1700, the British Isles were the only significant part of western Europe that still rejected the Gregorian calendar. Ships captains, merchants, and diplomats found it increasingly bothersome to conduct business overseas when their own year ended almost three months after another had already begun on the continent. A common practice consequently developed about 1670 to designate the period between January 1 and March 24 by hyphenating the overlapping years in various manners, as the following examples illustrate

January 1, 1684/1685
January 13, 1685–86
February 21, 1719/20
March 24, 17$^{07}/_{08}$

The Protestant Reformation led many English dissenters to insist on rejecting the Gregorian calendar as an article of faith. Puritans and the Society of Friends inculcated an especially hostile attitude toward the New Style; they also came to despise the traditional designations for the month, which had originated in pre-Christian Rome, as well as to detest the ancient folk names for weekdays, which originated from titles given to such Germanic pagan deities as Thor (Thursday), Woden (Wednesday), and the Moon Goddess (Monday). Many devout Congregationalists and Quakers devised a new calendrical vocabulary that substituted numbers for both days of the week and months of the year (with March still considered the first month). When writing out this system, they placed the weekday first, the month second, and the year last, in the manner of the examples below

24 12 mo 1725	March 24, 1725/26
25 i 26	March 25, 1726
13. 4. 40	June 13, 1740
4 7 51	September 4, 1751

England remained loyal to the Julian calendar through the mid-eighteenth century, by which time the discrepancy between Old Style and New Style dating had grown to eleven days. Parliament did not adopt the Gregorian calendar until the mid-eighteenth century. By law, the day following September 2, 1752, was declared to be September 14 in Great Britain and its overseas colonies, and the new year would thereafter begin on January 1.

The Gregorian calendar created widespread confusion among Anglo-American colonists. A large part of the population mistakenly assumed that dates prior to September 2, 1752, had to be adjusted forward by eleven days, even though Parliament never required them to be. George Washington, whose nativity occurred on February 11, 1732 (O.S.), evidently believed that he should consider his rightful birthday as February 22 (N.S.), and that date has erroneously been celebrated by grateful citizens of the United States ever since the winning of their independence.

Historians and antiquarians have subsequently developed a fetish for translating Old Style dates recorded in Anglo-American documents to New Style chronology whenever possible. Although often unnecessary, such conversions are essential when studying documents that involve foreign diplomacy or international trade. The following conversion table permits Old Style dates to be modernized into their proper New Style equivalents (all dates are inclusive).

From O.S.	To O.S.	Add
March 1, 1399/1400	February 29, 1499/1500	9 days
March 1, 1499/1500	February 18, 1699/1700	10 days
February 19, 1699/1700	February 17, 1751/1752	11 days

The Anglo-American colonies also inherited an idiosyncratic calendrical style by virtue of their relationship to Parliament, which registered its statutes according to the regnal system of enumeration. Provincial legislatures accordingly dated their laws with a numerical designation signifying the year of the current monarch's reign in which each measure took effect. Every colonial statute consequently bore the name of the king or queen whose governor signed it, preceded by the number of years in his or her reign, and a figure in Arabic numerals identifying its precedence in the laws signed during that regnal year. For example, the Parliamentary statute that adopted the Gregorian calendar was designated 24 George II, c. 23 (the twenty-third law passed in the twenty-fourth year since George II ascended the throne).

TABLE 16.2 TABLE OF BRITISH REGNAL YEARS, FOR REGISTERING COLONIAL LAWS BY DATE OF PASSAGE

Sovereign	Commencement of Reign	Last Regnal Year
George III	Oct. 25, 1760 (1 George III)	1820 (60 George III)
George II	Jun. 11, 1727 (1 George II)	1760 (34 George II)
George I	Aug. 1, 1714 (1 George)	1727 (13 George)
Anne	Mar. 8, 1702 (1 Anne)	1714 (13 Anne)
William & Mary[a]	Feb. 13, 1689 (1 William & Mary)	1702 (14 William III)
James II	Feb. 6, 1685 (1 James II)	1689 (4 James II)
Charles II	Jan. 30, 1649[b] (1 Charles II)	1685 (37 Charles II)[b]
Charles I	Mar. 27, 1625 (1 Charles)	1649 (24 Charles)
James I	Mar. 24, 1603 (1 James)	1625 (23 James)
Elizabeth	Nov. 17, 1558 (1 Elizabeth)	1603 (45 Elizabeth)

[a] At the death of Mary on December 28, 1694, William reigned alone under the style of William III.
[b] Although Charles II did not ascend the throne until May 29, 1660, his regnal years were computed to start on the day Charles I was executed, so that the restoration of Charles officially took place in the twelfth year of his own reign.
Source: Cortlandt F. Bishop, *History of Elections in the American Colonies* (1893), 296.

TABLE 16.3 PERPETUAL CALENDARS FOR HISTORICAL DATES UNDER THE JULIAN (O.S.) AND GREGORIAN (N.S.) SYSTEMS

Calendar		
Year	O.S.	N.S.
1799	…	3
1798	…	2

Calendar		
Year	O.S.	N.S.
1797	…	1
1796	…	13
1795	…	5
1794	…	4
1793	…	3
1792	…	8
1791	…	7
1790	…	6
1789	…	5
1788	…	10
1787	…	2
1786	…	1
1785	…	7
1784	…	12
1783	…	4
1782	…	3
1781	…	2
1780	…	14
1779	…	6
1778	…	5
1777	…	4
1776	…	9
1775	…	1
1774	…	7
1773	…	6
1772	…	11
1771	…	3
1770	…	2
1769	…	1
1768	…	13
1767	…	5
1766	…	4
1765	…	3
1764	…	8
1763	…	7
1762	…	6
1761	…	5
1760	…	10
1759	…	2
1758	…	1
1757	…	7
1756	…	12
1755	…	4
1754	…	3
1753	…	2
1752	11	14
1751	3	6
1750	2	5
1749	1	4
1748	13	9
1747	5	1
1746	4	7
1745	3	6
1744	8	11
1743	7	3
1742	6	2
1741	5	1
1740	10	13
1739	2	5
1738	1	4
1737	7	3
1736	12	8
1735	4	7
1734	3	6
1733	2	5
1732	14	10
1731	6	2
1730	5	1

(continued)

TABLE 16.3 (continued)

	Calendar	
Year	O.S.	N.S.
1729	4	7
1728	9	12
1727	1	4
1726	7	3
1725	6	2
1724	11	14
1723	3	6
1722	2	5
1721	1	4
1720	13	9
1719	5	1
1718	4	7
1717	3	6
1716	8	11
1715	7	3
1714	6	2
1713	5	1
1712	10	13
1711	2	5
1710	1	4
1709	7	3
1708	12	8
1707	4	7
1706	3	6
1705	2	5
1704	14	10
1703	6	2
1702	5	1
1701	4	7
1700	9	6
1699	1	5
1698	7	4
1697	6	3
1696	11	8
1695	3	7
1694	2	6
1693	1	5
1692	13	10
1691	5	2
1690	4	1
1689	3	7
1688	8	12
1687	7	4
1686	6	3
1685	5	2
1684	10	14
1683	2	6
1682	1	5
1681	7	4
1680	12	9
1679	4	1
1678	3	7
1677	2	6
1676	14	11
1675	6	3
1674	5	2
1673	4	1
1672	9	13
1671	1	5
1670	7	4
1669	6	3
1668	11	8
1667	3	7
1666	2	6
1665	1	5

	Calendar	
Year	O.S.	N.S.
1664	13	10
1663	5	2
1662	4	1
1661	3	7
1660	8	12
1659	7	4
1658	6	3
1657	5	2
1656	10	14
1655	2	6
1654	1	5
1653	7	4
1652	12	9
1651	4	1
1650	3	7
1649	2	6
1648	14	11
1647	6	3
1646	5	2
1645	4	1
1644	9	13
1643	1	5
1642	7	4
1641	6	3
1640	11	8
1639	3	7
1638	2	6
1637	1	5
1636	13	10
1635	5	2
1634	4	1
1633	3	7
1632	8	12
1631	7	4
1630	6	3
1629	5	2
1628	10	14
1627	2	6
1626	1	5
1625	7	4
1624	12	9
1623	4	1
1622	3	7
1621	2	6
1620	14	11
1619	6	3
1618	5	2
1617	4	1
1616	9	13
1615	1	5
1614	7	4
1613	6	3
1612	11	8
1611	3	7
1610	2	6
1609	1	5
1608	13	10
1607	5	2
1606	4	1
1605	3	7
1604	8	12
1603	7	4
1602	6	3
1601	5	2
1600	10	14
1599	2	6
1598	1	5
1597	7	4
1596	12	9
1595	4	1

Calendar

Year	O.S.	N.S.
1594	3	7
1593	2	6
1592	14	11
1591	6	3
1590	5	2
1589	4	1
1588	9	13
1587	1	5
1586	7	4
1585	6	3
1584	11	8
1583	3	7
1582	2	6
1581	1	…
1580	13	…

Note: To locate annual calendar under Old Style (Julian), find year under O.S. and consult calendar with number given at right; to locate annual calendar under New Style (Gregorian), find year under N.S. and consult calendar with number given to its right.

Source: Jennifer Mossman, ed., *Holidays and Anniversaries of the World* (1990), xvi, xvii.

perpetual calendar 1

january

sun	mon	tue	wed	thu	fri	sat
1	2	3	4	5	6	7
8	9	10	11	12	13	14
15	16	17	18	19	20	21
22	23	24	25	26	27	28
29	30	31				

february

sun	mon	tue	wed	thu	fri	sat
			1	2	3	4
5	6	7	8	9	10	11
12	13	14	15	16	17	18
19	20	21	22	23	24	25
26	27	28				

march

sun	mon	tue	wed	thu	fri	sat
			1	2	3	4
5	6	7	8	9	10	11
12	13	14	15	16	17	18
19	20	21	22	23	24	25
26	27	28	29	30	31	

april

sun	mon	tue	wed	thu	fri	sat
						1
2	3	4	5	6	7	8
9	10	11	12	13	14	15
16	17	18	19	20	21	22
23	24	25	26	27	28	29
30						

may

sun	mon	tue	wed	thu	fri	sat
	1	2	3	4	5	6
7	8	9	10	11	12	13
14	15	16	17	18	19	20
21	22	23	24	25	26	27
28	29	30	31			

june

sun	mon	tue	wed	thu	fri	sat
				1	2	3
4	5	6	7	8	9	10
11	12	13	14	15	16	17
18	19	20	21	22	23	24
25	26	27	28	29	30	

july

sun	mon	tue	wed	thu	fri	sat
						1
2	3	4	5	6	7	8
9	10	11	12	13	14	15
16	17	18	19	20	21	22
23	24	25	26	27	28	29
30	31					

august

sun	mon	tue	wed	thu	fri	sat
		1	2	3	4	5
6	7	8	9	10	11	12
13	14	15	16	17	18	19
20	21	22	23	24	25	26
27	28	29	30	31		

september

sun	mon	tue	wed	thu	fri	sat
					1	2
3	4	5	6	7	8	9
10	11	12	13	14	15	16
17	18	19	20	21	22	23
24	25	26	27	28	29	30

october

sun	mon	tue	wed	thu	fri	sat
1	2	3	4	5	6	7
8	9	10	11	12	13	14
15	16	17	18	19	20	21
22	23	24	25	26	27	28
29	30	31				

november

sun	mon	tue	wed	thu	fri	sat
			1	2	3	4
5	6	7	8	9	10	11
12	13	14	15	16	17	18
19	20	21	22	23	24	25
26	27	28	29	30		

december

sun	mon	tue	wed	thu	fri	sat
					1	2
3	4	5	6	7	8	9
10	11	12	13	14	15	16
17	18	19	20	21	22	23
24	25	26	27	28	29	30
31						

perpetual calendar 2

january

sun	mon	tue	wed	thu	fri	sat
	1	2	3	4	5	6
7	8	9	10	11	12	13
14	15	16	17	18	19	20
21	22	23	24	25	26	27
28	29	30	31			

february

sun	mon	tue	wed	thu	fri	sat
				1	2	3
4	5	6	7	8	9	10
11	12	13	14	15	16	17
18	19	20	21	22	23	24
25	26	27	28			

march

sun	mon	tue	wed	thu	fri	sat
				1	2	3
4	5	6	7	8	9	10
11	12	13	14	15	16	17
18	19	20	21	22	23	24
25	26	27	28	29	30	31

april

sun	mon	tue	wed	thu	fri	sat
1	2	3	4	5	6	7
8	9	10	11	12	13	14
15	16	17	18	19	20	21
22	23	24	25	26	27	28
29	30					

may

sun	mon	tue	wed	thu	fri	sat
		1	2	3	4	5
6	7	8	9	10	11	12
13	14	15	16	17	18	19
20	21	22	23	24	25	26
27	28	29	30	31		

june

sun	mon	tue	wed	thu	fri	sat
					1	2
3	4	5	6	7	8	9
10	11	12	13	14	15	16
17	18	19	20	21	22	23
24	25	26	27	28	29	30

july

sun	mon	tue	wed	thu	fri	sat
1	2	3	4	5	6	7
8	9	10	11	12	13	14
15	16	17	18	19	20	21
22	23	24	25	26	27	28
29	30	31				

august

sun	mon	tue	wed	thu	fri	sat
			1	2	3	4
5	6	7	8	9	10	11
12	13	14	15	16	17	18
19	20	21	22	23	24	25
26	27	28	29	30	31	

september

sun	mon	tue	wed	thu	fri	sat
						1
2	3	4	5	6	7	8
9	10	11	12	13	14	15
16	17	18	19	20	21	22
23	24	25	26	27	28	29
30						

october

sun	mon	tue	wed	thu	fri	sat
	1	2	3	4	5	6
7	8	9	10	11	12	13
14	15	16	17	18	19	20
21	22	23	24	25	26	27
28	29	30	31			

november

sun	mon	tue	wed	thu	fri	sat
				1	2	3
4	5	6	7	8	9	10
11	12	13	14	15	16	17
18	19	20	21	22	23	24
25	26	27	28	29	30	

december

sun	mon	tue	wed	thu	fri	sat
						1
2	3	4	5	6	7	8
9	10	11	12	13	14	15
16	17	18	19	20	21	22
23	24	25	26	27	28	29
30	31					

perpetual calendar 3

january

sun	mon	tue	wed	thu	fri	sat
					1	2
3	4	5	6	7	8	9
10	11	12	13	14	15	16
17	18	19	20	21	22	23
24	25	26	27	28	29	30
31						

february

sun	mon	tue	wed	thu	fri	sat
	1	2	3	4	5	6
7	8	9	10	11	12	13
14	15	16	17	18	19	20
21	22	23	24	25	26	27
28						

march

sun	mon	tue	wed	thu	fri	sat
	1	2	3	4	5	6
7	8	9	10	11	12	13
14	15	16	17	18	19	20
21	22	23	24	25	26	27
28	29	30	31			

april

sun	mon	tue	wed	thu	fri	sat
				1	2	3
4	5	6	7	8	9	10
11	12	13	14	15	16	17
18	19	20	21	22	23	24
25	26	27	28	29	30	

may

sun	mon	tue	wed	thu	fri	sat
						1
2	3	4	5	6	7	8
9	10	11	12	13	14	15
16	17	18	19	20	21	22
23	24	25	26	27	28	29
30	31					

june

sun	mon	tue	wed	thu	fri	sat
		1	2	3	4	5
6	7	8	9	10	11	12
13	14	15	16	17	18	19
20	21	22	23	24	25	26
27	28	29	30			

july

sun	mon	tue	wed	thu	fri	sat
				1	2	3
4	5	6	7	8	9	10
11	12	13	14	15	16	17
18	19	20	21	22	23	24
25	26	27	28	29	30	31

august

sun	mon	tue	wed	thu	fri	sat
1	2	3	4	5	6	7
8	9	10	11	12	13	14
15	16	17	18	19	20	21
22	23	24	25	26	27	28
29	30	31				

september

sun	mon	tue	wed	thu	fri	sat
			1	2	3	4
5	6	7	8	9	10	11
12	13	14	15	16	17	18
19	20	21	22	23	24	25
26	27	28	29	30		

october

sun	mon	tue	wed	thu	fri	sat
					1	2
3	4	5	6	7	8	9
10	11	12	13	14	15	16
17	18	19	20	21	22	23
24	25	26	27	28	29	30
31						

november

sun	mon	tue	wed	thu	fri	sat
	1	2	3	4	5	6
7	8	9	10	11	12	13
14	15	16	17	18	19	20
21	22	23	24	25	26	27
28	29	30				

december

sun	mon	tue	wed	thu	fri	sat
			1	2	3	4
5	6	7	8	9	10	11
12	13	14	15	16	17	18
19	20	21	22	23	24	25
26	27	28	29	30	31	

perpetual calendar 4

january

sun	mon	tue	wed	thu	fri	sat
			1	2	3	4
5	6	7	8	9	10	11
12	13	14	15	16	17	18
19	20	21	22	23	24	25
26	27	28	29	30	31	

february

sun	mon	tue	wed	thu	fri	sat
						1
2	3	4	5	6	7	8
9	10	11	12	13	14	15
16	17	18	19	20	21	22
23	24	25	26	27	28	

march

sun	mon	tue	wed	thu	fri	sat
						1
2	3	4	5	6	7	8
9	10	11	12	13	14	15
16	17	18	19	20	21	22
23	24	25	26	27	28	29
30	31					

april

sun	mon	tue	wed	thu	fri	sat
		1	2	3	4	5
6	7	8	9	10	11	12
13	14	15	16	17	18	19
20	21	22	23	24	25	26
27	28	29	30			

may

sun	mon	tue	wed	thu	fri	sat
				1	2	3
4	5	6	7	8	9	10
11	12	13	14	15	16	17
18	19	20	21	22	23	24
25	26	27	28	29	30	31

june

sun	mon	tue	wed	thu	fri	sat
1	2	3	4	5	6	7
8	9	10	11	12	13	14
15	16	17	18	19	20	21
22	23	24	25	26	27	28
29	30					

july

sun	mon	tue	wed	thu	fri	sat
		1	2	3	4	5
6	7	8	9	10	11	12
13	14	15	16	17	18	19
20	21	22	23	24	25	26
27	28	29	30	31		

august

sun	mon	tue	wed	thu	fri	sat
					1	2
3	4	5	6	7	8	9
10	11	12	13	14	15	16
17	18	19	20	21	22	23
24	25	26	27	28	29	30
31						

september

sun	mon	tue	wed	thu	fri	sat
	1	2	3	4	5	6
7	8	9	10	11	12	13
14	15	16	17	18	19	20
21	22	23	24	25	26	27
28	29	30				

october

sun	mon	tue	wed	thu	fri	sat
			1	2	3	4
5	6	7	8	9	10	11
12	13	14	15	16	17	18
19	20	21	22	23	24	25
26	27	28	29	30	31	

november

sun	mon	tue	wed	thu	fri	sat
						1
2	3	4	5	6	7	8
9	10	11	12	13	14	15
16	17	18	19	20	21	22
23	24	25	26	27	28	29
30						

december

sun	mon	tue	wed	thu	fri	sat
	1	2	3	4	5	6
7	8	9	10	11	12	13
14	15	16	17	18	19	20
21	22	23	24	25	26	27
28	29	30	31			

perpetual calendar 5

january

sun	mon	tue	wed	thu	fri	sat
				1	2	3
4	5	6	7	8	9	10
11	12	13	14	15	16	17
18	19	20	21	22	23	24
25	26	27	28	29	30	31

february

sun	mon	tue	wed	thu	fri	sat
1	2	3	4	5	6	7
8	9	10	11	12	13	14
15	16	17	18	19	20	21
22	23	24	25	26	27	28

march

sun	mon	tue	wed	thu	fri	sat
1	2	3	4	5	6	7
8	9	10	11	12	13	14
15	16	17	18	19	20	21
22	23	24	25	26	27	28
29	30	31				

april

sun	mon	tue	wed	thu	fri	sat
			1	2	3	4
5	6	7	8	9	10	11
12	13	14	15	16	17	18
19	20	21	22	23	24	25
26	27	28	29	30		

may

sun	mon	tue	wed	thu	fri	sat
					1	2
3	4	5	6	7	8	9
10	11	12	13	14	15	16
17	18	19	20	21	22	23
24	25	26	27	28	29	30
31						

june

sun	mon	tue	wed	thu	fri	sat
	1	2	3	4	5	6
7	8	9	10	11	12	13
14	15	16	17	18	19	20
21	22	23	24	25	26	27
28	29	30				

july

sun	mon	tue	wed	thu	fri	sat
			1	2	3	4
5	6	7	8	9	10	11
12	13	14	15	16	17	18
19	20	21	22	23	24	25
26	27	28	29	30	31	

august

sun	mon	tue	wed	thu	fri	sat
						1
2	3	4	5	6	7	8
9	10	11	12	13	14	15
16	17	18	19	20	21	22
23	24	25	26	27	28	29
30	31					

september

sun	mon	tue	wed	thu	fri	sat
		1	2	3	4	5
6	7	8	9	10	11	12
13	14	15	16	17	18	19
20	21	22	23	24	25	26
27	28	29	30			

october

sun	mon	tue	wed	thu	fri	sat
				1	2	3
4	5	6	7	8	9	10
11	12	13	14	15	16	17
18	19	20	21	22	23	24
25	26	27	28	29	30	31

november

sun	mon	tue	wed	thu	fri	sat
1	2	3	4	5	6	7
8	9	10	11	12	13	14
15	16	17	18	19	20	21
22	23	24	25	26	27	28
29	30					

december

sun	mon	tue	wed	thu	fri	sat
		1	2	3	4	5
6	7	8	9	10	11	12
13	14	15	16	17	18	19
20	21	22	23	24	25	26
27	28	29	30	31		

(continued)

TABLE 16.3 (continued)

perpetual calendar 6

january

sun	mon	tue	wed	thu	fri	sat
					1	2
3	4	5	6	7	8	9
10	11	12	13	14	15	16
17	18	19	20	21	22	23
24	25	26	27	28	29	30
31						

february

sun	mon	tue	wed	thu	fri	sat
	1	2	3	4	5	6
7	8	9	10	11	12	13
14	15	16	17	18	19	20
21	22	23	24	25	26	27
28						

march

sun	mon	tue	wed	thu	fri	sat
	1	2	3	4	5	6
7	8	9	10	11	12	13
14	15	16	17	18	19	20
21	22	23	24	25	26	27
28	29	30	31			

april

sun	mon	tue	wed	thu	fri	sat
				1	2	3
4	5	6	7	8	9	10
11	12	13	14	15	16	17
18	19	20	21	22	23	24
25	26	27	28	29	30	

may

sun	mon	tue	wed	thu	fri	sat
						1
2	3	4	5	6	7	8
9	10	11	12	13	14	15
16	17	18	19	20	21	22
23	24	25	26	27	28	29
30	31					

june

sun	mon	tue	wed	thu	fri	sat
		1	2	3	4	5
6	7	8	9	10	11	12
13	14	15	16	17	18	19
20	21	22	23	24	25	26
27	28	29	30			

july

sun	mon	tue	wed	thu	fri	sat
				1	2	3
4	5	6	7	8	9	10
11	12	13	14	15	16	17
18	19	20	21	22	23	24
25	26	27	28	29	30	31

august

sun	mon	tue	wed	thu	fri	sat
1	2	3	4	5	6	7
8	9	10	11	12	13	14
15	16	17	18	19	20	21
22	23	24	25	26	27	28
29	30	31				

september

sun	mon	tue	wed	thu	fri	sat
			1	2	3	4
5	6	7	8	9	10	11
12	13	14	15	16	17	18
19	20	21	22	23	24	25
26	27	28	29	30		

october

sun	mon	tue	wed	thu	fri	sat
					1	2
3	4	5	6	7	8	9
10	11	12	13	14	15	16
17	18	19	20	21	22	23
24	25	26	27	28	29	30
31						

november

sun	mon	tue	wed	thu	fri	sat
	1	2	3	4	5	6
7	8	9	10	11	12	13
14	15	16	17	18	19	20
21	22	23	24	25	26	27
28	29	30				

december

sun	mon	tue	wed	thu	fri	sat
			1	2	3	4
5	6	7	8	9	10	11
12	13	14	15	16	17	18
19	20	21	22	23	24	25
26	27	28	29	30	31	

perpetual calendar 7

january

sun	mon	tue	wed	thu	fri	sat
						1
2	3	4	5	6	7	8
9	10	11	12	13	14	15
16	17	18	19	20	21	22
23	24	25	26	27	28	29
30	31					

february

sun	mon	tue	wed	thu	fri	sat
		1	2	3	4	5
6	7	8	9	10	11	12
13	14	15	16	17	18	19
20	21	22	23	24	25	26
27	28					

march

sun	mon	tue	wed	thu	fri	sat
		1	2	3	4	5
6	7	8	9	10	11	12
13	14	15	16	17	18	19
20	21	22	23	24	25	26
27	28	29	30	31		

april

sun	mon	tue	wed	thu	fri	sat
					1	2
3	4	5	6	7	8	9
10	11	12	13	14	15	16
17	18	19	20	21	22	23
24	25	26	27	28	29	30

may

sun	mon	tue	wed	thu	fri	sat
1	2	3	4	5	6	7
8	9	10	11	12	13	14
15	16	17	18	19	20	21
22	23	24	25	26	27	28
29	30	31				

june

sun	mon	tue	wed	thu	fri	sat
			1	2	3	4
5	6	7	8	9	10	11
12	13	14	15	16	17	18
19	20	21	22	23	24	25
26	27	28	29	30		

july

sun	mon	tue	wed	thu	fri	sat
					1	2
3	4	5	6	7	8	9
10	11	12	13	14	15	16
17	18	19	20	21	22	23
24	25	26	27	28	29	30
31						

august

sun	mon	tue	wed	thu	fri	sat
	1	2	3	4	5	6
7	8	9	10	11	12	13
14	15	16	17	18	19	20
21	22	23	24	25	26	27
28	29	30	31			

september

sun	mon	tue	wed	thu	fri	sat
				1	2	3
4	5	6	7	8	9	10
11	12	13	14	15	16	17
18	19	20	21	22	23	24
25	26	27	28	29	30	

october

sun	mon	tue	wed	thu	fri	sat
						1
2	3	4	5	6	7	8
9	10	11	12	13	14	15
16	17	18	19	20	21	22
23	24	25	26	27	28	29
30	31					

november

sun	mon	tue	wed	thu	fri	sat
		1	2	3	4	5
6	7	8	9	10	11	12
13	14	15	16	17	18	19
20	21	22	23	24	25	26
27	28	29	30			

december

sun	mon	tue	wed	thu	fri	sat
				1	2	3
4	5	6	7	8	9	10
11	12	13	14	15	16	17
18	19	20	21	22	23	24
25	26	27	28	29	30	31

perpetual calendar 8

january

sun	mon	tue	wed	thu	fri	sat
1	2	3	4	5	6	7
8	9	10	11	12	13	14
15	16	17	18	19	20	21
22	23	24	25	26	27	28
29	30	31				

february

sun	mon	tue	wed	thu	fri	sat
			1	2	3	4
5	6	7	8	9	10	11
12	13	14	15	16	17	18
19	20	21	22	23	24	25
26	27	28	29			

march

sun	mon	tue	wed	thu	fri	sat
				1	2	3
4	5	6	7	8	9	10
11	12	13	14	15	16	17
18	19	20	21	22	23	24
25	26	27	28	29	30	31

april

sun	mon	tue	wed	thu	fri	sat
1	2	3	4	5	6	7
8	9	10	11	12	13	14
15	16	17	18	19	20	21
22	23	24	25	26	27	28
29	30					

may

sun	mon	tue	wed	thu	fri	sat
		1	2	3	4	5
6	7	8	9	10	11	12
13	14	15	16	17	18	19
20	21	22	23	24	25	26
27	28	29	30	31		

june

sun	mon	tue	wed	thu	fri	sat
					1	2
3	4	5	6	7	8	9
10	11	12	13	14	15	16
17	18	19	20	21	22	23
24	25	26	27	28	29	30

july

sun	mon	tue	wed	thu	fri	sat
1	2	3	4	5	6	7
8	9	10	11	12	13	14
15	16	17	18	19	20	21
22	23	24	25	26	27	28
29	30	31				

august

sun	mon	tue	wed	thu	fri	sat
			1	2	3	4
5	6	7	8	9	10	11
12	13	14	15	16	17	18
19	20	21	22	23	24	25
26	27	28	29	30	31	

september

sun	mon	tue	wed	thu	fri	sat
						1
2	3	4	5	6	7	8
9	10	11	12	13	14	15
16	17	18	19	20	21	22
23	24	25	26	27	28	29
30						

october

sun	mon	tue	wed	thu	fri	sat
	1	2	3	4	5	6
7	8	9	10	11	12	13
14	15	16	17	18	19	20
21	22	23	24	25	26	27
28	29	30	31			

november

sun	mon	tue	wed	thu	fri	sat
				1	2	3
4	5	6	7	8	9	10
11	12	13	14	15	16	17
18	19	20	21	22	23	24
25	26	27	28	29	30	

december

sun	mon	tue	wed	thu	fri	sat
						1
2	3	4	5	6	7	8
9	10	11	12	13	14	15
16	17	18	19	20	21	22
23	24	25	26	27	28	29
30	31					

perpetual calendar 9

january

sun	mon	tue	wed	thu	fri	sat
	1	2	3	4	5	6
7	8	9	10	11	12	13
14	15	16	17	18	19	20
21	22	23	24	25	26	27
28	29	30	31			

february

sun	mon	tue	wed	thu	fri	sat
				1	2	3
4	5	6	7	8	9	10
11	12	13	14	15	16	17
18	19	20	21	22	23	24
25	26	27	28	29		

march

sun	mon	tue	wed	thu	fri	sat
					1	2
3	4	5	6	7	8	9
10	11	12	13	14	15	16
17	18	19	20	21	22	23
24	25	26	27	28	29	30
31						

april

sun	mon	tue	wed	thu	fri	sat
	1	2	3	4	5	6
7	8	9	10	11	12	13
14	15	16	17	18	19	20
21	22	23	24	25	26	27
28	29	30				

may

sun	mon	tue	wed	thu	fri	sat
			1	2	3	4
5	6	7	8	9	10	11
12	13	14	15	16	17	18
19	20	21	22	23	24	25
26	27	28	29	30	31	

june

sun	mon	tue	wed	thu	fri	sat
						1
2	3	4	5	6	7	8
9	10	11	12	13	14	15
16	17	18	19	20	21	22
23	24	25	26	27	28	29
30						

july

sun	mon	tue	wed	thu	fri	sat
	1	2	3	4	5	6
7	8	9	10	11	12	13
14	15	16	17	18	19	20
21	22	23	24	25	26	27
28	29	30	31			

august

sun	mon	tue	wed	thu	fri	sat
				1	2	3
4	5	6	7	8	9	10
11	12	13	14	15	16	17
18	19	20	21	22	23	24
25	26	27	28	29	30	31

september

sun	mon	tue	wed	thu	fri	sat
1	2	3	4	5	6	7
8	9	10	11	12	13	14
15	16	17	18	19	20	21
22	23	24	25	26	27	28
29	30					

october

sun	mon	tue	wed	thu	fri	sat
		1	2	3	4	5
6	7	8	9	10	11	12
13	14	15	16	17	18	19
20	21	22	23	24	25	26
27	28	29	30	31		

november

sun	mon	tue	wed	thu	fri	sat
					1	2
3	4	5	6	7	8	9
10	11	12	13	14	15	16
17	18	19	20	21	22	23
24	25	26	27	28	29	30

december

sun	mon	tue	wed	thu	fri	sat
1	2	3	4	5	6	7
8	9	10	11	12	13	14
15	16	17	18	19	20	21
22	23	24	25	26	27	28
29	30	31				

perpetual calendar 10

january

sun	mon	tue	wed	thu	fri	sat
		1	2	3	4	5
6	7	8	9	10	11	12
13	14	15	16	17	18	19
20	21	22	23	24	25	26
27	28	29	30	31		

february

sun	mon	tue	wed	thu	fri	sat
					1	2
3	4	5	6	7	8	9
10	11	12	13	14	15	16
17	18	19	20	21	22	23
24	25	26	27	28	29	

march

sun	mon	tue	wed	thu	fri	sat
						1
2	3	4	5	6	7	8
9	10	11	12	13	14	15
16	17	18	19	20	21	22
23	24	25	26	27	28	29
30	31					

april

sun	mon	tue	wed	thu	fri	sat
		1	2	3	4	5
6	7	8	9	10	11	12
13	14	15	16	17	18	19
20	21	22	23	24	25	26
27	28	29	30			

may

sun	mon	tue	wed	thu	fri	sat
				1	2	3
4	5	6	7	8	9	10
11	12	13	14	15	16	17
18	19	20	21	22	23	24
25	26	27	28	29	30	31

june

sun	mon	tue	wed	thu	fri	sat
1	2	3	4	5	6	7
8	9	10	11	12	13	14
15	16	17	18	19	20	21
22	23	24	25	26	27	28
29	30					

july

sun	mon	tue	wed	thu	fri	sat
		1	2	3	4	5
6	7	8	9	10	11	12
13	14	15	16	17	18	19
20	21	22	23	24	25	26
27	28	29	30	31		

august

sun	mon	tue	wed	thu	fri	sat
					1	2
3	4	5	6	7	8	9
10	11	12	13	14	15	16
17	18	19	20	21	22	23
24	25	26	27	28	29	30
31						

september

sun	mon	tue	wed	thu	fri	sat
	1	2	3	4	5	6
7	8	9	10	11	12	13
14	15	16	17	18	19	20
21	22	23	24	25	26	27
28	29	30				

october

sun	mon	tue	wed	thu	fri	sat
			1	2	3	4
5	6	7	8	9	10	11
12	13	14	15	16	17	18
19	20	21	22	23	24	25
26	27	28	29	30	31	

november

sun	mon	tue	wed	thu	fri	sat
						1
2	3	4	5	6	7	8
9	10	11	12	13	14	15
16	17	18	19	20	21	22
23	24	25	26	27	28	29
30						

december

sun	mon	tue	wed	thu	fri	sat
	1	2	3	4	5	6
7	8	9	10	11	12	13
14	15	16	17	18	19	20
21	22	23	24	25	26	27
28	29	30	31			

perpetual calendar 11

january

sun	mon	tue	wed	thu	fri	sat
			1	2	3	4
5	6	7	8	9	10	11
12	13	14	15	16	17	18
19	20	21	22	23	24	25
26	27	28	29	30	31	

february

sun	mon	tue	wed	thu	fri	sat
						1
2	3	4	5	6	7	8
9	10	11	12	13	14	15
16	17	18	19	20	21	22
23	24	25	26	27	28	29

march

sun	mon	tue	wed	thu	fri	sat
1	2	3	4	5	6	7
8	9	10	11	12	13	14
15	16	17	18	19	20	21
22	23	24	25	26	27	28
29	30	31				

april

sun	mon	tue	wed	thu	fri	sat
			1	2	3	4
5	6	7	8	9	10	11
12	13	14	15	16	17	18
19	20	21	22	23	24	25
26	27	28	29	30		

may

sun	mon	tue	wed	thu	fri	sat
					1	2
3	4	5	6	7	8	9
10	11	12	13	14	15	16
17	18	19	20	21	22	23
24	25	26	27	28	29	30
31						

june

sun	mon	tue	wed	thu	fri	sat
	1	2	3	4	5	6
7	8	9	10	11	12	13
14	15	16	17	18	19	20
21	22	23	24	25	26	27
28	29	30				

july

sun	mon	tue	wed	thu	fri	sat
			1	2	3	4
5	6	7	8	9	10	11
12	13	14	15	16	17	18
19	20	21	22	23	24	25
26	27	28	29	30	31	

august

sun	mon	tue	wed	thu	fri	sat
						1
2	3	4	5	6	7	8
9	10	11	12	13	14	15
16	17	18	19	20	21	22
23	24	25	26	27	28	29
30	31					

september

sun	mon	tue	wed	thu	fri	sat
		1	2	3	4	5
6	7	8	9	10	11	12
13	14	15	16	17	18	19
20	21	22	23	24	25	26
27	28	29	30			

october

sun	mon	tue	wed	thu	fri	sat
				1	2	3
4	5	6	7	8	9	10
11	12	13	14	15	16	17
18	19	20	21	22	23	24
25	26	27	28	29	30	31

november

sun	mon	tue	wed	thu	fri	sat
1	2	3	4	5	6	7
8	9	10	11	12	13	14
15	16	17	18	19	20	21
22	23	24	25	26	27	28
29	30					

december

sun	mon	tue	wed	thu	fri	sat
		1	2	3	4	5
6	7	8	9	10	11	12
13	14	15	16	17	18	19
20	21	22	23	24	25	26
27	28	29	30	31		

perpetual calendar 12

january
sun	mon	tue	wed	thu	fri	sat
				1	2	3
4	5	6	7	8	9	10
11	12	13	14	15	16	17
18	19	20	21	22	23	24
25	26	27	28	29	30	31

february
sun	mon	tue	wed	thu	fri	sat
1	2	3	4	5	6	7
8	9	10	11	12	13	14
15	16	17	18	19	20	21
22	23	24	25	26	27	28
29						

march
sun	mon	tue	wed	thu	fri	sat
	1	2	3	4	5	6
7	8	9	10	11	12	13
14	15	16	17	18	19	20
21	22	23	24	25	26	27
28	29	30	31			

april
sun	mon	tue	wed	thu	fri	sat
				1	2	3
4	5	6	7	8	9	10
11	12	13	14	15	16	17
18	19	20	21	22	23	24
25	26	27	28	29	30	

may
sun	mon	tue	wed	thu	fri	sat
						1
2	3	4	5	6	7	8
9	10	11	12	13	14	15
16	17	18	19	20	21	22
23	24	25	26	27	28	29
30	31					

june
sun	mon	tue	wed	thu	fri	sat
		1	2	3	4	5
6	7	8	9	10	11	12
13	14	15	16	17	18	19
20	21	22	23	24	25	26
27	28	29	30			

july
sun	mon	tue	wed	thu	fri	sat
				1	2	3
4	5	6	7	8	9	10
11	12	13	14	15	16	17
18	19	20	21	22	23	24
25	26	27	28	29	30	31

august
sun	mon	tue	wed	thu	fri	sat
1	2	3	4	5	6	7
8	9	10	11	12	13	14
15	16	17	18	19	20	21
22	23	24	25	26	27	28
29	30	31				

september
sun	mon	tue	wed	thu	fri	sat
			1	2	3	4
5	6	7	8	9	10	11
12	13	14	15	16	17	18
19	20	21	22	23	24	25
26	27	28	29	30		

october
sun	mon	tue	wed	thu	fri	sat
					1	2
3	4	5	6	7	8	9
10	11	12	13	14	15	16
17	18	19	20	21	22	23
24	25	26	27	28	29	30
31						

november
sun	mon	tue	wed	thu	fri	sat
	1	2	3	4	5	6
7	8	9	10	11	12	13
14	15	16	17	18	19	20
21	22	23	24	25	26	27
28	29	30				

december
sun	mon	tue	wed	thu	fri	sat
			1	2	3	4
5	6	7	8	9	10	11
12	13	14	15	16	17	18
19	20	21	22	23	24	25
26	27	28	29	30	31	

perpetual calendar 13

january
sun	mon	tue	wed	thu	fri	sat
					1	2
3	4	5	6	7	8	9
10	11	12	13	14	15	16
17	18	19	20	21	22	23
24	25	26	27	28	29	30
31						

february
sun	mon	tue	wed	thu	fri	sat
	1	2	3	4	5	6
7	8	9	10	11	12	13
14	15	16	17	18	19	20
21	22	23	24	25	26	27
28	29					

march
sun	mon	tue	wed	thu	fri	sat
		1	2	3	4	5
6	7	8	9	10	11	12
13	14	15	16	17	18	19
20	21	22	23	24	25	26
27	28	29	30	31		

april
sun	mon	tue	wed	thu	fri	sat
					1	2
3	4	5	6	7	8	9
10	11	12	13	14	15	16
17	18	19	20	21	22	23
24	25	26	27	28	29	30

may
sun	mon	tue	wed	thu	fri	sat
1	2	3	4	5	6	7
8	9	10	11	12	13	14
15	16	17	18	19	20	21
22	23	24	25	26	27	28
29	30	31				

june
sun	mon	tue	wed	thu	fri	sat
			1	2	3	4
5	6	7	8	9	10	11
12	13	14	15	16	17	18
19	20	21	22	23	24	25
26	27	28	29	30		

july
sun	mon	tue	wed	thu	fri	sat
					1	2
3	4	5	6	7	8	9
10	11	12	13	14	15	16
17	18	19	20	21	22	23
24	25	26	27	28	29	30
31						

august
sun	mon	tue	wed	thu	fri	sat
	1	2	3	4	5	6
7	8	9	10	11	12	13
14	15	16	17	18	19	20
21	22	23	24	25	26	27
28	29	30	31			

september
sun	mon	tue	wed	thu	fri	sat
				1	2	3
4	5	6	7	8	9	10
11	12	13	14	15	16	17
18	19	20	21	22	23	24
25	26	27	28	29	30	

october
sun	mon	tue	wed	thu	fri	sat
						1
2	3	4	5	6	7	8
9	10	11	12	13	14	15
16	17	18	19	20	21	22
23	24	25	26	27	28	29
30	31					

november
sun	mon	tue	wed	thu	fri	sat
		1	2	3	4	5
6	7	8	9	10	11	12
13	14	15	16	17	18	19
20	21	22	23	24	25	26
27	28	29	30			

december
sun	mon	tue	wed	thu	fri	sat
				1	2	3
4	5	6	7	8	9	10
11	12	13	14	15	16	17
18	19	20	21	22	23	24
25	26	27	28	29	30	31

perpetual calendar 14

january
sun	mon	tue	wed	thu	fri	sat
						1
2	3	4	5	6	7	8
9	10	11	12	13	14	15
16	17	18	19	20	21	22
23	24	25	26	27	28	29
30	31					

february
sun	mon	tue	wed	thu	fri	sat
		1	2	3	4	5
6	7	8	9	10	11	12
13	14	15	16	17	18	19
20	21	22	23	24	25	26
27	28	29				

march
sun	mon	tue	wed	thu	fri	sat
			1	2	3	4
5	6	7	8	9	10	11
12	13	14	15	16	17	18
19	20	21	22	23	24	25
26	27	28	29	30	31	

april
sun	mon	tue	wed	thu	fri	sat
						1
2	3	4	5	6	7	8
9	10	11	12	13	14	15
16	17	18	19	20	21	22
23	24	25	26	27	28	29
30						

may
sun	mon	tue	wed	thu	fri	sat
	1	2	3	4	5	6
7	8	9	10	11	12	13
14	15	16	17	18	19	20
21	22	23	24	25	26	27
28	29	30	31			

june
sun	mon	tue	wed	thu	fri	sat
				1	2	3
4	5	6	7	8	9	10
11	12	13	14	15	16	17
18	19	20	21	22	23	24
25	26	27	28	29	30	

july
sun	mon	tue	wed	thu	fri	sat
						1
2	3	4	5	6	7	8
9	10	11	12	13	14	15
16	17	18	19	20	21	22
23	24	25	26	27	28	29
30	31					

august
sun	mon	tue	wed	thu	fri	sat
		1	2	3	4	5
6	7	8	9	10	11	12
13	14	15	16	17	18	19
20	21	22	23	24	25	26
27	28	29	30	31		

september
sun	mon	tue	wed	thu	fri	sat
					1	2
3	4	5	6	7	8	9
10	11	12	13	14	15	16
17	18	19	20	21	22	23
24	25	26	27	28	29	30

october
sun	mon	tue	wed	thu	fri	sat
1	2	3	4	5	6	7
8	9	10	11	12	13	14
15	16	17	18	19	20	21
22	23	24	25	26	27	28
29	30	31				

november
sun	mon	tue	wed	thu	fri	sat
			1	2	3	4
5	6	7	8	9	10	11
12	13	14	15	16	17	18
19	20	21	22	23	24	25
26	27	28	29	30		

december
sun	mon	tue	wed	thu	fri	sat
					1	2
3	4	5	6	7	8	9
10	11	12	13	14	15	16
17	18	19	20	21	22	23
24	25	26	27	28	29	30
31						

CHAPTER 17 Popular Life and Recreation

Popular Life

No subject brings a modern reader closer to the most central aspects of popular life in early America than an examination of how individuals married and raised children. Enormous variety distinguished the conditions under which families developed in New England and the South during the seventeenth century, even though both began as societies of transplanted English émigrés. The typical household in each region set down roots and transmitted itself across generations under fundamentally dissimilar conditions. In order to appreciate how greatly the domestic experiences of northerners and southerners diverged from one another during the formative period before 1700, some insight can be gained from briefly comparing two families broadly typical of their respective communities: the Holts of Andover, Massachusetts, and the Burks of Middlesex County, Virginia.

Nicholas Holt, a tanner, landed at Massachusetts in the early 1630s as a bachelor and became one of Andover's earliest settlers a decade later. He delayed marriage longer than usual and did not take a wife until his late thirties. He then fathered five sons and three daughters who survived to adulthood, married, and eventually divided the 400 acres allocated to their father as his share of the town's common land. Nicholas matured into an aged patriarch who could delight after 1657 in the first arrivals of a steady stream of grandchildren, who would ultimately number more than sixty. Holt's lifespan easily surpassed the biblical standard of "three-score and ten" for a respectable old age, and he did not die until 1686 when he was in his eighty-fourth year. His wife survived him, and his children inherited their parents' longevity and passed it on to their descendants.

The long-lived, prolific Holts could not have been more different from the Burks of Middlesex County, Virginia. The family's founder was an expatriate from England (the name was properly spelled *Bourke*) who migrated to the Old Dominion at about the same time Nicholas Holt helped found Andover. Burk became one of Middlesex County's early settlers in the 1650s. The elder Burk married about 1655, enjoyed the birth of his only child John in 1657, and died well short of his fortieth year about 1659. Young John Burk grew up in the household of his mother's second husband, Thomas Tuggle, with four stepbrothers; John Burk's own mother evidently died before he married and so never saw any of her grandchildren. When his stepfather Tuggle passed away in 1684, John Burk became his family's eldest male at the relatively young age of 27. He took a bride, who died; married another, who also died; and then found a third wife, all within the span of less than twenty years. John Burk himself barely survived into middle age, and he never lived to see any of his own grandchildren before he left a widow and seven orphans, going to the grave in 1699 at age 42.

The Burks and Holts serve as dramatic illustrations of how much the character of an early American's life cycle depended on whether he or she lived in New England or the Chesapeake. The dominant factor influencing life cycle was the disease environment, which was remarkably benign in New England (and also the Mid-Atlantic colonies) but highly lethal in Virginia, Maryland, and the Carolinas' coastal plain. (For a detailed explanation of this phenomenon, refer to Chapter 6, "Diet and Health," under "Life Expectancy and Mortality.") Death's brooding presence long sapped the vigor from southern households, which remained stunted, fragile, and notably deficient in family traditions until well into the early eighteenth century.

In the North

Northerners, however, lived longer lives, begat more children, and saw greater numbers of their offspring reach adulthood to carry on the cycle than southerners generally did during the seventeenth century. Northern family life betrayed a marked sense of stability, which was reinforced by the traditions and ancestral lore that grandchildren learned at the knees of their parents' aged fathers and mothers. New England households, in the main at least, reflected the idealized structure and authoritarianism of English families, wherein fathers exercised dominion over their children, not only while they matured, but also during adulthood. The extent of these patriarchs' intragenerational influence showed itself most strikingly in their ability to influence their offspring to marry in birth order, from eldest to youngest, and to block sons or daughters from marrying spouses of whom they disapproved, either through emotional pressure, refusing their assent to a marriage settlement, or withholding some other financial assistance.

Courtship and Marriage

Puritan parents replicated much of this system of generational control in New England. Both the Massachusetts Bay and Plymouth legislatures enacted statutes obliging children to obtain their fathers' permission for a first marriage. (Massachusetts gave its courts the option of not only having the guilty parties fined but also whipped, although corporal punishment seems never to have been invoked.) These laws were not idle measures, for surviving judicial archives record prosecutions of young people—including the daughter of a Plymouth governor—in both colonies for the crime of "self-marriage."

Laws against "self-marriage" did not have to be invoked very often because fathers found economic inducements to be far more effective in manipulating their children's emotional life. Younger sons often delayed marriage for years (during which they labored instead to expand output on the parental homestead through the slow process of clearing more acres for cultivation) because they were promised either a generous marriage settlement or legal title to enough land for themselves to be financially independent, if they would only stay at home through their midtwenties to work on the family farm.

Outright threats could ensue when children did not accede to their parents' wishes. Robert Young of Plymouth Colony, for example, faced stiff opposition from his mother Abigail over his choice of a bride. Abigail Young did all in her power to pressure Robert into abandoning his marriage plans by threatening to divide his share of her deceased husband's estate among her two other sons. "My mother," testified her son Nathaniel in 1692, "told me that if Robert had that girl which there was a talk about[,] she would not give him a penny." Robert was at his mother's mercy, unless he was unusually nonchalant about being disinherited.

Such considerations were a major factor in restraining large numbers of Puritan men from marrying as early as they might have been able. Although New England was a region with a severe shortage of labor where healthy, young, and thrifty laborers could expect to accumulate quickly the savings necessary to negotiate a mortgage on agricultural land, its second- and third-generation sons started families at a relatively late age. In seventeenth-century Andover, Massachusetts, just 4% married prior to their twenty-first birthday, while half of all men did not take wives until they had reached the approximate age of twenty-seven; nearly a quarter did not marry until age thirty or older.

New England wives did not delay marriage as long as their husbands, but neither were they teenage brides. Among the second generation of Andover's settlers, just one of every eight women became brides before age eighteen (the youngest was fourteen), and only a third married prior to reaching twenty-one. The average bride was almost twenty-three (22.8) at the time of her wedding, and three of every ten were twenty-five or older when they first married. Like their spouses, New England wives brought a significant level of maturity and several years of practical, workplace experience to their households.

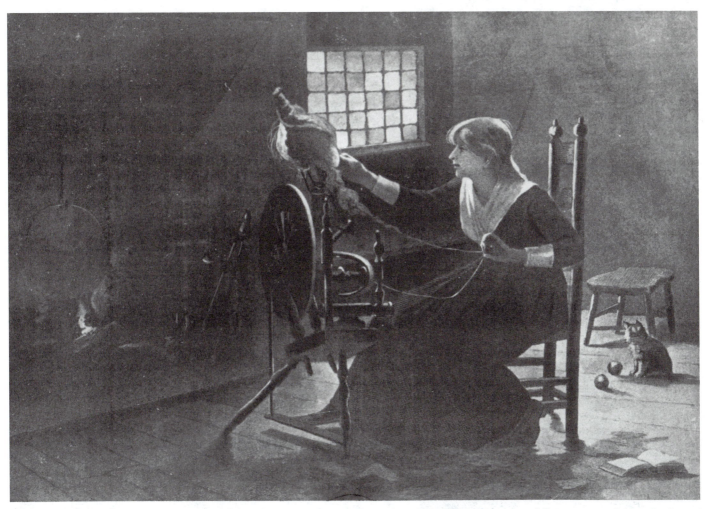

G. R. Barse's painting of Priscilla Mullins, one of the *Mayflower's* passengers, is a bit sentimental but still has the virtue of illustrating one of the major domestic responsibilities for a colonial woman. (Courtesy Library of Congress)

TABLE 17.1 AVERAGE AGE AT FIRST MARRIAGE FOR HUSBANDS AND WIVES IN NEW ENGLAND (WHITE FAMILIES ONLY)

Community	Date of Marriage	Age at First Marriage	
		Men	Women
Andover, Mass.	1644–1674	26.8	19.0
	1675–1699	26.7	22.8
	1700–1730	27.1	24.5
	1731–1749	25.3	23.2
Boxford, Mass.	1701–1725	26.9	22.8
	1726–1750	26.6	23.7
	1751–1775	25.5	22.8
Bristol, R.I.	pre-1750	23.9	20.5
	post-1750	24.3	21.1
Concord, Mass.	1750–1770	25.1	21.1
Dedham, Mass.	1640–1690	25.5	22.5
Guilford, Conn.	1720–1740	26.2	22.6
Hingham, Mass.	1641–1700	26.8	22.6
	1701–1720	27.8	24.3
	1721–1740	26.3	23.3
	1741–1760	25.7	22.5
Ipswich, Mass.	1652–1700	27.2	21.1
	1701–1725	26.5	23.6
	1726–1750	24.0	23.3

Community	Date of Marriage	Age at First Marriage	
		Men	Women
Plymouth	1621–1645	27.0	20.6
	1646–1670	26.0	20.2
	1671–1695	25.4	21.3
	1696–1720	24.6	22.3
Sturbridge, Mass.	1730–1759	24.8	19.5
Topsfield, Mass.	1701–1725	28.3	23.3
	1726–1750	27.8	25.3
Wenham, Mass.	1701–1725	24.8	22.8
	1726–1750	24.0	23.6
	1751–1775	24.7	23.7
Windsor, Conn.	1660–1670	25.1	19.8
	1670–1680	25.4	20.6
	1680–1690	26.4	21.8
	1690–1705	26.3	23.0

Sources: Maris A. Vinovskis, *Fertility in Massachusetts from the Revolution to the Civil War* (1981), 44. Philip J. Greven, "Family Structure in Seventeenth-Century Andover, Massachusetts," *William and Mary Quarterly,* XXIII (1966), 241, 242. Marc Harris, "The People of Concord: A Demographic History, 1750–1850," in David Hackett Fischer, ed., *Concord, The Social History of a New England Town, 1750–1850* (Waltham, 1983), 89. David Hackett Fischer, *Albion's Seed: Four British Folkways in America* (1989), 76. John J. Waters, "Family, Inheritance, and Migration in Colonial New England: The Evidence from Guilford, Connecticut," *William and Mary Quarterly,* XXXIX (1982), 66.

Puritan patriarchs not only induced their boys to remain at home until their late twenties but also inveigled them to accept the antiquated custom that male heirs should marry according to the order in which they were born. Nicholas Holt, mentioned above, enforced this dictum among his sons by threatening to withhold grants of land from any who might try to defy him and set off on their own. In Holt's town of Andover, the age at which men started households largely depended on their order of birth. Eldest sons married at an average age of 25.6 years, while the average for second sons was almost two years later (27.5 years), and the average for youngest sons lagged by almost two-and-a-half years (27.9) behind first sons. Only a minority of sons rebelled against parental tyranny by starting life anew in another frontier town; in Andover, for instance, 80% of the founders' sons never left home. However blissful love may have been in Puritan New England, most sons had to wait their turn before enjoying it.

In most communities where it is common to delay marriage well beyond the onset of adulthood, a large portion of people tend to remain single all their lives. In Old England, where men of that time also married in their late twenties, more than a quarter of them seem never to have wedded. New England differed markedly from this general tendency. In seventeenth-century Hingham, Massachusetts, which seems typical of demographic patterns in the colony, 94.7% of women and 97.4% of men eventually married. There seems to have been just one bachelor who resided in Rowley, Massachusetts, during its first generation of settlement. As in virtually all times, females who never married found themselves stigmatized in early New England; spinsters were derided as "thornbacks," and Puritan children snickered that women who died as old maids spent their afterlife dancing with apes through the fires of Hades.

Parents influenced their children to delay marriage, and they could exercise a veto over a prospective son- or daughter-in-law, but they did not choose their offspring's spouses. Couples initiated their own relationship but had to spend much of their time getting to know one another at their parents' homes because there were few other places to socialize in small New England villages. In order to allow a couple individual space for sharing personal thoughts, two unique courtship customs took root in New England: bundling and use of the courting stick.

Bundling originated in Europe as a practical solution to the problem of giving a couple an opportunity for privacy when they met in a small house with numerous relatives. Parents would escort the man and woman to a bed or mattress in the most distant corner of the home's great hall away from the hearth, or in a small room as houses became larger, and let them lie down together fully clothed. To ensure modest decorum, the father placed a plank lying upright between them and the mother might enclose the woman's legs in a form-fitting shroud sewn up like a stocking. The couple then covered themselves with enough blankets to keep warm (for bundling was invariably a cold-weather ritual) and spoke in hushed tones for as long as they wished to keep each other's company.

Courting sticks provided another expedient for creating privacy. This device was a hollow tube, several feet long, to which cow horns or carved, bell-shaped snouts were attached at both ends. The couple

Much of the interaction in a colonial family occurred around the fireplace. This hearth scene was photographed at the Joseph Gilpin house, near Chadd's Ford, Delaware County, Pennsylvania. (Historic American Buildings Survey, courtesy Library of Congress)

spoke to each other through this device, creating privacy. It provided an alternative to bundling during winter when a man and woman would find it awkward to talk freely while shivering around a hearth with many relatives trying to overhear their conversation. The courting stick allowed the couple to spend several hours whispering personal thoughts by the fireplace or somewhere else in the great hall while giving their parents the satisfaction of seeing the courtship develop under their own, very watchful eyes.

If courtship culminated in a desire to become man and wife, then the next step for a Puritan couple was to announce their intention at a public espousal ceremony. Espousals represented that time's equivalent of a formal engagement; they took place at one of the parties' home so that relatives could act as witnesses. Espousals customarily included a short sermon that emphasized marriage as a divinely ordained relationship based on a voluntary covenant between man and woman; after this the families undoubtedly toasted the prospective union with rum or wine. Connecticut law forbade espousals to take place until after the intended match had been publicly announced at least eight days prior. Although the other New England colonies passed no similar legislation, all of them viewed an espousal as a legally binding contract, and if either party broke it—such as by refusing to wed the other or marrying someone else—without just cause, he or she could be sued for breach of promise. Once espoused, furthermore, either the man or the woman having sex with another person was considered as adultery (which could be punished by death in Massachusetts, Connecticut, and New Haven colony) rather than simple fornication (which was not a capital offense). (Three executions did indeed take place for adultery, although in every case the crime occurred after marriage.)

Sexual Relations

An espousal represented such an irrevocable commitment to one another that popular sentiment viewed the couple as married for all practical purposes, even though the official ceremony had not yet happened. So strong was this view that if an espoused man and woman were later found to have surrendered to their sexual impulses and had intercourse before being married, their sin was considered as less serious than if no engagement had taken place. In Plymouth Colony, for example, the law forbade all sexual contact between unmarried persons, but the fine for this offense was four times higher for single persons than for an espoused couple. (The antifornication statute was nevertheless rarely employed in cases of prenuptial pregnancy; during the forty-five years prior to 1691, when Plymouth's population stood at 15,000, the colony's courts punished an average of less than two couples a year for having conceived a child prior to being married.) This rather indulgent view derived from traditional European folkways, which were at odds with the strict Puritan denunciation of fornication.

The usual custom in western Europe was that sex should never occur during courtship when no commitment to marry existed and that chaperones should accompany a couple to ensure that it did not. Once a couple had publicly announced their betrothal, however, they could meet without chaperones and had the opportunity to become intimate. If an engaged man and woman had intercourse between their espousal and marriage, their behavior was widely condoned and not considered a serious violation of sexual norms (although it was not entirely respectable either).

Premarital intercourse occurred at a far lower rate in New England than other parts of the Christian world. About 92% of first children born through 1680 were delivered nine months or more after their parents' marriage. (About every fifth baby that arrived less than nine months after its mother's marriage was born at least eight-and-a-half months later, and a significant number of these children were certainly premature infants of brides who had not been pregnant before their wedding night.) England's rate of premarital conception was about 21%, or almost three times as high. In a few towns, such as Andover

TABLE 17.2 PERCENT OF FIRST BABIES BORN LESS THAN NINE MONTHS AFTER PARENTS' WEDDING IN COLONIAL NEW ENGLAND

| Community | When Married | Percent of First Births Occurring | | | |
		Under 6 Months	Under 8.5 Months	Under 9 Months	After 9 Months
Andover, Mass.	1655–1674	0.0%	0.0%	0.0%	100.0%
	1675–1699	…	…	12.5%	87.5%
	1700–1730	…	…	11.5%	88.5%
	1731–1749	…	…	17.3%	82.7%
Boston, Mass.	1651–1655	3.6%	6.0%	14.3%	85.7%
	1690–1692	0.0%	17.9%	23.1%	76.9%
Coventry, Conn.	1711–1740	…	…	20.2%	79.8%
Dedham, Mass.	1662–1669	…	…	4.8%	95.2%
	1671–1680	2.8%	8.5%	11.1%	88.9%
Hingham, Mass.	1641–1660	0.0%	0.0%	0.0%	100.0%
	1661–1680	5.0%	11.2%	11.2%	88.8%
	1681–1700	3.5%	12.8%	18.6%	81.4%
	1701–1720	7.3%	13.8%	17.4%	82.6%
	1721–1740	11.6%	22.7%	27.3%	72.7%
	1741–1760	13.2%	31.2%	38.2%	61.8%
Hollis, N.H.	1741–1760	2.6%	12.8%	17.9%	82.1%
Ipswich, Mass.	1650–1687	3.8%	6.0%	8.2%	91.8%
	1701–1725	…	…	5.6%	94.4%
	1726–1750	…	…	6.3%	93.7%
Mansfield, Conn.	1700–1739	…	…	12.3%	87.7%
	1740–1769	…	…	19.2%	80.8%
Salem, Mass.	1651–1670	…	…	5.3%	95.7%
	1671–1700	…	…	8.2%	91.8%
	1701–1730	…	…	5.8%	94.2%
	1731–1770	…	…	12.5%	87.5%
Topsfield, Mass.	1660–1679	…	…	7.7%	92.3%
	1680–1699	2.3%	4.5%	6.8%	93.2%
	1738–1740	12.0%	24.0%	24.0%	76.0%
Watertown, Mass.	pre-1660	0.0%	11.1%	11.1%	88.9%
	1661–1680	0.0%	8.6%	8.6%	91.4%
	1681–1700	6.8%	9.1%	13.6%	86.4%
	1701–1720	7.9%	19.8%	25.1%	74.9%
	1721–1740	4.2%	18.7%	25.8%	74.2%
	1741–1760	10.9%	21.8%	23.6%	76.4%

Source: Daniel Scott Smith and Michael S. Hindus, "Premarital Pregnancy in America, 1640–1971," Journal of Interdisciplinary History, V (1975), 561–564.

and Hingham, Massachusetts, virtually all women were virgins on their wedding day during the period before 1680.

Rates of premarital pregnancy rose after 1680. The highest increases occurred in seaport towns rather than in more-traditional rural farming villages. Even so, for the entire period from 1641 to 1700, slightly more than 92% of first children were born at least eight-and-a-half months after their mother's wedding.

During the eighteenth century, however, premarital conception rose significantly in New England. The proportion of pregnant brides varied according to locale by the 1750s but seems to have ranged from lows of around 18% in Hollis, New Hampshire, to a high of 38% in Hingham, Massachusetts, with rates of 25%–30% being most typical. (Premarital conception also rose in England from about 21% in the early 1600s to about 35% during the last half of the eighteenth century.) By engaging more frequently in sex before marriage, New Englanders were not so much declining morally as resuming practices more akin to traditional European folk attitudes that tolerated intimate behavior between a couple formally engaged to be married.

New Englanders had no tolerance for illegitimacy, however. Because the overwhelming majority of couples abstained from intimacy at least until they were betrothed if not married, children born out of wedlock were almost nonexistent among seventeenth-century Puritans. (Illegitimacy was also exceedingly rare in contemporary England, where less than 2% of births occurred to unwed mothers during the period 1661–1720.) New England evidently maintained the lowest rate of illegitimacy not only in America but perhaps in Christendom; at the end of the colonial era, in 1764, for example, only one of every 130 births in Boston and surrounding Middlesex County, Massachusetts, were delivered to single mothers.

After their espousal ceremony, a couple would publicize through banns of matrimony their intention of marrying. Unless some knowledgeable persons offered any compelling information as to why the proposed union should not take place, they would then be wed after a betrothal period that usually lasted two or three months. Civil magistrates performed all weddings in early New England because although Puritans believed that marriage originated in the will of God, they did not accord it the status of a sacrament as did the Church of England, and they defined it primarily as a civil contract. Ministers did not receive authority to marry persons until 1686 when a reissue of the Massachusetts Bay charter gave them that power. Most Puritan ministers initially refused to perform the ceremony out of theological scruples, but many clergy were beginning to preside at weddings by the 1720s; this practice then spread from Massachusetts throughout New England.

Weddings

Having freed themselves from interference by the Church of England, Puritans no longer had to abide by its prohibitions against conducting marriages during Advent (the period from the fourth Sunday before Christmas to December 25) and Lent (the four-week interval from Ash Wednesday to Easter in spring). The peak season for weddings in New England was the three-month period encompassing the Christmas season—November, December, and January—with November being the most popular. April and May, which partly overlapped the Lenten season, were the next most-common months that couples chose for tying the knot.

Weddings remained unpretentious in New England during the colonial era. They were carried out by a justice of the peace at the bride's home. The actual ceremony entailed no exchange of vows, which Puritans considered unnecessary, nor of rings, which they rejected as a remnant of ancient pagan rituals. No preordained script existed for magistrates to follow while marrying couples, and so each justice made up his own, probably on the spur of the moment according to his familiarity with the families involved. This spontaneous event rarely lasted long and centered on the couple answering affirmatively that they would take one another as husband and wife, upon which they were declared married.

This brief ceremony, by custom, called for a wedding feast to celebrate the event. Although dancing and riotous merrymaking had no place in Puritan entertainment, no compelling barrier existed to savoring the moment with generous portions of rum and wine—for New Englanders were notoriously hard drinkers. The tradition of eating a special wedding cake, which dated back to medieval times, was a hallmark of New England weddings. On one occasion when a grain shortage induced the Massachusetts legislature to ban temporarily the baking and sale of luxury items like cakes and buns, a special exemption was made for wedding cakes.

While the spouses' families continued socializing, the bride's sisters, female cousins, and friends "chambered" her in a private room. A similar entourage then escorted her husband to her. The couple's escorts then retired outside and serenaded the newlyweds with a lusty shivaree that included whooping, whistling, clanging, and more than a few suggestions as to how the spouses might profitably use their time together. (While Puritans believed in decorum, they were not forerunners of the prudish Victorians and could be quite earthy under the right circumstances, such as a wedding night.)

The wedding night launched a couple into the central activity of families: begetting and raising children. New England produced a bumper crop of youngsters. Offspring appeared at a fairly regular interval of two years through the midforties. Infant mortality reduced the number of children who survived to adulthood but only by about 15% to 20%, a rate perhaps half that prevailing in densely populated Europe where deadly contagious diseases easily spread among vulnerable youngsters. This combination of relatively low mortality (by seventeenth-century standards) and a high birthrate (by any standard) generated an explosive rate of natural population growth, which was far in excess of the norm for western Europe.

Children

Large families became the norm in New England beginning with the first colony organized at Plymouth. By the 1670s, Plymouth households were raising an average of more than nine children who would reach adulthood; while birthrates in Plymouth were a bit higher than average, historical demographers have now verified beyond the shadow of any

TABLE 17.3 NUMBER OF CHILDREN BORN TO NEW ENGLAND FAMILIES IN COLONIAL AMERICA

Community	Date of Marriage	"Completed" Families[a]	All Families[b]
Andover, Mass.	1655–1674	8.3	8.3
	1675–1699	8.7	8.1
	1700–1730	7.6	7.2
Brookline, Mass.	1710–1810	7.2	6.5
Concord, Mass.	1750–1770	7.1	5.4
Hampton, N.H.	1638–1674	8.6	7.5
	1675–1699	7.3	6.7
	1700–1724	7.7	6.4
	1725–1749	7.2	6.9
Hingham, Mass.	to 1660	7.5	6.4
	1661–1680	7.9	7.7
	1681–1700	6.0	5.5
	1701–1720	5.6	4.8
	1721–1740	6.8	5.7
	1741–1760	7.2	6.3
Milford, Mass.	1660–1710	8.4	…
	1710–1740	7.4	…
	1740–1750	7.4	…
	1750–1760	7.8	…
	1760–1770	8.3	…
Nantucket, Mass.	1680–1739	7.2	…
Plymouth Colony	1621–1645	8.3	…
	1646–1670	8.7	…
	1671–1695	9.3	…
Sturbridge, Mass.	1730–1759	8.8	…
Waltham, Mass.	1671–1680	9.0	…
	1691–1700	8.3	…
	1701–1710	8.4	…
	1711–1720	8.5	…
	1721–1730	9.0	…
	1731–1740	9.7	…
Windsor, Conn.	1640–1659	7.7	…
	1660–1679	8.0	…
	1680–1699	7.2	…
	1700–1719	6.2	…
	1720–1739	7.6	…
	1740–1759	6.6	…
	1760–1779	7.1	…

[a] Families in which wife lived to age 40 (about 80% of families).
[b] All families, including those whose wife died before age 40.
Source: David Hackett Fischer, *Albion's Seed: Four British Folkways in America* (1989), 71.

doubt that high rates of fertility (averaging seven to eight offspring each) were the norm for New England families during the entire colonial period. The reproduction rate in New England, in fact, came very close to the biological maximum any early modern population could have attained given the medical profession's limited abilities to extend life in the 1600s.

A significant consequence of high birthrates was that as families multiplied exponentially across generations, the pool of potential spouses for young persons included an ever greater proportion of relatives in small towns. This situation conflicted with the Puritans' disapproval of cousins being married, based on the Mosaic prohibition in the Bible. Reality inevitably triumphed over theology, however, for after several generations, such complex and extensive kinship networks permeated rural society that a large minority of adults could not find compatible mates who were not connected in some way with their own families. In Guilford, Connecticut, during the mid-eighteenth century, 27% of parents had at least one child who took a cousin as a spouse, while an additional 12% of parents married two of their children to another pair of siblings. There was indeed a kernel of truth to the joking remark made about eighteenth-century Pepperell, Massachusetts, by Rev. Joseph Emerson, who said he "sometimes regretted that he did not marry a Shattuck, for he should then have been related to the whole town."

Another significant consequence of high birthrates was that children were almost evenly distributed within a family in a period of twenty to perhaps twenty-five years, unlike twentieth-century American households in which the offspring generally cluster together in the first six to eight years after marriage. This situation subtly affected a child's perception of generational differences. Unlike today, when the young can readily see a gulf between their own siblings and friends versus their parents and others of that age group, colonial youths saw a continuum in which the youngest children were toddlers, while elder brothers and sisters were adults who might even have children the same approximate age as their own youngest siblings. Under such circumstances, there was little opportunity for the sort of generation gap based on a self-conscious youth culture to emerge, as it has since the 1920s. Children spent most of their time in their parents' home rather than associating with others of their own age and so were less shaped by the influence of peer groups than are modern adolescents.

"It is striking that the seventeenth century (indeed all cultures before our own) had no real word for the period of life between puberty and full manhood," wrote historian John P. Demos, who also noted that the "term 'adolescence' is little more than seventy-five years old, at least in the sense of having a wide currency." Only *childhood* was seen to merit recognition as a unique phase in early personal development that entailed special consideration. Puritans hated idleness, but even they saw nothing untoward in letting youngsters "spend much time in pastime and play," for, as Rev. John Cotton explained, "their bodyes are too weak to labour, and their minds to study are too shallow."

New Englanders nevertheless judged their offspring to be fit enough for productive work at a far more tender age than modern sensibilities would ever allow. Three was the generally accepted birthday at which a child could start doing something useful around the house or barnyard. Although such chores were light, they served as a means of educating boys and girls into the rhythms of keeping a home and tending a garden. Boys began to dress in the fashion of adults about the age of six or seven, so they looked like miniature men and likewise began to assume more-important responsibilities around their father's farm or workshop.

Few New England fathers had sufficient land to leave all their sons some inheritance in real estate, so many tried to place younger boys as apprentices with craftsworkers whose children had already left home. Apprenticeship offered children upper mobility, but it also ripped many boys from their parents at a very young age. One such individual was Joseph Billington, who had been placed to learn a trade from John Cooke in Plymouth Colony about 1643. In that year, the General Court issued the following order pursuant to Cooke's complaint that he was being deprived of the value of young Joseph's labor with the connivance of his parents.

> Whereas Joseph, the son of Francis Billington ... was ... placed with John Cooke the younger, and hath since been inveagled, and did oft departe his said masters service, the Court, upon longe heareing of all that can be said or alleadged by his parents, doth order and appoynt that the said Joseph shalbe returned to his said master againe immediately, and shall so remaine with him during his terme; and that if either the said Francis, or Christian, his wyfe, do receive him, if he shall againe depart from his master without his lycence, that the said Francis, and Christian, his wyfe, shalbe sett in the stocks ... as often as he or shee shall so receive him

Behind the formalistic, legal language of that verdict lay the truly tragic dimension of this case: Joseph Billington was no mere truant defying his master's discipline; he was just a five-year-old boy.

Children imperceptibly but rapidly evolved into adults after age seven. According to English Common Law, girls might be married (with their parents' consent) as early as twelve because that was the youngest age at which a queen had become a bride. Boys began to train with the local militia company at sixteen, although they would not be sent to the field for combat until eighteen except in cases of extreme emergency. At eighteen, boys were universally acknowledged as having the right to leave their fathers' home and earn wages in their own right; in this way, they could begin to acquire the savings needed to buy the tools and possessions that would allow them to rent and operate a farm, which constituted the first step toward building savings to negotiate a mortgage.

Aging
As Puritan couples advanced in age, they gave increasing thought to their own mortality. "If a man is favored with long life," wrote Cotton Mather, one of New England's most respected ministers, "it is God who has lengthened his days." Of all the striking facets of popular life in early New England, one of the most underappreciated today concerns longevity among its settlers and the surprising appearance of grandparents in large numbers.

Few people today realize how unusual it was for western European adults to become grandparents centuries ago. In England, for example, most men wed just before age thirty and died in their early fifties, before their own children were likely to have wed and produced any offspring. Aged people were highly unusual, at least in social circles below the level of the gentry, whose wealth enabled them to live longer due to superior nutrition and better access to medical care.

Early New England diverged radically from those demographic patterns. Men and women were likely to live four decades or more after they married in their mid- or late-twenties and so became the first collective group in western society whose life cycle routinely included witnessing the arrival of several babies born to their own children. "New England," John M. Murrin has shrewdly pointed out, "might have been responsible for a simple but tremendously important invention, at least in terms of scale—grandparents."

In the South
The typical New England household possessed strength and nurtured tradition during the seventeenth century, but adverse socioeconomic and environmental conditions stretched the fabric of married life to the breaking point in the early South. A heavy imbalance of men over women kept a large part of the population from forming households. Low population density and poverty seem to have caused traditional marriage customs to fall into disuse for a long period before

1700. Rates of illegitimacy rose to levels far in excess of European norms. A ferocious disease environment moreover greatly weakened family structure through the premature death of parents.

Marriage

Unlike New England, where marriage was almost universal for adults, a large minority of colonists to the early South found it impossible to find spouses. Immigrants formed the vast majority of Virginia and Maryland's population until near the end of the 1600s, and for every three men who crossed the Atlantic to the Chesapeake, there was just one woman. This situation forced most males to delay marriage by a significant number of years while they waited their turn for a spouse to become available. So many men were never able to find a mate that in southern Maryland from 1650 to 1699, more than a quarter of all male property owners died unmarried.

At least three of every four immigrants came to the South as indentured servants. Before these individuals could marry, they had to wait for their terms of service to expire (usually four or five years), and then they had to spend several more years accumulating the savings necessary to set themselves up as a crafts worker or farmer. Ex-servants consequently had to delay marriage until their late twenties, often until twenty-seven or twenty-eight. American-born men were able to take brides two or three years sooner, at the usual age of twenty-four based on Darrett and Anita Rutman's study of late seventeenth-century Middlesex County, Virginia.

The scarcity of women greatly enhanced their status and allowed them to marry earlier than men. Female indentured servants still had to complete their contract, however, and most seem not to have become brides until age twenty-four or twenty-five in Maryland. American-born women could find husbands much earlier, and it was not unusual for them to wed as early as seventeen or eighteen prior to 1700. Native-born females married at a much earlier age in the South than in New England. Lois Green Carr and Lorena S. Walsh have reported that prior to 1670, first marriages of American-born women in Somerset County, Maryland, took place at an average age of 16.5, with the youngest bride being just twelve.

The Chesapeake endured a stagnant economy through most of the seventeenth century, and the area's low standard of living seems to have influenced its residents to dispense with many customs of courtship and marriage as unnecessary luxuries. The county courts rarely issued marriage licenses or kept a register of weddings. Banns of marriage were posted only in the most irregular fashion. Even wedding celebrations seem to have been rare, and almost no mention of marriage feasts can be found in surviving archival sources until after 1700.

A severe shortage of clergy kept many residents from being wed by a minister. This problem seems to have been greatest in Maryland, and it was compounded by the fact that justices of the peace lacked authority there to conduct marriages until the 1690s. A large proportion of couples simply wed themselves before 1720. It became customary to recognize any union as legitimate so long as its members lived together peacefully, pooled their labor and other economic resources for the household's support, and maintained an exclusive sexual partnership with each other. In other words, a sizable minority of people simply began to live together, said that they had been married in private, and succeeded in winning the larger community's acknowledgment of themselves as having formed bona fide households.

Sexual Relations

In a society where many people simply declared themselves husband and wife without benefit or clergy or any license from a magistrate, it is not surprising that rates of illegitimacy and prenuptial pregnancy reached high levels. Approximately one of every five female servants imported to Charles County, Maryland, came before the county court on charges of bearing a bastard child from 1658 to 1705. Most such "natural children" were evidently born by young female servants, but this problem also extended into the general population to a far greater degree than exclusively in New England and Great Britain. The best study of illegitimacy for this period has found that in Somerset County, Maryland, the rate of births to unwed mothers ranged between 6.3% and 11.8% during the years from 1666 to 1695. By contrast, illegitimacy was negligible in New England and very uncommon in old England where just 1% or 2% of children were born outside marriage from 1581 to 1720.

Premarital conception was even more common in the seventeenth-century Chesapeake. In Somerset County, Maryland, about a third of immigrant brides (mainly ex-servants) were pregnant when they married, although only a fifth of American-born women were expecting a child at the time of their wedding; these rates approximated levels of prenuptial pregnancy in old England, where the proportion of children born less than nine months after their parents' wedding ranged between 21% and 32% from 1550 to 1750.

Attitudes toward premarital sex were far more casual in the early South than in New England. Although legal presentments for conceiving a child before marriage were rare in New England, the Puritans there at least brought charges against women whose babies arrived within a scandalously short time after their marriage in order to make examples of them. Researchers have been unable to identify any prosecutions against married women for fornication prior to their wedding in Maryland's courts before 1700, and such cases also seem to have been extremely rare in Virginia.

TABLE 17.4 AVERAGE AGE AT FIRST MARRIAGE FOR HUSBANDS AND WIVES IN THE SOUTHERN AND MID-ATLANTIC COLONIES (WHITE FAMILIES ONLY)

Community	Date of Marriage	Age at First Marriage	
		Men	Women
Tidewater, Md.	1650–1700	…	16.8
	1700–1750	23.0	18.6
	1750–1800	25.0	22.2
Middlesex Co., Va. Former Servants	1680–1689	26.2	22.6
	1690–1699	28.1	19.6
	1700–1709	27.0	20.3
	1710–1719	27.3	…
Nonservants	1650–1669	28.2	18.0
	1670–1679	25.0	17.0
	1680–1689	24.1	17.0
	1690–1699	25.0	18.0
	1700–1709	24.0	18.7
	1710–1719	23.3	19.5
	1720–1729	24.5	19.7
	1730–1739	23.1	20.5
	1740–1749	26.4	21.3
Perquimans Co., N.C.	1720–1740	23.0	20.0
Chester Co., Pa.[a]	1681–1745	27.0	23.0
Lancaster Co., Pa.	pre-1741	25.0	20.9
	1741–1770	24.0	20.0

[a] Quakers only.

Sources: James M. Gallman, "Relative Ages of Colonial Marriages," *Journal of Interdisciplinary History*, XIV (1983–84), 613. Darrett and Anita Rutman, *A Place in Time: Explicatus* (1984), 64. Roger C. Henderson, "Demographic Patterns and Family Structure in Eighteenth-Century Lancaster Co., Pennsylvania," *Pennsylvania Magazine of History and Biography*, CXIV (1990), 357. Barry Levy, *Quakers and the American Family* (1988), 273. Allan Kulikoff, *Tobacco and Slaves: The Development of Southern Cultures in the Chesapeake, 1680–1800* (1986), 50, 60.

Children

Seventeenth-century southern families were smaller in size than New England households, even though Chesapeake women started to have babies at a younger age than their northern counterparts. At various times and places in Virginia and Maryland, the average family produced nine offspring, which equaled fertility among the Puritans. A high death rate (primarily due to complications from malaria) nevertheless snuffed out the lives of perhaps a quarter of all infants in their first year and then prevented up to 40% of all children from reaching age twenty. High mortality furthermore reduced average family size far below its biological potential by carrying off so many wives while they were still fertile. In seventeenth-century Middlesex County, Virginia, the typical mother died at age thirty-nine, and most women in Somerset County, Maryland, likewise did not live to age forty.

TABLE 17.5 PERCENT OF FIRST BABIES BORN LESS THAN AND MORE THAN NINE MONTHS AFTER PARENTS' WEDDING IN SOUTHERN AND MID-ATLANTIC COLONIES.

Community	When Married	Percent of First Births Occurring			
		Under 6 Months	Under 8.5 Months	Under 9 Months	After 9 Months
Gloucester Co., Va.	1749–1780	10.3%	21.8%	24.2%	75.8%
Middlesex Co., Va.	1720–1736	9.4%	15.2%	16.8%	83.2%
Richmond Co., Va.	1730–1749	...	33.3%[a]	...	66.7%
	1750–1759	...	38.5%	...	61.5%
Somerset Co., Md.					
Immigrants	1665–1695	23.7%	34.2%	36.8%	63.2%
Native-born	1665–1695	9.5%	19.0%	20.6%	79.4%
Bergen, N.J.	1665–1680	0.0%	5.6%	5.6%	94.4%
	1681–1700	...	...	19.4%	80.6%
	1701–1720	...	18.7%	25.0%	75.0%

[a] Measured in source as under 8.0 months.
Sources: Daniel Scott Smith and Michael S. Hindus, "Premarital Pregnancy in America, 1640–1971," *Journal of Interdisciplinary History,* V (1975), 561–64. David Hackett Fischer, *Albion's Seed: Four British Folkways in America* (1989), 298.

TABLE 17.6 NUMBER OF CHILDREN BORN TO FAMILIES IN THE SOUTHERN AND MID-ATLANTIC COLONIES

Community	Period	"Completed" Families[a]	All Families[b]
Middlesex Co., Va.	1650–1654[c]	7.0	...
	1655–1659	8.1	...
	1660–1664	9.6	...
	1665–1674	6.2	...
	1675–1679	5.9	...
	1680–1689	7.3	...
	1690–1694	7.4	...
	1695–1699	7.2	...
	1700–1704	7.3	...
	1705–1709	6.2	...
Somerset Co., Md.			
Immigrant whites	1665–1695[d]	6.1	3.9
Native-born whites	1665–1695	9.4	6.1
Tidewater, Md.	1650–1700[d]	9.4	3.3
	1700–1750	9.0	5.0
Virginia			
Elite Families	pre-1700[d]	8.5	...
	1701–1720	6.7	...

Community	Period	"Completed" Families[a]	All Families[b]
Germantown, Pa.	1680s[e]	...	5.8
New Paltz, N.Y.	1750–1774[d]	7.3	...
	1774–1779	8.9	...
New Jersey and New York Dutch	1685–1689[d]	8.9	...
	1760–1789	7.0	...
Pennsylvania Schwenkfelders	1735–1764[d]	5.3	...
	1765–1789	6.1	...
Quakers in Pennsylvania and New Jersey	before 1730[c]	7.5	6.7
	1731–1755	6.2	5.7
	1756–1785	5.1	5.0
Philadelphia, Pa. Elite Families	1700–1775[d]	9.2	7.5

[a] Families in which wife lived to age 40.
[b] All families, including those whose wife died under age 40.
[c] Cohort defined by date of birth.
[d] Cohort defined by date of marriage.
[e] Cohort defined by date of settlement.
Source: David Hackett Fischer, *Albion's Seed: Four British Folkways in America* (1989), 277, 483.

Death

The level of family disruption reached horrific dimensions in the Chesapeake and touched everyone, both rich and poor. In southern Maryland during the late 1600s, 67% of married men died before *any* of their heirs had reached adulthood; only 6% lived long enough to see all their children reach age twenty-one. In seventeenth-century Middlesex County, Virginia, a quarter of all children lost one (or both) parents before age five, more than half before age thirteen, and almost three-quarters before reaching twenty-one. Forty-one percent of Middlesex County families produced orphans who had lost both their natural parents before age twenty-one.

Parental authority withered under such circumstances. In sharp contrast to New England, where patriarchs exercised enormous influence over their offspring's marriage plans, Chesapeake parents rarely lived long enough to meddle in their adult children's lives. The South's high rate of premarital conception stemmed in part from the freedom that adolescents enjoyed over their private affairs. In seventeenth-century Somerset County, Maryland, for example, the proportion of brides already pregnant on their wedding day was 10% for those with fathers still alive but 30% for those who were orphans.

Survivors of a spouse's death quickly remarried and generally chose a partner who was also a widow or widower, but this step did little to reinforce parental authority because so many of these matches were subsequently shattered by premature death. Young William Hollis of Baltimore County, Maryland, for example, lost his father and then had three new stepfathers in just seven years. By the age of ten, Agatha Vause of Middlesex County, Virginia, had experienced the deaths of her father, two stepfathers, her mother, and finally a guardian uncle. A very large proportion of children thus experienced what could only be described as serial parentage.

Boys and girls probably matured quickly in the Chesapeake as they learned to deal with death and other realities of an uncertain future. "Before I was ten years old," wrote William Fitzhugh of Stafford County, Virginia, in 1698, "I look'd upon life here as but going to an Inn, no permanent being." Children began to work at household and farmyard chores about age three; they may have enjoyed less play than northern youngsters—aside from fighting. Scholars who have analyzed seventeenth-century southern probate records have noted that one can read through volumes of highly detailed inventories and yet find no mention at all of toys.

In a world where orphanhood was the common experience, and stepfathers stood a strong chance of dying shortly after marrying a widow, adoption was superfluous. Adoption did not exist, at least as it is known today, and children simply entered new households as wards. Orphans retained their surnames when they joined a new household or were put out as apprentices to learn a trade. Robert Beverley's household at Middlesex County, Virginia, for example, included not only several of his biological offspring but also two stepchildren named Keeble (by his first wife) and another named Hone (by his second wife). Children matured in a complex genealogical web of quasi-kinship, populated by half-siblings, quarter-cousins, and affinal relatives acquired by virtue of sequential marriages.

These fragile kinship ties steadily became stronger through the marriage of cousins and in-laws. One study of pre-existing kinship between spouses has shown that the percentage of cousins marrying one another doubled in Prince George's County, Maryland, during the period from 1700 to 1760. Pairs of brothers and sisters also became more likely to unite during that time. In the sparsely settled South, one of the major consequences of these interrelated matrimonial patterns was a tendency for kindred families to socialize primarily with themselves and in effect to acquire a sense of exclusivity from the larger community. This development served to fragment the rural

TABLE 17.7 KINSHIP TIES BETWEEN SPOUSES IN MARRIAGES OF PRINCE GEORGE'S COUNTY, MD., 1700–1760

Type of Marriage	1700–1730	1730–1760
Marriage Between Blood Relatives	...	...
Between first cousins	3%	6%
Between second cousins	...	4%
Between More Remote Blood Relatives	7%	12%
Totals	10%	22%
Marriage Between In-Laws or Other Affinal Relatives		
Between brother-in-law & sister-in-law	3%	6%
Between step-sibling & sibling's cousin	...	2%
Between more remote affinal relatives	5%	10%
Totals	8%	19%
Total With No Known Kinship Ties	81%	59%

Source: Allan Kulikoff, *Tobacco and Slaves: The Development of Southern Cultures in the Chesapeake, 1680–1800* (1986), 254.

South into extended clans, defined by both bloodline and marriage alliances, that provided an important source of security and mutual help but also increasingly turned inward upon themselves. Unlike the North, where a wide range of interrelatedness among families tended to promote cohesion within society, kinship networks in the South would often engender narrowness and divisiveness. In their most extreme form, they would later provide the tinder that would explode into the family feuds of the southern Appalachians during the late nineteenth century. Through such extended and tangled rings of cousinry, southern families eventually managed to establish their own individual identities and traditions, even if the results were somewhat socially dysfunctional.

Southern society evolved under agonizing circumstances during its first century of settlement. Life changed dramatically as the eighteenth century progressed, however. The proportion of males and females became roughly even, and this allowed nearly all adults the chance to marry if they wished. Once the population became predominantly native-born, its ability to withstand the local disease environment improved, life expectancy lengthened, and birthrates climbed upward.

Aging

Increasing health and longevity were especially notable among the people who settled the Piedmont from western Maryland to the Carolina backcountry after 1710. In this elevated terrain, they escaped the ravages of malaria, which infested the tidewater, and enjoyed a level of health that their grandparents could scarcely have imagined. Adults lived into their sixties—if not older—so that for the first time, large numbers of native southerners experienced the satisfaction of being grandparents. The number of children raised by southern families steadily grew through the eighteenth century until, by 1790, the first national census revealed that average family size in Virginia (6.0) exceeded the comparable figure for New England (5.7). By the end of the colonial era, then, the differences between family life in the North and South, which had been drastic during the 1600s, had largely converged so that households in both halves of Anglo-America basically resembled one another.

Recreations

Human nature has certainly undergone little basic change through the ages, but the manner in which its idiosyncrasies have manifested themselves through history has evolved significantly. Colonial Americans spent their leisure time in many activities still popular in the twentieth century, but the cultural context in which their behavior took place was often different. The subject of humor is one such example.

While it cannot be doubted that early Americans appreciated a good laugh, they do not seem to have enjoyed many of them. The stereotype of Puritans as incorrigibly stolid and dour appears to have been rooted in a grain of historical truth. Few jokes survive from early New England, of which the most ancient seems to be the following mock exchange, allegedly between a tax collector from Boston and an "Honest, Ingenious Countryman," that Lawrence Hammond of late seventeenth-century Charlestown, Massachusetts, preserved in his diary.

"What Newes Countryman?" the exciseman inquired.
"I know none," the rustic responded.
"I'll tell you som," came the reply.
"What is it?" said the countryman.
"The Devil is Dead," came the reply.
"How! I believe that not," the rustic insisted.
"Yes, he is dead for certaine," the tax collector assured him.
"Well then," the countryman drawled, "if he be dead, he hath left many fatherless Children in Boston."

It should go without saying that the early Yankees were not exactly awash in knee-slappers.

Drinking

The most common diversion among early Americans was certainly drinking. Whether functioning more as a pleasure or a vice, it was ubiquitous. One of the Virginia Company's earliest projects for developing Virginia's economy was to establish vineyards so that wine could be fermented. The colonists generally preferred stronger beverages, however, and they gave much immediate attention to sowing grains from which whiskey could be distilled and to planting orchards that would guarantee a source of brandy and cider.

In contrast to modern times, no religous groups condemned the consumption of alcohol on theological grounds. Puritan scholars carefully distinguished between the legitimate use of spirits, which they recognized as a gift from God to help relieve humanity's morose condition, and their abuse through drunkenness. Puritans considered each individual to be charged morally with using alcohol responsibly and viewed its temptations as one of many trials a saint would have to overcome in achieving salvation. They consequently never advocated prohibition, only self-restraint.

Quakers were one of the most moralistic sects ever to arise in Christendom, but they took the same position as Puritans did. The Society of Friends did not hesitate from forbidding access to a wide range of human pleasures, ranging from fashionable silk clothes to painted portraits of themselves, but it allowed members to imbibe alcoholic beverages so long as they did not abuse them. In one of his pamphlets written to encourage Quakers to emigrate from England to Pennsylvania, William Penn specifically promised that they would find plenty of beer to slake their thirst because one of the city's first enterprises was "a large brewhouse [built] in order to furnish the people with good drink, both there and up and down the river."

The trustees of Georgia believed that hard liquor would present insurmountable temptations to the discharged debtors with whom they wished to colonize that colony, so they banned all alcohol but highly expensive Portuguese Madeiras that an ordinary settler could not afford. This experiment in prohibition drew howls of protest from exasperated pioneers who only wanted to ameliorate the tedium of life on a sparsely inhabited frontier. One resident denounced this policy by asserting that the inhabitants lived under such extreme privations that they deserved the right to choose whether to be "quite Forlorn without hopes or Mad with Liquor." Seven years after outlawing alcohol, the trustees reversed themselves and ordered local authorities to allow the importation of whiskey, lest the prohibition would deter so many people from moving there that Georgia's population would stagnate or decline.

Early Americans consumed spirits at a prodigious rate. Yearly consumption has been estimated for each adult (aged fifteen or older) at 3.8 gallons of distilled liquor, 0.2 gallons of wine, and 34 gallons of fermented cider as of 1710 for an annual total of 5.1 gallons of absolute alcohol each. By the late 1760s, the white population of the thirteen colonies apparently guzzled about 7,750,000 gallons of rum annually, or more than 4 gallons for every man, woman, and child. Converting this figure into 21 gallons per adult white male—the group responsible for downing nearly all the total—it would appear that this volume of drinking could have only been sustained if every white male over age fifteen drank 3 pints of rum each week, or an average of seven one-ounce shots daily. It has become a cliche among early American economic historians to say that the thirteen colonies floated their oceanic trade in a sea of rum, but as John McCusker has reminded them, the colonists did not float in that sea of rum—*they drank it.*

Gambling

Drinking usually begot gambling. New Englanders catagorized alcohol among the gifts bestowed on humanity by a generous deity, but they denied that gambling came under the same heading. Puritans denounced gaming as a refusal to accept the station that the Lord seemed to intend for an individual to occupy at any moment in his life; they believed that it constituted an arrogant rejection of God's will. Dealing cards or rolling dice represented an attempt to rely on fortune rather than divine providence and as such bordered on blasphemy. On a more practical level,

A rising standard of living allowed American colonists to enjoy more sociable amenities during the eighteenth century. Tea was considered a luxury in the late seventeenth century, but its use had become widespread among the middle classes by the 1760s. High teas, like the one portrayed above, were starting to become a diversion among the wealthiest circles of Americans by that time, although they were still rare. By enjoying their refreshment on a rooftop, this smart set seems to be taking the term *high tea* to its most literal of meanings. (Courtesy Library of Congress)

gambling also undermined character by tempting the weak to seek prosperity through easy wagers rather than cultivating the self-discipline required for a life of thrift and hard, steady work. Massachusetts outlawed gambling entirely not only in public venues like taverns but also in the privacy of one's home. Its magistrates even attempted to suppress shuffleboard and apparently looked with disfavor on skittles. By the mid-eighteenth century, however, New England's opposition to gambling had withered considerably, and Boston newspapers carried notices of purses to be wagered on horseraces, which were evidently being held in the open, although they were still illegal.

TABLE 17.8 LEGALLY LICENSED LOTTERIES HELD IN THE BRITISH COLONIES, 1744–1762

Year	Number (Value)	Distribution by Colony
1762	17 (£33,350)	1 Conn. (£250); 1 Mass. (£1,000); 2 N.J. (£3,400); 1 N.Y. (£3,000); 12 R.I. (£25,700)
1761	10 (£26,300)	1 Conn. (£300); 1 Mass. (£2,000); 1 N.J. (£1,000); 2 N.Y. (£5,000); 1 N.C. (unknown); 4 R.I. (£18,000)
1760	13 (£40,410)	2 Conn. (£800); 6 Mass. (£7,410); 2 N.H. (£6,000); 3 R.I. (£26,200)

Year	Number (Value)	Distribution by Colony
1759	10 (£10,844)	2 Conn. (£100); 3 Mass. (£3,494); 1 N.H. (£600); 1 N.J. (£1,800); 1 N.C. (£450); 2 R.I. (£4,400)
1758	4 (£63,450)	2 Mass. (£31,200); 1 N.Y. (£2,250); 1 R.I. (£30,000)
1757	4 (£15,615)	1 Conn. (£8,000); 1 Mass. (£1,215); 2 N.H. (£6,400)
1756	5 (£14,275)	1 Mass. (£3,000); 3 N.Y. (£1,275); 1 R.I. (£10,000)
1755	2 (£290)	1 Conn. (unknown); 1 Mass. (£290)
1754	3 (£7,785)	1 Conn. (£660); 1 N.Y. (£1,125); 1 Va. (£6,000)
1753	4 (£34,250)	1 Conn. (£2,000); 2 N.Y. (£2,250); 1 R.I. (£30,000)
1751	1 (unknown)	1 Conn. (unknown)
1750	3 (£38,264)	2 Mass. (£27,900); 1 R.I. (£10,364)
1749	1 (£4,900)	1 Mass. (£2,500); 1 R.I. (£2,400)
1748	2 (£4,800)	1 N.Y. (£1,800); 1 R.I. (£3,000)
1747	2 (£17,500)	1 Conn. (£7,500); 1 R.I. (£10,000)
1746	2 (£5,625)	2 N.Y. (£5,625)
1744	2 (£10,500)	1 Mass. (£7,500); 1 R.I. (£3,000)

Source: John S. Ezell, *Fortune's Merry Wheel: The Lottery in America* (1960), 55–59.

Billiards appeared as a popular diversion during the eighteenth century, but their use was still largely limited to taverns in the cities and larger market towns. This eighteenth-century sketch suggests that habitués of the game did not enjoy much public esteem. (Courtesy Library of Congress)

Aside from Quakers, other colonial Americans found enormous excitement in gambling. By the 1760s, not only cards and dice but also billiard tables were standard equipment at a large number of taverns. Virginia's courts defined a gambling bet as a type of legal contract that was enforceable at law.

Southerners in particular embraced games of chance with true gusto, as a French visitor named Durand discovered while visiting Jamestown, Virginia, in 1686. After taking lodgings at a tavern with several members of the House of Burgesses, he found that his companions started to gamble soon after dinner and were still hard at it past midnight. When one of the planters noticed that the Frenchman was politely waiting for them to conclude their card game before going to bed, he advised him to retire and get his sleep. "'For,'" as Durand quoted him, "'it is quite possible that we shall be here all night,' and in truth I found them still playing the next morning."

Lotteries also achieved widespread popularity among the colonists. Early Virginia's settlement had been heavily financed by national lotteries operated in England under terms of the Virginia Company's charter of 1612. Similar drawings did not become common in Anglo-America until the mid-eighteenth century, however. Private individuals began to use them as a means of paying off debts or raising capital for some major investment. The assemblies uniformly moved to prohibit unlicensed drawings but allowed promoters to hold them if they obtained prior legislative approval.

Legally sanctioned lotteries started to appear on a regular basis during the late 1740s. Of the eighty-five drawings licensed from 1747 to 1762, sixty-five were held in New England and twenty-nine in Rhode Island alone. Even provincial governments sponsored lotteries when they were pressed for cash. Connecticut, Massachusetts, Rhode Island, and Virginia all raised money for military expenses through lotteries during the Seven Years' War, although not on a regular basis. Harvard, King's College (now Columbia), and the College of New Jersey (now Princeton) also received permission to raise funds through drawings during this period and so anticipated the widespread use of lotteries by modern American states to help defray the cost of their school systems.

Sports and Games

Few colonists could indulge in sports and other games as often as western Europeans might because the low population density made it extremely difficult to form teams on a regular basis. The most-frequent sporting activity seems to have been matches that involved individual competition, such as wrestling, boxing, running, jumping, throwing knives, hurling tomahawks, and shooting at marks with guns. There is no record of women or girls engaging in athletic games, and it seems that the female role in sports then consisted in watching the boys display their prowess, much as it unfortunately continued to be among Americans until the late twentieth century.

As population density swelled, some Americans, especially those in New England, could play team sports imported from England. The "Boston game" was one such diversion; it primarily entailed scoring points by kicking a leather ball through ones' opponents and then past some defined goal line. New Englanders added their own rules to this game, which achieved much popularity as a schooltime diversion during the late eighteenth century, when it was also known popularly as football.

New Englanders also refined another sport of English origin, rounders, which was variously called town ball, round ball, or the Massachusetts game in the colonies. In town ball, two teams took turns trying to score points earned by players who could hit a ball thrown by an opposing pitcher and then run around a square marked by four bases about 50 feet apart before being intercepted by an opponent carrying the ball. This Massachusetts game increased widely in popularity during the late 1700s among schoolboys; it first seems to have been referred to by its modern title in 1786 when a student at Princeton wrote about it using the name "baste ball." "What is now the American national game was originally a New England folk sport," David Hackett Fischer has shrewdly observed. "It still preserves a combination of order and action, reason and emotion, individuality and collective effort which was characteristic of Puritan culture."

CHAPTER 18 Crime and Violence

Law Enforcement and Crime

Early proponents of English colonization had encouraged their countrypeople to settle North America by intimating that refuge might be found across the Atlantic from the Old World's iniquity and crime. John Winthrop, the first governor appointed for Massachusetts Bay, for instance, had begun to refer to England as "this sinfull lande" as early as 1622. Seven years later, on sadly concluding that his country had grown "weary of her Inhabitants," Winthrop decided to forsake his native land, which seemed overrun by fraud and petty criminals driven to desperation by poverty.

None of the earliest colonists were so naive as to imagine that the New World would be free of sin, crime, or violence, but they harbored strong hopes that vice could be kept well below levels that prevailed in western Europe. "Many who in *England* have been lewd and idle," wrote John Hammond in 1656 while describing Virginia and Maryland, "... not onely grow ashamed of their former courses, but abhor to hear of them, and in small time wipe off those stains they have formerly been tainted with." "[Y]et I cannot but confesse, there are people wicked enough (as what Country is free) for we know some natures will never be reformed," Hammond conceded, "but ... if any be known, either to prophane the Lords day or his Name, be found drunk, commit whoredome, scandalize or disturb his neighbour, or give offence to the world by living suspiciously in any bad courses; there are for each of these, severe and wholsome laws and remedies made." Anglo-Americans could not entirely escape the legacy of original sin, but they would strive to restrain its effects.

Law Enforcement Officers

The thirteen colonies contained no full-time cadre of hired officers comparable in any way to a modern police force. Sheriffs were the only officials who held a full-time position responsible for keeping order, but none of them devoted much of their time to either crime prevention or suppression. A sheriff functioned primarily to oversee county government, particularly in regard to assessing property, collecting taxes, and conducting elections. His chief involvement with law enforcement stemmed from his role as an agent of the courts, which primarily entailed delivering writs to summon jurors, defendants, and jurors for trials and enforcing legal verdicts through the distraint of property or carrying out public punishments like whippings or executions.

Constables were the officials whose duties most approximated that of modern police officers; they neither worked full-time nor earned a regular salary, however. Each county court appointed its own constables, who acted as the sheriff's deputies whenever he found need for their services during their year's tour of duty. In lieu of pay, constables obtained reimbursement on a per diem basis for being called from their fields or shops to execute warrants, post legal notices at distant points, and attend court sessions. They also ranked as "conservators of the peace," a position that authorized them to disarm individuals deemed dangerous, suppress fights or tumults, and take unruly persons into custody for violations of public order. The job's fees barely compensated its holder for the many inconveniences incurred while carrying out its unpredictable obligations, so constables had little incentive to act as vigilant keepers of the peace, especially when doing so would engender ill-feeling by neighbors and relatives—much less to risk serious bodily harm. Few constables held the office beyond their year's appointment, and it was common for prosperous men to avoid serving by paying a designated fine instead.

Large cities augmented their constabulary forces with a nightwatch. New York established its own in 1698 and charged the personnel with perambulating "round the Citty Each Hour in the Night with a Bell and there to proclaime the season of the weather and the Hour of the Night and if they Meet in their Rounds Any people disturbing the peace or lurking about Any persons house or committing any theft they take the most prudent way they Can to Secure the said persons." The earliest of such watches went unpaid, and even after compensation was granted, their services were still undervalued relative to the trouble and potential danger. Most nightwatchmen consequently did their duties without enthusiasm or efficiency, and the greatest benefit of their service lay in being able to detect and stop any nocturnal fires before they might consume an entire neighborhood in a general conflagration.

Jailors constituted virtually the sole, full-time, paid law-enforcement officials in colonial America. Their jails primarily functioned as a place of pretrial and presentencing custody for people unable to post sufficient bond. Jails also served as a place of confinement for debtors until they sold off enough assets to satisfy their creditors. The threat of being locked up provided a major incentive to avoid transgressing the law or falling into debt, for conditions were abysmal. Patrick Mulvany, awaiting trial from a cell in New York City, lamented in 1766 that he had "nothing but the bare floor to lay on—no covering—almost devour'd with all kinds of Vermine." Winter was especially brutal on inmates in places like New York City's jail, where debtors and other prisoners had to supply their own firewood. In 1751, the detainees there arranged for the *New-York Gazette* to print an entreaty begging the public for charity funds because they did not have "one Stick to burn in freezing weather."

Punishment

Incarceration performed the purpose of coercing behavior (either to guarantee appearance at trial or to compel debtors into making full restitution) rather than serving as a legal punishment. Early Americans were extremely loathe to place criminals behind bars for long periods because the public would have to bear the cost of feeding and guarding them. No pentitentiaries consequently existed for long-term punishment of felons until Connecticut's legislature acted to finance one in 1773, and as late as 1800, prisons for long-term detention of convicted criminals existed in only half the states.

Instead of imprisonment, colonial courts relied most heavily on fines and corporal punishment. Fines predominated as the most common penalty for misdemeanors such as breach of the peace, public drunkenness, prophaning the sabbath, and such minor morals offenses as fornication. Judges had the option of forgiving fines for many such crimes if the malefactor publicly acknowledged the error of his or her ways and appeared likely to avoid similar trouble in the future. For those people who seemed less genuinely repentant, the courts might alternately compel them to post a bond for good behavior, which (unlike a remitted fine) could be forfeited at any later date when its conditions were broken.

Individuals who could neither pay their fines and fees nor reimburse people they had injured might also be sold into indentured servitude. The court and their victims would then obtain restitution from the price paid for their labor. During the seventeenth century, courts on the North American mainland also commonly banished persistent criminals overseas to the West Indies, and in the Seven Years' War, some justices gave guilty parties the choice of accepting an unusually onerous punishment (like whipping) or enlisting in a royal regiment for the conflict's duration.

Corporal punishment existed for more-serious offenses like theft, counterfeiting, prostitution, and vicious assaults. Flogging was the most frequently used penalty of this type; nearly all such sentences were set at thirty-nine lashes or less. Whipping was especially ignominious because it was always done publicly and invariably attracted substantial crowds. In 1743, one Philadelphia felon found the prospect of being beaten bloody in front of a large throng, which would certainly include nearly all his acquaintances, so intolerably humiliating that on reaching the whipping post, he drew a knife hidden within his clothing and cheated the court out its sentence by slitting his own throat.

When the courts wished to deter particular crimes that were either hard to detect or had recently risen to the level of a major nuisance, they usually sent the perpetrators to be pilloried on a date when the maximum number of people would be able to observe their fate, such as a market day or when the next court convened. The least part of enduring the pillory involved being locked in stocks for an hour while the assembled crowd jeered and pelted one's head and torso with everything from rocks to animal waste. The worst part only came after this preliminary ordeal had passed and the crowd began to cheer while the sheriff sliced off one or both of the prisoner's ears.

Capital punishment constituted law enforcement's ultimate sanction. Significant differences existed between legislation regarding death sentences in Anglo-America and Great Britain. Most colonies in New England enacted legal codes reflecting the orthodox Puritan belief that execution should not be imposed without a "warrant from God's word." New Englanders consequently prescribed death for extremely few crimes against property, even when the same transgression would merit execution under English law. Under the twenty-five statutes authorizing execution passed by Massachusetts Bay from 1630 to 1684, for example, death could only be imposed for two felonies concerning property, namely upon a third conviction for either robbery or burglary. By premising their legal code on Mosaic law, however, New Englanders made many crimes into capital offenses that did not merit death in Old England. Capital violations unique to the Puritan colonies included blasphemy, bestiality, incest, adultery, perjury that placed another's life in jeopardy, and stubborn disobedience toward one's father.

After 1700, however, New England's governments brought their legal codes into closer conformity with Britain's by establishing noncapital punishments for virtually all the Mosaic offenses that were previously subject to the death penalty (although each of them remained outlawed). Like other Anglo-American governments in the Mid-Atlantic and southern colonies, New England's legislatures also made a growing number of crimes against property punishable by death. The mainland colonies nevertheless reserved the death sentence for genuinely serious violations

Stocks and pillories were almost ubiquitous features of eighteenth-century courthouse yards. This stock and pillory are reconstructions built at Williamsburg, Virginia. (Courtesy Library of Congress)

against property and kept the list short. In Massachusetts, for example, the only additions to the register of capital crimes were several types of counterfeiting (after 1703), a second conviction for robbery (1711), first-time burglary (1715), a third conviction for theft (1737), and first-time robbery (1761). The spareness of this list contrasts sharply with the example set by Britain's Parliament, which attempted to counter a perceived increase in crime by extending the death penalty almost willy-nilly in regard to property crimes until there were an estimated 154 offenses for which British courts might execute someone by 1770, including any theft valued over twelve pennies (which included some articles as minor as a handkerchief), cutting down trees in an orchard, and breaking a pond dam so that fish escaped.

Judicial System

Final responsibility for law enforcement lay with each county's justices of the peace. These magistrates could issue summary decisions in cases of a minor nature, such as debt suits and a wide range of misdemeanors including public drunkenness or sabbath breaking, at private hearings termed petty sessions. To punish felonies like assault or burglary, three or more were required to deliberate collectively at monthly meetings of the county court or at quarter sessions where they would be joined by a judge from their province's highest court of appeal.

The court system's effectiveness was undermined by the fact that the overwhelming majority of magistrates were essentially part-time amateur jurists. Most members of the bench were wealthy landowners who obtained their positions through the political influence of family or other close associates. Not surprisingly, this situation led to a significant number of unsuitable or unmotivated men being placed on the courts. Of the 328 men serving as justices of the peace for the province of New York in 1763, one study concluded that at least 59% of them possessed neither legal training nor experience. Research into the functioning of local justice in Richmond County, Virginia, has found that in most years from 1714 to 1747, its court failed to convene for almost half of its required monthy sessions (missing an average of five out of twelve) because too few members attended to make a quorum. An examination of North Carolina's eighteenth-century legal system has determined that, at a minimum, one of every ten justices appeared in court—at some point in their adult lives—to face charges of criminal conduct, including assault, trespass, theft, extortion, and even a few murders.

Trial proceedings differed significantly from modern practices in most colonies during much of the colonial period. Judicial hearings did not follow the principles of today's well-developed, adversarial system but operated by a process more accurately described as inquisitorial. Whereas modern courtrooms attempt to insulate judges from any bias toward defendants by establishing a strict division of responsibilities between judge and prosecutor, it was the colonial justices of the peace who themselves assembled evidence against the accused, prosecuted the case by interrogating both the defendant and all witnesses, rendered a judgment, and passed sentence. The only real check on the judges came from grand juries, which possessed the sole authority to make an indictment.

Another serious disadvantage to criminal defendants was the absence of any recognized right for the accused to be represented by a lawyer. The colonies experienced such a shortage of attorneys during the colonial era, especially before 1720, that it would have been impossible for defendants to find counsel to all defendants, even assuming that their services could be paid for—because no public defenders existed. Most attorneys, moreover, preferred to practice property law, which was highly lucrative, and avoided criminal cases. The career of William Livingston, one of New York's most eminent

TABLE 18.1   DISTRIBUTION OF CRIMINAL CASES TRIED IN COLONIAL AMERICAN JURISDICTIONS COMPARED TO MODERN UNITED STATES

Crimes	New York[a] 1691–1776	North Carolina 1750–1759	Richmond Co., Va. 1714–1749	Chester Co., Pa. 1726–1755	United States 1995[e]
Violence Against Persons					
a) assaults	21.5%	38.5%	30.3%[b]	27.7%	14.1%
b) murder	...	1.8%	4.3%	...	0.1%
Property Crimes					
a) theft-burglary	13.7%	11.6%	21.1%	20.8%	15.6%
b) fraud	1.9%	...	...	1.1%	3.8%
c) trespass	...	6.8%	...	0.9%	...
Offenses Against Public Order					
a) disturbing the peace	18.8%	2.2%	[c]	4.5%	5.0%
b) contempt of authority	5.9%	2.8%	...	1.3%	...
c) prostitution	3.6%	...	...	1.2%	0.7%
d) illegal conduct with slaves	1.9%	...	...	...	...
e) misc. morals offenses	...	6.1%	...	22.9%	6.4%
f) breach of licensing & economic laws	...	...	44.3%[d]	2.3%	3.9%
Crimes by Public Officials	3.8%	...	...	...	...
Others	28.9%	30.2%	...	17.4%	50.4%

[a] Colony.
[b] Includes breaking the peace.
[c] Tabulated under assault.
[d] Includes keeping disorderly houses.
[e] Based on arrests, not crimes tried.
Sources: Douglas Greenberg, *Crime and Law Enforcement in the Colony of New York, 1691–1776* (1976), 21, 88. Donna J. Spindel, *Crime and Society in North Carolina, 1663–1776* (1989), 46. Peter C. Hoffer, ed., *Criminal Proceedings in Colonial Virginia* (1984), lvi. Alan Tully, *William Penn's Legacy: Politics and Social Structure in Provincial Pennsylvania, 1726–1755* (1977), 190–91. Federal Bureau of Investigation, *Uniform Crime Reports, 1995* (1996), 209.

lawyers, seems to have been entirely typical of the legal profession. While a member of the bar from 1741 to 1772, he argued more than 600 cases before New York's Supreme Court, but only sixteen of these (less than 3%) concerned criminal proceedings.

Jury trials were also employed far less in the colonial era than in subsequent times. The colony of New Haven operated its legal system solely according to summary, inquisitorial justice and dispensed with juries entirely. All other colonies guaranteed juries for crimes meriting the death sentence, but most failed to utilize them for lesser felonies and virtually all misdemeanors. Connecticut, to cite just one instance, held just seventeen jury trials prior to 1663, and none of these were for what would be considered an ordinary crime. (In civil cases involving debts or disputed property, however, juries were generally called, and this anomaly would indicate that early Americans placed a higher value on protecting their property than affording any advantages to accused criminals.) It became more common for courts to impanel juries in noncapital cases after 1700, but the practice continued to be rare in some jurisdictions. In Richmond County, Virginia, for example, juries decided just six cases involving people accused of crimes that did not carry the threat of execution for the accused during the entire period from 1711 to 1754.

Conviction rates were exceptionally high during the seventeenth century. Courts in New Haven convicted 90% of the accused prior to that colony being annexed by Connecticut. For much of the period before 1690, conviction rates in Massachusetts and Connecticut were just as high. Fewer defendants seem to have been found guilty as the eighteenth century advanced, at least outside of New England. North Carolina's county courts convicted just 45% of the accused during the century prior to 1776. During the period from 1691 to 1775, New York's courts found 52% of all defendants guilty.

Most sentences handed down by courts were monetary rather than corporal or capital. In North Carolina, from 1663 to 1776, the courts punished 75.7% of all defendants found guilty with fines, 10.1% with flogging, 1.7% with being pilloried, 6.6% with death, and 5.9% with other exactions. The number of executions was far less than the conviction rate might indicate because colonial judges allowed persons to cheat the hangman by entering the ancient plea of "benefit of clergy," in which a death sentence was canceled for any person able to read a prescribed—and universally known—verse from the Bible. (This custom dated from the Middle Ages when priests and monks composed the overwhelming majority of literate persons.) This plea was only valid once in a lifetime, however, and anyone using it was branded with a "C" on the thumb for identification. Through benefit of clergy or outright pardons, 35% of death sentences were apparently set aside in North Carolina, as were 52% of capital convictions in New York province.

Relatively few executions seem to have taken place in the colonies. There were twenty-five offenses for which death could be imposed in seventeenth-century Massachusetts, but capital punishment was only imposed under nine of them before 1693. Between 1630 and 1692 in Massachusetts, the number of executions totaled about forty (not counting another twenty-three hung as witches) and averaged less than one per year. Even as late as the period 1750–96, when the population of Massachusetts had grown to exceed a half-million, hangings averaged less than three a year.

Crime Rates

The most common crimes tried by the courts concerned offenses against people, property, and public order. These three categories generally composed more than two-thirds of the courts' docket. In Massachusetts, the bench most often heard cases involving slander, fornication, assault (either threatened or actual), and disorderly conduct. The proportion of trials concerned with assault was twice as high in the colonial period as in the modern United States, while the pro-

portion of cases involving larceny, trespass, and other property offenses was roughly the same in both periods.

Morals offenses composed a larger portion of court actions in seventeenth-century New England than elsewhere in Anglo-America. Most such charges concerned nonattendance at church, offensive behavior such as inordinate swearing, or sexual misconduct. Serious morals offenses, like adultery or prostitution, were generally rare, however. During the eighteenth century, grand juries gave greater latitude to individual behavior and indicted fewer people for moral lapses that did not pose a direct threat to society. Prosecutions declined for offenses like premarital conception or fornication, and when charges were brought for bearing an illegitimate child, the rationale increasingly came to be seen as identifying the father so that he—not the community—would be financially responsible for the child's welfare. In Richmond County, Virginia, for example, the grand jury ceased bringing charges for adultery or fornication the late 1730s, and it limited its presentments to instances of bastardy. In effect, its actions demonstrated that although it intended to avoid any unnecessary expansion of local poor relief, it no longer accepted the burden of serving as the arbiter of public morality.

Historians so far have accomplished relatively little in ascertaining crime rates in the thirteen colonies, but despite the meager extent of knowledge about this subject, it seems undeniable that the incidence of lawbreaking was dramatically lower in the British provinces than in the modern United States. In Richmond County, Virginia, for example, the courts heard an average of less than three cases involving serious property offenses (robbery, horse stealing, grand larceny, burglary, or arson) per year between 1720 and 1754. In nearby Westmoreland County, the usual number of such trials before was generally two each year from 1731 to 1746.

After comparing crime rates calculated from prosecutions or convictions in colonial courts with recorded arrests in 1995—figures that are not entirely equivalent but meaningful nevertheless—it would appear that prevailing levels of property crimes and violence against persons probably stand six to ten times higher today than prior to 1760. These data indicate that whereas a modern American adult (aged eighteen and above) stands better than a one-in-four chance of being victimized by a violent act or property crime during any ten-year period, the corresponding likelihood for a colonial adult was only perhaps one in sixteen over a decade. In terms of crime, modern Americans live in a society four times more threatening than the one inhabited by their colonial forebears.

Violent Crime

Although the murder rate was lower in colonial times than in the 1990s, it varied greatly by locale. Homicide occurred twice as frequently in Maryland as in Massachusetts during the late seventeenth century. Maryland's rate of 0.7 per 10,000 population approached modern levels of 0.9 per 10,000. In Massachusetts, however, killings took place at just one-third the level prevailing in United States today. Homicide and other violent crimes seem to have been far less of a social problem in New England than in the southern and Mid-Atlantic colonies.

Although the lawless element of the colonial population was much smaller than today, it contained enough hardened, remorseless criminals to send periodic shivers up the spines of law-abiding folks. The *Boston Weekly News-Letter* in its issue for March 20–28, 1740, gave the following account of how one band of bloodthirsty scoundrels wiped out most of a family.

> We hear from East Jersey of the following horrible Tragedy; not long since, about Eight or Ten Men (Irish all) by Night went to the House of a particular Gentleman in that Country, who was noted for a Man of Substance; and having call'd at the Door, diverse of the Family went out to see what the Matter was,

TABLE 18.2 ANNUAL RATES OF CRIMINAL PROSECUTION AND CONVICTION IN COLONIAL AMERICA COMPARED TO ARREST RATES IN MODERN UNITED STATES (PER 10,000 PERSONS)

Crime Region	Date	Theft & Other Crimes Against Property	Assaults & Other Violence Against Persons	Homicide	Breach of Peace	Others[a]	Total
Middlesex Co., Va.							
Prosecutions	1676–1750	...	...	...	...	...	29.0
Convictions	1676–1750	...	...	...	...	...	16.0
Maryland	1657–1680	...	...	0.7	...	...	...
Massachusetts	1657–1680	...	...	0.3	...	...	...
Richmond Co., Va.							
Prosecutions	1714–1716	13.4	8.0	2.7	...	...	24.2
Prosecutions	1729–1731	31.6	6.5	0.7	...	...	25.2
Prosecutions	1747–1749	11.2	6.3	0.6	...	...	11.9
New York, N.Y.							
Prosecutions	1703	...	...	...	...	...	30.0
Convictions	1703	...	...	...	...	...	17.0
Prosecutions	1723	...	...	...	...	...	15.0
Convictions	1723	...	...	...	...	...	8.0
Essex Co., Mass.							
Convictions	1651–1655	17.4	[b]	[b]	2.6	64.6	84.6
Convictions	1661–1665	20.4	[b]	[b]	6.0	103.0	129.4
Convictions	1676–1680	18.4	[b]	[b]	5.4	58.8	82.6
United States							
Arrests	1995	117.7	80.3	0.9	28.6	343.5	571.0

Note: All data was adjusted to measure rates per 10,000 population.
[a] Includes such charges as morals offenses, crimes against church (including nonattendance), contempt of authority.
[b] Source included this category with crimes against property.
Sources: Darrett B. and Anita H. Rutman, *A Place in Time: Middlesex Co., Virginia* (1984), 253, n. 27. Peter C. Hoffer, ed., *Criminal Proceedings in Colonial Virginia* (1984), lx. Kai T. Erikson, *Wayward Puritans: A Study in the Sociology of Deviance* (1966), 173, 175. Douglas Greenberg, *Crime and Law Enforcement in the Colony of New York, 1691–1776* (1976), 136. David Hackett Fischer, *Albion's Seed: Four British Folkways in America* (1989), 191, n. 6 (source gives William Buttenweiser's data as rates of incidence). Federal Bureau of Investigation, *Uniform Crime Reports, 1995* (1996), 209.

whom the Men without immediately fell upon and murder'd; the Gentleman of the House perceiving some Disturbance, went out himself, and was murder'd also. Upon which the Gentleman's wife in the utmost Distress ran up [the] Garret, leaving her young Child behind her, and hid herself in a Hogshead of Feathers, and so escap'd their bloody Hands. The Rogues having entered the House, in a most barbarous Manner murder'd the child, after they had tortur'd it in order to find the Mother, saying, *Make the Calf Blair, and the Cow will come.* After they had rifled the House, and pick'd up all the Money and Plate they could meet with, they made off, whilst one of them, in the Hurry, left his little Dog behind him, shut up in the House. The poor distressed Gentlewoman perceiving they were gone, ventur'd down Stairs, and then was presented with the most awful Spectacle that ever her Eyes beheld; her Husband, child, and Servants, all weltering in their Blood. The Authority being inform'd of this amazing and almost unparalled'd Piece of Vilany, order'd officers with proper Attendants, to pursue and make Search after the Murderers, who turning out the little Dog before mentioned, were led to an House, where they found seven Men, who appearing suspicious, were immediately apprehended and order'd to Prison.

Violent crime was not the sole province of marauding outlaws, however. Just as today, a high proportion of homicides were perpetrated against family members by relatives driven to murderous rage by extreme emotional pressure or mental instability. Females composed almost one-third of all those accused of murder or manslaughter in Massachusetts from 1674 to 1774, and in 84% of the cases,

they stood charged with killing their own children. Women made up about one-fifth of all individuals indicted for crimes prior to the Revolution, and infanticide was the most frequent offense committed by them.

Mentally imbalanced husbands also went beserk and turned on their families. The *Boston Weekly News-Letter's* issue of May 21–28, 1741, carried an account of an officer of the provincial land bank who gouged out his wife's eyes with a stick and left her in a forest several miles from the closest town. The *Pennsylvania Chronicle* reported a similar incident committed on October 19, 1769, at the home of a prosperous, slaveowning farmer (he owned a herd of forty cattle) near Gloucester, New Jersey.

About 4 o'clock in the Morning, the Man (a Person in good Circumstances) got out of Bed, and went up Stairs to a Negro Wench, and inquired after some Leading Lines, telling her that he intended to have a Butcher that Day in the House; he then went down Stairs, and shot his Wife with some Buckshot, which not immediately killing her, the Wound being in the Shoulder, he beat her Brains out with the But End of the Musket. The Report of the Musket alarmed the Negro Wench, who directly sprang out of a Window, one Story high, rushed into the Room, where she saw her Mistress wallowing in her Blood; she forced the Musket out of her Master's Hands, and ran to the first Neighbour's House, seven Miles distant, whom she informed of this dreadful Affair. When they came to the House, they found the Woman lying as the Negro had left her, and tracing a Track of Blood into the Barn, they found the Man hanging. ... Jealousy, we hear, was the Occasion of this fatal Affair. The Man bore the Character of being very desperate, and had twice before attempted to shoot his Wife.

On the whole, nevertheless, spousal abuse and other violent offenses occurred at a far lower rate more than two centuries ago than in modern times. Scholars who have researched crime in the colonial South have observed that, in particular, sexual assaults against women appear to have been far less common than in late-twentieth-century America, and reports of them were quite rare. "[W]e have no such trades carried on," wrote William Byrd of Virginia in 1726, "as that of house-breakers, highway-men, or beggars. We can rest securely in our own, with all our doors and widows open, and yet find every thing exactly in place the next morning."

Transportation of Convicts

No European empire ever made such extensive use of its overseas possessions for the systematic deportation of its prison population as Great Britain did prior to 1775. British courts had begun to sentence

This broadside was published as a souvenir for the large crowd expected to attend the public punishment of a man (Seth Hudson) convicted of counterfeiting in Boston. Although not mentioned in the broadside, the usual sentence for counterfeiting included having an ear sliced off. (Goodspeed Collection, courtesy Worcester Art Museum)

criminals to banishment for a period of years across the Atlantic according to makeshift arrangements as early as 1614. (Some individuals may have been bundled off to America simply for being unpopular, such as Roger and Robert Bates who were condemned to be sent to Barbados in the late 1600s "for wandering the country as vagabonds with other lewd persons calling themselves Egyptians and pretending to tell fortunes.") Exile emerged as the preferred solution for Britain's growing crime problem not only because that nation failed to create an efficient system of local police to prevent lawbreaking but also because its judges lacked any effective methods of punishing felons aside from either execution or lesser sentences that spared life but made no contribution toward reforming character.

Seventeenth-century English judges gradually came to view transportation across the seas as one of their discretionary sentencing powers. They applied the punishment on an ad hoc basis without any firm Parliamentary guidance and frequently acted in a high-handed, arbitrary manner. In January 1665, for example, the shire justices of Middlesex offered Henry Baker the unenviable choice of agreeing to be transported or being sentenced to both a whipping and time in prison. Sarah Browne found herself facing an even more unpleasant dilemma in August 1720, when a London court gave her the option "to be transported [to America] at her own expense or else [be] executed." In this fashion, English and Welsh courts dispatched perhaps 18,000 malefactors to America, primarily to the West Indies, from 1614 to 1717.

Parliament greatly stimulated the export of convicts overseas through its Transportation Act of 1718. This law regularized the mechanics of expelling criminals from the realm, which had been so haphazard that prisoners sometimes arranged their own passage; it furthermore subsidized the trade in selling them as field laborers through a bounty of £3 per individual as a means of encouraging merchants to accept prisoners who might be difficult to market as agricultural workers due to poor health or age. Transportation's primary goal was neither rehabilitating offenders nor deterring crime but to remove dangerous offenders from society while avoiding both the costs of an expensive incarceration system and the unsettling prospect of overreliance on the death penalty.

The Transportation Act gave judges the option of sentencing criminals to be sold into overseas labor for periods ranging from seven years (for noncapital offenses) to fourteen years (in lieu of being executed). At London's famous Old Bailey prison, 40% of felons condemned to hang escaped the gallows by accepting a pardon conditional on transportation as an indentured laborer. The overwhelming majority of England's transported criminals had committed grand larceny, a capital offense defined as theft of goods valued at a shilling (twelve pence). Relatively few beggars, vagrants, or prostitutes went into legal exile from England and Wales, although a high proportion of people deported by Irish courts fell into those categories. Given the British legal system's many opportunities for clemency and the apparent displeasure most judges felt in ordering banishment, it would appear that few first offenders were sent to America and that persistent offenders made up the bulk of transported felons. The death penalty eliminated Britain's most dangerous outlaws, so few of them arrived in the colonies, but transportation sent many hardened criminals overseas.

Legal exile, even if temporary, struck judges and criminals alike as a harsh fate. It was not unknown for noncapital offenders to write petitions requesting that they be allowed to undergo a flogging instead or to enlist in the army or navy. On being sentenced to transportation by a Middlesex court in 1735, Ann Blackerby flew into blind rage and screamed at the judge, "My curse and God's curse go with ye, and the prayers of my children [for ill fortune] fall upon ye."

One prisoner remembered the dreary hold of the ship carrying him away from England in 1734 and said that being confined there en route to America seemed like "Going to Hell in a Cradle." The number of convicts making this journey swelled to unprecedented proportions during the eighteenth century. At least 32,000 felons left England and

TABLE 18.3 CONVICTS TRANSPORTED TO THE THIRTEEN COLONIES FROM ENGLAND AND WALES, 1718–1775

Year	Number
1775	790
1774	1,180
1773	1,010
1772	1,080
1771	900
1770	830
1769	670
1768	830
1767	840
1766	900
1765	700
1764	800
1763	530
1762	290
1761	280
1760	320
1759	490
1758	670
1757	550
1756	600
1755	420
1754	590
1753	650
1752	720
1751	770
1750	820
1749	550
1748	350
1747	220
1746	310
1745	360
1744	420
1743	420
1742	670
1741	610
1740	610
1739	360
1738	440
1737	390
1736	620
1735	300
1734	340
1733	370
1732	460
1731	470
1730	520
1729	620
1728	310
1727	420
1726	520
1725	580
1724	350
1723	440
1722	300
1721	480
1720	380
1719	320
1718	170
TOTAL	31,900

Note: Approximately 13,000 other convicts were transported from Ireland during this period, plus almost 1,000 from Scotland.
Source: Compiled from sample of felons listed in Peter Wilson Coldham, *The Complete Book of Emigrants in Bondage, 1614–1775* (1988).

Wales involuntarily from 1718 to 1775. Another 13,000 were banished from Ireland. Scotland made little use of transportation and evidently sent just 700 of its own convicts across the ocean. The number of felons deported to the thirteen colonies was so large between 1718 and the Revolution that they amounted to one-fifth of all migrants to North America from the British Isles.

The Chesapeake colonies constituted the largest market for purchasing convict laborers. The best estimates indicate that Virginia and Maryland absorbed at least four of every five felons sold in North America, with an equal number going to each. The impact of criminals was greatest on Maryland, whose population was much smaller than Virginia. According to a special census taken of Maryland in 1755, one of every twenty white males above the age of sixteen was under sentence as a transported felon.

Convicts proved far less socially disruptive for colonial society than anyone might have imagined from their backgrounds. Studies of the surviving Chesapeake court dockets have revealed that felons from Britain made only infrequent appearances on suspicion of evildoing. The primary reason why convicts committed so few offenses was that the low population density of rural America offered fewer chances for the types of crime for which most had been banished, namely thefts and burglaries. To make a profit from larceny, a thief required not only victims but a fencing network to find ways to dispose of stolen property safely and profitably. Such criminal infrastructures invariably clustered around urban centers where crime rates were highest and were becoming highly sophisticated in Great Britain during the 1700s. Colonial society and economy, however, were still unsuited for a high level of concentrated criminal activity before the Revolution, and they did not offer transported convicts the same chance to engage in property crimes available near London, Liverpool, Bristol, and other major cities. "In the Colonies," explained an English justice in 1754, "where a great part of the white Tenants are Transports, Thieving is never heard of … The Reason is plain, there are no Receivers [of stolen property]."

The convicts' main illegal activity was breaking their indentures and running away from their masters. When convicts appeared before the bar for theft and other offenses, they had generally committed them while carrying out an escape. Research into advertisements for runaway felons indicates that about one in every ten transportees escaped before their sentence had ended, in the course of which they often pilfered food, stole clothes, and picked pockets.

Runaway criminals usually departed their masters to return to Britain early. "Great Numbers have been come back," observed one Englisman in 1725, "before half their time was expired." This tendency accelerated as the century passed, and by 1773, a London alderman could assert, "There are more returned transports at this time in the Kingdom than known before." The great majority of transported convicts likewise seem to have left America as soon as their terms had ended and sailed to England, in large part because the stigma against them was so great that they remained social outcasts for as long as they stayed in the provinces. Most convicts were transients who went back to Britain, legally or illegally, as soon as possible and left little imprint on colonial society.

Most Americans nevertheless viewed transportation as a major grievance. Typical of public sentiment was the opinion of Benjamin Franklin, whose feelings undoubtedly were influenced by having once found his home burglarized. Writing under the pseudonym Americanus, he castigated the policy in an essay published in the *Pennsylvania Gazette* on May 9, 1751. Franklin noted that because the shipment of felons to America was conducted as a business by the merchants who sold them, the colonists ought to send some commodity back in order to keep the balance of trade even. He suggested that his countrymen pay for the criminals disgorged at their wharves with cargoes of rattlesnakes. Even then, Franklin ruefully observed, the mother country would get the better part of the bargain, for "the rattlesnake gives warning before he attempts his mischief, which the convict does not."

Slave Unrest and Conspiracies

Slave unrest posed the greatest internal challenge to Anglo-American society. The threat of insurrection surfaced often during the colonial era in both northern and southern communities. Actual rebellions with pitched battles were rare, but slaves hatched numerous intrigues to take back their freedom.

At a minimum, there occurred twenty-seven conspiracies involving at least a half-dozen slaves in attempts to win liberty through violence; ten of these episodes culminated in armed fights of some kind. Resistance peaked during the period from 1687 to 1741, when a plot was either discovered or erupted into bloodshed on an average of once every two-and-a-half years somewhere in British North America. These struggles left about fifty whites and fifty blacks dead on isolated fields of combat, and they fanned a white backlash that led to at least 118 blacks being executed as rebels.

Slavery did not emerge as a significant part of Anglo-America's labor system until the late seventeenth century. The first blow for freedom struck by African Americans in the South fell at Gloucester County, Virginia, in 1663 when several blacks joined with white servants to secure their liberty (evidently by murdering their masters). After one of the white participants betrayed them all, local authorities executed the leaders and draped chimneys with their severed heads as a warning to all others.

Even as the number of slaves increased rapidly in the Carolinas and Chesapeake during the late 1600s, no insurrections occurred in which any white lives were lost. Ironically, the first instance of whites being killed by African Americans evidently took place in the North. Early in 1708, a group of black and Indian slaves rose up against their masters at Newtown, Long Island, New York. Seven whites died in the fighting, after which three blacks and an Indian were executed.

The earliest, large-scale slave conspiracy also took place in the North. In early 1712 in New York City, about three dozen slaves pledged to fight for freedom on an oath sealed by sucking blood from one another's hands. They set fire to a structure in April, attacked all whites who came to investigate the blaze, and killed or wounded a total of fifteen men. The authorities condemned twenty-seven persons to death, of whom six—including a pregnant woman—were pardoned. Gov. Robert Hunter described the modes of execution as follows: "Some were burnt others hanged, one broke on the wheele, and one hung live in chains in the town."

New York City was also the scene of the largest conspiracy identified in the North almost three decades later. Hysteria broke out in 1741 when word spread that slaves were planning to poison the water supply, and authorities arrested 200 persons for questioning about that allegation and several suspicious fires. A fair amount of interracial fraternizing had become common in New York's taverns, and so the dragnet led to the detention of several whites as well. Through coerced confessions and much circumstantial evidence, the courts found more than 100 persons guilty of conspiracy, of whom eighteen were hanged (including two white males and two white females), thirteen burned to death, and seventy banished. The panic also spread to nearby New Jersey where 150 blacks were rounded up for interrogation and five were executed.

Authorities in New York and New Jersey may have reacted so severely to rumors of slave intrigue because the bloodiest revolt in early Anglo-America had erupted just two years earlier in South Carolina. African Americans grew encouraged to strike out for freedom because they expected officials in St. Augustine, Florida, to welcome any escaped slaves after the War of Jenkins' Ear began between Spain and Britain in 1739. On September 9, 1739, ten slaves killed two guards at a storehouse that contained guns and ammunition at Stono Creek, about 20 miles southeast of Charles Town. They then started to head south toward Florida and grew to a force of about 100 men, who

TABLE 18.4   SLAVE CONSPIRACIES AND UNREST WITHIN THE PRESENT BOUNDARIES OF THE UNITED STATES, 1657–1774

Date	Location	Description
Nov. 1774	St. Andrews Parish, Ga.	After slaves killed 4 whites and wounded 3 others, 2 of the rebels were executed
1772	Perth Amboy, N.J.	Conspiracy discovered
Late 1767	Alexandria, Va.	Several overseers poisoned by conspirators, for which 4 slaves were executed
Apr. 1741	Elizabeth and Hackensack, N.J.	Over 150 slaves arrested for conspiracy to rebel, and 5 executed
Spring 1741	New York, N.Y.	Several hundred slaves arrested as conspirators, of whom 70 were deported and 31 executed
Jun. 1740	Charles Town, S.C.	After a conspiracy by more than 100 slaves was discovered, 50 slaves were executed
Sep. 9, 1739	Stono Creek, S.C.	About 100 slaves arose, burned 7 plantations, and killed 25 whites before being defeated
1739	Prince George's Co., Md.	After discovery of conspiracy involving up to 200 slaves, one was executed
Jan. 1734	New Brunswick, N.J.	Thirty slaves tried for conspiracy to revolt, and one of them was hanged
Aug. 1730	South Carolina	Conspiracy to revolt discovered among slaves, and leaders killed
1730	Counties of Princess Anne and Norfolk, Va.	Four slaves executed for organizing 200 persons into a conspiracy to rebel
1729	Virginia	After establishing a small village in the Shenandoah Valley, escaped slaves were recaptured in an armed fight
Spring 1723	Counties of Gloucester and Middlesex, Va.	Seven slaves deported for conspiring to incite rebellion
Late 1722	Rappahannock Valley of Va.	Three slaves deported for conspiring to incite rebellion
Early 1720	South Carolina	After a slave conspiracy was discovered, 14 slaves ran away to Florida but were captured by Indians and returned
1713	Goose Creek, S.C.	Plot to rebel was betrayed by one of the slave conspirators
Apr. 7, 1712	New York, N.Y.	Two dozen slaves killed 9 whites and wounded 6 others, for which 18 slaves were executed
Spring 1711	South Carolina	Sebastian led several escaped slaves in spree of theft until he was killed by Indians
Spring 1710	Counties of James City and Surry, Va.	Two slaves executed for trying to incite rebellion
Early 1709	Counties of James City, Surry, and Isle of Wight, Va.	Authorities arrest several leaders trying to organize revolt by black and Indian slaves
Feb. 1707	Newtown, N.Y.	Slaves killed 7 whites, for which 4 slaves were executed
1700	South Carolina	Authorities arrested Indian slaves for conspiring to rebel
Fall 1691	Rappahannock River valley of Virginia	Mingo formed band of escaped slaves who survived by stealing livestock from farms
1687	Northern Neck of Virginia	Discovery of slave conspiracy resulted in several leaders being arrested and hanged
1672	Virginia	Unknown number of slaves rebelled and escaped
Sep. 1663	Virginia	Unknown number of slaves and white servants were discovered plotting to gain freedom by killing their masters, for which several were executed
Spring 1657	Hartford, Conn.	Slaves assisted Indians in burning several buildings

Source: Herbert Aptheker, *American Negro Slave Revolts* (1943), 162–202.

organized themselves like a military company by marching behind a makeshift flag and two drummers. As they proceeded south, they looted and burned seven plantations and almost captured the governor, who was riding alone in their direction and was almost upon them before he realized his danger and fled. The slaves traveled about 10 miles before the militia overtook them. In the ensuing skirmish, the insurgents broke ranks after losing fourteen men in the first volley, and the rebellion collapsed. Heads cut from dead rebels' bodies were left spiked on top of every milepost on the main road to Charles Town to terrorize blacks into submission.

The Stono revolt of 1739 and the New York conspiracy of 1741 marked the last major instances of slave insurrection during the colonial period. No significant plots were discovered for a quarter-century after 1742, during which time slave resistance overwhelmingly took the form of individual acts of defiance, especially running away. No further outbreaks of violence on the scale of the Stono revolt would occur in Anglo-America until Nat Turner's Rebellion in 1831.

Piracy

Piracy has been termed the world's third-oldest profession, behind prostitution and medicine. However true that may be, robbery on the high seas was a problem that bedeviled North Americans from the time of their earliest settlements. The Pilgrims lost the entire value of their first year's labor, £500 worth of clapboards and furs that would have paid off a large part of their debt to English creditors, when a French corsair hijacked the shipment off the west coast of England. Piracy would continue to influence the colonial economy until Britain's navy extirpated the last crews of Jolly Rogers in the late 1720s.

European warfare spilled over into the West Indies during the seventeenth century, and it turned the Caribbean into a boiling cauldron of unrestrained piracy in which English, French, and Dutch seafarers coalesced into a conspiracy to loot Spanish commerce. These gadflies of the Spanish Main called themselves buccaneers, a term that originated on the island of Hispaniola where several squatter communities of herders and woodsmen subsisted primarily on a diet of wild hogs that were "boucanned," that is, barbecued. Many of these buccaneers turned to sea roving after being harassed by the Spanish who claimed Hispaniola, and they formed some of the Western Hemisphere's earliest pirate crews.

Maritime warfare accelerated after England seized Jamaica in 1655. That island lay in the heart of Spain's Caribbean holdings, and it became the base from which swarms of English sea dogs preyed on Spain's shipping or sacked its coastal ports. The buccaneers insisted they were not pirates because they directed all their depredations against the Spanish and not against ships or settlements of their own or other nationalities. English officials found them useful; they not only issued commissions authorizing them to attack Spanish targets but even gave both a knighthood and the lieutenant-governorship of Jamaica to Henry Morgan, the preeminent freebooter of that strife-torn era.

Many mariners began to slide down that slippery slope described by Rev. Cotton Mather of Boston, who cautioned New England's sailors in 1704 that "the privateering stroke so easily degenerates into the piratical, and the privateering trade is usually carried out with an unchristian temper and proves an inlet into so much debauchery and iniquity." These renegades continued to ravage Spanish ships and settlements in times of truce when their commissions no longer sanctioned such acts. For many captains brutalized by years of warfare and numerous sailors alienated by the merchant marine's harsh discipline and meager pay, it was impossible to withstand the temptation to grab sudden riches from captured prizes; they fanned out through the Atlantic and Pacific oceans to sail against the flags of all nations, even their own. Such marauders were most numerous during the decades from 1690 to 1730, a period often considered the golden age of piracy.

Piracy affected the economy of England's mainland colonies like a doubled-edged sword: it made oceanic commerce more risky, but it also created opportunities for many merchants to profit by doing business with buccaneers. Pirates needed many articles to outfit their ships after a voyage, and they paid for food, gunpowder, and other provisions with coins of gold and silver, which were in short supply in North America. Because their overhead was low, pirates could make money by selling expensive plunder at far less than its market value, and American merchants could then turn a good profit by fencing the goods at their actual worth to regular customers (or smuggling them to Europe). Shopkeepers and tavern owners extended a hearty welcome to pirate crewmen, for the rogues had plenty of cash and spent it with reckless abandon. Many high-ranking, royal officials, who all considered themselves underpaid, profited by accepting bribes from pirates in exchange for extending clemency for crimes committed on the high seas or issuing unauthorized privateer commissions.

Piracy flourished during its golden age in large part because it was allied with many Anglo-American merchants, protected by important public officials, and condoned by a large segment of the general population in the English colonies. New York City became notorious as a pirate haven in the 1690s, and its merchants were the most important source of provisions for the British sea robbers who plucked the Indian Ocean's fabulously rich trade routes. In Pennsylvania, the royal surveyor of customs groaned that buccaneers flouted the law shamelessly. "All these parts swarm with pirates," he wrote and added that they "walk the streets with pockets full of gold and are the constant companion of the chief in the Government." Large numbers of pirate members came from port cities of the Mid-Atlantic and New England provinces, as did some of their officers. The legendary Capt. William Kidd was a resident of New York City where he was raising his two daughters when he began his fateful voyage in 1695 on the *Adventure Galley* (a ship in which New York's governor, Lord Bellomont, was a secret investor, along with several high-ranking members of Britain's government).

The possibility of quick money and enormous profits drew men to piracy like moths to a flame. Each sailor following Capt. Bartholomew Roberts swore to abide by articles that obligated him to stay with the ship until he had earned at least £1,000, equal to $75,000 in modern currency. Captain Kidd's total haul probably equaled at least £28,000 on his last voyage, or $2,100,000. When two pirate crews seized the *Cassandra,* an East India Company vessel, in 1720 they won a cargo worth £75,000, or $5,625,000 today. One of the captains who took the *Cassandra,* John Taylor, pulled off the greatest coup of any British pirate; in 1721, he captured the Portuguese merchantman *Cabo,* carrying freight valued at £1,000,000, or $75,000,000 in modern money. Each of Taylor's crew received booty worth £4,000 ($300,000) *plus* forty-two diamonds apiece for a day's work in which none of them was killed or seriously wounded. Whereas common sailors in the merchant marine were often lucky to make £20 in a year, many pirates had sea chests holding £500 to £1,000 when they were captured by the Royal Navy.

Because buccaneers belonged to a fast-living, fast-dying subculture, money slipped through their fingers rather quickly. No sailors outdid them in "playing the king" by bacchanalian revels that combined trysting with prostitutes and gambling at high stakes until everyone had drunk themselves into oblivion. When fourteen pirates found themselves bemoaning their common fate in having earned too little plunder on a voyage to Madagascar, they decided to place the booty in one pile, divide into two sides, and fight with cutlasses until one group killed everyone on the other; when the affray ended, the victorious side had only two men left alive to divide the loot left by the twelve corpses lying on the ground. Capt. Bartholomew Roberts best expressed their devil-may-care mentality: "In an honest service there is thin rations, low wages and hard labor," Roberts stated, "in this [piracy], plenty and satiety, pleasure and ease, liberty and power; and

The most notorious pirate spawned by the North American colonies was Capt. William Kidd, whose last venture in plundering occurred after he had moved to New York City and had begun to raise a family there. This sketch shows him on the deck of his most famous ship, the *Adventure Galley.* (Howard Pyle Collection, Delaware Art Museum, Wilmington, Delaware)

who would not balance creditor on this side, when all the hazard is run for it, at worst, is only a sour look or two at choking [in a hangman's noose]. No, a merry life and a short one shall be my motto."

Life may have been merry in port while spending one's ill-gotten gains, but it was grim at sea. Rations sometimes became so rank with vermin and rot that the crew preferred to eat only at night when they could not see the maggots. Because so many hands were needed to man cannon and form a boarding party, corsairs carried three or four times the number normal for a merchant-marine crew (about eighty sailors for ship of 250 tons). Overcrowding sometimes left mariners no choice but to sleep packed together tightly, so that in one captain's memory they seemed to be "kennelling like hounds on the deck." Lights went out on shipboard about eight o'clock to avoid giving away their position to merchantmen or naval vessels, and any hands wishing to drink after then had to do so in the dark sitting on the open deck. Besides alcohol, their only relief from tedium came from listening to jigs played by the ship band, amateurs (often impressed from captured prizes) who beat out tunes with a motley collection of fiddles, fifes, drums, oboes, and even bagpipes.

It was perhaps because their voyages were filled with such hardships and monotony that when pirates had a chance to give full vent to their emotions, they could explode into blind rage and abuse their prisoners—or one another—with sadistic torments. They mercilessly pistol-whipped or otherwise beat captains and merchant sailors who resisted their boarding parties. If a merchant captain were identified by his crew as cruel and overbearing, pirates often subjected him to a ritual called "sweating," in which he was driven at a run round a mast while a fiddler played a jig; a solid circle of pirates enlivened his dance with jabs from their knives and cutlasses.

Those who only sweated got off easy. Some ships officers were marooned stark naked on deserted islands. Captains who objected too strenuously to their cargo's capture might find their mouth stuffed with some dry, combustible material that was then set afire. When the pirate Dirk Chivers tired of listening to complaints by the master of a vessel he had taken in 1695, he had the fellow's lips sewed together.

The beginning of the end for European piracy came in 1713 when Britain, France, and Spain finally made a conclusive end to their dynastic warfare and inaugurated a full generation of peace to the Atlantic world. Pirates could no longer cloak their crimes under the subterfuge of privateering against their country's enemies. The end of the War of the Spanish Succession nevertheless drove many mariners into piracy out of sheer economic desperation because the demobilization of tens of thousands of sailors and privateers led to both widespread unemployment and a calamitous drop in wages for deckhands. Hardened by so many years of warfare that they scarcely knew any other life, thousands of privateers hands went "on the account" under "pistol proof" captains and became marauders.

Economic hardship produced a piratical subculture that was far more deeply alienated from social norms than at any time in the past. Pirates of this period were unusually bloody-minded, and many appear to have degenerated into violence for its own sake. (See, for example, the sketch of Edward Teach [Blackbeard] in Chapter 11.) Their behavior verged on a caricature of the old buccaneering ethos as they denounced all restraints on their own behavior and refused to acknowledge any higher authority than the power of the sword. A flavor of their orientation can be glimpsed in a diatribe spoken by pirate leader Charles Bellamy as he raged at the captain of a captured merchantman who refused his offer to join him in a life of crime. "Damn ye," screamed Bellamy, "you are a sneaking puppy, and so are all those who will submit to be governed by laws which rich men have made for their own security, for the cowardly whelps have not the courage otherwise to defend what they get by their knavery. ... They villify us, the scoundrals do, then there is only this difference, they rob the poor under the cover of law, and we plunder the rich under the protection of our own courage."

Pirates became more of a self-conscious community of outcasts than ever before. Many refused to accept married men into their crews because they wanted no one with any residual loyalties to the shore and its traditional social values. They drastically increased the level of violence toward officers and mariners on board captured prizes. Abuse by pirates previously demonstrated elements of ritual torment that would not proceed beyond a certain level or had the practical purpose of forcing individuals to reveal where especially valuable cargo lay hidden. Ships captains were now frequently put to death if their crews denounced them as cruel; even mariners might be beaten, tortured, or killed for resisting impressment onto the pirate crew, whereas buccaneers formerly had respected decisions by ordinary mariners not to join their ranks. Cold-blooded killing now became a more frequent aftermath of the assault on commerce, and one pirate captain, Philip Lyne, boasted that he had murdered thirty-seven masters of vessels before being brought to justice in 1726. It was significant that not until after 1713 did pirates adopt the skull-and-crossbones flag, with its glorification of death, in place of the formerly favored crimson or "bloody" flag.

Pirates now indiscriminately attacked all shipping, even vessels from harbors like New York City; Newport, Rhode Island; and Charles Town, South Carolina, that had long fenced their goods and sheltered them from the law. As public opinion turned intolerant toward sea brigands, the freebooters became increasingly isolated and driven to the fringes of the Atlantic world. The growing hostility toward buccaneers led many of their former allies to turn against them and provide the Royal Navy with the information it needed to track them down to their hiding places in the Outer Banks of North Carolina and the Bahamas.

These circumstances enabled the navy to accomplish one of the most successful anticrime campaigns in history as it relentlessly ran down the rogues crew by crew. That task was formidable. In 1717 when the navy had been demobilized to just 6,240 sailors, an estimated thirty companies of Anglo-American pirates with a total 2,400 men in their crews were plying the seas. Pressure from the merchant communities of both Britain and North America helped convince Parliament to expand the navy to 16,200 in short order, and this augmented force kept the pirates under pressure for the next dozen years.

The navy waged a slow war of extermination, while the courts stopped showing leniency toward pirates and began to schedule mass executions. Twenty-six buccaneers were hanged in Newport, Rhode Island, on a single day in 1726. Thanks to a 1696 statute that enabled pirates to be tried at summary hearings by seven naval officers rather than having their cases decided under common-law safeguards that made it harder for the government to convict them, large numbers of scoundrels were executed on distant coasts, as many as fifty in a single day, after being condemned by drumhead courts-martial composed of seven naval officers from the same ships that had just captured them. By 1730, piracy had virtually ceased to exist as a threat to the British Empire's commerce.

Of the 5,000 Anglo-American sailors engaged "on the account" robbing ships on the high seas at various times from 1713 to 1730, probably 500 to 600, as many as one in every eight, finished their life swinging at a rope's end. Some of them died as audaciously defiant as they had lived, such as six pirates who sullenly stood on a Virginia gallows in 1720. Their leader "called for a Bottle of Wine, and taking a Glass of it, he drank Damnation to the Governour and Confusion to the Colony, which the rest pledged."

Witchcraft

In the seventeenth century, witchcraft was understood as a compact by which a human being agreed to sell his or her soul to the devil. The conventional view held that the victim sealed the bargain with Satan by adding his or her name to a black book listing all the ungodly host who had become wizards (if men) or witches (if women); he or she then had intercourse with the Devil, who temporarily assumed physical shape for that purpose. Witches and wizards held covens to celebrate the Black Mass and might inflict evil on their neighbors with Satan's assistance.

Western European nations all treated witchcraft as a crime that civil rulers had an obligation to punish. "The Bible teaches that there are witches," wrote John Calvin, "and that they must be slain." James I of England, who regarded himself to be God's anointed, once became convinced that a conspiracy of witches had almost succeeded in brewing up a tempest that nearly drowned him while he was at sea, as he related in a pamphlet he wrote on the subject titled *Demonologie* in 1597.

Belief in witchcraft was universal among Christians in the seventeenth century. While virtually no one doubted that the Devil had enlisted a significant following on Earth, no consensus existed on how many disciples followed Satan, whether the righteous could correctly identify them, or exactly how dangerous they might be. Of all European peoples, the English had always shown the least interest in ferreting out

Howard Pyle's painting, titled *They Questioned Him with Malevolent Persistence,* conveys a chilling sense of the deadly seriousness with which witchcraft inquisitions were conducted. (Howard Pyle Collection, Delaware Art Museum, Wilmington, Delaware)

the Devil's minions, and they were virtually alone in never having experienced a major outbreak of hysteria over witchcraft. Prosecutions for sorcery were small in number and quite isolated among the English, who also showed a more levelheaded attitude than other Europeans by refusing to burn witches. (In England, witches were hanged; only heretics and women who murdered their husbands were burned.)

It was in Virginia and other southern colonies where behavior concerning witchcraft came closest to the customs of old England. Virginians took the existence of sorcery for granted, and they accepted that the state had an obligation to protect its citizens from being victimized by people who could cast spells or use the Devil's powers to molest their neighbors. Witchcraft was one of many folk traditions about the supernatural world that had been transplanted from the old country. Belief in magic was also nearly universal, among both the common people and wealthier planters. Numerous superstitions remained unquestioned, such as the idea that if a person had died violently, the corpse would tremble if it were stroked and do so with noticeable agitation if the hand of its murderer passed over it; on at least three occasions, Virginia coroners or justices of the peace actually followed this procedure while trying to determine whether someone had died from foul play.

Virginians acted as if that they could take witchcraft in stride as matter-of-factly as they dabbled in "white" magic such as fortune-telling,

astrology, and finding water with a forked stick. Their courts sent no witches to their deaths: When officials at Jamestown learned in 1659 that a ship captain had hanged an old woman named Katherine Grady as a witch en route to the colony (because she was feared to be conjuring a gale that threatened to sink his ship), they summoned him before them to justify his conduct. The only person found guilty of witchcraft was William Harding of Northumberland County in 1655, and his punishment was relatively light for being convicted of a capital crime: ten lashes and orders to leave the colony by the end of two months.

Virginia courts showed an unmistakable awareness that charges of sorcery posed an enormous potential for gross miscarriages of justice. The magistrates of Lower Norfolk acted in 1655 to halt a recent spate of "dangerous and scandalous speeches" making allegations of witchcraft; the justices decreed that if anyone henceforth entered such a complaint and could not prove it, they would pay a heavy fine. That same year, the assembly followed their example by enacting penalties to punish "slander and scandall" by people who called others witches or wizards. Numerous individuals won lawsuits alleging defamation of character under the 1655 law, for Virginia courts invariably responded with a healthy dose of skepticism toward accusations of sorcery.

Unlike Virginia, New England contained a volatile mix of Calvinistic fervor and widespread belief in folk magic. The mental universe of orthodox Puritans created a worldview in which God's church was continually under siege by the Devil, whose forces would certainly triumph unless the righteous exercised constant and uncompromising vigilance to defend the faith. Such a perspective was not likely to take sorcery lightly, much less to recognize that a balance had to be struck between a Christian's obligation to combat Satan vigilantly and the necessity to prevent perversions of justice during witchcraft investigations.

It was easy for Puritans to imagine that witchcraft might be all around them in New England because numerous people practiced magic in their society. Known as wise folk, conjurors, or cunning men and women, they claimed to possess supernatural powers. They offered their services for healing the sick, divining the future, warding off injury through countermagic, and—in rare cases—inflicting revenge on enemies. Cunning folk were neither witches nor reprobates, for the vast majority of them seem to have attended church regularly and kept all the commandments. They simply carried on ancient folkways that had preserved—and slowly added to—a vast lore of superstition inherited from pre-Christian times. The clergy, however, viewed them as dangerously similar to "white witches" or wizards and warned that magic was a snare designed by the Devil to beguile the foolhardy into succumbing to his blandishments and signing the black book.

Cunning folk were disturbingly ubiquitous in New England, at least to orthodox Puritans. They may have been a tiny minority, but at least one of them was sure to live within a day's journey of almost every town, big or small. They were probably encountered less often than in the old country, but because they were not supposed to be found at all in New England, their very existence seemed like a fifth column undermining John Winthrop's "city upon a hill." Because almost every New Englander would have been acquainted with a "wise" man or woman, at least by reputation, virtually the entire population was prepared to believe that if "white" magic flourished in their community, then "black" magic could rear its ugly head at any moment. It was this dichotomy between Calvinist ideals and the reality of white magic in their midst that fueled the emotional tension behind New England's seventeenth-century witchcraft persecutions.

By the standards of the old country, New Englanders were unusually diligent in bringing witches to trial. When considered as a ratio of the total population, indictments for witchcraft were twenty-five times more frequent in New England than in the mother country; executions occurred at a per capita rate ten times higher than in old England. Even heavily Puritan regions of old England like East Anglia

TABLE 18.5   KNOWN CASES OF WITCHCRAFT IN ENGLISH COLONIES, 1638–1697

Year	N. Hamp. Male	N. Hamp. Female	Mass. Male	Mass. Female	Conn. Male	Conn. Female	Rh. Is. Male	Rh. Is. Female	N.Y. Male	N.Y. Female	Va. Male	Va. Female
1697	...	...	...	...	...	2[a]	...	...	...	...	...	...
1692	...	...	41[k]	115[l]	1	7[d]	...	...	...	...	...	...
1688	...	...	...	1[b]	...	...	...	...	...	...	...	...
1683	...	...	1[a]	1[a]	...	...	...	...	...	...	...	...
1681	...	...	...	1[a]	...	...	...	...	...	...	...	...
1680	...	3[a]	...	1[a]	...	...	...	...	...	...	...	...
1679–80	...	...	...	1[c]	...	...	...	...	...	...	...	...
1679	...	...	1[a]	...	...	...	...	...	...	...	...	1[a]
1676	...	...	...	1[a]	...	...	...	...	...	...	...	...
1674–75	...	...	...	1[a]	...	...	...	...	...	...	...	...
1673	...	...	...	1[a]	...	...	...	...	...	...	...	...
1670?	...	...	...	1[a]	...	...	...	...	...	...	...	...
1669	...	...	1[a]	3[a]	...	...	...	...	...	...	...	...
1668–69	...	...	...	...	...	1[a]	...	...	...	...	...	...
1665	...	...	1[a]	...	...	1[c]	...	...	1[a]	1[a]	...	1[a]
1663	...	...	...	...	...	3[e]	...	...	...	...	...	...
1662–63	...	...	...	...	1[b]	1[b]	...	...	...	...	...	...
1662	...	...	1[a]	...	...	4[f]	...	...	...	...	...	...
1661	...	...	...	...	1[a]	1[a]	...	...	...	...	...	...
1659	...	...	1[a]	3[a]	...	...	...	...	...	...	...	1[j]
1658	...	...	...	...	...	...	...	...	...	1[a]	...	1[a]
1657	...	...	...	...	...	...	...	...	...	...	...	1[a]
1656	...	...	...	3[e]	...	...	...	...	...	...	...	...
1655	...	...	...	...	1[a]	2[a]	...	...	...	...	1[h]	...
1654	...	...	...	...	...	1[g]	...	...	...	...	...	...
1653?	...	...	...	1[b]	...	...	...	...	...	...	...	...
1652	...	...	1[a]	...	...	...	...	...	...	...	...	...
1651	...	...	1[c]	2[i]	1[b]	2[b]	...	...	...	...	...	...
1648	...	...	...	1[b]	...	1[b]	...	...	...	...	...	...
1647	...	...	...	...	...	1[b]	...	...	...	...	...	...

Note: This list includes only cases that went to trial and came to final judgment. For indictments that did not reach trial (24), and for complaints of witchcraft that did not result in any indictment (59), see John Demos, *Entertaining Satan: Witchcraft and the Culture of Early New England* (1982), 402–409.
[a] Acquitted.
[b] Convicted and executed.
[c] Convicted and verdict reversed.
[d] One acquitted, other convicted, but verdict reversed on appeal.
[e] One person tried and acquitted twice, other convicted and executed.
[f] Two acquitted, one escaped jail, one convicted and probably executed.
[g] Convicted and probably executed.
[h] Convicted and banished.
[i] One acquitted, other convicted and executed.
[j] Executed summarily on board ship en route to Virginia.
[k] Five broke jail, six convicted and executed, one pressed to death, one died in jail.
[l] Four broke jail, thirteen convicted and executed, ten convicted and later reprieved (mostly for confessing), one convicted and then broke jail, three died in jail.
Sources: Richard Godbeer, *The Devil's Dominion: Magic and Religion in Early New England* (1992), 235–242. Philip A. Bruce, *Institutional History of Virginia in the Seventeenth Century*, 2 vols. (1910), I: 280–281.

experienced lower rates of prosecution for sorcery than did the Puritans' settlements in America.

Between 1647 and 1691, fifty-seven trials for witchcraft took place in New England. These cases evidently proceeded with due regard for the victims' rights, for the overwhelmingly majority, 72%, won acquittals (including several convictions reversed on appeal), whereas New England courts usually acquitted only about 10% of defendants. Juries nevertheless found sixteen persons guilty of sorcery, of whom at least fourteen (and probably all) suffered death. Four of the sixteen persons convicted had admitted to being witches, however, and under the law, their confessions left the courts no alternative but to send them to the gallows. None of these episodes ever resulted in widespread panic anywhere in the region, however, for prior to 1692, New Englanders seemed capable of accepting the presence of witches within their midst with reasonable equanimity.

Massachusetts had come under heavy stress by 1692, however, and its citizens were still reeling from several recent shocks. The colony had not yet recovered from the devastation of King Philip's War in the 1670s. It had lost its charter in 1684 and then lived under five years of military government, which had been finally overthrown by a coup in 1689. War had erupted with the French and Indians in 1689, and the conflict was not going well for the Yankees, whose attempt to capture Quebec in 1690 had failed miserably. The clergy was constantly harping on the theme that these misfortunes represented God's displeasure with a people whose piety was declining. Massachusetts was notably lacking in that collective sense of self-assurance that every community needs to prevent outbreaks of social hysteria.

The times were perfect for a witchcraft craze in Salem Village (now Danvers), an agricultural community lying 6 miles west of the Essex County seat at Salem Town. Salem Village was a factious place, divided between the supporters of its two leading families, the Putnams, whose fortunes were falling, and Porters, whose star was rising. Several Salem Village men had died on recent forays against the French. Its congregation was uneasy with its young, rigid, and ineffectual minister.

In this atmosphere, several young girls began to gather regularly at the minister's kitchen to hear tales of voodoo and have their fortunes told by Tituba, a slave from the West Indies. Two of the girls began to act oddly in early 1692, and they attributed their "odd postures" and "foolish, ridiculous speeches" to being under a witch's spell. Local matrons at first tried to allay their symptoms with "white" magic, by feeding a witch's cake made from rye and the girls' urine to a dog, but this expedient brought no relief from their symptoms. Within a month, another half-dozen girls began to behave as if they were also afflicted.

Adults forced the girls to name their tormentors by late February, and warrants went out for Tituba and two old women. All the accused held low status in the community: One was a slave, while the white women were poor, decrepit, and unpopular. The two old women denied the charges, but Tituba confessed eagerly, even saying that she had met the Devil, whom she described as "a thing all over hairy, all the face hairy, and a long nose." All three were found guilty and sentenced to death.

The Salem Village outbreak began to diverge from the typical pattern for New England witchcraft incidents. Having singled out a handful of deviant individuals and tried them, the life of Salem should have gone back to normal. Three more accusations came out in March, however, including the seven-year-old daughter of one of the accused witches and two women who were not only wives to prosperous farmers but also church members. From this point on, indictments for witchcraft began to climb the social ladder until no one was safe. The Salem hysteria also differed from previous witchcraft episodes in that everyone accused was found guilty, whereas prior to then, about three of every four persons charged with sorcery had been acquitted.

Of all the characteristics of this legal panic, the most striking aspect was how it pitted women against one another on a generational basis. Three-quarters of the accused witches were female, predominantly married or widowed women aged forty-one to sixty. All but a handful of their accusers were likewise female, but they were overwhelmingly single girls or adolescents aged eleven to twenty. This general pattern seems to suggest that the trials stemmed from the antics of an immature set of teenage girls frustrated by the social control exercised over them by their mothers (with whom they primarily interacted at home), who found an opportunity to strike back at the adult world and become the center of attention by labeling women of their mother's age group as witches and seeing them punished.

Once the trials began, they proceeded with a momentum of their own. The authorities placed great pressure on the accused to tell them who else were witches, and many did so that they might obtain a sentence other than death or at least stave off execution by having to testify at later trials. The whole process ballooned into an epidemic of multiplying charges as the newly accused witches also caved in and fingered innocent people as the Devil's disciples.

By the end of September 1692, legal proceedings for witchcraft had been initiated against 156 persons from twenty-four different towns, but perhaps another 250 had been mentioned as witches and faced arrest. The court at Salem had convicted thirty persons, of whom nineteen had already been executed. The death toll also included one man pressed to death in an attempt to make him answer the charge against him, four prisoners who died in jail, and two dogs who were killed after witnesses said they had been bewitched.

Doubts about the trials spread through the Puritan clergy, nearly all of whom had been passive observers as the mania mounted. A consensus grew among most ministers that the proceedings should be reexamined, and they provided Gov. William Phips, whose own wife's name had been dropped as a witch, with the pretext he needed to suspend the trials and order all accused persons set free from jail. When the trials resumed in 1693, the atmosphere had changed and the verdicts turned to acquittals.

The Salem trials largely discredited witchcraft prosecutions in the public mind. On October 11, 1711, the Massachusetts legislature passed a special act reversing the convictions at Salem. As late as 1720, however, the town of Littleton, Massachusetts found itself in turmoil when three little girls accused a neighbor of tormenting them by witchcraft because large numbers of adults found their statements credible. The girls eventually admitted that they had made up the entire story. The last death attributable to witchcraft hysteria occurred in July 1787 when a mob in Philadelphia dragged an old woman from her home and stoned her as a sorceress.

CHAPTER 19 A Documentary Sampler of Colonial America, 1492–1763

The following documents describe important events, reproduce manuscripts concerning the origins of Anglo-American political institutions, or portray the experience of settling a new continent, illustrating various social and cultural aspects of colonial life. The original spelling, punctuation, and capitalization have been altered when necessary to prevent undue difficulties for the modern reader; minor changes necessary for clarity's sake are otherwise shown in brackets.

Exploration: Europeans Reach the Americas

Logbook of Christopher Columbus's Flagship, Santa Maria

Thursday, October 11, 1492

The course was W.S.W. [west by southwest], and there was more sea than there had been during the whole of the voyage. They saw sandpipers, and a green reed near the ship. Those of the caravel *Pinta* saw a cane and a pole, and they took up another small pole which appeared to have been worked with iron; also came another bit of cane, a land-plant, and a small board. The crew of the caravel *Nina* also saw signs of land, and a small branch covered with wild roses. Every one breathed afresh and rejoiced at these signs. ...

As the caravel *Pinta* was a better sailer, and went ahead of the Admiral, she found the land, and made the signals ordered by the Admiral. The land was first seen by a sailor named Rodrigo de Triana. ... At two hours after midnight the land was sighted at a distance of two leagues [eight miles]. ...

Friday, October 12, 1492

The vessels were hove to, waiting for daylight; and on Friday they arrived at a small island of the Lucayos, called in the language of the Indians, Guanahani. Presently they saw naked people. The Admiral went on shore in the armed boat, and Martin Alonso Pinzón, and Vicente Yáñez, his brother, who was captain of the *Nina*. The Admiral took the royal standard, and the captains went with two banners of the green cross, which the Admiral took in all the ships as a sign, with an F and a Y [for Ferdinand and Ysabella] and a crown over each letter, one on one side of the cross and the other on the other. Having landed, they saw trees very green, and much water, and fruits of diverse kinds. The Admiral called to the two captains, and to the others who leaped on shore, and to Rodrigo Escovedo, secretary of the whole fleet, and to Rodrigo Sánchez of Segovia, and said that they should bear faithful testimony that he, in presence of all, had taken, as he now took, possession of the said island for the King and for the Queen his Lords, making the declarations that are required, as is now largely set forth in the testimonies which were then made in writing.

Presently many inhabitants of the island assembled. What follows is in the actual words of the Admiral in his book of the first navigation and discovery of the Indies. "I," he says, 'that we might form great friendship, for I knew that they were a people who could be more easily freed and converted to our holy faith by love than by force, gave to some of them red caps, and glass beads to put round their necks, and many other things of little value, which gave them great pleasure, and made them so much our friends that it was a marvel to see. They afterwards came to the ship's boats where we were, swimming and bringing us parrots, cotton threads in skeins, darts, and many other things; and we exchanged them for other things that we gave them, such as glass beads and small bells. In fine, they took all, and gave what they had with good will. It appeared to me to be a race of people very poor in everything. They go as naked as when their mothers bore them, and so do the women, although I did not see more than one young girl. All I saw were youths, none more than thirty years of age. They are very well made, with very handsome bodies, and very good countenances. Their hair is short and coarse, almost like the hairs of a horse's tail. They wear the hairs brought down to the eyebrows, except a few locks behind, which they wear long and never cut. They paint themselves black, and they are the color of the Canary Islanders, neither black nor white. Some paint themselves white, some red, others of what color they find. Some paint their faces, others the whole body, some only round the eyes,

Replica of Christopher Columbus's flagship, the *Santa Maria*, formerly known as *La Gallega,* a merchant ship of about 70 tons. (Courtesy Library of Congress)

others only on the nose. They carry nor know anything of arms, for I showed them swords, and they took them by the blade and cut themselves through ignorance. They have no iron, their arrows being reeds without iron, some of them having a fish's tooth at the end, and others being pointed in various ways. They are all of fair stature and size, with good faces and well made. I saw some with marks of wounds on their bodies, and I made signs to ask what it was, and they gave me to understand that people from other adjacent islands came with the intention of seizing them, and they defended themselves. I believed, and still believe, that they come here from the mainland to take them prisoners. They should be good servants and intelligent, for I observed that they quickly took in what was said to them, and I believe that would easily be made Christians, as it appeared to me that they had no religion. I, our Lord being pleased, will take hence, at the time my departure, six natives for your Highnesses, that they may learn to speak. I saw no beast of any kind except parrots, on the island.' The above is in the words of the Admiral.

Source: Samuel E. Morison, ed., *Journals and Other Documents on the Life and Voyages of Christopher Columbus* (Boston: Heritage Press, 1964), 62–67.

Experiences of the Earliest European Colonists

Virginia's Starving Time, October 1609–May 1610

Following the evacuation of Capt. John Smith after he was wounded from a gunpowder explosion, lack of discipline and Indian hostility combined to produce a crisis of subsistence at Jamestown, Virginia. The colony's population stood at approximately 500 in October 1609, but by the following May barely 100 remained alive. In this document, which John Smith later published with his own writings, a survivor recounted that winter.

Now we all found the losse of Captain *Smith,* yea his greatest maligners could now curse his losse: as for corne provision and contribution from the Salvages, we had nothing but mortall wounds, with clubs and arrowes; as for our Hogs, hens, Goats, Sheepe, Horse, or what lived, our commanders, officers and Salvages daily consumed them, some small proportions sometimes we tasted, till was devoured; ...

Nay, so great was our famine, that a Salvage we slew and buried, the poorer short tooke him up againe and eat him; and so did divers[e] [persons eat] one another boyled and stewed with roots and herbs: And one amongst the rest did kill his wife, powdered [that is, salted] her, and had eaten part of her before it was knowne; for which hee was executed, as hee well deserved: now whether shee was better roasted, boyled or carbonado'd [charbroiled], I know not; but of such a dish as powdered wife I never heard of.

This was that time, which still to this day [1624] we called the starving time; it were too vile to say, and scarce to be beleeved, what we endured:

Source: Edward Arber and A. G. Bradley, eds., *The Travels and Works of Captain John Smith, President of Virginia, and Admiral of New England, 1580–1631,* 3 vols. (Edinburgh: J. Grant Publishers, 1910), II, 498–499.

The Pilgrims Depart from Leyden and Contemplate the Unknown

Gov. William Bradford eloquently described the farewells exchanged by the Pilgrims as they left Leyden, their home in exile from England, en route to America. (Bradford's spelling has been simplified in certain instances for modern readers.)

At length, after much travail and these debates, all things were got ready and provided. A small ship was bought, & fitted in Holland, which was intended as to serve to help to transport them, so as to stay in the countrie and attend upon fishing and such other affairs as might be for the good & benefite of the colonie when they came there. Another was hired at London, of burden about 9. score; and all other things gott in readiness. So being ready to departe, they had a day of solemn humiliation, their paster taking his texte from Ezra 8.21. *And there at the river Ahava, I proclaimed a fast, that we might humble ourselves before our God, and seeke of him a right way for us, and for our children, and for all our substance.* Upon which he spente a good parte of the day very profitably, and suitable to their presente occasion. The rest of the time was spente in pouring out prayers to the Lord with great fervencie, mixed with abundance of tears. And the time being come that they must departe, they were accompanied with most of their brethren out of the citie, unto a town sundrie miles of called Delfes-Haven, where the ship lay ready to receive them. So they lefte that goodly & pleasante citie [Leyden], which had been ther resting place near 12. years; but they knew they were pilgrims, & looked not much on those things, but lift up their eyes to the heavens, their dearest countrie, and quieted their spirits. When they came to the place they found the ship and all things ready; & such of their friends as could not come with them followed after them, and sundrie also came from Amsterdame to see them shipte and to take their leave of them. That night was spent with little sleepe by the most, but with friendly entertainment & christian discourse and other reall expressions of true christian love. The next day, the wind being faire, they wente aboard, and their friends with them, where truly dolefull was the sight of that sad and mournfull parting; to see what sighs and sobbs and prayers did sound amongst them, what tears did gush from every eye, & pithy speeches pierced each heart; that sundry of the Dutch strangers that stood on the key as spectators, could not refraine from tears. Yet comfortable & sweete it was to see such lively and true expressions of dear & unfained love. But the tide (which stays for no man) calling them away that were thus loath to departe, their Reverend pastor falling downe on his knees, (and they all with him,) with watery cheeks commended them with most fervent prayers to the Lord and his blessing. And then with mutuall embraces and many tears, they took their leaves one of an other; which proved to be the last leave to many of them.

... Having arrived off Massachusetts, William Bradford described New England's stark winter coast as follows.] ...

Being thus passed the vast ocean, and a sea of troubles before in their preparation (as may be remembred by that which wente before), they had now no friends to wellcome them, nor inns to entertaine or refresh their weatherbeaten bodys, no houses much less townes to repaire too, to seeke for succoure. ... And for the season it was winter, and they that know the winters of that country know them to be sharp & violent, & subject to cruell & feirce stormes, deangerous to travill to known places, much more to search an unknown coast. Besides, what could they see but a hidious & desolate wilderness, full of wild beasts & wild men? and what multitudes there might be of them they knew not. ... For summer being done, all things stand upon them with a wether-beaten face; and the whole country, full of woods & thickets, represented a wild & savage hue. If they looked behind them, there was the mighty ocean which they had passed, and was now as a maine barr & gulfe to seperate them from all the civill parts of the world. ... What could now sustaine them but the spirite of God & his grace? May not & ought not the children of these fathers, rightly say: *Our fathers were Englishmen which came over this great ocean, and were ready to perish in this wilderness.*

Source: William Bradford (Harvey Wish, ed.), *Of Plymouth Plantation* (New York: Capricorn Books, 1962), 52–53, 59–61.

Political Development

The Virginia Company's Instructions for Establishing an Elected Legislature in Virginia, 1618

Prior to this document, officials appointed from London held all political power in Virginia. The following document ordered the creation of a representative assembly, the House of Burgesses, to make necessary laws with the governor and his appointed council of advisors. Self-government in Anglo-America can be said to have begun in 1619 with the implementation of these instructions.

To all people to whom these presents shall come bee seen or heard, the Treasuror, Council and Company of Adventurers and planters of the Citty of London for the first Collony in Virginia send greetings. Knowe yee That ... by authoritie directed to us from his Majestie under his great seale upon mature deliberation doe hereby order and declare, That from hence forward ther bee towe Supreame Counsells in Virginia for the better government of the said Colony as Aforesaid. The one of which Counsells to bee called the Counsell of State and whose office shall Cheiflie bee assisting with ther Care advise and circomspection to the said Governor shall be Chosen nominated placed and displaced from tyme to tyme by us the said treasurer Counsell and Company and our successors, which Counsell of State shall Consiste for the present only of those persons whose names are here inserted vizt. ... Which said Counsellors and Counsell wee Earnestlie Pray and desier, and in his Majesties name strictlie charge and Comand, That all factious parcialties and sinester respects laid aside they bend ther care and Endeavors to assist the said Governor first and principallie in advancement of the honor and service of almightie god, and the Enlargement of his kingdom amongste those heathen people, And next in the erecting of the said Colonie in one obedience to his Majestie and all lawfull Authoritie from his Majestie dirived, And lastlie in mayntayning the said people in Justice and Christian Conversation among themselves and in strength and habillytie to with stand ther Ennimies, And this Counsell is to be alwaies or for the most part resident about or neere the said Governor, The other Counsell more generall to be called by the Governor and yeerly of Course and no oftener but for very extreordynarie and Important occasions shall consist for present of the said Counsell of State and of Two Burgesses out of every towne [,] hunder [hundred,] and other particuler plantation to be respetially Chosen by the inhabitants. Which Counsell shallbee called the generall Assemblie, wherin as also in the said Counsell of State, all matters shall be decyded determined and ordred by the greater part of the voyces then present, Reserving alwaies to the Governor a negative voyce, And this generall assembly shall have free power, to treat Consult and conclude as well of all emergent occasions concerning the puplique weale of the said colony and everie part thereof, as also to make ordeine and enact such

generall lawes and orders for the behoof of the said colony and the good government thereof as shall time to tyme appeare necessarie or requisite. Wherin as in all other things wee requier the said generall Assembly, as also the said Counsell of State to imitate and followe the policy of the forme of government, Lawes Custome manners of loyall and other administration of Justice used in the Realme of England as neere as may bee even as ourselves by his Majesties Letters patente are required. Provided that noe lawes or ordinance made in the said generall Assembly shalbe and continew in force and validytie, unlese the same shalbe sollemlie ratified and Confirmed in a generall greater Court of the said Court here in England and so ratified and returned to them under our seale. It being our intent to affoord the like measure also unto the said Colony that after the government of the said Colony, shall once have been well framed and settled accordingly, which is to be done by us by authoritie derived from his Majestie and the same shall have bene soe by us declared, No orders of our Court afterwarde shall binde the said colony unlese they bee ratified in like manner in ther generall Assembly.

Source: Susan M. Kingsbury, ed., *The Records of the Virginia Company of London,* 4 vols. (Washington, D.C.: U.S. Government Printing Office, 1906–35), III, 482–484.

The Mayflower Compact, 1620

Having intended to settle near modern New York, then within the territory controlled by the Virginia Company, the Pilgrims lacked legal sanction for establishing a community at Cape Cod. To create legitimacy and ensure future cooperation, they signed this covenant that laid a legal basis for a civil society. The Mayflower Compact served as the foundation for the Plymouth Colony's government until it was annexed by Massachusetts Bay in 1691.

IN THE NAME OF GOD, AMEN, WE, whose names are underwritten, the Loyal Subjects of our dread Sovereign Lord King *James,* by the Grace of God, of *Great Britain, France,* and *Ireland,* King, *Defender of the Faith,* &c. Having undetaken for the Glory of God, and Advancement of the Christian Faith, and the Honour of our King and Country, a Voyage to plant the first Colony in the northern Parts of *Virginia;* Do by these Presents, solemnly and mutually, in the Presence of God and one another, covenant and combine ourselves together into a civil Body Politick, for our better Ordering and Preservation, and Furtherance of the Ends aforesaid: And by Virtue hereof do enact, constitute, and frame, such just and equal Laws, Ordinances, Acts, Constitutions, and Officers, from time to time, as shall be thought most meet and convenient for the general Good of the Colony; unto which we promise all due Submission and Obedience. IN WITNESS whereof we have hereunto subscribed our names at *Cape-Cod* the eleventh of *November,* in the Reign of our Sovereign Lord King *James,* of *England, France,* and *Ireland,* the eighteenth, and of *Scotland,* the fifty-fourth, *Anno Domini,* 1620.

Mr. John Carver	Mr. Samuel Fuller	Edward Tilly
Mr. William Bradford	Mr. Christopher Martin	John Tilly
Mr. Edward Winslow	Mr. William Mullins	Francis Cooke
Mr. William Brewster	Mr. William White	Thomas Rogers
Isaac Allerton	Mr. Richard Warren	Thomas Tinker
Myles Standish	John Howland	John Ridgdale
John Alden	Mr. Steven Hopkins	Edward Fuller
John Turner	Digery Priest	Richard Clark
Francis Eaton	Thomas Williams	Richard Gardiner
James Chilton	Gilbert Winslow	Mr. John Allerton
John Craxton	Edmund Margesson	Thomas English
John Billington	Peter Brown	Edward Dotey
Joses Fletcher	Richard Britteridge	Edward Liester
John Goodman	George Soule	

Source: Henry S. Commager, ed., *Documents of American History* (Engle-wood Cliffs: Prentice-Hall, Inc., N.J., 1973), 15–16.

Maryland Statute for Religious Toleration, 1649

Hoping to reassure the Protestant majority within Maryland that their religious principles were not threatened by the Catholic beliefs of the colony's highest officeholders, Maryland's assembly passed an act for religious toleration. Although it neither separated church and state nor protected the rights of non-Christians, the law represented the first official expression of religious freedom as an ideal in American society.

Forasmuch as in a well governed and Christian Common Wealth matters concerning Religion and the honor of God ought in the first place to bee taken, into serious consideration and endeavoured to be settled. Be it therefore ordered and enacted … That whatsoever person or persons within this Province and the Islands thereunto belonging shall from henceforth blaspheme God, that is Curse him, or deny our Saviour Jesus Christ to be the sonne of God, or shall deny the holy Trinity the Father some and holy Ghost, or the Godhead of any of the said Three persons of the Trinity or the Unity of the Godhead, or shall use or utter any reproachfull Speeches, words or language concerning the said Holy Trinity, or any Speeches, words or language concerning the said Holy Trinity, or any of the said three persons thereof, shalbe punished with death and confiscation or forfeiture of all his or her lands and goods to the Lord Proprietary and his heires … And whereas the inforceing of the conscience in matters of Religion hath frequently fallen out to be of dangerous Consequence in those commonwealthes where it hath been practised, And for the more quiett and peaceable government of this Province, and the better to preserve the mutuall Love and amity amongst the Inhabitants thereof. Be it Therefore … enacted (except as in the present Act is before Declared and sett forth) that noe person or persons whatsoever within this Province, or the Islands, Ports, Harbors, Creekes, or havens thereunto belonging professing to beleive in Jesus Christ, shall from henceforth bee any waies troubled, Molested or discountenanced for or in respect of his or her religion nor in the free exercise thereof within this Province or the Islands thereunto belonging nor any way compelled to the beleife or exercise of any other Religion against his or her consent, soe as they be not unfaithfull to the Lord Proprietary, or molest or conspire against the civill Government established or to be established in this Province under him or his heires. And that all & every person and persons that shall presume Contrary to this Act and the true intent and meaning thereof directly or indirectly either in person or estate willfully to wrong disturbe trouble or molest any person whatsoever within this Province professing to beleive in Jesus Christ for or in respect of his or her religion or the free exercise thereof within this Province other than is provided for in this Act that such person or persons so offending, shalbe compelled to pay trebble damages to the party soe wronged or molested, and for every such offence shall also forfeit 20£ sterling in money or the value thereof, half thereof for the use of the Lord Proprietary, and his heires Lords and Proprietaries of this Province, and the other half for the use of the party soe wronged or molested as aforesaid, Or if the partie soe offending as aforesaid shall refuse or bee unable to recompense the party soe wronged, or to satisfy such Fine or forfeiture, then such Offender shalbe severely punished by publick whipping & imprisonment during the pleasure of the Lord Proprietary, or

his Leiuetenant or cheife Governor of this Province for the tyme being without baile or maineprise.

Source: William H. Browne, et al., eds., *Archives of Maryland,* 65 vols. (Baltimore: Maryland Historical Society, 1883–1952), I, 244, 246.

Massachusetts Bay Rejoinder to England's Attorney General, 1678

The Massachusetts Bay legislature rejected royal charges that it had not upheld Parliamentary laws by asserting that its charter of 1629 conveyed the right to legislative self-government. The colony insisted that although its citizens owed allegiance to the crown, Parliament held no authority over them because Massachusetts voters elected no representatives to the House of Commons. This document thus rehearsed the same essential argument later used by colonial leaders to reject Parliamentary taxes and then to justify independence during the revolutionary crisis of 1763–76.

[Answer to Mr. Solicitor's Objections] … To obj. 7. Your answer also therein being aprooved, the [General] Court [the legislature] adds, viz, That for the acts passed in Parliament for incouraging trade and navigation, wee humbly conceive, according to the usuall sayings of the learned in law, that the lawes of England are bounded within the fower seas, and doe not reach America. The subjects of his majestie here being not represented in Parliament, so wee have not looked at ourselves to be impeded in our trade by them, nor yet wee abated in our relative allegiance to his majestie. However, so soone as wee understood his majesty's pleasure, that those acts should be observed by his majesties subjects of the Massachusetts, which could not be without invading the liberties and propperties of the subject, untill the Generall Court made provission therein by a law, which they did in October, 1677, and should be strictly attended from time to time, although the same be a discouragement to trade, and a great damage to his majesties plantation, untill we shall obteyne his majesties gracious favour for that liberty of trade, which wee are not without hopes but that his majestie will see just occasion to grant to us, for the encouraging of his good subjects in a wilderness & hard country, …

Source: Nathaniel B. Shurtleff, ed., *Records of the Governor and Company of the Massachusetts Bay,* 6 vols. (Boston: W. White Printers, 1853–54), V, 200–201.

The Albany Plan of Union, 1754

The Albany congress met to discuss Indian affairs and the growing prospect of war with the French in mid-1754; its members recommended that Britain's colonies establish a governmental system with jurisdiction over military defense and Indian negotiations. Largely drafted by Benjamin Franklin and Thomas Hutchinson, the Albany Plan of Union failed to win support from any province after the Congress requested approval from the legislatures. Despite its rejection, the Plan of Union ranks as the first proposed constitution for an American confederated government and so marks the first hesitant attempt of British colonists to overcome their traditional provinciality when confronted by a common threat.

It is proposed, that humble application be made for an act of Parliament of Great Britain, by virtue of which one general government may be formed in America, including all the said colonies, within and under which government each colony may retain its present constitution, except in the particulars wherein a change may be directed by the said act, as hereafter follows.

President-General and Grand Council. That the said general government be administered by a President-General, to be appointed and supported by the crown; and a Grand Council, to be chosen by the representatives of the people of the several colonies met in their respective Assemblies.

Election of Members. That within [to be determined] months after the passing of such act, the House of Representatives that happens to be sitting within that time, or shall be especially for that purpose convened, may and shall choose members for the Grand Council in the following proportion— that is to say:

Massachusetts Bay	7
New Hampshire	2
Connecticut	5
Rhode Island	2
New York	4
New Jersey	3
Pennsylvania	6
Maryland	4
Virginia	7
North Carolina	4
South Carolina	4
	48

Place of First Meeting. [blank name] who shall meet for the first time at the city of Philadelphia in Pennsylvania, being called by the President-General as soon as conveniently may be after his appointment.

New Election. That there shall be a new election of the members of the Grand Council every three years; and on the death or resignation of any member, his place should be supplied by a new choice at the next sitting of the Assembly of the colony he represented.

Proportion of Members after the First Three Years. That after the first three years, when the proportion of money arising out of each colony to the general treasury can be known, the number of members to be chosen for each colony shall from time to time, in all ensuing elections, be regulated by that proportion, yet so as that the number to be chosen by any one province be not more than seven, nor less than two.

Meetings of the Grand Council, and Call. That the Grand Council shall meet once in every year, and oftener if occasion require, at such time and place as they shall adjourn to at the last preceding meeting, or as they shall be called to meet by the President-General on any emergency, he having first obtained in writing the consent of seven of the members to such call, and sent due and timely notice to the whole.

Continuance. That the Grand Council have power to choose their speaker and shall neither be dissolved, prorogued, nor continued sitting longer than six weeks at one time, without their own consent or the special command of the crown.

Members Allowance. That the members of the Grand Council shall be allowed for their service ten shillings sterling per diem during their session and journey to and from the place of meeting; twenty miles to be reckoned a day's journey.

Assent of the President-General and His Duty. That the assent of the President-General be requisite to all acts of the Grand Council, and that it be his office and duty to cause them to be carried into execution.

Power of President-General and Grand Council; Treaties of Peace and War. That the President-General, with the advice of the Grand Council, hold or direct all Indian treaties in which the general interest of the colonies may be concerned; and make peace or declare with Indian nations.

Indian Trade. That they make such laws as they judge necessary for regulating all Indian trade.

Indian Purchases. That they make all purchases, from Indians for the crown, of lands not now within the bounds of particular colonies, or that shall not be within their bounds when some of them are reduced to more convenient dimensions.

New Settlements. That they make new settlements on such purchases, by granting lands in the King's name, reserving a quitrent to the crown for the use of the general treasury.

Laws to Govern Them. That they make laws for regulating and governing such new settlements till the crown shall think it fit to from them into particular governments.

Raise Soldiers and Equip Vessels, &C. That they raise and pay soldiers and build forts for the defence of any of the colonies, and equip vessels to guard the coasts and protect the trade on the ocean, lakes, or great rivers; but they shall not impress men in any colony without the consent of the legislature.

Power to Make Laws, Lay Duties, &C. That for these purposes they have power to make laws, and lay and levy such general duties, imposts, or taxes as to them shall appear most equal and just (considering the ability and other circumstances of the inhabitants in the several colonies), and such as may be collected with the least inconvenience to the people; rather discouraging luxury than loading industry with unnecessary burthens.

General Treasurer and Particular Treasurer. That they may appoint a General Treasurer and Particular Treasurer in each government, when necessary; and from time to time may order the sums in the treasuries of each government into the general treasury, or draw on them for special payments, as they find most convenient.

Money, How to Issue. Yet no money to issue but by joint orders of the President-General and Grand Council; except where sums have been appropriated to particular purposes, and the President-General is previously empowered by an act to draw such sums.

Accounts. That the general accounts shall be yearly settled and reported to the several Assemblies.

Quorum. That a Quorum of the Grand Council, empowered to act with the President-General, do consist of twenty-five members, among whom there shall be one or more from a majority of the colonies.

Laws to Be Transmitted. That the laws be made by them for the purposes aforesaid shall not be repugnant, but, as near as may be, agreeable to the laws of England, and shall be transmitted to the King in Council for approbation as soon as may be after their passing; and if not disapproved within three years after presentation, to remain in force.

Death of the President-General. That in case of the death of the President-General, the Speaker of the Grand Council for the time being shall succeed, and be vested with the same powers and authorities, to continue till the King's pleasure be known.

Officers, How Appointed. That all military commission officers, whether for land or sea service, to act under this general constitution, shall be nominated by the President-General; but the approbation of the Grand Council is to be obtained before they receive their commissions. And all civil officers are to be nominated by the Grand Council, and to receive the President-General's approbation before they officiate.

Vacancies, How Supplied. But in case of vacancy by death or removal of any officer, civil or military, under this constitution, the Governor of the province in which such vacancy happens my appoint, till the pleasure of the President-General and Grand Council can be known.

Each Colony May Defend Itself on Emergency, &c. That the particular military as well as civil establishments in each colony remain in their present state, the general constitution notwithstanding; and that on sudden emergencies any colony may defend itself, and lay the accounts of expense thence arising before the President-General and General Council, who may allow and order payment of the same, as far as they judge such accounts just and reasonable.

Source: Francis N. Thorpe, ed., *Federal and State Constitutions' Colonial Charters, and Other Organic Laws,* 7 vols. (Washington, D.C.: U.S. Government Printing Office, 1909), I, 83–86.

Immigration and the Mix of Peoples

The Earliest Reported Arrival of Blacks in Anglo-America. John Rolfe of Virginia to Sir Edwin Sandys in England, January 1620.

About the latter end of August, a Dutch man of Warre of the burden of a 160 tunes arrived at Point-Comfort, the Comandors name Capt Jope, his Pilott for the West Indies one Mr Marmaduke an Englishman. They mett with the Tre[asure]r in the West Indyes, and determyned to hold consort shipp hetherward, but in their passage lost one another. He brought not any thing but 20. and odd Negroes, which the Governor and Cape Marchant [Abraham Piersey] bought for victuall (whereof he was in greate need as he p[re]tended) at the best and easyest rate they could. He hadd a lardge and ample Comyssion from his Excellency to range and take purchase in the West Indyes. [No evidence exists concerning the exact status of these individuals, who may have been sold as slaves for life or as indentured servants who would gain freedom after several years' labor.]

Source: Susan M. Kingsbary, ed., *The Records of the Virginia Company of London,* 4 vols. (Washington, D.C.: U.S. Government Printing Office, 1906–1935), III, 244.

The First Jewish Community Established in North America. Rev. Johannes Megapolensis to Amsterdam Ministers, March 18, 1655.

[New Amsterdam] Some Jews came from Holland last summer, in order to trade. Later a few Jews came upon the same ship as De Polheymius; they were healthy, but poor. It would have been proper, that they should have been supported by their

The first Africans known to have been imported as laborers to the thirteen colonies arrived at Jamestown, Virginia, in 1619 on a Dutch warship, as pictured here by Howard Pyle. Because no law provided a legal basis for chattel slavery at that date, it is not definitely known whether these individuals held the status of slaves for life or were sold as servants obliged to serve for a specified number of years before being set free. (Courtesy Library of Congress)

After first becoming established at New Amsterdam in the 1650s, the Jewish community eventually established synagogues in five cities by 1763. The only one of these colonial buildings still standing is the simple but stately Touro Synagogue in Newport, Rhode Island. (Historic American Buildings Survey, courtesy Library of Congress)

own people, but they have been at our charge, so that we have had to spend several hundred guilders for their support. They came several times to my house, relating and bemoaning their misery. If I directed them to the Jewish merchant [Jacob Barsimon], they said he would not even lend them a few stivers. Some more have come from Holland this spring. They report that many more of the same lot would follow, and then they would build here a synagogue.

Source: Hugh Hastings, ed., *Ecclesiastical Records, State of New York,* 7 vols. (Albany: J. B. Lyon Printers, 1901–16), I, 335.

An Indentured Servant's Contract for a Scottish Girl, 1733

This Indenture made at Edinburgh the Twenty eight day of Aprile One thousand seven hundred and thirty three years Betwixt David Ferguson Mer[chan]t in Edinburgh on the one part and Ann Hill residenter in Ed[inburgh] on the other part. Witnesseth that the Said Ann Hill doeth Covenant and agree with the Said David Ferguson or his Assignees for the Space of four years from and after the Said Ann Hill her first and next arrival at Philadelphia or any other of his Majesties plantations in America. There to serve the said David Ferguson or his assigneys in what service & employment they shall think fitt to imploy her in during the space forsaid. In Consideration whereof the Said David Ferguson doth Covenant & agree to pay for the said Ann Hill her passage to Philadelphia & to find for & allow her meat drink apparell, lodging & all other necessarys

from the date hereof during the Space of this Indenture and to give her the Ordinar allowance of the Country after the Expiration hereof according to the Custome of the Country in the like kind. In witness whereof this Indenture is written upon Stamped paper by Robert Gray. . . .

Robert Gray, N.P. [Notary Public]

Source: Manuscript Collections of the Monmouth County, New Jersey, Historical Society, Freehold, N.J.

Gottlieb Mittelberger, Journey to Pennsylvania in 1750

[The journey from Germany to Pennsylvania] lasts from the beginning of May to the end of October, fully half a year, amid such hardships as no one is able to describe adequately with their misery.

The cause is because the Rhine-boats from Heilbronn to Holland have to pass by 36 custom-houses, at all of which the ships are examined, which is done when it suits the convenience of the custom-house officials. In the meantime the ships with the people are detained long, so that the passengers have to spend much money. The trip down the Rhine alone lasts therefore 4, 5 and even six weeks.

When the ships with the people come to Holland, they are detained there likewise 5 or 6 weeks. Because things are very expensive there, the poor people have to spend nearly all they have during that time. Not to mention many sad accidents that

German immigrants, like those whose experiences were related by Gottlieb Mittelberger, gained a reputation as especially careful and efficient agriculturalists. Unlike Anglo-Americans who used ordinary mold plows (see page 64), many Germans kept using central European wheeled plows, like this 77-inch one owned by Henry Kloch of Palatine, New York, in the 1760s. (Courtesy National Museum of American History, Smithsonian Institution, negative 42163-A)

occur here; having seen with my own eyes how a man, as he was about to board the ship near Rotterdam, lost two children at once by drowning.

Both in Rotterdam and in Amsterdam the people are packed densely, like herrings so to say in the large sea-vessels. One person receives a place of scarcely 2 feet width and 6 feet length in the bedstead, while many a ship carries four to six hundred souls; not to mention the innumerable implements, tools, provisions, water-barrels and other things that likewise occupy much space.

On account of contrary winds it takes the ships sometimes 2, 3 and 4 weeks to make the trip from Holland to Cowes in England. But when the wind is good, they get there in 8 days or even sooner. Everything is examined there and the custom-duties paid, whence it comes that the ships ride there 8, 10 to 14 days even longer at anchor, till they have taken in their full cargoes. During that time every one is compelled to spend his last remaining money and to consume his little stock of provisions that had been reserved for the sea; so that most passengers, finding themselves on the ocean where they would be in need of them, must suffer from hunger and want. Many suffer want already on the water between Holland and Old England.

When the ships have for the last time weighed their anchors near the city of Cowes in England, the real misery begins with the long voyage. For from there the ships, unless they have good wind, must often sail 8, 9, 10 to 12 weeks before they reach Philadelphia. But even with the best wind the voyage lasts 7 weeks.

But during the voyage there is on board terrible misery, stench, fumes, horror, vomiting, many kinds of sea-sickness, fever, dysentery, headache, heat, constipation, boils, scurvy, cancer, mouth-rot, and the like, all of which come from old and sharply salted food and meat, also from very bad and foul water, so that many die miserably.

Add to this want of provisions, hunger, thirst, frost, heat, dampness, anxiety, want, afflictions and lamentations, together with other trouble, as for example the lice abound so frightfully, especially on sick people, that they can be scraped off the body. The misery reaches the climax when a gale rages for 2 or 3 nights and days, so that every one believes that the ship will go to the bottom with everyone on board. In such a nightmare the people weep and cry most piteously …

I myself had to pass through a severe illness at sea, and I best know how I felt at the time. These poor people often long for consolation, and I often entertained and comforted them with singing, praying and encouragement; and whenever it was possible and the winds and waves permitted it, I kept daily prayer-meetings with them on deck. Besides, I baptized five children in distress, because we had no ordained minister on board. I also held divine service every Sunday by reading sermons to the people; and when the dead were sunk in the water, I commended them and our souls to the mercy of God …

No one can have an idea of the sufferings that women in confinement have to bear with their innocent children on board these ships. Few of this class escape with their lives; many a mother is cast into the water with her child as soon as she is dead. One day, just as we had a heavy gale, a woman in our ship, who was to give birth and could not deliver under the circumstances, was eased through a [port-hole] in the ship and then fell into the sea, because she was far in the rear of the ship and could not be brought forward. Children from 1 to 7 years rarely survive the voyage; and many a time parents are compelled to see their children miserably suffer and die from hunger, thirst and sickness,

and then to seem cast into the water. I witnessed such misery in no less than 32 children in our ship, all of whom were thrown into the sea. The parents grieve all the more since their children find no resting-place in the earth, but are devoured by the monsters of the sea. It is a notable fact that children, who have not yet had the measles or smallpox, generally get them on board the ship, and mostly die of them …

That most of the people get sick is not surprising, since, in addition to all other trials and hardships, hot food is served only three times a week, the rations being very poor and very little. Such meals can hardly be eaten, on account of being so unclean. The water that is served out of the ships is often very black, thick and full of worms, so that one cannot drink it without loathing, even with the greatest thirst … Toward the end we were compelled to eat the ship's biscuit that had spoiled long ago; though in a whole biscuit there was scarcely a piece the size of a dollar that had not been full of red worms and spiders' nests. …

At length, when, after a long and tedious voyage, the ships come in sight of land, so that the promontories can bee seen, which the people were so eager and anxious to see, all creep from below on deck, to see the land from afar, and they weep for joy, and pray and sing, thanking and praising God.

Source: Carl T. Eben, ed. and trans., *Gottlieb Mittelberger's Journey to Pennsylvania* (Philadelphia: J.Y. Jeanes, 1898), 18–24.

A Swedish Visitor Describes American Slaves. Peter Kalm, Travels in North America (1753–1761)

The servants which are made use of in the English American colonies are either free persons or slaves; … Formerly the Negroes were brought over from Africa, and bought by almost everyone who could afford it. The Quakers alone scrupled to have slaves, but they are no longer so nice, and they have as many slaves as other people. However, many people cannot conquer the idea of its being contrary to the laws of Christianity to keep slaves. There are likewise several free Negroes in town [Philadelphia], who have been lucky enough to get a very zealous Quaker for their master, who have them their liberty, after they had faithfully served him for some time.

At present they seldom bring over any Negroes to the English colonies, for those which were formerly brought thither have multiplied considerably. In regard to their marriage they proceed as follows: In case you have not only male but likewise female Negroes, they must intermarry, and then the children are all your slaves. But if you possess a male Negro only, and he has an inclination to marry a female belonging to a different master, you did not hinder your Negro in so delicate a point; but it is no advantage to you, for the children belong to the master of the female. It is therefore advantageous to have Negro women.

…The Negroes in the North American colonies are treated more mildly and fed better than those in the West Indies. They have as good food as the rest of the [white] servants, and they possess equal advantages in all things, except their being obliged to serve their whole lifetime, and get no other wages than what their master's goodness allows them. They are likewise clad at their master's expense. On the contrary, in the West Indies, and especially in the Spanish Islands they are treated very cruelly; therefore no threats make more impression upon a Negro here than that of sending him over to the West Indies, in case he would not reform. …

In the year 1620 some Negroes were brought to North America by a Dutch ship, and in Virginia they bought twenty of them. These are said to have been the first that came hither. When the Indians, who were then more numerous in the country than at present, saw these black people for the first time, they thought they were a true breed of devils, and therefore they called them "Manitto" for a great while; this word in their language signified not only God, but likewise the devil. Some time before that, when they saw the first European ship on their coasts, they were perfectly persuaded that God himself was in the ship. This account I got from some Indians, who preserved it among them as a tradition which they received from their ancestors; therefore the arrival of the Negroes seemed to them to have confused everything. But since that time, they have entertained less disagreeable notions of the Negroes, for at present many live among them, and they even sometimes intermarry, as I myself have seen.

Source: Mortimer J. Adler, ed., *The Annals of America,* 18 vols. (Chicago: Encyclopedia Britannica, Inc., 1968), I, 476–479.

The Social and Cultural Milieu of the Colonies

The Massachusetts Bay Old Deluder Act, 1647

This law, popularly known for justifying itself as a foil to Satan's schemes, mandated the first system of publicly funded education created anywhere in the world. State-supported primary education spread throughout New England, which became the first society to attain near universal male literacy by about 1700.

It being one cheife project of the ould deluder, Satan, to keepe men from the knowledge of the Scriptures, as in former times by keeping them in an unknowne tongue [Latin], so in these latter times by perswading from the use of tongues, that so at least the true sence and & meaning of the originall might be clouded by false glosses of saint seeming deceivers, that learning may not be buried in the grave of our fathers in the church & commonwealth, the Lord assisting our endeavours.

It is therefore enacted, that every towneship in the jurisdiction, after the Lord hath increased them to the number of 50 householders, shall then forthwith appoint one within their towne to teach all such children as shall resort to him to write & reade, whose wages shall be paid either by the parents or masters of such children, or by the inhabitants in generall, by way of supply, as the major part of those that order the prudentials of the towne shall appoint; provided, those that send their children be not oppressed by paying much more than they can have them taught for in other townes; & it is further ordered, that where any towne shall increase to the number of 100 families or householders, they shall set up a grammer schoole, the master thereof being able to instruct youth so farr as they may be fited for the university, provided, that if any towne neglect the performance hereof above one yeare, that every such towne shall pay 5£ to the next schoole till they shall performe this order.

Source: Nathaniel B. Shurtleff, ed., *Records of the Governor and Company of the Massachusetts Bay,* 6 vols. (Boston: W. White Printers, 1853–54), II, 203.

Trial for Witchcraft, New York, 1665

At [th]e Court of Assizes held in New Yorke

[Oct. 2, 1665]

The Tryall of Ralph Hall and Mary his wife upon suspicion of Witchcraft.

The names of the Persons who served on the Grand Jury.

Thomas Baker, Foreman of [th]e Jury, of East Hampton

Mr Hall of Jamaica
Anthony Waters of Jamaica
Thomas Wandall of Marshpath Kills
Mr Nicolls of Stamford
Balthazer de Haart of New York
John Garland of New York
Jacob Leisler of New York
Anthonio de Mill of New York
Alexander Munro of New York
Thomas Searle of New York

The Prisoners being brought to the Barr by Allard Anthony, Sheriffe of New Yorke, This following Indictm[en]t was read, first against Ralph Hall and then ag[ain]st Mary his wife, vizt.

The Constable and Overseers of the Towne of Seatallcott, in the East Riding of Yorkshire upon Long Island, Do Present for our Soveraigne Lord the King, That Ralph Hall of Seatallcott aforesaid, upon [th]e 25th day of December; being Christmas day last, was Twelve Monthes, in the 15th yeare of the Raigne of our Soveraigne Lord, Charles [th]e Second, by the Grace of God, King of England, Scotland, France and Ireland, Defender of the Faith &c, and severall other dayes and times since that day, by some detestable and wicked Arts, commonly called Witchcraft and Sorcery, did (as is suspected) maliciously and feloniously, practice and Exercise at the said towne of Seatalcott in the East Riding of Yorkshire on Long Island aforesaid, on the Person of George Wood, late of the same place by w[hi]ch wicked and destable Arts, the said George Wood (as it is suspected) most dangerously and mortally sickned and languished, And not long after by the aforesaid wicked and destable Arts, the said George Wood (as is likewise suspected) dyed.

MOREOVER, The Constable and overseers of the said Towne of Seatalcott, in the East Riding of Yorkshire upon Long Island aforesaid, do further Present for our Soveraigne Lord the King, That some while after the death of the aforesaid George Wood, The said Ralph Hall did (as is suspected) divers times by [th]e wicked and destestable Arts, comonly called Witchcraft and Sorcery, Maliciously and feloniously practise and Exercise at the said Towne of Seatalcott, in the East Riding of Yorkshire upon Long Island aforesaid, on the Person of an Infant Childe of Ann Rogers, widow of [th]e aforesaid George Wood deceased, by w[hic]h wicked and detestable Arts, the said Infant Childe (as is suspected) most dangerously & mortally sickned and languished, and not long after by the said Wicked and destestable Arts (as is likewise suspected) dyed, And so [th]e said Constable and Overseers do Present, That the said George Wood, and the s[ai]d Infante s[ai]d Childe by the wayes and meanes aforesaid, most wickedly and maliciously and feloniously were (as is suspected) murdered by the said Ralph Hall at the times and places aforesaid, ag[ain]st [th]e Peace of Our Soveraigne Lord [th]e King and against the Laws of this Government in such Cases Provided.

The like Indictm[en]t was read, against Mary the wife of Ralph Hall.

There upon, severall Depositions, accusing [th]e Prisonrs of [th]e fact for which they endicted were read, but no witnesse appeared to give Testimony vive voce [by voice].

Then the Clarke calling upon Ralph Hall, bad him hold up his hand, and read as followes.

Ralph Hall thou standest here indicted, for that having not [th]e feare of God before thine eyes. Thou did'st upon the 25th day of December, being Christmas day last was 12 Moneths, and at sev'[er]all other times since, as is suspected, by some wicked and destestable Arts, commonly called witchcraft and Sorcery, maliciously and feloniously practice and Exercise, upon the Bodyes of George Wood and an Infant Childe of Ann Rogers, by which said Arts, the said George Wood and the Infant Childe (as is suspected) most dangerously and mortally fell sick, and languisht unto death. Ralph Hall, what dost thou say for thyselfe, art thou guilty, or not guilty?

Mary the wife of Ralph Hall was called upon in like manner.

They both Pleaded not guilty and threw themselves to bee Tryed by God and the Country.

Where upon, their Case was referr'd to the [th]e Jury, who brought in to the Court, this following verdict, vizt.

Wee having seriously considered the Case committed to our Charge, against [th]e Prisonrs at the Barr, and having well weighed [th]e Evidence, wee finde that there are some suspitions by the Evidence, of what the woman is Charged with, but nothing considerable of value to take away her life. But in reference to the man wee finde nothing considerable to charge him with.

The Court there upon, gave this sentence, That the man should bee bound Body and Goods for his wives Appearance, at the next Sessions, and so on from Sessions to Sessions as long as they stay w[i]thin this Government, In the meane while, to bee of [th]e good Behavior. So they were return'd into the Sheriffs Custody, and upon Entring into a Recognizance, according to the Sentence of the Court, they were released.

Source: Edmund B. O'Callaghan, ed., *The Documentary History of the State of New York,* 4 vols. (Albany: Weed, Parsons, & Co., 1849–51), IV, 133–136.

Rev. Increase Mather, An Arrow Against Profane and Promiscuous Dancing Drawn out of Quiver of the Scriptures (Boston, 1684)

Concerning the controversy about dancing, the question is not whether all dancing be in itself sinful. It is granted that pyrrhical or polemical saltation, *i.e.,* when men vault in their armor to show their strength and activity, may be of use. Nor is the question whether a sober and grave dancing of men with men or women with women be not allowable; we make no doubt of that, where it may be done without offense, in due season and with moderation. The Prince of Philosophers [Jesus Christ] has observed truly that dancing or leaping is a natural expression of joy; so that there is no more sin in it than in laughter or any outward expression of inward rejoicing.

But our question is concerning gynecandrical dancing, or that which is commonly called mixed or promiscuous dancing, viz., of men and women (be they elder or younger persons) together. Now this we affirm to be utterly unlawful and that it cannot be tolerated in such a place as New England without great sin.

Ant that it may appear that we are not transported by affection without judgment, let the following arguments be weighed in the balance of the sanctuary.

That which the Scripture condemns is sinful. None but atheists will deny this proposition; but the Scripture condemns promiscuous dancing. This assumption is proved from the Seventh Commandment. It is an eternal truth to be observed in expounding the Commandments that whenever any sin is forbidden, not only the highest acts of that sin but all degrees thereof and all occasions leading thereto are prohibited. Now we cannot find one orthodox and judicious divine that writes on the Commandments but mentions promiscuous dancing as a breach of the Seventh Commandment, as being an occasion and an incentive to that which is evil in the sight of God. ...

The unchaste touches and gesticulations used by dancers have a palpable tendency to that which is evil. Whereas some object that they are not sensible of any ill motions occasioned in them, by being spectators or actors in such saltations, we are not bound to believe all which some pretend concerning their own mortification. ...

A Christian should do nothing wherein he cannot exercise grace or put a respect of obedience to God on what he does. This in lawful recreations may be done. ... But who can seriously pray to the Holy God to be with him when he is going to a promiscuous dance? It is that which hinders religious exercises, especially for persons to go immediately from hearing a sermon to a gynecandircal dance. It is a high degree of profaneness, an impudent contempt put upon the Gospel. The devil thereby catches away the good seed of the Word, and the former religious exercise is rendered ineffectual. ...

But will you that are professors of religion have your children to be thus taught? The Lord expects that you should give the children who are baptized into His name another kind of education, that you should bring them up in the nurture and admonition of the Lord. And do you not hear the Lord expostulating the case with you and saying, you have taken my children, the children that were given unto me; the children that were solemnly engaged to renounce the pomps of Satan; but is this a light matter that you have taken these my children and initiated them in the pomps and vanities of the wicked one, contrary to your covenant? What will you say in the day of the Lord's pleading with you?

Source: Mortimer J. Adler, ed., *The Annals of America,* 18 vols. (Chicago: Encyclopedia Britannica, Inc., 1968), I, 272–273.

Antislavery Petition of the Germantown, Pennsylvania, Quakers, 1688

These are the reasons why we are against the traffic of mensbody as follows: Is there any that would be done or handled at this manner, viz., to be sold or made a slave for all the time of his life? How fearful and fainthearted are many on sea when they see a strange vessel, being afraid it should be a Turk, and they should be taken and sold for slaves in Turkey. Now what is this better done as Turks do? Yea, rather it is worse for them which say they are Christians, for we hear that the most part of such Negroes are brought hither against their will and consent, and that many of them are stolen. Now, though they are black, we cannot conceive there is more liberty to have them slaves as it is to have other white ones. There is a saying that we shall do to all men like as we will be done ourselves, making no difference of what generation, descent, or color they are. And those who steal or rob men, and those who buy or purchase them, are not they all alike? Here is liberty of conscience, which is right and reasonable. Here ought to be likewise liberty of the body, except of evildoers, which is another case. But to bring men hither, or to rob and sell them against their will, we stand against.

In Europe there are many oppressed for conscience sake; and here there are those oppressed which are of a black color. And we, who know that men must not commit adultery in others, separating wives from their husbands and giving them to others, and some sell the children of those poor creatures to other men. Oh! do consider well this thing, you who do it, if you would be done at this manner, and if it is done according [to] Christianity? You surpass Holland and Germany in this thing. This makes an ill report in all those countries of Europe, where they hear of that the Quakers Do here handle men like they handle the cattle. And for that reason some have no mind or inclination to come hither.

And who shall maintain this your cause or plead to it? Truly we cannot do so except you shall inform us better hereof, viz., that Christians have liberty to practise these things. Pray! What thing in the world can be done worse toward us than if men should rob or steal us away and sell us for slaves to strange countries, separating husbands from their wives and children.

Being now this is not done at that manner we will be done at, therefore, we contradict and are against this traffic of mens-bodies. And we who profess that it is not lawful to steal must likewise avoid to purchase such things as are stolen, but rather help to stop this robbing and stealing if possible and such men ought to be delivered out of the hands of the robbers and set free as well as in Europe. Then is Pennsylvania to have a good report; instead it has now a bad one for this sake in other countries. Especially whereas the Europeans are desirous to know in what manner the Quakers do rule in their province, and most of them do look upon us with an envious eye. But if this is done well, what shall we say is done evil?

If once these slaves (which they say are so wicked and stubborn men) should join themselves, fight for their freedom and handle their masters and mistresses as they did handle them before, will these masters and mistresses take the sword at hand and war against the poor slaves, like we are able to believe some will not refuse to do? Or have these Negroes not as much right to fight for their freedom as you have to keep them slaves?

Now consider well this thing, if it is good or bad. And in case you find it to be good to handle these blacks at that manner, we desire and require you hereby lovingly that you may inform us herein, which at this time never was done, viz., that Christians have liberty to do so, to the end we shall be satisfied in this point, and satisfy likewise our good friends and acquaintants in our native country, to whom it is a terror or fearful thing that men should be handled so in Pennsylvania.

Source: Pennsylvania Magazine of History and Biography, IV (1880), 28–30.

Revivalism Becomes Part of American Culture. Benjamin Franklin Describes Rev. George Whitefield, 1739

In 1739 arrived among us from England the Reverend Mr. [George] Whitefield, who had made himself remarkable there as an itinerant preacher. He was at first permitted to preach in some of our churches; but the clergy, taking a dislike to him, soon refus'd him their pulpits, and he was oblig'd to preach in the fields. The multitudes of all sects and denominations that attended his sermons were enormous, and it was matter of speculation to me, who was one of the number, to observe the extraordinary influence of his oratory on his hearers, and how much they admir'd and respected him, notwithstanding his common abuse of them, by assuring them they were naturally *half beasts and half devils.* It was wonderful to see the change soon made in the manners of our inhabitants. From being thoughtless or indifferent about religion, it seem'd as if all the world were growing religious, so that one could not walk thro' the town [Philadelphia] in an evening without hearing psalms sung in different families of every street. . . .

He had a loud and clear voice, and articulated his words and sentences so perfectly, that he might be heard and understood at a great distance, especially as his auditories, however numerous, observ'd the most exact silence. He preach'd one evening from the top of the Court-house steps, which are in the middle of Market-street, and on the west side of Second-street, which crosses it at right angles. Both streets were fill'd with his hearers to a considerable distance. Being among the hindmost in Market-street, I had the curiosity to learn how far he could be heard, by retiring backwards down the street towards the river; and I found his voice distinct till I came near Front-street, when some noise in that street obscur'd it. Imagining then a semicircle, of which my distance should be the radius, and that it were fill'd with auditors, to each of whom I allow'd two square feet, I computed that he well might be heard by more than thirty thousand. This reconcil'd me to newspaper accounts of his having preach'd to twenty-five thousand people in the fields. . . .

By hearing him often, I came to distinguish easily between sermons newly compos'd, and those which he had often preach'd in the course of his travels. His delivery of the latter was so improv'd by frequent repetitions that every accent, every emphasis, every modulation of voice, was so perfectly well turn'd and well plac'd, that, without being interested in the subject, one could not help being pleas'd with the discourse; a pleasure of much the same kind with that receiv'd from an excellent piece of musick. This is an advantage itinerant preachers have over those who are stationary, as the latter can not well improve their delivery of a sermon by so many rehearsals.

Source: Albert H. Smyth, ed., *The Writings of Benjamin Franklin,* 10 vols. (New York: The Macmillan Co., Ltd., 1905–07), I, 354–359.

The Dynamics of Explosive Population Growth. Benjamin Franklin's "Observations Concerning the Increase of Mankind" (1751)

Europe is generally full settled with husbandmen, manufacturers, etc., and therefore cannot now much increase in people. America is chiefly occupied by Indians, who subsist mostly by hunting. But as the hunter, of all men, requires the greatest quantity of land from whence to draw his subsistence (the husbandman subsisting on much less, the gardener on still less, and the manufacturer requiring least of all), the Europeans found America as fully settled as it well could be by hunters. Yet these, having large tracts, were easily prevailed on to part with portions of territory to the newcomers, who did not much interfere with the natives in hunting, and furnished them with many things they wanted.

Land being thus plenty in America and so cheap that a laboring man that understands husbandry can in a short time save money enough to purchase a piece of new land sufficient for a plantation, whereon he may subsist a family, such are not afraid to marry; for, if they even look far enough forward to consider how their children, when grown up, are to be provided for, they se that more land is to be had at rates equally easy, all circumstances considered.

Hence marriages in America are more general, and more generally early, than in Europe. And if it is reckoned there that there is but one marriage per annum among 100 persons, perhaps we may here reckon two; and if in Europe they have but four births to a marriage (many of their marriages being late), we may here reckon eight, of which if one half grow up, and our marriages are made, reckoning one with another, at twenty years of age, our people must at least be doubled every twenty years.

But notwithstanding this increase, so vast is the territory of North America that it will require many ages to settle it fully; and, till it is fully settled, labor will never be cheap here, where no man continues long a laborer for others, but gets a plantation of his own; no man continues long a journeyman to a trade, but goes among those new settlers and sets up for himself; etc. Hence labor is no cheaper now in Pennsylvania than it was thirty years ago, though so many thousand laboring people have been imported. …

Thus, there are supposed to be now upward of 1,000,000 English souls in North America (though 'tis thought scarce 80,000 have been brought over sea), and, yet, perhaps, there is not one the fewer in Britain, but rather many more, on account of the employment the colonies afford to manufacturers at home. This 1,000,000 doubling, suppose but once in twenty-five years, will, in another century, be more than the people of England, and the greatest number of Englishmen will be on this side of the water. [*Note:* This prediction that the thirteen colonies' future population would exceed that of England by the 1840s proved correct.]

Source: Jared Sparks, ed., *The Works of Benjamin Franklin,* 10 vols. (Boston: Hilliard, Gray & Co., 1840), II, 311–314, 319–320.

Frontier Life. Joseph Doddridge's Notes on the Settlement and Indian Wars of Virginia and Pennsylvania (Wellsburg, 1824)

Many of the sports of the early settlers of this country [Pennsylvania] were imitative of the exercises and stratagems of hunting and war. …

[An] important pastime of our boys was that of imitating the noise of every bird and beast in the woods. This faculty was not merely a pastime, but a very necessary part of education, on account of its utility in certain circumstances. The imitations of the gobbling and other sounds of wild turkeys often brought those keen eyed and ever watchful tenants of the forest within the reach of the rifle. The bleating of the fawn brought her dam to her death in the same way. The hunter often collected a company of mopish owls to the trees about his camp, and amused himself with their hoarse screaming; his howl would raise and obtain responses from a pack of wolves, so as to inform him of their neighborhood, as well as guard him against their depredations.

Throwing the tomahawk was another boyish sport, in which many acquired considerable skill. The tomahawk with its handle of a certain length will make a given number of turns in a given distance. Say in five steps it will strike with the edge, the handle downwards; at the distance of seven and a half, it will strike with the edge, the handle upwards, and so on. A little experience enabled the boy to measure the distance with his eye, when walking through the woods, and strike a tree with his tomahawk in any way he chose.

The athletic sports of running, jumping and wrestling, were the pastimes of boys, in common with the men. A well grown boy, at the age of twelve or thirteen years, was furnished with a small rifle and shot pouch. He then became a fort soldier, and had his port hole assigned him. Hunting squirrels, turkeys and raccoons soon made him expert in the use of his gun.

Dancing was the principal amusement of our young people of both sexes. Their dances, to be sure, were of the simplest forms. Three and four handed reels and jigs. Contra dances, cotillions and minuets, were unknown. I remember to have seen, once or twice, a dance which was called the Irish trot, …

Dramatic narrations, chiefly concerning Jack and the giant, furnished our young people with another source of amusement during their leisure hours. Many of these tales were lengthy, and embraced a considerable range of incident. Jack, always the

The dress of many frontier residents, like the Pennsylvanians described by Joseph Doddridge, resembled this long hunter, shown here with the hunting dogs he kept to help run down game and give early warning of Indians. (Ink drawing by David Wright, available from Gray Stone Press of Nashville at 1-800-252-2664)

hero of the story, after encountering many difficulties, and performing many great achievements, came off conqueror of the giant. Many of these stories were tales of knight errantry, in which some captive virgin was released from captivity and restored to her lover. These dramatic narrations concerning Jack and the giant bore a strong resemblance to the poems of Ossian, the story of the Cyclops and Ulysses, in the Odyssey of Homer, and the tale of the giant and Great-heart, in the *Pilgrim's Progress.* They were so arranged, as to the different incidents of the narration, that they were easily committed to memory. ...

Singing was another, but no very common, amusement among our first settlers. Their tunes were rude enough, to be sure. Robin Hood furnished a number of our songs, the balance were mostly tragical. These last were denominated "love songs about murder;" as to cards, dice, back-gammon and other games of chance, we knew nothing about them. ...

The furniture for the table, for several years after the settlement of this country, consisted of a few pewter dishes, plates and spoons; but mostly of wooden bowls, trencher and noggins. If these last were scarce, gourds and hard shelled squashes made up the deficiency. The iron pots, knives and forks, were brought from the east side of the mountains along with the salt and iron on pack horses. These articles of furniture corresponded very well with the articles of diet on which they were employed. "Hog and hominy" were proverbial for the dish of which they were the component parts. Johnny cake and pone were at the outset of the settlements of the country the only forms of bread

in use for breakfast and dinner. At supper, milk and mush was the standard dish. When milk was not plenty, which was often the case, owing to the scarcity of cattle, or the want of proper pasture for them, the substantial dish of hominy had to supply the place of them; mush was frequently eaten with sweetened water, molasses, bear's oil, or the gravy of fried meat.

Every family, besides a little garden for the few vegetables which they cultivated, had another small enclosure containing from half an acre to an acre, which they called a *truck patch,* in which they raised corn for roasting ears, pumpkins, squashes, beans and potatoes. These, in the latter part of summer and fall, were cooked with their pork, venison and bear meat for dinner, and made very wholesome and well tasted dishes. The standard dinner dish for every log rolling, house raising and harvest day was a pot pie, or what in other countries is called *sea pie.* This, besides answering for dinner, served for a part of the supper also. The remainder of it from dinner, being eaten with milk in the evening, after the conclusion of the labor of the day.

...Yet our homely fare, and unsightly cabins, and furniture, produced a hardy veteran race, who planted the first footsteps of society and civilization in the immense regions of the west. Inured to hardihood, bravery and labor from their early youth, they sustained with manly fortitude the fatigue of the chase, the campaign and scout.

Source: Alden T. Vaughan, ed., *America Before the Revolution, 1725–1775* (Englewood Cliffs: Prentice-Hall, Inc., N.J., 1967), 68–69, 162–163.

Bibliography

The most comprehensive bibliography of book-length works on the colonial period is David L. Ammerman and Philip D. Morgan, *Books About Early America: 2001 Titles* (Williamsburg, Va.: Institute of Early American History and Culture, 1989). Researchers seeking to supplement this source should consult the bibliographies contained in David Hawke, *The Colonial Experience* (Indianapolis: Bobbs-Merrill, 1966), Jack P. Greene and J. R. Pole, eds., *Colonial British America: Essays in the New History of the Early Modern Era* (Baltimore: The Johns Hopkins University Press, 1984), and Richard Middleton, *Colonial America: A History, 1607–1760* (Cambridge, Mass. and Oxford, Eng.: Blackwell Publishers, 1992). A recently published source of basic facts about the colonial period is John Mack Farragher, *The Encyclopedia of Colonial and Revolutionary America* (New York: Facts On File, 1990). Extensive citations of scholarship in this field can also be found in Frank Freidel, ed., *Harvard Guide to American History* (Cambridge, Mass.: Harvard University Press [rev. 2d ed.], 1974).

An overview of New England's climatic conditions, which serves as a model for reconstructing the impact of weather upon other colonial regions, can be found in Karen Ordahl Kupperman's "Climate and Mastery of the Wilderness in Seventeenth-Century New England," in Colonial Society of Massachusetts, ed., *Seventeenth-Century New England* (Charlottesville, Va.: University Press of Virginia, 1984), 3–37. Another valuable monograph is David M. Ludlum's *Early American Winters, 1604–1820* (Boston: The American Meteorological Society, 1966). The most complete collections of temperature and precipitation records are in Charles A. Schott, ed., *Tabulations of Resulting Mean Temperatures from Observations Extending Over a Series of Years ... for Stations in North America* (Washington, D.C.: Smithsonian Institution, 1874) and the work of Helmut E. Landsberg as published in "Preliminary Reconstruction of a Long Time Series of Climatic Data for the Eastern US," *Technical Note BN–571* (Sep. 1968) of the University of Maryland's Institute for Fluid Dynamics and Applied Mathematics, and in H. H. Lamb, ed., *Climate: Present, Past, and Future*, 2 vols. (London: Methuen and Co., 1977), II, 577, 625, 626.

Among the best examinations of environmental change during the colonial era are William J. Cronon, *Changes in the Land: Indians, Colonists, and the Ecology of New England* (New York: Hill and Wang, 1983), Stephen J. Pyne, *Fire in America: A Cultural History of Woodland and Rural Fire* (Princeton: Princeton University Press, 1982), and Michael Williams, *Americans and Their Forests: A Historical Geography* (Cambridge, Eng.: Cambridge University Press, 1989). Jay R. Nash has provided the most complete listing of natural disasters in his *Darkest Hours: A Narrative Encyclopedia of Worldwide Disasters from Ancient Times to the Present* (Chicago: Nelson-Hall, 1976). Earthquakes occurred more frequently along the Atlantic seaboard during the seventeenth and eighteenth centuries than at present, and the U.S. Coast and Geodetic Survey has documented their activity in its *Earthquake History of the United States* (Washington, D.C.: U.S. Government Printing Office, rev. ed., 1965).

Donald W. Meinig currently sets the standard for scholarship on historical geography during colonial times in *The Shaping of America: A Geographical Perspective on Five Hundred Years of History, I, Atlantic America, 1492–1800* (New Haven: Yale University Press, 1986), the footnotes of which will refer readers to a wealth of sources on all aspects of this subject. Stella H. Sutherland compiled the best statistical data on the expansion of Anglo-America's settled area in her *Population Distribution in Colonial America* (New York: Columbia University Press, 1936). The best maps depicting population density were prepared by Herman R. Friis for publication as "A Series of Population Maps of the Colonies and the United States, 1625–1790," *Geographic Review,* XXX (1940), 463–470.

The Smithsonian Institution has long been engaged in a project to publish a definitive reference series titled *The Handbook of North American Indians,* with William C. Sturtevant as general editor. Of those volumes relevant to a study of colonial America, the following are currently in print: Wilcomb E. Washburn, ed., *History of Indian-White Relations* [vol. IV.] (Washington, D.C.: Smithsonian Institution, 1988); Bruce G. Trigger, ed., *Northeast* [vol. XV] (Washington, D.C.: Smithsonian Institution, 1978); Ives Goddard, ed., *Languages* [vol. XVII] (Washington, D.C.: Smithsonian Institution, 1996). Forthcoming volumes of this series will include *Introduction* [vol. I], *Environment, Origins, and Population* [vol. III], and *Southeast* [vol. XIV].

Other highly valuable reference works on Native Americans are John U. Terrell, *American Indian Almanac* (New York: New World Publishing Co., 1971), Carl Waldman, *Atlas of the North American Indian* (New York: Facts On File, 1985), and Frederick E. Hoxie, *Encyclopedia of North American Indians* (Boston: Houghton Mifflin, 1996). Among the best, specialized works evaluating interaction between Native Americans and Europeans are James Axtell, *The Invasion Within: The Contest of Cultures in Colonial North America* (New York: Oxford University Press, 1985), Alden Vaughan, *The New England Frontier: Puritans and Indians, 1620–1675* (Boston: Little, Brown, 1965), Allen W. Trelease, *Indian Affairs in Colonial New York: The Seventeenth Century* (Ithaca, N.Y.: Cornell University Press, 1960), Daniel K. Richter, *The Ordeal of the Longhouse: The Peoples of the Iroquois League in the Era of European Colonization* (Chapel Hill: University of North Carolina Press, 1992), and James H. Merrell, *The Indians' New World: Catawbas and Their Neighbors from European Contact through the Era of Removal* (Chapel Hill: University of North Carolina Press, 1989). A challenging (some would say provocative) approach to Native American history can be found in Martin Calvin's *Keepers of the Game: Indian-Animal Relationships and the Fur Trade* (Berkeley: University of California, 1978).

For those beginning a study of colonial trade, finance, or business affairs, the best starting point is Edward J. Perkins, *The Economy of Colonial America* (New York: Columbia University Press, 2d rev. ed., 1988). The most detailed review of this topic is John J. McCusker and Russell R. Menard, *The Economy of British America, 1607–1789* (Chapel Hill: University of North Carolina Press, 1985), which concludes with a seventy-seven-page bibliography that lists every significant monograph and article concerning every aspect of its subject. A very valuable synthesis of this field's scholarship is provided by James F. Shepherd and Gary M. Walton's *The Economic Rise of Early America* (New York and Cambridge, Eng.: Cambridge University Press, 1979).

Among the broadest studies of colonial agriculture are Percy W. Bidwell and John I. Falconer, *History of Agriculture in the Northern United States, 1620–1860* (Washington, D.C.: Carnegie Institution of Washington, 1925), Max C. Schumacher, *The Northern Farmer and His Markets During the Late Colonial Period* (New York: Garland Publishing Co., 1975), and Lucius C. Gray, *History of Agriculture in the Southern United States to 1860,* 2 vols. (Washington, D.C.: Carnegie Institution of Washington, 1933). Important studies of the maritime industries and overseas trade include Harold A. Innis, *The Cod Fisheries: The History of an International Economy* (Toronto: University of Toronto Press, rev. ed., 1954), Bernard Bailyn, *The New England Merchants in the Seventeenth Century* (Cambridge, Mass.: Harvard University Press, 1955), Arthur P. Middleton, *Tobacco Coast: A Maritime History of Chesapeake Bay in the Colonial Era* (Newport News, Va.: Mariners' Museum, 1953), and James F. Shepherd and Gary M. Walton, *Shipping, Maritime Trade, and the*

Economic Development of Colonial North America (Cambridge, Eng.: Cambridge University Press, 1972). Price movements are detailed in Arthur H. Cole, *Wholesale Commodity Prices in the United States, 1700–1861,* 2 vols. (Cambridge, Mass.: Harvard University Press, 1938) and Anne Bezanson, et al., eds. *Prices in Colonial Pennsylvania* (Philadelphia: University of Pennsylvania Press, 1935). The best data on imports and exports from Anglo-America were culled from unpublished and published research of specialists like Lawrence A. Harper and Jacob M. Price, and printed in the Bureau of the Census's *Historical Statistics of the United States: Colonial Times to 1970,* 2 vols. (Washington, D.C.: U.S. Government Printing Office, 1975), 1176–1194. (Before using this source, careful scholars should read Price's communication in *William and Mary Quarterly,* XXXIV (1977), 516, in regard to Series Z227–244.) Two other important sources colonial overseas trade are John J. McCusker, "The Current Value of English Exports, 1697–1800," *William and Mary Quarterly,* XXVII (1971), 607–628, and Thomas M. Truxes, *Irish-American Trade, 1660–1783* (New York and Cambridge, Eng.: Cambridge University Press, 1988). Exchange rates and other information on colonial money can be located in John J. McCusker, *Money and Exchange in Europe and America, 1660–1775: A Handbook* (Chapel Hill: University of North Carolina Press, 1978), Curtis P. Nettels, *The Money Supply of the American Colonies before 1720* (Madison: University of Wisconsin Press, 1934), Leslie V. Brock, *The Currency of the American Colonies, 1700–1764: A Study in Colonial Finance and Imperial Relations* (New York: Garland Publishing Co., 1975), and John J. McCusker, "'How Much is That in Real Money?': A Historical Price Index for Use as a Deflator of Monetary Values in the Economy of the United States," in the American Antiquarian Society's *Proceedings,* CI (1991–92), 297–373.

A large number of censuses from the colonial era were printed in Bureau of the Census, *A Century of Population Growth: From the First Census of the United States to the Twelfth, 1790–1900* (Washington, D.C.: U.S. Government Printing Office, 1909), 149–185. Other sources for demographic data, such as tax lists and muster rolls, can be consulted in Evarts B. Greene and Virginia D. Harrington, *American Population Before the Federal Census of 1790* (New York: Columbia University Press, 1932). Robert V. Wells has analyzed many of the more important sources in *The Population of the British Colonies in America before 1776: A Survey of Census Data* (Princeton: Princeton University Press, 1975). An overview of the trends shaping colonial population growth is available in Jim Potter's "Demographic Development and Family Structure," in Jack P. Greene and Jack R. Pole, eds., *Colonial British America: Essays in the New History of the Early Modern Era* (Baltimore: The Johns Hopkins University Press, 1984), 123–156. Quantitative research into the impact of immigration and the slave trade on population growth can be found in Aaron Fogelman, "Migrations to the Thirteen British North American Colonies, 1700–1775: New Estimates," *Journal of Interdisciplinary History,* XXII (1992), 691–709, David W. Galenson, *White Servitude in Colonial America: An Economic Analysis* (New York and Cambridge, Eng.: Cambridge University Press, 1981), and Philip D. Curtin, *The Atlantic Slave Trade: A Census* (Madison: University of Wisconsin Press, 1969).

Significant works on medicine and health in the thirteen colonies include Richard H. Shryock, *Medicine and Society in America, 1660–1860* (New York: New York University Press, 1969), John Duffy, *Epidemics in Colonial America* (Baton Rouge: Louisiana University Press, 1953), John B. Blake, *Public Health in the Town of Boston, 1630–1822* (Cambridge, Mass.: Harvard University Press, 1959), and William H. Williams, *America's First Hospital, The Pennsylvania Hospital, 1751–1841* (Wayne, Pa.: Haverford House, 1976).

For those seeking a general introduction to the religious complexity of early Anglo-America, a wealth of valuable information can be gleaned from Patricia U. Bonomi, *Under the Cope of Heaven: Religion,*

Society, and Politics in Colonial America (New York and Oxford, Eng: Oxford University Press, 1986), Sydney E. Ahlstrom, *A Religious History of the American People,* 2 vols. (New Haven: Yale University Press, 1972), and Edwin E. Gaustad, *Historical Atlas of Religion in America* (New York: Harper and Row, 2d ed., 1976). Two insightful surveys of scholarly trends within this topic are available in Jon Butler, "Magic, Astrology, and the Early American Religious Heritage, 1600–1760," *American Historical Review,* LXXXIV (1979), 317–346, and in David D. Hall, "Religion and Society: Problems and Reconsiderations," in Jack P. Green and Jack R. Pole, eds., *Colonial British America: Essays in the New History of the Early Modern Era* (Baltimore: The Johns Hopkins University Press, 1984), 317–344.

Carl Bridenbaugh has cast a long shadow over early American urban history with two, thick volumes titled *Cities in the Wilderness: The First Century of Urban Life in America, 1625–1742* (New York: Ronald Press, 1938) and *Cities in Revolt: Urban Life in America, 1743–1776* (New York: Alfred E. Knopf, 1955). The only other comparative study based on extensive research into the social and economic development of the largest seaports is Gary B. Nash, *The Urban Crucible: Social Change, Political Consciousness, and the Origins of the American Revolution* (Cambridge, Mass.: Harvard University Press, 1979).

The outstanding work about the foundation of America's school system remains Lawrence A. Cremin, *American Education: The Colonial Experience, 1607–1783* (New York: Harper and Row, 1970), the first volume of his magisterial trilogy. Although less extensive in scope, several other fine monographs also cover this subject, including James Axtell, *The School upon a Hill: Education and Society in Colonial New England* (New Haven: Yale University Press, 1974), Robert Middlekauff, *Ancients and Axioms: Education in Eighteenth-Century New England* (New Haven: Yale University Press, 1963), Samuel Eliot Morison, *Harvard College in the Seventeenth Century,* 2 vols. (Cambridge, Mass.: Harvard University Press, 1936), Richard Warch, *The School of the Prophets: Yale College, 1701–1740* (New Haven: Yale University Press, 1973), and Walter Crosby Eells, *Baccalaureate Degrees Conferred by American Colleges in the Seventeenth and Eighteenth Centuries,* U.S. Office of Education Circular No. 528 (Washington, May 1958).

A recent survey of scholarly activities in the field of colonial American literature has been published as Philip F. Gura, "The Study of Colonial American Literature, 1966–1987: A Vade Mecum," *William and Mary Quarterly,* XLV (1988), 305–341. Emory Elliott has edited two useful reference sources: *American Colonial Writers, 1606–1734* and *American Colonial Writers, 1735–1781,* vols. XXIV and XXXI of *Dictionary of Literary Biography* (Detroit: Gale Research Co., 1984–85). Also see Everett Emerson, ed., *Major Writers of Early American Literature* (Madison: University of Wisconsin Press, 1972), Wayne Franklin, *Discoverers, Explorers, Settlers: The Diligent Writers of Early America* (Chicago: University of Chicago Press, 1979), Kenneth Silverman, ed., *Colonial American Poetry* (New York: Hafner, 1968), and J. A. Leo Lemay, "Calendar of American Poetry in the Colonial Newspapers and Magazines and in the Major English Magazines through 1765," in the American Antiquarian Society's *Proceedings,* LXXIX (1970), 291–392; LXXX (1971), 71–222, 353–455.

Bibliographies of all known colonial imprints are contained in Charles Evans, ed., *American Bibliography: A Chronological Dictionary of all Books, Pamphlets, and Periodicals Printed in the United States … 1630 … to 1820,* 12 vols. (New York: Peter Smith, 1903–34), as amended by Roger P. Bristol, *Supplement to Charles Evans' American Bibliography* (Charlottesville, Va.: Bibliographical Society of the University of Virginia, 1970). On imprints with German text, see Karl R. Arndt and Reimer C. Eck, "The First Century of German Language Printing in the United States of America," *Publications of the Pennsylvania German Society,* XXI (1989). A complete enumeration of newspapers and magazines, with details on their publication histories, is available in

Clarence S. Brigham, *History and Bibliography of American Newspapers, 1690–1820,* 2 vols. (Westport, Conn.: Greenwood Press, rev. ed., 1947), Edward C. Lathem, *Chronological Tables of American Newspapers, 1690–1820* (Barre, Mass.: American Antiquarian Society, 1972), and Frank L. Mott, *A History of American Magazines, 1741–1850* (New York: Appleton, 1957). Also see Arthur B. Berthold, *American Colonial Printing as Determined by Contemporary Cultural Forces* (New York: Carnegie Corporation of New York, 1934), and John Tebbel, *A History of Book Publishing in the United States, I, The Creation of an Industry, 1630–1865* (New York: Bowker, 1972).

Works on early American science and its leading practitioners include: Raymond Phineas Stearns, *Science in the British Colonies of America* (Urbana: University of Illinois Press, 1970); Edmund and Dorothy Smith Berkeley, *Dr. John Mitchell: The Man Who Made the Map of North America* (Chapel Hill: University of North Carolina Press, 1974), idem, *John Clayton: Pioneer of American Botany* (Chapel Hill: University of North Carolina Press, 1963); idem, *The Life and Travels of John Bartram: From Lake Ontario to the River St. John* (Tallahassee: University Presses of Florida, 1982); Joseph and Nesta Ewan, *John Bannister and His Natural History of Virginia, 1678–1692* (Urbana: University of Illinois Press, 1970); Randolph Shipley Klein, ed., *Science and Society in Early America: Essays in Honor Whitfield J. Bell, Jr.,* published as American Philosophical Society, *Memoirs,* CLXVI (1986); and Herbert Leventhal, *In the Shadow of the Enlightenment: Occultism and Renaissance Science in Eighteenth-Century America* (New York: New York University Press, 1976).

Among the more significant works on colonial architecture are Cary Carson et al., "Impermanent Architecture in the Southern American Colonies," *Winterthur Portfolio: A Journal of Material Culture,* XVI (1981), 135–196, Abbott Lowell Cummings, *The Framed Houses of Massachusetts Bay, 1625–1725* (Cambridge, Mass.: Harvard University Press, 1979), James Deetz, *In Small Things Forgotten: The Archaeology of Early American Life* (Garden City, N.Y.: Doubleday, 1977), William H. Pierson, Jr., *American Buildings and Their Architects, I, The Colonial and Neoclassical Styles* (New York: Doubleday, 1970), and Daniel D. Reiff, *Small Georgian Houses in England and Virginia: Origins and Development through the 1750s* (Newark, Del.: University of Delaware Press, 1986).

Among the better studies that convey a sense of the everyday realities of life in early America are: Philip Greven, Jr., "Family Structure in Seventeenth-Century Andover, Massachusetts," *William and Mary Quarterly,* XXIII (1966), 234–256; John Demos, "Notes on Life in Plymouth Colony," *William and Mary Quarterly,* XXII (1965), 264–286; Daniel Scott Smith, "Parental Power and Marriage Patterns: An Analysis of Historical Trends in Hingham, Massachusetts," *Journal of Marriage and the Family,* XXXV (1973), 406–418; Daniel Scott Smith and M. S. Hindus, "Premarital Pregnancy in America, 1640–1971: An Overview and Interpretation," *Journal of Interdisciplinary History,* V (1975), 537–570; John P. Demos, *A Little Commonwealth: Family Life in Plymouth Colony* (New York and Oxford, Eng.: Oxford University Press, 1970); Ivor Noel Hume, *Martin's Hundred* (New York: Alfred E. Knopf, 1982); Darrett and Anita Rutman, *A Place in Time: Middlesex County, Virginia, 1650–1750* (New York: W. W. Norton, 1984), Edmund S. Morgan, *Virginians at Home: Family Life in the Eighteenth Century* (Williamsburg: Colonial Williamsburg Foundation, 1952); Allan Kulikoff, *Tobacco and Slaves: The Development of Southern Cultures in the Chesapeake, 1680–1800* (Chapel Hill: University of North Carolina Preess, 1986); Lois Green Carr and Lorena S. Walsh, "The Planter's Wife: The Experience of White Women in Seventeenth-Century Maryland," *William and Mary Quarterly,* XXXIV (1977), 542–571; Roger Thompson, *Sex in Middlesex: Popular Mores in a Massachusetts County, 1649–1699* (Amherst: University of Massachusetts Press, 1986); and Rhys Isaac, *The Transformation of Virginia, 1740–1790* (Chapel Hill: University of North Carolina Press, 1982). David Hackett Fischer has conceptualized the most compre-hensive and ambitious delineation of the full range of regional subcultures within Anglo-America in his encyclopedic *tour de force, Albion's Seed: Four British Folkways in America* (New York and Oxford, Eng.: Oxford University Press, 1989).

The study of crime and criminal behavior—as opposed to an analysis of lawmaking—is relatively new, with the first major monograph being Douglas Greenberg, *Crime and Law Enforcement in the Colony of New York, 1691–1776* (Ithaca, New York: Cornell University Press, 1974). Now available are David Thomas Konig, *Law and Society in Puritan Massachusetts: Essex County, 1629–1692* (Chapel Hill: University of North Carolina Press, 1979), Donna J. Spindel, *Crime and Society in North Carolina, 1663–1776* (Baton Rouge: Lousiana State University Press, 1989), N. E. H. Hull, *Female Felons: Women and Serious Crime in Colonial Massachusetts* (Urbana: University of Illinois Press, 1987), and Peter C. Hoffer and William B. Scott, eds., *Criminal Proceedings in Colonial Virginia: Richmond County, Virginia, 1710–1754* (Athens, Ga.: University of Georgia Press, 1984). Major studies of sentencing and punishments are Edwin Powers, *Crime and Punishment in Early Massachusetts, 1620–1692* (Boston: Beacon Press, 1966), Adam J. Hirsch, *The Rise of the Penitentiary: Prisons and Punishment in Early America* (New Haven: Yale University Press, 1992), and John M. Murrin, "Magistrates, Sinners, and a Precarious Liberty: Trial by Jury in Seventeenth-Century New England," in David D. Hall, et al., eds., *Saints And Revolutionaries: Essays on Early American History* (New York: W. W. Norton, 1984).

Book-length studies about the law and African-Americans are Philip J. Schwarz, *Twice Condemned: Slaves and the Criminal Laws of Virginia, 1705–1865* (Baton Rouge: Louisiana State University Press, 1988) and Herbert J. Aptheker, *American Negro Slave Revolts* (New York: Columbia University Press, 1943). Convict laborers are examined in A. Roger Ekirch, *Bound For America: The Transportation of British Convicts to the Colonies, 1718–1775* (Oxford, Eng.: Clarendon Press, 1987), and Peter W. Coldham, *Emigrants in Chains: A Social History of Forced Emigration to the Americas of Felons, Destitute Children, Political and Religious Non-Conformists, Vagabonds, Beggars and Other Undesirables, 1607–1776* (Stroud, Eng.: Alan Sutton, 1992).

Classic sources for piracy's golden age are John Exquemeling, *The Bucaniers of America* (London: William Crooke, 1684) and Captain Charles Johnson [Daniel Defoe], *A General History of the Robberies and Murders of the Most Notorious Pirates* (London: Charles Rivington, 1724). Contemporary analyses include Robert C. Ritchie, *Captain Kidd and the War Against the Pirates* (Cambridge, Mass.: Harvard University Press, 1986) and Marcus B. Rediker, *Between the Devil and the Deep Blue Sea: Merchant Seamen, Pirates, and the Anglo-American Maritime World, 1700–1750* (New York and Cambridge, Eng.: Cambridge University Press, 1987).

The best collection of primary source material concerning witchcraft is the three volumes edited by Paul Boyer and Stephen Nissenbaum, *The Salem Witchcraft Papers: Verbatim Transcripts of the Legal Documents of the Salem Witchcraft Outbreak* (New York: Da Capo, 1977). Among the most illuminating studies of this subject about New England are Paul Boyer and Stephen Nissenbaum, *Salem Possessed: The Social Origins of Witchcraft* (Cambridge, Mass.: Harvard University Press, 1974), John P. Demos, *Entertaining Satan: Witchcraft and the Culture of Early New England* (New York and Oxford, Eng.: Oxford University Press, 1982), and Richard Godbeer, *The Devil's Dominion: Magic and Religion in Early New England* (New York and Cambridge, Eng.: Cambridge University Press, 1992). Virginia's treatment of sorcery is summarized in Philip A. Bruce, *Institutional History of Virginia in the Seventeenth Century,* 2 vols. (New York and London: G.P. Putnam, 1910), I, 278–289.

APPENDIX: List of Tables

Index

This index is arranged alphabetically letter by letter. Page numbers in *italic* indicate illustrations or captions. Page numbers followed by *t* indicate tables, by *m* indicate maps, by *n* indicate notes, and by *b* indicate biographical profiles.

balance of nature *see* environmental change

balance of payments 122

Ball, John 103*t*

Ballard, Thomas 218

Ballendine, John 102*t*

Baltic Europe 83

Baltimore, barons of and Lords Proprietary 41–42, 45
  see also Calvert family and Henry Harford

Baltimore, Md.
  shipbuilding 99
  strategic location 14

Baltimore County, Md.
  censuses (1704, 1755) 153*t*–155*t*
  commodity prices 58*t*, 61*t*, 77*t*
  ironworks 102*t*
  persons taxed (1694–1700) 153*t*

Bamper, Ludwick 107*t*

Bampfield, George 189*t*

banking *see* land banks

Bannister, John 268

baptism (first) 38

Baptist Church
  Brown University 182
  historical sketch 182
  increase in churches 181*t*
  location of churches: (1650) 179*t*; (1750) 181*t*
  revivalism 180
  rising influence 182

bar association (first) 46

bar iron
  defined 100
  imports, exports 106*t*–107*t*
  prices 105*t*

Barbados
  anti-Semitic riot 230
  Carolina settlers from 215

Barber, Luke 203

barbers
  in workforce 111*t*–113*t*
  among indentured servants 166*t*

Barbourville, Ky. 13*t*

Barclay, David 201

Barclay, David Jr. 189*t*

Barclay, Robert
  proprietor 201
  governor 201

Bard, Peter
  ironmaster 103*t*

Barefoote, Walter 206

Barham, Henry 274*t*

Barker, Thomas
  agent 189*t*
  proprietor 201

Barkhamsted, Conn.
  census 147*t*

barks
  in merchant marine 81*t*
  type of sailing rig 99*t*

barley
  caloric intake 171*t*
  yields and value 54*t*–55*t*
  wages for mowing 114*t*

barns
  construction expenses 110*t*
  grain barns 76
  tobacco barns 73
  valuation 52*t*–53*t*

Barnstable, Mass.
  census (1764) 139*t*
  frigid weather 3
  merchant marine 81*t*
  militia (1690) 139*t*

Barnstable County, Mass.
  census (1764) 139*t*, 141*t*
  militia (1690) 135*t*
  Plymouth Colony 213

barrels
  carpentry costs 110*t*, 115*t*
  hoops 85*t*
  number exported 110*t*
  staves 84*t*–85*t*

Barrington, N.H.
  census (1767) 143*t*

Barsimon, Jacob 42, 324

barter economy 117

Bartlet, Benjamin (gentleman) 219

Bartlet, Benjamin (merchant) 219

Barton, Benjamin 214

Bartram, John 45, 269

baseball 303

basket manufacturing 57*t*

Bass, Captain 105*t*

Basse, Jeremiah 202, 218

Basse's Choice, Va.
  census (1625) 156

Bate, William 219

Bates, Amos 105*t*

Bath, earl of *see* Grenville, John

Bath, N.C.
  pirate haven 237
  Bay Psalm Book 252, 263

Bayard, Nicholis 226

Bayard, Samuel 107*t*

Bayard, Stephen 227

Baylis, Nicholas 104*t*

Bayogoula Indians
  linguistic stock 22*t*
  location 27*t*
  population 35*t*

beads (trade good) 95*t*, 97*t*

Beale, Henry 219

Beaman, David 104*t*

beans
  dietary staple 168
  earliest cultivation 38
  Native American staple 20
  protein source 20
  in rations 169*t*

Bear River Indians
  location 25*t*
  treaties 33*t*

bears
  natural distribution of 7*t*
  overkilling of 8
  peltry trade 91–94*t*

Beaufort, S.C.
  rice exports 68*t*

Beaufort County, N.C.
  militia (1756, 1766) 158*t*–159*t*

persons taxed (1748–1767) 158*t*–159*t*

beaver *see also* beaver and peltries trade
  exchange value 93*t*, 95*t*
  giant species of 7
  overkilling of 8
  hat industry 91, 94*t*

beaver and peltries trade
  business expenses 92*t*–93*t*; 95*t*
  coureurs de bois 91
  deerskins 91, 93*t*, 95–97*t*
  depletion of wildlife 8, 91
  European sources 90, 94*n*
  exports: peltries 91–94*t*; deerskins 95–96*t*
  material for hats 91
  prices: in currency 93*t*; in trade goods 93*t*, 95*t*
  regional specialization 91, 95
  shipping costs 93*t*
  trade goods 92*t*–93*t*, 95*t*
  traps 95*t*, 97*t*
  Treaty of Lancaster 46
  wars over 30–32*t*, 42, 47

beaver hats
  British exports 91, 94*t*
  colonial manufacture 91
  trade good 97*t*

Beaver Wars 31*t*–32*t*, 41, 91

Bedford, Conn.
  census 144*t*

Bedford, Mass.
  census (1764) 137*t*

Bedford, N.H.
  census (1767) 143*t*

Bedford County, Va.
  Native Americans 37*t*
  persons taxed (1749–1755) 157*t*

Beecham, John 105*t*

beef *see also* cattle
  caloric intake 171*t*
  dietary staple 58, 168–170*t*
  prices 55*t*–56*t*, 58*t*–59*t*
  fishermen's rations 80*t*
  weekly consumption 169*t*

Beekman, Christopher 104*t*

Beekman, Gerardus 209

Beekman, Henry 149*t*

beer
  cost of barrels 110*t*
  first brewed 39
  dietary staple 98
  malt content 171*t*
  as rations 169*t*

Beer, George 219

bees 55*t*–56*t*

Beggar's Opera 265

Beissel, Conrad 252

Bel Air, Md. 46

Belcher, Jonathan
  governor: Mass. 205; N.J. 207

Belchertown, Mass.
  census (1764) 138*t*

Belfast, Me.
  census (1764)

Bell, Nicholas 219

Bell, Tom 230–231*b*

Bellamy, Charles 314

Bellers, John 219

Belleborne, Jean Nicolet de 13*t*

Belleville, N.J. 110*t*

Bellingham, Mass.
  census (1764) 136*t*

Bellingham, Richard 204

Bellomont, earl of *see* Coote, Richard

bellringers 112*t*

benefit of clergy 307

Benin 167*n*

Bennett, Richard 217

Bennett family (Md.) 183

Berdt, Dennys de 189*t*

Berdt, Dennys de, Jr. 189*t*

Bergen, N.J. 200, 207, 299

Bergen County, N.J.
  censuses (1726–1745) 150*t*–151*t*
  ironworks 103*t*–104*t*
  occupational distribution 112*t*

Bering, Vitus 46

Bering Strait 2*m*, 20, 38

Berkeley, John Lord 42, 200, 207, 215, 218–219

Berkeley, William
  governor 217
  Greenspring mansion 281
  proprietor 215

Berkeley County, S.C. 160*t*
  persons taxed (1693–1760) 151*t*

Berkley, Mass.
  census (1764) 140*t*

Berks County, Mass.
  census (1764) 141*t*

Berks County, Pa.
  ironworks 102–103*t*
  paper milling 108*t*
  persons taxed (1693–1760) 151*t*

Berkshire County, Mass.
  census (1764) 141*t*

Bermuda
  merchant shipping 82
  immigration to 164*t*

Bernard, Francis
  governor: Mass. 205; N.J. 207

Bernardstown, Mass.
  census (1764) 138*t*

Berry, Charles 210

Bertie County, N.C.
  militia (1756, 1766) 158*t*–159*t*
  persons taxed (1753–1767) 158*t*–159*t*

Berwick, Me.
  census (1764) 140*t*

Bethlehem, Pa.
  chamber orchestra 46
  first girls' school 46
  musical center 265
  printing press 252*t*
  water system 47

Beverley, Mass.
  census (1764) 136*t*
  merchant marine 81*t*
  militia (1690) 135*t*

Beverley, Peter 218

holidays 46, 284–286
Holland *see* Netherlands
Holland, Edward 227
Hollis, N.H.
    census (1767) 143*t*
    premarital conception 295*t*
Hollis, William 299
Holliston, Mass.
    census (1764) 137*t*
    diphtheria epidemic 173
Holloway, John 218
Holme, Thomas 228
Holmes, Jonathan 105*t*, 214
Holmes, Obadiah 107*t*
Holt, Nicholas 292, 294
Holt, Ryves 200
Honniasont Indians
    linguistic stock 22*t*, 28*t*
    location 23*m*, 28*t*, 211
    population 35*t*
Hooker, John 200
Hooker, Henry 204
Hooker, Robert L. 207
Hooker, Thomas 199
Hooten, Thomas 219
Hopewell, N.J. 230
Hopewell Culture 20, 38
    see also Adena and Mississip-
      pian Cultures
Hopkins, Edward 199
Hopkins, Stephen
    governor 214
    chief jusitice 214
    speaker 214
Hopkins, Steven 320
Hopkinton, Mass.
    census (1764) 137*t*
Hopkinton, N.H.
    census (1767) 142*t*
Hornblower, Joshua 47
hornbooks 241
Hornigold, Benjamin 236
Horse Creek, S.C. 160*t*
horses
    accidental deaths by 177*t*
    exported 63
    fodder requirements 55*t*
    horseshoeing costs 115*t*
    ownership 52*t*–54*t*
    prices 63*t*
    Spanish 39
Horsmanden, Daniel 209
hospitals *see also* medicine
    cure rates 177*t*
    first general 46
    first mental 45
Houghton, Robert 273
Houma Indians
    linguistic stock 22*t*
    location 23*m*, 27*t*
    population 35*t*
Housatonic Indians 33*t*
house construction
    architectural types 275–283
    construction expenses 110*t*
    volume 109*t*
House of Burgesses 320
households *see* families
houses

number in Mass. (1764) 141*t*
Houstaqua Indians 27*t*
Houston, Tex. 13*t*
Houstoun, William 274*t*
Howard, Francis Lord 217
Howard, Martin 210
Howes, Job 216
Howland, John 320
Hoy, Thomas 274*t*
Hubbard, Joshua 205
Hubbard, Thomas
    moderator 222
    speaker 205
Hubbard, William 270
Huber, John Jacob 103*t*
hucksters 113*t*
Hudson, Henry 13*t*, 40, *208–209,*
    269
Hudson, Seth *309*
Hudson, William 229
Hudson Bay, Canada 91
Hudson River valley
    discovered 13*t*, 40, *208*
    frozen over 1–2
    fur trade 91
    settled 19, 40–41, 131*m*
    warfare 32*t*
Hudson's Bay Company 91
Hughes, Griffith 274*t*
Huguenots
    earliest settlement 215
    persecution 163
    numbers immigrating 164*n*
    silk production 68
Hull, England
    merchant marine 81*t*
Hull, Mass.
    census (1764) 136*t*
    militia (1690) 135*t*
Hume, Robert 216
Humphreys, Solomon 103*t*
Humphreys, Whitehead 103*t*
Hunking, Mark 206
Hunlike, Edward 218
Hunter, Robert
    authors play 45, 256
    governor: N.J. 207; N.Y. 209
    proprietor (W.J.) 219
    Royal Society 274
Hunterdon County, N.J.
    censuses (1726–1745)
      150*t*–151*t*
    ironworks 104*t*
    occupational distribution 112*t*
    voter turnout 195*t*
hunter's stew 169
Huntington, Jabez 200
Huntstown, Mass.
    census (1764) 138*t*
Huron Indians *see also* Wyandot
    Indians
    First Beaver War 31*t*, 41
    location 23*m*
    smallpox 34
hurricanes 10–12*t*
Hussey, Christopher 79
Hutcheson, George 219
Hutchinson, Anne 41
Hutchinson, Thomas

chief justice 205
    governor 205
    moderator 222
    proprietor (W.J.) 219
    speaker 205
Hutchinsons, Ga. 160*n*
Hyannis Indians 24*t*
Hyde County, N.C.
    militia (1756, 1766) 158*t*–159*t*
    persons taxed (1748–1767)
      158*t*–159*t*
Hyde, Edward 209–210
hypochondria 177*t*

I

Ibitoupa Indians 27*t*
Icafui Indians 27*t*
Ice Age 2*m*, 20, 38
    see also little ice age
illegitimacy 295*t*–296, 298
Illinois
    exploration 13*t*
    first settled 44
    fur trade 8
    missionaries 42
    Native Americans 23*m*, 28*t*,
      44
Illinois Indians
    linguistic stock 22*t*
    location 23*m*, 29*t*
    population 35*t*
    warfare 32*t*, 42, 44
    warriors 37*t*
Illinois River 13*t*
immigrant ship disasters
    11*t*–12*t*
immigration *see also* slave trade
    Acadians 13, 47
    Baltic 86
    convicts 45
    demographic consequences
      130, 148, 153, 162–164
    Dutch 40–41, 107, 163–164*n*
    English 13, 39, 41–42, 44, 99,
      130, 148, 153, 163–164*n*
    French 141*t*, 163
    German 107–108, 148,
      163–164*t*
    "great migration" 13, 163
    indentured servants 153, 216
    Irish: 148, 163–164*n*
    Italian 107
    Jewish 42
    to mid-Atlantic colonies 148
    to New England 130,
      162–164*t*
    Polish 86, 107
    rations 169*t*
    Scottish 44, 163–164*n*
    sex distribution 133, 148, 153,
      162, 164
    to South 153, 162–164*t*
    Swedish 41
    Swiss 107
imperial administration
    agents 188–190*t*
    Board of Trade 128–129, 188,
      193
    governors 188, 191, 193

Parliament 188–189
    Privy Council 188, 193
indentured servants
    age distribution 164*t*
    contract 324
    convicts among 154*t*
    immigration 153, 163
    literacy 248
    marriage prospects 298
    mortality among 153
    occupations 164*t*
    sex ratios 164*t*
    slaves replace 216
Indiana
    French outposts 45
    Native Americans 23*m*, 28*t*
Indian corn *see* corn
Indian peas *see* lima beans
Indians *see* Native Americans
indigo
    acreage sown 65
    bounties 65*t*
    exports 64–65
    labor requirements 65
infant mortality 174
influenza
    epidemics 173*t*–174
    high mortality 174
Ingersoll, Jared 189*t*
Ingle, Richard 41, 202, 207
Ingoldsby, Richard
    governor: N.J. 207; N.Y. 209
inner light 186
innkeepers
    book ownership 249*t*
    in workforce 111*t*, 113*t*
insects
    natural distribution of 7*t*
inside plumbing 45
insurance coverage 45
Inuit migration 38
inventions 273
Iowa Indians
    linguistic stock 22*t*
    population 35*t*
Ipswich, Mass.
    census (1764) 136*t*
    earthquake 11*t*
    married life 293*t*, 295*t*
    merchant marine 81*t*
    militia (1690) 135*t*
Ireland
    flax imports 62*t*–63*t*, 127*t*
    height, average 171*t*
    merchant marine 80
    trade with 122*t*–127*t*
Irish colonists
    Charitable Irish Society 46
    immigration 148, 163–164*n*
    marriage with Indians 29
    Northern 164*t*
    religion 185
    St. Patrick's Day 46
    southern 164*t*
Iron Act (1750) 98
iron industry
    bloomeries: described 100;
      locations 101*t*, 103*t*–104*t*
    bog ore 98